Introduction to Media Production
The Path to Digital Media Production
Third Edition

Introduction to Media Production
The Path to Digital Media Production
Third Edition

GORHAM KINDEM

ROBERT B. MUSBURGER

AMSTERDAM • BOSTON • HEIDELBERG • LONDON
NEW YORK • OXFORD • PARIS • SAN DIEGO
SAN FRANCISCO • SINGAPORE • SYDNEY • TOKYO

Focal Press is an imprint of Elsevier

ELSEVIER

Focal Press is an imprint of Elsevier
30 Corporate Drive, Suite 400, Burlington, MA 01803, USA
Linacre House, Jordan Hill, Oxford OX2 8DP, UK

Library of Congress Cataloging-in-Publication Data
Application submitted

British Library Cataloguing-in-Publication Data
A catalogue record for this book is available from the British Library.

ISBN: 0-240-80647-6

For information on all Focal Press publications
visit our website at www.books.elsevier.com

04   05   06   07   08   09   10 9 8 7 6 5 4 3 2 1

Printed in the United States of America

For Nancy and Pat

In return for their patience, understanding, and support

Table of Contents

Preface to the Third Edition

This third edition completely revises and updates *Introduction to Media Production: From Analog to Digital.* Recent developments in digital media technologies are discussed in each chapter. The text has been streamlined and bulleted for added readability and improved access to key concepts. Photographs and illustrations that illustrate important recent developments have been added where they best facilitate understanding. Finally, while analog technologies still figure prominently in certain areas of media production, digital media technology clearly predominates in others, and the structure and content of the third edition of *Introduction to Media Production* reflects these important changes. The authors are grateful to the external reviewers for their valuable suggestions and to Elinor Actipis, Cara Anderson, Christine Tridente, Jamey Stegmaier, and Eric De Cicco, for their encouragement and strong support for this edition. A special thanks to Tengah Nguyen and Larrizza Sanqui for the new photographs.

1

The Production Process: Analog and Digital Technologies

TOPICS FOR DISCUSSION

- What are the three stages of production?
- What are the differences between digital and analog production techniques?
- How has the history of production developed?
- Why is production terminology different?
- Who makes up the production team?
- What is production aesthetics?

INTRODUCTION

Media production requires both analog and digital technologies. The advent of digital technologies stimulated a number of important changes in media production, including the convergence of technologies as well as corporate integration. This chapter explores significant developments encouraged by digital media at the same time that it confirms the continuing value of analog technologies and provides an overview of the media production process. The digital revolution describes a process that started several decades ago. Technicians developed uses for the technology based on "1" and "0" instead of an analog system of recording and processing audio and video signals. Rather than a revolution, it has been an evolution, as digital equipment and techniques have replaced analog equipment and processes where practical and efficient. Digital equipment may be manufactured smaller, requiring less power, and producing higher-quality signals for recording and processing. As a result, reasonably priced equipment, within the reach of consumers, now produces video and audio productions

that exceed the quality of those created by professional equipment of two decades ago. But every electronic signal begins as an analog signal and ends as an analog signal, since the human eye and ear cannot directly translate a digital signal (Figure 1.1).

STAGES OF PRODUCTION

The production process can be organized into three consecutive stages: preproduction, production, and postproduction. Everything from the inception of the project idea to setting up for actual recording is part of the preproduction stage. This includes the writing of a proposal, treatment, and script, and the breakdown of the script in terms of production scheduling and budgeting. The second major phase of production is the production stage. Everything involved in the setup and recording of visual images and sounds, from performer, camera, and microphone placement and movement, to lighting and set design, makes up part of the production stage. Postproduction consists of the editing of the recorded images and sounds, and all of the procedures needed to complete a project.

Preproduction

Preproduction consists of the preparation of project proposals, premises, synopses, treatments, scripts, script breakdowns, production schedules, budgets, and storyboards. A *proposal* is a market summary used to promote or sell a project. A *premise* is a concise statement or assertion that sums up the story or subject matter. For example, the basic premise of Joan Didion's

Figure 1.1 Digital equipment and technologies have entered all phases of audio, video, film, and multimedia production. While digital production techniques are basically the same as analog techniques, there have been marked increases in efficiency, flexibility, and, in some cases, reproductive quality. (Courtesy Mackie Designs, Inc.)

film *The Panic in Needle Park* (1971) is "Romeo and Juliet on drugs in New York's Central Park."

A *synopsis* is a short paragraph that describes the basic story line. *Treatments* are longer plot or subject-matter summaries in short-story form, which often accompany oral pitches of a premise or concept, and *scripts* are virtually complete production guides on paper, specifying what will be seen and heard in the finished product. One can break down a script by listing all equipment and personnel needs for each scene so that a production can be scheduled and budgeted. A *budget* describes how funds will be spent in each production category. A *storyboard* provides a graphic visualization of important shots that will eventually be recorded by a camera.

Production

Production begins with setup and rehearsal. The film, video, or multimedia director stages and plots the action by rehearsing scenes in preparation for actual recording. Charting the movement of talent on the set is known as *performer blocking*, while charting the movements of the cameras is called *camera blocking*. Every camera placement and movement of the talent must be carefully worked out prior to recording. If the action cannot be controlled, as in the live transmission of a sporting event or the production of a documentary, the director must be able to anticipate exactly where the action is likely to go and place the camera or cameras accordingly. During actual production, the entire project is essentially in the hands of the director. In multiple-camera studio or location production, for example, the director often selects the shots by commanding the technical director (TD) to press certain buttons on a device called a *switcher*, which makes instantaneous changes from one camera to another. In single-camera production, the director remains on the set and communicates directly with the talent and crew. The script supervisor or continuity person watches the actual recording session with a sharp eye to ensure that every segment in the script has been recorded. Perfect continuity between shots, in such details as a consistent left-to-right or right-to-left direction, and identical flow of performer movements (matched action) from one shot to the next, must be maintained so that these shots can be properly combined during editing.

In an audio production or recording session, the producer maintains the same authority and responsibilities as a video or film director: rehearsing the musicians, instructing the engineer, and supervising the actual recording session. In a digital *multimedia* production, whether for a computer game, CD-ROM, or DVD recording, the producer's authority and responsibilities are the same except that the producer may be gathering and working totally with digital material instead of people. In multimedia production sessions, the producer may very well perform all aspects of the production—from writing through the entire process to creating the graphics and entering code in order to create the program in a digital form.

Postproduction

Postproduction begins after the visual images and sounds have been recorded. Possible edit points can be determined during the preview stage, when the recorded images and sounds are initially viewed. Pictures and accompanying sounds are examined and reexamined to find exact edit points before various shots are combined. Separate sound tracks can be added later to the edited images, or the sounds can be edited at the same time as the pictures. The postproduction stage ties together the audio and visual elements of production and smoothes out all the rough edges. The visual and audio elements must be properly balanced and controlled. Sophisticated analog and digital devices help editors and technical specialists mold sounds and images into their final form.

In audio postproduction the emphasis is placed on choosing the best of the many sound takes and combining the various tracks onto one, or in the case of stereo, two finished tracks, or as in the case of audio for high-definition television (HDTV), as many as six or more tracks. In motion picture production, the sound editor may use as many as 64 or more tracks to complete the production. Signal processing, including equalization, adding effects, and balancing tracks against each other, is often performed during the sound mix, that is, during the final process of combining various sound tracks. Such processing operations may be performed either in an analog or in a digital format. The tendency is to manipulate audio in a digital format in order to avoid any degeneration or degradation of the signal.

The three stages of production are separate only in a chronological sense. Proficiency in one stage of the production process necessarily requires some knowledge of all other stages. A director or writer cannot visualize the possibilities for recording a particular scene without having some awareness of how images can be combined during editing. In short, while the overall organization of this text into three stages (preproduction, production, and postproduction) follows a logical progression, mastery of any one stage demands some familiarity with other stages as well.

DIGITAL VERSUS ANALOG TECHNOLOGY

While all three stages of media production have been affected by the advent of digital technologies, analog technologies continue to play important roles in each stage as well. For many years, equipment used in media production was exclusively analog, and many analog technologies, including motion picture film, are still used widely today. In fact, the size and quality of images recorded by some film technologies have never been surpassed. The potential screen size and image detail, or resolution, of projected large-format film images, such as IMAX, Omnivision, and even standard 35mm film, are still superior to video projection systems, including digital HDTV projection systems, and it is likely to remain so for some time. The look of film, the softness of the film image, the intense saturation of colors, and film's superior reflectance contrast range (from bright white to dark black) over electronic media (200+:1 vs. 50:1) translate into a very sophisticated and subtle visual medium. As Nicholas Negroponte, MIT Media Lab founder and author of *Being Digital*, said about 10 years ago, "The subtlety and nuance of film is so far out of reach right now. Film is still by far the highest, best-resolution medium we have" (*American Cinematographer*, May 1995, p. 79). But advances in digital equipment and technology have made the visible differences to the audience less discernible between the two media. The increased efficiency in production, creative options, and distribution make digital techniques in feature film and commercial productions much more attractive to producers.

New media technologies rarely eliminate older technologies, although they often make the use of older technologies more specialized. The use of film has become more and more specialized with every advance in electronic imaging technology. For example, advances in videotape recording and editing made it less advantageous for television news operations to use news film during the 1970s, but many prime-time dramatic programs used film and have continued to do so. Today, digital editing systems offer a number of advantages over conventional film editing, and digital technologies have virtually replaced analog audiotape and videotape recording and editing technologies in most situations as well.

Digital systems encode audio and video information as a series of ones and zeros, or "on" and "off" signals. A full range of sounds (from loud to soft and from high pitch to low) and images (from bright to dark and from high color saturation to low) can be digitally encoded as a series of zeros and ones. Analog audio and video information, on the other hand, contains a vast range of incremental electrical or photochemical values that are analogous to the sound and image spectrum.

Digital recordings are more permanent and are much less likely to experience a loss in quality when they are copied from one generation to the next than are analog recordings, because only one value is used for encoding "on" or "off," one or zero. Digital encoding also offers increased flexibility and efficiency in terms of manipulating and shaping recorded sounds and visual images during post-production editing and special effects, because it is easier to manipulate a single value (one or zero) than a vast range of incremental values (Figure 1.2).

Digital technologies have increased the speed, efficiency, and flexibility of film and TV production. It is important to recognize some of the contributions that digital technologies have made to each stage of media production, including preproduction writing, producing, and storyboarding; production recording and lighting; and postproduction editing and special effects. Overall, digital technologies have significantly increased production efficiency in each of these areas, and they have also begun to alter conventional notions of reality and history through a proliferation of imaginative and realistic special effects.

Figure 1.2 Digital signals are determined by periodically sampling the values of comparable analog signals: the greater the number of samples per second, the higher the quality of the digital signal.

Digital Technologies Used in Preproduction

Film and TV preproduction stages consistently use digital computers. Scriptwriting and word-processing computer software programs help writers efficiently format and revise scripts. Producers and production managers use scheduling and budgeting software programs to quickly break down scripts and preplan their productions. Breakdown sheets list all equipment and personnel needs for each scene in a film or TV script. The cost of each of these items can quickly be totaled up to produce an overall budget, while the duration and sequence of recording each scene can be used to create an overall production schedule. Digital computers quickly and efficiently make changes in a script, a budget, or a schedule.

Computer graphics software facilitates the creation of storyboards, which can provide visual guidelines for camera shots, editing, and overall storytelling. A storyboard consists of a series of graphic images that indicate the camera framing and composition for each shot in a film or TV program. Other graphics programs allow sets and costumes to be visualized and coordinated before they are actually made. Lighting plots can be revised quickly when computer programs offer the potential to visualize the lighting effects on simulated characters and settings prior to actually hanging the lights.

Computerized casting networks and performer databases help talent agencies to promote actors they represent and casting directors to find them. Location scouting has been facilitated by computer databases, and the World Wide Web's ability to provide pictures of possible locations via computer networks offers the potential to both cut down on travel expenses and shorten preproduction schedules. The ability to capture and send images and sounds as well as text around the world via digital computer networks, such as the Internet and the World Wide Web, offers tremendous potential regarding the international flow of information. The Internet and its developing potential for video streaming also offers a new means of marketing motion pictures, and as Negroponte has suggested, "the Net will perhaps be the primary form of world commerce. . . . And the cinematography community will enjoy an extraordinary new marketplace" (*American Cinematographer*, May 1995, p. 80).

Digital Technologies Used in Production

New digital recording devices for video cameras offer a number of advantages for news recording. For example, a computer hard disk, digital disk, or solid-state RAM chip or a digital videotape recorder can be built into a portable video camera to record news stories for television. Dockable (camera-attachable) hard disks, digital disk, or RAM chips, or a digital videotape recorder, allow 30 minutes or more of professional-quality video to be recorded. Digital images and sounds can be edited immediately on a digital nonlinear editing system, greatly speeding up the production of news stories. Just as analog videotape recording and editing offered significant advantages over news film in the 1970s, digital recording and editing devices offer potential advantages over conventional analog videotape recording and editing news stories today.

Computerized digital lighting boards facilitate production by allowing a cinematographer or lighting director to preprogram a lighting setup and hang several lighting setups simultaneously using different computer files on the same lighting board program. Special lighting effects, such as projecting images and graphics on the walls of sets to add atmosphere or create laser light shows, can also be preprogrammed into a computerized lighting board and software program. Virtual sets created in a computer program inserted behind performers bypass the time-consuming and expensive process of set construction, assembling, and lighting. For example, the lighting director for a popular American film, *Batman Forever* (1995), made extensive use of digital lighting techniques and equipment during production in order to control more complicated lighting setups and changes than would be possible using conventional analog technology. This film returned to the original 1939 comic-book source of the mythical crime fighter, the Caped Crusader, to create a more active and action-oriented hero than the 1989 version of *Batman*, as well as active comic-book villains. In one scene at a circus, where the villain, Two-Face (played by Tommy Lee Jones) staged a deadly threat to Batman (played by Val Kilmer), more than 225 Xenon lamps were controlled by a computerized lighting board so that they could do color changes and chases. In another "pan-Asian" sequence within Gotham City, the lighting director used computer-controlled lighting to project saturated colors and Chinese motifs onto the sides of the buildings on Figueroa Street in downtown Los Angeles, where filming was done. The lighting director's extensive experience with rock and roll concerts and theatrical shows greatly facilitated his use of computerized lighting equipment in the film.

Sound recording has been greatly facilitated by digital audiotape (DAT) direct to MiniDisk, CD-ROM, and Audio-DVD recording processes and equipment. Digitally recorded sounds can be filtered more effectively and efficiently on location than analog recordings, for example, to remove unwanted background sounds. Digital sound recordings also minimize hiss as well as generational loss in sound quality when they are copied and dubbed for editing purposes, and they blend well with digitally recorded sound effects, music, and Automatic Dialogue Replacement (ADR) recorded in a sound studio during postproduction. Multimedia audio stays in the digital domain throughout the production process.

Digital Technologies Used in Postproduction

Some of the most significant contributions of digital technology to film and TV production have come in the postproduction area. Digital videotape recorders and direct-to-digital servers facilitate the creation of special effects during final or online editing by allowing images to be layered on top of one another in successive recordings without loss of quality.

Digital editing systems make editing and revising a film or video as simple and quick as operating a computer word processor. In addition to increasing postproduction efficiency, digital editing systems allow an editor to visualize a final edited program. Special effects such as conforming and answer printing or on-line videotape editing may be previewed prior to the final stages of film or video postproduction.

Both film and TV postproduction use digital editing systems throughout the processes. Most digital editing systems employ computer hardware that is capable of processing and storing vast amounts of visual and audio information. A digital editing system may include a central processing unit (CPU) that has a processing system with more than two gigahertz (GHz), eight *or more* gigabytes (GB) of random access memory (RAM), a keyboard, a mouse, one or two computer monitors, a videotape recorder, an amplifier and loudspeakers, and one or more hard disk drives designed for audiovisual (AV) use.

Digital editing software offers several advantages over conventional means of editing film, audiotape, and videotape, including increased flexibility, as well as potential time and cost savings. A common cliche is that digital editing is the equivalent of word processing and desktop publishing for audio, film, and video postproduction. The analogy holds for many aspects of editing that are shared by word processing and various digital editing software programs. For example, most word processing software programs allow a writer to cut, copy, paste, and delete words, paragraphs, and pages of text. Digital editing affords an editor similar flexibility in terms of instantaneously changing the order and duration of sounds and images. For example, clips of video or audio information can be cut, trimmed, copied, pasted, inserted, and deleted along a time line (Figure 1.3).

A *clip* is usually the smallest unit of digital video (or audio) information that can be stored and manipulated during editing. It can range in duration from just one frame to an entire movie, but it often consists of a single shot, that is, a continuous camera

Figure · 1.3 Digital equipment may be used to record, control, or edit audio, video, or lighting signals. (Courtesy Akai, Lexicon, Nagra, Colortran, and Yamaha.)

recording or take. Digitized clips are usually imported (or copied) into a particular editing project file, where they are edited along a time line with other images and sounds. Images and sounds from each clip are often displayed as a series of representative still frames along the time line. Clips can be copied and inserted at various points along the time line, and they can also be deleted from the time line and the remaining images and sounds attached to one another.

Every edit made using a digital software program is usually a virtual edit. No digitized material is discarded when clips are trimmed, cut, or deleted along an editing time line, since each clip is usually stored separately outside the time line window. Every clip stored on a disk drive is instantaneously accessible in its entirety and can be grabbed in the project or clip window and reinserted at any point along the time line. Many alternative versions of a scene or sequence can thus be quickly edited and examined without prematurely eliminating material that may be needed later. Transitions from one shot to another can be previewed, as can the superimposition of titles and various digital video effects without ever actually cutting, discarding, eliminating, or deleting any originally digitized video or audio.

The ability to manipulate clips of video and sound along a time line not only adds flexibility to the editing process; it can also make editing more efficient and cost-effective. Clips can be very rapidly trimmed, cut, inserted, and deleted. Digital editing is extremely fast compared with physically cutting and splicing a conventional feature film, and the time it takes to find and insert videotape images and sounds from a source onto a master videotape can be dramatically reduced by using instantaneously accessible digital clips along a time line. The amount of time scheduled for postproduction editing can be significantly diminished, facilitating the editing of projects that require a short turnaround time, such as topical news magazine segments and mini-documentaries. Increased editing efficiency can also translate into cost savings that affect the overall budget of longer-term projects when an editor's time and salary can be reduced. Clearly, digital editing offers a number of advantages in terms of flexibility and efficiency over conventional videotape and film editing.

Digital editing systems can be used at many different production levels. Some low-end digital editing systems are designed for use on home computers, and the range of graphics and special effects that are available on relatively inexpensive consumer programs to edit home videos is truly remarkable. Inexpensive digital editing systems also provide an excellent means of teaching video and sound editing, graphics, and special effects to students at a variety of educational levels. High-end professional systems can be used to efficiently edit feature films, relying upon Kodak film KeyKode numbers and SMPTE time-code numbers (discussed in Chapter 11, "Sound Editing") as references for film conforming and on-line editing. Large corporations whose video production units use high-end digital editing systems sometimes finish their programs in digital form, avoiding the added time and cost of on-line videotape editing. A large number of audio tracks can usually be edited initially using digital editing software, and additional editing, mixing, and sound "sweetening" can be done later using a compatible digital audio workstation (DAW).

Special effects techniques have been greatly expanded and enhanced by digital technologies, and the Academy of Motion Picture Arts and Sciences recently granted full-branch status (similar to the acting and cinematography branches of the Academy) to visual effects supervisors and artists. Digital effects are often combined with miniatures (smaller copies of objects) and models (full-size mockups) to produce startlingly realistic special effects in Hollywood feature films, such as J.R.R. Tolkien's *Lord of the Rings* series. (Miniatures and models are discussed more fully in Chapter 12, "Animation and Special Effects.") Computer graphics hardware and software have played an important role in the creation of special effects.

Many of the special effects used in the Hollywood film *Apollo 13* (1995), for example, were achieved by compositing (combining digital images) miniatures and models using computer graphics and digital video effects. *Apollo 13* focuses upon the nearly tragic story of the Apollo 13 astronauts: an accident occurred onboard their spacecraft in April of 1970 that forced their moon landing to be aborted and nearly left them stranded in space. These events took place at the height of the space race and the Cold War competition between the United States and the Soviet Union.

The ability to manipulate and control individual pixels (single dots of colored light on a dimensional graphic image) has led to a proliferation of effects that challenge conventional conceptions of history and reality. For example, the NASA space program astronaut who advised the producers of *Apollo 13* regarding the authenticity of various space-launch procedures and restagings asked the producers where they had obtained actual documentary footage of the launch of the Apollo 13 spacecraft, when in fact the images were digital special effects created on a computer.

The Hollywood film *Forrest Gump* (1994) placed the fictitious main character inside the frame of an actual documentary recording of former President Lyndon B. Johnson, while President Johnson's lips were animated and he appeared to speak to Forrest Gump. These examples illustrate the power of digital special effects to potentially rewrite history and to create artificial worlds that sometimes seem more real than authentic documentary recordings. Film history has itself been revised and manipulated through the digital colorization of old black-and-white feature films. Colorizing old (and sometimes new) Hollywood films has clearly distorted the original artist's intentions and has altered film history. In the hands of media moguls, such as Ted Turner, who acquired the MGM library for use on Turner Network television, it has also significantly added to the television markets and viewing audiences for older films. Digital film and TV technologies have had a significant impact upon conventional notions of history and reality, and they have challenged traditional legal, ethical, and aesthetic conceptions as well.

Digital technologies that offer potential connections to film and video are CD-ROM, DVDs, computer games, and other interactive software. Many Hollywood film companies work with CD-ROM producers to create interactive computer games in conjunction with the release of feature films to theaters. The same settings or locations used in a feature film can be recorded in virtual 360-degree space using several film cameras. These images can then be mapped three dimensionally via various computer programs so that a CD-ROM player can move throughout the space, interacting with characters and situations from the film. CD-ROMs that incorporate film and video material also offer tremendous potential in education, including interactive film and TV production training, such as learning how to operate specific pieces of equipment. Films and television programs released on DVDs include many extra features and supplementary materials, which expand the information on how and why a production was completed. Digital technologies have clearly increased the speed, efficiency, and flexibility of media production in all three stages of film and TV production: preproduction, production, and postproduction. While they have not yet eliminated superior analog technologies, such as film recording and theater screenings, digital devices have made the use of traditional analog technologies more specialized. In addition, digital technologies have begun to alter conventional notions of history and reality through the use of sophisticated computer graphics and special effects. Finally, as we begin the twenty-first century, new digital technologies, such as CD-ROMs, DVDs, the Internet, and the World Wide Web (WWW), will undoubtedly provide new markets for films and videos and new educational opportunities for film and TV students and scholars.

The advent of digital technology has blurred many traditional distinctions in media production, such as off-line versus on-line editing, film versus video production, and (active) artists versus (passive) viewers. Traditionally, videotape editing occurs in two stages, often referred to as off-line and on-line editing. During off-line editing, the sequential order of visual images and sounds is arranged and rearranged using small-format dubs or copies of the original videotape recordings. During on-line editing, the final decisions resulting from off-line editing are performed again using the original, high-quality videotape or digital recordings and more sophisticated equipment. Today a high-quality digital editing system can perform both functions; that is, it can be used for both (preliminary) off-line editing and for (final) on-line editing, making the passage from one stage to the next less distinct. In addition, the flexibility afforded by digital editing systems is similar to the flexibility of traditional film-cutting techniques but much more efficient. For example, a digital editing system allows an editor to reduce the overall length or duration of a program by deleting or removing images and sounds along a time line and simply bringing the remaining images and sounds together so that they directly precede and follow one another. This technique is similar to the removal of frames of film or a shot and accompanying sound from the middle of a film. The potential to change the overall program duration at will is often referred to as a nonlinear approach to editing because the order of shots and sounds can be reordered at any time. The overall program length or duration cannot be shortened or lengthened at will in linear videotape analog editing systems without reediting the entire program from the point at which something is removed. Digital systems can be used to edit productions that were originally recorded on either film or videotape using a nonlinear approach. In so doing, digital editing equipment has brought film and video editing closer together.

Digital HDTV cameras capture electronic images that have an aspect ratio (width to height ratio) and resolution (clarity and amount of detail in the image) that more closely approximates some wide-screen theatrical film formats than it does traditional television or video images. Professional as well as consumer HDTV cameras are designed to operate in either 16:9 or 4:3 aspect ratios and in a variety of scan formats (see Chapter 8, "Recording"). Finally, computers and interactive multimedia software allow traditionally passive media viewers and listeners to analyze and manipulate audio, video, and film productions and to actively recreate their own versions of existing media texts, as well as to learn new skills interactively or play computer games. Traditional distinctions between (active) artists versus (passive) viewers or listeners, film versus video production, and off-line versus on-line editing are becoming less and less meaningful as digital technologies bring traditional forms of media production closer together.

A SHORT HISTORY OF AUDIO, FILM, AND VIDEO PRODUCTION TECHNOLOGY

The basic technology for the eventual development of radio, audio recording, motion pictures, and television was available as early as the beginning of the nineteenth century. The predecessors for motion pictures may be considered to be still photography; for audio systems, the telegraph and telephone; and for television, the electrical discharge of light-sensitive materials. Each of these was discovered or invented before 1840 (Figure 1.4).

From 1839 to the end of the nineteenth century, experiments and practical models of both selenium-based electrical systems and rotating disc-based systems were developed to convert and transmit visual images. By 1870, Thomas Edison had produced a primitive mechanical cylindrical audio-recording device called the Gramaphone. During the last half of the nineteenth century, a variety of toylike machines, such as the Thaumatrope, Phenakistoscope, Zoetrope, and lantern shows with delightful titles such as Phantasmagoria and Magasin Pittoresqueó were used to display projected pictures that appeared to move.

Before the introduction of film, a perceptual mechanism or illusion on which motion pictures depend was discovered and called "an instance of the phi phenomenon" by the early twentieth-century perceptual psychologists, Wertheimer and Termus. Gestalt psychologists were fascinated by perceptual tricks and illusions because they provided a convenient means of studying the way our brains process sensory information. The phi phenomenon produces apparent motion out of stationary lights or objects. It occurs when two lights, separated by a short distance, are flashed or strobed very rapidly. Above a certain threshold of flashes per second, the human eye is deluded into thinking that one light is moving, rather than those two stationary lights flashing. This

A   **B**

Figure 1.4 Early media production equipment by today's standards was primitive and ineffective. But production techniques that were developed to produce shows on that early equipment still provide the basis for today's digital media production. (A) An early twentieth-century film camera compared with (B) a modern 35mm camera. (Courtesy Arri USA, Inc.)

same phenomenon helps to explain the perception of apparent motion from rapidly flashed still photographs. The mind's eye fills in the gaps between frames and produces apparent, not real, motion.

A period of invention at the end of the nineteenth century brought about the telephone, the electric telescope that was designed to convert moving images into an electrical signal, and early carbon, crystal, and ceramic microphones. Before the turn of the century, the disc record player and recorder were improved in France. In this country, Edison and W.K.L. Dickson developed a workable motion picture camera and projector, and George Eastman invented the flexible film base that made motion pictures possible. The century ended with the first "wireless" broadcasts, film projected on a screen for an audience, and a working model of a wire recorder.

Television experiments continued into the early twentieth century, alternating between rotating disc and electrical scan systems. Motion picture sound systems early in the century utilized sound recorded on discs with primitive methods designed to maintain synchronization between picture and sound. Many of the frustrations of workers in all three industries—motion pictures, radio, and television—were partially solved by Lee De Forest's invention of the triode-amplifying vacuum tube. This invention provided the means to send voices over the air for the first time and for the motion picture industry to use sound-reinforcing systems for theatres.

In 1908 the all-electronic television system now in use was described, but it took 17 years before a practical model became operational. Television technology is based on light coming through a camera lens and striking a light-sensitive surface on a camera pickup tube or surface of a charged couple device (CCD) chip. Fluctuations in current on the face of the tube or the surface of the chip are read by the circuitry of the camera as direct variations in the light striking the surfaces. These fluctuations in electrical current are then fed to a television picture tube or flat screen, which reverses the process. Bright light striking specific points on the camera pickup tube correspond to bright light emitted by the phosphors of the television receiver's picture tube or flat-screen monitor. A television screen is scanned completely 30 times every second; thus the images move at a speed of 30 frames per second, rather than the 24 frames per second of sound film. Television, like film, depends on the phi phenomenon to produce apparent motion, but it also relies on persistence of vision to fuse the continuous scanning of the picture tube into complete frames of picture. *Persistence of vision* refers to the temporary lag in the eye's retention of an image, which can fuse one image with those that immediately precede or follow. This phenomenon does not explain apparent motion, because the fusion of images in the same position within the frame would result in a confused blur, rather than the coherent motion of objects.

The first two-color, two-negative Technicolor film process was developed in 1917. It was followed three years later by the first AM radio stations in the United States receiving licenses and some experimental television stations being licensed to use the spinning disc system. By the early 1920s, the Hollywood motion picture industry had become pervasive enough to dominate foreign screens and to be threatened with domestic censorship. The first sound-on-film system was developed by De Forest the same year that Vladimir Zworykin invented the iconoscope television camera tube, which opened the way for an all-electronic television system. Within that same decade, the recording industry moved from acoustical recording to electronic methods, and AT&T started the first radio network. Twentieth Century Fox first used the Movietone sound-on-film system for newsreels. Warner Bros. used the Vitaphone disc system for their first sound features.

During the 1930s, modern dynamic and ribbon microphones were invented, and both British and American inventors continued to experiment with audio wire recorders. By 1932, Technicolor introduced their three-color, three-negative film process, and FM radio continued to be developed. German scientists perfected an audiotape recording system based on paper coated with iron oxide, and Eastman Kodak introduced 16mm film as an amateur format. The format quickly became popular with professional military, educational, and industrial filmmakers, as well as documentary producers.

Immediately preceding the entry of the United States into World War II, RCA promoted their all-electronic television system with the FCC, who later approved that system over the CBS rotating disc system in 1953.

Although World War II interrupted the rapidly expanding field of electronics, many developments in communication technology came from the war effort. The use of higher frequencies, miniaturization of equipment and circuits, and advances in radar that were used in television, and eventually computers, were all perfected. Following the war, magnetic tape became a standard for recording audio, television stations and receivers increased in number rapidly, and motion picture studios experimented with theater TV and close relationships with television stations and networks. The Paramount 1948 decree by the U.S. Supreme Court motivated the film industry to divorce the motion picture production and distribution from theater exhibition, bringing an end to the major studio era and stimulating greater independent production. The transistor was invented, CBS developed the 33⅓ long-playing (LP) records, and RCA followed with the 45 rpm.

Television saved the record business by forcing radio stations to turn to all-music formats, and the motion picture industry felt compelled to turn to wide-screen, 3-D, and all-color films to compete with the small-screen, black-and-white television systems of the 1950s. Eventually, greater interaction occurred between film and television as film studios produced television series and feature films that were shown on television. By the middle of the decade, the FCC approved the National Television Standards Committee (NTSC) color-TV standard, and stereo recordings on tape were marketed, leading to the development of multitrack recording techniques. Within the next two years, all three industries moved forward: television with the invention of the quadraplex videotape recorder, motion pictures with the Panavision camera and lens systems, and audio with the perfection of stereo discs.

The beginning of the rapid acceleration of technical developments occurred in 1959, when the integrated circuit was invented, leading to the development of computer chips. For the next twenty years computers moved from room-sized operations that could perform limited calculations (by today's standards) to pocket-sized computers and a variety of other applications priced for small companies and individuals. Within the next ten years, professional helical videotape recorders and electronic editing of videotape were developed; satellites were launched to permit transmission of audio, visual, and digital information instantaneously worldwide; the FCC approved a stereo standard for FM; quadraphonic and digital sound systems were developed; and cable moved from the country to the cities. During the period of these great advances in the electronic communication fields, motion pictures also utilized the same inventions to improve sound recording, lighting and editing systems, and theater exhibition systems. The expansion of cable television brought television to many rural areas that were out of reach of the TV stations of the time.

During the 1970s, miniaturization produced smaller cameras, recorders, and receivers, leading to new production techniques in both radio and television. Videotape formats began to proliferate, with systems both for the home (Betamax and VHS) and for the professional (U-matic and 1-inch). Cable became a major player in distributing both films and video productions as pay channels took to the satellites.

HBO provided movies, ESPN sports, and CNN 24-hour news.

Technical advances continued through the 1980s, with two events setting the stage for massive changes in all communication fields: in 1981, HDTV was first demonstrated, and in 1982, a consent decree between the Department of Justice and American Telephone and Telegraph (AT&T) separated the long-distance and equipment-supply portions of the corporation from the individual local telephone systems. Less earth-shattering but still important developments were the authorization of Lower-Power TV (LPTV) stations, Direct Broadcast Satellite (DBS) systems, the invention and rapid spread of compact discs (CDs), and the agreement on a Musical Instrument Digital Interface (MIDI) standard. The FCC approved a stereo TV standard, and RCA introduced the Charge Coupled Device (CCD) camera, which used computer chips in place of camera tubes. By the middle of the 1980s, digital systems were used in new videotape formats, motion picture editing and synchronizing systems, and digital audio decks and editing systems. (Figures 5-1A and 5-1B)

Fox, Universal-Paramount (UPN), and Warner Bros. (WB) television networks began operations as the other three networks (ABC, CBS, and NBC) changed ownership. Experiments with teletext and videotext found limited use, and a once-failed system, videodisc, returned and began making inroads in the home market. Professional videotape formats shrunk in size as half-inch BetaCam and Recam were followed by BetaSP and MII, which become the standards of the production and broadcast studios before digital cameras and recording formats were developed.

In the 1990s, computer workstations and DAT integrated audio production into a complete digital world, and nonlinear digital editing systems for video programs became the standard. The motion picture industry turned to digitized video for postproduction and special effects, as the two visual industries began to share many more technologies. Black-and-white movies were colorized, and graphics were created through the expanded use of digital systems. Interactive multimedia production of CDs incorporated audio, video, text, and graphics into interactive computer programs. The computer slowly encompassed virtually the entire field of communications in rapid sequences of developing technologies.

At the beginning of the twenty-first century, each of the production areas—audio, video, and motion pictures—has continued to merge, overlap, and grow closer together through the use of digital technology and equipment. A fourth area of production, multimedia, emerged during the last decade of the twentieth

A **B**

Figure 1.5 (A) Television camera tubes passed through a series of modifications and shapes and sizes from the 1930s until chips replaced tubes. From left to right: an Image Orthicon (IO) tube, the first practical camera tube used until the mid-1960s. The original color cameras required four IOs, one each for red, green, and blue colors, and a fourth for luminance. Later cameras used the green tube for luminance. Next to the IO are a series of vidicon, saticon, and newvicon tubes, each smaller and offering higher resolution, requiring lower power, and allowing a smaller camera. (B) The Image Orthicon tube's two-inch, light-sensitive surface compared to the one-half-inch, light-sensitive surface of a camera chip.

century and has become a dominant force in media production of the twenty-first century. By FCC ruling, broadcasters are required to use digital TV and HDTV by 2006. By the end of the first quarter of 2004, over 99% of all television homes had access to digital television broadcasts over the air. More than 1,000 TV stations were broadcasting some programs in digital format. Whether the TV signal may be viewed and heard in its full digital format depends on the television receiving equipment in each individual home. This transition from analog to digital by a portion of the audience at a time is comparable to the conversion from monochrome to full-color television in the 1950s. The availability of digital TV and HDTV equipment and consumer interest will increase during the first decade of the century. Distribution of home video on Digital Video Disk, or Digital Virtual Disk, (DVD) quickly surpassed that of VHS videocassettes. The high quality of audio and video information contained on DVDs, as opposed to VHS cassettes, including Dolby Digital five- and six-track audio for home theater sound and component video for various widescreen and HDTV formats, stimulated the proliferation of DVDs. The vast number of VHS decks in homes has kept VHS as a relatively popular home video recording system, but the ability to record (burn) directly onto DVD and/or CD-ROM disks on many personal computers makes the future of VHS uncertain. By late 2003, high-quality, easy-to-operate digital recording and editing equipment and software became a reality. Radio stations had begun to convert to all digital equipment, graphics,

and animation, and postproduction techniques all relied heavily on digital technology.

The problem of copyright violations through the use of MP3 equipment for downloading and distributing music reached a legal stalemate in 2003. As music producers lowered their prices and the Recording Industry Association of America (RIAA) filed hundreds of civil lawsuits, the number of illegal downloaded records began to fade. Apple computers and others began paid download systems that provided a practical and affordable alternative to illegal downloading of music. A comparable system eventually will appear for video programs.

The wars fought in the first five years of the century saw the development of miniaturized cameras, direct-to-satellite video and audio feeds from cell phones, and other digital technologies that were used by both the military and news-gathering organizations.

PRODUCTION TERMINOLOGY

Acquiring basic media production terminology is crucial to understanding the entire production process. The use of production technology and techniques requires a rather specialized vocabulary. As key words are introduced in this text, they are usually defined. When chapters are read out of sequence, the reader can refer to the Glossary and Index at the end of the book to find a specific definition or the initial mention of a term. We almost intuitively understand the meaning of such words as television, video, audio, and film, but it is important to be as precise as possible when using these and other terms in a production context. *Television* refers to the electronic transmission and reception of visual images of moving and stationary objects, usually with accompanying sound. The term *television* has traditionally referred to images and sounds that are broadcast through the air-waves. Electronic television signals can be broadcast by impressing them on a carrier wave of electromagnetic energy, which radiates in all directions from a television tower and is picked up by home receivers. Electrical energy travels in waves, much like ocean waves that crash on the sand at the beach. A carrier wave is usually rated in thousands of watts of power channeled through a television transmitter (Figure 1.6).

Electromagnetic energy ranges from sound to long radio waves to very short radio waves and on to light and gamma rays. The radio waves can travel through the atmosphere, the sea, and the earth, and they can be picked up by receivers. Television signals can also be sent through closed-circuit or cable television systems, that is, along electrical wires rather than through the airwaves. Prior to the 1930s, experimental television was primarily closed-circuit, but the commercial exploitation of this technology as a mass medium and as a means of distributing television to large numbers of private homes, known as *cable television*, did not occur until much later. Since the 1960s it has been possible to transmit television signals via satellites across continents and around the world. *Satellites* are communications relay stations that orbit the globe. Line-of-sight microwave (i.e., high-frequency) transmissions of television signals are frequently used for live, nondelayed, real-time news reports in the field and for sending signals to outlying areas where broadcast signals are not well received.

The terms *television* and *video* are sometimes used interchangeably, but it is generally agreed that television is a means of distributing and exhibiting video signals, usually over the air. *Video*, on the other hand, is a production term. Also, the term *video* is used very narrowly to refer to the visual portion of the television signal, as distinguished from the audio or sound. The more general definition of *video* as a production term refers to all forms of electronic production of moving images and sounds. This is the preferred use in this text. The term *video* can refer to a three- to five-minute popular song with accompanying visuals on a videotape or a CD-ROM, and it is actually a shortened form of the term *music video*. A *video* can also refer to a videotape copy of a feature film available at a video rental store. *Videotape* refers to magnetic tape, which is used to record both the video and the audio portions of the television signal. Videotape, digital servers, and other digital media allow television signals to be transmitted on a time-delayed basis, rather than live, and when used with various electronic editing devices, they allow recorded images and sounds to be changed and rearranged after they have been recorded. A videotape and a DVD also allows feature films to be played at home on a *VCR* (video cassette recorder) or a DVD player, respectively. Videotape (VTR) traditionally has meant the tape is mounted and played from an open reel. A VCR is a tape that has been encased in a closed cassette from which the tape is withdrawn as it is played. DVDs are disks containing video and audio recorded using a laser beam to embed the digital information in the surface of the disk. (There is more information about DVDs in Chapter 13, "Distribution and Exhibition.")

BROADCAST ELECTROMAGNETIC SPECTRUM

VERY LOW & LOW FREQUENCIES LONG WAVE 3 kHz – 300 kHz	MEDIUM FREQUENCIES MEDIUM WAVE 300 kHz – 3 MHz	HIGH FREQUENCIES SHORT WAVE 3 MHz – 30 MHz
Audio – 10 Hz/20 kHz Military & Experimental Broadcast	AM Broadcasting	Marine, Air, Land mobile Amateur (Ham) radio International Shortwave
VERY HIGH FREQUENCIES 30 MHz - 300 MHz	ULTRA HIGH FREQUENCIES 300 MHz – 3 GHz	SUPER & EXTREME HIGH FREQUENCIES 3 GHz – 300 GHz
Television channels 2-13 FM Broadcast	Television channels 14 – 69 L-Band satellites Land mobile	Microwave C, Ku, & Ka Band Satellites Radar

Figure 1.6 Broadcast carrier frequencies share space on the international electromagnetic spectrum with a variety of other signals and broadcast users.

Film has a variety of meanings in production. Defined very narrowly, it simply refers to the light-sensitive material that runs through a motion picture camera and records visual images. When film is properly exposed to light, developed chemically, and run through a motion picture projector, moving objects recorded on the film appear to move across a movie screen. In a more general sense, the term *film* can be used interchangeably with such words as *motion picture(s), movie(s),* and *cinema.* The first two words in the singular refer to specific products or works of art that have been recorded on film, while in the plural they can also refer to the whole process of recording, distributing, and viewing visual images produced by photochemical and mechanical, that is, non-electronic, means.

Audiotape refers to magnetic tape that is used to record sounds. *Digital audiotape* (DAT) is used to record audio signals in digital form on high-density magnetic tape in a DAT recorder. *Compact discs (CDs)* are digital audio recordings that are "read" by a laser in a CD player for high-quality audio reproduction.

Making clear-cut distinctions between video and film is becoming increasingly difficult, especially in the context of new digital technologies. For example, when a feature film, a television series, a music video, or a commercial advertisement is initially recorded on film but edited in digital form and distributed on videotape, broadcast on television, satellite transmitted, or sold or rented as a CD-ROM, DVD, or videodisc, is this a video, a film, or a new type of digital hybrid? Using a single video camera to record a program in segments, rather than using multiple video cameras to transmit it live or to record it live on tape, has frequently been called *film-style video production* because the techniques used in single-camera video production are often closer to traditional film practice than to those of multiple-camera studio or remote video production. On the other hand, the techniques of multiple-camera film production used to record stunts in feature films are often closer to traditional multiple-camera studio television practice than to traditional single-camera film practice. As mentioned earlier, digital editing techniques often combine traditional film and videotape editing techniques at the same time that they mimic computer word processing. All of these developments make it difficult to make firm distinctions between film, video, and digital media today. The term *electronic motion pictures* refers to distributing films to a theatre via electronic means rather than physically shipping the film to each theatre. (There is more on this subject in Chapter 13, "Distribution and Exhibition.")

Multimedia refers to the creation of works that combine video, audio, graphics, and written text.

Combining these media involves digitizing all of the various elements so that they can be computer controlled and stored in a variety of forms, such as on hard disk drives and CD-ROMs. *Interactive media* refers to various forms of viewer/reader/listener manipulation of and interaction with computer-controlled multimedia forms. Multimedia and interactive media have both been widely used in training and education, as well as computer games, but they are also developing into important new art forms and means of personal expression, especially as distributed on the Internet and the World Wide Web. These terms are often used in combination, with *interactive multimedia,* referring to works that are interactive and involve the use of multimedia.

New forms of media are constantly being developed and existing media forms are constantly changing. Thus, while it is important to be as precise as possible in the use of media terms, it is equally important to realize that the meanings of these terms can change over time, reflecting changes in the technology on which these media are based and the ways in which that technology is used.

SINGLE-CAMERA VERSUS MULTIPLE-CAMERA PRODUCTION, AND STUDIO VERSUS LOCATION PRODUCTION

A producer or director of a live-action production must make two basic decisions before production begins. First, he or she must decide whether one or more than one camera should be used to record or transmit images. Using one camera is called *single-camera production,* while using more than one camera is referred to as *multiple-camera production.* Second, a decision must be made about whether the images should be recorded inside or outside the studio. Recording inside the studio is known as *studio production,* while recording outside the studio is called *location production* in film and *remote production* (involving cable/microwave links to the studio) or *field production* in video.

Multiple-camera production techniques are used to record continuous action quickly and efficiently without interruption. Such techniques are the basis for television news programs, entertainment programs involving a studio audience, as well as much corporate, educational, and religious programming. Remote coverage of sporting events almost always requires multiple cameras. Multiple film cameras are frequently used to record dangerous stunts simultaneously from a variety of angles for feature films. Multiple film cameras also are used to film some television situation comedies.

In single-camera production, each separate shot is set up and recorded individually. The main artistic advantage of single-camera production is that few compromises have to be made in lighting or microphone placement in order to accommodate the viewing requirements of several different cameras. Logistically, only one camera needs to be set up or carried into the field at a time. Single-camera production of dramatic fiction usually begins with the recording of a master shot, which covers as much of the action in a scene as possible from a single camera position. Then the same actions are repeated and recorded again with the camera placed closer to the action. The resulting material is combined during postproduction editing. Single-camera production techniques are used to record feature films, documentaries, and television commercials, as well as in news recording. Except for live coverage of sports events, single-camera production is the norm for location and remote production situations.

In some production situations it is simply impossible to record events inside a studio, even though studio production facilities and techniques are usually more efficient and economical. Lighting and sound recording are more easily controlled in a studio than at a remote location. Most production studios are designed to provide ideal recording conditions by insulating the recording space from outside sounds, reducing the echo of interior sounds, and allowing easy overhead or floor positioning of lights and access to power supplies. Location production can give a film or television production a greater sense of realism or an illusion of reality.

Exterior locations often create a sense of authenticity and actuality. But location settings rarely provide ideal lighting and acoustical environments. Extraneous sounds can easily disrupt a production. Confined settings often create sound echo and make it difficult to position lights and to control the shadows they create. Inclement weather conditions outdoors can delay the completion of a project. Since location production sometimes increases production risks and costs, a producer must have strong justification for recording outside the studio. Of course, the construction of sets inside a studio can also be extremely expensive, in addition to creating an inappropriate atmosphere, and location production in this case is easily justified on the basis of both costs and aesthetics.

Planning for Positive Production Experiences

Everyone wants to have positive production experiences. Although no secret formula for success exists, a thorough understanding of production principles and a positive attitude toward the overall production process is certainly helpful. Exuding confidence in a project enlists the support of others. This requires knowing what is needed and how to get it. Making good creative choices demands careful advance planning of every logistical and conceptual aspect of production.

Many production techniques can be mastered through practice exercises, such as those recommended at the end of each chapter in this book, and through actual production experience. Truly benefiting from these experiences requires taking risks and learning from one's mistakes. Learning to work within present levels of ability, avoiding unnecessary or repeated errors through careful planning, and the development of strong conceptualization skills are also essential.

Avoiding Negative Production Experiences

The first law of production is Murphy's Law: **Anything that can go wrong, will go wrong.** Every production person has vivid memories of his or her first encounter with Murphy's Law, such as an essential piece of equipment that the camera crew forgot to take on location or one that failed to work properly. The second law of production is an antidote to Murphy's Law: **Proper prior planning prevents poor productions.**

Many production problems are preventable. Ignoring conceptual and aesthetic considerations, failing to learn how to operate a camera properly, forgetting to bring necessary equipment, and having no backup or replacement equipment are preventable mistakes. No one is beyond the point of needing to think carefully about what he or she is doing or learning how to use new equipment. Everyone should use detailed equipment checklists, specifying every necessary piece of equipment, which are checked and rechecked prior to going into the field. Every production needs to have some backup equipment and contingency plan to turn to when things start to go other than planned.

Some production problems are not preventable. No one can precisely predict the weather or when a camera will stop working. But everyone must have an alternative or contingency plan if such a problem occurs. Equipment should be properly maintained, but not everyone can or should try to repair equipment in the field. Certainly, the option to record another day, if major problems should occur, must be available. Good quality productions are rarely made in a panic atmosphere, and careful planning is the best anecdote to panic, Murphy's Law, and negative production experiences.

Quality productions are shaped and reshaped many times on paper before they are recorded and edited. Preproduction planning is extremely important. It is always cheaper and easier to modify a project before actual recording takes place than to do so after production is under way. The organization of this text reflects the importance of preproduction planning and the development of conceptualization skills. The first section is devoted entirely to preproduction planning. Some degree of advance planning and conceptualization is implicit in later stages of production and postproduction as well.

THE PRODUCTION TEAM IN AUDIO, VIDEO, FILM, AND MULTIMEDIA PRODUCTION

The production team can be organized hierarchically or cooperatively. In a hierarchical situation, the commands flow downward from the producer to the director, and from her to the rest of the creative staff or production crew. In a cooperatively organized production, every member of the production team has equal authority and control, and decisions are made collectively. Most production situations combine aspects of both the hierarchical and the cooperative models, although the former approach is clearly dominant in the commercial world. Combining approaches, the producer and/or director makes most of the important decisions, but the help, support, guidance, and input of all the creative staff and some of the technical crew is actively sought and obtained (Figure 1.7).

Production is rarely a purely democratic process, but it is almost always a collective process that requires the support and cooperation of large numbers of people. The members of any media production team usually can be divided into two distinct groups: the creative staff and the technical crew. This basic division is often used for budgeting purposes. Dividing the team and costs into above-the-line creative aspects and below-the-line technical aspects allows for a quick financial comparison between investments in the creative and technical sides of a production. The costs of paying the producer, director, scriptwriter, and performers are considered above the line, while those for equipment and the crew are below the line. The two should be roughly equivalent in terms of the allocation of financial support to ensure that neither the creative nor the technical side of the production is being overemphasized (Figure 1.8).

Creative Staff in Media Production

The creative staff in audio, video, multimedia, and film production includes the producer, director, assistant director, scriptwriter, designers, and the talent or performers.

The Producer
There are many different types of television and film producers: executive producers, independent producers, staff producers, line producers, and producer hyphenates (e.g., producer-writer-directors). The exact responsibilities of the producer vary greatly between different commercial and noncommercial production

STAGES OF MEDIA PRODUCTION

PREPRODUCTION	PRODUCTION	POST PRODUCTION
PRODUCER	DIRECTOR	EDITOR
Research	Visualization	Off-line
Writing	Interpretation	On-line
Law/Ethics	Selection	Titles
Budgets	Visual/Sound	Visual Effects
Scheduling	Integration	Narration
Production	Graphics	Sound Effects
Management	Lighting	Sweetening
	Casting	Integration
	Blocking	Distribution
	Rehearsing	
	Recording/Airing	

Figure 1.7 Each of the three stages of media production fulfills critical facets of the production process. Each of the three stages relies upon the professional completion of the other two stages. No one stage is more important than any other.

COMPARISONS BETWEEN MEDIA PRODUCTION TEAMS

PERSONNEL CLASSIFICATIONS	MOTION PICTURES	AUDIO	VIDEO	GRAPHICS
ABOVE THE LINE				
EXECUTIVE	Executive Producer Producer Production Manager	Producer	Executive Producer Producer Production Manager	Developer Publisher Producer
CREATIVE	Director Writer Art Director	Arranger Director	Director Writer Art Director	Designer Writer Video Director
PERFORMANCE	Actor Narrator	Musician Announcer	Actor Announcer	Voice Talent
BELOW THE LINE				
TECHNICAL	Stage Manager Lab Technician Sound Engineer	Operator	Technical Director Technician Audio Director Lighting Director	Computer Technician
PRODUCTION	Director/Photography Camera Operator Recordist Editor Mixer Grip-Gaffer	Mixer Board Assistant	Camera Operator CG/Graphics Operator Audio Operator Assistant Director Editor Stage Manager Stage Crew	Art Director Graphic Artist Animator Programmer

Figure 1.8 Parallels exist between the organization of production teams, depending upon the media used, but each medium has unique personnel categories for each level depending on whether the classification is above the line or below the line.

categories and levels. In general, the producer is responsible for turning creative ideas into practical or marketable concepts. The producer secures financial backing for a television or film production, and manages the entire production process, including budgeting and scheduling, although production managers often handle many of these tasks at major studios. Some producers become directly involved in day-to-day production decisions, while others function as executive managers who largely delegate production responsibilities to others. The producer ensures that the financial support for a production is maintained and usually represents the views of his or her clients, investors, or superiors, as well as those of prospective audiences, throughout the production process. The producer in radio or in an audio recording session also may hire the musicians, arrange for facilities and studio time, and in some cases actually operate the audio board or other recording medium (Figure 1.9).

The Director

The director creatively translates the written word or script into specific sounds and images. He or she visualizes the script by giving abstract concepts concrete form. The director establishes a point of view on the action that helps to determine the selection of shots, camera placements and movements, and the staging of the action. The director is responsible for the dramatic structure, pace, and directional flow of the sounds and visual images. He or she must maintain viewer interest. The director works with the talent and crew, staging and plotting action, refining the master shooting script, supervising setups and rehearsals, as well as giving commands and suggestions throughout the recording and editing.

The director's role changes with different types of production situations. In live, multiple-camera video, the director usually is separated from the talent and crew during actual production, remaining

Figure 1.9 The organization of motion picture companies varies with the number of films in production at any one time. Some company services are shared between productions, and others are unique to each individual production.

inside a control room. In the control room, the director supervises the operation of the *switcher*, a live-television editing device that controls which picture and sound sources are being recorded or transmitted. The director also gives commands to the camera operators from the control room. A stage manager or floor manager (FM) acts as the live television director's representative in the studio, cueing the talent and relaying a director's commands. In single-camera production, the director remains in the studio or on the set or location, and works closely with the talent and the director of photography (DP) (Figure 1.10).

The Assistant/Associate Director

The assistant or associate director helps the television or film director concentrate on his or her major function, controlling the creative aspects of production. In feature film production, the assistant director (AD) helps break down the script into its component parts prior to actual production for scheduling and budgeting purposes. The AD then reports to the production manager, who supervises the use of studio facilities and personnel. During actual production, the AD becomes involved in the day-to-day paperwork and record-keeping, sometimes actually taking charge of a shooting unit, but always making sure that the talent and the crew are confident, well-informed, and generally happy. In studio video production the associate director (AD) keeps track of the time, alerts the crew members and performers of upcoming events, and sometimes relays the director's commands to the camera operators, video switcher, and other crew members.

The Scriptwriter

The scriptwriter is a key member of the production team, particularly during preproduction. A scriptwriter outlines and, in large part, determines the overall structural form of a production project. He or she writes a preliminary summary of a production project, called a *treatment*. A treatment lays the groundwork for the script and is written in the third person, present tense, much like a short story. The script provides a scene-by-scene description of settings, actions, and dialogue or narration, and functions as a blueprint that guides the actual production.

The Production Crew in Media Production

The production crew in media production includes the director of photography, camera operator, lighting director, art director or scenic designer, editors, and

TELEVISION STATION ORGANIZATION

Figure 1.10 The organization of a television station varies considerably depending on the size of the market and whether the station is a network affiliate, network owned and operated, or a totally independent operation.

perhaps a number of specialized engineers and technicians, depending on the size and sophistication of the production. Figures 1.9 and 1.10 illustrate a more complete breakdown of the organization of a motion picture company and a television station.

The Director of Photography

The overall control of film lighting and cinematography, or the creative use of a movie camera, is usually given to one individual, the director of photography (DP). A DP supervises the camera crew, who are sometimes called *cameramen* (referred to as *camera operators* in this text), assistant camera operators, grips, and the electrical crew, who are sometimes called *engineers* or *gaffers* and who actually control the lighting setup. The DP works very closely with the director to create the proper lighting mood and camera coverage for each shot.

The DP is considered an artist who paints with light. He or she is intimately familiar with composition, as well as all technical aspects of camera control, and is frequently called on to solve many of the technical and aesthetic problems that arise during film recording. The DP rarely, if ever, actually operates the camera.

The Lighting Director

In video production the camera operation and lighting functions are usually kept separate. The lighting director is responsible for arranging and adjusting the lights in the studio or on location according to the director's wishes or specifications. The lighting director supervises the lighting crew, who hangs and adjusts the various lighting instruments.

The Camera Operator

The camera operator controls the operation of the film or video camera. Many adjustments of the video camera must be made instantaneously in response to movements of the subject or commands from the director, such as changing the positioning of the camera or the focus and field of view of the image. The director's commands come to the camera operator in the studio via an intercom system connected to the camera operator's headset. The camera operator must smoothly, quietly, and efficiently control the movement of the support to which the camera is attached in the studio and avoid any problems with the cable, which connects the camera to the switcher or videotape recorder. A film camera operator works much more independently than a video camera operator, following the directions that the DP and the director give before the camera rolls. While shooting, it is the operator's responsibility to maintain framing and follow the action.

The Art Director or Scenic Designer

The art director (film or graphics) or scenic designer (video) supervises the overall production design. He or she determines the color and shape of sets, props, and backgrounds. Art directors frequently work very closely with costume designers and carpenters to ensure that costumes and sets properly harmonize or contrast with each other. In feature film, the art director delegates the supervision of set construction and carpentry to the set designer, and in video the scenic designer often supervises both the abstract design of a set on paper and its actual construction.

The Technical Director

The technical director (TD) operates the switcher, a multiple-video-camera editing device, in the control room. At the director's command, the TD presses the buttons that change the television picture from one camera or playback device to another. In some television studios, the technical director supervises the entire technical crew, including relaying the director's commands to the camera operators, while also operating the switcher.

The Editor

In video postproduction, the editor operates an editing system that electronically connects the individually recorded segments into a sequential order. A film editor physically cuts together various pieces of film into a single visual track and an accompanying soundtrack. The sound editor is a specialist who constructs and organizes all the various sound elements so that they can be properly blended or mixed together into a final soundtrack. In film, the sound segments can be physically spliced together, but in video they are edited electronically. Film and film audio can also be transferred to videotape and audiotape for electronic editing.

The Audio Engineer or Mixer

In video production the individual responsible for all aspects of initial audio recording is called the *audio engineer*. In film production this person is referred to as the *mixer* or *audio (or sound) recordist*. In studio video production the audio engineer sits behind a large audio console in the control room, where he or she controls the sound from the microphones and playback units. The audio engineer also supervises the placement of microphones in the studio. The film mixer or audio recordist, like the audio engineer in video, adjusts and controls the various audio recording devices, but unlike the audio engineer, remains on the set rather than in the control room. The film mixer usually operates an audiotape recorder that runs synchronously with the film camera. The mixer tries to record a consistent, balanced audio signal throughout all the different single-camera setups so that a smooth, even soundtrack can be created during subsequent editing and mixing.

The Video Engineer or Laboratory Color Timer

The quality of video and film images depends on technical specialists who can control image, color, brightness, and contrast levels. In video production a video engineer usually controls the setting and adjustment (shading) of camera recording and transmission levels. The engineer is responsible for ensuring that all cameras are functioning properly and that

multiple cameras all have comparable image qualities. A video engineer can also make color corrections to individual shots during postproduction. The color timer at a film laboratory performs a similar role, but does so after the film has been edited and before copies are made. In video postproduction and in film that has been transferred to video, the color in each shot can be adjusted using special digital equipment. Color can also be adjusted within individual frames using computer-controlled colorizing equipment, which digitizes images and allows a colorist to control individual pixels in the frame. Many digital editing programs contain a wide range of image-control devices, allowing precise adjustments of the color, brightness, and contrast of scenes, sequences, shots, and individual frames during postproduction.

The Production Team in the Recording Industry

The employees involved with the actual production of audio programs in the recording industry may be as few as one: the producer/operator working with the musician or performer. Or the team may be as complex a group as arrangers, producers, engineers, operators, as well as the musicians and/or performers (See Figure 1.11).

The Producer and Operator

The producer and operator function the same as in a video production, except that they are concerned only with the sound of the program.

The Arranger

Arrangers work with the musicians to assemble the best possible musical composition. Often the musicians will arrange their own music or arrive at a recording session with the composition ready to record.

The Production Team in Interactive Multimedia Production

The interactive multimedia creative staff and production team includes the developer, publisher, producer, designer, writer, video director, graphic artist/animator, and programmer.

The Developer

The developer is the individual or corporation that creates an interactive multimedia product. The developer oversees program content and programming and delivers the product to the publisher. Developers are analogous to the production side of the film and video business. Production companies are developers.

RECORDING STUDIO ORGANIZATION

```
                              ┌─────────────────┐
                              │ President-Owner │
                              └─────────────────┘
     ┌───────────────────────────────┼───────────────────────────────┐
┌──────────────────┐          ┌──────────────┐                ┌──────────────┐
│ BUSINESS MANAGER │          │ LEGAL COUNSEL│                │  MARKETING   │
└──────────────────┘          └──────────────┘                └──────────────┘
    │                    ┌────────┼────────────────┐              │
┌────────────┐      ┌────────┐  ┌───────┐    ┌──────────┐   ┌───────────┐
│ Accounting │      │ Agents │──│ Unions│    │ Licensors│   │ Promotion │
└────────────┘      └────────┘  └───────┘    └──────────┘   └───────────┘
    │               ┌──────────┐               ┌──────────┐      │
┌─────────────────┐ │ Managers │               │  ASCAP   │ ┌────────────────┐
│ Human Resources │ └──────────┘               │   BMI    │ │ Public Relations│
└─────────────────┘                            │  Sesac   │ └────────────────┘
    │                                          └──────────┘      │
┌───────┐                                                   ┌──────────────┐
│ Sales │       ┌──────────┐   ┌──────────┐  ┌───────────┐  │ Art Director │
└───────┘       │ Composers│   │ Arrangers│  │ Publishers│  └──────────────┘
    │           └──────────┘   └──────────┘  └───────────┘
┌──────────────┐
│ Distribution │   ┌──────────┐  ┌──────────┐  ┌──────────┐
└──────────────┘   │ PRODUCER │  │ PRODUCER │  │ PRODUCER │
                   └──────────┘  └──────────┘  └──────────┘
                        │                           │
                   ┌──────────┐                ┌──────────┐
                   │ Engineer │                │ Musician │
                   └──────────┘                └──────────┘
          ┌────────────────────┐  ┌──────────────────────┐
          │ Assistant Engineer │  │ Maintenance Engineer │
          └────────────────────┘  └──────────────────────┘
```

Figure 1.11 The organization of a recording studio varies depending on the size of the studio, the type of recordings that are made in that facility, and the number of artists using the facility on a regular basis.

The Publisher

The publisher provides financial backing and ensures that the product will be successfully distributed. Publishers are analogous with the distribution side of the film and video business.

The Producer

The producer manages and oversees a project, interacts with the marketing people and executives in the publishing company, and coordinates the production team. The producer is sometimes referred to as a project director, project leader, project manager, or a director.

The Designer

The designer is basically a writer who visualizes the overall interactive multimedia experience and then creates the design document that specifies its structure, that is, a product's necessary and unique attributes. In an interactive computer game, for example, the design document may include the basic elements of the story, locations, and problems to be solved by the person playing the game. Animation, music, and sound effects are included in the design document, which is then handed over to a producer, who coordinates the creation of the design elements into a product.

The Writer

The writer may consult with the designer who initially envisioned a particular product but is usually hired by the producer to help create and develop design elements and to shape them into their final form. The writer may flesh out the characters, dia-logue (which may appear as text in one platform but be spoken in another), music, sound effects, and possible scenarios envisioned by the designer, or he or she may invent entirely new material. Interactive multimedia writers are generally very skilled at nonlinear storytelling.

The Video Director

If a video recording is needed to add live-action material to an interactive multimedia experience, a video director is brought in to handle staging the action, actors, and crew.

The Art Director

The art director is responsible for converting the written script into a visual production. Usually the art director draws or supervises the production of the storyboards that guide the production from conception to completion. The art director develops the basic concept of color, style, and character design before assigning the work to individual artists.

The Graphic Artist/Animator

The graphic artist and/or animator draws and animates characters, backgrounds, and computer environments, which make up the visual elements of an interactive multimedia product.

The Programmer

The programmer is the person who develops computer programs that integrate the various aspects of a multimedia product and facilitate interaction with it on various computer platforms, such as on a

Macintosh computer. Several computer programmers may be involved in the creation of interactive multimedia, which will be used on different platforms or computer environments, such as Windows, Mac, and NT. Programmers are sometimes referred to as engineers (See Figure 1.12).

Visualization: Images, Sounds, and the Creative Process

Visualization can be defined as the creative process of translating abstract ideas, thoughts, and feelings into concrete sounds and images. This demands strong conceptualization skills and a thorough understanding of media production methods and techniques. Scriptwriters and directors must have something significant to say and the technical means to say it. Quality production work requires an ability to organize one's creative thoughts and to select and control many devices that record, edit, and transmit visual images and sounds. Scriptwriters and directors must acquire a basic understanding of the overall production process before they can fully develop their visualization skills. A knowledge of production principles and practices stimulates the search for innovative ways to translate abstract ideas into concrete sounds and images. It also sets limits on a writer's creative imagination. A scriptwriter must be practical and realistic about production costs and logistics. An imaginative script may be too difficult or expensive to produce. A scriptwriter must also have some knowledge of camera placement, graphics design, composition, timing, and editing, even though his or her work is basically completed during the preproduction stage.

To visualize means to utilize the full potential of audio, video, film, and multimedia for creative expression. Film, video, audio, and multimedia communicators must be constantly open to new ideas, technologies, and techniques, because these media are constantly changing. But they cannot ignore traditional communicative practices and ways of structuring messages. Other media and older forms of communication provide a wealth of information about the communication process.

In a sense, the attempt to use visual images and sounds to communicate with others is as old as the human species. Early human beings, for example, drew pictures of animals on the walls of caves. Cave drawings may have been created out of a desire to record a successful hunt for posterity, to magically influence the outcome of future hunts by controlling symbolic images, or to express the feelings and thoughts of an artist toward an animal or hunt. These three purposes of communication can be summarized as conveying information, rhetorical persua-

Figure 1.12 The organization of a multimedia operation varies widely depending on the type, number, and budgets of the projects the individual studio specializes in within its specialized field.

sion, and artistic expression. To some extent, these explanations are also applicable to contemporary uses of video, film, audio, and multimedia.

Conveying Information

Communicating with pictures and sounds may have a single purpose, to convey information. What is communicated, the specific content or meaning of the message, consists of informative signs and symbols, images and sounds, which are transmitted from one person to another. We tend to think of certain types of films, television, and multimedia programs, such as documentaries, educational films, videotapes, audio recordings, news programs, and interactive programs, as primarily intended to convey information. Few media messages are exclusively informational, however. Other types of communication are needed to arouse and maintain audience interest and to enliven an otherwise dull recitation of facts.

Rhetorical Persuasion

Rhetoric is the art of waging a successful argument. Persuasive devices and strategies are designed to shape opinions, change attitudes, or modify behavior. The term *rhetoric* has been applied to the use of stylistic as well as persuasive devices and techniques in artistic works such as novels. An artist can select a rhetorical device, such as the point of view of a specific character, to tell or stage a story, so that the reader or audience becomes more emotionally involved. Rhetorical devices often stimulate emotions. They can make a logical argument more persuasive and a work of fiction more engaging and emotionally effective. In television, radio, film, and multimedia we tend to think of editorials, commercials, political documentaries, and propaganda as rhetorical forms of communication. Many fictional dramas can also be thought of as rhetorical in structure and intent.

Artistic Expression

Artistic works often communicate an artist's feelings and thoughts toward a person, object, event, or idea. Sometimes artistic expressions are extremely personal, and it is difficult for general audiences to understand them. At other times the artist's thoughts and feelings are widely shared within or even between cultures. An artistically expressive film, graphic, television, audio, or multimedia program can convey a culture's ethos and ideology, its shared values and common experiences, in unequaled and innovative ways. Works of art can communicate an artist's unique insight into his or her own self, culture, and medium of expression. Artists often experiment with new expressive

techniques and devices, presenting ordinary experiences in new and provocative ways. They can challenge a viewer's preconceptions and stimulate a serious and profound reexamination of personal or cultural goals and values. They can also reinforce traditional conceptions and cultural values.

PRODUCTION AESTHETICS

Media production requires more than a mastery of technology and techniques. It is also an artistic process that demands creative thinking and the ability to make sound aesthetic judgments. How should you approach a specific topic? What techniques should you use? Important aesthetic choices have to be made. To make these decisions you must be aware of many different possibilities and approaches. Every production choice implicitly or explicitly involves aesthetics. Some production techniques go unnoticed and enhance an illusion of reality, for example, while others are devices that call attention to themselves and the production process. The aesthetic alternatives from which you must choose at each stage of the production process can be divided into three basic categories: realism, modernism, and postmodernism.

Realism

A realist approach to production creates and sustains an illusion of reality. Realist techniques rarely call attention to themselves. Spaces seem to be contiguous to one another within a specific scene, and time seems to flow continuously and without interruption, similar to our experience of the everyday world.

Many Hollywood films, for example, sustain an illusion of reality and make us forget that we are watching a movie. This illusion of reality in Hollywood films is based, however, on stylistic conventions that audiences readily accept as real. Conventional editing techniques, such as matching a character's action over a cut from one shot to the next shot in traditional Hollywood films, help to sustain an illusion of reality, and are often referred to as realist conventions of classical Hollywood cinema (Figure 1.13).

As William Earl has suggested in his cogent description of modernism as a revolt against realism in films, realist films, which include many classical Hollywood films, define reality as familiar, recognizable, and comprehensible. Realist art feels most at home living among familiar things in their familiar places, or among persons with recognizable characters acting or suffering in comprehensible ways (Earl, "Revolt Against Realism in the Films," *The Journal of Aesthetics and Art Criticism*, Winter, 1968, Volume 27, #2).

Figure 1.13 A realist production strives to create an illusion of reality through spatial and temporal continuities that mirror real life experiences, as Tom Hanks and his platoon are depicted in the Dreamworks' production of *Saving Private Ryan*. (Courtesy of Dreamworks Pictures.)

Modernism

A modernist approach to production, which is reflected by many avant-garde works of video and film, often calls attention to forms and techniques themselves. Modernist works fail to create a realistic world that is familiar, recognizable, and comprehensible. A modernist media artist instead feels free to explore the possibilities and limitations of the audio, video, or film medium itself without sustaining an illusion of reality (Figure 1.14).

As viewers of modernist works, we often see familiar objects and events portrayed in a new light through the use of innovative techniques. Modernist art often appears less objective than realist art. Modernist works sometimes probe the subjectivity or inner psychological world of the individual artist/creator. In addition to self-expression, modernist productions often reflect feelings of ambiguity, as opposed to objective certainty. Time is not always continuous, and space is not always contiguous. Modernist art tends to be more elitist and private, as opposed to popular and public. The surrealist, dreamlike images in paintings by Salvador Dali, and early avant-garde films such as Salvador Dali's and Luis Bunuel's *Un Chien Andalou* or *Andalusian Dog* (1929), illustrate these aspects of modernism, as do some experimental dramatic films, such as the begin-

ning of Swedish film director Ingmar Bergman's film *Persona* (1966). Many other European art films and some contemporary music videos are distinctly modernist in approach as well.

Postmodernism

The emergence of digital technologies coincides with the rise of postmodernist films, videos, and audio art. Postmodernism literally means "after" or "beyond" modernism. While modernist art emphasizes the individual artist's self-expression and the purity of artistic form, postmodernist art is anything but pure. It often features a collage or grab bag of past styles and techniques, rather than a pure or simple form. What emerges from this menagerie of styles and grab bag of techniques is not an individual artist's self-expression but rather a hodgepodge of different expressive forms from different periods and artists.

The absence of a single artist as a controlling presence (controlling what a piece of art means or how it should be viewed) encourages the viewer or listener to act with the artwork, to play with it, and re into another form. The artist doesn't control meaning of a postmodernist text; the viewer or listener does. Postmodernist works often question human subjectivity itself. Sometimes they seem to suggest that the world is made of simulations

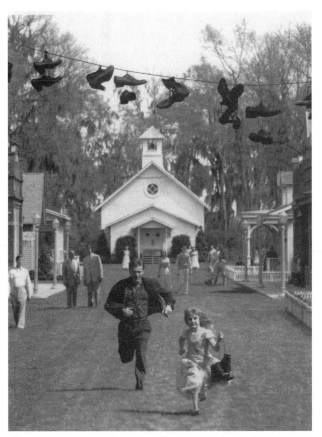

Figure 1.14 A modernist production goes beyond realism to create an artist's symbolic or imaginative world, as is depicted in Tim Burton's production of *Big Fish* in which Ewan McGregor tries to come to an understanding of his past life and relationship with his father. (Courtesy of Columbia Pictures.)

rather than real experiences. Human characters can become indistinguishable from cyborgs in postmodernist films, just as individual artists become less distinguished by their unique styles and somewhat indistinguishable from audiences who create their own texts through viewer/listener free play.

Postmodernist films and television programs often combine popular culture with classical and elite art, mixing a variety of traditionally distinct genres or modes, such as documentary and dramatic fiction, and encouraging viewer and listener interaction with (if not the actual recreation of) art works. Postmodernist art borrows images and sounds from previous popular and classical works of art with which most viewers and listeners are often already familiar. Rather than inventing entirely new and perplexing original forms (modernism) or trying to establish explicit connections to the real world (realism), postmodernist art plays with previously developed images and sounds and recreates a self-contained, playfully simulated world of unoriginal forms, genres, and modes of expression. Interactive multimedia works, such as Peter Gabriel's CD-ROM music

videos, allow viewers and listeners to adjust the volume and remix separate music tracks, creating their own versions of his music. A modernist piece of music would never allow the viewer/listener to freely play in this way with the work of art, since the artwork is presumed to have been perfected and completed by the artist. (See Figure 1.15.)

Postmodernism may be more difficult to define than realism or modernism because it is a more recent development, and it is still evolving. Nonetheless, some of the main characteristics associated with postmodernism are already apparent. These include the production of open-ended works that encourage viewer participation and play, rather than a concern for the human subjectivity of either the individual artist or the main character in a fictional drama or a social actor in a documentary or docudrama. Postmodernist art frequently offers a pastiche or collage of simulated images and sounds drawn from a variety of different modes and genres (both fiction and nonfiction, for example), a feeling of nostalgia for the past, a plundering of old images and sounds from previous works, simulations rather than "real experiences," and a mixture of classical and contemporary forms as well as popular and elite culture.

Combining Aesthetic Approaches

Obviously the three aesthetic movements and choices that have just been described (realism, modernism, and postmodernism) are neither definitive nor exhaustive. Many projects combine aesthetic approaches in various ways. Modernist sequences can be incorporated into realist movies, such as dream sequences in classical Hollywood cinema. Some Hollywood movies, such as *The Lord of the Rings* series (2001–4), *The Triplets of Belleville* (2003), and *Last Samurai* (2003), seem to combine realism with postmodernism. The choice of one aesthetic approach is neither absolute nor irreconcilable with other approaches. But although different approaches can be combined, the decision to combine them should be a matter of conscious choice.

Because aesthetic decisions are basic to different stages of the production process, many of the chapters in this text begin with a discussion of realist, modernist, and postmodernist approaches. This is followed by a discussion of production practices that are relevant to the use of digital and analog technologies. Combined with actual hands-on production experience, this text provides the basic information needed to make valid production decisions with the confidence that many possible alternatives have been explored and the best possible approach and techniques have been selected.

Figure 1.15 A postmodernist production far exceeds realism and modernism by suggesting that the audience must contribute to the production by mixing genres, such as science fiction and hard-boiled detective, as well as other styles. A postmodernist production may question, for example, what it means to be a human by making cyborg simulations indistinguishable from "real" people, such as the character depicted by Harrison Ford in the Ladd Company's production of *Blade Runner*. (Courtesy of the Ladd Company.)

SUMMARY

Production is divided into three stages: preproduction, production, and postproduction. Preproduction designates all forms of planning that take place prior to actual recording, including producing, production management, and writing. Production begins with the director's preparations to record sounds and images. It includes all aspects of sound and image recording. Postproduction refers to the last stage of production, when the editing of recorded images and sounds begins and the completed project is distributed and exhibited.

Digital technology has revolutionized media production and is replacing analog technology in a number of media production areas, but analog technologies, such as film, continue to play important roles in each stage of production. Digital technology has opened up a wide range of fascinating production and postproduction techniques, such as special effects that have begun to alter conventional notions of history and reality. Digital technology significantly reduces, if not eliminates, the degradation of sounds and images when copies are made. It has also blurred traditional distinctions and has brought media technologies closer together.

The histories of film, television, and audio technology are interrelated and overlap. Film is a nineteenth-century technology based on photochemical means. Television and video technology, developed commercially somewhat later, reproduces images by elec-tronic means. Audio technology developed simultaneously with film and television because both visual media eventually required sound to match their pictures. All three media underwent substantial changes during the twentieth century. During the twenty-first century, all media will continue to converge within the realm of a digital format.

Careful advance planning during the preproduction stages is the best way of avoiding negative production experiences. A producer initiates a project by drafting a proposal, obtaining financial support, and attempting to circumvent the operation of Murphy's Law: Anything that can go wrong, will go wrong.

Production can take place either in a studio or on location, again depending on the nature of the events to be recorded.

The production team is usually organized somewhat hierarchically, in the sense that a producer or director is in charge, and everyone is accountable to a staff head, who specializes in a particular area. But to work together effectively, a production team should also be cooperatively organized, so those individual specialists function collectively as a team.

Visualization is the creative process of image and sound construction. Video, film, and multimedia record moving images and sounds. These recordings can be edited. Writers and directors must be skilled at visualization. They must understand the relation between abstract words in a script and the concrete sounds and images that are recorded and edited.

There are three basic aesthetic approaches to media production: realism, modernism, and postmodernism. A realist approach relies on techniques that enhance an illusion of reality, a modernist approach emphasizes the artist's active shaping and manipulation of his or her material, and a postmodernist approach offers a pastiche of simulated images and sounds, questioning human subjectivity and the centrality of the individual artist. The choice of an aesthetic approach guides the selection of specific production techniques.

EXERCISES

1. Find examples of realistic, modernistic, and postmodernistic films. Compare how each tells its story, and describe why each fits in the category you have chosen.

2. Find examples of television/cable programs that fit the three aesthetic categories. Compare how each tells its story, and describe why each fits in the category you have chosen.

3. Using both the Internet and your library, find references to the early development of technologies that led to modern-day motion picture, television, and audio production techniques. Arrange your findings in chronological order.

4. Watch an evening of network programming on one network. Make a list of the programs, and determine by watching whether each program was originally produced on film or video (or totally digitally) and whether the production used a single camera or multiple cameras.

5. Call a local television station and ask to visit the station for a tour. While there, ask if an organizational chart of the station is available, or if someone would explain while you take notes how the station is organized by departments and what each department is responsible for.

6. Do the same as #5 for a recording studio, a film studio, and/or a graphics studio.

ADDITIONAL READINGS

Benedeti, Robert. *From Concept to Screen: An Overview of Film and TV Production.* Boston: Allyn and Bacon, 2002.

Bordwell, David, and Kristin Thompson. *Film Art*, 5th ed. New York: McGraw-Hill, 1996.

Cook, David A. *A History of Narrative Film*, 3rd ed. New York: W.W. Norton & Company, 1996.

Earl, William. "Revolt Against Realism in the Films." *The Journal of Aesthetics and Art Criticism* 27, no. 2 (Winter 1968). Page numbers not available.

Ellis, Jack C. *The Documentary Idea: A Critical History of English-Language Documentary Film and Video.* Englewood Cliffs, NJ: Prentice-Hall, 1989.

Everett, Anna and John T. Caldwell, eds. *New Media: Theories and Practices of Digitexuality.* New York: Routledge, 2003.

Hofstetter, Fred. *Multimedia Literacy.* New York: McGraw-Hill, 1995.

Mast, Gerald, Marshall Cohen, and Leo Braudy. *Film Theory and Criticism*, 4th ed. New York: Oxford University Press, 1992.

Orlik, Peter B. *Electronic Media Criticism: Applied Perspectives*, 2nd ed. Mahwah, NJ: Lawrence Erlbaum Associates, Inc., 2001.

Roberts-Breslin, Jan. *Making Media: Foundations of Sound and Image Production.* Boston: Focal Press, 2003.

Shuman, James E. *Multimedia in Action.* Belmont, CA: Wadsworth Publishing, 1997.

Sterling, Christopher H. and John Michael Kitross. *Stay Tuned: A History of American Broadcasting*, 3rd ed. Mahwah, NJ: Lawrence Erlbaum Associates, Inc., 2002.

Udelson, Joseph H. *The Great Television Race: A History of the American Television Industry, 1925-1941.* Tuscaloosa, AL: University of Alabama Press, 1982.

Wasko, Janet. *Hollywood in the Information Age.* Cambridge: Polity Press, 1994.

2 Producing and Production Management

TOPICS FOR DISCUSSION

- Who is a producer, and what does this person do?
- What is preproduction paperwork, and why is it needed?
- What are the laws, restrictions, and ethics of production?
- What is production management?

INTRODUCTION

A producer is often the only key member of the production team who guides a project through all phases of production, from preproduction planning through postproduction editing and distribution. A producer initiates a project by drafting a proposal, obtaining financial support, assembling the necessary personnel, and then managing and overseeing the entire production process. He or she also ensures that the completed project reaches its target audience and satisfies people who have financially supported it. A producer provides the necessary continuity between one stage of production and the next, and tries to ensure consistency in the final product. While the producer plays an important part in all three production stages, this chapter focuses on the producer's role during preproduction and production. The producer's role during postproduction is covered in the final chapter, Chapter 13, "Distribution and Exhibition."

PRODUCING

The Role of the Producer

A producer is a risk-taker, someone who seizes an idea, runs with it, and convinces others to participate in a project. Producers are creative administrators who act as links between the corporate executives, managers, financial concerns, investors, or distributors who finance video and film productions and the artists who create them. Such productions can require large sums of money, which come in the form of bank loans, outright grants, risk capital, and governmental or corporate "in-house" budget allocations. These productions also require a great deal of logistical planning and administration. Creative artists rarely have the time or the desire to deal with many of these administrative tasks, such as financing, budgeting, scheduling, and overall production management. Producers try to create high-quality products as efficiently as possible.

They know how to turn unappealing or extravagant ideas into workable material and marketable concepts. They understand the diverse needs of creative people, corporate executives, investors, product buyers, and audiences. Producers tread a fine line between the creative talent's need for artistic expression and the necessity of providing concrete returns on production investments.

Good producers must be effective decision-makers and people-managers. A producer's ability to understand and work with many different individuals is constantly tested throughout the entire production process. Ultimately, the production buck stops with the producer, who assumes responsibility for the successful completion of the project. If the production runs over schedule or over budget–that is, beyond the initial guidelines in terms of production time or money–it is the producer who must step in and decide what to do. Should production be terminated, a key individual replaced, or additional time and funds allocated to complete the project? These decisions can be extremely difficult. If a problem develops with a particularly unruly and disruptive actor or staff member, the producer or the director must try to resolve the dispute amicably or take disciplinary action.

Producers often specialize in particular types of programs. Specialists who work with television commercials, dramas, sports news, or interactive multimedia, for example, rarely work outside of their program type because success in one type of production does not guarantee success in another. Producers are further typed into at least four different categories according to the nature and extent of their responsibilities: staff producers, independent producers, executive producers, and producer hyphenates.

Staff producers are employed on a continuing basis by a production company or organization. Producers are often assigned to specific projects in a small video or film production company. Local television station staff producers often work in several areas simultaneously, sometimes floating from news to sports to public affairs. At the network television level, staff producers are assigned to specific divisions, such as news or sports, and they work exclusively within these domains. Staff producers in film often specialize in the production of feature films, educational films, commercials, documentaries, sports films, or industrial films. Unit production managers at major Hollywood studios are staff producers who are intimately involved with and extremely knowledgeable about almost every aspect of production. They are directly involved in production decisions on a daily basis. Staff producers of interactive multimedia productions and computer games coordinate a team of artists, designers, programmers, and writers for a developer or publisher.

Independent producers put together and sell production ideas to studios, film distributors, network and cable television executives, syndicators, and publishers. Independent producers are responsible for the bulk of all theatrically released entertainment films and prime-time television programming. They put together marketable story, staff, and talent packages. An independent producer is not employed on a continuing basis by a film studio or a television network or station. She or he works on a specific project or freelance basis.

Executive producers are often less involved in day-to-day production decisions than other types of producers. They may delegate many production tasks to others and focus on project development and evaluation instead. In television, production executive producers are sometimes legendary figures, such as Norman Lear, Grant Tinker, Michael Crichton, Steven Botchco, or David E. Kelly, who have supervised several productions simultaneously and are

constantly developing and promoting new program concepts and ideas. In feature film production, executive producers vary from people whose participation ensures sufficient funding to peripheral non-participants whose involvement in any aspect of production is minimal. Co-producers of feature films are rarely if ever involved in production in a major way or on a daily basis.

Finally, producer "hyphenates" combine the role of producer with those of writer and/or director. Writer-producer-directors immerse themselves in pre-planning and the day-to-day production process, almost totally controlling the quality of the final product and preserving the integrity of their original idea.

Production Strategies

Producers often rely upon production strategies to help ensure that a project is successful in obtaining necessary funding, fulfilling its purposes, and reaching an audience. The development of a production strategy involves at least four steps:

1) Turning a provocative idea into a funded and marketable media package
2) Defining the goals and objectives of the project
3) Researching the topic
4) Assessing the potential audience

Market Research

Where do media production ideas come from? Creative minds? Obviously creativity is a necessary asset in production, but it is not sufficient in itself to guarantee success. Producers must also be sensitive to the needs, preferences, and desires of potential funding sources, investors, executives, managers, buyers, distribution channels, and audiences. Project ideas can arise from a variety of sources, including personal experiences, such as a chance encounter with an impressive human being, an unusually committed or effective organization, or a compelling social problem. An idea might be generated by a current event in a newspaper; a pre-sold property, such as a successful book or play that suddenly becomes available; a desire to make a statement or to explore a specific issue for the public good; a need expressed by a corporate executive, government administrator, or a consumer or labor group; or a previously successful television program, film, or computer game. Exactly where an idea comes from is not as important (unless it involves copyrighted material whose media rights have already been secured and are unavailable) as what is done with that idea to make it appeal to potential funding sources, distribution channels, and audiences. Successful producers are people who not only develop or recognize good ideas but also know how to package, promote, and execute their ideas and to communicate them to others.

To transform good ideas into funded, marketable, and doable material, producers put together marketable packages featuring components of known or presumed value to reduce the uncertainty that sponsors and investors feel about whether or not a proposed project will be successful. Many people believe that the prior success of a similar venture or previous productions by members of the creative staff enhances the chances of success for a new project. According to this view, a producer, writer, director, or star performer who has recently had successful films or television programs is likely to be successful again. Obtaining production financing for proven talent is always easier than for unproven talent. The prior success or notoriety of the subject of a documentary or of a novel or play upon which a dramatic film or television program is based is also presumed to provide some guarantee of success.

Noncommercial projects initiated by people who have been previously successful are also more likely to receive funding than those undertaken by neophytes, but inexperienced producers can overcome this problem by involving at least a few experienced creative staff members in their project. Previous success in production can be defined in terms of awards, published reviews, specialized showings, and satisfied clients, as well as in terms of profits. In any case, an attractive media idea and package plays on prior success to appease sponsors and partially reduce financial risks inherent in production support and investments.

Unfortunately, producers rarely have the luxury of waiting for prior success of a similar project or property to be amply demonstrated before they initiate a project. Screen rights to novels and plays are often secured prior to publication or staging. A hot topic may have lost its popularity before a project is actually completed due to the long lead time between project initiation and completion. Successful producers anticipate trends almost before they happen, but they are also able to package these new concepts and ideas in traditional ways that help a sponsor or investor to see how appealing or marketable a new concept can be.

Production Goals and Objectives

Defining the goals and objectives for a project begins with the formation of a project idea, which must be refined as it is transformed into workable material.

The importance of defining the goals and objectives of a project cannot be overestimated. (Figure 2.1)

For example, when major film producers and directors David O. Selznick, who had previously produced "Gone With The Wind" (1939), and Alfred Hitchcock, who subsequently directed "Psycho" (1960), vehemently disagreed about how literal the adaptation process, that is, how true to the novel, a film should be, the initial result was a major success, "Rebecca" (1940), which won the Academy Award for Best Picture. But subsequently they produced a complete disaster, "The Paradine Case" (1948). Bitter disagreements over goals, objectives, and methods of producing and directing films led to major headaches and problems for everyone involved in the production process during all of their "collaborations," and despite their early success, they parted ways soon after experiencing failure, and Selznick in fact closed down his production studio (Figure 2.1).

Members of the production team need to be aware of a program's overall objectives and to share common goals to prevent unnecessary conflicts from arising during the production process. Obtaining financial support for a project is much easier when the goals and objectives of the project are clearly specified. Any potential sponsor or funding source wants to know what you are trying to accomplish. If your goals and objectives remain vague and unspecified, your project is unlikely to generate much support. While the goal or objective of a project may be primarily a commercial one, it is rarely exclusively to make money. Project goals may be quite specific, such as winning a particular award, or they may be more general, such as reaching a new level of artistic expression. They may involve a political agenda, such as changing people's minds about an important issue or problem, or motivating concrete actions,

PRODUCTION GOALS & OBJECTIVES

PRODUCTION GOALS (General Assertions and Statements of Purpose)

GOAL #1	
GOAL #2	
GOAL #3	

PRODUCTION OBJECTIVES (Specific, Concrete Anticipated Results)

OBJECTIVE #1	
OBJECTIVE #2	
OBJECTIVE ##	

Figure 2.1 Precisely conceived and researched production goals and objectives keep a production on track and moving toward a complete and finished production.

including voting for a particular candidate or buying a specific product. The goal might be primarily educational, such as teaching students to use a new computer program through the production of an interactive CD. On the other hand, the goal might be to produce pleasure by allowing someone to play a challenging computer game, listen to emotive music on an audio CD, or view a compelling or exciting story on videotape. It might be to increase public appreciation of work undertaken by a fascinating person or a highly committed organization. It might also be to increase public awareness about compelling social problems, such as hunger, disease, and violent conflict at home or abroad, or to serve the needs of children or a minority group for nonviolent entertainment and educational programming.

Whatever the goals and objectives of a project may be, it is important to write them down so that they can be clarified, carefully considered, and discussed prior to developing a script or recording and editing a project. Enumerating the goals and objectives of a project will help to galvanize support and to ensure that everyone on the production team is using the same playbook. It will help to reduce future conflicts and to increase the appeal of a project to potential funding sources.

Researching a topic is another important step in the development of a production strategy. Topic research allows a producer to gather accurate information about a specific film or television topic. Careful research ensures that productions do not misinform. The quality of the research directly affects the integrity of the entire project. A hastily produced, poorly researched production can generate a great deal of antipathy from its audience. Sometimes pressure groups are aroused and legal actions, such as libel suits, are taken against the producer or production company. Careful research can make the difference between promoting misinformation versus carefully examining the key issues and stimulating a reasonable debate. Exciting action and intense, well-acted performances contribute a great deal to the impact and success of any dramatic production, but thorough topic research gives a project significance, depth, and lasting value and promotes the long-term interests of the producer.

Topic research requires imagination and determination. New sources of information are only uncovered with extreme diligence and persistence. Research can involve the collection and inspection of at least four different types of data or material records: written, visual, oral, and digital. Data banks of information are produced daily as vast quantities of information of all types are collected and released in digital form, either on disc, CD-ROM, or through the Internet or various Web sites. Producers or their researchers can save many hours traditionally spent in libraries by using digitized sources. Books, magazines, newspapers, diaries, and private correspondence are written materials that often need to be uncovered, read, and analyzed. Good producers read extensively about their subject in preparation for production. Unlike scholars, producers may perform their research with a broad brush and with little attention to footnotes and minute details in order to get an overall understanding of their topic. This will facilitate the presentation of information in an accessible and logical manner.

Visual records may include photographs, and drawings of relevant settings, props, and costumes may also need to be examined. Actual locations may need to be visited as well. Historical visual and audio records and stock footage may need to be examined. Performing research in archives often requires considerable time and effort. Location scouts may use the World Wide Web (WWW) and electronic mail (e-mail) to provide a rapid method of corresponding with location sources and interviewing subjects without waiting for mail service and/or a telephone response. Stock footage of historical events is expensive, since rights to duplicate this material must be obtained.

It is often important to examine or conduct oral interviews with people who are knowledgeable about specific topics. Interviews might be conducted with actual participants in events or recognized experts in a field. Interview questions should be written down and carefully planned, but the interviewer should not read them, but rather remember them as a guide so that a more lively and spontaneous interview can be recorded. In some cases experts, who are interviewed during preproduction may be retained as consultants throughout the production phase. Sometimes consultants are supplied by specific organizations, such as the American Medical Association, which do not want to be slighted by improper or inaccurate information. In any case, extensive topic research often helps a producer make intelligent production decisions, while impressing potential sponsors and funding sources with her or his knowledge of the subject, adding program depth, and avoiding a variety of ethical pitfalls and problems.

Audience Analysis

An accurate estimate of the size, demographic makeup, and needs of a prospective audience is essential for the development of workable, funded projects and marketable media ideas. What media should a producer use to reach a specific audience?

How large is the potential audience? What size budget is justified? What needs and expectations does a particular audience have? What film or television format should be used? These questions can only be answered when the prospective audience is clearly defined. Even in noncommercial productions, the overall budget must be justified to some degree on the basis of the potential size and demographics of the audience.

AUDIENCE ANALYSIS
- **Choice of Medium**
- **Size of Audience**
- **Budget Justification**
- **Audience Expectations**
- **Choice of Medium Format**

Audiences differ in size and demographics. The age and gender of the members of an audience are often just as important as the overall number of people who will see the production. Television advertisers, for example, often design television commercials to reach specific demographic groups. Even documentary filmmakers, such as George Stoney, who headed the undergraduate production program at New York University for many years, often pretest films on audiences to see how effective they are in generating and maintaining interest and waging arguments. The process of assessing audience preferences for and interest in specific projects has become more scientific in recent years, but it inevitably requires an experienced and knowledgeable producer to interpret and implement research findings.

AUDIENCE DEMOGRAPHICS
- **Age**
- **Gender**
- **Income**
- **Education**
- **Religion**
- **Culture**
- **Language**

Detailed audience information can facilitate later stages of the production process by giving the audience input into production decisions. The nature and preferences of the audience can be used to determine a project's format, subject matter, and structure, as well as its budget. For example, the feature film *The Life and Times of Grizzly Adams* (1975) was targeted specifically for working-class families interested in outdoor-adventure dramas. Everything from the actual locations to specific character types was selected on the basis of audience pretesting. While the artistic merit of using audience-survey research to make production decisions may be questionable, since it can produce a hodgepodge of styles and content rather than a unified work, its success has to some degree validated the technique in the commercial marketplace. It has also proved vital for noncommercial productions, where audience response is a primary measure of program effectiveness. Research can also be used during postproduction to assess the impact and effectiveness of a project. While audience research is no substitute for professional experience, it can give scientific, statistical validity to production decisions that might otherwise be based solely upon less reliable hunches and guesses.

Estimating the size and demographics, for example, the age, gender, and other characteristics, of the potential audience for a prospective media project can be quite complicated. Sometimes a project's potential audience can be estimated from the prior success of similar productions. For example, the A.C. Nielsen and Arbitron ratings for television audiences drawn to previous programming of the same type can be consulted. Television ratings provide audience information in the form of program ratings, shares, and demographic breakdowns for national and regional television markets. *Ratings*, or rankings, refer to the percent of all television households, that is, of all households with a television set, regardless of whether that set is on or off at a particular time, that are tuned to a specific program. If there are 80 million television households and 20 million of them are tuned to a specific program, then that program has a rating of 25, which represents 25 percent of the total television population.

Shares indicate the percent of television households with the television set on at a specific time that are actually watching a specific program. Thus if 20 million households are watching something on television at a particular time and 10 million of those 20 million households are watching the same program, then that program has an audience share of 50, which represents 50 percent of the viewing audience. Demographic breakdowns of the television audience help advertisers and media-time buyers and sellers to target programs for specific audiences. Consulting ratings data about earlier programs of the same general type provides only a rough estimate of the potential drawing power of a future program, since audience interest in that type of programming can increase or decrease with time and repetitive presentations.

Commercial producers and distributors often rely on market research to estimate audience size and the preferences of audiences that might be drawn to a particular project. The title of the project, a list of the key talent, the nature of the subject matter, and a synopsis of the story line, for example, might be given to a test audience, and the audience members' responses can be recorded and evaluated. Research has shown that by far the best predictor of feature film success is advertising penetration, that is, the number of people who have heard about a project, usually through advertising in a variety of media. Other significant predictors of success appear to be the financial success of the director's prior work, the current popularity of specific performers or stars, and the interest generated by basic story lines pretested in written form.

Audience research has been used for a variety of purposes in commercial production. Sometimes prior to production, researchers statistically compare the level of audience interest (the "want-to-see" index) generated by a synopsis, title, or credits of a production to the amount of audience satisfaction resulting from viewing the completed project. A marketing and advertising strategy is often chosen on the basis of this research. A film that generates a great deal of audience interest prior to production, but little audience satisfaction after viewing a prerelease screening of the completed film, might be marketed somewhat differently from a film that generates little interest initially but is well received in completed form. The former might be marketed with an advertising blitz and released to many theaters before "word of mouth" destroys it at the box office, while the latter might be marketed more slowly to allow word of mouth to build gradually.

Some television programs and commercials will be dropped and others aired solely on the basis of audience pretesting. Story lines, character portrayals, and editing are sometimes changed after audience testing. Advertising agencies often test several versions of a commercial on sample audiences before selecting the version to be aired. A local news program may be continuously subjected to audience survey research in an attempt to discover ways to increase its ratings or share. A sponsor or executive administrator may desire concrete evidence of communication effectiveness and positive viewer reaction after a noncommercial production has been completed.

Audience research has to be recognized as an important element in the production process. While it is no substitute for professional experience and artistic ability, research nonetheless can provide some insurance against undertaking expensive projects that have no likelihood of reaching target audiences or generating profits. Informal assessments of viewer responses to media products, such as viewer letters of praise or interest, or having audiences fill out questionnaires after viewing, can provide some index of success. Even a film or video project whose main purpose is self-expression and aesthetic pleasure can benefit from or be harmed by audience response in the form of published criticism.

Noncommercial audience research often focuses on assessments of audience needs and program effectiveness. A project that is not designed to make money often justifies production costs on the basis of corporate, government, or cultural needs, as well as audience preferences and size. Sponsors need to have some assurance that the program will effectively reach the target audience and convey its message. Audience pretesting can help to determine the best format for conveying information and reaching the audience. Successful children's programs are often based on audience research that assures program effectiveness. For example, the fast-paced, humorous instructional style of *Sesame Street*, which mirrors television commercials and comedy programs, was based on exhaustive audience research. Whether it is used during preproduction or postproduction, audience research can strengthen a program and widen its appeal.

Proposal Writing

A proposal is a written document designed to help raise money and obtain other kinds of support for a project. It may be submitted to a group of investors, a private foundation, or a government agency, such as the National Endowment for the Arts or a regional, state, or local arts council. An effective proposal generates enthusiastic support. It should be written in clear and engaging language that any nonspecialist can understand, but it should also be sufficiently thorough to meet the expectations of media and subject area specialists.

Good proposals usually contain the following elements: a provocative opening statement of purpose; a rationale of the need for such a project; its structure, organization, and approach; a preliminary budget and schedule; specific information concerning the anticipated audiences and the means of reaching them; and short, paragraph-length summaries of the careers of the producer, director, and other key creative personnel. Proposals are sometimes accompanied by videotape "show reels" containing clips from previously successful works by members of the creative staff (Figure 2.2).

The opening statement of purpose for any proposal is extremely important. It should provide a concise summary of the goals and objectives of your project. It should also generate interest and enthusiastic support. Try to imagine that you have just read about 100 proposals, and, although some of them are

SAMPLE PROPOSAL FORMAT

TITLE:	Safety Training	PAGE: 1
WRITER:	T. Bartlett	LENGTH: 10 mins
CLIENT:	Mountain Industries	DATA: 10-10-96

Rivers and Streams Productions, Inc. will produce a ten minute, color videotape to be used as a training medium for new and present employees of Mountain Industries. The tape will target specific safety procedures necessary to be followed in the unique operation of logging in the mountains of Montana. The tape will emphasize personal safety actions and procedures required by the Occupational Safety and Health Administration.

The shooting schedule will last for ten days, weather and other acts of nature not withstanding. Postproduction will last for four weeks following the completion of principle videography. Taping will start within two weeks of final script approval. Research and preparing of the treatment will last three weeks following the acceptance of the proposal. The final script will be prepared within three weeks of acceptance of the proposed treatment.

The budget will be approximately $35,000.00, depending on specific technical requirements of the script. Because the script calls for a series of dangerous actions requiring stunt actors and technicians, some allowances for costs and shooting overruns may be required.

The format will be semi-documentary/instructional with the tape narrated and techniques explained by an actor representing a skilled and knowledgeable logger. Both incorrect and correct operational procedures will be illustrated. Employees, equipment, and facilities of Mountain Industries logging operation will be required for the production of this tape.

Figure 2.2 A proposal is a sales tool that needs to be written clearly and to describe completely the intended project, including all critical or unusual aspects of the production involvement in this project.

stimulating, you are becoming quite bored with the whole process. Suddenly something hits you like a breath of fresh air. One proposal stands out above the others. The writer is particularly clever, insightful, or committed. The proposal generates a contagious feeling of excitement. This is what you must try to accomplish in your opening statement of purpose. What is it that has stimulated your own interest? Now encapsulate this feeling and communicate it to someone else by putting it into powerful prose that relies upon active rather than passive verbs in every sentence.

The opening statement usually includes a tentative title for the project. It also identifies the subject matter and convinces the reader of its importance and impact, often by providing a taste and flavor of the story that will unfold, including at least a hint of the conflicting forces and elements of dramatic structure that stimulate and propel it. Try to specify what you want your project to accomplish and who you hope will be moved by it.

What important need justifies the expenditure of the money and resources required to undertake and complete your project? Will it serve the public good? How? Will it be commercially successful? Why? Does it help to solve a social problem or promote greater understanding among and between different groups of people? Does it have a particular appeal to young or old people?

Proposal writers often provide some essential background information so that nonspecialists can begin to understand why this need is so compelling. Background statements provide the reader with sufficient grounding in a subject area to be able to understand and accept a basic premise and to make informed judgments concerning the importance, feasibility, and effectiveness of your project. They should be very concise, providing basic and essential information. Writers use computers to access data and information sources during proposal writing to gather accurate and comprehensive information. Two of the resources are Lexis and Nexis. Lexis is a legal database, containing court cases and other legal information in the United States. Nexis is a news retrieval system, listing most major newspaper, magazine, and newsletter contents. Both systems are designed for searching under a variety of methods to quickly reach the specific information that the research requires.

The approach, organization, and structure of a proposal indicate how you plan to tell your story and from whose point of view. For example, you might classify your project as a serious drama about an imminent separation and divorce, told from a child's view, or as a documentary portrait of an artist exploring an upbeat former stage designer's views on his pending blindness as he creates wall hangings and fabric designs that are enriched by his newly stimulated tactile senses. A documentary may consist of vérité sequences, "talking-head" interviews, and traditional voiceover narration. Or it may present dramatic reenactments of what "witnesses" convinced themselves happened at a violent crime scene, such as those presented in Errol Morris's *The Thin Blue Line*. Each of these descriptions of a project characterizes its approach and structure.

The anticipated audience may be quite narrow or very broad, but it should be described in specific terms. The primary audience for a documentary might be a specific ethnic group, such as African-American communities in northern urban areas. A dramatic Appalachian folktale might be aimed at young Anglo-American teenage girls. In the latter case, the means of reaching that audience, or the specific distribution channel, might be motion picture theaters, prime-time public television, or afternoon commercial television. The former project might be designed for prime-time commercial or public television broadcast, as well as for rental to schools and universities through a nontheatrical distributor.

A proposal should also contain short biographies of the primary creative staff, written in paragraph form. These should highlight previous productions that are most closely related in content and approach to the project being proposed. Citing earlier works that have received major awards or national distribution will encourage potential funding sources to believe that prior success will ensure continued success. If you have a limited track record yourself, you should enlist the participation and support of creative staff members who have extensive experience and impressive track records, if at all possible. Letters of endorsement and support from highly regarded individuals, especially from people with whom the funding source is already familiar, should also be included with a proposal whenever possible. You should also try to make personal contact with the funding source, which, one hopes, will lead to an oral presentation of your project proposal. Writers use computers to prepare all written preproduction materials, such as proposals, treatments, and scripts. A computer allows the writer flexibility to make changes, deletions, and additions quickly and efficiently. Working in the digital domain allows information to be distributed to all involved personnel in either digital or hard-copy form (Figure 2.3).

Project Presentations

A producer who has interested a potential funding source usually tries to make a personal, face-to-face, oral presentation to the investor, sponsor, or executive who is considering funding the project. Sometimes the

PROPOSAL REQUIREMENTS

- Concise statement – indicate what you hope to say

- Background and need (Purpose and Objectives)

- Your approach, structure, and style

- Preliminary budget

- Shooting schedule

- Equipment list

- Summary of credits, experiences

TREATMENT REQUIREMENTS

- Written in third person, present tense

- Describe all action sequences

- Describe main characters

- Indicate conflicts and resolutions

- List stylistic features

- Limit dialog

Figure 2.3 A proposal and a treatment together are key tools that a producer uses to sell a production in order to gain financing. They must be concise and accurate to be understood by a nontechnical client.

presentation will be made over lunch or dinner. At other times it will be a more formal presentation in an office. At the very least, it will consist of a telephone conversation. Regardless of the setting, it is essential that the producer capitalize on any interest generated by a written proposal during the presentation. A producer who lacks enthusiasm in presenting his or her project to a prospective sponsor or investor is destined to fail. Sometimes the acceptance of a dramatic project hinges on the availability of a well-known creative staff member or star performer. If a producer has some well-known talent under contract before the face-to-face presentation, that presentation is more likely to solidify funding support. The presentation also offers a producer the opportunity to present additional, less fully developed, future project ideas to a funding source, to gauge his or her interest, and to make adjustments later based on some of the funding source's reactions and recommendations. You should always go to a "pitch" or presentation with another idea in your back pocket, just in case you are given the opportunity to present it.

Legal Rights and Concerns

Producers are often involved in legal matters, many of which require the involvement of a qualified enter-tainment lawyer. Music and written materials are usually protected by copyright. Any use of copyrighted materials is usually secured on the basis of a royalty fee that is paid to the owner of this property. Legal releases free the producer from threat of lawsuits from people who appear in a film or television program, and must be secured before that work is publicly exhibited. Private citizens can sue for libel, slander, invasion of privacy, or defamation of character if they believe they have been unfairly portrayed. The law is somewhat different for public figures, but they are still protected to some extent, and, as noted earlier, producers must exercise great care in the treatment of human subjects to avoid lengthy and expensive legal actions. The large number of legal services that are often required for commercial production has resulted in legal specialists, known as entertainment lawyers, who cater to the specific needs of the industry.

Producers are generally responsible for obtaining permissions and releases. Permissions to use personal property and copyrighted works, such as specific locations and music, require negotiations with the property owners. For example, a student who wishes to use a piece of popular music in a film or video needs to obtain permission from both the owner of the musical recording or CD, such as Sony music, AND the publisher of the music, such as ASCAP or BMI. Personal releases signed by people appearing in the film or video inhibit subsequent legal suits brought by them against the producer, especially when they are dissatisfied with the final product or outcome.

Some producers maintain their own music libraries, so that they do not have to commission expensive original music for every production need. These music libraries are collections of musical recordings that are available from organizations such as the American Society of Composers, Authors, and Publishers (ASCAP) and Broadcast Music Incorporated (BMI). These music recordings on CDs or digital tape require royalty payments in the form of needle-drop fees, which simply means that every time a cut from the CD or tape is used, a specific fee must be paid, regardless of how long the recording runs. Production music libraries are available on CD, Audio DVD, digital and analog tape. Regardless of the medium, including downloading from the Internet, the needle-drop fee still applies.

Unions, Guilds, and Nonunion Working Conditions

Talent and technicians in many states are protected by union or guild contracts that have been worked out with major producers and production companies. Union or guild-negotiated contracts specify salary scales, working conditions and policies, and many other factors, such as residual payments. The unions or guilds with which a producer may work, or at least honor in terms of salary and working conditions, represent the highest level of professionals in the entertainment industry.

Some states, of course, have right-to-work laws, which prohibit the formation of completely closed shops; that is, they prevent unions from requiring all workers to join their union, pay dues, and abide by union-negotiated contracts. Texas and Florida are examples of such states.

MEDIA GUILDS and UNIONS

- AFTRA   American Federation of Radio and TV Artists
- SAG   Screen Actors Guild
- WGA   Writers Guild of America
- DGA   Directors Guild of America
- AFM   American Federation of Musicians
- IATSE   International Alliance of Theatrical & Stage Employees
- NABET   National Association of Broadcast Employees and Technicians
- IBEW   International Brotherhood of Electrical Workers

Production in most metropolitan areas is heavily unionized, especially at the highest levels of production, such as network and broadcast station television, feature films, and 35mm film commercials. In these areas, salary levels must meet or exceed certain specified minimum levels. A union member who fails to abide by these conditions and works for less pay is vulnerable to disciplinary fines or expulsion from the union, and the producer or production company may have to renegotiate a union contract, since its violation of the agreement makes the document null and void. In right-to-work states, union contracts of this type do not always exist, and salaries and working conditions are often negotiated on an individual basis.

Nonunion productions are often difficult to distribute or air at the highest, most lucrative levels. It is well known, for example, that the major Hollywood feature film distributors cannot purchase or distribute more than one nonunion-produced film per year without jeopardizing their union contracts. Most producers of feature films and network television programs must face the added costs of union salary scales during production or accept the added difficulties of finding an effective means of national distribution. Although the highest levels of television and film production are heavily unionized, except in right-to-work states, a great deal of commercial and noncommercial production is accomplished without union talent and crews throughout the country. Much public, cable, local, corporate, government, educational, and religious television and film production takes place in nonunion or partially unionized work environments. It is often easier to obtain initial production experience and employment in these nonunionized production settings.

The "illusion of reality" inherent in nonfiction programming and films, it has been argued, gives television and film producers the power to shape as well as reflect public opinion. Some nonfiction programming, such as network news broadcasts, functions as a primary source of public information about current events. Since nonfiction media producers can influence public opinion, they have an ethical responsibility not to intentionally mislead the public. The fact that many nonfiction film and television producers are concerned with making a profit as well as performing a useful social function often means that individuals will be tempted to compromise their ethical responsibilities. Although it is true that nonfiction works must have entertainment or dramatic value to attract audiences and prove cost-effective, there is a point at which a shortsighted pursuit of profit forces abandonment of long-term social goals and values. Self-serving creators of nonfiction programming have the potential to do harm to individuals and our democratic institutions. The Federal Communications Commission (FCC) attempts to ensure that broadcasters operate in "the public interest, convenience, and necessity." The concept of equal time, requiring broadcasters to provide equal time for presenting alternative points of view, is an attempt to compensate for limited channels of television information.

Private citizens are protected from media abuse by the possibility of bringing libel, slander, or invasion of privacy suits. Documentary filmmakers, for example, must obtain written permission (releases) from private citizens before they can publicly exhibit television or film recordings of them. Public figures are less well protected than private citizens, and even private citizens who are involved in bona fide, public news events may legally be filmed or taped without their permission. Generally speaking, in a court of law public figures need to prove a producer's "intent" to do them harm, but private citizens only need to demonstrate a harmful "effect."

Beyond the legal and public policy limitations and implications of their work, writers and producers of films and television programs have an ethical responsibility to use the "illusion of reality" inherent in nonfiction and fiction formats wisely and to treat their human and nonhuman subjects fairly. From a production standpoint, documentary and news people must be concerned about the potentially negative effects a publicly exhibited work may have on the people who are photographed or recorded. What is done to a human being when his or her picture is shown to thousands or millions of viewers, especially when that person is a private citizen rather than a public figure?

Lance Loud, the gay son who appeared along with the rest of his family before a national public television audience when *An American Family* (1973) was broadcast on PBS, made a public exhibition of coming out of the closet. In 2001, PBS broadcast a follow-up after Lance had died of AIDS, entitled *"Lance Loud! A Death in an American Family,"* which explored some of the benefits and burdens of being publicly exposed, as well as the ethical implications of the earlier documentary. Ross McElwee's probing and insightful but also highly personal explorations of Southern culture, such as *Sherman's March* (1986) [his most recent Southern adventure is entitled *Bright Leaves* (2003)], sometimes exposed Southern women to possible humiliation or embarrassment as he pursued romantic relationships with them on camera. However, some of McElwee's documentary subjects have been performers who were actively seeking exposure and public recognition. In the latter cases, who was using whom? Are we talking about exploitation or the pursuit of mutual self-interest?

Other questions to consider include, how are releases to use the images of private citizens obtained? Are people coerced into signing a release, or do they freely choose to be publicly exhibited? Does the unannounced appearance of a news or documentary camera crew at a private citizen's home or office constitute a form of coercion? Does the subject's initial permission allow the producer or editor to use the recordings in any manner that he or she sees fit, or does a writer, editor, director, or producer have some responsibility to show the completed work to the subject before it is publicly shown, so that a follow-up permission can be obtained? These are ethical questions that should concern documentary and news writers, directors, and producers, who must weigh the public's right to know against the citizen's right to privacy. These questions frequently arise in many different types of nonfiction programming, not only documentaries and news stories, but also commercials and educational programming.

PRODUCTION MANAGEMENT

Producers are usually responsible for production management. Production management includes the supervision, acquisition, use, and scheduling of the production staff, equipment, and facilities. The producer, or another member of the staff under the producer's direction, such as a production manager for a major film studio (often called a unit production manager or unit manager) breaks a script down according to its component locations and settings. The personnel and facilities needed for each scene are easily specified by an experienced individual who is intimately familiar with essential production equipment needs, budget limitations, personnel contracts, and salary scales.

Script Breakdown

A script breakdown helps a producer estimate and follow realistic schedules and budgets by providing a complete record of all equipment, personnel, and facilities needed for every scene or sequence. It also makes it possible to shoot the production efficiently out of continuity, that is, ignoring the chronology of sequences in the script and shooting all the scenes that take place in one setting at the same time, regardless of where they will appear in the finished product. This procedure is obviously more efficient than returning to the same settings or locations several times in the course of production. After the script has been broken down according to its settings and locations, breakdown sheets are filled out. Each sheet lists the cast members, staff, sets, props, costumes, and equipment needed at one setting or location. An overall shooting schedule and equipment and personnel list can be made and total costs estimated from all the breakdown sheets put together. All of the production management forms are now available as computer programs, allowing for such forms to be manipulated as easily as any word processing program. Shooting schedules, script breakdowns, production reports, and budgets all may be processed in a digital format (Figure 2.4).

Shooting Schedule

A shooting schedule indicates the total number of days of recording that will actually be required to complete the project. Shooting schedule information is often assembled using a computer program that segments a schedule into units of one day's shooting at a specific location or studio. An individual segment indicates all major personnel and equipment needs for one day at one place. The segments can be moved around if the production schedule must be altered. Since shooting is scheduled primarily on the basis of scenes and locations, the segments for all the days of shooting of the same scene or location usually appear sequentially on a schedule board.

The expense or lack of availability of key production personnel at a certain period can compli-

SCRIPT BREAKDOWN

PRODUCTION TITLE _____ **PAGE:** _____

SET: _____ **SEQUENCE:** _____

SOUND: _____ **SILENT:** ____ **LOCATION** ____ **DAY/NIGHT:** _____

CAST	SCENE NUMBERS & SYNOPSIS
WARDROBE	
SPECIAL EFFECTS & CONSTRUCTION	**SET DRESSING & PROPS**
MUSIC	**MISCELLANEOUS**

Figure 2.4 The script breakdown form needs to indicate everything that will be used on a production during a specific shooting period, usually a day or a single location.

cate scheduling, sometimes forcing a producer to return to a location or studio more than once during actual production. Once the shooting schedule is finalized, the production schedule for a feature film at a major studio, for example, can be fitted into a master production schedule governing a production company's overall use of facilities and personnel for several simultaneous or overlapping projects. Scheduling computer software can generate as many hard copies as needed and allow instantaneous changes to be made in production scheduling (Figure 2.5).

Production Budget

Production budgets are usually divided into above-the-line and below-the-line costs. *Above-the-line* costs include the salaries of the creative staff members, such as the producer, the director, the designer (in interactive multimedia production), and the scriptwriter, and the fees paid to performers or talent, such as actors or narrators. *Below-the-line* costs cover technical facilities, equipment, and personnel, such as production engineers and crew. When below-the-line costs are approximately equal to above-the-line costs, the production values, or overall level of sophistication of the equipment and crew, are usually appropriate for the investment in creative talent.

Running time, the total duration (as well as the complexity) of a completed project, is an important determinant of overall budget. While it is generally true that longer running times require larger budgets, the case of high-budget, network-level television commercials suggests that there are some exceptions to this rule. Running times for specific types of programs are often standardized. A public television program might run for about twenty-six or fifty-two minutes, whereas the same program would be only about twenty-three or forty-six minutes long if it were to be commercially broadcast, to allow time for the commercials. Theatrical films, those that are shown in commercial theaters, are rarely more than three hours in duration, because it is difficult for a theater owner to show films longer than this more than twice a day: once in the afternoon and once in the evening. Film length can directly affect box-office revenues.

Shooting ratios represent the ratio of footage shot during production to footage actually used in the final edited version. Such ratios vary considerably from format to format. Shooting ratios for a cinema verité, a documentary approach in which a single camera is used to record unstaged events, can range anywhere from 20:1 to more than 100:1 of recorded material shot to material used. An efficiently produced, sponsored film or videotape, on the other hand, may be produced at a 4:1 or 5:1 shooting ratio

SHOOTING SCHEDULE				

DATE:_____

DIRECTOR: PROD.NO.:   PROD. TITLE:

Date	No. of Days	Name of Set & Scene Numbers	Cast	Location

Figure 2.5 The shooting schedule form lists the key requirements for an entire production broken down by shooting days or portions of days if more than one location is scheduled in any one day.

of footage shot to footage used. An average feature film or television action drama requires a shooting ratio of 15:1 or more. Television commercials can easily run up shooting ratios as high as 50:1 or more. In some categories, such as certain soft drink commercials, as much as 50,000 feet of 35mm film may be originally exposed in order to produce just 45 feet (thirty seconds) of final product.

SHOOTING RATIOS

FOOTAGE SHOT :	FOOTAGE USED
• Sponsored Film/Video	4:1 – 5:1
• Feature or Drama	15:1 – 20:1
• Documentary	20:1 – 100:1
• Commercials	50:1 – 1,000:1

Producers must determine the exact cost of almost every production item, from equipment rental or purchase to union salary scales, talent residuals, and copyright royalty fees. Television and film equipment can be rented from businesses that specialize in these services, or it can be purchased by a studio or individual and amortized, that is, depreciated in value for tax purposes on a yearly basis over the period of time that it is actually used. *Residuals* are payments that performers and talent receive for repeat uses of productions in which they appear that continue to earn money (Figure 2.6).

Every final budget should include a contingency fund that represents from 10 percent to 30 percent of the estimated budget. The contingency fund permits some latitude for error, which can arise in a number of areas, for unpredictable circumstances such as inclement weather that delays production, and for talent or labor difficulties. A budget that does not include a contingency fund is unlikely to attract any but the most naive sponsors or investors.

There are many different ways to organize and structure production personnel and the production process, but most approaches can be placed somewhere along a continuum from a strict hierarchy to a loose cooperative. A hierarchical model is basically a pyramid structure. Authority flows downward from the producer to the director and other members of the production team. In short, everyone has an immediate supervisor who is responsible for making production decisions. These decisions flow downward from the top. A cooperative model divides production tasks and responsibilities equally among each of the various areas of specialization. A different individual or group is responsible for each aspect of production, and all decisions are made cooperatively and collectively within and between different divisions.

Few actual production situations are exclusively hierarchical or cooperative in approach. Television

and film production is necessarily a cooperative, collective process to some extent. In large-scale productions, specialization forces producers and directors to delegate responsibility to experts, whose cooperation and creative innovation is essential to the completion of a quality product. But media production is rarely a purely democratic art. Most productions are organized somewhat hierarchically around the funding source or the producer, who represents that source. Responsibility for daily decisions is frequently delegated to the director, and by the director to specialists in each area, such as the stage manager, the art director, and the lighting director. The producer and the director must coordinate and supervise the overall production. They must create an effective communication network that ensures that information flows freely from the bottom up as well as from the top down.

One means of ensuring adequate communication among the various staff and crew members is to schedule regular production meetings before, during, and after actual production. Coordinating the overall production minimizes the risk that continuity will be lost, that costumes will clash with sets, that lighting will be inappropriate to the mood of a particular scene, or that staff members will simply misunderstand the overall purpose and design of the production. Involving people in production decision-making encourages their support and cooperation. A production meeting may also require some exercise of authority on the part of the producer or director to ensure production efficiency and consistency. In general, the more time allocated to production meetings (provided that these are not simply drink fests or "bull sessions"), the less time and money the production team will later need to spend on costly reshooting.

Producers must constantly evaluate the efficacy of procedures being used in production. Short-term evaluations focus on gathering daily information. The producer fills out daily production reports, based on information received from each production area. Accurate records are kept for financial purposes, and some secretarial or clerical skills are essential. The forms to be filled out concerning a feature film production, for example, are almost endless. There are daily call sheets, weekly budget summaries, revised shooting schedules, lab reports, and work orders. The producer must supervise a staff of assistants and secretaries who are able to organize and maintain production records and quickly respond to daily production needs. Long-term evaluations focus on applications to future projects.

The producer often works in concert with the director in casting the major talent for a specific production. Many variables must be considered before

```
                              PRODUCTION  BUDGET
        TITLE:                DATE:
        PRODUCER:             DIRECTOR:
        CLIENT:               PHONE:
        ADDRESS:              MEDIUM:          FORMAT:
        CONTACT:              PHONE:
        ALTERNATE:            PHONE:


   1. SCRIPT (Rights, research, writing, duplication)          _____

   2. STAGING (Sets, costumes, location fees, props)           _____

   3. EQUIPMENT (Rental, lease, use fees)                      _____

   4. SPECIAL EQUIPMENT (Mounts, aerials, submarine)           _____

   5. RAWSTOCK                                                 _____

   6. DUPING (Time code copies, off-line copies)              _____

   7. AUDIO (Effects, fees, rights, sweetening, looping, etc.) _____

   8. MUSIC (Fees, rights, performance)                        _____

   9. GRAPHICS (Titles, animation, art)                        _____

  10. EDITING                                                  _____

  11. PERSONNEL:    Staff      _____
                    Crew       _____
                    Talent     _____                      _____

  12. TRAVEL (Transportation, lodging, per diem)               _____

  13. DISTRIBUTION (Dubs, promotion)                           _____

  14. POSTAGE/INSURANCE                                        _____

  15. OTHER                                                    _____


                                            SUB-TOTAL          _____
        OVERHEAD        _____  0

        CONTINGENCY     _____  0
                                            GRAND TOTAL        _____
```

Figure 2.6 The production budget form must indicate all costs, regardless of how small, and if unknown, a professional estimate must be made. This is the summary page; each of the categories indicated necessitates one or more pages to include every category of funds required for the production.

casting decisions are made. Selections from the available talent pool are sometimes suggested by individual agents, but actors are finally selected and tested at auditions, in which they read segments of the script in the presence of the director, the producer, and sometimes the casting director. The actor's appearance, voice quality, talent, and salary have to be carefully considered. Sometimes an inexperienced actor or

"real" person from the actual locale will offer a more authentic portrayal than a professional actor.

Producers often consider the box-office appeal (theatrical film popularity) or TVQ (television quotient, an index of popularity that is based on the star's fame and popularity and that is used by television networks) of specific star performers as a means of justifying the added expense of acquiring proven talent. Directors are often more concerned about aesthetic values, such as whether or not a particular actor or individual is perfectly right or natural for the role, than is the producer, who also worries about salaries and box-office appeal. The producer is often the funding source's sole representative during production and must therefore consider many financial, as well as aesthetic, factors.

Staff producers in small corporate, government, educational, and local cable television production units function much the same way as other producers. Their budgets may be smaller, and the people they work with are fewer in number, but the same basic skills are required. To illustrate the fact that all producers perform essentially the same role, let us consider a student production made in an academic setting. A student who is producing an assigned project for a grade must obtain funding for the project, either by earning the money, negotiating with parents, or finding a sponsor who can use the finished product. The student producer must procure the necessary equipment, supplies, and personnel to make the best possible film or video project with limited resources. Scheduling the production and acquiring talent within an academic environment is often extremely difficult, since students have different class schedules and responsibilities.

Once the actual shooting is scheduled, the weather may not cooperate and the shoot may have to be rescheduled. Perhaps special costumes or props are needed, and the student must undertake delicate negotiations with the drama department or the head of buildings and grounds on campus. If the work is to be publicly screened or used on a local cable channel, the producer must be sure to pay all copyright fees for prerecorded music or commission original music from a friend in the music department. Release forms should be obtained from people who appear in a work that will be publicly exhibited. Finally, when the project is finished, the student must evaluate feedback from a number of people, including an instructor's unexpectedly high or low grade. The producer, then, has to be an effective supervisor of people, an administrator, a salesperson, a sensitive but objective critic, and, above all, a good fund raiser and money manager. These diverse skills, which combine business acumen and organizational ability with creativity and sensitivity to people, are not plentiful in the profession, nor are they easily acquired. Good producers should be recognized for their unique value to both the artistic and the business sides of the production process.

SUMMARY

Producers plan, organize, and supervise the production process from the initial idea to its eventual dis-tribution and exhibition. Producers adopt conscious production strategies to turn creative ideas into marketable concepts. A production strategy involves at least four steps: generating funded and workable ideas, defining the goals and objectives of the project, researching the topic, and assessing the potential audience. Producers must also estimate the production budget and make a proposal to a potential source of funding during a face-to-face presentation of the project's ideas and goals.

Effective producers possess a variety of supervisory skills, from the ability to manage people and resolve disputes, to strong organizational skills, which facilitate the flow and recording of information as well as budgetary decisions. Production team interaction can be structured hierarchically and/or cooperatively. Together with the director, the producer becomes involved in casting decisions. The producer is frequently the sponsor's or investor's sole representative during actual production.

Production management involves breaking down the script into its component parts so that the project can be shot cost-effectively out of continuity and coordinating the use of facilities, personnel, and equipment. Script breakdown sheets aid in the preparation of a budget and the scheduling of production facilities and personnel.

EXERCISES

1. Rent four movies. Watch each until the end credits have finished. List the number of producers and their titles, including associate and assistant producers for each production. Also list the first assistant director(s), since they are responsible to the producers.

2. Watch four major television programs, and list the producers, associate, and assistant producers on each production. Compare the number with your list of movie producers from question 1.

3. Write a concept of a production that you would like to produce. Create a budget. Decide where you can get funding, and attempt to do so. If unsuccessful, decide what was wrong with your approach to gaining funding.

4. Find a complete script of a movie (some are available on the Web). Break down the script based on how you would organize the shooting of the script.

5. For the exercise of question 4, decide what would be the most efficient order in which to shoot

the scenes and how to most efficiently use your cast and crew.

6. Hold a casting call among your friends and fellow students. Cast the script above as objectively as possible. Keep in mind that the perfect cast might not exist, and create the best choices you can.

ADDITIONAL READINGS

Albarran, Alan B. and Angel Areese. *Time and Media Markets*. Mahwah, NJ: Lawrence Erlbaum & Associates, Inc., 2003.

Alberstat, Philip. *Independent Producer's Guide to Film and TV Contracts*. Boston: Focal Press, 1999.

Alberstat, Philip, ed. *Law and the Media*, 4th ed. Boston: Focal Press, 2001.

Block, Peter, William Houseley, and Ron Southwell. *Managing in the Media*. Boston: Focal Press, 2001.

Cartwright, Steve R., and G. Phillip Cartwright. *Designing and Producing Media-Based Training*. Boston: Focal Press, 1999.

Chater, Kathy. *Research for Media Production*. Boston: Focal Press, 2001.

Cleve, Bastian. *Film Production Management*. Boston: Focal Press, 1999.

Curran, Trisha. *Financing Your Film: A Guide for Independent Filmmakers and Producers*. New York: Praeger, 1986.

DiZazzo, Ray. *Corporate Media Production*. Boston: Focal Press, 2000.

Gates, Richard. *Production Management for Film and Video*, 3rd ed. Boston: Focal Press,1999.

Gripsrud, Justein. *Understanding Media Culture*. New York: Oxford University Press, 2002.

Jacobs, Bob. *The Independent Video Producer*. Boston: Focal Press, 1999.

Kindem, Gorham. *The American Movie Industry*. Carbondale, IL: Southern Illinois University Press, 1982.

Kindem, Gorham, ed. *The International Movie Industry*. Carbondale, IL: Southern Illinois University Press, 2000.

Koster, Robert. *The On Production Budget Book*. Boston: Focal Press, 1997.

Lazarus, Paul N. *The Film Producer: A Handbook for Producing*, 2nd ed. New York: St. Martin's Press, 1992.

Lee, John J., Jr. *The Producer's Business Handbook*. Boston: Focal Press, 2000.

Pryluck, Calvin. "Ultimately We Are All Outsiders: The Ethics of Documentary Filming." *Journal of Film and Video* 28, no. 1:21–29.

Radford, Marie L., Susan B. Barnes, and Linda R. Barr. *Web Research: Selecting, Evaluating, and Citing*. Boston: Allyn and Bacon, 2002

Rosenthal, Alan. *Writing, Directing, and Producing Documentary Films*, 3rd ed. Carbondale, IL: Southern Illinois University Press, 2002.

Singleton, Ralph S. *Film Budgeting: Or, How Much Will It Cost to Shoot Your Movie?* Los Angeles, CA: Lone Eagle Publishing, 1996.

Stone, Chris, and David Goggin. *Audio Recording for Profit: The Sound of Money*. Boston: Focal Press, 2000.

Warnick, Barbara. *Critical Literacy in a Digital Era*. Mahwah, NJ: Lawrence Earlbaum and Associates, Inc., 2002.

Weise, Michael. *Film and Video Budgets*. Boston: Focal Press, 2001.

3 Scriptwriting

INTRODUCTION

Scriptwriting can be divided into two basic categories: fiction and nonfiction. Many feature films, television series, miniseries, serials, made-for-TV movies, and interactive games originated from works of fiction, and most documentaries, news programs, commercials, corporate videos, and interactive educational or training productions are works of nonfiction. Fiction scripts generally present dramatic stories imaginatively invented by the scriptwriter. Nonfiction scripts often convey information or rhetorical arguments concerning various topics regarding issues and actual historical events.

The line separating fiction from nonfiction is not always clear and distinct, however. Some projects fall into a gray area between the two. For example, historical dramas and docudramas are often based upon actual events, and some documentaries involve staged or dramatized reenactments. Dramatic and narrative structures associated with fiction are sometimes relevant to the presentation of historical or contemporary events in works of nonfiction, and rhetorical structures associated with nonfiction are sometimes relevant to the presentation of characters and themes in fiction.

Every scriptwriter should be familiar with the basic elements of both fiction and nonfiction writing. Principles of dramatic structure that are used in fiction may also be applicable to the development of audience interest in a documentary or news story. Principles of rhetorical persuasion and expository structures used in documentaries and commercials can be helpful in terms of presenting a social issue or problem in a dramatic production, such as a children's afternoon special program or a made-for-TV movie.

This chapter provides an introduction to visual thinking and a sequential overview of the scriptwriting process. It also examines some of the ways in which fiction and nonfiction scripts can be effectively organized. The focus is on elements of dramatic, narrative, rhetorical, and expository structure, which are of practical value to scriptwriters working in a variety of areas and formats.

VISUAL THINKING

A script that guides the production of a film, video, audio, or interactive multimedia program can be compared with an architectural drawing or blueprint. A script orients the director and other key members of the creative staff to the overall story or topic. It provides a preliminary sketch or outline for a project that is to be constructed and gives it concrete form. Just as an architect must be knowledgeable about building construction methods and materials, a scriptwriter must understand the entire production process. Scriptwriting cannot be completely divorced from the other preproduction, production, and postproduction activities discussed in this book.

A scriptwriter should only write what he or she is confident can actually be staged and recorded. Abstract concepts and ideas have a more limited place in scriptwriting than they do in forms of writing that are not intended to be performed or pictorially rendered. Thinking visually demands that a scriptwriter think in practical terms of actual settings, concrete actions, and specific dialogue that will actually be performed or observed and recorded. A good feature film scriptwriter or screenwriter, for example, often begins a script visually with an image that will give the audience a strong sense of place, atmosphere, mood, and even the theme of the picture.

Television, film, audio, and interactive multimedia are visual and acoustic media. A fiction scriptwriter establishes settings, describes actions, and defines characters through concrete sounds and visual images. Settings are established very economically as specific buildings, locations, and props. Characters are defined by their actions and reactions, as well as by what they say to other characters. The emotional texture of settings, actions, and characters is developed through the actual performance and recording of concrete sounds and visual images. A sound or image does not speak in terms of "people" or "screams" in general, but of this specific person and this specific scream.

Unlike a playwright, a scriptwriter does not need to rely exclusively or even primarily upon dialogue or just a few settings to tell a story. Dialogue can be substantial or it can be practically nonexistent. A scriptwriter can use a variety of settings to reflect different moods, atmospheres, and aspects of a character, or just one setting to provoke a feeling of confinement. Actions can occur outdoors or indoors, in quick succession at different times and at a variety of geographic locations, or slowly at one time and place. A stage play is usually restricted to just a few settings, which must be set up quickly between different scenes or acts. Time is usually continuous within each scene. Time and place in a film, television program, audio recording, or interactive game can be continuous or discontinuous. A media production can depict many existing settings around the world, reconstruct them in a studio, or create a purely imaginative acoustic or animated environment. Actions occurring in a character's past can be intercut with those in the present or future.

Economy of expression is one of the hallmarks of good scriptwriting. Every setting, prop, or character in a fictional story, for example, can only be briefly described. Its presence in the script indicates that it is an essential and integral part of the story or topic, rather than a peripheral detail. Unlike a novelist or short story writer, a scriptwriter rarely writes long passages describing the setting or a character's state of mind and feelings.

One of the skills that scriptwriters must develop is visual thinking. A script facilitates the recording of specific moving images and sounds, and it is based on a firm understanding of the production process. By reading the production and postproduction sections of this book, especially those chapters that focus on the aesthetics of generating, recording, and editing sounds and images, a beginning scriptwriter can acquire some understanding of the creative potential of moving images and sounds, or visual thinking. Quality scriptwriting demands a firm grasp of production aesthetics and the entire production process.

PREPARATION FOR SCRIPTWRITING

The scriptwriting process has several distinct stages, beginning with the research phase. Before a script is written, considerable research must be carried out. Research provides insurance against presenting implausible stories or conveying factually incorrect information. It also provides a source of inspiration and creative ideas.

A premise, synopsis, and several story outlines may be drafted after the research phase before a treatment is prepared. A treatment is a plot description in short-story form and is used primarily as part of a proposal submitted to a potential funding source. It is often submitted to a funding source or producer as an accompaniment to an oral presentation or pitch. It provides a guide for the writing of a complete script.

The next stage in the scriptwriting process is the writing of the script itself. A script may go through several drafts and involve the participation of several writers before it is completed and production can begin. The final stage is the preparation of a shooting script, which indicates all camera placements, transition devices, and various types of effects. These are usually added by the director (or the designer in multimedia production).

STAGES OF SCRIPTWRITING
- Research
- Premise, Synopsis
- Story Outline
- Treatment
- Proposal
- Rough Draft
- Final Draft
- Scene Script
- Shooting Script

The first stage of scriptwriting is the research phase. Every aspect of the topic should be carefully and thoroughly researched before the script is written. Whether the project is to be primarily entertaining, informative, or persuasive, its overall quality directly depends on the quality of research that has gone into the development of the script. The more carefully documented the information contained in a script is, the more realistic, authentic, accurate, and responsible the finished product will seem to be. A digital word processing or scriptwriting program is the most efficient method to research and write proposals, treatments, and scripts.

Careful research is both a form of insurance and a source of inspiration. Carefully documenting sources of information can protect a producer from legal prosecution. News and documentary writers, for example, have an obligation to research their stories carefully. It is often necessary to find hard evidence from reliable sources in order to support a basic statement or argument. Thorough investigation of a subject frequently leads to the revelation of information that stimulates the creative process and challenges and excites the viewer.

Research

Research is a creative process of uncovering new sources of information. A project researcher or scriptwriter begins by acquiring a general background in the area on which the project will focus. She collects as many books and articles as possible that deal with the general topic area and reads those that seem to be most helpful and pertinent to the specific issues at hand. Searching computer files and systems such as Lexis and Nexis, as well as other databases, is one of the fastest and most accurate methods of acquiring the basic information needed when researching a project. Armed with this general knowledge, the researcher progresses by focusing more narrowly on specific problems and concerns. General understanding of the topic stimulates the creation of insightful questions that can be raised during interviews with an expert or a participant in the events. The more knowledgeable a writer or researcher becomes, the more information she will elicit from additional sources of information. Like a good detective, a writer learns that one piece of evidence leads to the discovery of another.

Production research is usually either novelistic or journalistic in approach. A fiction writer or novelist conducts research in order to find details that stimulate reader interest and authenticate events and settings. A fictional film, television program, or computer game is often researched in this manner. Strict authenticity is sometimes sacrificed for dramatic interest and action. Journalistic research, on the other hand, aims at uncovering sources of documentary evidence that can be used to support the presentation of information and editorial arguments (Figure 3.1).

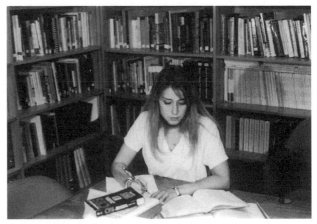

Figure 3.1 The beginning of any media production is the research stage. Information must be gathered, facts checked, and information documented before the script is written.

Premise, Synopsis, and Outline

Every good treatment is preceded by the writing of a simple idea or concept, called a *premise*. A premise is basically a "what if" statement, which describes the basic story idea. For example, "what if" Romeo and Juliet sang and danced, and were caught between rival gangs and ethnic groups in New York City? This is the basic premise of *West Side Story* (1961). "What if" Romeo and Juliet were involved with drugs in Central Park? A feature film entitled *The Panic in Needle Park* (1971) operates on the basis of this simple premise. A good treatment is always based on a simple but interesting concept. The premise can be used later as a strong opening "pitch" of a script or screenplay to a producer by providing a concise label for the project.

The next preparatory step prior to writing a treatment is to compose a synopsis, which consists of one or more paragraphs that describe the basic *story line*: "Tony and Maria fall in love, but because they are associated with rival gangs, the Sharks and the Jets, there are many obstacles placed in the path of their love. After Maria's brother is accidentally killed by Tony in a fight, their relationship is filled with suffering and frustration."

On the basis of this synopsis of *West Side Story*, an *outline* can be written, developing the major plot lines and characters in the story. This outline also defines all major actions and character reactions. Usually several outlines are written and revised before the treatment is created.

Treatments

A treatment is an important step in the development of a script. Usually written in the third person, present tense, it provides a narrative summary of the basic story lines. A treatment visualizes the story as it will unfold on the screen and gives a play-by-play of all major actions and scenes in reduced form. A writer composes a treatment so that he or she can receive an approval or commission to write a fictional script or undertake a documentary project. When a producer initiates a project, the treatment sometimes accompanies a proposal, which is submitted to a funding source. Scriptwriters (and their agents) often initiate a film or television project by writing a treatment.

The major portion of the treatment is devoted to a highly visual, but concise, narrative presentation of characters and events. Some examples of dialogue spoken by characters are usually included, and the treatment adopts a short-story format. A good treatment adopts a lively prose style that dramatizes the basic premise and effectively communicates the tone and flavor of a piece. Camera directions and shot descriptions are used very sparingly, if at all. Resonant images are conveyed by highly visual nouns or adjectives and action verbs. A treatment is not a legal document fashioned with dry regularity and precision. It must excite and interest a producer or funding source, and serve as a thorough and helpful guide for the writing of a script or screenplay. A treatment provides some protection against future writing problems by forcing the writer to resolve many difficulties prior to actual scriptwriting.

How long should a treatment be? A treatment for a feature-length film screenplay, which will run about two hours, usually has about 20 to 70 double-spaced, typewritten pages. The finished screenplay will be 100 to 140 pages, since each page of a screenplay usually translates into about one minute of actual screen time. A treatment for a work of short fiction should probably be from 5 to 10 pages in length. It is always preferable to err on the side of brevity, since verbose, overwritten treatments are not likely to be read with interest and enthusiasm.

Nonfiction treatments, such as a documentary treatment that is included in a proposal submitted to a potential funding source, are concise narrative descriptions of what the viewer will see and hear written in the present tense. Like dramatic fiction treatments, the purpose is to evoke interest, excitement, and, if possible, the same emotional response from the reader that you hope your production will elicit from the viewer or listener. A separate paragraph is usually devoted to each sequence that will appear in the completed project (Figure 3.2).

SCRIPTWRITING FORMATS

After the preliminary stages of scriptwriting have been completed, a writer or group of writers begins to write a fill script. The script conforms to one of the following formats: split-page, full-page, or a semi-scripted format, such as a script outline. Scriptwriters rely on a basic set of terms as well as these common formats in order to effectively communicate with other members of the creative staff, such as the director. A discussion of three standard scriptwriting formats, full-page, split-page, and semi-scripted, is presented in the following sections.

Full-Page Master Scene Script Format

A full-page master scene script format is frequently used in dramatic fiction programs, including single-camera film and video productions, such as live-action dramas and feature films, and multiple-camera live-on-tape productions, such as television situation comedies. In a full-page master scene script format, a single column, which is devoted to both visuals and audio, fills the entire page. The script is organized into scenes, which are numbered in consecutive order. The location and time of day of each scene are specified. Actions and camera movements are described in full paragraphs. Scriptwriting computer programs are available for all computer operating systems. These programs format the script in a professional layout, relieving the scriptwriter of the tedium of worrying about margins and spacing while attempting to create a workable script (Figure 3.3).

Because a full-page master scene script is organized by scenes, it can easily be reorganized so that all the scenes requiring a single set or location can be shot consecutively. As we noted in the previous chapter, producers and production managers try to organize production so that all the scenes at a specific location can be shot at one time, because it is usually more efficient and cost-effective than recording the scenes in chronological order as they appear in the script.

Every scene presented in a master scene script usually begins with a "scene heading," indicating an indoor/interior (INT.) or outdoor/exterior (EXT.) setting, the name of the specific location, and the time of day. There may be a number of different setups, dialogue sequences, and descriptions of actions and characters until the location, time of day, and interior or exterior setting change.

SAMPLE TREATMENT FORMAT

TITLE: Safety Training   PAGE: 1
WRITER: T. Bartlett   LENGTH: 10 mins
CLIENT: Mountain Industries   DATE: 10-10-96

The ten-minute training tape will open with a montage of incorrect logging operations followed in each case by the possible disastrous and life-threatening results of such actions. Examples of such scenes are:

A logger without a safety belt steps back and falls from a tree stand.

A chainsaw jams and flips back into the logger.

A tractor tips over on the driver because it exceeded its tilt limit.

A logging truck driven too fast forces an on-coming car from the road.

A log falls from a truck being loaded and strikes a logger who was standing too close to the truck.

A logger refuels his saw improperly, causing a fire.

A truck or tractor becomes a runaway when left improperly locked down.

A logger dumped into the river and crushed by logs.

A log avalanche occurs because of careless blocking of a log stack.

This series of accidents will be enhanced with sound effects and dramatic music as well as the actual sound of each accident.

Following this montage, the narrator will walk into the scene and describe in general the dangers and reasons for following OSHA safety requirements for those working in dangerous occupations such as the

(continued)

Figure 3.2 The treatment of a production is, along with the proposal, another sales tool. Potential funding sources need to be able to accurately visualize in their minds, while reading the treatment, exactly what the producer has in mind. If the treatment is not clear and complete, funding is highly unlikely.

MASTER SCENE SCRIPT FORMAT

(Margins and tabs set as indicated below, assuming 80 space wide paper)

| 5 | 10 | 20 | 25 | | 55 | 60 | 70 | 75 |

FADE IN:

1.   INT./EXT.   DAY/NIGHT   1.
        BRIEF SCENE OR SHOT DESCRIPTION, CAM. ANGLE.

        In upper and lower case, a more detailed description of the scene giving setting, props, and CHARACTERS position if needed with margins set at 10/70.

                              CHARACTER
                    (Mode of delivery, upper and
                    lower case, margins at 25/55)

                The dialog is typed in upper and lower case
                centered within 20/60 margins.

        Any other descriptions of shot framing, movement of CAMERA or CHARACTER is at margins set at 10/70.

                                              (TRANSITION)

2.   INT   WS   UNIVERSITY CLASSROOM   DAY   2.

        Classroom is full of students, some wide awake, gossiping, others sleeping or nodding off as they wait for the professor to arrive.

                              JANE
              (Quietly so only Jack can hear her.)
           Are you sure there isn't going to be an exam
              during tomorrow's class?

                            JACK
           (With a bravado, all-knowing tone)
          Of course not, have I ever lied to you?

        The professor enters the room, downstage right, walks to the lecturn and the room becomes quiet.

                        PROFESSOR
           (Emphatically as a reminder)
          If I am forced to repeat myself again, I WILL
          be forced to give you your first examination in
          tomorrow's class.

(DISSOLVE TO)

3.   EXT   WS   CAMPUS   DAY   3.

        The clouds suddenly darken the sky as rain, thunder and lightning start and the lights go out plunging the room into darkness.

        (A scene script describes the entire scene in very general terms, a shooting script contains much more detailed descriptions and shot instructions)

Figure 3.3 A master scene script gives the screenwriter the opportunity to notify the director of the writer's intent without limiting the director to specific shots. But the script must include enough information so that the director understands what the writer had in mind and wants the actors to say and do.

EXT. XANADU—NIGHT—EXTREME LONG SHOT—
    FENCE AND MANSION

The full-page master scene script describes few, if any, camera movements and shots. It is much more common for the director to select and indicate specific shots during the preparation of the final shooting script immediately prior to production. A director's shot descriptions often specify camera-to-subject distance, angle of view, and camera movement when they are incorporated into the stage directions following the scene heading. Rather than providing shot descriptions, a scriptwriter can artfully visualize the scene in prose following the header without specifying camera-to-subject distances, angles, and so forth. In any case, camera shots, angles, movements, transition devices, times of day, interior and exterior settings, specific character names, and sound effects are generally typed in uppercase letters, while actions, events, and specific stage directions, including sets, props, characters, and actions, as well as dialogue, are usually in lowercase letters. Dialogue to be spoken by a specific character normally follows the stage directions and has the character's name listed in the middle of the page immediately above his or her lines of dialogue, which are slightly indented from the paragraph descriptions of actions and camera movements. The end of a scene is usually indicated by a "scene close," such as CUT TO: or DISSOLVE TO:, which indicates the transition to the next scene.

The information highlighted in UPPERCASE LETTERS throughout a master scene script is emphasized for the convenience of the producer or production manager, who will break down the script into its component parts for scheduling and budgeting. Each scene is numbered for easy reference, and each revision of a master scene script is dated, to ensure that all performers, creative staff, and crew members are using identical copies of the script during production.

Split-Page Script Format

In a split-page script, the visual information appears in one column on a sheet of paper and the audio information in the other column. The split-page script format is often used for commercials and other forms of nonfiction production, such as documentaries. The dialogue and narration are written out fully on the audio side of the page. Visual images are indicated on the opposite side of the page. The latter are sometimes described quite sparingly in live multi-camera productions, such as awards ceremonies and performances, leaving wide margins, so that the director or assistant director can make copious notes about specific cameras and shots in these blank areas. Visual cues and segment durations are written in full uppercase letters in the visual column, and any information in the script that should not be read on-air is circled (Figure 3.4).

The obvious advantage of the split-page format is that visual and audio elements can be directly compared and coordinated. An empty column suggests that one aspect is being focused on to the exclusion of the other. A rough equality in terms of space devoted to these two tracks or creative elements ensures that both will be fully utilized in the completed project.

Semi-Scripted Formats

Many types of nonfiction television programs and films do not need to be fully scripted in advance of production. A talk show, game show, or even a documentary film or videotape may only be partially or semi-scripted. A semi-scripted format may consist of a simple rundown sheet, which is a basic outline of the show from beginning to end, indicating what material or performer is needed at specific times. It is organized on the basis of the running time of each segment and of the entire program. Different electronic sources of material, such as remote feeds and videotape playbacks, are also specified (Figure 3.5).

A script outline is another semi-scripted format. Portions of a script outline may be fully scripted, such as the opening or closing segments of a news, talk, or game show that remain the same from show to show. Other elements are simply outlined in rough form, either because they must be ad-libbed during recording, or because the exact information to be read may not, in fact, be available until just prior to air or recording time, such as with quiz and game shows. Documentary, sports, and talk show directors often use a script outline because it is difficult to precisely script live or uncontrolled events. The questions to be asked during an interview show can be written down in advance, but the answers cannot, unless the interview is staged. A director or camera operator must be able to respond instantly to unpredictable events as they happen. The actual selection of shots to be used may be delayed to later stages of production, such as postproduction editing. Only the general type of shot or action may be specified in a script outline.

FICTION SCRIPTWRITING

Drama and narrative are fictional art forms that have a basis in everyday life. A drama is basically a

DUAL COLUMN SCRIPT FORMAT

TITLE: PAGE:
WRITER: LENGTH:
CLIENT: DATE:

VIDEO	AUDIO
1. SINGLE SPACE VIDEO INSTRUCTIONS	1. ANNCR: Audio copy is lined up directly across the page from its matching video.
2. TRIPLE SPACE BETWEEN EACH SHOT	2. Double space between each line of audio copy.
3. EACH SHOT MUST BE NUMBERED ON THE SCRIPT	3. The audio column's number must match that of its video.
4. EVERYTHING THE VIEWER IS TO SEE; ALL VISUALS, VIDEO TAPES, CG, CAMERA SHOTS, ARE INCLUDED IN THE LEFT-HAND COLUMN.	4. Everything the viewer is to hear; all sounds, music, voices, sound effects, narration and all audio cues are included in the right-hand column.
5. EVERYTHING ON THE VIDEO SIDE IS TYPED IN CAPITAL LETTERS.	5. Everything spoken by the talent is typed in upper and lower case letters. All instructions in the audio column are typed in capital letters.
6. THE TALENT'S NAME STARTS EACH NEW LINE, BUT DOES NOT HAVE TO BE REPEATED IF THE SAME PERSON OR SOUND SOURCE CONTINUES.	6. SAM: Note--the name is in caps, what Sam says is in upper and lower case.
7. AVOID SPLITTING SHOTS AT BOTTOM OF THE PAGE.	7. Avoid splitting words or thoughts at the end of the line.

Figure 3.4 A split-page format defines clearly how each shot is to be framed, the action within that shot, and the accompanying audio.

| Client: | WEMPLE'S DUTCH MILL | DATE: | 7-7-94 |
| JOB: | #WDM-94-7-3 | MEDIA: | TV |

SCENE 1:

SCENE:	Kitchen, middle class	MOM:	A little more mustard?
TALENT:	Mom and Male kid		
ACTION:	Mom busily fixing lunch	KID:	That's great, you make the best cheeseburgers in the whole world

SCENE 2:

SCENE:	Backyard	KID:	But I'd rather be eating at Wemple's
TALENT:	Male kid		
ACTION:	Kid runs out of back door		

SCENE 3:

SCENE:	Mom in kitchen		
TALENT:	Mom	MOM:	Never mind burgers, I'd rather be eating at Wemple's
ACTION:	Mom puts away lunch, hurries out front door		

☐
SCENE 4:

| KEY LOGO & TAG | VO: | Everybody'd rather be eating at Wemple's |

Figure 3.5 A semi-script provides the director with a rough outline of the production, allowing much greater freedom for deciding on shots. The form also is used for productions that cannot be scripted: sporting events, game shows, and special events.

series of actions performed by actors, such as a stage play. A narrative is a chain of events, which is told or narrated, such as a novel or short story. While most dramas and narratives draw upon everyday life and experience, effective works of fiction are often shaped and refined by carefully organizing and structuring these actions and events, and removing the dull moments of life so that viewer, listener, or reader interest can be intensified. The organization of dramatic actions and narrative events is often referred to as the elements of dra-matic and narrative structure. Fiction scriptwriting has the potential to combine certain elements of dramatic and narrative structure, and a successful work of fiction, be it a film, video, audio, or multi-media production, is usually one that makes effective use of these basic structural elements.

Dramatic Structure

Dramatic films and television programs can be plotted into a framework that consists of a basic three-act structure and a series of rising and falling actions, which culminate in a climax and resolution. Act One of a drama usually sets up the main plot by establishing the central characters, their goals and conflicts, as well as the basic time, place, and situation of the story. Act Two and Act Three each begin with a turning point, such as a major shift in the main plot, which moves the drama in a different direction from the previous act, generating audience interest and maintaining story momentum. Secondary as well as primary characters and themes are usually more fully developed through both main plot and subplot actions in Act Two. Conflicts and problems eventually reach a climax and are resolved as the main plot and subplot are brought together near the end of Act Three.

Rising actions include build sections, where conflicts build into a series of crises, and a final climax. Falling and horizontal actions include temporary resolutions or pauses in the action following crises, which allow the audience to catch its breath before proceeding to the next crisis or climax. Then the final resolution of the conflicting elements that led to the climax are revealed bringing the drama to a close.

These classic forms of dramatic structure ensure that actions build in a logical and exciting way on the basis of major conflicts that must be resolved. A drama may have very limited or extensive expositions of characters, situations, and settings; few or many complications, reversals, and crises; but it almost always relies upon internal or external conflicts, which build toward a climax and resolution, if it is to sustain interest, arouse excitement, and evoke a sense of fulfillment. Political dramas, such as *The West Wing,* crime dramas, such as *CSI* and *CSI Miami,* and medical dramas, such as *ER,* illustrate classic dramatic structure.

Act One

Act One usually begins with powerful images that convey the essential focus, pace, and style of the film or television program. We not only sense the time and place of the story, but we are often introduced to a major theme as well. Generally without writing any dialogue, the scriptwriter is able to convey the basic ideas, thoughts, and feelings that the unfolding story will eventually develop in great detail through character actions, dialogue, and/or interior monologue.

The main plot action is usually initiated and propelled by a precipitating event or catalyst in Act One. The precipitating event may consist of an action, such as a murder; a piece of dialogue, such as one character informing another that they have found the secret to eternal life; or a situation, such as the appearance of a young unmarried woman who is obviously pregnant. The precipitating event helps to establish the basic spin or direction of the main plot.

Learning more about the characters in Act One might require some back story, such as flashbacks into a character's past or some discussion of a particular character's life by other characters. The plot unfolds in Act One as a series of dramatic beats or actions that reveal who characters are by what they do and say. A dramatic scene, that is, a series of actions or events occurring at one time and place, may consist of several *beats* or dramatic moments.

Act Two

Act Two usually begins with the first turning point. A turning point substantially changes or reverses the direction of the plot. For example, one character may believe that another character is her best friend, but new information reverses her opinion and suggests that her supposed friend is really someone to be feared and avoided. During Act Two the subplot is more fully developed than in Act One. For example, the main plot of the story may focus on a woman whose career objective is to succeed as an executive in a major corporation, while the subplot may focus upon her romantic involvement with the chief executive at a rival company. In Hollywood films, subplots often focus upon romantic love and develop important themes, while main plots often focus upon characters' pursuit of material goals, actions, and concrete objectives.

During Act Two, secondary as well as primary characters are more fully developed, along with resulting conflicts between characters. Subsequent events, such as the eventual death of a particular character, are often foreshadowed, although the payoff may not occur until Act Three. Complications develop, which sometimes act as barriers to a character's successful accomplishment of his or her goals. For example, a long-distance runner who is very religious may discover that a major competition is scheduled to take place on an important religious holiday, and his participation in that event violates his own ethical and religious standards.

Act Three

The second turning point usually initiates Act Three and speeds up the action. Act Three provides a sense of urgency and propels the story toward its conclusion. Actions build toward a climax, where the conflicts originating in Act One are resolved and the main plot and the subplot come together.

Rising Action: Crises and Climax

Dramatic action that has progressed through several complications inevitably builds to a crisis. A drama may have several crises, in which the conflict that has stimulated the action intensifies to the point that something or someone is threatened. We all encounter crises in our lives, but drama removes most of the dull moments between these crises, so that characters' actions and emotions, and viewers' interest and involvement, are intensified. The major character or characters may have to make an important decision. Perhaps it is a life-and-death situation. Should a risky surgical procedure be performed? Can a murderer be identified and sacrificed? Should a character choose between a lover or a spouse? The dramatic action usually builds through several important crises that finally culminate in a major crisis or climax.

A climax is the most decisive point of confrontation in a drama. It simply demands some form of resolution. One side must win or a compromise must be reached. The climax brings the major conflicting forces together so that they may be openly confronted and resolved. The climax is usually the highest, most intense emotional peak of the drama.

Falling Action: Resolution

Overcoming the basic conflict or fulfilling the goals and motivations that have stimulated the dramatic action is known as a resolution. The defeat of the antagonist, the death of the hero, the marriage of the loving couple, or the attainment of the major goal may each represent the culmination of the action. A resolution is considered a falling action compared with the rising action of a crisis or climax. The resolution section of the drama considers the implications of the climactic actions and gives the audience time to contemplate what has just transpired before new actions are initiated or the drama ends. Emotionally, the audience may need sufficient time to recuperate from the emotional experience of the climax. A drama that ended immediately after the climax might leave some of the audience's expectations unfulfilled.

The resolution of a drama can be ambiguous or unambiguous. An ending can appear to resolve all major conflicts or allow the hero to achieve his or her major goals. In a mystery story, the discovery of a secret can answer all questions. But an ending can also be ambiguous. Conflicts can persist and goals remain unachieved. Some dramatic forms have virtually no resolution at all. Soap operas rarely, if ever, reach any resolution. They consist of a series of crises. Any apparent solution, such as a marriage, is usually the source of another conflict. The absence of any resolution establishes a new convention that is unique to the open-ended, serial dramatic form. A closed dramatic form uses resolution to enforce a sense of finality or closure at the end. The drama is essentially self-contained, although the dramatic action may continue in the form of a sequel.

Text and Subtext

A good writer not only plays with the surface text of the dialogue while telling a story but often develops a subtext through character actions and reactions. The subtext defines what the characters are really feeling, that is, the feelings that underlie their dialogue. For example, a man and a woman may be discussing something rather innocuous, such as the weather. Their dialogue defines the text. "Don't you think that it's getting warmer?" "Yes, but my hands are freezing." "There's still a touch of winter in the air, but the ice is melting." The text indicates that the characters are aware that spring is coming and the weather outside is getting warmer. But by staging the action so that the characters gradually get closer together and begin holding hands and touching one another, the subtext (and double entendre of the dialogue) is that they are gradually warming up to each other romantically.

Narrative Structure

In addition to having dramatic structure, the structure of action, scripts also have narrative structure, the structure of time and point of view. A story can follow an uninterrupted chronological structure from beginning to end, or it can have flashbacks and flashforwards, which disrupt the continuous flow of time. A great deal of screen time can be devoted to some events and very little to others. For example, a character in a soap opera can go upstairs in one scene and come down in the next, having aged several years (and sometimes having been replaced by another actor). On the other hand, it may take several episodes or even several weeks of episodes to develop all the intrigues occurring at a party that supposedly lasted for only two hours on one day. The difference between the actual screen time and the supposed story or historical time devoted to specific events is sometimes referred to as *narrative duration*, and the difference between the actual order of presentation and the supposed historical chronology of specific events in the story is sometimes referred to as *narrative order*. Scriptwriters can manipulate narrative order and duration to effectively relate one event to another, such as providing character back story by using a flashback to break the chronological order of the narrative and to relate a character's history to his or her present actions.

A fictional work can also be narrated by someone. A story can be told from a specific point of view. An omniscient or effaced (hidden) narrator tells the story but does not appear as a character within it, while a dramatized narrator is a specific character who also tells the story. In media production the director can use the camera to enhance the point of view of a specific character whom the scriptwriter is using to tell the story by placing the camera in that character's approximate physical position on the set. We, the audience, then see and understand what that character sees and understands from his or her point of view throughout the story. An effaced or omniscient narrator acts as a substitute for the scriptwriter. He or she is an unseen person who presents the story when no character takes responsibility for it. An effaced narrator selects what we will see and understand by adopting a more "objective" point of view, and a director can use the camera more "objectively" by not placing it in the approximate spatial position of any specific character.

Narrative point of view is an extremely important structural component. How something is presented is just as important as what is presented. If we experience a series of events through the eyes of a character as opposed to omnisciently through an effaced narrator, our experience of these events is quite different. Adopting the point of view of a particular character makes a difference in terms of how actions, events, and their meanings are perceived. Imagine, for example, the presentation of the Battle of the Little Big Horn through the eyes of a Sioux warrior versus those of a U.S. cavalryman. Arthur Penn's film *Little Big Man* (1970) presents a shifting point of view on General Custer through the ambiguous cultural identity and affiliation of its main character/narrator. The adoption of a specific point of view colors and even distorts events in a particular way, and such a perspective must be carefully and thoughtfully selected.

A well-known short film called *An Occurrence at Owl Creek Bridge* (1964), based on the short story of the same name by Ambrose Bierce, illustrates most major aspects of narrative structure. It tells the story of a southerner during the Civil War who is about to be hanged from a bridge by Union soldiers. The story is generally presented from the victim's point of view. The victim dreams about his wife as he is about to be hanged, and the images intercut pleasant memories of the past with the present horror of imminent death as he watches the Union soldiers prepare for his execution. We are shown his memories of his wife as the victim narrates historical time. Cutting back to his present predicament, the camera often assumes his physical position within the setting at the bridge. Just when he seems about to die, the rope snaps and he falls into the river. Writer-director Robert Enrico expands historical time underwater. It takes the victim more than three minutes of film time to free himself underwater from the ropes that bind him and swim to the surface. Enrico then condenses the time it takes him to swim away down the river, eluding the gunfire of the soldiers along the shore. But when he gets home and is about to embrace his wife, the scene cuts directly to his hanging at the bridge again. In retrospect, the escape scenes can be interpreted by the audience as a wish fulfillment of the victim's hope of escaping death, which is shattered by the reality of his death. The events of the escape have only occurred in the victim's mind. They have been narrated by the victim and exist as a dream outside of the normal "present" time of the dramatic scenes of the hanging.

Characterization and Theme

There are almost as many ways to initiate the writing of an original piece of fiction as there are works of fiction. Some writers begin with specific characters. Once they have these characters firmly in mind, they begin to imagine specific, exciting situations within which these people find themselves. Conflicts arise from interactions among characters who have different goals and values. Certain themes begin to emerge as the characters initiate or become involved in specific actions. This "organic" approach to fiction writing tries to ensure that actions and themes flow "naturally" out of "real" characters (Figure 3.6).

Another approach to writing fiction begins with a basic theme, idea, or message. In some ways it is more difficult to begin with the theme and then find three-dimensional characters who can initiate actions to reinforce the theme. There is a real danger that the theme will become overbearing. The opposite danger faced by the "character-first" approach is that the actions undertaken by certain characters will not be thematically significant or interesting.

A third way to initiate a fictional script is to begin with the plot or story structure, and then work in both directions, that is, toward characters who can carry out those actions and the themes that those actions reflect or represent. In using this method, there is a danger that characters will simply become pawns to carry out actions and that themes will be tacked on from the outside.

Where a scriptwriter begins is probably less important than paying attention to the development of all three fictional aspects: plot, characters, and themes. Plot, that is, the telling or presentation of specific actions and events, has already been discussed in terms of dramatic and narrative structure, but characterization and theme need further consideration.

Figure 3.6 A dramatic production should draw the audience into the story through a combination of quality acting, directing, and production values. Universal Pictures' production of *Apollo 13* provided the audience with such an experience. (Courtesy of Universal Pictures.)

Developing strong, believable, and interesting characters is just as important as creating an exciting series of actions and events. Complex characters give a story depth and three-dimensionality. A character's values and beliefs lead to conflicts with other characters who hold opposing values. If these values are significant and strongly held, the entire fictional experience is enhanced.

Character can be revealed through two primary vehicles: actions and words. What characters do and say reveals in large part who they are. But actions and behavior are usually more important than dialogue. Characters should show us what they believe through their actions. The important thing for the writer to remember is that communication takes place through concrete sounds and images. A character is largely created through external appearances, actions, and speech. But the external surface of a character must reflect a complex internal value system and a set of abstract thoughts, beliefs, and feelings. An external surface that is not based on a solid psychological foundation lacks depth, understanding, and true artistic potential.

Characters can be roughly divided into egories: central characters, principal charac secondary or incidental characters. The cent. acter or characters figure prominently in a ...ory. They are the primary sources of audience satisfaction, interest, and identification. The decisions they make and the actions they initiate propel the drama. Their values, beliefs, feelings, and goals determine, to a great extent, how meaningful and significant the entire drama will become. The principal characters are usually friends or foils to the central character(s). They can offer support to the actions and thoughts of the central character, or they can present significant obstacles to the attainment of his or her goals. In a longer drama there is usually enough time to give most or all of the principal characters sufficient depth so that their interactions with the central character become important and convincing.

Secondary and incidental characters may help create a situation that provokes a conflict, but they are contributors to (rather than initiators of) major actions. There is rarely time to fully develop all the minor characters in a drama into complex individuals. They have certain traits and mannerisms that distinguish them in a crowd and add spice to the drama, but these can easily deteriorate into stereotypes or cliches. Stereotyping secondary or incidental characters often runs the risk of stereotyping certain occupational or ethnic groups and minorities. Some reliance on character types (as opposed to stereotypes) ensures immediate audience recognition of the most important aspect of a character and contributes to the drama as a whole. What minor characters say about any major character helps to develop the latter's characterization. A good deal of information about the central character can be communicated to the audience through the words of secondary and incidental characters, sometimes reinforcing and sometimes contradicting the central character's own speech and actions.

A *theme* is basically a significant statement that a work of fiction asserts or an important issue that it raises. Themes generally emanate from the values, beliefs, and goals of the central characters, but a general theme may be much broader and universal than the attitudes of any single character. The film *Citizen Kane* (1941) has several broad themes, for example. The portrayal of Kane's life focuses on such issues as the absence of love in his life and his pursuit of fame, fortune, and power. Images, symbols, and motifs, such as "Rosebud," suggest, perhaps, that the absence of a happy childhood or family or parental love and guidance can lead to an inability to love and a meaningless pursuit of money and power. This film also develops other themes concerning democracy, politics, and the press, including, perhaps, a criticism of American society and capitalism in general. Of course, not all films are so heavily thematic, but the greatness of this film is that it does not sacrifice characterization and dramatic structure in order to make meaningful statements. Important themes coexist with strong characters and a complex plot. The themes are not the sole interest of the story (Figure 3.7).

Adaptation

An adaptation is a relatively faithful translation of a play, short story, a novel, or even a comic strip into a film or television program. The scriptwriter is usually very familiar with the original literary work and makes every attempt to translate it into a different medium with the central characters and themes virtually intact. A television or film script that is less faithful to the original is frequently said to be based on that source, while a work that uses the original written piece as a springboard for essentially new ideas is said to be freely adapted or simply suggested by the original (Figure 3.8).

The adaptation process usually begins with a consideration of the author's intent. What is the basic theme and point of view from which the story is told? Which characters are particularly memorable and/or attractive, disturbing and/or sympathetic? The plot must be analyzed in detail, using some of the basic elements of dramatic and narrative structure discussed earlier as a guide to good storytelling technique in media production. Does the story have a basic three-act structure? Does it build logically and dramatically toward a climax and resolution? Does the story have a plot and a subplot, and do the two coalesce at the denouement, that is, at the point of their final solution and clarification? Are there dead spots that can be eliminated or conflicts that need to be intensified? How many different scenes and settings are required? Is the story told from an omniscient or a specific character's point of view? Is there substantial dialogue and action, or will a character's interior monologue need to be dramatized and shown rather than simply told? Does the story follow a chronological structure, or does it involve flashbacks and/or flash forwards in time?

After completing a careful analysis of the basic plot, subplot, characters, and themes, the scriptwriter who is adapting a work from one medium to another will write a treatment and then a screenplay that usually provides a number of changes from the original work. These changes may include the following: creating or eliminating subplots; eliminating, combining, adding, or altering (usually secondary or minor) characters; cutting, shortening, or expanding and enhancing specific scenes; adding, subtracting, or altering settings. The scriptwriter makes these changes to improve a story's dramatic and narrative structure; to enhance the characterization and theme of the original

Figure 3.7 The acclaim of *Citizen Kane* is based in part upon its strong characters, complex plot, and important themes. (Courtesy of RKO Pictures.)

Figure 3.8 The *Spider-Man* films produced by Columbia TriStar were adapted from the original Spiderman cartoon strip and an animated television series. (Courtesy of Columbia TriStar Pictures.)

novel, play, or short story; and to increase the efficiency and often decrease the cost of actual production.

A full and complete adaptation of a lengthy novel, for example, could substantially exceed the normal time restrictions of most media productions. A scriptwriter must then decide which elements are crucial to the story, which will be the most dramatic, what scenes or portions of the plot can be eliminated entirely, and how others can be shortened. Sometimes characters can be combined, so that the ideas and values they espouse are not lost but simply condensed. Dialogue or action scenes may have to be added, however, in order to dramatize information that was presented in the novel as pure description or characters' inner thoughts. The story should be shown not just told. Literary dialogue must work well as spoken dialogue, and dialogue should not become so lengthy and informative that it substitutes for action. An adaptation scriptwriter must understand the production problems and costs involved in composing a faithful adaptation of an original piece of writing. He or she must also understand the needs and expectation of the audience so that an effective, exciting, and interesting presentation of characters, actions, and themes will be created on the screen (Figure 3.9).

Before the adaptation process commences, the rights to a published and/or copyrighted work must be secured, of course. An original novel, short story, play, history, or biography may be protected by copyright for up to 75 years, and any television or film producer who attempts to adapt it, however freely, without paying for the right to do so can be held liable for damages to the value of that property.

Figure 3.9 The *Harry Potter* films produced by Warner Bros. were adapted by a series of books written by J. K. Rowling. (Courtesy of Warner Bros.) HARRY POTTER AND THE SORCERER'S STONE © 2001 Warner Bros., a division of Time Warner Entertainment Company, L.P. All Rights Reserved.

...tion forms, such as television situation ...ly require different treatment, including ...alternative dramatic and narrative struc-tu... story construction, from that of longer forms, such as feature films. For example, half-hour episodes in a television situation comedy series present the same set of characters in a slightly different situation each week. The relatively short duration of an individual episode encourages a different organization and approach.

A sitcom episode is usually organized into two acts with three scenes per act and a tag or epilogue after the last commercial to keep the audience tuned in and to reinforce any message or theme. The opening of an episode must grab the attention of the audience to prevent viewers from switching channels. A major conflict or problem must be presented in the first five minutes (Act One, Scene One), prior to the first commercial break. The dramatic device that grabs the audience is called a *hook*. It often takes the form of a problem or conflict that excites the viewer and foreshadows events that occur later in the story. A specific object or idea introduced early in a drama, which becomes an important factor during the final resolution, is called a *plant*. Planting and foreshadowing are effective devices in terms of hooking the audience. The conflict builds through a series of complications or misunderstandings until the end of Act One, where a new complication is introduced. In Act Two things begin to get sorted out, and the main conflict is resolved in Act Two, Scene Three. With the opening credits, closing tag, and commercials between scenes, a series episode writer only has about twenty minutes to quickly develop the basic conflict or situation, add a few complications, and then neatly resolve it. The structure of a situation comedy follows this basic formula, regardless of the exact setting and characters. There is a constant need for imagination and creativity within this tight, somewhat restrictive format.

Other types of short fiction are not as formulaic as situation comedy, but they nonetheless demand tight dramatic structure. There simply isn't enough time to develop many minor characters or a complicated subplot. A short drama usually has a short exposition section. New characters and situations must be developed very quickly and efficiently. A few lines of dialogue can establish who new characters are and their basic motivations. The plot must develop several complications to promote interest and variation, but it must also build toward a climax. Loose ends are quickly tied up and resolved.

Interactive scripts differ from traditional dramatic and narrative scripts in a number of ways. Traditional noninteractive scripts tend to be linear in terms of narrative structure. There may be flashbacks and flash-forwards in time, but dramatic narratives follow a relatively fixed linear progression. Interactive stories and game scripts, on the other hand, are distinctly nonlinear. Players can select characters and a variety of story paths to pursue during a game.

Scriptwriters and programmers use one of two types of logic systems for interactive story construction: branching and artificial intelligence. *Branching* refers to a structure that is similar to the structure of a tree or a series of highways that intersect. Choosing a specific action sends the player character along a path that consists of a series of branches off the initial road or tree trunk. Branches may intersect, bringing the character back toward the center, or they may send the character further and further away from the center. A scriptwriter specifies various branches by placing single words in brackets, such as [ATTACK] or [RETREAT], which indicate actions the player or PC (player character) has chosen. Actors and computer characters (CCs) then respond to the player character's actions with various forms of text-based or spoken dialogue, and in so doing the story proceeds along various paths or branches.

Artificial intelligence (AI) refers to the ability to insert variables into a text so that a wide variety of text-based dialogue can be created and displayed very efficiently. Using standard terms, such as computer character (CC) and player character (PC), the scriptwriter uses a % mark to indicate a variable set of dialogue that can be accessed elsewhere. A # mark is used to locate the name of a set of dialogue and instructions, and a series of "if/then" statements indicates actions and dialogue that will be inserted as the PC makes various choices and the CC responds.

One method of organizing scenes for interactive stories is a flowchart, which is also discussed in more detail later in this chapter in reference to interactive educational scriptwriting under "Interactive Learning and Training." Flowcharts allow writers and programmers to visualize various branches and variables that can be followed throughout a game. Computer programs are available that allow a standard full-page master scene script to be married to a flowchart program.

An interactive script consists of a series of instructions to programmers concerning player characters, computer characters, text-based and spoken dialogue, actions, and responses, which follow a branching or artificial intelligence logic system for story construction. An interactive story or game may be designed for one or more platforms, including CD-ROM, Sega, Genesis, floppy disk, or on-line. Dialogue is usually written as text or spoken dialogue to be recorded using actors. In either case, it is usually very brief. Writers need to be conscious of the limitations of various platforms, such as CD-ROM, in terms of storage space for both graphics and text.

Every line of dialogue needs to have a specific purpose in terms of moving the story forward, and this restriction makes it somewhat more difficult to build character through dialogue in interactive than in motion picture and television scripts. There should be enough variety that a player is not bored by endless repetitions of the same line of dialogue. If the dialogue will appear on the screen in written form, remember that the screen is generally restricted to 80 characters of 12-point type per line or less. Scripts are often written in ASCII unformatted style so that they can be directly input into the computer. Full caps are used to emphasize the most important information, such as if/then statements, character names, and actions the player character may choose. Notation and style are generally based upon a standard computer programming language known as C++.

NONFICTION SCRIPTWRITING

Many different types of nonfiction programs and films are used as informative or persuasive media devices. Documentaries, news stories, instructional programs, and commercials are examples of nonfiction films and television programming. These types of products seem to share some common characteristics. There is usually an emphasis on actuality or the presentation of real people, things, situations, actions, and problems. They are often structured or organized to transmit information or to motivate people to change their attitudes or behavior. They make frequent use of expository and rhetorical structures to convey information and to make persuasive appeals to an audience.

Nonfiction shares certain characteristics with dramatic fiction. All scriptwriters attempt to stimulate viewer interest through the portrayal of dramatic conflicts. The theorist Kenneth Burke has argued that all media presentations (both fictional and nonfictional) are essentially dramatic social devices. Reuven Frank, as executive producer of the NBC Evening News in the 1960s, sent the following memorandum to his news staff: "Every news story should, without any sacrifice of probity or responsibility, display the attributes of fiction, of drama. It should have structure and conflict, problem and denouement, rising action and falling action, a beginning, a middle, and an end. These are not only the essentials of drama; they are the essentials of narrative."

In short, elements of dramatic and narrative structure are important to nonfiction scriptwriters, and the material presented earlier in this chapter concerning fiction scriptwriting is relevant to nonfiction scriptwriting as well. In addition, nonfiction scriptwriters utilize rhetorical and expository structure to present argument and convey information.

Rhetorical and Expository Structure

Nonfiction scriptwriters know how to wage effective arguments and to present information in a logical manner that facilitates understanding. Arguments are fashioned on the basis of rhetorical strategies. An argument can take the form of inartistic or artistic proof. Inartistic proofs are dependent upon factual material available to the writer, editor, or speaker, such as interviews with various participants, witnesses, and observers. There are three main types of artistic proof: ethical, emotional, and demonstrative. An ethical proof relies quite heavily on the moral integrity and credibility of the speaker. An emotional proof relies on the appeal to audience emotions and feelings. A demonstrative proof relies on a series of expositions (showing, not just telling), which have recourse to actual events or opposite/alternative points of view. A specific script might rely on all of these different forms of proof and argument.

We can also distinguish rhetorical strategies and approaches on the basis of whether the argument focuses upon its source, its subject, or the viewer. The credibility of the source of an argument in part determines its effectiveness. For example, a highly trusted or reliable person, such as a news anchor or a narrator with a commanding voice, carries a certain persuasive power. Utilizing widely shared beliefs about a subject can also be highly persuasive, such as the idea that all politicians are corrupt or that many large corporations are insensitive to environmental issues. Other arguments focusing on the subject include leaving out various alternative solutions to a problem and implying that the solution presented is the only one possible. This form of argument conceals its basic premise. Emotional arguments, such as waving the flag or castigating someone as a communist, on the other hand, focus more upon viewers (and the assumption that certain emotional responses are widely shared) than upon the subject or the source of the argument.

A nonfiction scriptwriter relies upon expository structures that help to organize information in a logical manner. Widely used expository structures include effects-to-causes, problem/solution, enumeration, classification into logical categories, and theme/countertheme. Many network television documentaries, for example, begin with scenes that dramatize the effects of a particular social problem. These highly charged, emotional scenes act as a hook to grab the audience's attention. A dispassionate narrator then begins to explore some of the causes that have produced these effects. In a classic documentary, such as *The River* (1936) or *Harvest of Shame* (1960), the film or television program ends with proposed solutions to the problem. Specific goals are cited, and specific courses of action are recommended to viewers concerning flood control (the Tennessee Valley Authority) and migrant worker welfare (federal legislation), respectively. Each documentary is structured as an argument for the elimination of a pressing social problem, and the information is logically presented through a problem/solution and effects-to-causes organization (Figure 3.10).

Visual and audio information can also be edited to compare and contrast different opinions and points of view. This can take the form of a theme/countertheme structure, where one idea or point of view clashes repeatedly with another, much like a theme and countertheme in a piece of music. For example, the documentary film *Hearts and Minds* (1975) uses a theme/countertheme structure to alternate between anti-Vietnam War and pro-Vietnam War interviews and statements. *Enumeration* refers to a listing of

various possibilities or realities, while logical categories might consist of different aspects or approaches to a subject. For example, an educational documentary about a Latin American country might examine political, social, economic, cultural, and artistic aspects of that country.

A nonfiction scriptwriter uses dramatic as well as expository structure. Events in a documentary, for example, can be considered to be rising and falling actions. The overall structure of a documentary can obtain emotional power by building toward a climax where a central problem or conflict is resolved. The pace of a non-fiction work is extremely important in terms of maintaining audience interest. The pace should vary to provide an effective emotional (as well as a logical) flow of events. Pacing is difficult to control during the writing stage, because it depends on so many factors that are evident only when the actual sound and image recordings are available. While the writer must exhibit some concern for pacing during the scriptwriting phase, it is really the documentary director and editor who finally determine the pace of specific elements and of the documentary film or videotape as a whole. Pacing is affected by the editing together of long- and short-duration camera shots as well as the speed of actions within shots, dialogue, and narration.

The opening of a nonfiction film or video should define what the piece is about and where it is going. It should serve as a hook to grab the viewer's attention, pique his or her curiosity, and generate a sense of expectation. Presenting a problem or conflict in dramatic, human terms is one of the best ways of gaining immediate audience attention. Presenting a particularly exciting segment of scenes or vignettes, which will be shown in their entirety somewhat later, acts as a teaser that can stimulate interest. Short segments from longer interviews can be edited together to dramatize a conflict or to present alternative points of view at the start. The writer's job is to find a way in which the documentary's main idea, theme, point of view, or conflict can be concisely dramatized in human terms that the intended audience will immediately understand. Later, near the conclusion of the piece, a sense of completion and fulfillment can be achieved by providing a definitive ending that leaves few questions raised in the opening sequence unanswered.

Figure 3.10 A documentary, such as *The River* (1936), not only needs to tell a coherent story, but must make a specific point or argument for or against a social issue.

Voice and Point of View

Many nonfiction and documentary scripts establish a particular point of view. A point of view is an important angle or perspective from which an issue or problem can be productively approached. Television documentaries and news magazines such as *60 Minutes*, for example, sometimes adopt the point of view of a person in an underdog role, such as an individual consumer, as opposed to a large anonymous corporation or bureaucracy. Establishing a specific point of view helps to dramatize and humanize the problem. The audience frequently identifies with the individual, underdog, or injured party, and this can be used to increase the audience's emotional involvement in the problem.

Nonfiction scriptwriters and directors often assert their own voices and opinions. The assertion of a voice can be direct and explicit, such as when a narrator states an opinion, belief, or argument. It can also be indirect and implicit in the expository structure and order in which information is presented. For example, the film *Hearts and Minds* (1975) shows a Vietnamese woman crying over a family member's grave immediately after General William Westmoreland states that Vietnamese people don't value life as dearly as Americans do. Here the expository structure and order of presentation undercuts General Westmoreland and asserts the filmmaker's editorial opinion.

Direct or indirect assertions of a voice are associated with a variety of nonfiction and documentary approaches. Classic rhetorical and expository documentaries, such as *The River* (1937) and *Harvest of Shame* (1960), for example, rely upon direct address through an authoritative narrator or reporter/anchor person. Observational approaches to nonfiction film and video, such as the so-called cinema Everité approach, on the other hand, generally suppress the voice of the filmmaker, avoid using a narrator, and require little, if any, scriptwriting. Events are recorded as they happen in long, continuous camera and sound takes. Nonetheless, the order of presentation of these events, which is determined during editing and postproduction, can rely upon indirect means of asserting the filmmaker's opinion, such as the order of presentation cited earlier with respect to *Hearts and Minds*. An interactive approach encourages the subjects of a documentary to assert their own voices, often highlighting their interaction with the filmmaker. In this case the subjects directly assert their own voices, while the filmmaker relies upon both direct and indirect means of asserting his or her voice. Finally, a self-reflexive approach makes a filmmaker's implicit assertions explicit by self-consciously analyzing his or her own role in the filmmaking process. A self-reflexive approach turns the filmmaker's voice into the subject of the nonfiction film or video.

Narration and Interviews

A nonfiction scriptwriter needs to tell an interesting story in a gripping and imaginative way, using facts, anecdotes, and opinions collected during research. Sometimes narration facilitates telling a story. At other times it gets in the way. If a nonfiction story effectively unfolds through compelling sounds and images, leave it alone. There is no need to retell the story with narration. Narration should clarify images and provide important additional information rather than redundantly describing what sound and images themselves convey. Narration can also emphasize and explain important points and details.

Narration needs to be written so that it can be spoken by a narrator rather than read silently as text by the viewer. It should be colloquial and down to earth. It should also be personalized whenever possible. Narration written in the first person, which will be spoken by a participant in the events that the sounds and images depict, for example, usually works much more effectively than narration written in the third person, which will be spoken by someone who has no connection to the events.

A nonfiction scriptwriter should use simple sentences and action verbs. Words should be particular rather than general, concrete and specific rather than abstract and indefinite. Narration should be factual and informative, directing the viewer's attention to specific details or enhancing the mood and atmosphere by using adjectives that create a more vivid and memorable experience. Using long lists of data, recitations of statistics, and difficult specialized terminology rarely provide narration that is sufficiently informal, subtle, and effective (Figure 3.11).

Interviews often add emotion and personalize events. They should be carefully planned by writing down questions on a piece of paper after carefully and thoroughly researching the subject, but the interviewer should memorize these questions and never simply read them during the interview. An interviewer needs to maintain eye contact with the interviewee and use questions to facilitate rather than disrupt a personal or emotional response to questions. Interview questions should not be able to be answered by a simple "yes" or "no" from the interviewee. They should be specific and directive rather than rambling or excessively general. They should encourage the interviewee to divulge information through personal anecdotes as well as through the expression of attitudes, feelings, and opinions that generate enthusiasm or emotional power. An interviewer should come prepared with a

Figure 3.11 The writer or producer must gather information before the script is written. Interviewing the sources of information provides basic and accurate information upon which to base the script.

bevy of specific questions whose order of presentation will be determined in large part by the interviewee's responses.

Short Nonfiction Forms and Formats

Many scriptwriting principles used with longer nonfiction forms, such as documentaries, are also applicable to shorter forms, such as news stories, talk shows, instructional programs, and commercials, but each of these shorter forms of nonfiction writing has its own principles and practices as well.

News Stories

A television newswriter, for example, writes *copy* or narration to be spoken by on-camera or off-camera news anchors and reporters. Most reporters write their own stories. Only in larger markets do news anchors generally read copy written by a newswriting specialist. Network and most local station newscasters are generally involved in writing their own copy. Whether one is working as a news anchor, reporter, producer, or director, some knowledge of basic newswriting is essential.

Unlike print journalism, television newswriting does not begin with a who, what, when, where, and why approach. There isn't time to answer all of these

questions immediately. Television *story leads* quickly identify the situation. Key information is usually delayed until the second sentence delivered by the newscaster. The first sentence orients the viewer to the general issue to be discussed. "Another accusation of voter fraud surfaced today" leads into a story about a close senatorial election. "Candidate Sherlock Holmes accused the committee to reelect Senator Moriarty of foul play in Baskerville County" then provides the specific information. News copy generally plays a subservient role to accompanying sounds and pictures. Like good documentary narration, good newswriting doesn't try to compete with visual information, but rather sets a context for its interpretation (Figure 3.12).

Newswriting does not have to describe what happened, when news clips are available. The writer simply sets a context for the viewing experience, establishes links or transitions between different stories, and provides a limited summary or conclusion. When commentary accompanies images and sounds, it should identify key participants. Since the camera cannot jump from one participant to another as quickly as they can be verbally identified, a descriptive phrase about each person allows sufficient time for close-ups to be edited together. The alternative to this practice is to use a less dramatic long shot, which includes all participants at once and allows them to

Figure 3.12 Many television news stories are produced and shot in the field. A crew of a reporter, a producer, and a camera operator make up the basic electronic news gathering (ENG) crew. In some markets a crew as small as one person or as large as five persons may make up the ENG crew.

be quickly identified as a group or, in any case, by no more than three individual identifications.

Newswriting should be simple and conversational, so that a newscaster can clearly and concisely communicate the essential information as though he or she is talking to a friend. Remember that a newscaster is an invited guest in private homes. A writer must use discretion when discussing difficult issues. Shocking or disturbingly violent visuals should be clearly identified in advance, giving children and sensitive adults an opportunity to avoid them.

Newswriters, like print reporters, must be careful to attribute information to specific sources and to protect themselves from charges of falsehood. All too often, careless TV news reporters present suppositions as facts. False broadcast news reports can have an immediate and profound effect on viewers.

The first component of a field-recorded news story to be written and recorded is usually the reporter's on-camera commentary. This commentary introduces the subject, provides bridges between various segments, and offers a summary at the end. It is used as voiceover narration to order dramatic visual images and sounds that illustrate what the reporter is talking about.

A newswriter must be concerned with pace. Numerous stories are presented during a half-hour newscast (actually 23 minutes plus commercials).

Each must be cut down to minimal length in a way that retains excitement, interest, and essential information. Although a newscaster often seems calm and in control, the delivery and pace of the entire newscast must be both rapid and smooth. A television newswriter emphasizes active rather than passive verbs to increase pace and viewer interest. The sources of information must be given at the beginning of a sentence rather than at the end of a sentence for better oral communication. The order of words should result in an unambiguous interpretation of events. The purpose of a television newscast is to describe events rather than to interpret them or editorialize about them.

Each story is written as a separate computer file so that the producer can assemble the show as she or he sees fit. When the producer determines the best order of the stories, the computer files can be arranged in that order. Stories must be accurately timed. A good average reading speed is about 150 words of copy per minute. The combination of written copy and edited visuals and sounds must be precisely timed so that the total program fits into the allotted time slot. The completed script indicates if and when commercials will be inserted, and functions as a timing and source guide to live production for the entire staff and crew. A copy of the script goes to the producer, the director, and all on-set newscasters, often called talent. The copy to be read should include phonetic spellings, so that pronunciation is understood. The script is automatically formatted in news script format and is also sent to the teleprompters on the cameras for the anchors to read. It is possible and often necessary to make last-minute changes to the script while the newscast is on the air, moments before the story being changed is seen by the anchors on the prompter.

The material a newswriter edits, rewrites, condenses, or originates comes from a variety of sources. Broadcast news often relies on wire services, such as the Associated Press. Some stories are simply downloaded from computer files provided by wire services. However, using these stories verbatim fails to establish a unique news style. Although wire services usually offer different story renditions for print and broadcast news clients, it can be quite risky to present unedited copy written by print-oriented wire-service journalists. Relying on wire-service copy also fails to provide viewers with news of local or regional interest. Assigning print journalists who have no experience with broadcast journalism to write broadcast copy can also be disastrous. Network news and the most comprehensive local news usually originate from experienced reporters in the field who are investigating specific events, issues, and topics, and who receive tips from interested participants. Local stations also keep a close eye on the print media and competing newscasts to catch up on stories they might otherwise miss. Follow-ups on major stories from preceding days are another important news source.

The news producer must determine the significance of each story and the viewer interest it is likely to arouse so that the lead story, or most important beginning segment, can be selected and the other stories coherently ordered. Which stories will actually be aired depends on a number of factors, including program length, the availability of accompanying still images or videotape, the number of major events that have occurred that day, and the producer's own preferences and priorities. A large number of stories will be written each day; some of those will actually be aired and others either presented later, if they have accompanying visuals of continuing interest, or abandoned entirely. The selected stories are usually presented in blocks that reflect geographical or topical relationships. Innate interest and importance to the audience are equally valid considerations. Many producers try to end a news program with a humorous or human interest story.

Many factors, including the quality of the news writing, affect the selection and placement of news stories for a particular broadcast. Ordering stories in a newscast can be somewhat subjective and quite complex. The trend in commercial television broadcasting is toward many short items, rather than a few long reports on selected topics, and significant use of actual footage and flashy graphics. While a fast-paced structure and format for a news broadcast raises many questions about the quality of in-depth understanding available to the American public on any single topic through commercial television, this approach is obviously economically advantageous to commercial broadcasters, since it attracts many viewers.

Talk Show

News and entertainment functions are combined on many talk shows. There are basically two types of interviews conducted on these shows: celebrity interviews and authority interviews. Celebrity interviews are frequently seen on afternoon and evening entertainment programs. Comedy or singing performances often accompany such interviews. Celebrity interviews generally try to explore the human side of guests and coax them into revealing more about themselves than they may have initially intended. The interview can be purely a performance to entertain the audience or an occasion for self-disclosure, depending on the interviewer's success in gaining the confidence of the celebrity. Celebrity interviews almost always have a commercial purpose. The guest is often promoting a recent book, film, or television program when they appear on the *Tonight Show* or on *The Letterman Show*. Sometimes he or she simply wants to become better known to the general public. Authority interviews focus for the most part on issues, information, ideas, and attitudes rather than personalities. The interviewer's purpose is often to play devil's advocate and force the guest to clarify and substantiate a position and possibly to reveal some important detail that has been omitted in previous reports and interviews. It is not the authority's personality that is of primary interest, but his or her knowledge of and opinion on some significant topic. The authority interview comes perilously close to the celebrity interview, however, when the primary objective is simply to find a political skeleton in the guest's closet.

Writers and researchers must carefully prepare the interviewer for his or her interaction with the guest. A good interviewer is at least as well informed as the audience, and has anticipated what questions audience members would ask if they could. Interviewers often write the questions they plan to ask on note cards. They then go over these cards, paring them down to a reasonable number of questions that they are confident will appeal to their audience. A good interviewer is less concerned with impressing the audience with brilliant questions than with functioning as an effective representative of the audience during the interview. Background information on the guest and topic must be thoroughly researched. But the interviewer must also be a glib respondent to unpredictable events, a careful and sensitive listener, at times a cajoler, and at other times a provocateur or a catalyst.

Although a tremendous amount of writing may be compiled prior to the interview, only a small fraction of it will actually be used during the interview. The interview must appear to be unrehearsed and spontaneous. Questions cannot be read from a sheet of paper. They must be presented as though they are spontaneous. A written script provides a general outline of guests to be interviewed and topics to be discussed. Introductions and background material can be written out and displayed at the appropriate time on a teleprompter, which projects copy on a see-through mirror in front of the camera lens. Cue cards are also created for the interviewer's use. A script also indicates when commercials will appear and the precise timing of the segments of a show.

Talk-show writers and interviewers, like good documentarians and newswriters, are concerned about ethical issues, such as the potential conflict between the public's right to know and the citizen's right to privacy. When a sensitive topic or personal problem is to be discussed, the interviewer must satisfy the audience's curiosity without embarrassing the guest or placing him or her in an awkward position. A good interviewer knows how to phrase questions in a tactful manner so that the guest is not offended, although the audience's curiosity and expectations are fully satisfied. Indirect methods of questioning can be quite effective, and they raise fewer ethical dilemmas about pressuring a private citizen into revealing more personal details than he or she really cares to have the public know.

Barbara Walters, in discussing her celebrity-interviewing techniques, has said that she often uses indirect methods of questioning. For example, she felt that it would be in bad taste to ask Mamie Eisenhower, the former President's widow, any direct question about her supposed problem with alcohol. Instead, she simply asked Mrs. Eisenhower if there was ever a time that she felt concerned about her public impressions in the White House. Mrs. Eisenhower revealed that she had an inner ear problem that sometimes caused her to lose her balance, and that the press had misinterpreted this as a sign of alcoholism.

Commercials and Public Service Announcements

Commercials are brief messages that advertise products, company names, and services. Unlike many other types of nonfiction, commercials aim directly at modifying audience behavior and attitudes. The chief test of a commercial's success is not whether people watch and enjoy it. The true test is whether people buy a specific product or are positively predisposed toward a particular company. Commercials are primarily persuasive; they are informative only to the extent that audiences become aware of the existence of new products and services or corporate goodwill.

Commercials vary considerably in terms of their production values and formats. Network commercials and national spot commercials (network-level commercials aired on local stations in major markets) are generally written and controlled by major advertising companies, such as Leo Burnett, J. Walter Thompson, and McCann-Erickson. These companies oversee all aspects of the creation of a commercial from writing, through storyboarding, to actual production by an independent production company. They are often shot on 35mm film, and budgets can run as high as several hundred thousand dollars. On the local level, commercials are usually made on videotape by a television station or by a small production studio. The people who produce local commercials often write them as well. Many regional and local commercial producers use digital production effects and transitions as well as computer graphics, whether the commercial was originally shot on film or videotape.

The first step in writing a commercial is to establish the main goal. In most cases the goal is to sell a specific product or service, but some commercials sell corporate goodwill. Public utilities do not always compete directly with other companies supplying the same type of power or service. They nonetheless need to maintain a positive public image, if only to obtain periodic rate increases. Targeting a goal for products, services, or corporate goodwill is helpful in terms of selecting a specific selling strategy.

Commercial scriptwriters rely quite heavily on advertising research to determine the best way to sell a product or service. The look and selling approach of a television commercial are often dictated by audience testing and positioning. Positioning refers to the most effective means of reaching prospective buyers for a product or service. Audience testing and positioning determine the overall approach that a writer should take, how a commercial will look, and how it will communicate to a selected target audience. Market research reveals the best selling strategy.

Writers of commercials try to define three things before they begin writing the script: the intended audience, the major selling points of the product, and the best strategy or format with which to sell the product. The audience can be defined generally or very specifically in demographic terms of sex, age, race, socioeconomic status, and so on. Airtime for the presentation of the commercial can be selected on the basis of this well-defined target audience. The writer must be familiar with the types of expressions and selling techniques that will appeal to the intended audience. Advertising agencies conduct research before actual writing begins, trying to ascertain why a particular group of people likes or uses a product and why others do not. A commercial is usually designed to broaden the appeal of the product without alienating the current users or consumers. Writing a commercial requires a firm understanding of the specific product or service that is being sold. Listing the major selling points of the product will help the writer to select those elements that appeal primarily to the main target audience and to determine the best selling format, whether it is a hard sell or a soft sell, a serious or a humorous tone, a testimonial, and/or a dramatization.

Both hard-sell and soft-sell commercials are used to promote specific products. They are usually based on a careful study of the nature of the product and its appeal. Consumer testing reveals that a hard sell works well with automobiles and soap products, for example. An aggressive pitch does not turn off potential customers. Many soap-product commercials present "real-life" dramatizations that end in a hard sell from a typical consumer who is satisfied with the product. Other products rely on a soft sell or less direct appeal. They create a particular image that entices consumers to seek beauty aids or brand-name clothing in order to have a more satisfying social life. A commercial can create an attractive image that is associated with the product and that the customer aspires to emulate. This approach often reinforces social stereotypes, such as traditional or emerging trends in male and female roles. Commercials generally reinforce the status quo because advertisers are afraid of offending potential customers. Testimonials, which are endorsements of a product or service made by celebrities, often rely on hard-sell techniques. Dramatizations, except in the soap products, usually offer a more direct approach. The viewer is left to his or her own conclusions about why someone is so attractive, successful, or satisfied.

Generally, humorous treatments work well in some cases but not others. Humorous treatments of products or services related to death, personal hygiene, or profound social problems are generally in poor taste and can be offensive to audiences and thus counterproductive. Humor can be used effectively to deflate the sophisticated image of a specialized foreign product, such as Grey Poupon Mustard, or to associate a product with fun and good times, as McDonald's commercials have done. Humor can create amusement and attention, but if poorly handled it can also distract attention form the product or company name. Appropriate use of humor generally requires talented performers. A variety of means can be used to help the audience remember the product or company name, such as simple name repetition or a song with a catchy phrase or slogan, called a *jingle*. Many commercials begin with the creation of a song to which the visual elements will be edited. The lyrics and music are frequently performed by top-name musicians and performers, and they often set the tone and pace for the entire commercial. The emphasis in jingles is on repeatable phrases that will help the consumer remember the product or company name.

Commercials are often extensively tested on audiences and potential consumers prior to any purchase of expensive airtime. The objective of most scientific tests is to determine the effect of the commercial on product recall or name retention. It is assumed that if viewers can recall the product or company name, they are likely to buy the product. Other tests examine actual or simulated purchasing behavior, such as the opportunity to select a soft drink from among several competing products after viewing commercials. Sometimes several versions of a commercial may be tested, only the most effective of which will actually be used.

Written or spoken advertising copy must be clear, succinct, concrete, and active. Clarity is of utmost importance. If the message is to be understood, it must be expressed in terms that the average viewer can easily comprehend. Time for commercials is both limited and expensive, so the message must be short and direct. There is no time for wasted words that distract attention from the central point. It is usually best to use very concrete nouns and adjectives, as well as active verbs. Passive verbs are too tentative and rarely help sell products. Writers of commercials try to use words that will be popular with the anticipated audience and consumer. Key words or *buzzwords*, such as "natural" or "no artificial ingredients," can increase the appeal of a product for potential buyers, despite the fact that chemists often consider such words to be imprecisely applied to soft drinks and food, since very few edible substances are actually artificial.

A *storyboard* is a preproduction tool consisting of a series of drawings and accompanying written information. In some ways a storyboard is similar to a comic strip. The storyboard tells the commercial story or message in still pictures. Narration or dialogue, camera movements, sound effects, and music are usually specified under or next to each frame. An advertising agency usually creates a storyboard to show clients and producers what a commercial will look like. The storyboard suggests how images and sounds will be ordered, the placement of the camera, and the design of the set. Today, computer storyboard programs or programs that combine both word processing and a storyboard segment provide a flexible and efficient method of creating and editing scoreboards.

Directors sometimes use storyboards along with the script as a guide to the actual recording of the finished commercial on film or videotape, and their use is highly recommended for any type of production for which step-by-step planning is possible. Many feature film directors compose their shots on storyboards prior to actual production. A television storyboard consists of four elements: hand-drawn sketches, camera positions and movements, dialogue or narration, and sound effects or music. Each hand-drawn sketch is composed within a frame that has the same proportions as a television screen (4 units wide by 3 units high, a ratio of 4:3). A frame is drawn for each shot. Camera positions and movements, lines of dialogue or narration, and sound effects (SFX) and music are specified under or next to each frame.

A public service announcement, or PSA, is produced much like a commercial. PSAs are usually aired free of charge by commercial broadcasting stations, and most noncommercial stations offer no other form of announcements. PSAs often promote nonprofit organizations. They can attempt to raise public awareness of specific social problems and social service agencies, and are usually persuasive in the sense that they have clear behavioral objectives, such as appeals for help or money. In the case of a social need or charity event, the emphasis is usually on developing audience empathy for people in need rather than on appealing to the audience's materialistic needs and drives.

The writing of a PSA is virtually identical to that of a commercial. The same steps and procedures can be followed, including researching the particular organization or cause, specifying the goal, matching the selling or promotional strategy to the intended audience, and creating a storyboard. PSAs offer an opportunity for students and beginning production people to obtain valuable experience in writing and production, because they are usually produced on very low budgets and incur few, if any, expensive airtime costs.

Instructional Films and Videos

Instructional films and videos often serve one of the following purposes: to supplement lectures in the classroom; to inform the public and government employees about new, government policies; or to inform employees and/or the public about corporate practices, policies, and points of view. These three purposes reflect the institutional needs of producers in educational, government, and corporate environments, respectively. Instructional programs are designed as either supplementary or primary materials. They may accompany an educational, government, or corporate speech, or they may have to stand on their own without the help of a person who can set a context for viewing or answer questions.

The most important factor in planning instructional programs is to understand the needs, expectations, and level of knowledge of the audience. Groups with different demographics (age, socioeconomic status, and educational level) often require entirely different instructional strategies. A four-year-old child requires a different approach than a 10-year-old. While the overall objective of any instructional program is to impart knowledge, effective communication depends on the writer's awareness of the audience's sophistication, age, and educational level. A writer must use terms with which the audience is already familiar or define new terms in words that the audience already understands.

Instructional information must be clear and well organized. Each step or concept must follow logically from preceding steps and concepts. Suppose, for example, that a program is designed to instruct beginning photography students about basic concepts of developing film. It is logical to begin with a description and graphic demonstration of a piece of film, showing the various light-sensitive layers and substances. The camera can be described next, along with the process of exposing the film to light. Finally, the stages of developing and printing the film, using different chemicals and pieces of equipment, can each be described sequentially. A short review of the fundamental steps then summarizes the overall process.

An instructional program must be more than clear and logical, however. It must graphically demonstrate concepts and ideas. Otherwise, what is the point of making a videotape or film? Cross-sections of a piece of film and the working parts of a camera can be drawn. Actual scenes might be shot in a photographic darkroom under red lights, which give the impression of a darkroom setting but provide sufficient light for recording purposes. A photographer can actually demonstrate the various stages of developing and printing photographic images, so that students are brought out of the classroom into an actual work environment. Educational films and videotapes present materials that cannot be easily demonstrated through a lecture or the use of other less-expensive media, such as slides, audiotapes, or graphic projections. Moving images should move. There is no justification for using film or videotape recording for something that can be done just as well and much less expensively with still pictures. Noted communications researcher Carl I. Howland's experiment comparing slides and lectures with movies as teaching devices demonstrated that slides and lectures were better, not just less expensive. Of course, motion is an important component of many educational subjects. The narration that accompanies this graphic material must be concise, clear, and easily comprehended. A sense of drama, like a sense of humor, can add interest and excitement, but it can also be overdone. The main objective is to show rather than tell. The narration should be authoritative, but not condescending. It must impart accurate information, link various parts of the demonstration, and establish a context within which the accompanying images can be clearly and completely understood.

Interactive Learning and Training

Writing for interactive multimedia educational applications is an important aspect of authoring. *Authoring* includes everything from designing a flowchart for the interactive learning or training process to writing actual text that will appear on a computer monitor when the application is run. Authoring begins with the development of an interactive training concept. An author clarifies the training concept and specifies the intended audience, the purpose of the application, and the basic subject matter by writing a treatment document, which provides a narrative description of the proposed project. The treatment may also indicate the anticipated platforms (Mac, PC, and so on), operating systems (Mac OS 10, 9; Windows 2000, NT, 98, 95; DOS; and so on), style (command or object), and interface (text-based or graphical). Like a treatment for an interactive game, the latter information defines the authoring environment, that is, the computer hardware and software that will be used to design the application as well as the intended avenues of its distribution. This aspect of authoring is also similar to a producer's development of a proposal and treatment for a (noninteractive) film or video. The author defines the objectives for a project and the means by which those objectives will be accomplished (Figure 3.13).

The scriptwriting phase of interactive educational multimedia production, similar in many respects to authoring or writing computer games and other forms

CUEING AUDIO TAPE DECKS

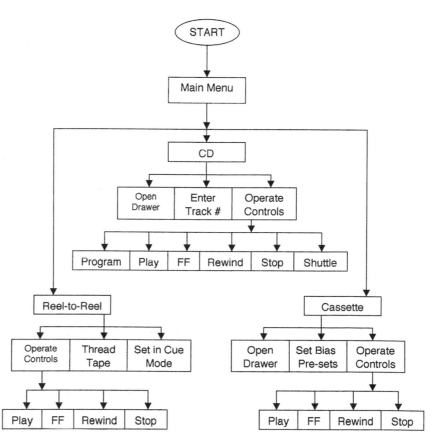

Figure 3.13 An interactive program diagram shows the various paths or choices that the person using the program has to follow. Arrows indicate directions that the paths may take in moving forward, retracing, or starting a new path.

of interactive entertainment, is sometimes referred to as the *design stage*. The purpose of the design stage is to provide an architectural blueprint for the overall project that will guide the selection and arrangement of content. Creating a design can take the form of flowcharting as well as actual scriptwriting. A flowchart indicates the possible avenues that a student can pursue to acquire information or to be trained in the use of various hardware or software. A fixed flowchart on paper can become very complex and somewhat confusing when there are many different interactive choices and options that result in numerous intersecting lines. Using computer software for authoring, which includes screen icons that move the flowchart to different levels by means of double-clicking a mouse pointer on an icon, can increase the clarity and flexibility of a flowchart.

The script for an interactive learning or training application indicates all the content that will appear in the completed project, including graphics, animation, video, and audio, as well as written text. The flowchart provides an overview of the program architecture and interactive training options, while script material added to the flowchart indicates in some detail all of the content that will appear at various points along the flowchart. Descriptions of visual images and sounds are generally kept to a minimum. Various icon symbols are often used to indicate repeated (as opposed to unique) sounds, graphic images, animation sequences, and live-action video that will appear at different points along the flowchart. Text may appear as spoken narration or written text that accompanies visual images and sounds. For example, CD-ROMs and videodiscs of music videos or feature films can include written text that provides additional information about its production. An interactive CD-ROM or videodisc can also allow a student to manipulate various components, such as remixing the sound or altering special effects in the image. In this case, a viewer/listener becomes an active participant in the creative process and learns how to control sounds and images through hands-on experience. Educational multimedia products can also provide written text in the form of specific questions and correct or incorrect answers to these questions, which test a student's knowledge, providing immediate feedback. Several incorrect responses might indicate to a student that he or she needs to repeat one section before going on to the next.

Interactive multimedia provides obvious educational advantages over published manuals and textbooks that an author or scriptwriter should utilize whenever possible. Since some students are primarily auditory learners, and others learn better through visual or tactile stimulation, authors should make some attempt to vary the form of media presentation. Sometimes media redundancy, that is, conveying similar information using audio, visual, and hands-on interaction, can be extremely effective for all types of learners. Authors should also allow for different learning rates or speeds of information acquisition. Flowcharts should provide enough options to facilitate the learning process for students who learn relatively quickly or slowly.

SUMMARY

Scriptwriting can be divided into two basic categories: fiction and nonfiction. Every scriptwriter should be familiar with the basic elements of both fiction and nonfiction writing. Principles of dramatic and narrative structure used in fiction may also be applicable to nonfiction, and principles of rhetorical persuasion and expository structures used in nonfiction can be helpful in a dramatic production. Elements of dramatic, narrative, rhetorical, and expository structure are of practical value to scriptwriters working in a variety of areas and formats.

Scriptwriting demands visual thinking. Scriptwriters know how to use the full creative potential of moving images and sounds. Preparation for scriptwriting includes performing research and writing a treatment. Research is a creative process of uncovering new sources of information. A synopsis of the story or subject matter is called a treatment. A treatment provides a summary of the project in short-story form. It provides an outline of the script that can serve as a guide for future writing.

There are three basic script formats: full-page master scene, split-page, and semi-scripted.

Dramatic films and television programs can be plotted into a framework that consists of a basic three-act structure and a series of rising and falling actions, which culminate in a climax and resolution. Dramatic structure includes rising actions and falling actions, text, and subtext.

Fictional stories are usually told or narrated by someone. Narrative structure has two basic elements: time and point of view.

Dramatic narratives develop characters and themes. Characters' values reveal themselves through actions and words. The writer's job is to externalize these values through speech, mannerisms, and actions.

Nonfiction scripts often convey information about actual events. Nonfiction scriptwriters work in a variety of formats, including documentary, news and talk shows, commercials, and educational programs, such as interactive multimedia applications. They make frequent use of expository and rhetorical structures to convey information and to make persuasive appeals to an audience.

Arguments are fashioned on the basis of rhetorical strategies. Rhetorical strategies and approaches can also be distinguished on the basis of whether the argument focuses upon its source, its subject, or the viewer.

A nonfiction scriptwriter relies upon expository structures that help to organize information in a logical manner. Widely used expository structures include effects-to-causes, problem/solution, enumeration, classification into logical categories, and theme/countertheme.

Narration needs to be written so that it can be effectively spoken.

Short nonfiction formats include news stories, talk shows, and commercials. A newswriter's job is to organize a story and to describe events in a straightforward, clear, and succinct way. There are basically two types of talk show interviews: celebrity interviews and authority interviews. Commercials are brief messages that are broadcast as persuasive appeals.

Instructional films and videos must be clear and well organized. Writers must rely on terms and concepts that will be easily comprehended by the appropriate educational level or demographic group to which the instructional material is directed.

The script for an interactive learning or training application indicates all the content that will appear in the completed project, including graphics, animation, video, and audio, as well as written text. A flowchart provides an overview of the program's architecture and interactive training options. Interactive multimedia can be tailored to meet the needs of students who are primarily auditory, visual, or tactile learners.

EXERCISES

1. Write a synopsis of a short, five-minute script of a simple drama.

2. Write the script from #1 in a single column full-master master script format. Second, reorganize the script in a two-column format. Finally, organize the material into a semi-scripted format.

3. Outline the script into three acts

4. Choose a favorite fairy tale or short story, and write a script adaptation.

5. Choose a controversial topic of the day, research the topic, and then write an eight-minute script in the model used by the CBS-TV program, *60 Minutes*.

6. Using a product you use, write three 30-second commercials. Each one should use a different selling strategy.

ADDITIONAL READINGS

Bonnet, James. *Stealing Fire from the Gods: A Dynamic New Story Model For Writers and Filmmakers*. Michael Wiese Productions, 1999.

Cartwright, Steve R., and G. Phillip Cartwright. *Designing and Producing Media-Based Training*. Boston, MA: Focal Press, 1999.

Cooper, Pat, and Ken Dancyger. *Writing the Short Film*, 2nd ed. Boston, MA: Focal Press, 1999.

De Abreu, Carlos, and Howard Jay Smith. *Opening the Doors to Hollywood: How to Sell Your Idea/Story*. Beverly Hills, CA: Custos Morum, 1995.

DiZazzo, Ray. *Corporate Media Production*. Boston, MA: Focal Press, 2000.

Emm, Adele. *Researching for Television and Radio*. New York: Routledge, 2001.

Em, Michele. "The Ever-Changing Story: Writing for the Interactive Market." *Journal of the Writers Guild of America West*, June 1994, pp. 16–21.

Field, Syd, *Screenplay: The Foundations of Screenwriting*. DTP, 1984.

Garrand, Timothy. *Writing for Multimedia and the Web*, 2nd ed. Boston: Focal Press, 2001.

Johnson, Claudia H. *Crafting Short Screenplays That Connect*. Boston, MA: Focal Press, 2000.

Luther, Arch C. *Designing Interactive Multimedia*. New York: Bantam Books, 1992.

Rabiger, Michael. *Developing Story Ideas*. Boston, MA: Focal Press, 2000.

Rosenthal, Alan. *Writing, Directing, and Producing Documentary Films*, 3rd. ed. Carbondale, IL: Southern Illinois University Press, 2003.

Rosenthal, Alan. *Writing Docudrama*. Boston, MA: Focal Press, 1995.

Seger, Linda. *Making a Good Script Great*, 2nd ed. New York: Dodd, Mead & Company, 1994.

Thompson, Kristin. *Storytelling in the New Hollywood: Understanding Classical Narrative Technique*. Cambridge: Harvard University Press, 1999.

Van Nostran, William J. *The Media Writer's Guide: Writing for Business and Educational Programming*. Boston, MA: Focal Press, 2000.

Whitcomb, Cynthia. *Selling Your Screenplay*. New York: Crown Publishers, 1988.

4

Directing: Aesthetic Principles and Production Coordination

TOPICS FOR DISCUSSION

- What are directing aesthetics approaches?
- How do shots vary?
- What does composition mean to a director?
- How are shots combined into sequences and scenes?
- How do single- and multiple-camera directing differ?

INTRODUCTION

Video and film directors are artists who can take a completed script and imaginatively transform it into exciting sounds and images. Directors creatively organize many facets of production to produce works of art. They know how and when to use different types of camera shots and have mastered the use of composition, image qualities, transition devices, and relations of time and space. Directors know when and how to use different types of sound and how to control sound and image interaction. They understand how to work with people, especially actors and various creative staff and crew members. Above all they know how to tell good stories. By using all of their creative powers, directors are able to produce films and video programs that have lasting value.

Directors prepare a shooting script by indicating specific types of images and sounds to be recorded within each scene. Armed with a final shooting script,

a director is ready to organize production. In order to record the different scenes and sequences described in the script, the director must organize the activities of many different people who are involved in production. The role of the director is quite different in multiple-camera versus single-camera productions. The director must be able to communicate precisely and quickly with cast and crew. A specific communication system and language must be understood and followed by each person as a command is directed at him or her. Each of these facets of the director's responsibility in the production process will be covered in this chapter. The director usually selects and organizes images and sounds according to one of the three basic aesthetic approaches introduced in Chapter 1, "The Production Process: Analog and Digital Technologies."

AESTHETIC APPROACHES

A convenient way to organize *aesthetics*, or approaches to the creative process, is to use three very general categories: realism, modernism, and postmodernism. Most artistic approaches reflect one or more of these three aesthetic tendencies, which differ in their emphases on function, form, and content. *Function* refers to why something is expressed: its goal or purpose. *Form* can be thought of as how something is expressed in a work of art. *Content* refers to what is expressed. Function, form, and content are closely connected aspects of any creative work.

AESTHETICS
- Function—Why
- Form—How
- Content—What
- Realism—Content Over Form
- Modernism—Form Over Function
- Post Modernism—Audience's Involvement Over Artist's Form & Content

Realism

Realism stresses content more than form. In realist works, artists use forms and techniques that do not call attention to themselves, or a so-called transparent style. Realist artists depict a world of common experience as naturally as possible. Smooth, continuous camera movements and actions, continuity of time and place, and the use of actual locations and real people (i.e., nonactors) help to sustain a sense of reality. Realist art relies on conventions that some artists and viewers believe will preserve an illusion of reality. Although realist techniques and conventions change, as in the shift from black-and-white to color images for added realism in photography, film, and television during the 1950s and 1960s, the mimetic tradition of art and literature imitating reality and the intent to preserve an illusion of reality in Western art has persisted over time. A realist artist is a selector and organizer of common experience, rather than a self-conscious manipulator of abstract forms, principles, and ideas.

Many prime-time network television dramas, such as *ER* and *The West Wing*, and nonfiction programs, such as *60 Minutes*, *48 Hours*, and *20/20*, select and organize common experience as naturally as possible. Continuity of space and time is evident even in the titles of some of these programs, such as *48 Hours*. Forms and techniques rarely call attention to themselves. Instead a transparent but very dramatic style helps to depict worlds of common experience and sustain an illusion of reality.

Modernism

Modernism stresses the idea that form is more important than function. Creators of avant-garde works of video and film art explore their medium beyond the usual restrictions and limitations of a realist approach without considering the illusion of reality. A modernist director's works show less objectivity, tend to explore feelings of ambiguity, and may lack continuity in space and time. Many music video productions and some science fiction programs may be classified as modernist.

Some European feature film directors, such as Ingmar Bergman in Sweden and Luis Bunuel in Spain and France, have used modernist aesthetics to guide their approaches to filmmaking. Bergman's film *Persona* (1966), for example, offers a collage of images that reflect the psychological states of mind of an actress who refuses to speak, and a nurse who is trying to take care of her both inside and outside a Swedish mental hospital. Their personalities and faces seem to merge during the course of the film. The editing of this film and the world that Bergman depicts often conform more closely to internal mental states than they do to an external illusion of physical reality. Space and time are often discontinuous. Luis Bunuel's early surrealist avant-garde film, *Un Chien Andalou* (*An Andalusian Dog*, 1929), which he co-directed with the surrealist painter Salvador Dali, and his later narrative feature films, such as *The Discreet Charm of the Bourgeoisie* (1973) and *Tristana* (1970) or *Viridiana* (1961), often defy logic and rational thought as well as continuity in space and time. The surrealist world that Bunuel depicts allows the irrational thoughts and unconscious feelings and desires of his characters to be freely exposed at the same time that it makes a satirical comment on social conventions and institutional religious practices. Ingmar Bergman and Luis Bunuel are strongly personal, modern artists who sometimes stress style more than content and explore feelings of ambiguity and interior states of mind in their films rather than present an external illusion of reality.

Postmodernism

Postmodernism stresses viewer participation within open-ended works with vaguely defined characteristics. A scattered blending or pastiche of new and old images, genres, and production techniques may intentionally confuse the audience, yet at the same time attempt to emotionally and sometimes interactively involve the viewer or listener in the creation of texts rather than treat them as passive consumers of entertainment. Film and video directing and production in the post-modernist mode continue to evolve, and their precise definitions remain somewhat elusive.

An example of a postmodernist work is Peter Gabriel's CD-ROM entitled *Explora 1 Peter Gabriel's Secret World* (1993), which was developed and directed by Peter Gabriel, Steve Nelson, Michael Coulson, Nichola Bruce, and Mic Large. This interactive CD-ROM contains Peter Gabriel's music and music videos as well as minidocumentaries about the artist and the production of his works, including information about performing artists with whom Gabriel has collaborated as well as other visual artists. Viewers and listeners control the sequence and duration in which the entertainment and information contained on this CD-ROM are presented in the "INTERACT" mode, while the "WATCH" mode takes them on a guided journey through the disk. Viewers and listeners have to correctly put together an image of Peter Gabriel to gain entry and to select different worlds to explore and different areas with which to interact. In one section, viewers and listeners can even add or subtract different musicians and control the sound levels of the audio mix for a selection from Peter Gabriel's music during an interactive recording session. The ways in which this CD-ROM combines animation, live action, and documentary recordings, information and entertainment, and "INTERACT" and "WATCH" modes of presentation clearly offer a postmodernist approach to directing that directly involves the viewer and listener in the creative process.

Realism, modernism, and postmodernism are not mutually exclusive, nor do they exhaust all aesthetic possibilities, but they offer a convenient means of organizing the field of aesthetics from the standpoint of production. The relation of expressive forms and techniques to program content and purposes often reflects these three general tendencies. They are applicable to all the aspects of production that will be covered in the following sections, including visualization, lighting, and set design, as well as postproduction editing.

VISUALIZATION

The director decides what types of pictures should be used to tell the story specified in a script by considering the choices available. The visualization process includes an analysis of the types of shots possible, composing those shots, and deciding how to combine the shots visually and with the proper sounds into a comprehensive whole.

A director's ability to select and control visual images begins with an understanding of specific types of shots. The camera can be close to or far away from the subject. It can remain stationary or move during a shot. The shots commonly used in video and film production can be described in terms of camera-to-subject distance, camera angle, camera (or lens) movement, and shot duration.

Types of Shots

Long Shot (LS)

The long shot orients the audience to subjects, objects, and settings by viewing them from a distance; this term is sometimes used synonymously with the terms *establishing shot*, *wide shot*, or *full shot*. An establishing shot (ES) generally locates the camera at a sufficient distance to establish the setting. Place and time are clearly depicted. A full shot (FS) provides a full frame (head-to-toe) view of a human subject or subjects (Figure 4.1).

Medium Shot (MS)

A medium shot provides approximately a three-quarter (knee-to-head) view of the subject. The extremes in terms of camera-to-subject distance within this type of shot are sometimes referred to as a *medium long shot* (MLS) and a *medium close-up* (MCU) (Figure 4.2). The terms *two-shot* and *three-shot* define medium shots in which two or three subjects, respectively, appear in the same frame.

Figure 4.1 A long shot (LS) may refer to the framing of a human figure from head to foot, or the longest shot in the sequence.

Figure 4.2 A medium shot (MS) may refer to the framing of a human from the head to just below the knees, or a shot framing two persons, sometimes called a two-shot.

Close Shot (CS) or Close-Up (CU)

The terms *close shot* and *close-up* are often used synonymously. A close-up refers to the isolation of elements in the shot and normally indicates the head and shoulders of a person. When someone is making an important or revealing statement or facial gesture, a close-up will draw the audience's attention to that event. Close-ups focus and direct attention and create dramatic emphasis. When they are overused, however, their dramatic impact is severely reduced. A very close camera position is sometimes called an *extreme close-up* (ECU). See Figures 4.1, 4.2, and 4.3 for illustrations of long, medium, and close-up shots, respectively. There are times when the standard nomenclature of framing is not appropriate. If the widest shot in a program is from a blimp and the tightest shot is of one football player, then the blimp shot would be the LS and the player shot would be a CU. Conversely, if the entire commercial is shot in close-ups, the tightest shot would be an ECU, and the widest shot would be an LS, even if it were only a shot of a hand holding a product.

Camera Angle

The camera angle is frequently used to establish a specific viewpoint, such as to involve the audience in sharing a particular character's perspective on the action. The goal may be to enhance identification with that person's psychological or philosophical point of view.

Point-of-View Shot (POV Shot)

A point-of-view shot places the camera in the approximate spatial positioning of a specific character. It is often preceded by a shot of a character looking in a particular direction, which establishes the character's spatial point of view within the setting, followed by a shot of that same character's reaction to what he or she has seen. The latter shot is sometimes called a reaction shot. A closely related shot is the *over-the-shoulder shot* (OS). The camera is positioned so that the shoulder of one subject appears in the foreground and the face or body of another is in the background. Another variation on the point-of-view shot is the *subjective shot*, which shows us what the person is looking at or thinking about. Like point-of-view shots, subjective shots offer a nonobjective viewpoint on actions and events, and can enhance audience identification with more subjective points of view (Figures 4.4 and 4.5).

Figure 4.4 A point-of-view (POV) refers to framing as if the observer were viewing from inside the camera or if the camera lens represented what a character would be viewing from their position in the set.

Figure 4.3 A close-up (CU) may refer to the framing of a person from the top of the head to just below the neck line, or if framing an object, filling the frame with the object.

Figure 4.5 An over-the-shoulder (OS) refers to a two-shot from behind one of the subjects who is facing the other subject. Generally the framing is a medium shot.

Reverse-Angle Shot

A reverse-angle shot places the camera in exactly the opposite direction of the previous shot. The camera is moved in a 180-degree arc from the shot immediately preceding it.

Low-Angle Shot

A low-angle shot places the camera closer to the floor than the normal camera height, which is usually at eye level. A low angle tends to exaggerate the size and importance of the subject (Figure 4.6).

High-Angle Shot

The high-angle shot places the camera high above the subject and tends to reduce its size and importance (Figure 4.7).

Overhead Shot

An overhead shot places the camera directly overhead and creates a unique perspective on the action. This can sometimes be accomplished by a set of periscope mirrors, an overhead track, or by attaching the camera to an airplane, helicopter, or crane (Figure 4.8).

Stationary Versus Mobile Camera Shots

An objectively recorded scene in a drama establishes a point of view that conforms to the audience's main focus of interest in the unfolding events. This objective placement of cameras can still be quite varied. A director can use a continuously moving camera gliding through the scene to follow the key action. This approach establishes a point of view that is quite different from recording a scene from several stationary camera positions. Both approaches can be objective in the sense that neither attempts to present a specific person's point of view, although a moving camera creates a greater feeling of participation and involvement as the audience moves through the setting with the camera.

A moving camera adds new information to the frame and often alters spatial perspective. A moving camera shot can maintain viewer interest for a longer period of time than a stationary camera shot. But a moving camera shot can also create difficulties. It is often difficult to cut from a moving camera shot to a stationary camera shot. The camera should be held still for a moment at the beginning and end of a moving camera shot so that it can easily be intercut with other shots. One moving camera shot can follow another so long as the direction and speed of movement remain the same. Both moving the camera and cutting from one stationary camera shot to another

Figure 4.6 A low-angle shot is the view from a camera positioned well below the eye level of the subject looking up at the subject.

Figure 4.7 A high-angle shot is the view from a camera positioned well above the eye level of the subject looking down on the subject.

Figure 4.8 Among many other means of mounting either film or video cameras is the gyroscope mount, which can be mounted on an airplane, helicopter, or any moving vehicle. The stabilizing system provides a solid, smooth picture, and the operator inside the vehicle can pan, tilt, and zoom the camera as the shot requires.

can give us a spatial impression of the setting from a variety of perspectives, but the former generates feelings of smoothness and relaxation, and the latter creates an impression of roughness and tension, which was used effectively to stimulate a feeling of disorientation in a film such as *Natural Born Killers* (1994). Many types of mobile camera shots can be recorded with the camera remaining in a relatively fixed position.

Pan Shot

A camera can be panned by simply pivoting it from side to side on a fixed tripod or panning device. This shot is often used to follow action without having to move the camera from its fixed floor position.

Tilt Shot

A camera tilt is accomplished by moving the camera up and down on a swivel or tilting device. This shot is also used to follow action, such as a person standing up or sitting down. It can also be used to follow and accentuate the apparent height of a building, object, or person.

Pedestal Shot

A camera can be physically moved up and down on a pedestal dolly. A hydraulic lift moves the camera vertically up and down within the shot, such as when a performer gets up from a chair or sits down. A pedestal shot allows the camera to remain consistently at the same height as the performer, unlike a tilt shot, where the camera height usually remains unchanged. Pedestal shots are rare, but a pedestal is often used to adjust the height of the camera between shots (Figure 4.9).

Zoom Shot

A zoom can be effected by changing the focal length of a variable focal-length lens in midshot. A zoom shot differs from a dolly shot in that a dolly shot alters spatial perspective by actually changing the spatial positioning of objects within the frame. During a zoom shot the apparent distance between objects appears to change because objects are enlarged or contracted in size at different rates. During a *zoom-in* objects appear to get closer together, and during a *zoom-out* they seem to get farther apart. Other types of mobile camera shots require camera supports that can be physically moved about the studio.

Dolly Shot

A dolly shot is a shot in which the camera moves toward or away from the subject while secured to a movable platform on wheels. It is often needed to fol-

Figure 4.9 A studio pedestal is designed to allow the heavy weight of a studio camera, lens, and prompter to be moved about the studio with relative ease. The direction of the wheels under the skirt of the pedestal can be changed to allow the camera to be guided in any direction. The vertical pedestal column is counter-weighted or controlled by compressed air to allow the operator to raise or lower the camera easily and smoothly. The pan head is mounted on the top of the pedestal column. (Courtesy Chapman/Leonard Studio Equipment, Inc.)

low long or complicated movements of performers, or to bring us gradually closer to or farther away from a person or object.

Trucking Shot

In a trucking shot, the camera is moved laterally (from side to side) on a wheeled dolly. The camera may truck with a moving subject to keep it in frame. If the dolly moves in a semicircular direction, the shot is sometimes referred to as an *arc* or *camera arc*.

Tracking Shot

A tracking shot uses tracks laid over rough surfaces to provide a means of making smooth camera moves in otherwise impossible locations.

Crane or Boom Shot

The camera can be secured to a crane or boom so that it can be raised and lowered or moved from side to side on a pivoting arm. This type of shot can create a dramatic effect when it places the subject in the context of a large interior space or a broad exterior vista.

COMPOSITION

Composition is a term used by painters, graphic artists, and still photographers to define the way in which images can be effectively structured within a frame. Frame dimensions or aspect ratio of the specific media format affected the composition. Two basic principles of composition that will be discussed in Chapter 9 are symmetry and closure. Composition is complicated by the fact that video and film images move in time. Therefore, composition is constantly changing.

Aspect Ratio

A frame limits the outer borders of the image to specific dimensions. The ratio of these dimensions, that is, the ratio of a frame's width to its height, is called the aspect ratio of the frame. Composition is obviously slightly different for different aspect ratios. If you were to put identical paintings in frames with different dimensions and aspect ratios, for example, the paintings would look very different: the relations between the shapes and objects or the composition within the frames would not be the same. Video, Super-8mm, 16mm, and standard 35mm film all have the same aspect ratio: 4:3 or 1.33:1. But feature films in Super-16, 35mm, and 65mm, which are made for wide-screen projection in theaters, have aspect ratios that vary from 1.85:1 to 2.35:1.

High-definition TV (HDTV) is set at 16:9, or 1.78, which closely approximates the 1.85:1 academy aperture feature film format or aspect ratio. Wide-screen images can enhance an illusion of reality by involving more of our peripheral or edge vision, but they also alter the aesthetics of object placement and composition within the frame. Consider the different impressions created by a wide gulf between two characters on a wide-screen frame, and the greater proximity of two characters in a video frame. It is difficult to copy or transfer visuals from one aspect ratio to another intact, as in copying magazine photographs with a video camera or showing a wide-screen film on television (Figure 4.10).

Essential Area

An important factor in terms of frame dimensions is the concept of essential area. The full video or film camera frame is rarely, if ever, viewed in its entirety. Part of the border or edge of the full frame is cut off during transmission and conversion in the home receiver. *Essential* or *critical area* refers to the portion of the full frame that will actually be viewed. All key information, actions, and movements must be safely kept within this essential area (Figure 4.10).

Rule of Thirds

One well-practiced theory of composition involves dividing the frame into thirds, both horizontally and vertically. If you mentally draw two vertical and two horizontal lines that divide the frame into thirds, objects can then be arranged along the lines. Important objects may be placed at the points where these lines intersect for added interest or emphasis. Following the rule of thirds allows a picture to be quickly comprehended in an aesthetically pleasing way. Placing subjects in this manner is more interesting than simply bisecting the frame. Other slightly more complicated forms of visual composition can also be used with success, but they are not always comprehended so quickly and easily. The framing composition changes radically with a 16:9 aspect ratio when the rule of thirds is applied. The vertical area remains the same, while much more space needs to be filled in the horizontal areas. Those areas increase the possibilities of using many more multiple images in a single frame than in a 4:3 ratio (Figure 4.11).

Symmetry

Symmetry is an important aesthetic principle of composition in any two-dimensional, framed visual medium. A director can create a symmetrical or balanced spatial pattern by using objects in the frame. A symmetrical frame appears stable and solid, but eventually uninteresting and boring as well. An asymmetrically or unbalanced frame is more volatile and interesting but can also be extremely distracting. When properly used, both symmetrically and asymmetrically organized frames can be pleasing and effective.

The key is to know when it is appropriate to use one form of composition rather than the other. Framing the head of one person talking directly into the camera in an asymmetrical pattern can be distracting. The audience's attention is supposed to focus on the spokesperson, but it is distracted by the lack of balance in the frame. An asymmetrical image of one or more people in the frame can suggest that someone or something is missing. The entrance of

ASPECT RATIO – ESSENTIAL AREA

Scan Area

Essential (Critical) Area

Y .8 Y

.8 X

X

Y = 3 units   X = 4 units

Standard 3:4 NTSC Ratio

Scan Area

Essential (Critical) Area

Y .8Y

.8 X

X

Y = 9 Units   X = 16 Units

Standard HDTV 9:16 ATSC Ratio

Figure 4.10 The aspect ratio is the ratio of the height (Y-axis) of a frame to the width (X-axis). The NTSC television and traditional film ratio is 3 units × 4 units. The HDTV aspect ratio is 9 units × 16 units, and wide-screen films range from 9 × 16 to 1 × 2. The critical or essential area is considered to be the portion within the frame outline by a 10% border of the full scanned area. This is true of both 3 × 4 and 9 × 16 aspect ratios.

another person or character then balances the frame (Figures 4.12 and 4.13).

An asymmetrical frame can suggest that something is wrong or that the world is out of balance. The concept of symmetry must be integrated with the rule of thirds and other concepts, such as lookspace, walkspace, and headroom. *Lookspace* refers to the additional space remaining in the frame in the direction of a performer's look or glance at something or someone outside the frame. *Walkspace* is the additional space in the frame remaining in front of a moving performer. When following the rule of thirds, the performer's face (in the case of a look or glance) or the performer's body (in the case of a walk or run) is placed on one of the trisecting vertical lines, leaving two thirds of the remaining space in the direction of the glance or movement. This asymmetrical compo-

sition is much better than having the performer in the exact center of the frame (Figure 4.14). *Headroom* refers to the space remaining in the frame above the subject's head, which is most pleasing visually when there is a slight gap between the top of the head and the top of the frame.

Closure

The concept of lookspace is related to another aspect of visual composition called *closure*. On-screen space, that is, space within the frame, often suggests continuity with off-screen space. An open frame suggests that on-screen space and objects continue into off-screen space. A completely closed frame, on the other hand, gives the illusion of being self-contained and complete in itself.

FRAMING RULE OF THIRDS

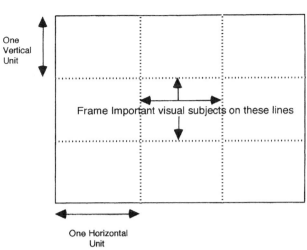

Figure 4.11 The rule of thirds divides the frame into nine areas by drawing two vertical lines one-third of the way in from each side and two horizontal lines one-third of the way from the bottom and the top of the frame.

ASYMMETRICAL FRAMING

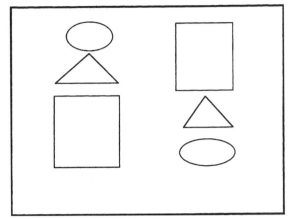

Figure 4.13 Symmetrical balance in composing the objects within a frame shows exactly the same items on each side of a line drawn down the middle of the frame. Asymmetrical framing can vary from an equal weight of objects on each side of the frame to totally unbalanced weight, as well as asymmetrical groupings of objects.

SYMMETRICAL FRAMING

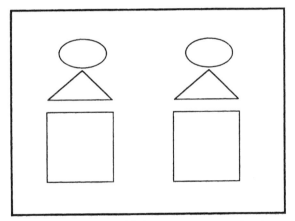

Figure 4.12 Symmetrical balance in composing the objects within a frame shows exactly the same items on each side of a line drawn down the middle of the frame. Asymmetrical framing can vary from an equal weight of objects on each side of the frame to totally unbalanced weight, as well as asymmetrical groupings of objects.

The way in which an image is framed and objects are arranged can create a sense of closure or a sense of openness. Symmetrically framing a performer's head in the center of the frame creates a sense of closure. The composition does not allude to parts of the body that are missing off-screen. Framing body parts between normal joints of an arm, leg, or waist, on the other hand, suggests continuity in off-screen space. Something appears to be missing, although our memories readily fill in the missing parts (Figure 4.15).

Figure 4.14 Any object, either moving in the frame or facing in an obvious direction, needs room to "move" and "look" within the frame. A common framing practice is to place such subjects on either of the lines splitting the frame into nine sections.

Figure 4.15 Logical cutoff points to keep in mind when framing subjects SHOULD NOT fall at the joints of the body. To allow for closure and the assumption that the body continues beyond the cutoff point, camera operators must frame the subject BETWEEN the joints, that is, between the ankle and knee, or between the waist and breast.

Depth and Perspective

Screen composition can enhance an illusion of depth and three-dimensionality. Lighting can add depth to the image by helping to separate foreground objects from their backgrounds. Placing the camera at an angle so that two sides of an object are visible at the same time creates three-dimensionality. Including foreground objects in a frame can enhance the illusion of depth by setting a yardstick by which the distance, size, and scale of the background can be determined. A person, tree branch, or object of known scale in the foreground can set a context for depth. Diagonal or parallel lines, such as those of a railroad track, can guide the eye to important objects in the frame and create a greater illusion of depth. Placing objects or people at several different planes of action within the frame, or creating frames within frames, such as a person standing inside a doorway, increases the perception of depth within the frame.

Of course, a certain degree of care must be exercised when using multiple planes of action so that two planes do not unintentionally connect to create one confused plane, as when a plant in the background appears to be growing out of a person's head. *Image perspective* refers to the apparent depth of the image and the spatial positioning of objects in different planes. Perspective can be affected by the type of lens that is used. Telephoto or long focal-length lenses often seem to reduce apparent depth, while wide-angle or short focal-length lenses seem to expand space and apparent depth. Lenses help an image look deep or shallow. A moving camera, as in a dolly shot, can also affect the apparent depth and perspective by changing the relationship between objects in the frame. Cutting from one camera angle to another can help create an illusion of three dimensionality out of two-dimensional video and film images.

Frame Movement

A moving frame changes visual composition. In video and film, composition is constantly in flux due to camera or subject movement. In this respect, film and video are quite unlike photography and painting, which present motionless images. One type of composition can quickly change to its opposite. A symmetrical frame can quickly become asymmetrical, or an open frame can appear closed. The illusion of depth can be enhanced by the movement of a camera or of objects within the frame. Objects that move toward or away from the camera naturally create a greater sense of depth than those that move laterally with respect to the camera. Diagonal lines of movement, such as diagonal lines within a static frame, add dynamism and force to the composition. A canted frame is created by tilting the camera to the left or right. This adds a sense of dynamic strength to an image, such as an exciting shot within a car chase, but a canted frame used in less-intense action sequences often looks out of place.

Image Qualities

A director must be conscious of subtle differences in image tonality, especially when editing or combining images. *Image tonality* refers to the overall appearance of the image in terms of contrast (gradations of brightness from white to black) and color. Image contrast can be affected by lighting and recording materials. Combining two shots that have very different contrast levels can be disconcerting to the viewer, but it can also arouse attention. A high-contrast scene, that is, one that has a limited range of gray tones with mostly dark black and bright whites, will look quite different from a low-contrast scene, which has a wide range of intermediate tones. Matching image tonalities in terms of contrast and color can help effect smooth transitions from shot to shot and scene to scene. Combining mismatched tones can have a shock or attention-getting value. Excessive contrast is a common problem in video production, especially field production, where outdoor lighting is difficult to control. High contrast is sometimes more of a problem in video than in film, due to the narrower range of contrasting shades or tonalities that video can record, but it is an important consideration in both media.

Scale and Shape

Scale refers to the apparent size of objects within the frame. Camera-to-subject distance, camera angle, and the type of lens used can affect the apparent size of objects. Lower camera positions and angles sometimes increase the apparent size of an object in the frame. The apparent size of an object can increase or decrease its importance.

Directors can create a balanced and symmetrical frame by arranging objects of equivalent size or similar shape in different parts of the same frame. Graphic similarities, such as similarities in the shape or color of objects, can create smooth transitions between shots. Graphic differences can be used to create an asymmetrical frame or to emphasize transitions from one shot to another.

Speed of Motion

Images can have different speeds of motion. *Speed of motion* refers to the speed at which objects appear to move within the frame. This speed can be changed by altering the film recording speed or the video playback speed to produce fast motion or slow motion. Editing many short-duration shots together can enhance the speed of motion, while using fewer shots of longer duration can help slow down actions and the speed of motion. The pace of editing is called *editing tempo*. The apparent motion of objects is also affected by camera placement, lenses, and the actual motion of the photographed objects. A long focal-length lens often slows down apparent motion by squashing space, while a wide-angle lens can speed up motion by expanding the apparent distance traveled in a given period of time.

COMBINING SHOTS

One of the director's key jobs, which is shared by the editor during postproduction, is to determine the precise duration of each shot. An exposition section may call for a number of long takes that slow down the action and allow the audience to contemplate character, situation, and setting. A dramatic cli-

max, on the other hand, may call for many different short-duration shots, which help intensify the action. The famous three-minute shower-scene murder in Alfred Hitchcock's *Psycho* (1960), for example, is made up of well over 100 separate pieces of film cut together to intensify the action. Modernist film aestheticians, such as Sergei Eisenstein, have sometimes advocated the use of many short-duration shots, while realist aestheticians, such as André Bazin, have often recommended the use of longer-duration shots.

A good director is usually a good editor; that is, directors know how and when to combine specific images. Editing begins with an understanding of composition, image qualities, and different types of shots. Shots can be combined using a variety of transition devices, including straight cuts, fades, dissolves, wipes, and digital transitions.

Straight Cut or Take

A *straight cut* or *take* is a direct, instantaneous change from one camera shot to another, say from a long shot of a scene to a close-up of a performer's face. Time is assumed to be continuous over a straight cut, except in the case of *jump cuts*, where actions are discontinuous and do not match from one shot to the next, suggesting a gap in time. If a cut is made from a shot of a person talking to someone on one side of a room to a second shot showing the same person talking to someone else on the opposite side, the result is a jump cut. Jump cuts are widely used in commercials, in which stories are condensed to thirty seconds by using rapid editing tempos, and in documentary and news interviews, where this procedure is sometimes considered more honest than using cutaways to mask deletions. It is becoming more and more common to use jump cuts to compress time in fiction as well.

Fade

The picture of a video program or film can fade in from blackness to image or fade out from image to blackness. A fade-out followed by a fade-in usually indicates a significant passage of time. A fade, like a curtain on the stage, can be used to mark the beginning and the end of a performance and to separate acts or scenes (Figure 4.16).

Dissolve

A dissolve is actually a simultaneous fade-out and fade-in. One scene or shot fades out at the same time that another shot fades in to replace it. For a very short duration, the two shots are superimposed on

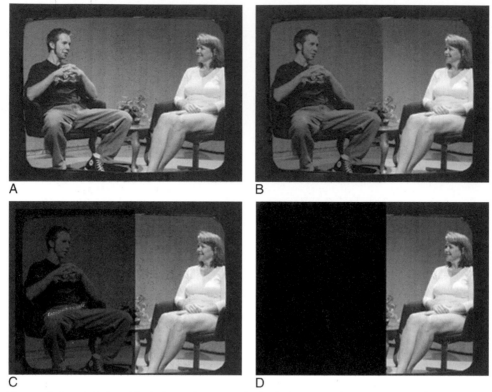

A B

C D

Figure 4.16 A fade to black shows the image slowly darkening until it disappears. A fade from black starts with a totally blank frame and then the first image slowly appearing. Frame A shows an image on both halves in full view. Frame B shows the left side of the frame beginning to fade to black. Frame C shows the left side of the frame nearly faded all the way to black, and Frame D shows the left side of the frame completely faded to black. The right side of the frame has remained at full level in each frame.

one another. Dissolves are frequently used to conceal or smooth over gaps in time rather than emphasizing them as in a fadeout and fade-in. A very rapid dissolve is sometimes called a *soft cut* or *lap dissolve*.

Wipe

A wipe is a transition device created on a switcher, a special effects generator, or an optical film bench whereby one image or shot is gradually replaced on the screen by another. A wipe may begin on one side of the screen and move across to engulf the opposite side. It can also begin in the middle of the frame and move outward. Ending one shot by dollying or zooming in to a black object that fills the frame and beginning the next shot by dollying or zooming out from a black object is sometimes called a *natural wipe*. (See Figure 4.17.)

Defocus

Placing one image out of focus and gradually bringing a replacement image into focus is called a *defocus* transition.

Swish Pan

A rapid movement of the camera on the tripod swivel or panning head causes a blurring of the image,

Figure 4.17 A wipe appears as one image is replaced by another with a straight line separating the two images. A wide number of different patterns separating the two images also may be used. A wipe stopped at midpoint creates a split screen.

which can be used as a swish pan transition from one scene to another. This transition is frequently accompanied by up-tempo music, which accelerates the sense of action and movement, rather than creating a pause.

Special Effects

Split Screen or Shared Screen

Having one image occupy a portion of the same frame with another image is called a *shared screen*. When the frame is split into two equal parts by the two images, it is called a *split screen*. Sometimes these techniques make it possible to show two different but simultaneous actions on the same screen.

Superimposition

Having two different shots occupy the same complete frame simultaneously is called a *superimposition*. One shot is usually dominant over the other to avoid visual confusion. The superimposed images should not be excessively detailed or busy. In effect, a superimposition looks like a dissolve that has been stopped while in progress. Combining a long shot and close-up of the same person from different angles sometimes creates an effective superimposition (Figure 4.18).

Keying and Chroma Key

A specific portion of a video image can be completely replaced with a second image using keying or chroma key techniques. Titles and graphics can be inserted into a portion of another image. A scene from a still photograph or slide can be inserted into a blue- or green-colored area (e.g., a green or blue screen on the set) in a shot using video chroma key. The monochrome blue or green portion of the latter shot is replaced with the inserted shot.

Matte and Blue Screen

A matte is used in film to black out an area in one image that will then be filled in with a second image. Matting is to film what keying is to video. Blue screening in film is equivalent to chroma key in video, since the blue screen area in one image is replaced by a second image.

Negative Image

A normal visual image is positive. A negative image reverses the brightness and darkness of the original image. Blacks become whites and whites become blacks. Colors turn into their complements. In television, this can be done by simply reversing the polarity of the electrical picture signal. In a film, a negative print can be made from a positive image.

Freeze Frame

A freeze frame is a continuing still image from one frame of a video or film shot created during postproduction. Usually the action stops by freezing the last frame of a shot, such as at the conclusion of a film or video program.

Digital Transitions

A wide variety of effects now can be created with a digital effects generator. Page turns, shots on each side of rotating blocks, a subject morphing into another subject, shots disintegrating into another shot, plus virtually any transition imaginable, are all possible through the use of digital switchers and effects. The specific language and naming of digital transitions remains in flux as the industry attempts to reach standards agreed upon among the many manufacturers of digital equipment. A caution for new directors: use a special effect only when needed, not just because the equipment is capable of performing such effects. A special effect is not special if overused (Figure 4.19).

Scene Construction

A *scene* is a series of shots of action occurring in continuous time at one place. It is important to ensure that significant changes in camera angle and/or camera-to-subject distance occur between two successive shots within a scene. The camera angle should change at least 45 degrees with respect to the subject from one shot to the next, unless there is a significant

Figure 4.18 A superimposition is a combination of two images created by stopping a dissolve at midpoint. Depending on the intensity of each image, part of one will bleed through the other.

Figure 4.19 A digital effect is any one of a number of transitions, such as page turns, unique patterns, or three-dimensional transitions.

change in camera-to-subject distance. A few aesthetic reasons for making a cut that involves a change of camera-to-subject distance are (1) to depict an action that was omitted in the previous shot; (2) to provide a closer look at an event or object; (3) to emphasize an object or action; and (4) to draw back and establish the setting. A cut from a medium shot to a close-up provides a closer look at an object or event, while a cut from a long shot to a close-up emphasizes an object or action. Cutting from a medium shot to a long shot helps to reestablish the setting and place the action in context or in broader spatial perspective.

A conventionally constructed scene might begin with a long shot or establishing shot to place the subjects within a specific setting. Then the camera gets progressively closer to the subject as the action intensifies, and finally the camera pulls back to reestablish the setting at the conclusion of the scene. An alternative approach is to begin a scene with a close-up and gradually pull back from shot to shot to reveal more and more of the setting as the action progresses. The latter approach is initially somewhat confusing and spatially disorienting, but it also arouses viewer curiosity.

Certain types of cuts involve quite severe changes in camera-to-subject distance, such as those from long shot to close-up or vice versa. In realist situations, these dramatic changes of scale should be used sparingly and primarily for emphasis, because they often have a distracting effect on the audience. More gradual changes of scale are less disruptive and provide a smoother transition. A new shot or image should serve a purpose different from that of the previous shot. It can anticipate the audience's next point of interest, that is, it can be psychologically moti-

vated on the basis of viewer expectations. It can present additional or contrasting information by revealing actions that were hidden from a previous angle. In general, every shot should be cut as short as it can be without inhibiting its function. A good director separates essential from nonessential information to determine how long a specific shot will maintain viewer interest.

Continuity Editing

Continuity editing usually means creating a smooth flow from one shot to the next. Actions that begin in one shot are completed in the following shot with no apparent gaps in time. There is continuity in the spatial placement and the screen direction of moving and stationary objects from shot to shot. Conventional continuity can, of course, be disrupted in time and space. Gaps or jump cuts in the action can be consciously edited into a scene. Actions can be repeated over and over again, slowed down, and speeded up. But it is important to learn the basics of continuity editing before attempting to disrupt it. Beginning video and film directors need to first acquire some appreciation of the difficulty inherent in trying to maintain continuity and in meeting conventional viewer expectations.

Pace and Rhythm

The selection of long- and short-duration shots affects the pace or rhythm of a scene. A director must be very sensitive to changes in pace and rhythm. To build a scene out of different shots, a director must match the tempo or rhythm of the editing to the subject matter and the audience's expectations. Rapidly cutting together many short-duration shots for a how-to film about woodworking, for example, distracts the audience's attention from the primary subject matter. Slow-paced editing for a soft drink commercial may be extremely boring and an ineffective persuasion technique. A fast-paced exposition and a slow-paced climax in a dramatic production usually fail to achieve the desired emotional effect and dramatic structure.

Compression and Expansion of Time

Directors can compress and expand time through editing, even while preserving the illusion of temporal continuity. For example, suppose that you wish to record the action of someone getting dressed and ready for work in the morning. A single shot of this activity that preserved exact temporal continuity might last 10 minutes or more in actual duration. But by recording different segments of action and editing them together, the essential elements of time activity can be preserved without creating any readily apparent gaps in time. How can this be done? Simply by cutting from a long shot of the action to a close-up of a hand or an object in the room, and then cutting back to a long shot in which the person is more completely dressed than could actually have occurred in the duration of the close-up.

A director can speed up an action by eliminating unimportant or repetitious actions between cuts. The action and time are condensed and compressed. The same technique can be used for someone crossing a street. For instance, we begin with a full shot or long shot of the person starting to step off one curb, then cut to a medium shot and then a close-up of his or her feet or face. Finally, we present a long shot of the person reaching the other side of the street. This edited version of the street crossing might last just five seconds, while actually walking across the street takes more than 20 seconds. Condensing or compressing action can increase the pace and interest of actions. Actions can also be expanded through editing. An action can be shown, followed by the thoughts of one or more of the characters as the action occurs. In reality, the action and the thinking would have occurred simultaneously, but in a media production each must be shown separately, lengthening the time it takes to depict the actual time of the incident.

Screen Directionality

Depicting a three-dimensional world in a two-dimensional medium presents the director with special problems of screen directionality. *Screen directionality* refers to the consistent direction of movements and object placement from one shot to the next. Inconsistent screen direction causes spatial confusion. What viewers actually see seems to contradict their expectations. This type of confusion can be effective in music videos and formative or modernist works of art. But, in general, maintaining directional consistency of looks and glances, object placements, and subject movements within the frame reduces viewer confusion by increasing spatial clarity in realist and functionalist works.

Directional Glances

It is important to record a consistent pattern of performers' spatial looks and glances within the frame to preserve an illusion of reality. The improper placement of a camera can result in confusing inconsistencies (which again can be useful in a modernist approach). A close-up of one character looking screen left at a second character is usually followed by a shot of the other character looking screen right to suggest that he is looking back at the first character. When one person looks down at another person, the other should look up within the frame of the second shot, and so on. The camera must be placed and the image framed so that there is directional consistency from one shot to the next.

The 180-Degree Axis of Action Rule

The 180-degree rule of camera placement ensures directional consistency from shot to shot. An imaginary line can be drawn to connect stationary subjects. Once the camera is placed on one side or the other of this axis of action, all subsequent camera placements must occur on the same side of the line to prevent a reversal in the placement of objects in the frame (Figure 4.20).

A moving subject establishes a vector line, and all camera placements are made on one side of this line or the other to maintain consistent screen direction of movement. If the camera crossed this line, a subject going from left to right in one shot would appear to be going in the opposite direction in the next shot. There are ways to break the 180-degree rule without creating spatial confusion or disrupting an illusion of reality. First, the camera can move across the line during a single shot, establishing a new rule on the opposite side of the line to which all subsequent shots must conform. A director can also cut directly to the line itself by placing the camera along the line and then cross over the line in the next shot to establish a new rule. Finally, the subject can change direction with respect to the camera during a shot and thus establish a new line.

SOUND AND IMAGE INTERACTION

An overvaluation of visual images can lead directors to neglect accompanying sounds, but sound is an extremely important aspect of video and film production. Sound can complement and fill out the image. It can also conflict with corresponding images or produce an independent experience. Sound can shape the way in which images are interpreted. It can direct our attention to a specific part of the image or to things not included in the image. Some sounds and music have the ability to stimulate feelings directly. Sounds can create a realistic background or a unique, abstract, impressionistic world.

Sound and image relationships can be divided into four oppositional categories:

(1) on-screen versus off-screen sounds, (2) commentative versus actual sounds, (3) synchronous ver-

180 DEGREE AXIS OF ACTION RULE

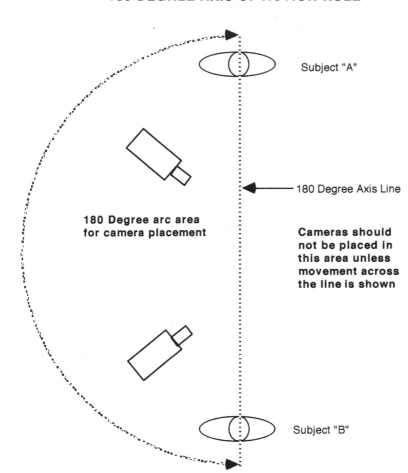

Subject "A"

180 Degree Axis Line

**180 Degree arc area
for camera placement**

**Cameras should
not be placed in
this area unless
movement across
the line is shown**

Subject "B"

Figure 4.20 A line drawn through the two main subjects in a scene divides the studio plot into two areas, one on each side of that line. Once shooting in that scene has started on one side of the line, the rest of the scene must be shot from that same side, unless a shot moves from one side to the other while recording.

sus asynchronous sounds, and (4) parallel versus contrapuntal sounds. Understanding each of these categories opens up a broad range of aesthetic possibilities. This section concludes with a separate consideration of combining music and visual images from two different standpoints: editing images to prerecorded music and composing original music for video and film.

SOUND AND IMAGE RELATIONSHIPS

• On Screen	Source is Visible
• Off Screen	Source is not Visible
• Commentative	No Obvious Visible Source (Music)
• Actual	Created from Visible Source
• Synchronous	Matched Visual Movement
• Asynchronous	Movement not Matched to Visual
• Parallel	Blends with Visual
• Contrapuntal	Contradicts Visual

On-Screen Versus Off-Screen Sound

A sound coming from a source that is visible within the frame is called an *on-screen sound. Off-screen sounds* come from sources assumed to be just outside the frame. The use of off-screen sounds can enhance spatial depth. Noel Burch, a media theorist, has pointed out that an off-screen sound can seem to come from six possible positions outside the frame: from the left, from the right, from above, from below, from behind the wall at the back of the frame, and from behind the camera. The precise spatial placement of an off-screen sound is not always discernible. Stereophonic or multichannel sound obviously helps us to determine the position of an off-screen sound, but the effect is the same. Our attention is directed off-screen to the source of the sound, particularly if on-screen performers are looking in the appropriate direction. By arousing our curiosity, off-screen sound can set up an expectation of the visual presentation of its source. It can also break down some of the limitations of a visual frame, opening it up as a realistic window on the world, as opposed to a more abstract, self-contained, modernist aesthetic world.

Commentative Versus Actual Sound

Sound and image relations also can be classified on the basis of the supposed actuality or artificiality of their sound sources. Commentative sound has no known source, while actual sound is presumed to come from some actual or real sound source either inside or just outside the frame. Spoken dialogue is usually actual sound. Narration is commentative sound, unless the narrator appears on-screen. Music can be either commentative or actual sound. Scoring is commentative sound, and source music is actual sound. Commentative sound effects, such as shrill metallic sounds that have no readily apparent source, can help to create an impressionistic, emotionally charged atmosphere. Commentative music, narration, and sound effects can be effectively used to reinforce specific feelings. Lush, romantic music, for example, might complement a romantic scene, such as the reunion of long-separated lovers, although such conventions easily become musical clichés.

Synchronous Versus Asynchronous Sound

Synchronous sounds match their on-screen sources. Lip sync sounds synchronize with the lip movements of the on-screen speaker. Sound effects match their on-screen sound sources. For example, the sounds of a runner's feet striking the pavement should be synchronized within the corresponding visual images. Music can also be said to be synchronous with visual actions or cuts that precisely follow the beat or rhythm. Asynchronous sound does not match its sound source. Poor quality lip-sync is asynchronous sound, such as a film dubbed into a foreign language that fails to match the lip movements of the speaker. But asynchronous sound is not always poor-quality sound. In fact, asynchronous sound offers many exciting aesthetic possibilities, such as providing a basis for contrapuntal sound. Commentative sound effects can be used asynchronously to contrast with their corresponding visuals. One example is the substitution of a train whistle for a woman's scream in Alfred Hitchcock's *The Thirty-Nine Steps* (1935). Commentative, asynchronous sound effects can produce emotional effects or meanings that counterpoint rather than parallel their accompanying visual images.

Parallel Versus Contrapu[ntal] Sound

The emotional effect or conceptua[l ...] and images can be virtually the [...] different. Speech, sound effects, and music can parallel the meaning or emotions of the visuals, or they can counterpoint them. The term *counterpoint* in music refers to two separate and distinguishable melodies that are played simultaneously. The same term has been applied to image and sound interaction in video and film. Contrapuntal sound has an emotional effect or conceptual meaning that is different from its corresponding visuals. Sounds and images are aesthetically separate and often contrast with one another.

Parallel sound, like musical harmony, blends together with its corresponding visuals. Like musical notes played simultaneously and in harmony, sounds and images can have parallel meanings or emotions that are mutually supportive. Suppose that the visually depicted events are sad or tragic but the accompanying music is upbeat and in a major key, so that it communicates a bright, happy, strong feeling. In this case the music counterpoints the corresponding visuals. The same thing happens when sad music accompanies a happy event. But when sad, minor key music accompanies a tragic scene, the sounds and images parallel one another in emotional tone.

Speech sounds and sound effects can parallel or counterpoint their corresponding images. For example, the film musical *Singin' in the Rain* (1952) begins with the main character, Don Lockwood, describing his path to Hollywood stardom. Lockwood gives a short autobiography to his fans in which he claims to have received his training and background at elite, high-class schools and cultural institutions. But what we see contradicts his voiceover narration. We see that he actually began his performance career in pool halls and bars, and gradually worked his way into the movies as a stuntman. His elitist posturing provides a pseudo-sophisticated, tongue-in-cheek commentary on Hollywood. The meaning of what we see contradicts the meaning of what we hear, producing a powerfully humorous effect.

Composing Images for Prerecorded Music

The use of music in video and film is a rather complex art. It is important for directors to understand some of the basic aesthetic possibilities inherent in two approaches to combining images and music: (1) editing visual images to preselected, prerecorded music; and (2) composing original music for video and film, even if the responsibility for the music is in the hands of a specialist, such as a music director, composer, or performer.

Visual images can be selected and ordered into a pattern that is prescribed by prerecorded music. For example, fast-paced music might be accompanied by rapid cutting of visual images and rapid action within the frame, and slow-paced music might call for less frequent cutting and slower movements. The visual action might reach its climax at the same time as a musical crescendo or swelling in the volume and intensity of the music. The timing of the visuals can be made to coincide with the timing of the music so that both begin and end at the same points and achieve a parallel structure throughout. Dancing and singing sequences require a high degree of synchronization and parallelism between the music and visuals. The music can be recorded in advance and used as a basis for the choreography. Pre-recorded music establishes a basic structure and timing to which the performance and editing of visual images must conform, unless conscious asynchronization or contrapuntal relations between the sounds and images is desired.

Composing Music for Prerecorded Images

MUSIC AND IMAGE INTERACTION
- Intensify the Action
- Intensify the Dramatic Tension
- Establish the Period or Location
- Set Atmosphere or Mood
- Stimulate Screen Emotion
- Fill Dead Air

Another approach to music and image interaction is to compose original music for specific film or video sequences. Music composed for video or film usually serves one or more of the following functions: (1) intensifying the action or dramatic tension, (2) establishing the period or place, (3) setting the atmosphere or mood, (4) stimulating a specific emotion in conjunction with a character or theme, and (5) avoiding screen silence. Music rhythm can intensify action and create dramatic tension. The pace of music can increase with the speed of the action, such as a crescendo that accompanies a dramatic climax or crisis. Music can communicate time and place by virtue of its source, period, and style. Selecting a specific mode of music affects the overall mood or atmosphere. A specific melody can develop an emotion in conjunction with an important character or theme. Leitmotifs can intensify audience identification with

specific people or characters and stimulate emotions. Finally, music can be used simply as a filler to cover silence or to attempt to create viewer interest during slow-paced visual action sequences.

Background music is all too frequently used to fill a void rather than to create a specific effect in conjunction with visual images. Careful selection and design of music is a much better approach to the problem. Original music for television and film can consist of sounds from a single instrument, such as a solo guitar or flute, or a fully orchestrated symphonic score. The number of musicians required and the complexity of the music can vary considerably depending on the specific needs and requirements of the project and the available budget. Sometimes a scarcity of materials and resources can be an advantage. Simple music and solo performers can be easier for beginning producers to obtain and control. New computer music programs and synthesizers make it easier to have original music composed, played, and recorded by one person. Apple's computer program "Soundtrack," which accompanies "Final Cut Pro 4," facilitates the creation of film and video music, especially for directors and editors with limited composing experience and low budgets. Regardless of the sophistication of the music, video and film directors should make every attempt to collaborate with composers and musicians so that the music can be designed and performed for their specific needs. Original music can be tailored to a video or film production much better than pre-recorded library music, but in some cases the latter is more cost effective.

PREPARING THE SHOOTING SCRIPT

Directors begin to apply aesthetic principles to concrete production problems when they plan a production. Production planning is usually done on paper. Directors specify shots and sound effects for each scene in the script as they prepare a final shooting script (Figure 4.21).

After the shooting script is completed, shot lists are often written up for camera operators. Sometimes a storyboard consisting of still-frame drawings of every shot in the final shooting script is drawn up as a visual guide to production.

After carefully analyzing the script, a director begins to prepare a final shooting script by indicating specific types of shots, transition devices, and sound effects. Directorial terms for specific types of visual images and sounds must be thoroughly learned before a shooting script can be created. Shots are continuous recordings of actions within a scene made by a single camera. Abbreviations are used to specify

---

SHOOTING SCRIPT

1.   INT   WS   UNIVERSITY CLASSROOM   DAY   1.

Classroom is full of students, some wide awake, gossiping, others sleeping or nodding off as they wait for the professor to arrive.

2-Shot of Jane and Jack, Jane turns around in her seat to whisper to Jack.

                                      JANE
                        (Quietly so only Jack can hear her.)
                     Are you sure there isn't going to be an exam
                     during tomorrow's class?

CU Jack, he leans forward toward Jane.

                                      JACK
                        (With a bravado, all-knowing tone)
                     Of course not, have I ever lied to you?

The professor enters the room, downstage right, walks to the lectern and the room becomes quiet.

MWS from back of classroom, students in foreground, Professor in background.

                                   PROFESSOR
                        (Emphatically as a reminder)
                     If I am forced to repeat myself again, I WILL
                     be forced to give you your first examination in
                     tomorrow's class.

MS Students as they react to Professor, groans, turning to each other in sympathy.

                                                            (DISSOLVE TO)
2.   EXT   WS   CAMPUS   DAY   2.

The clouds suddenly darken the sky as rain, thunder and lightning start and the lights go out plunging the room into darkness.

Figure 4.21 A shooting script should provide the director with enough information to shoot the scene as closely as possible to the vision the writer had when writing the script. If the script is not clear, then the director must make decisions on specifically how to shoot the scene.

camera placements and movements, such as ECU (extreme close-up) or MS (medium shot), which specify the desired distance of the camera from the subject. Where the camera is placed can have a considerable impact on what action is viewed or how a subject appears. Camera movements, such as CAMERA PANS RIGHT or CAMERA DOLLIES IN, are also specified in a shooting script, as are transitions between one shot and another, such as CUT, FADE OUT, FADE IN, and DISSOLVE. Camera movements add motion to the recording of a scene and can also change the perspective or point of view on a subject or action. Various transition devices are used to communicate changes of time and/or place to the audience. Sound effect designations, such as SFX (sound effect): PLANE LANDING, specify concrete sounds that should accompany specific images.

Preparing a final shooting script allows a director an opportunity to shoot and reshoot a video or film production on paper at minimal expense before actual recording begins. To compose a final shooting script, a director must understand a full range of aesthetic possibilities. There are many different ways to record a specific scene in any script. A director interprets the action and decides on the best shots, transition devices, and sound effects for each scene. Directors select specific recording techniques, such as different types of shots, for each scene on the basis of the aesthetic approach they have chosen. A director's overall aesthetic approach in large part determines the meaning of images and sounds by setting a context for interpretation. A realist approach often involves the use of techniques that help to preserve an illusion of reality through a transparent or unnoticed style. Modernist and postmodernist approaches call attention to techniques and highlight a director's manipulation and control over the recording medium and subject matter.

Some types and combinations of visual images and sounds can be realist in one context but modernist or postmodernist in another. For example, jump cuts are discontinuities in human actions or movements from one shot to the next. Since they disrupt the continuous flow of realist time and space, jump cuts are often considered a modernist technique, but they are also used in news and documentary interviews.

A jump cut indicates that something has been removed and is often considered more honest than using techniques that disguise the fact that editing has been done. From a modernist perspective, jump cuts, such as those in Jean-Luc Godard's *Breathless* (1959), call attention to directional control by breaking down the illusion of temporal continuity or the smooth, continuous flow of time from shot to shot. But from a realist perspective in news and documentary productions, jump cuts make it clear that the recording of an event has been edited.

PRODUCTION COORDINATION

Video and film directors are personnel managers as well as artists using the media of moving images and sounds. Directors coordinate production by working with their staff, crew, and performers. Frequent production meetings facilitate coordination. A cooperative, collective effort has to be carefully orchestrated and managed by the director if a quality product is to be achieved. The director must be a good judge of character.

Production Meetings

Frequent production meetings provide the director and the production staff with an opportunity to work out important details and problems collectively. Prior to actual production, the director usually meets with key staff members, such as the producer, the art director or scenic designer, and the lighting director. The overall goals and objectives of the film or video project are clarified during these meetings. Everyone must understand the overall purpose and design of the production to prevent members of the production team from working at cross-purposes. Everything must be worked out and all problems solved prior to actual live video production, since live production means that there is no postproduction and therefore little or no room for mistakes during production.

The director must be able to communicate effectively with the staff if these problems are to be quickly and efficiently resolved. The more talented, independent, and opinionated the staff, crew, and performers are, the more likely it is that problems and disputes will arise, unless a common purpose has been collectively determined or hierarchically imposed at the beginning. The director's authority may be questioned, and his or her status with the staff, crew, and other performers jeopardized, if an unruly participant is allowed to dominate the proceedings. The director must be explicit and authoritative about commands. The director must also listen to the needs, desires, and problems of the staff, crew, and talent. Production meetings provide the director with an opportunity to exercise authority and give commands, but also to listen to the ideas, needs, and problems of others. Effective managers are often good listeners.

Casting

To cast a specific performance effectively, the director must have a firmly established interpretation of each character or role. Each role, however small, is important in terms of the quality of the final product, and a video or film program is often only as good as its worst performer. It is often said that almost any director can evoke an excellent performance from an experienced, talented performer but that good direction is most evident in the quality of smaller roles and bit parts. Good casting depends on a director's understanding of at least three factors: the audience, the character or role, and the physical appearance of specific performers. The natural look and feel of a performer is probably the most important factor in terms of his or her appropriateness for a specific role, although skilled actors can drastically change their appearance and still appear naturally suited to a role. Robin Williams did in *Mrs. Doubtfire* (1993) (Figure 4.22).

Casting sessions often consist of actors reading a short scene from the script so that the director and producer can evaluate their suitability for a role. Sometimes several actors will be auditioned before a part is cast. Directors often have to deal with performers who have different levels and types of acting experience. Inexperienced actors need to be explicitly told what is wanted. Most fail to understand or prepare themselves for the rigors of video and film acting. Inexperienced performers have difficulty relating to an awkward, unfeeling camera. Constant feedback and praise from a director can greatly improve the quality of a performance. Experienced profes-

sionals, on the other hand, may require more freedom in some situations and a firmer hand in others. Most directors work somewhere in between two extremes of management styles: Either a director allows the actor to find his or her role, or the director takes an authoritative approach in order to develop a consistent interpretation.

Rehearsals

Once the performers have been selected, a director can begin a preliminary run-through of the production by helping the actors to develop their specific characters. Preliminary practices of a performance are called *rehearsals*. Rehearsals sometimes begin with reading sessions, in which actors sit around a table and read their respective parts prior to actually performing them. Many rehearsals may be necessary before the actors are fully prepared to perform unerringly before the camera(s). All the bugs have to be worked out before a performance can proceed without problems or disruptions. The final rehearsal,

A
B

Figure 4.22 The range actors can portray serves them well, especially if they are asked to take the part of someone as different from their own persona as Robin Williams was able to do in Twentieth Century Fox's production of *Mrs. Doubtfire* (A) and in Touchstone/Columbia Pictures *Bicentennial Man* (B). (Courtesy of Twentieth Century Fox and Touchstone/Columbia Pictures.)

which usually takes place with the sets fully dressed and the performers in costume, is called a *dress rehearsal*. It simulates the actual recording session in virtually every respect.

Multicamera and live productions usually demand more rehearsal time than single-camera productions, because entire scenes or programs are recorded at one time rather than broken up into segments for a single camera. The entire performance must be worked out to perfection so that even minor mistakes are avoided during actual recording. Actors in single-camera productions do not always know how one shot relates to another. Single shots are often recorded in isolation, and performers cannot build a performance in perfect continuity as they would on the stage or for a multiple-camera production. Close-ups are often recorded out of sequence, for example. The director must be able to provide the performer with a context that will help the actor achieve a proper performance level so that shots can be combined during postproduction editing. One of the director's primary responsibilities during rehearsal and production is to ensure that the actors maintain continuity in the dramatic levels of their performances from one shot to the next. Many directors prefer to have a complete rehearsal in advance.

Performer and Camera Blocking

The director usually stages and plots the action in two distinct stages: performer blocking and camera blocking. Prior to selecting final camera placements, angles, lenses, and so on, the director will frequently run through the basic actions to be performed by the talent. This is called *performer blocking*. A director must carefully preplan the entire performance in advance. Only rarely are the performer's movements precisely set during performer blocking alone. Instead, a general sense of the action is determined, which facilitates camera blocking and prepares the performers for actual recording.

Camera blocking refers to the placement of cameras so that they can follow the movements of the talent. Whether several cameras or a single camera will actually record the action, the director must be able to anticipate the types of shots that will provide adequate coverage, dramatic emphasis, and directional continuity from shot to shot. Shot lists can be drawn up and supplied to the camera operator(s). These lists are a helpful guide to camera operation during blocking sessions and actual production. Every consecutive shot in each scene for each camera is written on a piece of paper that the camera operator can tape to the back of the camera for easy reference. Shot lists indicate types of shots and camera movements called

for in the final shooting script. In some recording situations, there is minimal time to block the cameras and the performers separately, and the two stages are combined. During camera blocking, the performers, director, and camera operator(s) exchange ideas and discuss problems as the action is blocked or charted on the floor or on location. The director refines his or her conception and interpretation of the script, making notations of any deviations from previous shot selections. Performers not only learn and remember their lines, they must also remember their marks, that is, the precise points where they must position themselves during actual recordings (Figure 4.23).

MULTIPLE-CAMERA DIRECTING

Directing several cameras simultaneously requires a different approach from that of single-camera recording. The preproduction planning stages are always very extensive, because major changes are more difficult to make once recording has begun. Performers must learn the lines of dialogue for several scenes, since more script material will be recorded in a single session. Camera operators must anticipate what camera positions, lens types and positions, and framing they are to adopt for upcoming segments. Ample time and space must be provided for the cameras to be moved during recording. Every detail must be worked out in advance, and a detailed shooting script or camera shot sequence must be provided to each key member of the production team.

When the recording session has been properly planned and practiced, tremendous economies in time and expense can be accomplished by using multiple-camera recording. But a multiple-camera situation can also be extremely frustrating if a key individual is improperly prepared or the director has failed to anticipate all the problems that can arise. Murphy's Law—**If anything can go wrong, it will**—is an optimistic expectation in multiple-camera and live television recording situations where directors, crews, and talents are insufficiently prepared.

For multiple-camera recordings of uncontrolled events, such as sporting events, cameras are often placed in fixed positions. Each camera operator is responsible for covering a specific part of the action from one position. The director of a live production, such as coverage of a sporting event, may have to watch and control as many as 10 cameras, some of which are connected to slow-motion recorders. The director must be able to respond instantaneously to any action that occurs, rapidly cutting from one camera to another. The director selects from among the

Figure 4.23 A director blocks performers and cameras before and during rehearsal in order to determine the best placement of each to provide the framing and movement intended for each shot. A plot drawn as if looking straight down on the scene is helpful in visualizing where cameras and performers need to be blocked.

images displayed on a bank of television screens. Since only minimal scripting is possible, the action and atmosphere within the director's control room itself often become very intense during a sporting event or similar production. Accurate decisions must be made very quickly. To anticipate actions and cuts, directors must be intimately familiar with the particular sport.

Timing

An important function performed by the director is timing. The control of program pace in terms of the speed of dialogue, actions, and editing is one form of timing. As discussed in Chapter 3, "Scriptwriting," dramatic pacing is a subjective impression of time in video, film, and sound productions. Through effective editing, a sequence of action can be made to seem longer or shorter in duration to the audience. Other types of timing are equally important in the production process.

Running Time

A director is responsible for ensuring that the program length or actual running time of a completed program conforms to the required length. In video production, *running time* should be distinguished from *clock time*. The latter refers to the actual time of day on the studio clock. Each video or film program or program segment has its own running time, which is the exact duration of the program, regardless of what time of day it is actually shown. During live productions, a timer is used to calculate the running time of each program segment so that the total running time will conform to the scheduled overall length of the program.

Timing in Production

Television commercials, public service announcements, and broadcast or cablecast programming must be accurately timed during production. When recording a commercial, for example, a director must obtain shots that will add up to exactly 10, 30, or 60 seconds. The screen time of the various shots and vignettes must add up to the exact screen time of the commercial format that has been chosen. Live video production demands precise screen timing with a timer as well as a studio clock, since the show cannot be reedited, lengthened, or shortened.

Backtiming is the process of figuring the amount of time remaining in a program or program segment by subtracting the present time from the predetermined end time. Music is sometimes backtimed so that it will end at the conclusion of a live production. This means that if the music should last three minutes, you back-time three minutes from its end and start playing it three minutes before the end of the program, gradually fading it up. In other words, if you want it to end at 6:59, you backtime it three minutes and start it at 6:56. In multiple-camera video production, the talent is often told how much time remains by means of hand signals. Five fingers, followed by four, three, two, and one, indicate how many minutes of running time remain for that segment. Rotating the index finger in a circle indicates that it is time to wind up a performance, since the time is almost up. A cutoff signal (the hand cuts across the neck, as though the stage or floor manager's own head is coming off) indicates the actual end of a segment or show.

On-the-Air Timing

Prerecorded videotapes such as commercials, which will be inserted into a program as it is being broadcast or cablecast, must be accurately backtimed or cued and set up on a playback machine. A countdown leader displaying consecutive numbers from 10 down to 0 is placed just ahead of the prerecorded pictures and sound. The numbers indicate how many seconds are left before the start of the prerecorded material. The playback can then be *prerolled*, that is, begun at the appropriate number of seconds before the commercial is due to start.

Production Switching

In multiple-camera video production, the director supervises virtually all of the editing in the control room during actual production. Production editing is done by means of a switcher, a device that allows shots to be selected from among several different cameras instantaneously. The director usually commands the technical director (TD) to change the transmitted image from one camera to another. (In many local stations, the director actually operates the switcher.) The TD then pushes the correct buttons on the switcher. Each button on the switcher is connected to a different camera or image source. When the TD pushes a button, the switcher automatically substitutes one picture for another.

The TD and the director view these changes on television monitors as they are taking place. The images sent out of the switcher can either be directly transmitted and broadcast during live production or recorded on videotape. A videotape recording can be used for subsequent postproduction editing and delayed broadcast, cablecast, or closed-circuit showing. A switcher is both an electronic editing device and a special effects machine. The TD can not only cut from one image or camera to another, but also fade in, fade out, dissolve, wipe, key, chroma key, and superimpose images. Various transition devices can be used in changing from one image or camera to another.

A switcher consists of a series of buttons organized into units called *buses* (Figure 4.24). There are three types of buses: preview, program, and special effects or mix. Individual buttons within each bus are linked to specific sources, such as Camera 1, Camera 2, Camera 3, a videotape player, a remote source, still store, character generator, digital generator, and a constant black image.

Each bus has one button assigned to each of these image sources. Thus a bus allocated to previewing

VIDEO SWITCHER

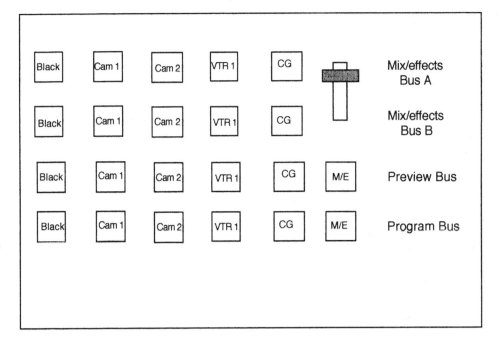

Figure 4.24 The simplest switcher would contain at least four busses—one for on-air (program), one to check shots ahead of time (preview), and two for mixing or wiping shots (mix/effect, or M/E). In addition to all other inputs to the switcher, the program bus must also contain a button for switching to the M/E bus.

images prior to sending them out of the board, called a *preview bus*, would have at least nine individual buttons connected to the nine image sources cited above: Cameras 1, 2, 3, videotape player, remote source, still store, character and digital generators, and a constant black image. When one of these buttons is pressed, the image from that source appears on the preview monitor. A second bus having the same number of buttons is assigned to the actual program feed; on a simple switcher, this is the signal that will actually be transmitted or recorded.

A switcher having just two buses would only allow the TD to preview images and to cut directly from one image to another. If any special effects are to be created, the switcher must have special effects or mix buses. These two effects or mix buses are usually designated "A" and "B." In order to send any visual signal on the effects buses out of the switcher, a button designating the effects buses must be activated on a secondary program bus called the master program bus.

The master program bus acts as a final selection switch, determining what will be transmitted by the switcher. The TD can select the program bus (which contains one of the nine visual sources) or the effects bus by depressing one of these two buttons on the master program bus. A master preview bus is also available on more sophisticated switchers, so that an effect, such as a split-screen or digital effect, can be previewed prior to recording or transmission via the master program bus.

Director's Commands

A director must communicate accurately with the entire crew in order to coordinate a production effectively, but communication with the TD is critical since the TD's response and action determine what pictures will be seen on air or fed to the tape. Operating the switcher during production requires careful preparation and infallible communication between the director and the operator of the switcher. The TD must know in advance exactly what switcher operations will be called for by the director and the order in which they will be called for. It is very easy to become confused and push the wrong button or misunderstand the director's commands. It is the director's responsibility to convey clear and distinct commands to the TD and to provide adequate time between the preparatory command and the command of execution.

Video and film directors have developed relatively precise terminology and methods with which to communicate with their cast and crew. The method is based on a two-step system of first warning of an impending command with a preparatory (prep) command, followed by a command of execution at the precise timing moment. A preparatory command always begins with either the words "*stand by*" or "*ready.*" This tells everyone that a new command is about to be announced, so pay attention. The prep command needs to be detailed and precise and clearly stated so that the crew and cast directly involved know what to prepare themselves for when the command of execution arrives a few seconds later. The command of execution needs to be as short and as precise as possible, since that command determines the precise moment when an action is to take place.

If the director wants Camera 3 to zoom in to a two-shot, for example, a typical command series would be as follows.

SIMPLE COMMAND SEQUENCE

PREPARATORY COMMAND: Camera 3, stand by to zoom into a two-shot.

COMMAND OF EXECUTION: Three-zoom.

More often a single command series is directed at more than one crew or cast member. The beginning command of a newscast might be directed at the TD (the switcher transition), the audio operator (to open a mic), the camera operator (who gets the opening shot), and the floor manager (to give the anchor a stand-by and a cue to start talking).

COMPLEX COMMAND SEQUENCE

PREPARATORY COMMAND: Stand by to anchor, ready mic, ready to fade in camera 2 on the anchor.

COMMAND OF EXECUTION: Mic, fade in 2, cue anchor.

The order of the commands and the precise nature of their execution is critical. Sloppy or inaccurate calls by a director will guarantee a sloppy production. Commands to the TD and camera operators are especially important because in both cases some preoperation activities may need to be carried out before the command can be followed. The switcher may need to have a complex set of buttons aligned or set up, or a camera or lens may need to be moved or adjusted before the shot is ready.

Live-on-Tape Recording

A live-on-tape (multiple-camera) director can use the techniques of live multiple-camera video to record events quickly and efficiently but also has the option to change the shot sequence during postproduction. This is accomplished by recording the images from several cameras simultaneously while at the same time making some editing decisions on the switcher that are recorded on a separate recorder. Editing decisions made during production can then be changed during postproduction by inserting different camera shots. This method gives the director maximum flexibility to produce a program economically in the shortest possible time without jeopardizing the quality of the final product, since changes can always

be made later. In this way multiple-camera recording techniques can be combined with the techniques discussed next, allowing the director to benefit from the advantages of both methods.

SINGLE-CAMERA DIRECTING

The number of cameras used and the order and time frame of recording or filming shots constitute the major differences between multiple- and single-camera directing. The types of shots are the same, but the physical arrangement and order of shooting those shots differ between the two production modes. Recording with a single camera usually takes longer than multiple-camera recording. The lighting, camera, and set are sometimes moved and readjusted for each shot. Better quality images are often obtained using this method, since fewer compromises have to be made in terms of recording logistics. Each shot is composed and the action repeated so that an optimal recording is made. But potential problems can arise in terms of discontinuity or mismatched action from one shot to the next. The director and the script continuity person must observe and duplicate every detail recorded or filmed in the master shot during the shooting of the inserts.

Both film and video use three different types of setups for one camera: (1) master shots, (2) inserts, and (3) cutaways. Single-camera recording normally begins with a shot of the entire action in a scene, or as much of the complete scene as it is possible to record in a single shot. This is often called a *master shot*. Master shots are usually, but not always, long shots. Specific actions occurring within the master shot are then repeated after the camera has been placed closer to the subject for shots known as *inserts*. Inserts are usually the medium shots and close-ups indicated in a script. Master shots and inserts may be rerecorded several times before an acceptable recording has been made. Specific recordings are called different *takes* of the same shot. A script continuity person then marks the shooting script (as shown in Figure 4.25) with the number of the exact shot specified in the script, and each take is circled at the beginning point of actual recording.

A line is drawn vertically through the script to the point where actual recording of that take ends. Inserts are normally extended before and after the exact edit points in the script to allow for overlapping action and a range of editing choices. A marked shooting script provides a complete record of actual recording in terms of master shots and inserts. *Cutaways* are additional close-ups and medium shots of objects or events that are not central parts of the

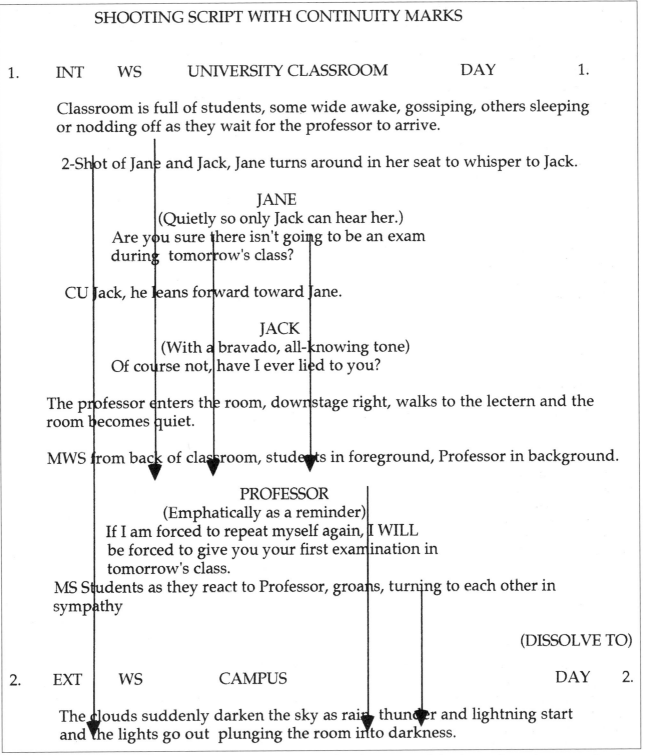

SHOOTING SCRIPT WITH CONTINUITY MARKS

1.   INT   WS   UNIVERSITY CLASSROOM   DAY   1.

Classroom is full of students, some wide awake, gossiping, others sleeping or nodding off as they wait for the professor to arrive.

2-Shot of Jane and Jack, Jane turns around in her seat to whisper to Jack.

> JANE
> (Quietly so only Jack can hear her.)
> Are you sure there isn't going to be an exam
> during tomorrow's class?

CU Jack, he leans forward toward Jane.

> JACK
> (With a bravado, all-knowing tone)
> Of course not, have I ever lied to you?

The professor enters the room, downstage right, walks to the lectern and the room becomes quiet.

MWS from back of classroom, students in foreground, Professor in background.

> PROFESSOR
> (Emphatically as a reminder)
> If I am forced to repeat myself again, I WILL
> be forced to give you your first examination in
> tomorrow's class.

MS Students as they react to Professor, groans, turning to each other in sympathy

(DISSOLVE TO)

2.   EXT   WS   CAMPUS   DAY   2.

The clouds suddenly darken the sky as rain, thunder and lightning start and the lights go out plunging the room into darkness.

Figure 4.25 Continuity marks on a script are made as the scene is shot. The continuity clerk indicates when a shot starts and ends with codes agreed upon with the editor. Often the codes will indicate the framing of a shot as well as its length and the number of takes. These kinds of markings are invaluable to the editor during postproduction.

action and are often not specified in the script. They can be inserted into a scene to bridge mismatched actions or to hide mistakes within or between a master shot and an insert. The master shot or long shot can act as a safety net in the event that matching medium shots or close-ups specified in the script do not prove satisfactory. A continuously running long shot or master shot can be quite boring in comparison with using several different long shots, medium shots, and close-ups for emphasis and variety. But the knowledge that the master shot covers the entire action and can be used at any point can be of some comfort to the editor.

Insert shots, which record some of the same actions as the master shot but from a closer camera position or a different angle of view, are called *inserts* or *cutins*, since they will be cut into the master shot. The director and the script continuity person must observe and duplicate every detail recorded in the master shot during the recording of the inserts. The actors must perform the same gestures, wear the same clothing, and repeat the same actions and lines of dialogue if actions are to overlap and match from one shot to the next. In extremely low-budget situations, where it is impossible to record several takes of each insert, a director is well advised to record a few cutaways for use in bridging mismatched actions between shots that are discovered during postproduction editing. It is the director's responsibility to provide adequate coverage of events and actions so that a program can be edited with minimal difficulty. Good coverage provides insurance against costly reshooting.

Cutaways

Cutaways are shots of secondary objects and actions that can be used to hide mismatched action and to preserve continuity, or simply to add depth and interest to the primary action of a film or television program. *Cut-ins* depict actions that appear within the frame of master shots, while *cutaways* depict actions and objects outside the master shot frame. In single-camera news recording, a reaction shot of the reporter or interviewer is sometimes used to bridge gaps or to avoid jump cuts in a condensed version of an interview, or simply to provide facial expressions to comment on what is being said. Close-ups of hands gesturing and relevant props can also be used as cutaways. They can be inserted at almost any point to bridge mismatched action in master shots and inserts, or simply to add more detail to the spatial environment. Cutaways provide an editor with something to cut away to when editing problems are discovered.

Shooting Ratios

All single-camera directors try to get an acceptable shot in as few takes as possible; nonetheless there can be considerable variation in shooting ratios from one production to another. *Shooting ratios*, which refer to the ratio of visual material shot to visual material actually used, can range from about 5:1 to 100:1 in different types of production situations. Obviously, more takes of each shot translate into higher shooting ratios. Network commercials often have the highest shooting ratios. At the other end of the spectrum, student productions often have shooting ratios as low as 5:1 or even 3:1, due to limited production funds. Low-budget situations call for highly efficient production methods.

Director's Terminology

Since a single-camera director is normally present on the set with the camera operator rather than isolated in a control room, as in multiple-camera production, he or she can communicate directly with the crew and talent. Directorial terminology for camera placements and movements is generally the same as that for multiple-camera recording, but a few commands are quite different. When the crew and the talent are ready to record a single shot, the director says "Roll tape" to the videotape (in video) or audio (in film) recordist, and "Roll film" to the film camera operator. When the tape or film is up to speed, the operator says "Speed" or "Camera rolling." The director then calls "Slate," and a grip or camera assistant slates the shot by calling out the scene, shot, and take numbers, which are also written on a board called a *slate*. In film, the slate has electronic or physical clapsticks that are brought together so that separate sounds and pictures can be synchronized later. The scene, shot, and take numbers displayed on the slate are used as a reference during postproduction editing. They are usually written down on a camera report sheet, which is sent to the film laboratory or used by the videotape editor.

When the talent is ready and the slate has been removed from the shot, the director says "Action" and the performance begins. When a shot is over or a problem develops in midshot, the director says "Cut." If the director wants a scene printed for later viewing, the command "Print" will be given. The "Print" command is noted on the camera report. Since editing can be done during postproduction, there is no need for the director to communicate with a technical director (switcher operator) during actual production. Editing decisions will be made later (Figure 4.26).

Figure 4.26 The director on a single-camera shoot stands next to the camera to give directions to both the camera operator and the talent. Either the director or a production assistant keeps an accurate record of each shot on a camera log.

SUMMARY

Video and film directors are artists who can turn a completed script into a shooting script and produce works of art from recorded visual images and sounds. To prepare a shooting script, a director must know when to use different types of shots. Shots can be categorized by camera-to-subject distance, camera angle, camera (or lens) movement, and shot duration. Directors also know how to control various aspects of visual composition and image qualities, such as tone, scale and shape, depth, and speed of motion, and the use of various transition devices and special effects.

In scene construction, conventional continuity often begins with a long shot and gradually moves closer to the subject as the action intensifies. Continuity suggests an uninterrupted flow of time, with no apparent gaps or mismatched actions from shot to shot. Video and film are temporal and spatial arts. Classical continuity refers to the continuity of time and continuity of space maintained in many classical Hollywood films (e.g., most films made in Hollywood between 1920 and 1960).

The aesthetic use of sound is extremely important. Although sound can be used simply to accompany and complement the visuals, it can also be treated as an independent aesthetic element. There are four basic categories of sound: speech, music, sound effects, and ambient noise. A director must be familiar with the basic elements of music, such as rhythm, melody, harmony, counterpoint, and tonality or timbre, as well as different types of music. Sound effects are sometimes used to enhance an illusion or reality, or to create imaginative sound impressions. Ambient noise, also called background sound, is present in any location and can be used to preserve temporal continuity and to create an illusion of spatial depth. A director can affect the perception of temporal continuity through the selection and ordering of sounds. Mismatched levels and gaps in the presentation of sounds can create discontinuity, thus disrupting the flow of time. It is possible to condense and expand time without disrupting the illusion of continuity, however.

Music composed for television or film often performs one of the following functions: intensifying the drama, establishing the period or place, setting the mood or atmosphere, stimulating a specific emotion in conjunction with a character or theme, or simply filling in and avoiding silence. The director and the composer should collaborate with one another, fully and creatively exploring the artistic potential of visual image and music interaction.

The director supervises the creative aspects of television and film production by coordinating the production team, initiating and chairing preproduction and production meetings, casting the film or television program with the producer and casting director, and organizing production rehearsals.

The director's function can vary considerably between multiple-camera and single-camera recording situations. The multiple-camera video director frequently sits in a control room isolated from the talent and crew during actual recording. In live and multiple-camera production, directors are usually directly involved in the selection of specific types of shots and in the creation of transition devices and special effects. The multiple-camera director supervises the movement of several cameras, using an intercom, and controls the editing by having the TD punch buttons on the switcher, changing the main signal from one camera or source to another. The single-camera director, on the other hand, is usually present on the set during the shooting and works directly with the talent and crew during the period of time between shots, when the camera is being moved and the lighting and sound recording devices reset. The editing of single-camera production is usually left to a specialist who cuts the film or electronically edits together videotape during postproduction.

EXERCISES

1. View a scene or sequence from a completed production repeatedly and write a postproduction shooting script or shot analysis for it based on actual shots in the finished product. Compare your shooting script or shot analysis for this segment to a published version to determine if you have made proper use of shooting script terms and concepts.

2. Take a segment from a completed and published script and attempt to transform it into a shooting script by adding specific shots, sound effects, and so on. Use techniques that are consistent with a realist, modernist, or postmodernist approach when creating your shooting script. Do this exercise for both a multiple-camera production and a single-camera production.

3. Record a television program without watching it. Then play it back without watching the screen. Determine if you are able to follow and understand the program without the visual side of the story line.

4. Record another program, only this time don't listen to it. Then play it back, and watch it with the sound turned down. Determine if you are able to follow and understand the program without the audio portion of the story line.

5. Using either of the tapes from # 3 or #4, carefully listen to the sounds: create a chart by time in seconds. On the chart indicate when there is music, sound effects, narration, wild sound, and dialog. Keep each type of sound in a separate column to determine how much of the audio portion of the program is music, SFX, narration, wild sound, or dialog.

6. Using either of the programs recorded in # 3 or #4, create a chart showing each transition between shots. List cuts, dissolves, wipes, digital effects, and fades to or from black. Total the number of transitions and how many of each type were used in the production.

ADDITIONAL READINGS

Andrew, J. Dudley. *Major Film Theories*. New York: Oxford University Press, 1976.

Armer, Alan A. *Directing Television and Film*, 2nd ed. Belmont, CA: Wadsworth, 1990.

Bate, Richard L. *The Film Director: A Practical Guide to Motion Picture and Television Techniques*. New York: Collier Books, 1971.

Benedetti, Robert. *From Concept to Screen: An Overview of Film and Television Production*. Boston: Allyn and Bacon, 2002.

Bernstein, Steven. *Film Production*, 2nd ed. Boston, MA: Focal Press, 1994.

Bordwell, David and Kristin Thompson. *Film Art: An Introduction*, 2nd ed. New York: Alfred A. Knopf, 1986.

Burch, Noel. *Theory of Film Practice*. Trans., Helen R. Lane. New York: Praeger, 1973.

Cury, Ivan. *Directing and Producing for Television: A Format Approach*. 2nd ed. Boston, MA: Focal Press, 2001.

Douglass, John S. and Glenn Harnden. *The Art of Technique: An Aesthetic Approach to Film and Video Production*. Needham Heights, MA: Allyn and Bacon, 1996.

Gordon, Clay. *The Guide to High Definition Video Production: Preparing for a Wide-Screen World*. Boston, MA: Focal Press, 1996.

Hickman, Harold R. *Television Directing*. Santa Rosa, CA: Cole Publishing, 1991.

Kindem, Gorham. *The Live Television Generation of Hollywood Film Directors*. Jefferson, NC: McFarland, 1994.

Kingson, Walter K. and Rome Cowgill. *Television Acting and Directing*. New York: Holt, Rinehart and Winston, 1965.

Lukas, Christopher. *Directing for Film and Television.* New York: Anchor Press/Doubleday, 1985.

Millerson, Gerald. *TV Production*, 13th ed. Boston, MA: Focal Press, 1999.

Rabiger, Michael. *Directing: Film Techniques and Aesthetics*, 3rd ed. Boston, MA: Focal Press, 2003.

Rabiger, Michael. *Directing the Documentary*, 3rd ed. Boston, MA: Focal Press, 1999.

Watkinson, John. *The Art of Digital Video.* Bosto Focal Press, 2000.

Weis, Elizabeth and John Belton. *Film Sound: The and Practice.* New York: Columbia University Press 1985.

Zettl, Herbert. *Sight, Sound, and Motion: Applied Media Aesthetics*, 3rd ed. Belmont, CA: Wadsworth Publishing, 1999.

Audio/Sound

TOPICS FOR DISCUSSION

- What are the aesthetics of sound?
- What types of mics are available?
- How are mics selected and placed?
- How is sound measured and controlled?
- What does sound perspective mean?
- How are sound signals connected?

INTRODUCTION

This chapter explores audio production techniques and equipment used to record and control high-quality sound and sound perspectives. Quality audio is extremely important in media production. Poor-quality sounds can destroy the impact of high-quality visuals. High-quality sounds not only enhance accompanying visuals. They can directly affect emotions and develop additional creative dimensions and responses.

Some directors feel that sounds and visual images should be almost completely independent of one another so that each component could stand entirely on its own, while others feel that sounds should reinforce accompanying visual images. The former approach is consistent with modernist aesthetics, while the latter reflects a realist approach to production. Some directors combine these approaches and suggest that high-quality sound should function well on its own as well as in combination with visual images.

Except for signal processing, editing, and distribution, no substantial difference exists between analog and digital audio production techniques. Greater care must be taken in all stages of digital audio production due to the increased frequency response and lower level of noise. Digital editing technologies are covered in Chapter 10, "Visual Editing," and Chapter 11, "Sound Editing." Digital distribution systems are covered in Chapter 13, "Distribution and Exhibition."

AESTHETICS OF AUDIO/SOUND

Audio/sound can be approached from the three aesthetic perspectives of realism, modernism, and postmodernism. A realist approach uses sound to stimulate an illusion of reality, reinforcing the temporal and spatial continuity of visual images. Modernist audio develops sound independently of accompanying visual images, breaking down realist conventions and stimulating more abstract impressions and visceral feelings. Postmodernist audio emphasizes listener participation within productions in order to emotionally involve the audience as much as possible.

TYPES OF MICROPHONES

The ability to duplicate quality audio in film, video, and audio-only situations depends on careful mic selection and placement. This means choosing a mic designed for the specific purpose at hand and positioning it properly. A microphone is a type of transducer. Transducers are devices that change one form of energy to another form of energy. Mics convert analog sound wave action into analog fluctuations in electrical voltage. A digital signal must be created by converting the analog signal through an analog-to-digital converter. Sound is created by the very rapid vibration of objects, and sound waves consist of rapidly contracting and expanding particles of air. A tuning fork, for example, causes air molecules to compress and expand as it vibrates, creating a sound pressure wave. As one arm moves forward, it pushes the air molecules, and as it moves backward, the air molecules, which are elastic or resistant to being pushed, expand again to fill the partial vacuum or void. Rapid vibration creates a pressure wave of alternately compressed and expanded air molecules. This pressure or sound wave moves in a relatively straight line and strikes other objects, such as the human ear or a microphone element. The eardrum vibrates in response to the sound wave and produces an auditory impression in the mind. A mic has an element that is sensitive to these air waves and converts the wave action into corresponding fluctuations in electrical current. The electrical signal thus becomes an analog, or copy, of the sound wave. Once an electronic equivalent of the audio signal has been created, that signal may be converted into a digital signal for processing and maintenance of the highest quality.

Mics can be classified on the basis of the type of transducer element they use into three basic categories: dynamic, ribbon, and condenser. One type of mic element may be better suited to a specific audio situation than another.

Transducer Elements

A dynamic mic consists of a moving coil attached to a vibrating diaphragm or disc suspended between two magnetic poles. As the diaphragm vibrates with the sound wave, the coil moves up and down within a magnetic field and changes the voltage of the electrical current flowing through the coil. In general, dynamic mics are very durable, not extremely susceptible to wind noise, and relatively inexpensive (Figure 5.1).

A ribbon mic contains a narrow strip of corrugated foil suspended in a magnetic field. This ribbon vibrates in response to the difference in air pressure in front and in back of it, and produces an alternating current along the length of a coil. The ribbon itself is quite fragile and can easily be damaged by simply blowing into the mic, although newer ribbon mics have been designed to be more durable but still are best confined to studio use. A ribbon mic usually produces a smooth, bass-accentuated sound, is preferred by many radio and television announcers for that reason, and is ideal for digital recording since its warm sound accentuates high frequencies. Most ribbon mics are priced at the top of the range of professional microphones.

Condenser mics are relatively complex, compared to dynamic or ribbon mics. The element is a capacitor that requires two charged plates: a diaphragm and a fixed backplate. As the diaphragm vibrates, the space between it and the fixed plate changes in capacitance, that is, in its ability to pass an electrical current or signal. The strength of the electrical sound signal increases or decreases accordingly. The signal is very weak, however, and a preamplifier is required to boost the signal to a usable level. Additional current may be supplied

MICROPHONE ELEMENTS

Dynamic (Moving Coil) Element

Ribbon Element

Condenser Element

Figure 5.1 The three transducer elements now used in microphones are dynamic, ribbon, and condenser. Dynamic transducer involves the movement of a thin diaphragm moving a coil of wires wrapped around a permanent magnetic. A ribbon transducer involves a thin corrugated strip of metal moving between the poles of a permanent magnet. A condenser transducer involves two thin plates of metal moving within a static charged capacitance field.

to the preamplifier by a battery in the mic handle or by a power supply located in the mixer called a *phantom supply*. An electret condenser mic is constructed with permanently charged plates, reducing the power needed to operate the mic. Condenser mics vary in price from relatively inexpensive to quite expensive, and some inexpensive cameras and cassette recorders have built-in condenser mics of lesser quality. A condenser mic generally reproduces high-quality sound, and with its built-in pre-amp can be considered quite sensitive.

Pickup Patterns

Mics can be classified according to their directional sensitivity or pickup patterns, as well as their transducer elements. Different recording situations require the use of mics that pick up sounds from a very narrow or a very wide area. Some mics pick up sounds coming from every direction, while others are sensitive to a very restricted area. The three basic categories of pickup patterns are as follows: omnidirectional, bidirectional, and unidirectional or cardioid.

An *omnidirectional mic* is equally sensitive to sounds from all directions, that is, from the entire 360-degree area surrounding it. A *bidirectional mic* is sensitive to sounds coming from two opposite directions. Its sensitivity drops off rapidly at 60 degrees on either side of these two opposite directional points. At 90 degrees (perpendicular to the two optimal sound source directions), it is almost totally insensitive to sound. Unidirectional mics are sensitive to sounds from one direction only (Figure 5.2).

Microphone Pickup Patterns

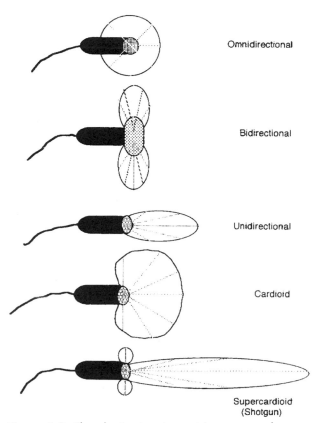

Omnidirectional

Bidirectional

Unidirectional

Cardioid

Supercardioid
(Shotgun)

Figure 5.2 Three basic microphone pickup patterns of omnidirectional, bidirectional, and unidirectional may be modified or combined to create two additional patterns: cardioid and/or supercardioid or shotgun pattern.

A *cardioid mic* is a type of unidirectional mic so named because its pickup pattern is heart shaped. A cardioid mic is somewhat more sensitive to sound emanating from directly behind it, but it is very sensitive to sound coming from directly in front of it. A supercardioid mic is somewhat more sensitive to sound coming from the rear of the mic but has an even narrower optimal response area (about 60 degrees as opposed to 120 degrees for a cardioid mic). Shotgun mics are long, narrow tubes; they frequently have a supercardioid pickup pattern.

Impedance A third characteristic of microphones that determines their use and placement is impedance. Impedance is a complex measurement of the property of wires and equipment that determines the ability of a signal to pass through that piece of equipment. It is critical that all audio equipment be designed to match input and output impedances. For microphones there are two basic impedance choices, high or low. High-impedance mics are low-cost amateur mics, whereas all professional mics are low impedance. High-impedance mics may be connected with wires that contain one conductor and a shield, which does not provide the maximum protection for the signal from outside interference. Low-impedance mics normally are connected with wires that contain two conductors and a shield, providing maximum protection for the signal.

MIC PLACEMENT AND SELECTION

Mic placement during recording can be either on-camera or off-camera. On-camera mics, such as a reporter's handheld mic, are visible to the viewer. Off-camera mics are not visible to the viewer. An off-camera mic can be hidden somewhere on the set or under a speaker's clothing, or it can be situated just outside the camera frame.

On-Camera Mics

Hand mics are the most common on-camera mics. Mics that are to be handheld should be shock mounted; that is, they should be well insulated so that noise is not created as the performer moves the mic. Since a hand mic can be moved and controlled by the performer, it does not always stay in a fixed position, and it generally has a relatively wide pickup pattern, such as omnidirectional or cardioid. It is wise to use a mic with a durable element, such as a dynamic or an electret condenser mic, in a handheld situation. An inexperienced performer should be instructed in how to keep the hand mic at a relatively constant distance from his or her mouth in order to keep the loudness relatively constant. A problem that frequently arises with the use of a hand mic is controlling the mic cable. Performers must learn to move the mic around without stretching the cable or tangling it (Figure 5.3).

Desk mics often have less durable elements than hand mics. If a desk mic is placed in a relatively permanent position, it does not have to be shock mounted. If a desk mic is to be removed from its mount and also function as a hand mic, as frequently occurs, it must have some of the same qualities as a hand mic. Most desk mics have cardioid pickup patterns and are placed one to two feet from the speaker. Sometimes a single bidirectional or omnidirectional desk mic can be used for two speakers to limit the number of mics needed (Figure 5.4).

A *stand mic* is supported on an adjustable pole in front of the performer; thus it offers a distinct advantage to a person who has his or her hands occupied with a musical instrument. The stand mic can usually be tilted and adjusted to a comfortable height for different performers. In general, more sensitive ribbon and condenser mics are used on a stand to record relatively soft sound sources such as stringed instru-

Figure 5.4 A desk stand is designed to hold a microphone in position to pick up people seated at the desk. It usually works best for one person, but can be placed between two people if their audio levels are nearly the same.

ments, while dynamic mics with omnidirectional or cardioid reception patterns are often used for singers and amplified instruments. Sometimes more than one mic may be attached to a single stand: perhaps a condenser mic positioned from below to pick up the sounds of a guitar and a dynamic mic above to pick up the singer's voice (Figure 5.5).

A *lavalier mic* also leaves a performer's hands free and does not require a stand that restricts his or her mobility. This type of mic, which is either hung around the performer's neck with a strap or clipped to a tie or outer garment, is relatively unobtrusive compared with a desk mic or a stand mic. Care should be taken in the placement of a lavalier mic to ensure that it will not create noise by rubbing against rough clothing or jewelry. Lavalier mics are often susceptible to cable problems because their cables are relatively thin and fragile. To guard against this on live broadcasts, performers such as newscasters often wear two lavaliers clipped together to create a dual-redundancy system, where one mic serves as a backup for the other. Only one mic at a time is live to prevent phasing problems, which are discussed later in this chapter. A lavalier microphone can be hidden or concealed behind clothing, although this can lead to added rubbing noise (Figure 5.6).

Some handheld and lavalier mics have battery-powered FM transmitters, which allow the speaker using the mic to move around quite freely without a

Figure 5.3 Hand microphones also may be mounted on a desk stand, floor stand, or boom, but must be designed to fit comfortably in the hand with reasonable sensitivity. (Courtesy of Shure.)

Figure 5.5 A stand mic is designed to allow one or more people to stand on each side of the microphone, depending upon whether the microphone is bidirectional, unidirectional, or omnidirectional. (Courtesy of Sony Corporation.)

transmitted signal. While wireless mics can be extremely helpful in many difficult recording situations, they also have a number of pitfalls. Like any FM radio, the wireless receiver can pick up interfering signals, such as noise from CB radios. Batteries can expire in the middle of a recording, especially when performers forget to turn them off. Finally, wireless mics are more expensive to rent or purchase than wired mics (Figure 5.7).

Figure 5.7 A wireless microphone may be designed as either handheld, a lavalier, or on a head-mount. The transmitter may be built into the base of the handheld microphone, or the lavalier and head-mount may be connected to a small transmitter fastened to the body of the performer. (Courtesy of Shure.)

restrictive mic cable. Wireless lavalier mics can also be used as hidden mics by concealing the mic and its transmitter under clothing. An FM receiver at the audio input of the recording machine receives the

Figure 5.6 A lavalier microphone is designed to be clipped to the clothing of the person speaking. The design of a lavalier compensates for the microphone resting against the chest of the speaker, and the microphone is located below the speaker's mouth. A lavalier should not be used as a handheld microphone away from the body.

Off-Camera Mics

Off-camera mics may be attached to a mic boom. A *mic boom* is a long pole that can be placed (usually above the heads of the talent) just outside the camera frame. It can also be hidden on the set. There are three different types of mic booms: fish-pole, giraffe, and perambulator booms. A *fishpole boom* is an aluminum pole with a mic-mounting device at one end. Some fishpoles can be telescoped to allow for maximum extension during shooting and contracted for compact storage. The fishpole's greatest asset is its portability. A fishpole and the attached mic are usually lightweight enough to be handheld for a relatively long period of time without excessively tiring the operator. One disadvantage of the fishpole boom is that the length generally cannot be changed during recording. The boom operator must move as the talent moves. Also, the entire pole must be twisted to change the positioning of the microphone, making it somewhat difficult to alternate the placement of a directional mic between two different performers. The portability and flexibility of a fishpole gain may be increased by using an FM mic instead of a wired mic.

A *giraffe boom* is somewhat more bulky and less portable than the fishpole, but it allows for greater mobility and flexibility during recording. The giraffe is basically a fishpole gain attached to a three-wheeled dolly. It can be quickly and easily moved around the studio. It also has the advantage of allowing the operator to rotate the mic on a swivel to which the pole is attached. It requires only one operator and can be extended to different lengths during camera setups (Figure 5.8).

The *perambulator boom* is the heaviest type of boom. It has a large pole, which can be telescoped during a camera take; a swivel mechanism for rotating the mic; an operator platform, which can be raised and lowered; heavy-duty rubber tires; a guide pole, which requires the presence of a second operator to push or pull the boom around the studio; and a boom pan-and-tilt control. The perambulator boom is designed primarily for studio use. It is not very portable. It is counter-weighted so that it can support a heavy microphone and a mounting device. Some perambulator booms allow an attached microphone to be panned or moved a full 180 degrees, so that a highly directional mic can be used to pick up a moving performer or to switch from one speaker to another.

Boom Operation

Operating a boom demands great care and manual dexterity. Movements of the mic and the boom must

Figure 5.8 A giraffe microphone is a small boom generally used to pick up the voice of one or two persons in fixed locations.

be smooth, precise, and carefully planned. Excessively rapid movements of the boom or mic will create objectionable noise. The movement of the talent must be fully anticipated by the boom operator. If the boom operator has not preplanned the movements of the boom so that it can follow the talent, it will be difficult to maintain a constant sound level or to avoid crashing into other equipment on the set. The boom operator's job is to keep a moving sound source within the mic's primary pickup pattern. The operator listens to the sounds on headphones, which serve the same function as a viewfinder for a camera operator.

Omnidirectional mics are rarely used on a boom; even though they might make it easier to follow the movements of the talent, because they simply pick up too much unwanted additional noise. Unidirectional mics seem to work best on a boom. They cut down on unwanted sounds by focusing on the sound source, and they provide good reception at a greater distance from the subject than mics with wider pickup patterns. This can be especially helpful when recording long camera shots with an off-camera mic.

Boom Placement

The optimum placement of a cardioid mic on a boom is one to four feet in front of and one to three feet above the speaking subject. In general, the boom operator should keep a uniform distance between the subject and the mic. Sometimes it may be necessary to vary this distance, however. To achieve proper sound perspective in single-camera recording, the mic may have to be slightly closer to the subject for close-ups and farther away for long shots (Figures 5.9 and 5.10).

An overhead boom can create harsh shadows that disrupt the image. The placement and movement of a boom must be carefully preplanned to prevent objectionable shadows on the set. Sometimes it is simply impossible to place the microphone directly overhead on a boom without noticeably affecting the lighting or camera and performer movements. In these situations, a fishpole boom may be placed at the bottom or side of the frame, or a hidden mic may be used.

Boom operators who are attempting to record the best-quality sound often place the mic as close to the subject as possible without entering the camera frame. In multiple-camera production, the audio operator informs the boom operator when the mic has entered an underscanned TV monitor, which shows a portion of the picture not viewed at home. In single-camera productions, the camera operator carefully monitors the frame area. One strategy boom operators sometimes use to obtain good-quality sound is to place the mic within the camera frame during a rehearsal or blocking session. This forces the director, audio operator, or camera operator to ask for the mic to be raised out of the frame. This strategy ensures that the mic will always be as close as possible to the subject and forces the director to consider whether the camera placement is compromising the quality of the sound. While directors usually are well aware of these limitations, a periodic reminder can go a long way toward preventing subsequent objections to the quality of the sound recording.

Hidden Mics

There are three different types of hidden or concealed mics: the hanging mic, the prop mic, and the concealed lavalier mic. *Hanging* and *prop mics* are stationary, but the concealed *lavalier* moves with the talent to whom it is attached. A stationary hanging mic can be attached to an overhead grid. It is usually an omnidirectional mic capable of covering a wide area of action. Its chief advantage is that it does not require a

Figure 5.9 A handheld microphone boom may be placed above the speaker's head or below, depending on the noise at the location or the type of shot. The mic may be placed closer to the speaker's mouth if the shot is a close-up rather than a wide shot.

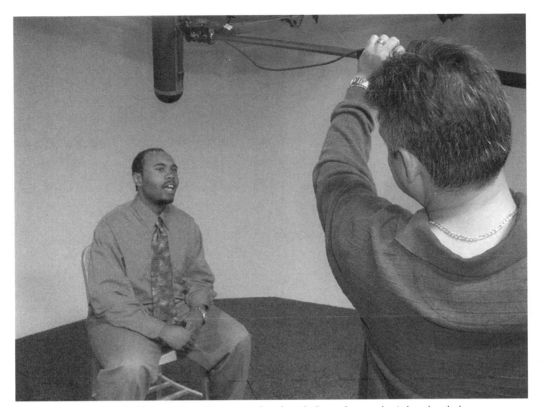

Figure 5.10 A handheld microphone boom may be placed above the speaker's head or below, depending on the noise at the location or the type of shot. The mic may be placed closer to the speaker's mouth if the shot is a close-up rather than a wide shot.

boom operator. Its obvious disadvantages are that it cannot be moved to vary or improve the audio during visual recording, and it often picks up ambient noises below it, such as footsteps and equipment being moved. Prop mics are microphones that are concealed on the set. A telephone at the center of a table around which several performers are seated can conceal a mic. Since a prop mic is stationary, it often has a relatively wide pickup pattern so that the talent does not have to stand immediately in front of the prop, calling attention to the presence of the mic or making it the focal point of a scene (Figures 5.11 and 5.12).

A *prop mic* can be extremely useful in situations in which it is difficult to use a boom, such as when the camera is shooting an extreme long shot or when the space is so confining that a boom necessarily affects the lighting. A concealed lavalier mic is frequently used as a hidden mic for extreme long shots and complicated movements of the camera or talent. The concealed lavalier mic may be wrapped in foam rubber and taped to the subject underneath his or her clothing. It should not be free to rub against garments or jewelry and create noise, and care must be taken to ensure that the sound reaching it is not muffled by heavy clothing.

Wireless (RF) Mics

As media productions become more mobile, a need for a system of connecting audio sources with recorders and mixers without entangling wires brought about the development of RF (radio frequency) wireless microphones. Each RF system consists of a microphone, a transmitter, and a receiver. Mics (usually electret) may be body mounted, head mounted, handheld, stand, or boom mounted. Each mic must be connected to a transmitter. A transmitter may be built into the base of the mic or plugged into the base of the mic, or a lavalier mic may be connected with a short cable to a body-mounted transmitter. The receiver may be a small, battery-operated unit mounted on a camcorder or a larger A/C-powered unit feeding a mixer, public address system, or recorder.

The transmitters are designed to operate on one of three frequency bands: VHF, UHF, or ultra UHF. VHF equipment offers lower-priced equipment but may suffer a greater chance for interference from taxis, police officers, or other RF users. Units operating on UHF frequencies are designed specifically for radio and TV broadcasters for high-quality communication systems. Newer digital units operate above the UHF band offering the highest quality but are

Figure 5.11 In an emergency, a microphone can be hung from a light batten over a sound source, but this works best if the person speaking stands in one position and the mic is a cardioid.

the most expensive. Antenna placement on both the transmitter and receiver is critical. Operation and positioning of all RF equipment should closely follow the manufacturer's recommendations.

Selecting the Best Mic

Selecting the best mic for a specific recording situation depends on an understanding of sound aesthetics and different mic characteristics. The more versatile and widely used mics are the *dynamic* and electret condenser cardioids. They have extremely durable elements and a pickup pattern about halfway between a full-range omnidirectional and a narrow unidirectional mic. An on-camera mic can be hand-held (in this case they should be shock mounted) or mounted on a floor or desk stand. An off-camera mic can be suspended overhead on a mic boom just outside the frame.

A cardioid mic works best when it is relatively close to the speaker or sound source; thus it is not always the best mic to use for long-distance pickup. Suppose an off-camera mic at some distance from the speaker must be used during the recording of an extremely long shot. A unidirectional condenser mic, such as a supercardioid shotgun mic, may be the best choice. The narrow pickup pattern isolates the primary signal from the surrounding space. The condenser element provides a stronger signal because of

Figure 5.12 If the production requires off-camera mics, a microphone also can be concealed in a set piece or hand prop on a set near where the actors will be talking.

its built-in preamplifier. Care must be exercised when using a shotgun mic, however, so that noise coming from directly behind the speaker is not amplified along with the primary voice signal.

A second concern with the dynamic cardioid mic is that it is difficult to make inconspicuous on camera. A lavalier condenser mic can be the size of a tie tack. It can be placed very close to the speaker without dominating the frame. It can also be completely hidden in a person's clothing. When connected to a tiny FM transmitter, it can even allow for freedom of movement without mic cables, or for extremely long-range camera shots with extremely high-quality voice sounds. This can be an advantage when recording functional sound, but realistic sound perspective is better achieved by using a shotgun mic. The ribbon mic is best left to completely stationary performance situations, such as talk shows, interviews, or dramatic radio productions. The ribbon mic can be quite versatile in such a situation, since it is capable of producing a very resonant sound. It can be set for an omnidirectional, bidirectional, or unidirectional pickup pattern so that it can be used by several speakers, a single speaker, or two performers facing each other. An omnidirectional dynamic or condenser mic is often used to record several speakers simultaneously. It can be suspended overhead in a fixed position or permanently positioned at a central location on the set.

Using Multiple Mics

Using a single omnidirectional mic is not necessarily the best way to record several different sound sources, such as several talk show performers. For one thing, even if the mic is centrally located, it will probably pick up a good deal of unwanted background sound along with the primary signals or voices. Using a different mic for each sound source provides better control and higher-quality sound recording, provided each mic can be placed close to its sound source. One advantage is that each mic can be selected for the particular characteristics of its sound source. For example, suppose that you are recording a singer on camera, while a band is playing off camera. If the singer moves with a handheld mic, the loudness of the band music will vary with the mic direction, unless one or more stationary mics are set up specifically for the band.

These two sound sources should be separately controlled and combined (or mixed together), using two mic inputs on a recorder or a device called a mixer. The music now maintains a constant loudness. The singer can use a dynamic cardioid, while an omnidirectional dynamic or ribbon mic is set up for

the band. Better yet, several different mics can be set up for different instruments in the band.

Separate mics can be set up for each individual speaker at a table. Each mic must be carefully placed, however, so that different mics do not pick up the same signals. This can lead to multiple-microphone interference, in which some of the sounds picked up simultaneously by two different mics cancel each other. Such cancellation is a phasing problem that occurs when similar sound waves passing through the same medium are 180 degrees out of phase with respect to each other. Phasing is sometimes used deliberately to create special audio effects, such as the noise of a robot, or to disguise a speaker's identity.

The best way to find out if multiple-microphone interference exists is to set one mic at its proper level and then turn on the other mic. If the volume goes down rather than up when both mics are on, there is interference, which must be corrected by changing the distance between the two mics and/or their directional placement. Some sophisticated audio consoles allow the audio engineer to eliminate phasing problems electronically. Multiple-microphone interference can be prevented by keeping live mics well separated, using directional mics, and having them directed at different sound sources. If two subjects are seated quite close together, a single mic should be used for both, either by swiveling an overhead mic or a boom, or by placing a stand mic or a desk mic with a relatively wide pickup pattern between them. When more than two people are involved, two or more mics should be set up so that they are at least three times as far apart as the subject-to-mic distances. This three-to-one rule ensures that there will be no phasing problems with multiple mics (Figure 5.13).

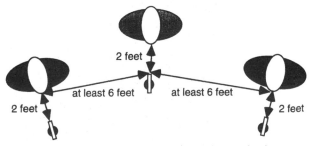

**MULTIPLE MICROPHONE PLACEMENT
THE 3-TIMES RULE**

2 feet

at least 6 feet   at least 6 feet

2 feet   2 feet

Figure 5.13 When using multiple microphones, the three-times rule should be followed. The rule indicates that each sound source (person) must be three times the distance from any other microphone as he or she is from his or her own microphone. Any closer and audio phasing may occur, causing distortion in the sound.

Another solution is multichannel recording, where each mic is fed to a separate recording channel on an audiotape recorder. Using multiple mics can also cause problems with excessive ambient noise. Each mic picks up the same ambient noise, and when more than one mic is used, the ambient noise adds up and can become disturbingly loud. Placing mics as close as possible to their sound sources so that loudness levels can be turned down helps reduce ambient noise in some instances. At other times different speakers can simply share the same mic.

Stereo Mic Placement

Stereo provides an additional spatial dimension by giving sound a directional placement from left to right. This is accomplished by recording sounds with at least two mics. Two cardioid mics can be arranged so that they crisscross one another, forming a 45- to 90-degree angle.

Each mic picks up sounds from a different direction. This setup works quite well for speech. Using two parallel cardioid mics separated by 10 to 15 feet and well in front of an orchestra or band works well for music. The sounds picked up by each mic are kept separate and recorded on different audio channels, which can then be played back through speakers that are spatially separated from one another. For proper balance, the mics must be adjusted so that a sound coming from a source directly between them creates a signal that is equally strong on both channels.

Cardioid mics are well adapted to stereophonic use because they are slightly more receptive to sounds directly in front of them than to sounds coming from the right or left. Stereophonic sound can be used to bring added realism or simply more spectacular audio effects to a film or television program. But stereo can also bring added production problems. In terms of production logistics, it is often difficult to record stereophonic sound on location. Handling additional mics and audio equipment inevitably leads to greater risks and problems. Stereophonic recording also complicates the postproduction process, since many additional sound elements must be smoothly combined and balanced during final mixing.

Digital Mic Placement
Most equipment, including microphones, originally designed for analog sound systems emphasizes high frequencies to compensate for losses. Digital systems do not suffer the same problem, so mics designed for analog systems used on digital systems tend to sound strident and shrill. Noises created in preamplifiers or other sources of noise that are not noticed in analog

systems may become obvious in digital systems. Therefore, mics must be positioned to avoid emphasizing high frequencies by placing them off-center rather than straight out from a sound source.

Setting mics close also may cause distortions or noise that would not be obvious in analog systems but that would be heard in digital systems, since there is little or no masking of tape- or amplifier-created noise in a digital system. Some digital systems are also sensitive to overmodulation, creating another type of distortion to guard against.

SOUND-SIGNAL CONTROL

Controling sound depends on understanding problems of level, signal to noise, and managing the signal as it passes through cables and operational equipment.

Audio Problems: Distortion and Noise

Distortion and noise are two different unwanted changes in an audio or video signal. *Distortion* is an unwanted change in a signal; *noise* is an unwanted addition to the signal. In both cases, audio may be distortion or noise in a specific production, or simply an additional audio element. Rock musicians often add distortion to their music for an effect. Someone trying to listen to a country-and-western recording would consider a classical music recording played simultaneously as noise. But, of course, to a classical music fan, classical music is not noise (Figure 5.14).

One of the most common problems encountered in audio recording is distortion. The most common type of distortion encountered by beginning media production students is loudness distortion, which occurs when a sound is recorded at a level that exceeds the limitations of the electronic system. The peaks or high points of the sound wave are flattened, and new, unwanted frequencies of sound are

Figure 5.14 There are two types of sound: noise or distortion. Noise is unwanted sound that's added to the original sound, and distortion is an unwanted modification of the original sound.

produced. The end result is a reproduction that sounds like there is some kind of variable interference or garble on the line. Loudness distortion is controlled by setting the volume so that it does not exceed the limits of the system. A volume unit or VU meter allows the recordist to set the volume controls as high as needed for a good-quality recording without distorting the sound.

There are basically two types of noise, ambient noise, discussed earlier, and system noise. *Ambient noise* comes from open mics fed into an audio console or tape recorder that pick up the sound of air ventilators, lights, cameras, or other devices. (Fluorescent lights frequently cause a hum or buzzing sound, for example.) A second type of noise is called *system noise*, which can come from the electrical recording system and equipment. Microphone lines placed too close to lights and electrical cables often create system noise, as do worn volume controls or bad circuit boards and cable connections. Tape hiss is inherent in any system using analog tape recordings. Most ambient noise and some system noise can be controlled, but most system noise is simply inherent in the recording equipment. A digital audio system cannot control ambient noise any differently than an analog system can, but a digital system does reduce system noise to a minimum level. Therefore, signal-to-noise ratios are less important in digital systems.

An important determinant of sound quality is a system's signal-to-noise ratio. This is the ratio of desired sounds to unwanted system noise. Many professional audio systems have signal-to-noise ratios of 55:1 or above; that is, the main signal is 55 times as loud as the system's noise level. Quality audio production requires the maintenance of high signal-to-

noise ratios throughout all stages of the process. At each stage of duplication or reproduction, an analog system's signal-to-noise ratio will decrease, increasing the noise level. In digital systems, duplication or reproduction will not normally change the signal-to-noise ratio, thereby maintaining the same low level of noise (Figure 5.15).

Sound Intensity Measurement

Many different devices for indicating the volume intensity or loudness of a sound signal are used today. A less expensive tape recorder often has a red light that flickers with volume peaks. Overmodulation or loudness distortion is indicated when the light stays brightly lit for a continuous period rather than flickering intermittently. Other recorders employ a needle device that indicates loudness distortion when the needle enters a red zone. These less-expensive meters are quite small and do not have precise volume scales. More expensive meters are calibrated in specific units of sound intensity, such as volume units or percentages of modulation. There are basically two types of professional sound intensity meters: volume unit (VU) meters and peak program meters (PPMs). The VU meter is the American standard. It is a special type of electrical voltmeter, which reads voltage shifts in electrical current as changes in sound intensity.

Needle readings are calibrated in both percentages of modulation and volume units or decibels (dBs). Approximately every 3 dB increase indicates a doubling of sound intensity. (A decibel is a logarithmic unit of sound intensity.) The modulation percentages are usually indicated on the lower scale

SIGNAL TO NOISE RATIO

Program Audio

Difference between program audio and noise = Signal to Noise Ratio (S/N Ratio)

Noise

DECIBELS

Figure 5.15 The ability to minimize the signal-to-noise ratio is one of the critical measures used to determine the quality of an electronic system. Noise inherent in magnetic-tape systems and noise picked up by cables are the leading creators of poor signal-to-noise ratios.

of a VU meter. They range from 9% to 100%, the thresholds of signal detection and distortion, respectively. The upper scale indicates volume units or decibels. A reading of 0 dB usually corresponds to 100% modulation or peak loudness before distortion occurs, and the scale reads down on the left side and up on the right side (+1, +2, +3, and so on) of 0 dB.

A VU meter provides an electrical analog to human hearing. It does not show instantaneous peaks and immediate distortion, but indicates the average sound intensity over a very short period of time. This average reading closely approximates the response of the human ear to peak sound intensities. In general, signals on a VU meter should register between 50% and 100% modulation, or between 6 dB and 0 dB. Below 50% modulation or 6 dB, the signal-to-noise ratio becomes relatively low. Above 100% modulation or 0 dB loudness, distortion occurs. Sounds that intermittently peak above 100% modulation, or 0 dB, for very short periods of time rarely cause noticeable distortion, but sounds that continuously pin the needle to its maximum above 100% modulation, or 0 dB, not only cause distortion but frequently cause meter damage as well. The audio operator continually watches the VU meter and makes minor adjustments in the sound level throughout a recording, using a volume-control mechanism such as a *potentiometer* (*pot*) or a sliding fader bar. Volume level adjustments should be made smoothly and slowly. Major shifts in volume level affect the noise levels and background sounds as well as the primary signal and change the sound perspective and dynamics of the recorded sounds.

The PPM (sometimes called a *modulometer*) is another type of loudness or voltmeter and is the European standard. Rather than averaging sound intensities, a PPM responds immediately to peak sounds. The human ear cannot perceive extremely rapid loudness distortion, but many PPM users believe that such distortion nonetheless affects a sound recording. Obviously an operator using a PPM or modulometer must respond to needle readings on the devices somewhat differently, probably more reservedly and slowly, than one would respond to a VU meter reading. Both types of meters facilitate sound signal control, however.

A third type of level monitoring is a series of light-emitting diodes (LED). The string of diodes lights as the level intensity changes, providing an accurate and easy-to-follow means of monitoring levels. The diodes usually are arranged in a row with at least two colors. A change in color indicates overmodulation. LEDs measure instantaneous peak voltages.

Some recorders have automatic gain controls (AGC) or automatic level controls (ALC) for mic input. An AGC prevents loudness distortion automatically. However, it also boosts the ambient noise level when primary sounds are at low levels, such as at pauses in dialogue. To avoid this problem, levels should be set manually using a VU meter with the AGC turned off, if possible. Peak limiters are sometimes more useful than AGCs, as these simply limit the upper level of loudness without automatically setting the basic recording level and running the risk of increasing ambient noise levels. But most professionals prefer to control recording levels manually. Volume levels on a digital recording must also be carefully set. Although digital signals are either off or on, they do vary in intensity. An over-modulated digital recording will suffer uncorrectable distortion or total loss of the recording (Figure 5.16).

Cables and Connectors

Professional mic cables have two conductor wire lines: a ground and a grounded shield. This type of balanced line is less susceptible to cable noise than an unbalanced line, which has a single conductor wire and a grounded shield. The two conductor lines are usually well insulated from each other, the ground wire, and the cable exterior in balanced lines. Poorly insulated cables are much more susceptible to interference from other electrical cables and devices. Mic cables should never be placed near lighting instruments or electrical power cables, which can cause interference. Nor should they be wound tightly together or twisted in any manner that will reduce their life expectancy and damage the wire conductors. A less-expensive recorder sometimes has a mic attached by an unbalanced line cable with a single-prong mini-plug at one end that is inserted into the front or side of the recorder. Balanced line cables are attached to three-prong XLR connectors, which can be plugged into mics, audio consoles, or tape recorders. These connectors have separate prongs for the two conductors and the ground. Male and female connector ends lock into each other so that they do not become disconnected easily (Figure 5.17).

It is probably a good idea to wrap two cables together in a very loose knot around the connectors, so that any pulling on the cables will pull the connectors together, rather than apart. Even though this procedure may place considerable stress on the cables in the case of an accident, such as someone tripping over a cable, it would undoubtedly be more expensive to reshoot the entire sequence in the event of a complete disconnection. Care should be taken,

Figure 5.16 Audio control boards vary from small portable boards (*top*) for field and postproduction facilities to large multi-input and multi-output boards (*bottom*) for motion picture mixing theatres and music recording studios. (Courtesy Fairlight USA, and Mackie Designs, Inc.)

of course, to minimize the amount of twisting and stress that occurs at the juncture of the cable and connector, since this part of the cable is extremely vulnerable to damage and wear. Also cables should be coiled carefully before storing. Two methods of coiling cables are the over-and-under method and the figure-eight method. Each system, when properly carried out, prevents internal twisting and damage to conductors inside the cable (Figure 5.18).

Mixing

An audio console or mixer is designed to combine sounds from several different sound sources, such as mics, tape recorders, and playback units. These devices can vary from an elaborate studio audio console to a simple multiple-input mixer, which allows for separate volume control over each input. Basically the audio console routes signals from sound

sources or playback units to a control device or recording unit. It can send a signal from a particular mic or a playback unit to a recorder, so that a duplicate copy or dub can be made, for example. It can combine or mix together several sound sources into one (monophonic) or onto two or more (multi-track) sound tracks or channels, which are recorded as a final or master audiotape. In a digital board, the analog signals originating from mics, tape decks, or other nondigital sources are converted to a digital signal as it enters a digital mixer. Digital inputs are then combined with the converted analog inputs. From that point until the signal must be converted back to analog to feed speakers or headphones, the signal may remain in the digital format for processing and editing. Digital boards also provide for digital outputs to feed other digital signals including a digital transmitter. Some digital boards contain their

Figure 5.17 Audio and video signals are carried through different cable types and connected by a variety of connectors. On the left: three video cables, RF or "F", UHF, and BNC. In the center: adapters, RCA to BNC, ¼-inch stereo to mini-plug, an XLR male-to-male barrel, UHF to BNC, and RCA to mini-plug. On the right: ¼-inch, XLR female, XLR male, RCA to ¼-inch adapter, and a micro-plug to mini-plug adapter.

Figure 5.18 In order to properly coil cables, an over-and-under method may be used. This system protects the cable from twisting and provides a clean, straight unwinding when uncoiled for use.

own recording media. A computer hard drive, solid-state memory, or digital tape deck may be built into the board. Since a digital board is in essence a computer with multiple inputs and outputs, the processing of the signals, depending on the software, follows that of computer word processing: cutting, pasting, adding, deleting, and modifying with simple user-friendly controls. There will be more on this subject in Chapter 10, "Visual Editing," and Chapter 11, "Sound Editing." Some digital boards are labeled digital audio workstations (DAW) (Figure 5.19).

An audio console consists of a series of faders, each of which controls the volume level of a single input. The inputs can come from microphones, turntables, analog and digital audiotape recorders, compact disc (CD) players, or audio playbacks from videotape recorders. The output is controlled by a single (or dual) master pot. Each pot or fader often has its own equalization controls for increasing or decreasing bass and treble (low frequencies and high frequencies) directly above or below it. In a digital board, signal control may be by faders or by computer controls or software operations (Figure 5.20).

Most audio consoles and mixers have two types of audio inputs: high impedance and low impedance. Impedance cuts down on the flow of alternating current; it is analogous with resistance in devices operated on direct current (batteries). Impedance and resistance are measured in ohms. High-impedance signals come from some nonprofessional mics, from playback machines, and from some signal-processing equipment. Low-impedance signals usually come from professional-quality microphones and other equipment. Professional mics usually have an impedance of about 50 ohms, while playback units and other high-impedance sources are above 600 ohms.

An impedance imbalance or mismatch between the sound source and the mixer or console input will result in a signal that is either too loud and distorted, or too soft and weak to be useful for recording purposes. Different sound sources can have different levels of sound intensity or signal strength (volts), as well as different impedances (ohms). These also require separate inputs or an audio console. Mic levels are usually lower than line levels from playback units. Preamplifiers in the audio console car boost a low-level signal to a higher level so that it equals that of other sound sources. When a high-level signal enters the console through a low-level input, distortion occurs. The level output of a mixer can be either high-level or mic (low) level, or, if amplified, the speaker level that is generally the highest level (Figure 5.21).

Any computer equipped with sufficient memory, a sound-processing board, and an audio-editing program can function as an audio postproduction board. The functions of mixing, equalizing, setting and varying levels, editing, and adding special effects are performed quickly with such a computer system.

Compression

The term "compression" in audio traditionally referred to a process of decreasing the dynamic range (loudest to quietest) of a signal. In the digital world, "compression" refers to a reduction in the amount of bandwidth required to record or transmit a digital signal. A compression system omits certain sounds unimportant or redundant in the over-all signal so

Figure 5.19 A digital audio workstation (DAW) is designed for quick editing for talk radio, call-in clips, news actualities, promotional announcements, and commercials. It is designed to edit like a word processor with cut/copy/paste and precision scrubbing functions. (Courtesy Fairlight, USA.)

that the human ear does not recognize the loss. The amount of compression is stated as a ratio of 2:1, which means the bandwidth has been cut in half.

The higher the compression ratio, the greater the possibility that the signal will lose enough of the signal that a discerning listener will detect a loss in quality. MP3 recordings are compressed to reproduce a signal lower in quality than a CD that is also compressed, but not as much.

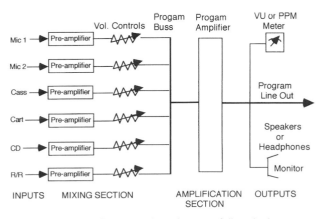

Figure 5.20 Audio mixing board circuits follow the basic pattern of pre-amplifying low-level inputs, mixing all inputs through a program buss and monitoring the program output signals by viewing a metering system and listening on headphones or through loudspeakers. A parallel set of circuits carries signals for cueing or monitoring purposes without placing those signals on air.

Figure 5.21 The three primary audio levels vary in voltage from the very weak signal directly from a microphone, turntable pickup arm, and magnetic recorder playback head, to a middle level of a preamplified signal (called line level), and lastly to the high level of the output of an amplifier intended to power a speaker or speaker system.

Console Operation

Once impedance and line levels of source and input match, the console operator can set the proper loudness levels for recording each sound source. To accomplish this on an audio console or mixer with a single VU meter or LED indicators, all of the faders should be closed, except for the one being set. If each input has its own VU meter, then it can be set independently from the others. The level for each input should be set between 80% and 100% modulation for an optimal signal-to-noise ratio. In some instances, such as background music and sounds, the level may be set somewhat lower for a proper overall balance between the sounds. Balance is an aesthetic concept that refers to the best proportion of sound intensities from the different elements, such as speech and music. Generally speaking, music must be toned or faded down to achieve a proper balance with accompanying dialogue or narration. In addition to balancing sounds, an audio operator should check for multiple-microphone interference by determining if the volume levels of specific sources increase as others are shut off. It is generally a good idea to label each fader with the number or name of the mic or sound source it carries for each sound source and fader in order to eliminate any confusion when adjustments have to be made during actual recording.

Recording and Mixing Commands

To perform well at the audio console or mixer, the audio recordist should be familiar with each of the following audio terms, cues, and commands:

Fade-in audio. The sound intensity is gradually raised to an audible level, and its proper volume setting is increased from an inaudible or nonexistent level.

Fade-out audio. The sound intensity is gradually lowered to an inaudible level.

Segue. One sound source is faded out while another is immediately faded in without any overlap or dead air in between the two sounds.

Cross-fade. One sound source is faded out while another is faded in over it. The sum of the two sounds should remain at a peak level.

Open mic. The fader or pot for a specific mic is raised immediately to its proper level or is simply switched on.

Cut sound or kill sound. The fader or pot is abruptly closed, or the channel switch is cut off.

Sound up and under (or *bed sound*). The sound is faded up promptly to its proper level and then is faded down to a lower level, at which level it is still audible but less prominent, to allow for a voice to be balanced over the original background sound, usually music (Figure 5.22).

Backtime. A prerecorded sound or music track is prepared so that it will end at a specified time. This requires a calculation that subtracts the length of the track from the end time of the production. The playback machine must begin at the exact backtime in order for the track to end correctly. The pot or fader assigned to it is not turned up until required, so that the sounds or music can be gradually faded in at the appropriate point. Many digital playback machines can be programmed to automatically backtime if data is properly entered.

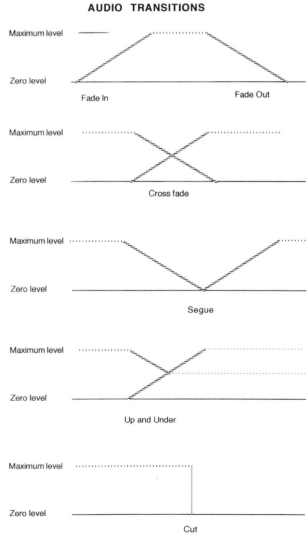

Figure 5.22 Audio transitions provide a means of mixing audio from two or more sources, or a means of switching from one audio source to another.

SOUND PERSPECTIVES

The relationship of sound to space parallels that of a picture with three dimensions: left-right, up-down, and in front of or behind the listener. In order to duplicate audio realistically, the perception of these dimensions must be duplicated. The characteristics to be duplicated are distance and directionality. Sound that appears to be originating close by or far away may be recorded by placing the mic(s) close to or at a distance from the sound source. The sound indicating the size of the environment will be determined by the reflective or absorption values of the walls, furniture, or other objects in the space, and the size of the room. The direction of the sound can only be determined through the use of one of several multichannel systems to give the audience the sense that the sound is to the left, right, in front of, or behind.

Stereo Sound

Both stereo and surround-sound systems and modifications are attempts to duplicate the three-dimensional aspects of a sound environment. Stereo offers two or three channels of sound: left, right, and, depending on the size of the theater, a center channel. Reproduction of sound through the left or right channel to match the objects originating the sound on the screen may add to the realistic effect, but also may become confusing if overdone. Now that stereo television receivers are available, the impulse to split sound into left and right must be weighed against the realization that television is a close-up medium that requires audio to be concentrated in the center of the screen or balanced between the left and right channels.

Wide-screen films, on the other hand, offer much greater opportunities to utilize sound originating from the side of the screen matching the source of the sound. Care must be taken not to overbalance sound to one side or another, or else the audience seated on the opposite side of the theater may miss some critical sounds. In the recording industry, music is recorded either to duplicate the physical arrangement of the group (symphonic orchestras) or to enhance the vocals or a solo instrument (rock groups). Today music is recorded with the assumption that it will be reproduced on a stereo rather than monaural system.

Surround Sound

Surround sound was the next logical step from stereo in creating the realistic three-dimensional sound environment. Mixing the sound into at least four channels to be reproduced through speakers located in the four corners of the listening space enhances the sense of the original recording, but such a process increases the complexity of mic placement, mixing, and speaker location. Surround sound in the past has not proved practical for the average home or video production. Modification of the theory has opened new avenues for film sound. Most theaters today are capable of reproducing sound recorded on as many as 10 channels using three to four speakers lining the side walls of the theater to supplement the normal stereo and center speakers located behind the screen. Multichannel sound increases the illusion of both the width and depth of the picture.

Dolby Digital 5.1 and 6.1 Sound

Dolby Digital 5.1 and 6.1 sound systems designed to compliment advanced television systems requires six or seven channels of audio and six or seven separate speakers. The usual four-corner speakers (left front, right front, left rear, and right rear) are supplemented by two or three additional speakers: one directly behind or under the screen for bass response, called a subwoofer, and the sixth directly behind or above the screen, called a front channel, and a seventh directly behind the audience, called a rear channel. The maximum effect of making the audience feel as if they are placed within the program occurs when each audio channel is properly programmed to carry the correct signal. Whether the complexity of Dolby Digital 5.1 or 6.1 will discourage consumers from installing such a system to match their HDTV system will be determined in the next five or 10 years. As a production situation, a 5.1 or 6.1 signal, consisting of six or seven channels, is complicated not only by the differences in apparent direction of the sources, but also by the differences in equalization of the individual channels.

SUMMARY

The aesthetic use of recorded sounds demands an understanding of realist, modernist, and postmodernist aesthetics as well as recording devices and their selection, placement, and control. A mic or microphone is a transducer that converts analog sound-wave energy into analog electrical energy. Mics can be classified into three different categories on the basis of their transducer elements: dynamic, ribbon, and condenser.

Mics can also be classified on the basis of pickup patterns: omnidirectional, bidirectional, and unidirectional mics, such as the cardioid and supercardioid or shotgun mic. Mics can be placed in on-camera and off-camera positions. Hand mics, desk mics, stand mics, and lavalier mics are examples of on-camera mic positions. Mics on booms, such as fishpole, giraffe, and perambulator booms, as well as various hidden mics, such as the hanging mic, prop mic, and concealed lavalier mic, are off-camera mics.

Selecting the best mic and mic position depends on an understanding of what mic characteristics and placements are best suited to a specific situation. Digital recording of audio requires greater care in mic selection and placement as well as noise reduction.

Sound signal control helps a sound recordist achieve the best-quality recorded sound by eliminating specific audio problems, such as loudness distortion and excessive ambient and system noise. A sound-measuring device, such as a VU (volume unit) meter or LED indicators, can be used to set the sound level as high as possible for optimal signal-to-noise ratio, while avoiding loudness distortion. Balanced mic cables should be used to minimize noise and electrical interference.

Audio mixing is done on an audio console, mixer, or DAW. Mixing refers to combining several different inputs, such as different mics or playback machines, into a single (monophonic) or dual (stereophonic) output, which is directed to a tape recorder or some digital recording medium. Faders on the audio console, mixer, or DAW are used to adjust the volume very gradually.

Audio operators using a console, mixer, or DAW must be familiar with basic audio terms, cues, and commands, so that they can effectively communicate with the rest of the staff and crew. Sound perspectives should match the perspectives of the matching visual as well as the requirements of the drama or music. Perspectives include both distance and dimensionality.

EXERCISES

1. Practice following a person moving and speaking with a cardioid mic on a mic boom as he or she walks around a studio on a precise, preplanned route. Try to keep the mic one to four feet in front of and one to three feet above the speaker. Record the sounds on audiotape or videotape without changing the pot or fader setting on the recorder so that the initial volume setting is used constantly. Change the mic to a supercardioid or shotgun mic, and perform the same exercise. Did you keep a constant distance between the mic and the speaker? Was the mic always in the best

position to pick up the speaker's voice? Listen to your recording critically for fluctuations in the loudness of the speaker's voice. Discuss what you could have done to improve recording consistency. Did the shotgun mic increase overall sound quality but make it more difficult to maintain a constant recording level?

2. Set up an on-camera narration videotape recording outdoors. Select a location that is relatively quiet. Bring along three mics: a cardioid hand mic, a small lavalier mic, and a supercardioid or shotgun mic. Record the same on-camera narration with the speaker looking directly into the camera three times, once with each type of mic. Make sure that each mic has a windscreen, and position the speaker with his or her back to the wind, if possible. When using the shotgun mic, make sure that there are no loud sounds coming from directly behind the person speaking. Position the shotgun mic as close to the edge of the camera frame as you can without entering the frame. Have the speaker hold the cardioid mic about six to nine inches from his or her mouth. Attach the lavalier so that no clothing or jewelry rubs against it and the mic cable is well hidden. Compare the three.

3. Place two microphones of the same type side by side and an equal distance from a subject. Open both mics, and have the subject speak evenly and continually while closing one mic slowly and noting if there is a decrease or increase in the level of the audio output. Separate the mics more than three times the distance from the subject to the mics, and again close and open one mic, noting the change in level while someone speaks evenly and continually.

4. Place a microphone near the speaker of a CD player. Feed the mic through a preamp and an amplifier to a recorder. Monitor the recording as you play back the CD. Raise the level to the maximum capability of the amplifier, then back to a normal level as shown on a meter, then to a level that barely shows on the meter. Rewind the recorder, and play the recording back at a set level and listen for distortion when the level is too high and an increase in noise when the level is too low.

5. Feed three audio sources through a mixer. Start with one source, set a normal level, then open another source and bring it to the same level. Open a third source and bring it to a normal level. When seeking to keep the sum of two sources at the previous level, note whether it was necessary to reduce the level on the first source as a second

source was brought up to. Note the same as the third source level is brought up.

6. Watch a DVD or videotape of a well-made motion picture. Note whether the audio always is at the same level, or whether it changes with the positioning of the source of the audio. If you have access to a multiple-channel audio system, note which channel carries which sound, again depending on the location of the source in reference to the camera.

ADDITIONAL READINGS

Alten, Stanley. *Audio in Media*, 6th ed. Belmont, CA: Wadsworth, 2002.

Bartlett, Bruce, and Jenny Bartlett. *On Location Recording Techniques*. Boston, MA: Focal Press, 1999.

Eargle, John. *The Microphone Book*. Boston: Focal Press, 2001.

Frater, Charles. *Sound Recording for Motion Pictures*. New York: A.S. Barnes, 1979.

Gross, Lynne S., and David E. Reese. *Radio Production Worktext*, 4th ed. Boston, MA: Focal Press, 2001.

Hausmann, Carl, et al. *Modern Radio Production*, 5th ed. Belmont, CA: Wadsworth Publishing, 2002.

Holman, Tomlinson. *5.1 Channel Surround Sound*. Boston, MA: Focal Press, 1999.

Huber, David Miles. *Modern Recording Techniques*. Boston: Focal Press, 2001.

Rumsey, Francis. *Audio Workstation Handbook*. Boston, MA: Focal Press, 1996.

Rumsey, Francis. *Spatial Sound*. Boston: Focal Press, 2001.

Watkinson, John. *The Art of Digital Audio*. Boston, MA: Focal Press, 2000.

Weis, Elisabeth. *The Silent Scream: Alfred Hitchcock's Sound Track*. Rutherford, NJ: Far-leigh Dickinson University Press, 1982.

Weis, Elisabeth, and John Belton. *Film Sound: Theory and Practice*. New York: Columbia University Press, 1985.

Yale French Studies. Special issue on "Sound in Film," 60, 1980.

6 Lighting

TOPICS FOR DISCUSSION

- What are the aesthetics of light?
- How do light and color interact?
- What types of lighting instruments are available?
- How is light measured and controlled?
- How are lighting instruments focused?

INTRODUCTION

One of the most creative and visually exciting tasks in video and film production involves lighting. Visual artists refer to lighting as painting with light. A lighting director or director of photography can use lights just as effectively and expressively as any painter uses color pigments to evoke a specific mood or visual impression. Lighting can be used to emphasize and dramatize a subject by bringing objects into sharp relief or contrast, or it can be used to soften and to harmonize. Lighting directly affects the overall impressions and feelings generated by recorded visual images. It is a complex art, but basic video and film lighting can be reduced to a limited number of concepts and techniques. This chapter provides an introduction to the basic aesthetic approaches, techniques, and equipment needed to design and control the lighting of moving images.

The expressive design and effect of a lighting setup can be described as realist, modernist, or postmodernist.

LIGHTING AESTHETICS

Realist Lighting

Realist lighting appears to come from actual light sources in a setting or location. It enhances an illusion of reality. Realist lighting conforms to the audience's expectations of how a scene should normally or naturally appear in real life. In conventional popular dramas, the lighting is usually realistic. The major problem for the lighting director is to determine the actual light source in the scene. The brightest lights are positioned according to the direction and intensity of the central or main source of light. Directional lighting continuity is maintained from one shot to the next in the same scene. If the main source of light is a window, the direction of the lights basically preserves the spatial positioning of the window on the set. The same holds true for firelight or candlelight. The lighting director tries to match the natural scene under normal vision using artificial lights. Multiple shadows should be minimized, if not eliminated, so that the lighting rarely calls attention to itself. There is a logical consistency to the direction and intensity of the lighting, which has a presumed cause or real source.

Few productions are completely realist. Some degree of modernist stylization is often needed to stimulate dramatic interest. Lighting directors use lighting to bring out and emphasize specific aspects of a personality or setting. They highlight details that add depth to performers and actions. Strict authenticity often fails to stimulate emotions and viewer interest, and a purely realist lighting setup often seems flat and boring.

Modernist Lighting

Modernist lighting has no real-life referent. The lighting director is much freer to design a lighting setup according to purely abstract or subjective emotional criteria, that is, to stylize the use of light. The lighting director literally paints with light to create emphasis and spatial impressions. Modernist lighting tries to achieve a specific emotional effect or abstract design through non-naturalistic patterns of light. The actual sources of light are often of little interest.

Modernist lighting stimulates emotions and creates a dynamic visual impression. For example, the lighting setup for a musical variety program may light an empty stage with pools of colored light, creating abstract patterns. The mood or atmosphere can coincide with the central theme or emotion expressed by a song or dance. Even in a realist drama, a dream sequence might call for highly stylized lighting that mirrors the internal state of mind of the central character. These are often highly abstract and unrealistic visual sequences, but they effectively convey the character's feelings, emotions, and state of mind. Excessive or inappropriate stylization calls attention to the lighting and distracts viewer attention from the central message or information of a nonfiction program. It can also destroy the illusion of reality in a realistic drama, but the absence of any stylization at all leads to viewer disinterest.

Postmodernist Lighting

Postmodernist lighting often mixes a variety of lighting styles drawn from different genres. For example, highly stylized Hollywood studio lighting is used to record interviews in Errol Morris's *The Thin Blue Line* (1987), a documentary. Postmodernist lighting often appeals to the emotions on a different level from modernist or realist lighting. At first glance, postmodernist lighting may not make any sense on a practical level, but by mixing concrete realism with abstract modernism, it can evoke an emotional response in the viewer. Some music videos and rock concerts use postmodernist lighting effects and styles, bombarding the viewer with powerful sensations unrelated to any realist action in the film or video or any specific thoughts or feelings inside the mind of a character. These lighting effects and styles reflect the complexity and diversity of contemporary life, art, and culture. Postmodernist lighting in *Batman Forever* (1995) relies on computerized lighting effects similar to those used at rock concerts to create a feeling of disorientation at a circus. By controlling the projection of Chinese symbols and motifs in exterior settings of Gotham City, the film combines different cultures, times, and places through lighting in distinctly postmodernist ways.

LIGHT AND COLOR

There are a variety of light sources that can be used for television and film recording. Each of these can be distinguished in terms of the color temperature of the light it emits. Color temperature is usually defined in technical terms of degrees Kelvin (K). *Degrees Kelvin* is a unit of measurement that refers to the type of light that would theoretically be given off by a perfect light radiator (what physicists call a black-box radiator) when it is heated to a specific temperature. White light is actually composed of relatively equal amounts of all the colors in the visible spectrum; but light sources with different color temperatures emit slightly different amounts of the various color wavelengths (red, green, blue light), which together make up white light and the visible spectrum. Sunlight has a relatively high color temperature, about 5,400 or 5,600 degrees Kelvin, while tungsten or incandescent light, such as that given off by many living room lamps and much professional lighting equipment, has a much lower color temperature, about 3,200 degrees Kelvin.

Sunlight has somewhat more blue light (short wavelengths) than does tungsten light, which has slightly more red light (long wavelengths.) As a result, a film stock or video camera designed or preset for tungsten light will record bluish images when it is exposed under sunlight, and a film stock or video camera rated or adjusted for daylight (sunlight) will record reddish images under tungsten light. Because video and film recording devices are often more sensitive to these differences in color temperature than our eyes, specific light sources must be carefully selected and controlled (Figure 6.1).

Sunlight

Sunlight is a natural light source. Burning gases on the sun's surface emit light that has a relatively high color temperature when it reaches the earth's surface, or 5,400 degrees K. Sunlight contains approximately equal proportions of all color wavelengths in the visible spectrum. Unless it is broken up and diffused by clouds, direct sunlight produces intense, harsh, contrasty light. This kind of light quality is called *hard* as opposed to *soft* light. It creates harsh shadows. Diffusion screens and reflectors can be used on location to reduce the intensity and contrast of direct sunlight and to create soft light. Indirect sunlight, often called *skylight*, has a higher color temperature than direct sunlight: from 6,000 degrees K to 20,000 degrees K. Indirectly lit shadow areas also contain a higher proportion of ultraviolet (UV) light than areas lit by direct sunlight. To reduce the bluish cast that is often produced by this ultraviolet light, an ultraviolet or skylight filter can be placed over the camera lens.

Tungsten Light

One of the earliest sources of electrical lighting was Thomas Edison's incandescent bulb. An incandescent bulb consists of a tungsten filament in a glass-enclosed vacuum. A strong electrical current encounters considerable resistance at the filament, generating both

COLOR TEMPERATURES OF LIGHT SOURCES

SOURCE	DEGREES KELVIN	MIREDS
Match flame	1700K	588
Candle flame	1850K	541
Sunrise or sunset	2000K	500
Consumer lamps	2650K-2990K	317-345
Standard Tungsten/Halogen	3200K	313
Photoflood	3400K	294
Early morning, late afternoon	4300K	233
Daylight photoflood	4800K	208
HMI	5600K	179
Typical noon	5400K-5800K	185
Carbon arc	5800K	172
Overcast sky	6000K	167
Summer shade	8000K	125
Full summer sun	10,000K-30,000K	100

Comparable Degrees Kelvin for Fluorescent Sources

Warm white	3050
White	3500
Natural White	3700
Cool white	4300
Daylight	6500

Figure 6.1 The differences in the actual color of light sources range from full summer sun to a candle flame. Fluorescent light sources also vary over a range, but not as widely as incandescent and natural light sources.

heat and light. In general, a tungsten light source produces somewhat more light of longer wavelengths, such as red and orange, than of shorter wavelengths, such as blue and violet. Professional tungsten light has a color temperature of 3,200 degrees K. Incandescent lamps in the home and office may emit a much lower color temperature.

The color temperature of all tungsten lamps decreases with age. Tungsten-halogen-quartz bulbs (usually called *quartz lights*) have become an important source of 3,200 degree K indoor lighting. Caution needs to he exercised in the handling of quartz bulbs, however. They should never be touched, since the oil in your skin breaks down the quartz-like glass and reduces the life of a bulb. Quartz lights are usually rated in terms of the watts of electrical energy they consume. The most common sizes are 650 and 1,000 watts.

Carbon Arc Light

Carbon arc lights produce intense light, which has very high color temperature. Light is produced by passing a spark between two carbon poles. Carbon arcs generally require vast amounts of DC electrical current and produce intense heat and noxious vapors and exhaust, which must be ventilated. The high intensity and high color temperature of arc lights make them useful for location production in combination with sunlight. However, they are extremely bulky and require special electrical generators on location.

Metal Halide Light

The latest development in location lighting is the metal halide light, three of which are in use today: HMI (Halogen-Metal-Iodide), CID (Compact Iodine Daylight), and CSI (Compact Source Iodide). HMI and CID lamps provide light at approximately 5,400 degrees Kelvin and now are replacing carbon arc lamps. HMI lamps, the most popular of the three, give almost four times the amount of light for the same electrical input as tungsten-quartz-halogen lamps. This light source produces high-intensity, high-color-temperature light (similar to daylight) with great efficiency. It generates little heat and operates on standard 120-volt, 60Hz AC current (although a few use 220-volt current). HMI lights are frequently used to raise the lighting level at outdoor locations, which may be partially lit by indirect sunlight. HMI lights are fully glass-enclosed arc lamps that require separate start and ballast mechanisms to control electrical current. HMI lights can also be filtered so that they duplicate 3,200 degree K tungsten light sources.

Fluorescent Light

Unlike all the other types of light sources discussed thus far, fluorescent light is discontinuous throughout the visible spectrum. Certain bands of colored light, such as bands of red, yellow, green, or blue light, are strong, while others are almost nonexistent in a fluorescent light source. Light is produced through phosphorescence rather than incandescence, and different phosphors produce different wavelengths of light. In film recording, color filters placed over the light source or camera lens can compensate for some of this spectral discontinuity, but there are so many differences between most fluorescent bulb types and brands that no simple filter or combination of filters will properly remedy every situation. Video recording devices can be at least partially adjusted for fluorescent light sources by white-balancing the camera under fluorescent lighting, but not for film. Professional fluorescent lighting instruments have been developed that produce highly intense but diffuse light of 3,200 degree K color temperature using minimal electricity. Although these instruments are expensive, they are also highly efficient sources of fill light and now are available in small tubes and mountings for location and hand-held shooting situations with the new small digital camcorders.

Conventional fluorescent lighting often produces humming and flickering. The alternating current mechanisms used to create fluorescent light can cause flicker in a recorded image and produce an audio hum, which is easily picked up by even distant microphones and affects the recorded sound track, but professional fluorescent systems are designed to avoid hum and flicker. Because of negative audio and visual effects, it is often advisable to shut off conventional fluorescent lights, if possible, and to use tungsten or HMI lighting instead. In some situations, such as certain industrial locations, it is virtually impossible to replace all the preexisting fluorescent lights with other artificial lighting. In this case, one type of light source is selected as primary, and all other light sources are reduced as much as possible in intensity. Light sources having different color temperatures should not be used simultaneously unless filters can be placed in front of light sources, including windows, to change and equalize different color temperatures.

White Balance

In order to adjust either video or film systems to various Kelvin temperatures, compensation must be provided. Video cameras can be adjusted to the degree Kelvin of the light source through the process of white balancing. Once the lighting has been determined and set, the camera(s) are pointed at the subject area, focused on a white card. A switch is thrown on the camera or camera control unit and held until an indicator shows that the camera has adjusted its electronic circuits to that lighting temperature. A video camera must be white balanced again each time the location or light source has been modified. Some new digital cameras now contain automatic white balance circuits that "read" the color temperature of a scene and adjust internal circuits to maintain proper light color relationships. Video cameras are designed to operate under 3,200-degree Kelvin tungsten lighting without filters. If operated under daylight or other 5,400-degree light sources, a filter must be inserted to compensate for the difference in light temperature. Normally an 85 (yellow-orange) filter is used (Figure 6.2).

Film systems, on the other hand, must match the film stock to the lighting temperature. If shooting under tungsten, a film balanced for 3,200 degree Kelvin must be used, or daylight film with an 80 blue filter can be used. If shooting under daylight conditions, a film balanced for 5,400 degrees Kelvin or tungsten film with an 85 filter must be used to compensate for the difference in Kelvin temperature (Figure 6.3).

LIGHTING INSTRUMENTS

The housing within which a light source or lamp is encased is called a *lighting instrument* or *luminaire*. Lighting instruments can be generally classified according to the directness or indirectness and hardness or softness of the light they emit. Sharply

Figure 6.2 With the proper filter placed between the video camera lens and pickup chips or tubes, the camera's internal circuits will automatically white balance when focused on a pure white card and when the white balance switch is thrown. Film camera white balance is dependent upon the type of film stock and filter arrangement, not the camera or the camera's internal operation.

MOTION PICTURE FILM EXPOSURE CHARACTERISTICS

NAME	LIGHT BALANCE	EI	FILTER
Color Negative			
Agfa XT 100	Tungsten	100/80	85
Agfa XT 320	Tungsten	320/200	85
Agfa XTS 400	Tungsten	400/250	85
Eastman EXR 50D	Daylight	12/50	80A
Eastman EXR 100T	Tungsten	100/64	85
Eastman EXR 200T	Tungsten	200/125	85
Eastman EXR 500T	Tungsten	500/320	85
Eastman HS Day	Daylight	80/250	80B
Fujicolor F-64	Tungsten	64/40	85
Fujicolor F-64D	Daylight	64	
Fujicolor F-125	Tungsten	125/80	85
Fujicolor F-250	Tungsten	250/160	85
Fujicolor F-500D	Daylight	64/250	80A
Fujicolor F-500	Tungsten	500/320	85
COLOR REVERSAL			
Eastman Ekta-day	Daylight	40/160	80A
Eastman Ekta-tung	Tungsten	125/80	85B
Eastman Ekta-HS-D	Daylight	100/400	80A
Eastman Ekta-HS-T	Tungsten	400/250	85B
Kodachrome 25	Daylight	6/25	80A
Kodachrome 40	Tungsten	40/25	85
BLACK & WHITE NEGATIVE			
Agfa Pan 250		200/250	
Eastman Plus-X		64/80	
Eastman Double-X		200/250	
Fuji FG		64/80	
Fuji RP		64/80	
BLACK & WHITE REVERSAL			
Eastman Plus-X Reversal		40/50	
Eastman Tri-X Reversal		100-125	

Figure 6.3 The design and manufacture of motion picture film stock determines whether the film is designed to be shot under daylight or tungsten light sources. The speed of film stock also is determined by the manufacturing process. Each of these characteristics can be modified with filters and processing modifications. (Courtesy of Eastman Kodak, Fuji Films, and Agfa Films.)

Figure 6.4A and B The light pattern from a Fresnel lighting instrument is controlled by moving the lamp inside the fixture closer or farther away from the stepped lens in the front of the instrument and by adjusting the barndoors mounted on the outside front of the lamp (*top*). The light pattern from an ellipsoidal lamp is controlled by adjusting shutters mounted inside the case of the lamp between the lamp and the front lens. Barndoors also may be mounted on ellipsoidal lamps (*bottom*). (Courtesy of Colortran.)

focused and concentrated light produces harsh shadows and high contrast.

Diffused or softened light minimizes shadows and reduces contrast. Lighting instruments with lenses that sharply focus light are referred to as spotlights. Lighting instruments without lenses that have reflectors that spread and soften light are called floodlights.

Spotlights

Fresnel and ellipsoidal lighting instruments are two different types of spotlights. *Fresnel* refers to a specific type of lens, which bends the light so that it travels in a relatively narrow path. The term *ellipsoidal* refers to the shape of a mirror or reflector at the back of the instrument that concentrates the light rays focused by a lens. Both types of spotlights concentrate the light emitted by a lamp or bulb into a narrow, intense band of light (Figures 6.4A and B).

Floodlights

The most commonly used types of floodlights are scoops, broads, soft lights, and strip lights. These open lights lack lenses and mirrors that focus light into a narrow beam. Instead, they diffuse or spread light, decreasing both its intensity and harshness. Scoops, broads, and soft lights usually consist of one, two, or three lamps, and have somewhat larger and more diffuse reflectors than spotlights. Strip lights have several bulbs, each with its own built-in reflector, placed close to one another so that they diffuse and soften the light in combination. Strip lights may be equipped with colored lenses to throw a "colorized" wash onto a cyc, or cyclorama (a large plain background scenery, usually stretched cloth), or other neutral background. Floodlights are frequently used to light wide areas. They are also used to fill in the shadows created by spotlights and thereby reduce contrast within a scene (Figures 6.5A and B).

Portable Lights

A wide variety of lighting kits are available for use on location. Portable lighting kits usually have open, nonlensed lighting instruments and quartz lamps rated from 500 to 2,000 watts. These instruments lack some of the controls of studio spotlights. Lighting kits contain several open-reflector quartz lights and collapsible light-mounting equipment, power cords, and other lighting accessories. Photofloods, such as Lowell Light units, are highly portable lamps with self-contained reflectors inside the bulb (see Figures 6.6B, C, and D). Some lightweight lighting instruments have their own portable power supply or rechargeable

Figure 6.5A and B Flood lamps are manufactured in a variety of shapes and sizes, but the purpose is to provide a soft, diffused light. Control of light from flood lamps is more difficult due to its diffused nature. (Courtesy of Colortran)

battery pack. Battery-powered lights, such as the Sylvania Sun Gun, can be used in moving vehicles or on remote locations, where a standard power supply is not available. The batteries should be fully charged, since the color temperature gradually decreases as the battery weakens and the voltage drops (Figure 6.6A).

With the increase of available power in newer battery designs, more efficient luminaires, and cameras and films that are more sensitive, battery-powered lighting has become more practical. Standard alternating current power sources are still preferable to batteries for lights, whenever possible.

Mounting Devices

Studio lighting is accomplished with overhead lighting instruments, which are attached to a grid. This makes it easier for cameras and performers to move about the studio floor without running into lights. The grid, which consists of a series of pipes suspended in parallel rows above the studio floor to which instruments are attached with C-clamps, is probably the most common type of grid. Safety chains or heavy-gauge wire loops ensure that no accident will occur if the C-clamp slips on the pipe. Another type of grid has a sliding track to which instruments can be attached and along which they can be moved (Figure 6.7).

A collapsible floor stand is one of the most frequently used light-mounting devices on location. The seven- or eight-foot stand telescopes for portability. Sandbags can be placed over the three legs of the stand for added stability. Lights can also be mounted on special clips and clamps, such as a spring-tension alligator clip, or simply taped to a wall with a strong adhesive gaffer's tape. The latter must be used with care as it sometimes damages paint or wallpaper on removal (Figures 6.8A and B).

Shaping Devices

Light can be shaped, manipulated, and controlled by a variety of devices, such as barndoors, scrims, diffusers, flags, gels, cookies, and reflectors. These are often attached to a lighting instrument. *Barndoors* are black metal flaps that can be attached to the top, bottom, and sides of a lighting instrument. When properly positioned, they prevent light from spilling into areas of the set where it is not wanted. *Screens* are pieces of wire mesh that can be placed over the front of a lighting instrument to cut down the amount of light transmitted. *Scrims* and *diffusers* are pieces of translucent material, such as spun glass, that break up direct light and spread it out in all directions. *Flags* are opaque pieces of metal, plastic,

Figure 6.6A, B, C and D Portable light kits are designed to provide the maximum amount of light output in small, easily moved and controlled lighting fixtures that also draw a minimum amount of amperage. The kits are designed to provide both spot light and flood light with a variety of designs or adjustments of the lamp fixtures. (Courtesy of Lowell Light.)

or cardboard that prevent light from spilling into an undesired area.

Gels are flexible sheets of transparent colored plastic that can act as color filters when they are placed in front of light sources, such as windows or lamps. A gel can be used to convert 5,400 degree K light coming through a window to 3,200 degree K light, which is the same color temperature as interior room lighting. A *cookie* or *cukaloris* is a piece of opaque material with holes in it, which patterns the light into shadowed and brightly lit areas. Cookies are built to be slipped into a slot between the lamp and the lens of the body of an ellipsoidal spotlight. Reflectors provide indirect, reflected light, which is usually less harsh than the primary direct light. Sunlight, for example, can be reflected to function as fill light outdoors,

FIGURE 6.7 The lighting grid in a studio is constructed to support both the batten, which carries the power to the pigtails, and the lighting instruments. The grid must be high enough to allow wide-angle shots, but it also must allow for space above the grid to dissipate the heat generated by the lighting instruments

Figure 6.8A and B The design of portable light fixtures allows them to be mounted on floor stands, anchored by sand bags, hung from doorways, or clipped to other handy positions on the set. (Courtesy of Lowell Light and Colortran.)

while direct, unreflected sunlight functions as a key light (Figure 6.9).

LIGHT CONTROL

Lighting Control in the Studio

Electrical lighting in a studio can be controlled by means of patch panels and dimmer boards operated either electronically or digitally. A patch panel or electrical distribution center consists of a series of plugs for specific electrical circuits to which lighting instruments can be connected.

The voltage carried by each circuit can be controlled by a dimmer board. Each circuit has a limited electrical capacity, varying from about 20 to 50 amps (Figures 6.10A and 6.10B). Using the formula watts = amps volts (W = A V), you can determine the maximum number of lamps that can be safely attached to each circuit without blowing a fuse or tripping a circuit breaker. For example, five 1000-watt, 110-volt lamps can be safely plugged into a 50-amp circuit, since each lamp will draw slightly more than 9 amps (watts/volts = amps; 1000/110 = 9.1 amps per lamp; 5 × 9.1 = 45.5 total amps) (Figure 6.11).

For quick reference for calculating wattage and amperage in your head, use 100 volts instead of 110 or 120. This allows approximately a 10% safety factor. In the examples above: 1000/100 = 10 amps; 10 × 5 = 50 amps.

The dimmer board is a useful means of reducing or adjusting light intensity for black-and-white production, but it is not very useful in this respect for color recording. A dimmer board reduces the light intensity by dropping the voltage, and dropping the voltage below 120 volts causes a consequent drop in color temperature, which is not acceptable in color production. In color production, lighting intensity is reduced by moving a lighting instrument or using a scrim. To determine the result of moving a lighting instrument, the inverse square law may be used. This law of physics states that the amount of light change

Figure 6.9 The control and shape of light as it falls on the set may be controlled by barndoors mounted on the front of the instrument, by reflecting light from a light surface such as an umbrella, or by placing scrims, flags, and diffusers between the lamp and the subjects. (Courtesy of Colortran and Lowell Light.)

Figure 6.9 *(Continued)*

caused by increasing the distance between the light source and the subject will decrease by the square of the inverse of the change in distance.

Conversely, the amount of light change caused by decreasing the distance between the light source and the subject will increase by the square of the inverse of the change. For example, if the incident light from a lamp 8 feet from the subject measures 100 foot-candles and then the lamp is moved to 16 feet away (doubling the distance), the light will decrease by the square of the inverse of the change: ½

squared is ¼, and ¼ of 100 foot-candles is 25 foot-candles. On the other hand, if the lamp's distance is cut in half to 4 feet, then the amount of light would increase by the square of the inverse of the change: 2/1 squared is 4/1 or 4; 100 × 4 is 400 foot-candles. It is obvious that it takes very small changes in the distance between the lamp and subject to make a major change in the amount of light reaching the subject (Figure 6.12).

Dimmer boards are useful for controlling entire banks of instruments simultaneously and for presetting

Figure 6.10A and B Light control patch bays may be designed to require physically placing patch cords into patch panels (*left*) or all connections can be performed through a computer program and computer-controlled distributor systems (*below*). (Courtesy of Colortran.)

a series of lamps for the next scene. Modern dimmer boards are computer controlled and allow an infinite number of individual instruments or series of instruments to be preset and changed at the press of a button. Computer control boards are designed to perform complex and rapidly changing light cues in variable combinations and number of cues (Figure 6.13).

Lighting Control on Location

Securing adequate electrical current for lighting on location presents more problems and hazards than does studio production. The most pressing problem is how and where to secure adequate power. If sufficient electricity is not available, portable gasoline generators are sometimes brought in. When using a private home or office, a lighting director and electrician may decide to tap the main power supply or to use the existing circuits. If the former course is taken, a qualified electrician must perform the operation of tapping into the 100 amp (or more) main supply, which can then be channeled to a portable circuit board for distribution to individual instruments. If you decide to use existing circuits in the home or office, you can determine which outlets are on the same circuits and how many amps each circuit can carry by simply checking and closing a circuit at the main circuit box or fuse box, and then testing outlets in the rooms where filming is to take place. Load demands should never exceed those specified at the circuit or fuse box, because excess power traveling along a line can melt the wires and start a fire. Any situation in which an extensive amount of lighting and electrical energy is required demands the expertise of a qualified electrician.

LIGHT MEASUREMENT

The basic unit of light intensity measure is the foot-candle. One foot-candle is an agreed-upon standard that represents the approximate light intensity produced by a candle one foot away. The normal measurement range of a light meter is from 1 to about 250 foot-candles. A light meter is extremely useful in both video and film production for determining lighting levels and contrast within a scene, as well as for properly positioning and setting individual lights. In film recording, a light meter must be adjusted to the proper sensitivity scale or EI (Exposure Index) number (DIN in Europe) so that it provides the correct f-stop readings for the specific sensitivity of the film stock (Figure 6.14).

The three major light sources are key light, fill light, and separation light. The *key light* is the brightest, hardest light. It provides modeling or texture. *Modeling* refers to the appearance of a textured surface that has shadows where there are indentations in the surface. A surface with good modeling looks three-dimensional. *Fill light* is softened, lower-intensity light that helps to fill in some of the shadows created by the key light and to reduce the contrast between light and shadow areas. *Separation light* comes from

---

OHMS LAW AS APPLIED TO LIGHTING SITUATIONS

The Wattage portion of Ohms Law is stated:

WATTAGE EQUALS VOLTAGE TIMES AMPERAGE
or
POWER = ELECTRICAL PRESSURE X ELECTRICAL FLOW

or stated as a formula:

W = V x A

a converse of the law is stated:

$$A = \frac{W}{V}$$

Either formula is simplified by using 100 V for Voltage although the normal Voltage in the U.S. is between 110 and 120 V, the difference provides a margin of protection.

The Wattage formula is used to determine how many Watts of lamps may be hooked to any one circuit once the Amperage of that circuit is known.

For example: typical electrical household or business building circuits provide 20 Amps of current, therefore:

W = V x A   W = 100 x 20   W = 2000 Watts

That means a total of 2000 watts of lamps and equipment could be connected to that one circuit.

If the total Wattage is known (total the wattage required to power all lamps & equipment) and then using the Amperage formula. If your location requires 2450 Watts of power then:

$$A = \frac{W}{V}\qquad A = \frac{2450}{100}\qquad A = 24.5\text{ Amps}$$

That means a circuit that provided at least 24.5 Amperage of current would be required. Neither a 15 Amp nor 20 Amp circuit would work, so either a 25 Amp circuit would need to be located, or the lamps would have to be split between a 15 Amp and a 10 Amp circuit or more likely two 15 amp circuits in order to provide enough current without blowing a fuse or breaker.

Using 100 for Voltage means that in most cases these calculations can be completed mentally, since it is easy to remember to multiple by 100 to obtain Wattage or divide by 100 to obtain Amperage.

Figure 6.11 As complicated as it may seem, calculating the amount of power required to power equipment and lighting instruments can be accomplished with simple formulas dividing or multiplying by 100.

behind the subject. It creates a halo effect, which outlines the subject and helps to separate it from the background.

Types of Light Meter Readings

There are two basic types of meter readings: incident and reflected. *Spot meters* are a specialized type of reflected meter. Another type of reflected reading may be gained through a meter built into the film camera or electronic circuits built into a video camera. This type of metering is called *through the lens* (TTL). Some light meters are capable of producing only one type of reading. Others can be used for several different types of readings. Each reading has a specific purpose in terms of lighting control. On some light meters a white hemisphere or flat circle is placed over the photoelectric cell so that the meter can measure the intensity of the light falling on the subject, or the *incident light*. This white surface gathers and diffuses light falling on the meter from several directions. For a reading of direct light falling on the subject, the meter is pointed at the camera from the position of the subject (Figure 6.15).

A reading of incident or direct light is called an *incident reading*. Because such a reading measures the light falling on the subject, it is not affected by the reflectance of the objects to be recorded (Figure 6.16).

A measurement of indirect light, that is, light reflected by the subject, is called a *reflected reading*. The white covering is removed from the photocell for a reflected reading, and the meter is pointed at the subject from the camera. A reflected reading of

---

INVERSE SQUARE LAW AS APPLIED TO LIGHTING SITUATIONS

The Inverse Square Law states that the light intensity falling on a subject will vary inversely by the square of the variation in the distance between the light source and the subject.

A simpler variation is that changing the distance between a source of light and the subject will result in a major change in the amount of light falling on the subject.

Stated as a formula:

$$I = \frac{1}{D^2} \, fc$$

When I is the change in light intensity and
D is the change in distance between the light source and subject

An example:

If the measured light at the subject is 100 foot candles (fc) when D = 10 feet, and the D changes from 10 to 20 feet which is double the distance then:

$$I = \frac{1}{2^2} \; 100 \qquad \text{(the distance doubled and the inverse of 2 is 1/2)}$$

$$I = \frac{1}{4} \; 100 \, fc$$

$$I = 25 \, fc$$

Or, if D changes from 10 to 5 feet, which is 1/2 the distance then:

$$I = 2^2 \; \text{(The distance is 1/2 inverse of 1/2 is 2)} \times 100 \, fc$$

$$I = 4 \times 100 \quad \text{or } 400 \, fc.$$

Just remember moving a luminaire or the subject in relation to each other will modify the light measurement on the subject radically. A small movement will result in a great change in the light on the subject.

Figure 6.12 Calculating the amount of light falling on a subject as the lamp is moved back and forth is accomplished with a simple formula based on dividing by the square of the light source if the change in distance is increased, or multiplying by the square of the light source if the distance is decreased.

the subject or whole scene averages the amount of light reflected by objects in the scene to determine the best overall exposure or base light level. A *spot meter reading* is the reflected light from a small isolated area within the frame. Spot meter readings are often used to take light readings of objects that are too far away to make an incident reading practical or from subjects that reflect far more or less light than the average subject in the area.

A *TTL* or *through-the-lens reading* provides a reflected reading of the exact image framed within the camera and can be used to adjust the lens automatically. Some TTL systems do not respond instantaneously to light changes, and the proper exposure lags slightly behind actual changes in light intensity. In essence a video camera is a TTL meter. The operator can determine the proper exposure by reading an oscilloscope attached to the camera output, or by gauging the contrast and exposure through the camera viewfinder, assuming the viewfinder is properly adjusted. The operator actually is viewing the reflected light in the viewfinder.

Determining Contrast Ratios

A light meter can be used in both video and film production to determine contrast within a scene. Apparent contrast within the image area can affect image clarity as well as the overall emotional mood. There are two important contrast ratios in any lighting setup: lighting ratio and contrast ratio. The mathematical relationship between light intensity in foot-candles or between f-stops on a light meter can be used to determine these specific ratios. (Foot-candles can be directly compared, whereas each higher f-stop number indicates a doubling and each lower f-stop a halving of the light intensity.)

Lighting Ratios

Key-to-Fill Ratio   Key-to-fill ratio indicates the proportion of key light to fill light in any lighting setup. This is called the *lighting ratio* but should not be confused with the inherent contrast ratio of a video camera or film stock, as will be discussed in Chapter 7, "Camera." Lighting contrast is caused exclusively by

Figure 6.13 A modern computer-operated lighting-control dimmer board allows all of the adjustment functions of lighting instruments (except for moving the lamps) from the control board. (Courtesy of Colortran.)

Figure 6.14 Handheld light meters may be designed for different functions. The one on the left is designed primarily to read incident light, and the one on the right is designed to read reflected light, although both meters will read either incident or reflected light.

lights. It is actually a comparison of key-plus-fill light to fill light alone.

Some fill light always spills over into the key light area and increases its intensity. An incident reading is taken of the key and fill lights together. Then the key light is shut off and a fill light reading is taken. A comparison of the two readings in terms of foot-candles or recommended f-stop readings indicates the key-to-fill light ratio. A key-plus-fill light reading of 250 foot-candles compared with a fill light reading

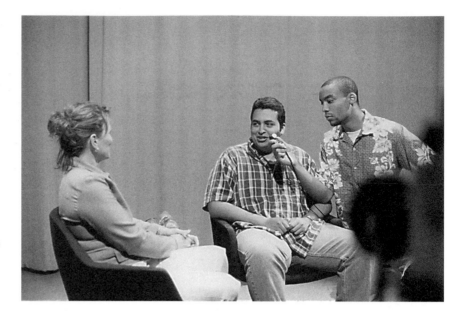

Figure 6.15 To take an incident light reading, the meter should be held close to the subject pointing toward the light source(s). A wide-angle light meter with a diffusion cap provides the most accurate incident meter reading.

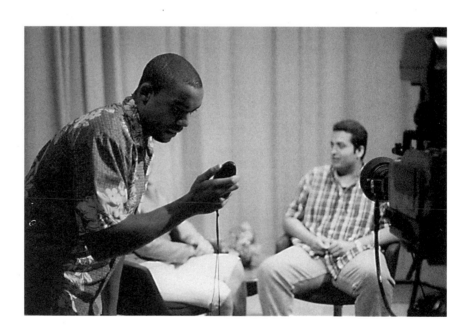

Figure 6.16 To take a reflected light reading, the meter is held close to the camera and pointed at the major subject. A narrow-angle meter provides the most accurate reflected meter reading.

of 125 foot-candles equals a 2:1 lighting ratio. One f-stop difference between the two indicates a 2:1 ratio, two f-stops a 4:1 ratio, three f-stops an 8:1 ratio, and so on. In most situations, video and film recording is done under a key-to-fill light ratio of 4:1 or less, unless a highly dramatic effect with high contrast is desired. Since video has less tolerance for contrast than film, it generally is advisable to use a 2:1 or lower key-to-fill light ratio in video recordings or film recordings that will be transferred to video. The key-to-fill ratio determines whether a high-key or low-key aesthetic of lighting is in effect. Low-key lighting has a high key-to-fill ratio, while high-key lighting has a low key-to-fill light ratio.

Key-to-Back Ratio The relative proportion of key light to backlight is called the *key-to-back ratio*. In most instances back lights and key lights should have approximately the same intensity. This ratio is usually kept at about 1:1 or 1:1.5. A weak backlight does little to separate the subject from the background or to create a halo effect. An extremely strong backlight, on the other hand, can cause an excessively bright halo to form around the subject's head and back.

Contrast Ratios

Contrast ratios can be determined by taking reflected light meter readings of the brightest and darkest reflecting objects in the scene. A spot meter is a great help in isolating a specific object, although moving a standard reflected light meter closer to an object without interrupting the light falling on it accomplishes the same goal. Again, a comparison of light meter foot-candle or f-stop readings indicates the contrast ratio between the brightest and darkest reflecting areas in the scene. Video cameras cannot record a reflectance contrast ratio greater than 30:1 or at most 40:1 (approximately five f-stops). Some standard film stocks, such as color negative, can often record reflectance contrast ranges as high as 100:1 (six or seven f-stops).

LIGHTING RATIOS
(Incident meter readings)
- Key to Fill Ratio = Lighting Ratio
  250 fc : 125 fc   = 2:1
- Key to Back Ratio = Key to Back ratio
  375 fc : 250 fc   = 1.5: 1
- Contrast Ratio (Reflected meter readings)
  Brightest area : Darkest area
  100 fc : 5 fc = 20:1

Adjusting Contrast

There are several ways of altering a scene's contrast to make it more acceptable for visual recording. Specific lights that are too strong or too weak can be moved farther from or closer to the subject. Scrims and diffusion materials can be used to cut down on the light intensity. Additional instruments can be focused on the subject, although care must be taken to keep these multiple keys and fills close together so that objectionable multiple shadows are not created. Altering the lighting contrast ratio can affect the reflectance contrast ratio since the two are interdependent: objects reflect key and fill light. In some cases, a change in the color or brightness of props, sets, or costumes may be required to increase or decrease light reflectance.

SETTING LIGHTING INSTRUMENTS

Three- and Four-Point Lighting

Three-point and four-point lighting are realist techniques that help create an illusion of three-dimensionality and depth in two-dimensional media such as video and film (Figures 6.17A, 6.17B, and 6.18A). Three-point and four-point lighting setups use three specific types of light, which have different directional placements, degrees of softness and hardness, and intensities.

Key Light

The key lights are the brightest and, in some ways, the most important lights on the set. The key light determines the overall recording or exposure level. The placement of a key light suggests the direction of the primary source of light within a scene, such as a window, an overhead light, the sun or moon, or even a candle or fireplace. When the key light strikes a subject directly from the front or camera side of the subject, few shadows or variations in surface texture are created and the result is a flat, uninteresting image. For optimal modeling and aesthetic effect, the key light should be 30 to 40 degrees away from the camera-subject axis, and it should light the short or narrow side of a face, that is, the side of the face that is least exposed to the camera. Moving the key light up and down, and from side to side, affects the direction and length of facial shadows and increases or decreases facial modeling.

Key light usually has a hard quality. The beam of light is narrowly focused and rarely if ever diffused or softened, except perhaps in a situation where softness is needed to create a romantic or light mood. The height of the key light affects the length of shadows falling on the set. Key lights should be placed high enough that long shadows do not spill onto the background from foreground subjects. The key light is usually placed much higher than the camera, unless a special effect is desired, such as the presentation of a flat, untextured image (in which case, the key light is at camera height) or a mysterious and horrifying face (in which case the key light is placed lower than camera height). In multiple-subject setups, the same light that functions as a key light for one subject can also function as the fill or back light for another. The term *key light* simply refers to the brightest light source striking a subject from the camera's viewpoint. The specific instrument designated as the key light can change as the camera or subject moves.

Fill Light

Fill light is used to provide general illumination on the set and to fill in the shadows created by the key lights. Fill light is usually softer than key light. It is frequently diffused by reflectors or translucent materials placed in front of the lighting instrument. The fill light is often placed at approximately camera height or just slightly above so that shadows created by overhead key lights can be properly filled in. It is usually on the opposite side of the camera from the key light. The intensities and physical placement of the key and fill lights will determine to a significant extent the emotional mood and lighting atmosphere within the scene.

Separation Light (Back Light)

One or two separation lights complete the three-point lighting triangle or four-point rectangle.

Figure 6.17A and B A subject lit with one harsh luminaire that represents the sun or major light source is called a key light. Such a lighting design is not flattering nor particularly revealing. A subject lit with both a key light and an additional softly diffused luminaire from the opposite side of the subject from the key light creates a more pleasant and useful subject.

Figure 6.18A and B To separate the subject from the background and to highlight the subject's hair, a luminaire is placed directly opposite the camera focused sharply down on the subject. A fourth luminaire may be used to throw a pattern on the background, erase unwanted shadows, or light the area not covered by the other three luminaires.

A backlight is usually placed above and behind the subject to create a halo effect that outlines the subject, separating it from the background. The backlight completes the three-point lighting setup, but it is not the only light that can be used to separate the subject from the background. In a four-point lighting setup, another separation light, called a *kicker*, may be placed exactly opposite the key light on the set. A kicker functions similarly to a backlight, but it is directed from the back and the side of the subject (usually opposite or facing the key light), rather than from directly behind and above the subject's back and head. Separation of subject and background through backlights and kickers is extremely important in black-and-white recording. The height of the backlight or kicker and its intensity in comparison with the key light affect the amount of separation that takes place (Figure 6.18B).

Background Light

Background light illuminates the background or set. It affects every lighting setup and is extremely important in the overall aesthetic appearance of a scene. While fill lights and key lights frequently spill over onto the background and partially illuminate it, it is important to light the background separately so that its appearance can be more carefully controlled. The amount of light cast on the background obviously affects subject/background separation. It can also affect visual emphasis within a scene. If the background is brighter than the subject, the viewer's attention will be distracted from the primary focus of interest. If the background is too dark, the set may look unnatural or the scene too contrasty. To add interest and texture to an otherwise flat, monochromatic background, patterns can be cast on the background to break it up and give it some modeling and texture. While too much patterning can be distracting, a flat, monochrome, evenly lit background looks dull and unimaginative. The use of different colors for the subject and background can effect much the same separation in color production, but separation lights have not been entirely abandoned in color production because they add so much texture, dimension, and depth to the visual image. In an optimal three-point lighting setup, the key, fill, and back lights form the points of a triangle or a Y. When a kicker and a backlight are used together, the four lighting points form a rectangle or an "X." Such ideal placements are rarely, if ever, consistently maintained. Only static, artificial, intensely boring still scenes with subjects and cameras that never move would allow for a permanent, perfectly triangular three-point or rectangular four-point lighting setup. A more typical situation is characterized by the constant movement of the subject(s) and cameras, and a complex, constantly varying relationship between keys, fills, and back lights or kickers. The three-point and four-point lighting procedures outlined earlier simply provide a starting point and an idealized model that is necessarily and continually manipulated in complex recording situations.

Controlling Shadows

Background light should not be used to try to burn out shadows from foreground performers that fall on the background. The most effective means of eliminating bad shadows is proper placement of the key lights. Key lights should be placed high enough above the performers so that prominent shadows are not cast on background walls as they move around the set. Performers should also be kept at a safe distance from the back wall whenever possible. Another complicating factor in three- and four-point television and film lighting is the creation of objectionable shadows by microphone booms. Since the key light creates the most noticeable shadows, microphone-boom placement and movement must be arranged to minimize interference with the key lights. Sometimes this can be accomplished by adjusting the barndoors of the key lights so that light does not spill into the microphone boom area. In other cases, the key lights may have to be placed higher overhead than normal, so that boom shadows fall on the floor, rather than on more noticeable parts of the set. A microphone-boom shadow can often be hidden in a part of the set that is already riddled with a shadow pattern. Obviously, the planning of the lighting setup must include consideration of the placement and movement of the microphone boom, before the key and fill lights are firmly positioned.

Cross Key Lighting

Cross key lighting uses two key lights to light two subjects equally. A fill light is not needed since the spill light from the key lights acts as fill.

Lighting Moving Subjects

The discussion of lighting to this point has assumed that the subject to be recorded is relatively stationary. A moving subject significantly complicates a lighting setup. The major problem inherent in lighting a moving subject is how to maintain relatively consistent light levels as the subject moves about the set. A moving subject in the studio must be lit by multiple key lights.

If a subject were to walk too close or too far away from a single key light, he or she would become too light or too dark, and realist continuity in lighting would be lost. Multiple key lights are hung at constant distances from the moving subject so that the subject can move from one key light to another without a noticeable change in lighting. Problems arise when key light beams overlap or when there are gaps of darkness between key lights. To prevent these problems, the barndoors or shutters on the key lights are adjusted so that key light beams are exactly adjacent to each other along the performer blocking line (where a subject will move on the set). As long as the talent follows this prearranged line of action and hits his or her marks, no gaps or overlaps of lighting will occur.

Low-Key Versus High-Key Lighting

The terms *low-key* and *high-key lighting* originated in the studio eras of feature film production in Hollywood. They seem counterintuitive, that is, the terms mean the opposite of what we think they should mean. Low-key lighting refers to the minimal use of fill light, that is, a relatively high key-to-fill ratio. This kind of lighting creates pools of light and rather harsh shadows. Many Warner Bros. gangster films and detective films produced in the 1930s and 1940s used low-key lighting for aesthetic effect. However, a whole genre of Hollywood films called film noir (literally, "black film" in French) relied on low-key lighting in the 1940s. Low-key lighting evokes a rather heavy and serious mood or feeling that enhances the emotional atmosphere of certain types of films. Low-key lighting is similar to an effect in painting known as *chiaroscuro*.

This technique is evident in the paintings of Rembrandt, for example, where shafts of light illuminate central figures in the painting, while the remaining parts of the scene are dimly lit and heavily shadowed. Low-key lighting can have a similar effect in video and film, although contrast ratio differences between video and film call for different lighting techniques to create the same effect in the two media.

High-key lighting presents a brightly lit scene with few shadow areas. It has been suggested that during the 1930s and 1940s, MGM (Metro-Goldwyn-Mayer) studios used high-key lighting for its lavish musicals so that no detail in its elaborate and expensive sets would be hidden in the shadows.

In any case, the use of high-key lighting in musical comedies is another example of form following function. The term *notan* is often applied to high-key lighting. The word *notan* refers to the bright, low-contrast paintings of the Japanese master painters. The light, happy atmosphere stimulated by high-key lighting contrasts with the somber, mysterious, or threatening atmosphere of low-key lighting. Thus, an important consideration in selecting either high- or low-key lighting styles is attempting to match the form of the lighting to the specific function it is intended to serve.

Lighting Plots

A specific lighting setup can be outlined or diagrammed on a piece of grid paper that represents an overhead scale diagram of the studio. This outline is called a *lighting plot*. The overhead lighting grid to which specific instruments can be attached is drawn onto the studio diagram. The basic elements of the set are added to this overhead view. The placements and movements of the talent and camera(s) can be added to the diagram after preliminary performer and camera blocking, so that the lights can be positioned accordingly. Lighting plots also may be created using specifically written computer programs that allow for manipulation of diagrams of sets, instruments, and performers. Such programs also allow for the printing of hard copies of the diagrams as well as storage of the files on discs for recall at a later time. The lighting director equipped with such computer programs uses the computer graphics to create these plots quickly and efficiently without tediously hand drawing each instrument and connection.

The program also will create lists of the instruments required and indicate patch-board connections. Several key lights may have to be arranged so that they maintain an even or balanced brightness on the moving performer throughout the set. Only

when the exact blocking line of the talent is known can these lights be properly placed. The distance of the key lights from the talent can be determined by relying on the inverse square law (light intensity changes according to the square of the distance of the light source from the object) and the scale dimensions of the grid paper. One-quarter inch on paper may equal one foot of actual studio floor space, for example (Figure 6.19).

Composing a lighting plot allows the lighting director to consider all relevant factors that can affect the selection and placement of lighting instruments prior to actual production. He or she must consider the placement and movement of the talent, cameras, and microphone booms, as well as the electrical and spatial capabilities and limitations of the studio or location environment. The lighting plot must also incorporate many aesthetic or stylistic variables. It can be low key or high key; realist, modernist, or postmodernist. The lighting director must develop a lighting setup that is both aesthetically satisfying and practical from an engineering standpoint.

Single-Camera Versus Multiple-Camera Situations

In single-camera recording situations, the lighting is sometimes changed for each shot or each major

TYPICAL LIGHTING PLOT

Figure 6.19 Lighting plots provide a means of carefully planning ahead of time for the placement of lighting instruments to avoid unnecessarily moving fixtures once the sets and blocking have been completed. The plot must be drawn to scale or it is of little value for accurate planning.

change in camera position. Of course, changing the lighting slightly for each separate shot can be extremely laborious and time-consuming. Subtle changes in lighting are made in realist productions, not drastic changes that call attention to the lighting. Lighting continuity from shot to shot and scene to scene will break down with too much shifting of lighting instruments. Feature films and network television commercials, which have big budgets, long shooting schedules, and large production crews, can better afford the luxury of lighting each separate shot perfectly than can lower-level productions.

The aesthetic expectations of audiences and the demands of clients make lighting a high priority in some single-camera productions. Still, the lighting for any single-camera production can benefit from the added time and care this production method affords. Since recording is continuous in multiple-camera production, the lights cannot be reset for different shots. Lighting decisions and compromises must be fully worked out prior to actual recording. The same lighting setup is used for long shots, medium shots, and close-ups. The lighting director must be able to anticipate every camera angle and placement that will be needed before arranging and setting up the lights on the set.

Lighting for Digital Cameras

Digital cameras see light in the same way as analog cameras. The digital signal maintains an apparently higher level of resolution because there are no defects added to the picture. For this reason many fine details lost with an analog camera will stand out visibly in the digital mode. It is imperative, then, that light falls only on areas that need to be lit, and that accurate lighting ratios are developed in the lighting plan. Sloppy work in all aspects of digital production will become obvious in areas that would not show in an analog production. Lighting for digital signals simply requires greater care for the small details than lighting for analog signals.

Aesthetic lighting setups can be divided into three categories: realist, modernist, and postmodernist lighting. Realist lighting attempts to recreate the presumed natural sources of lighting within a specific location. Key lights are used to maintain the consistent directional placement of the presumed central light source in a room, while fill lights reduce contrast to a normal or acceptable level. Lighting can also be used in a modernist or stylized manner to achieve a particular atmospheric effect, psychological mood, or abstract design.

SUMMARY

Light sources, such as the sun and incandescent, carbon arc, HMI, and fluorescent lamps, emit light of a specific color temperature. Daylight, carbon arc, and HMI light have higher color temperatures and a greater proportion of blue in comparison with red light than incandescent or tungsten light. Fluorescent light is discontinuous throughout the visible spectrum. Color film stocks must be selected and video cameras balanced for the color temperature of the primary light source if a normal color rendition is to be recorded.

Spotlights and floodlights are two different types of lighting instruments. Spotlights produce bright, narrow beams of light, and floodlights provide softer, more diffused lighting for wider areas. Lighting instruments can be secured to a variety of mounting devices, including overhead studio grids and lightweight portable light stands. Light-shaping devices, such as barndoors, scrims, flags, and cookies, help direct and control lighting and create shadow patterns.

Artificial lighting consumes significant amounts of electricity. Load limits for specific electrical circuits must be carefully observed to avoid dangerous overloading.

Light meters measure light intensity. An incident light meter reading measures the intensity of the light falling on a scene, while a reflected reading measures the intensity of the light reflected by objects in the scene. These readings help to determine image contrast, as well as the proper exposure level. Lighting ratios can be determined by using incident light meter readings to compare specific lights in terms of their intensity. Contrast ratios in a scene affect visual aesthetics and techniques such as low-key and high-key lighting.

Three-point and four-point lighting consist of a triangular or rectangular arrangement of three types of light: key light, fill light, and separation light. Basic three- or four-point lighting in television and film production is complicated by the movement of subjects and cameras, which gives a dynamic, constantly changing character to a lighting situation. Multiple key lights can be used to maintain consistent light levels as a subject moves through a scene.

A lighting setup should be carefully planned to avoid problems on the set, such as blocking difficulties, unbalanced light intensities, and microphone-boom shadows. A lighting plot, which presents an overhead view of the studio floor or actual location drawn to scale, can help a lighting director to organize and plan a lighting setup.

Low-key lighting refers to a relatively high key-to-fill light ratio that creates pools of bright light surrounded by dark shadow areas. It is frequently used to effect an atmosphere suitable for horror and gangster films and television programs, although it can be an effective dramatic device in many productions. High-key lighting, which has a low key-to-fill light ratio, presents few shadows and is frequently used in comedies and musicals.

Lighting for digital cameras requires greater care and control than lighting for analog cameras. The higher resolution of digital cameras (depending on their scan and line rate) reveals details in a picture that normally are not visible or obvious in an analog signal. For that reason greater care is needed to light well-balanced scenes with light falling only where it is necessary or important.

EXERCISES

1. Design two sets of lighting plots for a specific dramatic scene: one for single-camera recording and another for multiple-camera recording. Make subtle changes of light placements for close-ups in the single-camera production that will enhance the view of the subject without disrupting the overall appearance of the lighting when the camera is moved to another perspective. Find the best (compromise) position for lights used in multiple-camera production so that the subject looks reasonably good from many different camera perspectives at the same time.

2. Light a stationary, two-person interview, using cross-key lights and fill lights, creating a 2:1 key-to-fill ratio and a 1:1.5 key-to-back light ratio.

3. Set up multiple key, fill, and separation lights, which will keep a moving subject lit by relatively constant light intensity, while maintaining a 2:1 key-to-fill ratio and a 1:1 key-to-back light (or kicker) ratio.

4. If both film and video cameras are available, light a simple scene. Place the cameras side by side. Shoot several sequences after varying the light from high contrast to low contrast. Shoot some sequences with too much light, and some with not enough by normal standards. After the film is processed, compare the reaction of the two media to changing light values.

5. Light a scene with tungsten fixtures near an open door. Follow the talent as they walk from the interior to the exterior. Note the change in white balance and the change in light level and its effect on the recording.

6. Find the breaker box in your home, office, or class building. Note the amperage rating of each circuit. If the breaker box is well marked, it will indicate where each circuit is located. Calculate how many light fixtures and at what wattage you would be able to use in any one room of the building, without blowing a breaker.

ADDITIONAL READINGS

Alton, John. *Painting with Light*. Berkeley: University of California Press, 1995.

Bermingham, Alan. *Location Lighting for Television*. Boston, MA: Focal Press, 2001.

Box, Harry. *Set Lighting Technicians Handbook*, 3rd ed. Boston, MA: Focal Press, 2003.

Box, Harry. *Gaffers Handbook*. Boston, MA: Focal Press, 1999.

Brown, Blain. *Motion Picture and Video Lighting*, revised ed. Boston, MA: Focal Press, 1996.

Clark, Charles G. *Charles Clark's Professional Cinematography*. Hollywood, CA: ASC Press, 1964.

Hummel, Ed., ed. *American Cinematographer Manual*, 8th ed. Hollywood, CA: The ASC Press, 2001.

Ferncase, Richard K. *Film and Video Lighting Terms and Concepts*. Boston, MA: Focal Press, 1995.

Fitt, Brian, and Joe Thornley. *Lighting Technology: A Guide for the Entertainment Industry*. Boston, MA: Focal Press, 1997.

Gloman, Chuck and Tom LeTourneau. *Placing Shadows: Lighting Techniques for Video Production*, 2nd ed. Boston, MA: Focal Press, 2000.

Grotticelli, Michael, ed. *American Cinematographer Video Manual*, 3rd ed. Hollywood, CA: The ASC Press, 2001.

Jackman, John. *Lighting for Digital Video and Television*, San Francisco, CA: CMP Books, 2002.

Lyver, Des and Graham Swainson. *Basics of Video Lighting*, 2nd ed. Boston, MA: Focal Press, 1999.

Malkiewicz, Kris. *Film Lighting*. New York: Fireside, 1986.

Millerson, Gerald. *Lighting for Television and Film*, 3rd ed. Boston, MA: Focal Press, 1999.

North American Philips Lighting Handbook. Bloomfield, NJ: North American Philips Corp., 1984.

Viera, Dave. *Lighting for Film and Electronic Cinematography*. Belmont, CA: Wadsworth Publishing, 1993.

Wilson, Anton. *Cinema Workshop*, 4th ed. Hollywood, CA: The ASC Press, 1994.

7 Camera

- How do digital and analog cameras differ?
- What determines how a camera is placed and operated?
- What part do lenses and optics play in camera operation?
- How do film and video cameras differ?

INTRODUCTION

Camera operators try to provide directors with the best possible pictures that will enhance a particular aesthetic approach. To accomplish this they must know how to use basic image framing, composition, and camera movements, and how to control numerous technical devices of the camera and lens. To record clear and distinct images, for example, camera operators must understand how lenses work and then place key information in sharp focus. Significant image depth, that is, placing a wide range of objects at various distances from the camera in sharp focus, can be an effective realist approach to camera operation. Image depth enhances the perception of spatial continuity, which, like temporal continuity, is one of the hallmarks of realist aesthetics. Limiting or restricting image depth can help to create a modernist perspective on everyday objects by isolating them from their surroundings and temporarily "making them strange" (a formalist and modernist characteristic), often providing an unusual perspective upon them.

The differences between analog and digital cameras are subtle but important. These differences and comparisons will be explained later in this chapter. Film cameras also have benefited from the increased use of digital circuits. A professional film camera will have a video assist (video picture output) originated by one or more CCD chips. In addition, time-code signals may be recorded in a digital format for easier conversion in postproduction.

Some aesthetic aspects of camera use, such as composition and camera movement, were considered in terms of directing in Chapter 4, "Directing: Aesthetic Principles and Production Coordination," but they bear repeating here from the standpoint of camera placement and control. After reading this chapter and before attempting to use any camera, you should read the instruction manual carefully for the specific camera you wish to operate. Continual practice with the camera is necessary to make it an extension of your eyes and body. Basic camera exercises, such as those recommended at the end of this chapter, can significantly improve your skills as a camera operator.

Potential camera operators should be aware of the capability of studio systems to include remote controls for all of the camera operations: panning, tilting, zooming, and even dollying and trucking across the studio floor. The cameras used on major network newscasts now are all remote controlled from the control room. One of the functions of a camera operator may be to operate several cameras simultaneously with remote controls while seated in the control room. The traditional setting of the electronic controls of cameras by a camera control operator before each production also has been replaced by a computer built into the camera control unit. With a single press of a button, the computer runs a complete check of all electronic circuits and sets the camera controls for that particular production.

CAMERA PLACEMENT

Placing a camera in the best position for recording realist or modernist images consists of three camera operations: framing, positioning, and movement. *Framing* refers to the arrangement of actions and objects within the camera frame. *Positioning* includes the selection of camera-to-subject distance and angle, while *movement* of the camera is accomplished by means of various camera mounting devices.

Framing

Four key concepts help camera operators frame visual images: essential area, lookspace, walkspace, and headroom. *Essential area* refers to the safe recording area within the camera frame. All key information is placed within the essential area of the frame so it is not cut off by mistake. Objects and actions can be placed within the essential area by moving the camera closer to or farther away from the subject, or

by altering the focal length of a zoom lens. *Lookspace* is the frame area in front of an on-screen performer who is looking at an off-screen object or person. Leaving some space in the frame for the performer's look or glance creates the best spatial composition. Lookspace can be increased by panning the camera. *Walkspace* refers to the additional space left in the frame into which a performer can walk or run. When following a performer with a camera, as during a panning or trucking shot, walkspace should be placed in front of the subject within the frame. Otherwise, the edge of the frame acts as a restrictive border and the visual composition seems awkward (Figure 7.1).

ASPECT RATIO – ESSENTIAL AREA

Standard 3:4 NTSC Ratio

Standard HDTV 9:16 ATSC Ratio

FIGURE 7.1 Camera operators, whether of film or video, need to be aware that all viewers at home will not be able to see in their receivers the subjects exactly the same as operators see them in their viewfinders. There is a certain amount of loss of the picture around the edges through the conversion and transmission process. This trims off a border around the picture that could amount to as much as 20% of the total picture. To be safe, a camera operator should include within the central 80% all subjects that are critical to the shot, while still keeping in mind that some people may see virtually everything the operator is viewing. Regardless of the aspect ratio, 3 × 4 or 9 × 16, the critical area still needs to be observed. Also a production may be shot and recorded on a 9 × 16 aspect ratio camera with the intention of using the video for both 9 × 16 and 3 × 4 production, requiring the camera operator to frame for both aspect ratios simultaneously.

Another important aspect of composition is providing an appropriate amount of *headroom*, that is, space above the performer's head within the frame. Too little headroom creates a sense of confinement, while too much gives an impression of limitless space that sometimes dwarfs the performer. Of course, tight close-ups often have little or no headroom. Changes in headroom result from tilting the camera, moving the camera closer or farther away, or zooming the lens. The rules for framing in the 16:9 aspect ratio are the same as 4:3, except much more space is available on the sides of the frames that must be filled with some objects or filler. The frame still may be split into nine areas, and the rule of thirds still pertains. But the horizontal areas require greater planning and thought to maintain satisfactory composition, especially for objects that are predominately vertical in their individual framing.

Positioning

Camera operators also need to be familiar with the basic rules of camera placement and composition. For example, the 180-degree action-axis rule should be followed in camera placement, if the directional relationship of objects in the frame and subject movements is to remain spatially consistent from shot to shot. Crossing the line with the camera can reverse screen direction. In terms of composition, the rule of thirds, or dividing the frame into three parts both vertically and horizontally, allows the camera operator to place objects along the lines and at the intersection points to help achieve a satisfying frame composition. Additional compositional factors from the standpoint of aesthetics, such as symmetry or balance and closure, should also be considered (see Chapter 4, "Directing: Aesthetic Principles and Production Coordination").

Camera operators and directors control the placement and movement of cameras and put aesthetic principles into actual practice. A specific terminology is often used to refer to common types of camera placements and movements. Terms such as *medium shot, dolly, pan, pedestal,* and *crane shot* have specific meanings when they appear in a final shooting script and/or shot lists supplied to the camera operators by the director.

A *close-up* is basically a head-and-shoulders shot of a person. An *extreme close-up* fills the frame of the camera with a character's face, a part of the face, or some specific object. Close-ups are used for emphasis, to achieve a degree of intimacy or involvement, or to focus the audience's attention on a particular detail. Used sparingly, close-ups can be an effective way of achieving dramatic emphasis. Close-ups are created by moving the camera closer to the subject or by zooming in.

A *medium shot* includes one-half to three-quarters of a character's body. The camera is placed farther away from the subject or the lens is zoomed out from a close-up. This type of shot is a compromise between the long shot and the close-up. Some details and facial gestures are readily apparent, but many broad actions of several characters can sometimes be included within the frame as well. A *two-shot* is generally a medium shot that presents two people or characters within the same frame. Television and film directors frequently frame an image as a two-shot so that the audience can see the actions and reactions of two characters simultaneously.

A *long shot* gives a full-body image of a character or characters. An *extreme long shot* might include a broad exterior vista. Long shots allow audiences to see broad action but do not provide emphasis or subtle details. The long shot is often called an *establishing shot* when it sets the character(s) in the context of the setting or location. Many standard scenes begin with an establishing shot to set the context or physical location, and then cut to combinations of closer shots of specific actions and characters. A camera is normally placed at the subject's eye height in video and film production, but some shots call for a higher camera angle, while others call for a much lower camera position. These high- and low-camera angles can be used to simulate the spatial positioning and points of view of specific characters, or simply to provide perspectives that will exaggerate or reduce the apparent size of the object(s) in the frame.

Movement

Camera movements in midshot should be made only when they significantly improve our understanding of what is being presented. When overused, they can be visually distracting. Moving camera shots should begin and end with the camera stationary so that they can be intercut or combined with stationary camera shots.

When a camera is placed on a moving tripod or dolly, it can be moved toward or away from the subject. These camera movements are called *dolly shots*. They differ from *zoom shots*, which result from changing the focal length of a zoom lens. Dolly shots alter perspective; that is, they change the apparent spatial positioning of objects in a scene. They give the audience the feeling that they are actually moving through the scene, as well as shifting their perspective and focus of attention.

Physically moving the camera horizontally or laterally with respect to the subject is called a *trucking shot*. Trucking shots can be used to keep a moving subject in frame. A lateral movement of the camera in a semicircular path is called an *arc*. To perform a trucking shot or arc, the camera must be mounted on a wheeled dolly. Sometimes tracks are laid on the floor or ground so that the wheels of the dolly will follow a prearranged path. If the tracks are laid properly, minimal bounce of the camera will occur, even over rough terrain. During tracking, trucking, and dolly shots, it is often advisable to use a wide-angle lens to minimize the bouncing of the image. Telephoto lenses accentuate camera bounce.

A stationary tripod usually has a panning and a tilting device. A *pan action* slowly and smoothly rotates the camera from side to side on a tripod pivot, and a *tilt action* moves it up and down. These movements can be used to change the angle of view or to follow action. Panning too quickly can cause vertical lines or objects to strobe or flicker. Pans and tilts can also be used to follow performer movements. Tilts are often used to follow a performer sitting down or standing up. Like all camera movements, they usually begin and end with a well-composed stationary frame. A camera can also be physically moved up and down on a pedestal dolly. A hydraulic lift pushes the camera straight up or brings it straight down. This technique is called a *pedestal movement* and is used to adjust the camera for a high- or low-angle shot rather than to move the camera in midshot. A *crane shot* uses a long pivoting arm to move the camera up and down or from side to side in the studio or on location. It is usually reserved for wide establishing shots and is often used to move the camera in midshot.

Mounting Devices

Camera placements and movements usually require the use of specific camera-mounting devices in order to record steady images. Mounting devices for video cameras range from pistol grips to cranes. A *pistol grip* is used to hand hold a lightweight, portable, small-format camera (Figure 7.2). This device is rarely used for professional recording. The *crane* is a relatively large mounting device, which consists of a long counterweighted arm on a four-wheeled dolly or truck. It allows a camera to be raised to extreme heights in a studio or field situation, and usually requires several technicians to assist the camera operator in actually moving the camera. In between these two extremes we find the body mount, tripod dolly, and pedestal dolly.

Body Mount

A shoulder harness can be anything from a built-in camera mold or special body brace that fits perfectly over the operator's shoulder, to a more elaborate

Figure 7.2 The smallest and most flexible camera mount is a pistol grip mounted on either the camera body or the lens. Using such a mount requires upper-body strength, since all of the weight of the camera and lens rests on the operator's shoulder and right hand. Much practice is necessary to learn to hand hold a camera in order to provide a steady, unwavering shot.

servo stabilizer, such as a *Steadicam*, which minimizes vibration of the camera and allows the camera operator to move around freely. A Steadicam uses a complex system of springs and counterweights to smooth out the jerky movements of the operator and to simulate dolly or crane movements of the camera. The Steadicam can be used with a film camera as well as a video camera. (A Steadicam Jr. can be hand held with a lightweight video camera.) However, a Steadicam positions the camera in such a way that the normal film camera viewfinder cannot be used. The camera is usually at the operator's waist and is detached from his or her body. A video pickup is fitted into the camera viewfinder, and a video signal is fed to a small black-and-white monitor on the top of the camera, where it can be viewed by the operator. The video signal can also be fed to a recorder, so that immediately viewable television images are recorded at the same time as the film. Film, of course, cannot be screened until it is developed (Figures 7.3A and B).

Tripods

A tripod is a three-legged device upon which a stationary camera can be secured. The legs of the tripod can be extended to raise or lower the camera. Tripods are one of the most frequently used single-camera supports.

They usually consist of three extendible legs, with pointed spurs on the tripod shoes, a cradle and ball joint for leveling, a fluid head or other form of panning and tilting device, and a camera locking bolt. A *fluid head* allows the camera to be smoothly panned or tilted on the tripod. When used outdoors,

Figure 7.3A and B Body mounts are manufactured to carry either film or video cameras of all sizes. They are designed with a built-in spring and gyro system to maintain positioning on a level and even keel as the operator moves about the set. (Courtesy of Cinema Products.)

the spurs of the tripod can frequently be secured in soft ground, but on hard surfaces and indoors, the spur must be secured in a *spider* (sometimes called a *triangle* or *spreader*), which provides a device for locking down the shoes of a tripod to prevent them from slipping. Tripods for small-format video cameras often have flat rubber shoes rather than pointed spurs and are intended for both indoor and outdoor use without a spider (Figures 7.4A, B, C, and D).

The head of a tripod frequently has a bubble device for proper leveling of the tripod. *Leveling* a tripod refers to making the camera horizontally level, so that the horizontal frames of the image are parallel with the horizon outdoors or the lines formed by the floor and the back wall, or the ceiling and back wall in an interior setting. The nut that secures the head to the tripod cradle can frequently be removed to allow the tripod head to be secured to another support device, such as a high hat. The *high hat* places a camera just a few feet above the ground, but well below the lowest tripod height. When it is equipped with suction cups, a high hat can be secured to almost any flat surface, such as the hood

of an automobile or the top of a boat. A tripod can also be secured to a *hitchhiker*, which is a spider with wheels on it. The hitchhiker allows a tripod and attached camera to move around the studio and transforms a stationary tripod into a movable dolly.

Dollies

A *dolly* is a camera platform or support device on wheels, which allows the camera to move smoothly about a studio (Figures 7.5A and B). A *pedestal dolly* can be vertically moved up and down to raise or lower the camera in midshot. A tripod can be attached to a hitchhiker to create a dolly. The wheels of a hitchhiker, like those of a pedestal dolly, can usually be locked to prevent movement of the camera. Three wheels give the hitchhiker or pedestal dolly ample stability and ease of movement, although care must be taken to plan the movement of a camera so that the bulky coaxial cables connecting the camera to the camera control unit do not get in the way. A dolly should never roll over audio or video cables on the studio floor.

Figure 7.4A, B, C, and D Tripods vary in size to match the size and weight of the cameras to be mounted on them. Specialized accessories include spiders to hold the tripod feet; quick release mounts to allow the camera to be quickly placed on or off the tripod as necessary to move to the next setup; and a high hat to allow the camera to be mounted close to the ground or on the side or top of a vehicle. (Courtesy of Matthews Studio Equipment.)

Various types of dollies and other mobile mounts can be used with film and video cameras. A *crab dolly* allows up-and-down pedestal movements. Some dollies, like the *Elemac spider dolly*, are collapsible yet extremely versatile and stable. Sometimes a wheelchair or moving vehicle, such as a car or van, can serve as an excellent dolly. A special mount, such as the *Tyler mount*, can be used to record vibrationless images from a helicopter or an airplane in combination with a special fluid-filled lens called a *dyna*

lens. Finally, a *crane* can be used in studio or field productions to raise even the heaviest film camera to tremendous heights.

LENS CONTROL

Another way in which camera operators control the presentation of visual images is by using various camera lenses. A *camera lens* consists of one or more

Figure 7.5A and B Dollies are constructed in a variety of shapes and sizes. These two are designed to be operated by hand, rather than motorized. The dolly in the top photo is designed with the camera mounted in a yoke and with the operator and grip moving the camera and dolly as needed. The dolly in the bottom photo is designed for the camera operator to ride seated. (Courtesy of Chapman/Leonard Studio Equipment.)

pieces of glass that focus and frame an image within the camera. Lens control begins with an understanding of basic optics.

Basic Optics

A *lens* is a curved piece of glass that causes light rays to bend. Because glass is denser than air, light slows down at the point where it enters the lens. Lenses bend light so that it can be controlled and projected in proper focus and size at a specific point behind the lens, where a light-sensitive material can record or transmit the image. The curvature of the lens, as well as the type of glass from which it is made, affects how much the light bends and, to a certain extent, determines the classification and function of a specific lens. Simple, single lenses fall into two basic categories: concave and convex (Figure 7.6).

Concave lenses, which are thinner at the center than at the edges, bend light rays away from the center of the lens, causing them to diverge from each other. *Convex lenses*, on the other hand, are thickest at the center and bend light toward the center so that the light rays converge or intersect at a specific point behind the lens, known as the *focal point*. The distance from the optical center of a lens to its focal point is known as a lens's *focal length*. The curvature of a lens affects its focal length.

Lenses can be classified according to their focal lengths. For example, film and video lenses with short focal lengths are sometimes called *wide-angle lenses*. Beyond the focal point the light rays diverge

from each other, and at some area behind the lens, known as the *focal plane*, they form an inverted, reversed image of the objects that are reflecting light in front of the lens. Images at the focal plane are in acceptable focus; that is, the objects are clear and sharp. A piece of light-sensitive material, such as the front surface of a film or an electronic pickup chip, placed at the focal plane will record an inverted and reversed image of the original scene. Modern film and video lenses are composed of more than one piece of glass and are called *compound lenses* (Figures 7.7A and 7.7B).

Aberrations

Compound lenses combine several concave and convex lenses in various configurations to cut down on disruptions of, or imperfections in, light transmission, which are called *aberrations*. A simple convex lens, such as a magnifying glass, creates several types of aberration, including field curvature, distortion, and chromatic aberration. *Field curvature* refers to the fact that the image projected by a simple convex lens falls into best overall focus on a curved, rather than a flat, plane or image surface. Motion picture film and front surfaces of video pickup chips are flat, not curved.

Distortion is caused by changes in magnification that occur in different parts of the image projected by a simple, convex lens. *Chromatic aberration* refers to the fact that various color wavelengths bend at different angles when they enter a piece of glass, such as a prism or a simple lens.

A modern lens combines several concave and convex lenses to reduce these types of aberration. Modern lenses are also coated with substances such

Figure 7.6 Typical parts of a lens are: 1. Lens front surface; 2. Iris; 3. Concave element; 4. Convex element; and 5. Focal point.

Figure 7.7A and B Lenses for video and film cameras come in a wide variety of sizes and purposes. Pictured are various variable focal length studio and field lenses. (Courtesy of Fujinon Corporation.)

as magnesium fluoride that reduce the reflection of light entering the lens and therefore increase light transmission. The lens coating is usually placed on the outside element of a lens. Never touch the front surface of a lens with your finger. Body oils can etch the lens coating if they are not removed immediately with lens cleaning paper and proper cleaning solutions. Clean the lens with fluids infrequently, since repeated cleaning can wear down the lens coating. An air blower or camel-hair brush usually does a good job of cleaning loose dirt off a lens. Lenses must be handled carefully, and cleanliness is essential.

Lens Perspective

Focal Length and Angle of Acceptance

Lens perspective, or the way in which a lens presents the spatial relations between the objects it records or transmits, varies with a lens' focal length and angle of light acceptance. The *angle of acceptance*, or the angle at which a lens gathers light in front of a camera, is determined by the focal length of the lens and the format (size) of the recording medium. Shorter focal-length lenses generally have wider angles of acceptance than long focal-length lenses. Focal lengths usually range from 10mm (about ½ inch) or less to 200mm (about 8 inches) or more. Short focal-length lenses are usually called *wide-angle lenses*, while long focal-length lenses are frequently referred to as *telephoto lenses*. *Normal lenses* are so called because they present an image perspective that seems to approximate that of normal monocular (single-eye) human vision. (See Figure 7.8.)

Variable Focal Length Lens

A variable focal length lens (zoom) allows a camera operator to change the focal length of a lens from wide angle through normal to telephoto and vice versa by manually turning the zoom barrel (or by pushing the button for an electric zoom motor). Zoom-ins and zoom-outs in midshot are easily misused and overused by beginning students. A zoom-in should direct our attention to something within the frame, while a zoom-out presents new information, often clarifying the setting. A zoom-in or zoom-out during a shot should be made smoothly and precisely.

A zoom lens also makes it easier to change focal length between shots, since one lens does not have to be physically replaced by another on the camera. Changing the focal length magnifies and demagnifies the image. At a long focal length the objects in the frame seem to be closer together, and at a short focal length they seem to be farther apart. A zoom lens should first be focused at its maximum focal length (telephoto). This ensures proper focus at all other focal lengths, assuming the subject-to-camera distance does not vary, including the end point of a zoom-in. Zoom lenses are available in a variety of focal length ranges, with minimum focal lengths as short as 10mm and maximum focal lengths as long as 200mm.

Field of View

Field of view refers to the exact dimensions of the image framed by the camera. The field of view of an image captured by a specific film or video camera is largely determined by the focal length of the lens and the video or film format. Shorter focal-length lenses present a wider field of view than longer focal-length lenses when used in the same film or video format. But the field of view provided by any lens changes when the format of the recording medium changes. A 25mm or 1-inch lens provides a narrower field of view in 16mm film or ⅔-inch video camera pickup chips than it does in 35mm film, or the same lens provides a wider field of view for ½-inch or smaller chips. In short, lens classifications, such as wide-angle, normal, or telephoto, and fields of view for specific focal-length lenses vary from one format to another. Whether a specific lens is wide-angle, normal, or telephoto, and whether it has a wide or a narrow angle of acceptance and field of view, depends on both its focal length and the dimensions of the film or video format (Figure 7.9).

Image Depth

Image depth is a general term describing the overall range of distances and objects that appear to be in sharp focus within the frame. It can be affected by a variety of specific factors, including the type of lens used, various lens adjustments, the placement of the objects within the set (see Chapter 9, "Design and Graphics"), and the lighting (see Chapter 6, "Lighting"). In this chapter, depth is considered from the standpoint of specific lens factors that affect one aspect of image depth, called *depth of field*. The primary factors creating depth of field are focus

ANGLE OF ACCEPTANCE

10mm = 35 degrees
25mm = 15 degrees
50mm = 7 degrees
120mm = 3 degrees

Camera with 1/2" chips

Figure 7.8 The coverage that a lens allows the camera to cover is measured in the angle of acceptance. The shorter the focal length, the wider the angle of acceptance, and, conversely, the longer the focal length, the narrower the angle of acceptance.

FIELD OF VIEW

FOCAL LENGTH	1/2" CCD/S-8Film	16mm Film	35mm film
10mm	35 degrees	50 degrees	95 degrees
25mm	**15 degrees**	**30 degrees**	**45 degrees**
50mm	7 degrees	15 degrees	25 degrees
80mm	4.5 degrees	7 degrees	15 degrees
120mm	3 degrees	4.5 degrees	10 degrees
200mm	1.75 degrees	3 degrees	6 degrees

Note: a 25mm lens for a small format (1/2" CCD or S-8 film) is a telephoto lens while the same focal length in a medium format (1"tube or 16mm film) is a normal lens.
In a large format (35mm film) the 25 mm lens is a wide angle lens.

Figure 7.9 The field of view of a camera varies with the size of the chip or the aperture opening of the film, and the focal length of the lens. A 50mm lens on a small-format camera would provide a narrow-angle shot, on a medium-format camera a standard shot, and on a large-format camera a wide-angle shot.

distance, lens aperture, and focal length. It is easier to understand the concept of depth of field by first explaining the primary factors that can be used to control it on a lens.

Focus Distance

Focus distance refers to the distance of the subject from the focal plane of a camera. On film cameras, the focal plane is indicated on the outside of the camera by a line drawn through the center of a circle. Focus distance can be accurately measured with a tape measure stretched from the focal plane to the subject. The focus ring on the lens barrel is adjusted according to the exact distance in feet or meters. On a reflex camera or video camera, focus distances can be set by simply turning the focus ring while viewing the subject through a properly adjusted viewfinder.

The *viewfinder diopter* on the reflex film camera is a device that adjusts the focus of a lens to the eyesight of a particular camera operator. This can be done by setting the lens focus ring on infinity and then looking through the viewfinder at an object that is at least 50 feet away. Turn the diopter focus ring until the object appears in proper focus and then lock down the diopter. Now the focus ring on the lens can be turned to set the focus on any subject regardless of its distance from the camera. A video camera does not have a viewfinder diopter or focus adjustment, since the viewfinder is usually a small black-and-white monitor; but for accurate focusing, the contrast and brightness of the monitor must be set properly.

Lens Aperture

An aperture is an opening through which light is allowed to pass. A camera has a fixed rectangular aperture or frame with a specific aspect ratio, where the film or pickup chip actually is exposed to light. A lens has a variable, circular-shaped aperture or iris, which allows the amount of light passing through the lens to be increased or decreased. The amount of light a lens transmits to a recording device can be controlled by varying the diameter of the lens aperture.

Lens aperture settings are calibrated in sequential f-stops or T-stops. The most commonly used measure of light transmission are *f-stops*, which have been mathematically calculated from a lens' physical characteristics. Some lenses have both T-stops and f-stops. *T-stops* provide an accurate index of actual light transmission by a specific lens. They are often used with zoom lenses, because the complex elements within the lens and the many air-to-glass surfaces can absorb a great deal of the light before it finally reaches the film or pickup tube. The most commonly labeled f- and T-stops on an aperture setting ring are 1, 1.4, 2, 2.8, 4, 5.6, 8, 11, 16, and 22. The higher the number, the narrower the opening in the lens, and thus the less light that is actually transmitted through the lens. It is sometimes helpful to conceive of the increasing numbers as reciprocals or fractions, that is, 1.4 = 1/1.4 and 16 = 1/16. Each higher f-stop represents a 50% decrease in light transmission from the f-stop immediately below it in numerical scale and two times the f-stop above it. Thus, an f-stop of 2 transmits half as much light through a given lens as an f-stop of 1.4, and twice as much as an f-stop of 2.8 (Figure 7.10).

Deciding exactly which f-stop to use is complicated by the many other variables that can affect exposure, such as the sensitivity of film stocks and pickup chips, as well as the amount of available light. In the 1930s many Hollywood camera operators always tried to light a scene for an f-stop of 5.6. There were several reasons for this beyond mere habit. First, and most important in terms of image quality, every lens has an optimum aperture, which is usually two to three full stops down from wide open. At an optimum aperture, such as a midrange f-stop of 5.6, the objects in focus are at their maximum sharpness. When the iris is closed down to a tiny hole, diffraction occurs around the blades of the iris, causing the sharpness of the image to be reduced. Such diffraction is more severe with wide-angle than with telephoto lenses. Studio camera operators selected 5.6 because even with poorer quality lenses, it consistently produced sharp images. Second, certain studios simply wanted to preserve a theoretical normal depth of field. A great deal of studio video recording today follows the same practice of using an f-stop of 5.6 for similar reasons.

LENS APERTURES - F/STOPS

Figure 7.10 The numbers designating f-stops seem to act in reverse to their actual function. A small number, such as f 1.4, actually is a relatively large opening in the aperture, but f 22 is a relatively small opening, allowing very little light to enter the camera.

Depth of Field

Depth of field refers to the range of distances in front of the lens that are in acceptable focus at the focal plane. Depth of field depends on the lens factors described earlier: (1) focus distance (which is usually the same as camera-to-subject distance); (2) lens focal length; and (3) the lens aperture or f-stop number. It also varies with the size of the recording format. Depth of field increases as the camera-to-subject distance increases, the focal length of the lens decreases, and the lens aperture narrows within a single format. Moving to a larger recording format increases the depth of field of a particular lens. For example, a 25mm lens offers a greater depth of field when used with ⅔-inch diameter video camera pickup chips than when used with ½-inch pickup chips.

Depth-of-field charts for different focal-length lenses and film or video formats indicate the range of distances in front of a lens where objects will appear to be in focus at different lens settings. The range of distances is mathematically calculated from f-stop settings, focal lengths, and camera-to-subject distances. Obviously, focus does not immediately drop off beyond the nearest and farthest distances listed

for each combination of focal length, camera-to-subject distance, and lens aperture setting. But the chart recommendations provide a relative standard for gauging depth of field and acceptable focus range (Figure 7.11).

Changing the focal length, either by changing lenses or by zooming out or in, obviously changes the depth of field. So does moving the camera closer to or farther away from the subject and changing the focus distance setting of the lens. The same holds true if the subject moves and the focus setting is changed. If a subject begins to exceed the depth-of-field range, the camera operator may have to adjust the focus distance setting, which is known as *pulling focus*. Sometimes a camera operator may intentionally try to limit the depth of field, either to isolate the subject from the background by putting the background out of focus or to shift the viewer's focus of attention by pulling focus from an object or face in the background to another in the foreground or vice versa. Depth-of-field limitations are extremely important in terms of the placement and movements of the talent, who must be accurately informed about the range of distances within which they can safely walk and still hit their marks during

DEPTH OF FIELD RANGES
16mm FILM - 25mm LENS

Hyper-focal distance	134.6'	96.1'	62.3'	48.0'	33.6'	24.0'	16.8'	12.2'	8.4'	6.1'
f-stop	1	1.4	2	2.8	4	5.6	8	11	16	22
Lens Focus	Near Far	Near Far	Near Far	Near Far	Near Far	Near Far	Near Far	Near Far	Near Far	Near Far
50'	36' 80'	33' 104'	29' 195'	25' Inf.	20' Inf.	16' Inf.	13' Inf.	10' Inf.	7' Inf.	5' Inf.
10'	9'3.5" 10'9.5"	9' .5" 11'2"	8'9" 11'9"	8'3" 12'7"	7'9" 14'3"	7'1" 17'2"	6'3" 25'	5'6" 55'	4'7" Inf.	3'10" Inf.
3'	2'11.25" 3' 3/4"	2'11" 3'1.25"	2'10.5" 3'1.75"	2'9.75" 3'2.5"	2'9" 3'3.5	2'8" 3'5.25"	2'6.5 3'8"	2'5" 3.11.5"	2'2.5" 4'8"	2' 5'11"

Figure 7.11 The depth of field of a lens is determined by three factors: the f-stop, the focal length, and the hyper-focal distance, or the point of best focus. Each of these three can be manipulated to increase or decrease the depth of field, depending on the desires of the camera operator.

a shot. Controlling depth of field affects the perception and aesthetics of image depth within the frame, which was discussed more fully in Chapter 6, "Lighting." A camera operator who learns the basic principles of depth of field can fully exploit the creative and aesthetic potential of film and television images.

VIDEO CAMERAS

Video and film cameras are sophisticated pieces of electronic and mechanical equipment. There are many different types of video and film cameras, which must be fully understood before they can be artistically controlled. This section considers basic camera design, function, operation, and artistic control.

Basic Video Camera

A basic video camera consists of pickup chip(s), a black-and-white viewfinder, a tally light, a lens, and all the electronic and mechanical controls needed to operate each of these devices.

Color cameras have one or more light-sensitive pickup chips, while black-and-white cameras have only one pickup chip. Even on color cameras, most viewfinders present black-and-white images, which show the camera operator what is being recorded by the camera. The lens focuses light rays on the video camera pickup chips. Most modern cameras have a single zoom lens, which allows for power or manual control of the image size. Telephoto lenses magnify the image, while wide-angle lenses present a wide field of view and demagnify the image. The *tally light* is usually positioned on the top of the camera. It lights up to inform the talent and crew which of several cameras in multiple-camera production is actually being used for recording or transmission.

The Camera Chain

A basic video camera chain consists of five separate parts: (1) a camera; (2) a power supply; (3) a sync generator; (4) a camera control unit; and (5) an encoder, which combines the *luminance* (brightness or amount of light) and *chrominance* (saturation or amount of color and hue, or shade of color) channels of visual information into a single video signal. The power supply for American television systems consists of either 120-volt AC current for a studio camera or a 12-volt DC battery (usually) for a field camera (Figure 7.12).

A separate *sync generator* (which is housed inside a field camera) supplies the signal that ensures

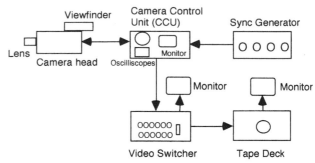

BASIC COMPONENTS OF A VIDEO CAMERA CHAIN

Figure 7.12 A basic camera chain consists of the following parts: the camera, its head, lens, and viewfinder. A camera control unit contains a vector scope, oscilloscope, and monitor. A sync generator provides synchronizing signals. If the camera is used in a studio setting, then the signal is fed to a switcher with monitors and to a recording medium with its monitor. A portable camera has the CCU and sync generator built into the camera body so that it can operate independently of any other equipment.

proper synchronization between the scanning of the camera pickup tube and the scanning of a videotape or a monitor or receiving picture tube, such as a video camera viewfinder. A *camera control unit* for a studio camera allows the video engineer to shade the camera, that is, to control the levels and color values in the video camera signal. This is done by adjusting the pickup chips' output levels and color. Multiple cameras must be shaded and white-balanced so that all shots will be comparable in brightness and color. Field cameras have built-in controls, which also allow the color signal to be properly set for white balance and brightness.

Video Camera Filters

There are two types of filter controls used on video cameras: a filter wheel or a filter switch. A *filter wheel* consists of several different filters arranged around the perimeter of the wheel so that each filter can be positioned between the lens and the camera pickup tube(s). One of the wheel settings has no filter for normal studio operation. A *cap filter* on the wheel is opaque. It is used to protect the pickup tube when the camera is not actually recording. *Color correction filters* on the wheel alter the color temperature of daylight so that it corresponds with the preset color sensitivity of the video camera. *Neutral density filters* reduce the intensity of excessively bright light. The amount of light or brightness in a signal can also be controlled by adjusting the lens aperture and/or the brightness control on a field camera. A *filter switch* is commonly used on a portable video camera in place of a filter wheel. This switch allows a color-correction filter to be positioned between the lens and the pickup tube(s) when recording under sunlight.

Types of Video Cameras

The most basic distinction between video cameras used to be that of color versus black and white. But due to the standardization of color for most video situations, the most important distinctions today are those between standard-definition (SD) and high-definition (HD) cameras and whether the cameras are capable of producing a picture in a 3:4 ratio and/or a 9:16 ratio or either of the scan systems: *interlace*–with two fields to a frame, or *progressive*–with a single frame made up of the total numbers of lines in the one frame. An additional consideration becomes important between those of field cameras, studio cameras, and convertible cameras, which can be converted for either field or studio use. Within each of these categories there is a variation in terms of image quality, and a distinction is often made between professional, prosumer, and consumer-quality cameras. *Prosumer* cameras are those designed for lower-level professional productions such as weddings and other social events, but higher quality than typical consumer equipment. Recorded images must be of high quality to be edited and duplicated for broadcast, and this usually requires more sophisticated and expensive equipment. The most sophisticated and highest-quality cameras are those that maintain the video signal in the digital domain from the pickup chips to the built-in digital recorder. Most modern cameras are capable of creating both 3:4 and 9:16 pictures with a flip of a switch. Since most of the circuits within the camera and camera control units now are digital-based, varying between standard-definition and high-definition signals is easily accomplished. With the coming of high-definition television (HDTV), scan rates also vary from 480 lines to 1,080, and the method of scanning from interlaced to progressive. The recorder could be either a digital videocassette recorder, direct to disc, either DVD or CD-ROM or a built-in computer with either a removable hard drive or RAM memory package.

The image quality of a video camera should be matched with the format and quality of the videotape recorder being used. It is as pointless to use an expensive, three-chip, studio camera to make a ½-inch VHS original videotape recording as it is to use a digital recording system with an inexpensive single-chip consumer video camera. The characteristics and image quality of both the video camera and recorder must be compatible with the production expectations and standards of the specific task at hand (Figure 7.13).

Figure 7.13 A professional video camera is a self-contained unit consisting of the camera head, lens, viewfinder, microphone, and built-in CCU and sync generator. The camera may be powered either by batteries or an adapter pack from 100-volt power. (Courtesy of Sony Corporation.)

DIGITAL CAMERAS

A digital camera contains three basic components: viewfinder, body, and optics. If the camera includes a recording medium, it is a camcorder, and the recording unit makes a fourth component.

Viewfinder

The viewfinder may be a small, 1.5-inch monochrome (black and white) monitor viewed through an eyepiece as film cameras and consumer cameras have been constructed, or a larger, 2.5-inch LCD color monitor that swings out from the side of the camera. This is also a common feature of consumer cameras. With an LCD monitor, the operator stands back from the camera and monitor rather than holding it on a shoulder close to the face. Each has advantages. The eyepiece monitor provides the opportunity for the operator to concentrate on what is visible in the viewfinder only and to not be distracted by other activities outside of the frame. For most shooting situations, the lack of a color monitor is not a handicap for the operator since framing, focus, and movement are prime concerns, not the color of the object in the frame. The monitor, either black and white or color, should be properly adjusted using color bars signal to set contrast, brightness, and chroma and not adjusted for the personal taste of the operator. All viewfinders show a certain number of functions or adjustments on the screen along with the subjects included in the frame. A tally light showing the camera is operating and recording, a zebra effect showing overmodulation, and battery and tape conditions generally are the minimum functions visible in the viewfinder. The viewfinder of a digital camera may show many more functions, often as a series of menus. Menus may indicate the adjustments for origin setup, display choices within the viewfinder, the recording medium setup, the camera setup, some possible shading and/or special effects available, and a series of switches required to operate the camera. Controls and choices of audio recording also are included in a menu. The operator must learn which menu contains the adjustments needed for a particular shot or setup and which adjustments are included in each menu. On the surface this makes operating a digital camera complicated, but at the same time it gives the operator of the camera/recorder a tremendous amount of flexibility in choosing how the recording will progress.

Body

The body of the camera contains the electronics starting with the Charge Coupled Device (CCD) chips that convert light to a video signal. Newer professional cameras replace the CCD chips with Complementary Metal-Oxide Semiconductor (CMOS) chips. A synchronous generator keeps all of the signals in proper alignment, and an analog to digital converter must be included since the light entering the lens is an analog variation making the first electronic signal analog. Digital Signal Processing (DSP) circuits within the camera may vary from simple amplifiers to complex special effects amplifiers and circuits to create a variety of output signals, both analog and digital. All cameras have audio input circuits for both microphones and high-level audio. Once again the analog signal from the mic must be converted to a digital signal for recording and distribution. A plug for a headset provides a means for monitoring the audio signal while recording and to check during playback. All professional and many consumer video cameras are multi-format output capable. That is, the output signal may be either analog or digital, a choice of line rate from 480 Interlaced (i) or progressive (p), 720i or p, 1080i or p, a frame rate of 24, 29.97, 30, 50, 59.97, or 60 fps, an aspect ratio of either 4:3 or 16:9. All of these variations are possible through the use of digital circuits within the camera body, yet the cost for such functions is minimal compared to analog cameras of 20 years ago.

Optics

The optic system for most digital cameras begins with a variable focal length (zoom) lens. Since the back focal distance is different in video cameras from film cameras, most video cameras are not able to use high-quality film lenses. The lenses are designed to

Figure 7.14A and B Video cameras are now equipped with all of the production accessories used in motion picture camera production. Such cameras are called Electronic Cinematography. (Courtesy JVC Broadcast Division.) A camcorders can now record directly onto a built-in hard drive or removable disk drive. (Courtesy of Ikegami Electronics, USA, Inc.)

vary their focal length at least over a 10 to 1 range, and some professional lenses vary as much as 100 to 1. The major differences between optics for analog cameras and optics for digital cameras relate to quality. Because the resolution and reproduction capabilities of a digital system are much higher, the smallest aberration or fault in the lens becomes noticeable and objectionable. Automatic iris, focus, and zoom controls are common on all levels of lenses, but are used sparingly in professional situations. Filters may be mounted between the lens and the prism blocks that split the light into the three primary colors, or a matte box may be mounted on the front of the lens to hold filters, scrims, and other light control devices. The prism block is considered part of the optic system, but is not physically attached to the lens. The block, through the use of filters between the sections of the block, either stops certain colors from passing, or reflects them in a different direction to separate the three colors to feed the three CCD or CMOS chips. The three colors are red, green, and blue. An equal combination of light of each of the three colors creates a white light. Any variation in the amount of each color creates any color of the spectrum.

Recording

The fourth segment of the camera is its recording section. This may be a tape deck, a CD or DVD laser burner, a solid-state chip, a memory card, a variety of floppy discs, or a digital hard drive. Each of these drives may be either removable or permanently mounted within the body of the camera. The design of each camera is somewhat dependent on the recording medium, and this area of camera design is rapidly changing. The subject of recording media will be covered in greater detail in Chapter 8, "Recording" (Figure 7.14B).

Types of Digital Cameras

Today there are four basic types of digital cameras: studio, field, hand-held, and box/pencil, although with the exception of box cameras, the other three often are interchangeable depending on their design adaptability.

Studio Digital Cameras

For the past few years all new studio cameras purchased have been designed for high definition television (HDTV) digital signal origination, but many still are used to feed a standard definition (SD) analog or digital signal to take advantage of the superior quality of the originating HDTV signal. Studio cameras are equipped with zoom lenses capable of approximately 20:1 focal length range. They are mounted on large, heavy, wheeled pedestal mounts. A pedestal mount with or without an operator is capable of dolling, trucking, panning, tilting, and/or zooming, and any combination of the movements. These cameras were originally designed to be operated by an operator standing behind the camera, but today many programs, such as news and game shows, have replaced the operator in the studio with a single operator in a control room remotely operating several cameras simultaneously. The controls for the camera movements are preset in a specialized computer program, allowing each camera to have a series of shot positions preset to change with a touch of a button on the computer. These same cameras are also used on sporting events with zoom lenses capable of as much as a 100:1 focal length range. Sports events cameras are seldom remote controlled, except for

specific shots with cameras mounted in positions impossible or difficult for an operator to occupy, such as behind the backboard of a basketball court. Studio cameras generally produce the highest-quality signals and are the most expensive, except for the higher quality and more expensive specialized electronic cinema (EC) cameras.

Electronic Cinema Cameras

EC cameras fall in the category of multipurpose because they are used both in the studio and in the field. EC cameras use either a much larger CCD/CMOS chip, or create a date stream instead of a video/audio signal, or operate totally in an uncompressed mode. None of the EC cameras are camcorders, since they are designed to feed either a large high-quality record system or a server rather than a portable media recording system (Figure 7.14A).

Field Digital Cameras

The major growth in cameras during the past five years has been in field cameras. As digital circuits assume responsibility for many previous manual functions, as the size decreased, as battery life increases, and as flexibility of operation increases, the field camera takes on a new, higher level of creativity for the operator and director. The increase in resolution and contrast range in field cameras moves them from handy production tools to truly high-quality creative tools. Depending on the attached or built-in recording medium, the signal far surpasses that of an analog camera of the turn of the century. The smaller size and weight allows the camera to be held on a body mount, on the shoulder, or on any number of portable camera mounts. Increased battery life permits longer shooting sessions without changing batteries, and also allows for the use of portable lighting fixtures powered by the camera battery. The flexible operation permits shooting under a wide variety of lighting conditions, instant changing of settings, and utilizing built-in effects and pre-editing functions. Most digital field cameras are camcorders with either built-in recording media, or the ability to attach a system to the camera feeding the signal directly to the attached system. The wide variety of new recording systems is covered in Chapter 8, "Recording." The recording system chosen must match the electronics of the camera, but many field cameras are designed with the flexibility to create an output that varies in line rate, frame rate, digital level, or aspect ratio with a flip of a switch.

Handheld Digital Cameras

As the size of digital cameras decreased, it became apparent that a camera could be designed that could be held in one hand much as a still camera is held. A series of such cameras have been designed primarily for the consumer market, but the quality of the output, especially if the camera uses three chips, makes the miniature camcorder useful for news, television sales, streaming, and prosumer productions. The handheld camcorders are designed with automatic focus, iris settings, white balance, and audio level controls. They come equipped with lenses that zoom in a range from 10:1 to 20:1. Most record on miniDV or Digital8 tapes, but there is a movement for direct recording onto discs or memory cards. At least one model is designed to output directly to the Internet for video streaming.

Box/Pencil Digital Cameras

Box cameras are sub-miniature cameras used for security, law enforcement, surveillance, and special shots to cover sports in hard-to-reach positions. Such cameras are small enough to be mounted on helmets, on race cars, skiers, and other fast-moving sports. A box camera has no viewfinder, all automatic operations, with remote-controlled zoom lens or a single fixed focal length lens. Despite their small size, digital circuits create a reasonably acceptable output for prosumer as well as professional productions. Few come equipped with attached recording media; instead, the camera is hard wired or connected wireless to a recorder at a safe, secure location or has a small transmitter attached similar to a wireless mic transmitter. Such cameras are labeled as pencil cams, doggie cams, and other names to fit their purpose.

FILM CAMERAS

Film cameras can also be differentiated on the basis of sound-recording capabilities. Mechanical or spring-wound cameras cannot run the film at a consistent speed and therefore cannot record synchronous or matching sounds. There are two basic systems by which electronic film cameras can record synchronous sounds: single system and double system. *Single-system* or *sound-on-film (SOF)* recording refers to the recording of synchronous sounds on the edge of the film as it runs through the camera. The camera records images and sounds at the same time. The sounds are recorded by a magnetic sound head, which is 18 (Super-8) or 26 (16mm) film frames ahead of the picture aperture, on magnetic tape striping on the edge of the film. During *double-system recording*, a separate high-quality audiotape recorder records sounds, which can be played back in perfect synchronization with the recorded film images. The camera and sound-recording motors for double-

system recording are usually crystal controlled for extremely accurate and precise recording and playback.

Types of Film Cameras

8mm Cameras

Most super-8mm cameras have reflex viewfinders and are used for recording home movies, but a few professionals prefer to work in this small format as well. Most Super-8 cameras are battery-powered with automatic focus and iris setting. Synchronous sound on some Super-8 cameras can only be recorded at 24 fps. Some sophisticated Super-8 cameras can be used with separate synchronous sound tape recorders. Super-8 cameras use single and double Super-8 film cassettes, which contain 50 to 100 feet of unexposed film.

16mm Cameras

There are many different types of 16mm cameras. Some lack the ability to record synchronous sound, such as spring-wound mainspring-driven cameras that create considerable camera noise and run at imprecise speeds. Cameras that have quiet-running, battery-powered electric motors and film advance mechanisms are called *self-blimped* film cameras. Single-system sound-on-film cameras were once widely used for recording news footage; they have been replaced by ENG (Electronic News Gathering) video camcorders. A few film cameras are capable of both single-system and double-system film recording. Many self-blimped, double-system cameras are driven by crystal-sync electric motors that allow the camera to be used without any cable connection between it and a separate synchronous sound recorder. The absence of a cable connection allows for more freedom of movement and is particularly helpful in documentary situations. The camera operator can move about independently of the sound recordist (Figure 7.15). With the advent of 9:16 aspect ratio, documentary and some commercial and dramatic cinematographers are using specially modified 16mm cameras, a format often referred to as super-16mm, to shoot wide-screen productions by using a wider aperture. The film stock used for super-16 productions is standard 16mm film, but the aperture in the camera exposes light in a path wider than a standard 16mm aperture. The extra space on the film stock is gained by using the sound track area used for standard 16mm films. Since the image size is larger than that of professional video camera chips, the quality is comparable for conversion to HDTV.

Unlike video cameras, whose viewing systems can be electronically controlled, the viewing system

Figure 7.15 16mm film cameras vary from lightweight, spring-wound, non-sync sound cameras to heavier cameras with built-in videotapes, crystal-sync systems, and sound-deadening blimp cases. They may be stripped down with few accessories, or fully equipped with the accessories found on 35mm feature film cameras. (Courtesy of Arri Corp.)

Figure 7.16 35mm film cameras may vary in size from simple handheld to large multi-format with a variety of accessories mounted to facilitate the best possible production. (Courtesy of Arri Corp.)

of a reflex film camera is often quite dim during actual recording. Film cameras are often focused with the aperture wide open (lowest f-stop) prior to actual recording; when the aperture is closed down to the proper f-stop for recording, less light is transmitted to the viewfinder. Some viewing systems reflect only 18% of the light to the viewfinder, and a camera operator must become used to recording under difficult conditions. Sometimes a video tap (an electronic feed from the camera's viewfinder to a videotape deck) is attached to a film camera to monitor the image and to provide immediately viewable results.

35mm Cameras

It is important to note that 35mm motion picture cameras differ quite dramatically from 35mm still cameras. Still cameras run 35mm-width film horizontally through the camera, but 35mm motion picture cameras run the film vertically through the camera, recording film frames that are not as wide as still-frame slides. The aspect ratio and image size of a 35mm motion picture frame are thus quite different from a still-camera frame. A 35mm still-camera frame has a much higher aspect ratio (2.35:1) than video or 35mm motion picture film (1.33:1 or 3:4); thus it is difficult to record complete slides on a motion picture or video camera (Figure 7.16).

Some smaller 35mm motion picture cameras, such as the Arriflex 35-3, are used exclusively for MOS ("mitt out" or without sound) nonsynchronous sound recording. Other, very bulky cameras, such as the Mitchell BNC and Panavision, are used

almost exclusively for studio synchronous sound recording situations. A Panavision camera is frequently used for wide-screen feature film recording in the studio. The latter has an extremely lightweight and portable stepchild, called the Panaflex camera, which is frequently used for feature film work on location. Only extremely high-budget feature films use 65mm cameras for original recording. Most 70mm feature film prints are not made from 65mm camera originals but rather from 35mm original recordings that have been blown up to this larger format. Most 35mm cameras are designed to shoot a variety of aspect ratios, from 4:3 to extreme wide-screen, depending on the design of the aperture or anamorphic lens. Professional motion picture camera recording in 16mm, 35mm, and 65mm sets a very high standard in image quality, which is gradually being rivaled by EC-35 and HDTV cameras.

Camera Accessories

Many cameras have attachable matte boxes or lens hoods that shade the lens from direct sunlight and allow filters to be attached to the lens for color correction or special effects. A frequently used film camera accessory is the *cable release*, which minimizes the vibration to the camera when single-frame images are exposed individually. Another important film camera accessory is a *changing bag*, which is a black, light-tight bag that can serve as a portable darkroom for loading and unloading longer rolls of film wound on open cores.

CAMERA CARE

Cameras consist of extremely delicate instrument parts. They must be handled with great care because they can be damaged very easily. Cameras should be kept clean and dry. Never leave a camera unprotected and exposed to elements, such as rain, sleet, snow, or sand. Never leave a camera unattended or in a hazardous position, where it is likely to fall or be stolen. Always make sure that you have sufficient battery power by charging batteries well before actual recording begins. Nothing is more frustrating than having a group of people waiting around for the batteries to be recharged (Figure 7.17).

If the video camera has a built-in recorder, use the same operating procedures that you would use for a separate VCR (discussed in Chapter 8, "Recording") to avoid having the tape jam within the recorder. Video cameras are even more sensitive to high heat and humidity than film cameras and therefore require shading under intense sunlight, insulation from the cold, and careful use of videotape in high humidity. Digital cameras using solid-state recording media prove to be much more rugged than those cameras equipped with tape decks.

Operating a film camera requires extreme care and sensitivity to every possible malfunction of the equipment. Since film is quite expensive to record, minor mistakes can translate into significant financial losses, as well as reshooting time. Digital and solid-state equipment, on the other hand, are immediately viewable and can be reused.

It is important to develop a checklist of camera operating procedures and to make sure that every item on the list is checked off before recording. First, make sure that the lens is clean and that there are no hairs or pieces of film stuck in the film gate of the camera where the film is exposed to light. On professional film shoots for commercials, the camera lens is usually removed from the camera periodically to check the film gate for hair or debris, since the image must be perfectly clean. If a filter must be placed in the camera or on the lens, make sure that the filter is completely clean so that there will be no spots or marks on the film and no loss of light.

Carefully load the film into the camera and its magazine, and then run the film with the camera and magazine cover open to make sure that it is running properly and not tugging at the film gate, which will cause jittery images. Finally, close the camera and the magazine where the film is exposed and stored, and listen to a properly running and loaded camera. It has a characteristic sound. If this sound changes during actual recording, stop shooting immediately! Something is wrong. The camera should be opened and the aperture area inspected for problems. The film will probably need to be reloaded. Potential problems with a videotape deck also may be determined quickly by listening carefully to the sound of the tape motor and drive movements. The same care should be followed in loading tape, discs, or cards in digital cameras.

SUMMARY

Camera operators must be thoroughly familiar with camera techniques and equipment to provide directors with the best possible visual images from the standpoint of a particular aesthetic approach. A camera operator controls image composition and camera placement by employing four key concepts: essential area, lookspace, walkspace, and headroom. Camera operators also employ the rule of thirds and realist conventions, such as the 180-degree action-axis rule.

Camera operators understand the best position and angle at which to place the camera in terms of camera-to-subject distance and high-angle versus low-angle camera positions. Camera movements alter spatial perspective and are often used to follow performer movements. Pans, tilts, and pedestal and crane movements can be made with a stationary tripod or camera-mounting device. Dollies, trucking shots, and arcs are accomplished using movable camera-mounting devices. Moving camera shots are used primarily to keep moving subjects within

CAMERA CARE

DOS

Keep clean and dry
Carefully clean the film gate with each film load
Clean lenses properly and periodically
Clean filters before each use
Check for proper filter before each take
Protect from elements such as snow, rain, dust, sand, dirt
Check for properly charged batteries
Allow time for adjustment to changes in temperature and/or humidity
Insulate from extremes in temperature
Check for proper film threading by visually watching with an open cover and
    then again by listening with the camera closed

DON'TS

Bump, drop or shake violently
Point a tube camera at a bright light, especially the sun
Leave unattended at ANY time
Leave exposed to public view in a vehicle
Leave tripod or pedestal head with pan or tilt controls unlocked
Expose to high heat, humidity, rain, or salt water
Ignore changes in sound when running
Assume anything

Figure 7.17 All cameras, whether video or film, must be treated as fine, sensitive pieces of expensive equipment. Careful handling requires knowledge of what can harm the camera and how to avoid damaging the camera either inadvertently or through ignorance.

the camera frame or to reveal new information by altering spatial perspective.

Camera operators must understand how lenses function in order to control them. Lenses are curved pieces of glass that bend light in a predictable manner. Lenses help a camera operator control an image's field of view, brightness, focus, perspective, and depth of field. Lenses can be categorized by their focal lengths within a specific video or film format into wide-angle, normal, and telephoto lenses. Zoom lenses allow an operator to manipulate field of view by varying the focal length of the lens. A zoom lens should usually be focused at its longest focal length (telephoto). Varying the aperture, or iris, of a lens changes the amount of light transmitted through the lens. The depth of field of an image, that is, the range of distances in front of the lens that remain in focus, will vary with changes in focal length, aperture, and camera-to-subject distance or focus distance within a specific film or video format.

A video camera contains one or more light-sensitive pickup chips. The camera chain consists of a camera, power supply, sync generator, and a camera control unit. Video cameras can be divided into three basic categories: field cameras, convertible cameras, and studio cameras. Field cameras are lightweight and portable. They can range from consumer cameras to sophisticated and expensive DVCPro or other digital video recording equipment that records the highest-quality images. Digital cameras are growing smaller, use less power, and at the same time produce a higher-quality signal for a lower cost than previous video cameras. The use of videotape in camcorders is being replaced with disc, solid-state circuits, and hard drive recording systems.

Film cameras can be divided into different levels of image quality on the basis of film formats, such as Super-8mm, 16mm, 35mm, and 65mm, which refer to the width of the film in millimeters. Professional film camera recording still sets a high standard of image quality, which is gradually being rivaled by digital video technology.

EXERCISES

1. Use a handheld or shoulder-mounted video camera to follow a person moving around in a random fashion outdoors. Maintain good framing and focus while following this unpredictable action. Move your body and the camera as slowly, smoothly, and deliberately as you can without missing any key action. View the recorded videotape to determine why problems occurred at certain points.

2. Use a dolly-mounted video camera to follow a person moving around in a random fashion within a studio. Maintain good framing and focus while following this unpredictable action. Move the dolly as slowly, smoothly, and deliberately as you can without missing any key action. View the recorded videotape to determine why problems occurred at certain points.

3. Select the best lens settings for each shot designated in a shooting script scene by determining the depth of field that will be necessary to keep the performers safely in focus throughout each shot. Remember that depth of field depends on the camera-to-subject distance, the focal length of the lens, and the aperture or f-stop opening of the lens.

4. Using a digital camera, open the menu and run through all of the possible settings, then set the camera for daylight shooting. Shoot a subject outdoors, then bring the camera under tungsten lights and shoot with the same daylight setting.

5. Record a short shot. Set the camera for a digital effect and then add another shot. Build a sequence with a variety of digital in-camera effects.

6. Handhold a camera while seated in a car or van. Hold the camera away from your body and try to anticipate bumps and changes in the motion of the moving vehicle while shooting subjects moving parallel to the vehicle.

ADDITIONAL READINGS

Bernstein, Steven. *Film Production*, 2nd ed. Boston, MA: Focal Press, 1994.

Burrows, et al. *Video Production: Disciplines and Techniques*, 8th ed. Boston, MA: Focal Press, 2001.

Compesi, Ronald. *Video Production and Editing*, 6th ed. Boston, MA: Allyn and Bacon, 2003.

Elkins, David E. *Camera Assistant's Manual*, 3rd ed. Boston, MA: Focal Press, 2000.

Grotticelli, Michael, ed. *American Cinematographer Video Manual*, 3rd ed. Hollywood, CA: The ASC Press, 2001.

Hodges, Peter. *The Video Camera Operator's Handbook*. Boston, MA: Focal Press, 1995.

Honthaner, Eve Light. *The Complete Film Production Handbook*, 3rd ed. Boston, MA: Focal Press, 2001.

Hummel, Ed., ed. *American Cinematographer Manual*, 8th ed. Hollywood, CA: The ASC Press, 2001.

Lester, Paul Martin. *Visual Communication: Images with Messages*. Belmont, CA: Wadsworth Publishing, Inc., 1995.

Mamer, Bruce. *Film Production Techniques*, 3rd ed. Belmont, CA: Wadsworth Publishing, Inc., 2003.

Mathias, Harry, and Richard Patterson. *Electronic Cinematography*, 2nd ed. Belmont, CA: Wadsworth Publishing, Inc., 1990.

Millerson, Gerald. *The Technique of Television Production*, 13th ed. Boston, MA: Focal Press, 1999.

Musburger, Robert. *Single Camera Video Production*, 3rd ed. Boston, MA: Focal Press, 2003.

Roberts-Breslin, Jan. *Making Media: Foundations of Sound and Image Production*. Boston, MA: Focal Press, 2003.

Samuelson, David. *David Samuelson's Hands On Manual for Cinematographers*, 2nd ed. Boston, MA: Focal Press, 1998.

Vineyard, Jeremy. *Setting Up Your Shots: Great Camera Moves Every Filmmaker Should Know*. Studio City, CA: Michael Wiese Productions, 2000.

Ward, Peter. *Digital Video Camerawork* Boston, MA: Focal Press, 2000.

Whitaker, Jerry. *Master Handbook of Video Production*. Boston, MA: McGraw-Hill, 2002.

Wilson, Anton. *Cinema Workshop*. Hollywood, CA: The ASC Press, 1983.

Zettl, Herbert. *Television Production Handbook*, 7th ed. Belmont, CA: Wadsworth, 2000.

8

Recording

TOPICS FOR DISCUSSION

- How do digital recording systems differ from analog systems?
- What makes up the video signal?
- How does digital video differ from analog video?
- What processes are used in recording film?

INTRODUCTION

Recording good-quality sound and images is extremely important, as poor-quality recordings can destroy the impact of a high-quality production. Some directors feel that sounds and visual images should be almost completely independent of one another so that each component could stand entirely on its own, and others feel that sounds should reinforce accompanying visual images.

Acquiring a basic understanding of media technology increases your ability to control aesthetic variables, whether they are realist, modernist, or postmodernist. If you understand the means by which images and sound are recorded, you can consistently obtain high-quality recordings of the intended production. Visual and aural media are based on digital and analog electronic, magnetic, and photochemical recording processes. This chapter provides an introduction to audio and video electronics, as well as film photochemistry.

ANALOG AUDIO

Analog recording produces a continuously varying magnetic copy of the electrical fluctuations stimulated by the original sound waves. The original sine wave variations of the audio signal are duplicated in sine wave magnetic variations, matching as closely as possible the original signal. Magnetic tape passes over a magnetic sound-recording head, consisting of a magnet with a coil wrapped around it, which carries the electrical sound signal. As the voltage in the electric sound signal fluctuates, the magnetic field through which the tape is passing changes, and the sound signal is recorded on tape. A bias signal (30,000 Hz or above, which is outside the range of human hearing) produced by a bias head aligns the signal to record on the linear portion of the magnetization curve. In the playback mode, the tape is passed over a playback head (in some recorders the same head is used for both recording and playback), which picks up the prerecorded tape's magnetic variations and causes a weak electrical current passing through the magnetic head to fluctuate accordingly. This signal is then amplified; that is, it is increased in strength and intensity so that it can be sent to a loudspeaker, headphones, or another tape recorder.

Audiotape Formats

Audiotape for either analog or digital recording is made up of particles of iron oxide or other metallic substances attached to a flexible support base. Tape formats can be categorized on the basis of two factors: the dimensions of the tape and the form in which it is packaged. Tape dimensions differ in terms of thickness and width. Audio quality generally increases with increasing tape thickness and head width, and the relative speed of the head to tape. The thickness of audiotape is measured in mils (thousandths of an inch). Tape thicknesses vary from 1½ to ¼ mil. Audiotape also comes in a variety of widths, from ⅛-inch to 2-inch. Multitrack analog and digital tape recorders (each track is a separate tape path) require wider audiotape. As many as 64 separate tracks can be recorded on some multitrack machines using 2-inch-wide audiotape (Figure 8.1).

Audio signals in video recording are usually recorded directly on videotape in a variety of formats, which are discussed later in this chapter. Film audio

AUDIO TAPE RECORDER TRACK LAYOUTS

Figure 8.1 The arrangement of audio tracks varies with the type of tape deck and the number of audio tracks, sync, pulse, or time-code tracks that need to be recorded.

may be recorded on a separate ¼-inch audiotape, onto fullcoat film stock, on a portable digital recorder, or directly onto the film itself. In the latter case, the edge of Super-8mm or 16mm film is coated with magnetic material; this is called *magnetically striped film* (Figure 8.2).

Analog Audio Recorders

The enclosures in which tape is packaged and the type of machines on which the recordings are made provide another means of differentiating recording formats. Analog tape can be obtained in the form of cartridges and cassettes, as well as in open reels. Cartridges con-

Figure 8.2 Magnetic film tracks are laid down on the edge of the film if a picture also is recorded on the same stock. If the film is to be used for sound only, the track can be laid down in one or more paths down the middle of film as magnetic fullcoat film.

sist of continuous loops of 1½-mil, ¼-inch audiotape, ranging from a few feet to several hundred feet in length and from a few seconds to several minutes in duration. Cassettes are pairs of small reels encased in a plastic housing. The standard width of cassette tape is ⅛ inch, and the normal cassette tape recorder speed is relatively slow: 1⅞ inches per second. Open reel tape has the advantage that it can be edited (see Chapter 11, "Sound Editing"), runs at higher speeds, and is available in a variety of tape sizes. Cartridges are quicker and easier to set up and recue, that is, to find the specified starting point (Figure 8.3).

Audiotape Speeds

The speed at which an audiotape is driven directly affects the amount of tape that is used and, more important, the quality of the tape recording. In general, faster recording speeds produce better-quality recordings. Analog tape recorders have a speed-control setting that can be adjusted to any of the following speeds: ¹⁵⁄₁₆, 1⅞, 3¾, 7½, 15, **or** 30 *inches per second (ips)*. Professional recordings of live music, if recorded on analog equipment, are usually made at tape speeds of 15 ips or above. Most multitrack sound analog recording is done at a speed of 30 ips. Simple voice recordings are frequently made at 7½ ips or even 3¾ ips.

DIGITAL AUDIO

A digital audio recorder samples or evaluates the electrical sound wave thousands of times every second and gives an exact numerical value to the electrical sound signal for each specific instant of time. The numerical values are coded into a series of on-and-off electrical pulses, known as *binary code*. These are the same types of signals used by computer systems. These electrical pulses are not an electrical copy or analog of the sound wave. The only signal that is recorded is electricity that is either entirely on or entirely off, rather than different gradations of electrical current, as is the case in analog recording.

The values of the recorded digital signal are determined by two factors: sampling and quantization. The analog signal is analyzed by periodically sampling its frequency. The more often the signal is sampled, the higher the quality of the digital signal. The rate must be at least twice the highest frequency to be reproduced. Today the standard sampling rates are 32 kHz, 44.1 kHz, and 48 kHz. In order to determine dynamic or loudness range, assigned binary bits determine how many different discrete audio levels can be recorded. Standards vary from a

Figure 8.3 The common analog audiotape decks are: ¼-inch reel-to-reel, broadcast cartridge, and a standard ⅛-inch cassette deck.

low of 8 bits to a high of 128 bits. In both sampling and quantization, the higher the rates, the better the quality; but at the same time, the cost and amount of memory required increase. (See Figure 8.4.)

Digital recording extends the recordable range of intensities and frequencies and virtually eliminates many other problems inherent in analog recording, such as tape noise, *cross-talk* (two recorded tracks on the same tape interfering with each other), and *print-through* (one layer of recorded tape bleeding through and interfering with another). *Flutter* (an unwanted fluctuation in pitch) is another common analog recording problem. Digital recordings can be duplicated without degradation of the signal and can produce a much more permanent record than analog recording. Fine gradations of analog signals can completely fade away and be lost forever, while a magnetic signal that is

completely *on* or *off* can easily be restored to its original state as the *on*s begin to fade. For these reasons, digital recording has replaced analog recording as the professional audio standard.

Digital Recorders

Today there are four types of digital audio recording media: digital audiotape (DAT), audio-DVDs, CDs, and tapeless systems. DAT recorders operate in two different methods: stationary head (S-DAT) and revolving head (R-DAT) (Figures 8.5, 8.6A and B).

The design and operation of the stationary-head *DAT recorders* are much like analog decks in that a tape is drawn across a head or series of heads, depending upon the number of tracks to be recorded at a set speed. A ¼-inch S-DAT recorder can record up to eight tracks plus sync tracks, and a 1-inch deck can handle up to 32 tracks.

The R-DAT machines borrow from helical videotape technology by mounting the record heads in a revolving drum and wrapping the tape part way around the drum. The heads in the drum rotate in the opposite direction of the tape movement and, as in VCR technology, this movement increases the tape-to-head relative speed, thereby increasing the quality of the recording. There are several different noncompatible S-DAT standards, but most R-DAT recorders are compatible, and because they can be manufactured in relatively small packages, they make ideal field recorders for video, film, and concert recording.

DAT was designed as a professional recording medium, and the two forms have found their niches

DIGITAL SIGNAL

Analog Signal

Digital Equivalent

Figure 8.4 An analog signal is a continuous signal equivalent to the frequency and level of the comparable audio signal. On the other hand, a digital signal is a series of pulses that "samples" the original sound at frequent intervals and then converts those samples to on-and-off digital signals that can be converted back to the original sound.

in the recording industry. R-DAT also has become a back tape format for non-linear computer editors. Although the video is compressed, the R-DAT recording matches the quality of DV, now the most common video recording format.

With the rapid increase in computer memory and the lowering of costs, *tapeless audio recording* will develop and find a place in the industry. Audio is simply fed into a computer and the digitized signal is recorded on one of three recording media: one or more computer hard drives or floppy disks, solid-state random access memory (RAM), or some form of optical disc. The most common form of the latter is a write-once-read-many (WORM) drive, which has a high memory capacity, a recordable compact disc (CD-R), or audio-DVD. With the advent of the Motion Picture Experts Group-Layer 3 (MP3), standard, audio may be downloaded from the Internet onto one of several digital music recorder/players. Each requires a digital signal input from either the Internet or any other digital source, such as a CD. Most of the small portable players play back from either disks or miniature memory chips for up to two hours at a time. It is clear that the question of copyright infringement using such technologies has become a major legal issue. Misuse of MP3 can bring heavy fines, prison penalties, and loss of the use of the Internet. The "free" use of downloading music from the Internet has been replaced with systems charging small fees for each download, a fair and equitable resolution of the problem.

It is possible today to feed a signal directly from a microphone into a computer, add any number of tracks, manipulate the signals in any manner desired, and output the finished signal to a digital format for distribution or playback without ever leaving the digital domain. Once the audio has been digitized, it may be edited as if the audio were a series of symbols in a word processor. The audio can be cut, rearranged, equalized, and mixed in any combination, depending on the complexity of the computer program. Once entered into the computer, the editing process is much more efficient than any other form of audio editing, but all of the audio must be entered into the computer in real time, which may be time-consuming if there is much original material.

Figure 8.5 Digital tape decks operate in either R-DAT or S-DAT format. Digital decks, like analog, can record several tracks simultaneously in any of the formats. (Courtesy of Nagra.)

Figure 8.6A and B Audio may be recorded without using tape by recording directly onto computer floppy disks, hard drive, or into RAM to be converted to another format. Audio can also be recorded directly or as a final format on CD discs. (Courtesy of Studer.)

Digital audio processes have nearly replaced analog processes, but just as magnetic recording replaced electronic disc recording, and electronic disc recording replaced acoustical recording (although the majority of audio recording and processing are now through digital means), some analog audio recording will always be needed.

ANALOG VIDEO

Composite Video Signal

Video cameras transform and transmit visual images by converting light energy into electrical energy. The composite video signal of a visual image can be transmitted along an electrical conduit or wire in a closed-circuit system to a video monitor or a video recorder. The composite (or complete) video signal must be made up of three major components in order to be accurately recorded. The three components are the video signal, synchronization pulses (sync), and control track (CT) pulses.

Video Signal

The portion of the composite video signal that actually carries the voltages that are transformed into picture elements in a monitor and are recorded on a tape deck is called the *video signal*. That signal varies in voltage in direct proportion to the intensity of the light striking the camera tube or chip. In the analog system, it is a constantly changing signal, varying from a fraction of a volt to a maximum of 1 volt (assuming proper levels are being maintained). In a composite color system, the video is more complex because there are three separate color signals combined out of phase, but the basic concept of an analog signal is the same.

Synchronization Signal

In order for a video recorder or monitor to use the electronic signal transmitted from a camera, it must have some reference for the scan and the field rates of the picture. A synchronizing or sync signal, which functions like electronic sprocket holes, is fed either to the camera or generated internally in the camera during recording.

The sync signal is necessary for stable reproduction of the original signal. There are actually two sync signals: horizontal sync and vertical sync. The *horizontal sync signal* controls horizontal scanning and blanking, while the *vertical sync signal* controls the rate of the vertical scanning and blanking. These sync signals are passed along within the composite video signal so that all recipients of the whole signal will reproduce the picture at the same rate and direction as the camera originating the signal.

Control Track Pulse

A video recorder records a pulse signal, called a *control track (CT) signal*, that guides the playback video heads into position to accurately follow or track the signal laid down by the record head at the time of recording. A *servo capstan*, that is, a rotating tape drive cylinder with an accurate motor, varies the speed of the playback so that proper synchronization is maintained. It also moves the videotape through the recorder at the correct speed and ensures that it is aligned properly by the CT (Figure 8.7).

Monochrome and Color Video

Thus far our description of the video process has only described the transmission of black-and-white images. A black-and-white system transmits only the brightness values of light, not hue or saturation. There are several different camera pickup systems for creating color video images. Some use only one pickup chip, and others use two or three. Light entering a video camera is divided into its red, green, and blue components by using color filters. The three-color information picked up by chips is then encoded as two chrominance or color signals, which are called the *I and Q signals*, and one luminance or brightness signal, which is called the *Y signal*.

This chrominance and luminance information is then transmitted to the recording medium, where it is recorded. Light, as explained in Chapter 6, "Lighting," can be analyzed and manipulated on the basis of its three characteristics: hue, saturation, and brightness. Different wavelengths of light are perceived as different colors, or *color hues*, such as red, green, and blue. Color video and film systems are capable of recording and projecting a wide range of color hues. Like our eyes, these systems depend on three basic hues: red, green, and blue, called the *additive color system*. Light can be described in terms of its color saturation and brightness as well as its hue. The saturation of a specific hue indicates its *color purity*, that is, the amount of grayness the color contains. A vibrant but pure color of red, such as on a stop sign, is heavily saturated. In video, saturation is translated into a chroma or chrominance signal. *Brightness* refers to a light's intensity, its lightness or darkness. Bright lights have strong intensities.

In video, brightness is reproduced in the luminance signal. Black-and-white video and film recording devices are only sensitive to the brightness or luminance of a light, not its hue or saturation. Two distinctly different colors may contrast with each other to the naked eye, but if they are equal in brightness, a black-and-white recording depicts them as virtually identical. When recording in black and white, hue and saturation can generally be ignored, since brightness values are paramount. Hue, saturation, and brightness play key roles in video and film

color recording processes. The basic principles of colored light, covered in Chapter 6, "Lighting," provide the basis for the recording processes of both video and film. An NTSC (National Television Standards Committee) video signal reproduces color by keeping the three signals (I, Q, and Y) separate, either by combining them in one signal with each of the components out of phase with each other (the composite system), or by actually using three circuits to keep the signals separate (the component system).

Analog Video Recorders

Scanning Systems

Before discussing the method of recording a video signal, an understanding of scanning systems is necessary. The United States and other countries that use NTSC standards for television use an *interlace system* of scanning to create and to reproduce the picture. Each picture is scanned twice: first the even lines are scanned, comprising one field, and then the odd lines are scanned, making up the second field. The two fields together make up a complete picture that is scanned every 1/30th of a second. Interlace is an efficient system, but it can introduce artifacts or distortions in the picture. Computer systems use a progressive system of scanning. Each frame is created by scanning every line in order to make a complete frame.

Improved modern technology has made *progressive scanning* a preferred system. Progressive systems can scan at the rate of 24, 25, or 30 frames a second. The recording process depends partly on the frame rate of the system in use since the recording and editing systems must match the scan rate and the scan system used. As analog and standard-definition systems are being replaced by high-definition systems, the number of lines and aspect ratios also are changing. The FCC has ruled that 9:16 is the accepted wide-screen standard, and the number of lines may be either 525 or 625 for analog systems, and 480, 720, or 1080 active lines for digital systems. The end result is that there are 18 different combinations of aspect ratio, line rates, and progressive or interlace scan system standards set by the Advanced TV Systems Committee (ATSC) for Advanced TV (ATV) systems.

Helical Scan Recording

All videotape recorders, either analog or digital, now use the helical scan method of recording. Helical scan recorders use two or more video heads, which continuously record electrical video signals. As magnetic tape travels from left to right across the recording heads, the heads rotate in a clockwise

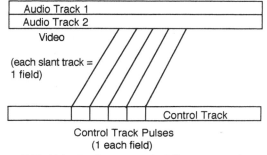

HELICAL TAPE TRACK POSITIONS

Figure 8.7 Helical videotape tracks follow a general pattern of several linear audio tracks, a linear control track, a linear time-code track, and video recorded at a steep angle in slashes across the tape by a video head rotating at a high speed in the opposite direction of tape travel. This method of recording video is necessary for the high head-to-tape speed necessary to record the high frequencies of video.

direction, opposite to the movement of the tape. On a two-head recorder, each time a single head passes over the tape it records a complete field of 262 half-lines of video in a 525-line system. At the exact instant that the first rotating head disengages from the tape, the second head engages it, so that a continuous recording of the television signal is made along the tape by consecutive heads. The passage from one head to the next corresponds to the *vertical blanking period* and is a crucial part of maintaining synchronization. The vertical blanking period is the time when the scan line is dropped to black and cannot be seen as it retraces to start a new scan line. The combined passage of the two heads records a complete frame of 525 lines (Figures 8.8 and 8.9). In a progressive scan system two or four heads alternate, each creating a single frame as they pass over the tape. Instead of alternating scan lines, as in the interlace system, the progressive system scans lines continuously from the top of the frame to the bottom to create a single frame.

The videotape is wrapped around a semicircular drum, and the heads maintain continuous contact with a semicircular wrap of tape around the drum, moving in a downward diagonal direction as they rotate past the tape. Because the recording is made in a slanting movement of the head across the tape, a *helical scan recorder* is sometimes called a *slant-track recorder*. The linear speed of the tape passing the rotating heads in a digital recorder varies from 100mm/second (approximately 250 ips) to 200mm/second (approximately 500 ips). Although the speed of initial recording cannot be varied, a helical scan

TRACK LOCATIONS ON VIDEOTAPE FORMATS

Figure 8.9 Each of the helical videotape formats records its signals in different paths, at different angles, and at different speeds. Each format historically was developed to provide a higher quality at lower cost. As time passes, the newer digital formats will replace the present analog formats.

recorder can be slowed down or speeded up in playback to create slow- or fast-motion action. During slow motion, scan lines are repeated, but during fast motion, some lines are skipped. The image can also be stopped and the action frozen by repeating one recording line or complete field of the video image, called a *freeze-frame*, which is often designated as the pause mode during playback. High-quality ½-inch helical scan recorders and digital recorders allow for special effects creation without sacrificing image quality.

Analog Videotape Formats

Videotape contains iron oxide or other metallic particles that store electrical information in magnetic form. These microscopic particles are attached to a flexible support base, such as cellulose acetate or polyester (Mylar) (Figure 8.10). Videotape recorders (VTR) or videocassette recorders (VCR) are capable

Figure 8.8 The video head of a helical recorder contains from two to eight different recording or erasing heads depending on the complexity of the format.

of both recording and playing back video information on reels or cassettes of videotape. The signals may be either analog or digitized video or audio signals.

The actual recording of video and audio signals is done by video and audio record heads, which also function as playback heads. The *audio* and *video heads* are usually separated from one another because the recording of a video signal requires a complex movement of the head with respect to the videotape, while an audio head remains stationary. Some tape decks record audio signals using rotating audio heads parallel to the video heads, or record digital audio embedded within the digital video signal. An erase head erases previous information stored on the videotape prior to recording new images.

The format, or width, of videotape ranges from 8mm to 19mm. Helical scan recorders use one of the following formats: 6.35mm (¼-inch), 8mm (⅓-inch), 12.5mm (½-inch), or 19mm (¾-inch) videotape. Small-format helical scan recorders use 6.35mm (¼-inch) or 8mm (½-inch) videotape. Digital recorders use tape from 6mm to 19mm wide. A variety of different helical scan systems have been developed for recording on ½-inch videocassettes: VHS, S-VHS, Betacam SP, Digital Betacam, BetacamSX, D-3, D-5, D-9, and digital VHS. These systems all use ½-inch videotape in closed cassettes and helical- or slant-tracking techniques, but the actual scanning of the videotape is sufficiently different so that they are noncompatible systems. As an example, a D-9 recording, which uses a slightly larger videocassette and a different loading mechanism, cannot be played on a BetacamSX machine and vice versa. As of this writing, four tape formats specifically designed for high-definition are available: D5-HD, based on D-5; D7-HD, based on DVCPro; D9-HD, based on Digital-S; and HDCAM, based on Betacam. Some analog and other digital formats are available with upgrades or modifications that allow playing and/or recording an HD signal. Each season new digital and HD equipment are designed and produced, making it difficult to keep up with the latest available equipment. At the same time, many of the present formats may not find a market and may disappear within a year or two of their first appearance.

The digital systems are all high-quality recording systems, but they are also incompatible with each other (except for D-3 and D-5; and Beta, Betacam SP, and Digital BetaSX) or with any other ½-inch system. Some consumer ½-inch videocassette recorders are capable of running at a variety of speeds, so anywhere from one to six hours of recording can be made on the same videocassette. Some videocassette recorders are capable of recording and playing back several different types of television signals, such as NTSC, PAL, and SECAM, using different types of electrical current. When large quantities of video and/or audio material need to be recorded and accessed in a nonlinear manner, computers with maximum digital storage capacities are used. These systems are called servers. (See Figure 8.11.)

High-quality ½-inch analog and digital tapes used for professional recordings allow sufficient

Figure 8.10 Audio and video recording stock is manufactured in a great variety of widths, thicknesses, and magnetic coatings depending upon the purpose for which the tape is intended. The recording media today moves from magnetic tape to disc and on to solid-state media. From top down on the left: Mini-VHS, DVCPRo, Hi8, M-II, BetaMax, BetaSP, Quarter-cam, U-matic, DV. On the right: 2″ quad cart, 2″ quad open real, EIAJ ½″, Type "C" 1″. In front of the reels, a DVD and a 2″ video floppy.

Figure 8.11 A video server that is designed to record and play back digital video/audio cuts on a nonlinear basis. It emulates videotape recorders, cart machines, and video storage systems. (Courtesy of Philips Broadcast Television Systems Company.)

space for a control track, up to four sound tracks, a time-code track, and one video track. One-inch, once the professional broadcast standard, has been replaced by digital and ½-inch formats. Smaller consumer format videotapes can be broadcast when they have been channeled through an image stabilizer, known as a *digital time-base corrector* or *TBC*. A TBC accurately synchronizes the scanning process by changing a conventional analog signal into a more easily controlled digital signal, thus providing high-quality video sync signals (see Chapter 10, "Visual Editing"). Minor variations in synchronization that cause a picture to jitter are eliminated using a TBC, which makes it possible for smaller format recordings to be broadcast directly or dubbed up to better-quality videotape formats.

Videotape Sound Synchronization

Synchronization between sounds and images is very simple to maintain in videotape recording. A single videotape recording machine may be used to record picture and sound elements simultaneously on the same tape. In most videotape recording, on-set or synchronous sounds are recorded on the track located away from the edge of the tape. There is a slight distance separating the points at which the sounds and the picture are recorded on the video-tape, due to the fact that on most types of videotape recorders the video record and playback heads rotate but sound heads remain stationary. During electronic editing, then, the corresponding sound and images must be picked up from slightly different points on the tape. However, since videotape is always played back on a machine that has the same gap between images and sounds, this distance creates no real problem in terms of synchronizing sounds and images. Control track recording (discussed in Chapter 10, "Visual Editing") is an important reference for postproduction editing, although some machines provide another type of reference, called SMPTE time code, which is discussed in Chapter 10, "Visual Editing."

DIGITAL VIDEO

Digital video technology is the same as digital audio, except that much higher frequencies and a greater quantity of recorded material must be handled. The original analog video signal is sampled and quantized, requiring up to 300 MB per second of recorded program, as compared with less than 100 KB per second for digital audio. Higher tape speeds and/or compression of the signal before recording allow suf-

ficient video to be recorded without consuming an impractical amount of tape stock (Figure 8.12).

Signal Compression

The compression process removes redundant or repeated portions of the picture, such as the blue sky or white clouds. As long as there is no change in the hue, saturation, or luminance value, the digital program "remembers" the removed portions, then decompresses and restores them when the tape is played back. This process saves space on the tape, disc, or chip, depending on the recording method. Compression allows a reasonable amount of programming material to be recorded, but the price is a slight degradation of picture quality.

The greater the compression, the greater the possible loss of quality. There are two basic systems now in use: JPEG, developed by the Joint Photographic Experts Group and originally intended for compression of still images, and MPEG, developed by the Motion Picture Experts Group and intended for compression of moving images. Each system offers advantages and disadvantages, and the possibility exists that new and better systems will be developed. Currently there are three MPEG systems: MPEG-1, MPEG-2, and MPEG-4. MPEG-2 was an improvement over MPEG-1, and MPEG-4 originally was written for interactive media intended for consumer use, but later developments have made the system applicable to HDTV and other high-quality and bandwidth-demanding formats (Figure 8.13).

Component Versus Composite Recording Systems

When a standard NTSC video signal is recorded—that is, the entire video signal made up of the three (red, green, and blue) color signals, blanking and sync signals are combined into one signal—it is called the *composite system*. This system allows the video and audio to be recorded, transmitted, and processed as a single signal. All D-2 (explained below) and analog NTSC formats (except S-VHS) are composite signals. Such a system has built-in negative factors that cannot be removed and become obvious in multigeneration editing and recording.

A system that delivers a higher-quality signal has been developed, called the *component system*. In this system the video signal is kept in its original three parts: the luminance signal and two chrominance signals. This maintains the highest quality possible in 525-line (or higher) systems. The negative factor is that a component system requires three of everything: wiring, special switching equipment, and more

DIGITAL VIDEOTAPE FORMATS

DESIGNATOR	DATE INTRODUCED	WIDTH	TAPE SPEED	COMPONENT/ COMPOSITE	TRACKS/SECTORS
D-1	1986	19mm 3/4"	286.588mps 12.74 ips	Component	V,CT,TC,Cue, 4 audio
D-2	1988	19mm 3/4"	131.7 mps 5.85 ips	Composite	V,CT,TC,Cue, 4 audio
D-3	1990	12.7mm 1/2"	83.2 mps 3.7 ips	Composite	V,CT,TC,Cue, 4 audio
Digital Beta	1993	12.7mm 1/2"	96.6 mps 4.29 ips	Component	V,CT,TC, Cue, 4 audio
D-5	1993	12.7mm 1/2"	167.2 mps 7.43 ips	Component or Composite	V,CT,TC,Cue, 4 audio
DV	1995	6.35mm 1/4"	33 mps 1.33 ips 18.3 mps .753 ips	Component	V, 2 audio No CT or TC or cue
D-6	1996	19mm 3/4"	497.4mps 19.9 ips	Composite	V,CT,TC,Cue, 10-12 audio
Digital-8	1998	8mm		Composite	V,CT,2 audio
D-7 DVCPro	1998	6.35 1/4"	33.8 mps	Composite	V,CT,CT 8 audio
D-9 Digital-S	1999	12.7 mm 1/2"	18.3 mps	Component	V,Ct,TC 8 audio
IMX	2000	12.7 mm 1/2"	16.7 mps	Component	V,Ct,TC, 8 audio

Figure 8.12 As of the writing of this text, the formats listed above are in use. Each year new formats are developed and perfected, in some cases replacing earlier formats. Compatibility between formats is rare for digital formats.

complex recording technology. Most digital recorders, except for D-2 and D-3 (discussed below), are component recorders. Despite the incompatibility between all of the digital recording formats, the number and layout of tracks is similar. Each records four digital audio tracks, a control track, a time-code track, a cue track, and, of course, a video track.

Digital Videotape Formats

D-1 was the first industry-accepted digital format. The Society of Motion Picture and Television

Engineers (SMPTE), the organization that sets standards in the visual fields, agreed upon the D-1 standards in 1986. It has become the universal, component digital standard. The signal is recorded on a 19mm oxide tape, offering the highest-quality and most flexible recording system, but also the most expensive. It is capable of recording compressed HDTV signals, but it does not compress standard signals. It is especially useful for multilayering graphics and animation.

D-2 was the second SMPTE standardized digital system, but it is a composite system. It also records

VIDEO COMPRESSION STANDARDS

LABEL	FUNCTION	ORIGINATING ORGANIZATION
H.261 or P64	Compressed video over telephone wires	Int'l Tele/Tele Consultative Comm.
JPEG	Compressed still images	Joint Photo Experts Group & ISO
Motion-JPEG	Edit moving video	Joint Photo Experts Group & ISO
MPEG-1	Compressed moving images, VHS quality	Moving Pictures Experts Group & ISO
MPEG-2	Compressed moving images, B-cast quality	Moving Pictures Experts Group &ISO
MPEG-2+	Edit moving video, Broadcast quality	Moving Pictures Experts Group & ISO
MPEG-3	Undeveloped	
MPEG-4	Video telephony	Moving Pictures Experts Group & ISO

Figure 8.13 In order to record and manipulate high-frequency video signals within a digital format, some method of compressing the signals needed to be developed to avoid requiring tremendous amounts of computer memory. Two basic systems and variations on those systems have been developed, JPEG and MPEG. Researchers constantly work at developing newer systems that require less memory yet maintain the highest quality possible.

on 19mm tape, but it requires special metal tape. D-2 is less expensive than D-1, can be modified to record in the component mode, and is very commonly used by broadcasters. Neither D-1 nor D-2 is practical for use in a camcorder due to the physical size of the tape transport system.

D-3 and *D-5* are compatible systems, even though D-3 was designed as a composite system and D-5 as a component system. Neither system compresses the video, and both use 12.5mm (½-inch) metal tape. D-3 has a four-hour capacity on one reel, and D-5 two hours. D-5 is designed to record HDTV signals when the standards for that format are agreed upon.

Two systems created by competing videotape companies have not received standardization from SMPTE as of this writing. Both are being manufactured and are finding their individual markets. Sony developed *Digital Betacam* and *BetacamSX* to record on the same 12.5mm metal tape stock as the Betacam SP recorder. They are also downward compatible with Betacam tapes. Digital Betacam is also a compressed component system compatible with the D-2 signal, but not the D-2 tape.

In the last decade nearly a dozen digital tape formats have been developed and marketed. *D-6* records on a 19mm tape designed for HDTV. *D-7* (DVCPro)

is one of the professional formats based on the consumer DV 6.35mm format. Others are *DVCAM* and *DVCPro50*. In some cases, depending on the tape deck, the DV formats are compatible. *Digital 8* is the digital version of the Hi8 format and is downward compatible with the 8mm formats. *D9*, or Digital-S, is based on the S-VHS format and in some cases is downward compatible with S-VHS. Tape formats will continue to proliferate until solid-state recording media replace the mechanical tape systems.

Tapeless Video Recording

Video and audio signals may be recorded in digital form without using magnetic tape. Digital pulses may be recorded on random access memory (RAM) chips within a computer. RAM chips are capable of recording as much as 128 MB per chip. With compression, over an hour of video material can be recorded on one chip. The advantages of impressing production information on computer chips are instant access, no moving parts, no maintenance, and no need to shuttle through other information. In addition, there are no physical aberrations, such as dropouts, tracking, or skewing, in digital pulses. There are no problems of compatibility, only possible differences in compression standards between computer programs. Expensive digital tape decks can be replaced by relatively inexpensive personal computers.

Many of the same advantages exist if the digital pulses are recorded on computer hard drives or floppy disks. A hard drive is now designed to hold multiple gigabytes (1000 MB) and can be disengaged from the computer, stored, and moved to another computer. The removable feature provides an advantage if more than one project is assigned to the same computer and for archiving the material. *Write-Once-Read-Many (WORM)* CD and DVD optical discs also offer the same advantages, except that once they are recorded they are not erasable. Erasable and reusable optical discs, called *Direct-Read-After-Write (DRAW),* exist. Prices for professional- and consumer-quality disc recorders have lowered to the point that CDs and DVDs are now an affordable and practical means of recording digital information on permanent or reusable discs.

FILM RECORDING

Basic Photochemistry

Photography uses light energy to transform the chemical properties of light-sensitive substances. Photographic film consists of light-sensitive materials, such as silver halide crystals or grains, attached to a flexible support base, such as cellulose acetate. Silver halide forms an invisible latent image when it is exposed to light in a camera. Light stimulates a chemical change in silver halide crystals, which can only be made visible and permanent by developing the image in certain chemical solutions. The film image appears dark or opaque where it was struck by light and clear where the light energy was not strong enough to stimulate the silver halide crystals. The resulting image is called a *negative image.* It inverts the whites and the blacks of the original scene. A white wall appears black and a black curtain appears white (Figure 8.14).

In order to get a positive image, which reproduces the whites and blacks of the original scene, the negative film must be printed or copied onto another piece of film on a device called a *contact printer.* When the copy is chemically developed in the same manner as the negative film from which it was printed, it reproduces the correct whites and blacks. The bright areas in the original scene are now white and the black areas are black. This method, in which a negative is copied to produce a positive image, is called the *negative/positive process.*

An alternative approach to this two-stage, negative/positive process is known as the *reversal process.*

The difference between negative/positive and reversal film is similar to the difference between snapshots and slides in still photography. Reversal recording is a single-stage process that produces a positive image after one development of the originally exposed film. The negative image resulting from initial exposure is converted to a positive image during several stages of development.

Reversal film produces a positive image immediately. It does not have to be printed to view the original scene, as does negative film. The size and composition of the silver halide crystals in large part determine the overall light sensitivity and graininess of the film stock.

Light sensitivity or film speed is rated in *EI,* which stands for exposure index. The American Standards Association rating, called *ASA* (or EI), or a German standard, called *DIN,* is often printed on the film package. These indices of a film's overall sensitivity to light provide a relative indication of how much light will be required to properly expose a specific film. Slower films, with lower numbers, require more light than those with higher numbers (Figure 8.15).

The term *graininess* refers to the size and visibility of particles in the film. A grainy image is one in which these particles are readily visible, and a fine-grain image is one in which they are not. Faster film stocks, which are more sensitive to light and therefore have higher EI numbers, generally have more visible grain structures than slower films, producing grainier images.

The size of the grain in the image can affect its *resolution* and *sharpness,* terms that refer to image clarity. Slower film tends to have higher resolution and sharpness than faster film. The size of the film grain also will determine the film's latitude, or the ability to reproduce a wide range of reflected light. Better films are able to reproduce an image in lighting with a 100:1 contrast range, but a standard video camera pickup tube has an effective contrast ratio of 30:1 and a video camera chip has a ratio of 50:1. If there is a wide range of dark to light reflecting objects in a scene, a video camera will not record as wide a range of greyscale as film. Many neutral tones will be recorded as completely black or completely white, rather than some shade in between. In film, a full range of tones may be recorded. The effect of contrast ratio on lighting and scene design is discussed more fully in Chapter 6, "Lighting," because the difference between lighting for film and video is important (Figure 8.16).

Color Film

We have so far considered only the recording of different brightness levels of light on black-and-white

BLACK AND WHITE FILM STOCK LAYERS

Emulsion
Base
Antihalation Backing

EMULSION RESPONSE TO LIGHT & PROCESSING

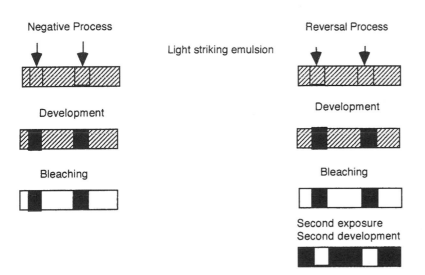

Negative Process

Light striking emulsion

Reversal Process

Development

Development

Bleaching

Bleaching

Second exposure
Second development

Figure 8.14 Black-and-white film consists of a layer of light-sensitive material, a flexible base, and an antihalation backing layer to prevent light from reflecting back through the base to the emulsion. Reversal film requires additional processing to create a positive image rather than a negative image.

Figure 8.15 The label on a film canister provides all of the information the camera operator or director of cinematography needs to adjust the camera and make exposure decisions. The EI numbers indicate the film speeds for daylight or tungsten lighting, and the other numbers indicate the type of film (the top can is 7278, a high-speed black-and-white reversal film sock), batch numbers, inventory, and order numbers.

film. Color film responds to different hues and saturations of light, as well as different levels of brightness. A color-film emulsion consists of a multilayered

suspension of light-sensitive particles and color dyes attached to a flexible support base, such as cellulose acetate. When light enters a camera, it strikes three different layers of color dyes and light-sensitive particles. These layers are sensitive to blue, green, and red light, respectively. Light first strikes the blue-sensitive layer, where only the blue light affects the particles and dyes. The other colors of light then pass through this layer and a yellow filter, which removes excess blue light, before striking the green- and red-sensitive layers. These layers are sensitive to blue light, as well as their own wavelength bands. The blue-sensitive layer thus records the blue component, the green-sensitive layer the green component, and the red-sensitive layer the red component of white light (Figure 8.17).

Film Exposure

Film is exposed inside a lightproof mechanism called a *camera body*. A basic film camera consists of a *lens*, which focuses an image on the film; a *viewfinder*, which allows the camera operator to see the image that is being recorded; a *film feed and take-up mechanism*, which supplies film to the exposure area and

LUMINANCE CONTRAST RATIOS

The difference between the brightest subject and the darkest subject for which detail can be seen is the contrast ratio. Different media are able to reproduce detail under different maximum contrast ratios.

Television camera tube	20:1
Television camera CCD	30:1 - 50:1
Average film	250:1
Human eye	1000:1

Different lighting situations provide a variety of contrast ratios.

Foggy day	10:1
Average daylight	130:1
Bright day	800:1
White object next to black velvet lit by bright direct sun	2000:1

Figure 8.16 The contrast ratio of a medium determines how wide a variation in light reflectance values that medium can reproduce without losing either the brightest or the darkest values. Any attempt to reproduce a subject or frame containing a higher contrast range than the medium is capable of reproducing will result in either muddy dark areas or flared-out white areas.

rolls it up after it has been exposed; a *motor*, which drives the film through the camera; a *rotating opaque shutter*, which rapidly opens and closes to expose each frame of film; an *aperture*, which determines the dimensions of the frame that is exposed; *pressure plate*, which holds the film flat against the aperture to ensure good focus; a *pulldown claw*, which intermittently grabs film sprocket holes or perforations to advance the film for each single frame or still photograph at the aperture; a *speed control*, which determines how many individual frames will be exposed each second; and a *run/stop button*, which turns the camera on and off.

Motion-picture film is perforated at regular intervals so that it can be driven intermittently by a camera and a projector. This intermittent movement allows a single frame of film to be held stationary while a rotating shutter opens up and allows light passing through the lens to expose the film. A projector uses the same mechanism to project recorded images through the lens onto a screen. The feed and take-up mechanisms push the film continually through the camera, while the claw pulls the film at the aperture. Film is constantly pushed and pulled through a 16mm camera at a rate of 36 feet per minute, or through a 35mm camera at 90 feet per minute. Normal sound speed exposes 24 frames per second (fps) in 35mm, 16mm, and Super-8.

The camera shutter and claw must be synchronized so that the shutter stays open when the claw disengages the film and retracts behind the aperture plate. At this point the film is stationary in the aperture. Sometimes it is held stationary by a device known as a *registration pin*, which holds the film in

COLOR FILM EMULSION LAYERS

Blue-sensitive Emulsion
Yellow Dye
Green-sensitive Emulsion
Magenta Dye
Red-sensitive Emulsion
Cyan Dye
Antihalation layer

Base

Figure 8.17 Color emulsion film layers alternate specific color-sensitive layers with opposite color-dye layers. This produces a negative reproduction of the image exposed to the camera. Color reversal film, like black-and-white reversal film, requires additional layers and processing. Like black-and-white film, color film stocks come in negative or reversal processes, and a variety of light sensitivities and contrast ranges.

firm registration, that is, it holds it very steady when it is not being pulled by the claw. The shutter must be closed when the registration pin retracts and the claw engages the film to advance it, or the film images will blur as they pass the light in the aperture.

The speed control allows the camera operator to alter the frames-per-second speed of the camera. Film recorded at speeds above 24 fps will reproduce images in slow motion when it is projected or played back at normal sound speed (24 fps). Camera images recorded at fewer than 24 fps will produce fast motion. Thus slow and fast motion are produced during actual recording in film, unlike video recording, which always occurs at 30 fps. Increasing the film recording speed also changes the synchronized shutter speed and affects the amount of light exposing the film. Faster recording speeds produce more rapid shutter speeds and less light reaches each frame during exposure, since the duration of each exposure is reduced. To compensate for these changes in exposure, the lens must be adjusted so that more light passes though it and strikes the film when the camera speed is increased.

Motion Picture Formats

Motion picture film, which is exposed to light inside a camera, is available in a variety of formats or film widths, including 8mm, 16mm, 35mm, and 65mm. These distinctions between various formats refer to the width of the film in millimeters. The width of the film affects image size and quality, as well as the cost of supplies and equipment. There used to be two 8mm formats: standard 8mm and Super-8mm. Super-8mm cameras record images that are 50% larger than those of standard 8mm cameras. Standard 8mm is now virtually obsolete. All subsequent references in this book are to Super-8, which is sometimes used for home movies, as well as for some independently produced, low-budget films.

The 16mm format has been widely used for professional recording of industrial, educational, governmental, and documentary films, as well as some commercials and low-budget feature films, but now videotape productions are competing for the same markets. Some resurgence in the use of 16mm film has come from new developments in Super-16. Such films are easily transferred to a video format for 16:9 wide-screen broadcast on television and cable. Network-level commercials and television programs are recorded in 35mm, as are most feature films. Some feature films are recorded on 65mm film, which is then printed onto 70mm film, with the added 5mm being the width of the sound track area, for projection in large, specially outfitted theaters. Other 70mm film prints for projection are enlargements or blowups from original 35mm recordings (Figure 8.18).

COMMON FILM FORMATS

Figure 8.18 Virtually all professional film is now one of three formats: 16mm, 35mm, or 70mm. Super-8 film is still available for consumer use, and special larger feature film formats also are in use, along with IMAX, a wide-screen format, film for specific purposes.

Film stocks are available in different film lengths and loading arrangements or configurations. Super-8mm film comes in a lightproof cartridge and is exactly 8mm wide. It is normally packaged in 50-foot lengths, which lasts for 2 minutes and 46 seconds. Sixteen-millimeter film is available on daylight spools, which contain 100, 200, or 360 feet of film. It is also available on plastic cores, which simply provide a firm center on which the film is wound but do not protect the edges of the film from light. Film that comes on a core must be loaded in complete darkness. The standard length of 16mm film cores is 400 or 1,200 feet. One hundred feet of 16mm film, when exposed at 24 fps, runs for 2 minutes and 46 seconds. Thirty-five-millimeter film comes on cores in standard lengths of 100, 200, 400, and 1,100 feet. Ninety feet of 35mm film runs for 1 minute at 24 fps.

Film stocks differ in terms of their perforation or sprocket-hole sizes and placements. Super-8 film has sprocket holes on only one side of the film, while 16mm films are available with single- or double-sided perforations, which are called *single-perf* and *double-perf*, respectively. Magnetically striped 16mm film has audio track in place of one row of sprocket holes. Thirty-five-millimeter film is always double-perf.

Film Sound Synchronization

Synchronous sounds match their visual sound sources and are usually recorded at the same time as the corresponding visual images. Many different systems have been developed to synchronize recorded visual images with recorded sounds. Early in the 1950s, portable ¼-inch reel-to-reel tape recorders had the capacity to record a sync signal that allowed them to be used in conjunction with a motion picture camera. Today, separate digital recorders are used since they run to absolute speed and do not have to be connected to either the video or film camera to maintain sync, as long as the film camera receives a sync signal from a crystal control or the video camera is locked to its sync signal. This allows the separate recording of sounds that are synchronous with their corresponding pictures.

Single-System Film Recording
There are basically two different systems of synchronous sound film recording in common use today: single system and double system. Single-system recording, as shown in Figure 8.19, puts sounds and images on the same piece of film; usually, the sound is recorded on the edge of original motion picture film.

This technique is called *sound-on-film* (SOF). As a general rule, 35mm film is not used for sound-

Figure 8.19 Cameras that record sound simultaneously with the exposing of the film are called single-system cameras. The sound-recording head must be located apart from the aperture, since the two cannot be physically located at the same place within the body of the camera. The sound head on a 16mm single-system is located 28 frames ahead of the aperture. This separation must be taken into consideration when shooting original film to edit without transferring the sound to another medium.

on-film or single-system original recording. Sixteen-millimeter magnetic sound-on-film is recorded 28 frames ahead of the picture gate or film aperture. (Sixteen-millimeter optical sound-on-film is 26 frames ahead of the picture. Optical sound is created by exposing the edge of the film to light.) Super-8mm sound-on-film is recorded 18 frames ahead of its corresponding pictures. These standard intervals allow the film driven through a camera to change from an intermittent movement at the film aperture, where a rapid series of still frames are recorded, to a continuous movement over the sound-recording head. The same 28-, 26-, or 18-frame advance of sound ahead of the picture is standard in most 16mm or Super-8mm film sound projectors.

Single-system sound is commonly used for exhibition purposes. The final film prints marry an optical or magnetic sound track with their corresponding pictures on the same piece of film.

Single-system recording is used extensively in small formats, such as Super-8mm film recording. Editing problems arise from the fact that the sounds are always a specific number of frames ahead of the corresponding pictures. Sound-on-film yields an initial sound recording that is decidedly inferior in audio quality to a double-system film sound recording. If SOF is to be edited, either it must be shot with pauses in the voice track, so edits can be made without losing portions of the sound, or the sound track must be dubbed to a separate piece of film for double-system editing.

Double-System Film Recording

In double-system synchronous sound recording, the sounds and images are recorded on separate materi-als. (This approach is normally used for production and editing but not for final projection.) Rather than recording sounds directly on the edge of the film during production, an independent tape recorder is used, which can record and play back sound in exact synchronization with the corresponding images. The system for synchronizing the recording of the separate sounds and pictures depednds upon both the camera and recoder's speed controlled by crystal sync (Figure 8.20).

Cable sync refers to the use of an electrical cable, which connects the camera to the tape recorder like an umbilical cord. The cable carries a 60-cycle-per-second sync signal, called *Pilotone*, which is generated by the camera. The Pilotone is recorded on the audiotape by a special sync head on the audiotape recorder. *Crystal sync* allows the camera and the tape recorder to be physically separated. This can be a distinct advantage because it increases the flexibility, mobility, and independence of sound and picture recording machines and operators, who are otherwise linked by an umbilical cable. For crystal sync, the speed of the camera is controlled by a crystal oscillator so that the film is driven at a precise speed of 24 fps. The analog audiotape recorder uses a separate crystal oscillator to place a sync signal on the audiotape, so that its original recording speed can be duplicated during playback and a digital recorder runs true to speed. Digital audiotape recorders also can be synchronized to film cameras using sync signals or the stable recording speed of a digital recorder to maintain sync.

Slating

Creating a common point where separately recorded elements of sound and picture match is called *slating*. In video recording this generally is not necessary since the audio is recorded directly onto the same tape as the picture, but it does provide a means of accurately logging scenes as they are shot. Normally a slate, sometimes called a *clapstick* or *clapboard*, is used for this purpose in motion picture production. The clapboard consists of a piece of wood with a hinged arm that makes a clapping sound when it strikes the bottom portion of the clapboard. This device produces a loud, recorded sound that can be matched to the corresponding visual image of the closing arm (Figure 8.21).

In the absence of a clapboard, a person can call out "Slate!" followed by a sharp handclap. If the separate sound and picture tracks are perfectly matched at the beginning of a shot, the editor can be reasonably sure that the entire cable or crystal-sync recorded shot will maintain synchronization. Slating is also used to identify the project title, director, and shot and take

Figure 8.20 The camera and sound recorder stay in synchronization because they are both running with internal crystal sync.

Figure 8.21 After both the camera and recorder have reached speed, a production assistant holds the clapboard in front of the camera. The board contains information indicating the shot and take numbers, director and camera operator's names, and other information critical to the shot. Once speed has been reached, the assistant snaps the clapper shut smartly, creating a sharp, intense sound and a visual record that will be used to sync the film and sound track later during the editing process.

numbers during single camera film or videotape recording. This information is written on the chalkboard surface of the slate or clapstick, and read aloud at the beginning of each camera shot. Thus each take is fully identified on the film or videotape and the audiotape.

Some film cameras are designed for documentary shooting in situations where the use of a clapboard is impractical. They have an electronic means of providing a reference synchronization point for editing, called an *automatic slate*. At the beginning of each camera take, the first few frames (usually the first eight) of picture are flashed or fogged with a small light inside the camera, and a signal that is separate from the Pilotone is sent to the tape recorder either by cable, if cable sync is being used, or by radio transmitter, if crystal sync is being used. This signal triggers a clap alarm, which creates an audible tone, known as the *bloop*. The proper flash frame of the picture can then be matched to the bloop at the beginning of the shot for editing synchronization.

Another development in slating is the *electronic clapboard*, which generates a tone that is fed to the camera and recorder and illuminates a continuously running SMPTE time code visible to the camera and recorded on the edge of the film or on the videotape.

SUMMARY

Understanding the technology that makes audio, video, and film recording possible helps us to obtain better-quality images. Recording media are based on digital, optical, electronic, and photochemical recording processes. Film uses a subtractive mixing process, with cyan, magenta, and yellow filters embedded in different layers of the film to subtract different color wavelengths from a white light source to produce a variety of colors on a screen. A video camera records and transmits visual images electronically using an additive color process of mixing red, green, and blue light to produce color video.

Film contains silver halide crystals, which form a latent image when they are exposed to light. These latent images become visible through chemical processing. There are two basic film development processes, negative and reversal, which are analogous to color prints and slides in still photography. Film generally has a wider contrast ratio than video. Some film stocks, such as color negative, can record and differentiate brightness levels that are more than 100 times as bright as the darkest object in a scene, yielding a contrast ratio of 100:1 or 200:1. The maximum contrast ratio in video is usually 30:1 or 50:1.

Videotape and film recording materials are available in a variety of formats. Among helical scan recorders, VHS videotape recorders use ½-inch (8mm) videotape, while others use 6.35mm (¼-inch), 8mm (⅓-inch), 12.5mm (½-inch), or 19mm (¾-inch) videotape. Digital recorders use tape from 6mm to 19mm wide. Super-8, 16mm (which includes Super-16mm), 35mm, and 65mm film require different cameras and recording equipment. Some ¼-inch videotape formats, such as DVPro, MiniDV, and DV CAM, reproduce high-quality images, but digital videotape recorders, from D-1 through D-9 and newer formats, provide even higher quality images.

Four tape formats specifically designed for high definition are available: D5-HD, based on D-5; D7-HD, based on DVCPro; D9-HD, based on Digital-S; and HDCAM HD, which provides the highest-resolution videotape images. IMAX provides the highest-resolution film images.

The aesthetic use of recorded sounds demands an understanding of recording devices and their selection. Audiotape is available in a variety of formats in terms of tape sizes (widths and thicknesses) and tape enclosures, such as audiocassettes. An analog audiotape recorder converts the electrical audio signal to magnetic pulses stored on magnetic recording material. Digital recordings consist of a series of on-and-off pulses, and are less susceptible to recording problems, such as cross-talk, print-through, and fading, than are analog signals, which record the entire electrical signal. Tape speed directly affects the amount of tape consumed, and higher speeds generally produce higher-quality recordings. In general, the larger the tape size and the faster the speed, the better the quality of the recorded sound.

There are several ways to obtain sounds and images that synchronize with each other. In videotape recording, sounds and images are recorded on the same piece of videotape. A control track, which is a recording of the sync signal, allows the videotape to be played back at the same speed at which it was recorded and synchronizes the playback head with the recording on the videotape. Film sound and images can be recorded on the same piece of film, which is called single-system sound-on-film (SOF) recording, or they can be recorded on separate sound and picture mechanisms, which is called double-system film sound recording. Double-system recording allows for more editing flexibility than single-system. Slating refers to the placement of a common starting point on the picture and sound recordings. It is also used to identify the project title, director, and shot and take numbers during single-camera recording.

EXERCISES

1. Find a CD recording and an audiocassette recording of the same music. Transfer both to a computer audio program and compare the frequency response and dynamic range. Then compare the two to the original CD recording for the same characteristics.

2. Record the same scene on videotape and film. Then transfer the film to a videotape that has the same format as the originally recorded videotape.

Compare the two videotape images in terms of image contrast, hardness and softness, and resolution.

3. Record and view several network television commercials. Try to determine which ones were originally recorded on videotape and which ones were recorded on film and then transferred to videotape. Do some commercials use the apparent contrast and hardness or softness of videotape and film to good effect? When might you prefer to use videotape or film for original recording?

4. Light a still life with subjects of various colors and reflectance values. Using both a film still camera and a digital still camera mounted side-by-side, shoot at least 10 exposures with various f-stop and shutter speeds. (The digital camera has equivalent shutter speeds.) Note the differences in the results.

5. Find at least two recorders that use different videotape formats, one analog, the other digital. Feed the same signal to both. Play back on the same or equivalent monitors to compare the differences.

6. Using the tapes in Exercise 2 above, dub each tape onto an equivalent recorder: the analog to an analog recorder, the digital to a digital recorder. Then play back on equal monitors and compare the results.

ADDITIONAL READINGS

Alten, Stanley. *Audio in Media*, 6th ed. Belmont, CA: Wadsworth, 2002.

Amyes, Tim. *Audio Post-Production in Video and Film*, 2nd ed. Boston, MA: Focal Press, 1999.

Ascher, Steven, Edward Pincus, and Carol Keller. *The Filmmaker's Handbook: A Comprehensive Guide for the Digital Age*. New York: Plume, 1999.

Collins, Mike E. *ProTools: Practical Recording, Editing, Mixing for MusicProduction*. Boston: Focal Press, 2001.

Derry, Roger. *PV Audio Editing from Broadcast to Home CD*. Boston, MA: Focal Press, 2000.

Hartwig, Robert L. *Basic TV Technology: Digital and Analog*, 3rd ed. Boston, MA: Focal Press, 2000.

Huber, David Niles. *Modern Recording Techniques*, 5th ed. Boston, MA: Focal Press, 2001.

Laycock, Roger. *Audio Techniques for Television Production*. Boston, MA: Focal Press, 2001.

Rumsey, Francis, and Tim McCormick. *Sound Recording: An Introduction*, 4th ed. Boston, MA: Focal Press, 2002.

Tolputt, Bob. *DV Filmmaking*. Boston: Focal Press, 2001.

Watkinson, John. *MPEG Handbook*. Boston, MA: Focal Press, 2001.

Watkinson, John. *The Art of Digital Audio*, 3rd ed.

Boston, MA: Focal Press, 2000.

Watkinson, John. *An Introduction to Digital Audio*, 2nd ed. Boston, MA: Focal Press, 2002.

Weis, Elizabeth, and John Belton. *Film Sound: Theory and Practice*. New York: Columbia University Press, 1985.

Wilson, Anton. *Cinema Workshop*, 4th ed. Hollywood, CA: American Society of Cinematographers Holding Corporation, 1994.

Yale French Studies. Special issue on "Sound in Film," 60, 1980.

Zettl, Herbert. *Video Basics,* 3rd ed. Belmont, CA: Wadsworth, 2001.

9

Design and Graphics

TOPICS FOR DISCUSSION

- What are the aesthetic choices of graphics?
- What are the elements of design?
- How do composition factors affect graphics?
- What are graphic applications in digital productions?
- How is scene design used in digital productions?

INTRODUCTION

Almost every object that human beings create reflects the product of a conscious design that organizes spatial forms. Graphic design involves the creation and coordination of many different production elements, including sets, properties, costumes, and performer makeup. It also involves computer-generated titles, backgrounds, and objects. Graphic designers rely on basic design principles, such as design elements, color, and composition. These basic design elements fulfill the requirements of a design, whether the designer uses a pen, pencil, paintbrush, or a computer-graphics application. Computer graphics programs have been written specifically for newscasts, election returns, costume and scene design, and animated sequences. Designers put these principles into practice when they approach specific production problems from the following aesthetic perspectives: realism, modernism, or postmodernism. This chapter examines aesthetic approaches to graphic design, principles, and applications. The chapter concludes with a consideration of the overall integration of graphic design with other production components, such as lighting, performance, and visual and sound recording.

AESTHETIC APPROACHES

Realist Design

A realist design simulates an existing setting, location, or graphic format. Although a realistic set may be filled with objects and furnishings that one would expect to find in such a place, emphasis is placed on the illusion of reality, not necessarily the depiction of reality itself. Maintaining basic principles of spatial perspective and proportional size are extremely important in realist design, since they help to sustain an illusion of reality. Sets are often constructed out of lightweight materials that give the impression of being real but are much easier to construct and move around than actual objects. Virtual sets and backgrounds are created or stored as computer files to be used on command and at the will of the director. Such virtual sets may take the form of interiors, exteriors, space, or any location within the imagination of the creative staff of the production. Realist designs are rarely defined by their supposed fidelity to nature or reality alone. Almost every realist design that has emotional impact has some degree of subjective stylization. A realistic setting, title, or illustration should convey a psychological impression that reinforces the central theme of a drama or the central message of an informational program. It can reflect warmth or coldness, tension or relaxation, simply by virtue of the colors, lines, and shapes it presents. It is even possible for a realistic setting to reveal a specific character's emotional state through the feelings that the design conveys.

Modernist Design

Modernist designs are much more abstract than realist designs. The subjective feelings they arouse and the subjective impressions they convey are rarely tied to actual experience or production efficiency alone. Modernist artists usually have much freer rein to explore specific design elements or subjective impressions for their own sake. A designer may decide to call attention to textures, shapes, lines, and colors themselves. Visual innovations often stem from such formative experiments, which can be incorporated into more conventional narrative, documentary, or instructional programs. Innovative television programs and films by many experimental artists have shown how a formative or modernist approach to scenic design can break down conventional illusions of reality by ignoring spatial perspective and using highly artificial, stylized sets, backdrops, and lighting, such as those used on the *Entertainment Tonight* program.

Postmodernist Design

Postmodernist designs leave much of the visual perception to the imagination of the viewer. Graphics, color, and movement can be juxtaposed in a series of apparently unrelated images. Postmodernist designs often mix a variety of design styles drawn from different genres and historical periods. For example, the settings in the film *Who Framed Roger Rabbit* (1988) suggested 1940s Los Angeles in a semi-realist way until the timeless, garish cartoon world of Toontown collided with the live-action world. The production design in *Chinatown* (1974) limited the color blue to appearances of the main theme, water, in 1930s Los Angeles, while pastel colors and art nouveau designs were reminiscent of the 1930s in the 1980s urban setting of the television series *Miami Vice*. Postmodernist designs sometimes appeal to the emotions and often are difficult to analyze or categorize, just as postmodernist paintings and writings are difficult to place in traditional categories. A blend of classical and modern, traditional and contemporary, elite and popular patterns and combinations of colors and textures can serve as the basis for postmodernist designs.

PRINCIPLES OF DESIGN

A designer works with three basic principles of design: design elements, color, and composition. The ways in which these elements are selected and combined determines the nature and success of the design. The selection of design elements must support the themes, plots, and characterizations of a drama or the central message of a nonfiction production. Their use conforms to one of the three aesthetic approaches discussed above as well as the following basic design elements.

Design Elements

The artist's design elements are line, shape, texture, and movement.

Line

Line defines the form of a design. An independent line can be straight, curved, or spiral. Edges are lines formed by shapes or objects that overlap each other, such as a foreground door and background wall. Lines can be repeated to create parallel lines or concentric circles. They create a path or direction of movement for the eye. Converging parallel lines create an illusion of depth or spatial perspective, for example. Straight lines are more dynamic than curved lines and circles. They create a strong sense of directional movement. Smooth curves and circles communicate a smoother, softer feeling of more gradual movement. Sergei Eisenstein's famous "Odessa Steps" sequence in *Potemkin* (1925), for example, associates straight-line diagonals with the merciless, advancing Cossack soldiers, and curved lines or circles with the defenseless women, children, and students who are attacked on the steps.

Shape

A combination of lines creates a shape. An infinite number of different shapes reflect specific objects, but some common, recurring shapes with which all designers work are circles, squares, rectangles, triangles, ellipses, trapezoids, octagons, and hexagons. Shapes can carry symbolic meaning. They can be repeatedly used in conjunction with specific people or settings to evoke specific themes. In the film *Ivan the Terrible* (1942), Eisenstein used circular shapes surrounding Ivan to connect the circular shape of the sun to the symbolic meaning of Ivan as the "Russian sun king." Basic design elements often reinforce specific themes.

Texture

Texture provides a tactile impression of form. Texture can be real or represented. Real textures are revealed by directional light, which creates shadows and modeling on a nonsmooth surface. Represented textures, such as granite, marble, or wood grains, have smooth surfaces that create a tactile impression. The texture of a surface affects our perception of depth. A rough texture with heavy shadows provides a greater sensation of depth than a smooth, flat surface. A heavily textured material used in drapes or costumes can create a richness that relates to a theme of opulence, splendor, or decadence. Texture, like shapes, can create a sense of space that affects our emotions and relates symbolically to the major themes of a story.

Movement

Movement can be real or imaginary. The movement of performers on a set indicates real movement, while the illusion of movement stimulated by a series of still drawings or stationary backgrounds appears imaginary. In design, imaginary movement is just as important as real movement. The illusion of movement can be enhanced by the use of parallel diagonals in a design, for example. It can also be limited or reduced by the use of verticals and horizontals. Specific shapes and lines, such as spirals, concentric circles, and radial designs, can generate significant movement in a static frame. Transference can take place between real or imagined movement and otherwise stationary objects. A simple figure placed against a pulsating background will appear to dance or vibrate itself. A moving background can transfer the illusion of movement to a stationary figure placed in front of it. Movement throughout a stationary image is carefully controlled through changes in color, shape, space, and direction that guide the eye through a design.

Color

The three aspects of color of primary importance to a designer consist of color harmony, color contrast, and the emotional or symbolic effect of color.

Color Harmony

Various relationships between color pigments on a two-dimensional color wheel in large part determine the degree to which specific colors will harmonize with each other. A two-dimensional *color wheel* is a series of different colored chips or samples arranged in a circle from colors that are cool (short wavelengths of light), such as violet, blue, and green, to colors that are warm (long wavelengths of light), such as yellow, red, and orange. Traditional color judgments indicate that colors distant from each other on the wheel harmonize better than close colors, which tend to clash with each other. Several harmonious colors for sets and costumes can be selected by laying an equilateral triangle or square on top of a color wheel and using the colors at the

points. As the triangle or square is rotated, the group of harmonious colors changes.

Color Contrast

Different colors help separate objects in a scene through their mutual contrast. If two objects or shapes did not contrast with one another, they would appear as one object or shape. Contrast can help us perceive spatial depth. If specific colors of foreground and background are different, we will perceive their separation and hence spatial depth. Adjacent colors tend to interact. If you place a gray object against different colored backgrounds, it will appear darker or lighter depending on the color and brightness of the background. A particular hue takes on a completely different feeling depending on the hues that are adjacent to it. Complementary colors of the same intensity should not be placed next to each other, unless the intense contrast is intentional.

Maintaining brightness and contrast between different lines, shapes, and masses is extremely important when designing graphic images for television and film. A television graphic designer cannot rely exclusively on color contrast, since a television program may be received in either color or black-and-white. Adjacent colors should have a gray-value brightness contrast of at least 30%; that is, each object or shape should be 30% brighter or darker than the one next to it. Brightness contrast between different shapes and objects can be determined by using a gray scale (see Figure 9.1). A *gray scale* consists of a sequential series of gray tones from white to mid-gray to black. Pure white has virtually 100% reflectance and video white approximately 90%, while pure black has 0% and video black approximately 3%. The midpoint on the gray scale is about 18% reflectance, that is, about 18% of the light falling on this shade of gray is actually reflected back to the eye. In order to maintain adequate brightness contrast, dark letters and shapes should be placed on light backgrounds, and vice versa (Figure 9.1).

Emotional Response to Color

Most designers believe that a general distinction can be made between warm colors and cool colors in terms of their emotional effect on an audience. Colors such as reds, oranges, and yellows create a sense of warmth in a scene. A romantic scene lit by firelight and surrounded by red, orange, and yellow objects on the set uses these warm colors to enhance a romantic mood. Caution should be used with reds and yellows in video recording, because video noise can occur in these colors on repeated generations of an analog videotape. Colors such as blue and green, on the other hand, are often considered to be cool

Figure 9.1 A gray scale chart contains 19 specifically designed chips ranging from TV-white to TV-black on two strips. The center chip is pure black. This chart provides a standard against which a technician may adjust a video camera for maximum quality under the lighting conditions present.

colors. They are sometimes used to enhance a sense of loneliness or aloofness in a character, or a general mood that is related to a lack of human as well as physical warmth.

Cool colors tend to recede, while warm colors tend to advance. For example, pure hues of greenish yellow, yellow, yellowish orange, orange, and orangish red tend to advance and call attention to themselves, while pure hues of violet, red violet, blue, and blue-green tend to recede. Warm colors can convey a mood of passion or action, while cool colors tend to reinforce a sense of passivity and tranquility. The colors of sets, costumes, and graphic images must be selected with an eye toward their visual prominence, whether they recede or advance, as well as the degree to which they contrast with other colors. Colors that are repeatedly associated with specific objects, people, and settings can take on symbolic or thematic meaning. The red dress of a character in a drama can be used to signify sensuous passion. This color might contrast with the cool green or blue colors associated with a competitor for the affections of a male character.

Cultural Response to Color
Color symbolism also varies with different cultures. For example, the color white (or lack of color) to Japanese may signify mourning, but for Western culture white often signifies purity and hope. The same color may have different connotations depending on its use in a specific film or television program. The color yellow may mean cowardice, sinfulness, or decay, yet it also can carry the meaning of spring, youthfulness, and happiness. Both blue and green

also carry various meanings depending on people's cultural backgrounds. The use of color must be carefully considered based on the expected or targeted audience and their cultural background and traditions.

Composition

A designer organizes basic design elements by using principles of composition within the limitations of the visual frame. These principles can be applied to any visual design problem, including computer graphics and the arrangement and selection of sets, props, furniture, and costumes. They are concepts employed by designers in many other fields as well.

Balance
A design is balanced when there is an equal distribution of visual weight on each side of an imaginary center line bisecting the image. Balance or equilibrium enhances unity and order. There are at least four different types of balance: symmetrical, asymmetrical, radial, and occult. *Symmetrical balance* consists of a mirror image of one half of a design in the other half. Identical but reversed elements are arranged on either side of the axis line, which seems to cut the design in two. *Asymmetrical balance* does not have completely identical elements or mirror reflections on either side of the axis line, but the weight or size of the elements on both sides is nonetheless equivalent. Asymmetrical balance permits a higher degree of variation and viewer interest than symmetrical balance. In *radial balance*, two or more similar elements are placed like the spokes of a wheel about a central point.

This creates a strong sense of motion or movement around this point, while preserving balance. *Occult balance* is a sense of equilibrium achieved through the placement of unlike elements. Balance is intuited without reliance on conventions or rules. There is usually a strong sense of movement and a dynamic quality to the design (Figure 9.2A).

Perspective
Perspective refers to the arrangement of various elements to draw attention to the most important aspect of the image, which is called the *focal center*. A common focal center is the performer, but more abstract aspects of a frame can also function as focal centers. Designers rely on a number of basic principles of perspective, such as proximity, similarity, figure/ground, equilibrium, closure, and correspondence. All of these principles are based on the common ways in which our eyes and minds attempt to organize visual images (Figure 9.2B).

Proximity

Objects placed near each other form common groupings. Conventional wisdom has it that graphic information should be grouped into common topics within the frame for greater intelligibility. It is unwise to try to pack too much information into a single graphic image. A second graphic frame is usually required when another topic is introduced or there is a great deal of information to convey about a single topic (Figure 9.2C).

Similarity

The perception of similarity between shapes and objects in a frame provides another means by which graphic images can be organized. Objects with similar shapes, sizes, colors, and directions of movement are united into common groups. Any deviation from this similarity, such as a runner moving in the opposite direction from the pack or a red object in the midst of green objects, draws immediate attention on the basis of its lack of similarity (Figure 9.2D).

Figure/Ground

Figure/ground refers to the relationship between backgrounds and foregrounds. Our eyes try to organize visual images into background fields and foreground objects. Some visual illusions are ambiguous, and we can alternate the foreground and background to create different shapes and objects from the same picture. A corporate logo or graphic marks that consist of letters and words, such as Eaton Corporation or PlayMakers Repertory Company, combine white and black letters that reverse figure and ground. The reversal in the PlayMakers' logo suggests a rising curtain that is consistent with its theatrical subject matter. Symbols and signs that use figure/ground relationships can be effective means of gaining audience attention and communicating ideas (Figure 9.3A).

Equilibrium

Another way in which our eyes try to organize graphic images is through a principle of equilibrium. An image in equilibrium is logically balanced and ordered. Equilibrium can be based on natural scientific laws, such as gravity or magnetic attraction, as well as a balancing of object weights and sizes on either side of a center line in a frame. This organizing principle reflects a well-ordered, logical universe. When images defy a sense of balance or accepted physical or scientific laws, they are in disequilibrium, which can arouse interest but also cause distracting confusion (Figure 9.3B).

Closure

Viewers have a natural tendency to try to complete an unfinished form, a principle that is called *closure*. An open form is ambiguous and leaves some questions unanswered. A partially hidden form can still be identified because we expect good continuation of a form off-screen or behind another object, but this is a projection of our need for closure onto the image. A designer can frustrate or fulfill our desire for closure by completing graphic forms or leaving them partially incomplete. The former seem stable and resolved, while the latter seem unstable, although they sometimes stimulate creative and imaginative impressions (Figure 9.3C).

Emphasis

Brightness and contrast, size and placement, and directionality are devices that help create emphasis. Generally, a bright object attracts attention more readily than a dark object. Our eyes are drawn immediately to the brightest part of a design. However, if the image is almost completely white, emphasis can be achieved by using contrasting darkness for an object. Objects in contrasting colors can create emphasis. Since warm colors advance and cool colors recede, emphasis can be created by using contrasting reds, oranges, or yellows for important objects.

The size or dimension of an object and its placement within the frame can also create emphasis. In general, large objects attract more attention than small objects. However, if most of the objects in an image are large, then a single small object is emphasized by virtue of its deviation from the norm. The placement of objects in a frame can also create emphasis. Closer objects are usually more prominent than distant objects. If several objects are grouped together, the one that is set apart acquires emphasis through variation and contrast. An isolated, individual object can be singled out from a group and thus be emphasized. If the single object outside the group is also different in size, brightness, or color from the members of the group, that emphasis is reinforced. One of the most common forms of directional emphasis is created by the use of converging parallel lines that direct the eye to a specific object. These lines enhance the illusion of perspective and depth at the same time that they add emphasis. The lines can be formed by natural objects, such as a row of trees or a road leading to a house, for example. Many different lines and shapes can direct the eye to various parts of the image, focusing attention in the desired direction.

EXAMPLES OF VARIOUS FORMS OF BALANCE

Symmetrical

Asymmetrical

Radial

Occult

A

PERSPECTIVE

B

PROXIMITY

C

SIMILARITY

D

Figure 9.2 (A) Graphic designs may be laid out in a variety of patterns. They may be symmetrical (exactly balanced on each side of the frame), asymmetrical (balanced visually on each side of the frame, but not exactly matched), radial (a pattern balanced around a central figure), or occult (without any obvious balance or symmetry) (B) Forcing perspective in a graphic design develops a feeling of depth along the Z-axis (leading in and out of the frame—toward and away from the viewer), which does not actually exist in a two-dimensional medium. A design appears to have three dimensions by making some objects look larger while others appear smaller, or by appearing to converge toward the background. (C) One way of graphically indicating that a group of objects belongs together is to group them close together in an obvious pattern. The cylinders appear to belong together, and the boxes do not. (D) By grouping similar objects together in an obvious pattern, any other object, even if similar, that is not in the pattern will appear to move away from or at least not belong to the similar grouping.

X-Y-Z Axis

The three-dimensionality of reality is created in either a video or film frame with a two-dimensional reproduction. In order to give the impression that the picture represents the 3-D world, an understanding of how the three dimensions relate to the frame is

necessary. The movement or composition along a line running from left to right or vice versa is considered the X-*axis*. Any movement or composition running from the bottom to top, or vice versa, is considered the Y-*axis*. The Z-*axis* does not actually exist in a two-dimensional medium, but it can be depicted or

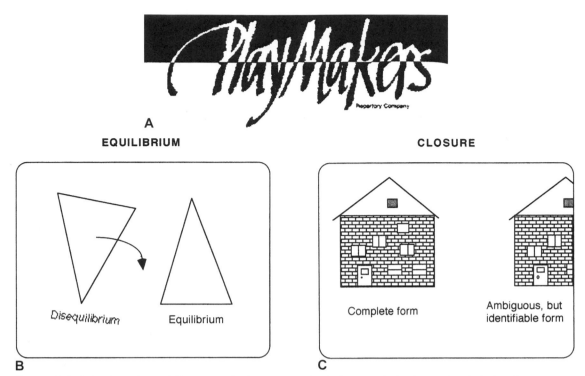

Figure 9.3 (A) A figure/ground illustration. The design conceals which part is the background and which is the foreground by alternating black and white within the type and the background. (Courtesy of the PlayMakers Repertory Company.) (B) A triangle or other object with a broad base indicates a graphic arrangement of equilibrium giving the arrangement a stable, firm graphic appearance. An arrangement with a smaller bottom or an object leaning without any visible support gives the audience a feeling of being off-balance or very unstable. (C) The psychological condition of closure actually arises from an ambiguous or incomplete graphic that is designed to allow the viewer to fill in the rest of the picture through prior or common knowledge. A single house by itself will appear to be just that, a single house; but a row of houses may be depicted by only two houses, one on each side of the frame only partly visible. The viewer will fill in the rest of the houses and assume that there are more houses out of sight on each side of the frame.

created through the use of compositional arrangements within the frame. If objects are arranged at an angle, instead of straight across the frame, or a series of objects diminish in size as they rise in the frame, a Z-axis is created. To avoid boring or static pictures, efforts should always be made to create a Z-axis in each sequence.

Readability

The size and amount of detail in an image affects *readability*, which refers to the ease of deciphering and comprehending graphic images. The size of a typeface or style of lettering, for example, is an important determinant of how easy it is to read a graphic image. Type of extremely small point size is usually avoided in video production because small titles are difficult to read on a film or television screen. *Point size* refers to the height of letters; the higher the point size, the larger the letter. (The text you are reading is in 10-point type.) Lettering sizes smaller than 1/15 of the full picture height should be avoided in television graphics (Figure 9.4).

MINIMUM TYPE SIZE

This type is less than 1/15 the height of the frame.

This type is too small for normal video graphics

This type is 1/15 the height of the frame

This type is larger than 1/15 the height of the frame

The video frame is 3 units high, 4 units wide—the smallest type should be larger than 1/15 the height of the scanned frame, 3/15 or 1/5 of a unit.

Figure 9.4 In television production, partly due to the relatively low resolution of a home television receiver, and partly because some of the audience may be watching on a small-screen receiver, graphic material in type form should not be smaller than 1/15th of the scanned height of the graphic.

Graphic artists also avoid finely drawn lettering and *serifs*, which are delicate decorative lines that are often difficult to reproduce. Because of the limited size, resolution, and sharpness of television images, boldface type is recommended for titles and subtitles. Plain backgrounds give prominence to foreground titles and lettering. A highly detailed or multitoned background is distracting. Good contrast between foreground and background tones and colors is essential for legibility. When titles are keyed over live-action images, bright lettering should be used, preferably with some kind of border, drop shadow, or edge outline, which gives greater legibility and three dimensionality (Figure 9.5).

Image Area

An important determinant of composition in visual graphics is the aspect ratio or frame dimensions of the recorded and displayed image. As noted earlier, frame dimensions vary in television and film. The aspect ratio, or proportion of height to width, of standard television images is 3:4 or 1.33:1. The aspect ratio specifications for HDTV is 9:16 or 1.85:1; projected film images vary somewhat in terms of their aspect ratios, from 1.33:1 to 2:1 (Figure 9.6).

A standard 35mm still-camera film frame has an aspect ratio of 2:3 or 1.5:1; digital still camera aspect ratio is 3:4. Graphic images must be composed for specific formats and aspect ratios. If an illustration is produced in an aspect ratio other than 3:4, as shown in Figure 9.6, some of the information recorded on the sides of the frame will be cut off by the narrower aspect ratio of the video camera, or additional background material will need to be added to fill the frame.

When HDTV images are viewed on a 3:4 standard television receiver or monitor, the viewer will either not see a portion of the image on both sides of the frame, or the signal will need to be broadcast in letter-box frame. *Letter-box framing* refers to a widescreen image shown in its full width, but a narrow

COMPARISON OF FRAME RATIOS

4:3 (1.33:1)
Academy Standard
Television, 35mm, 16mm,
and S-8mm film formats

3:2 (1.5:1)
35mm Slide format

16:9 (1.77:1)
HDTV format

(1.85:1)
American Widescreen
format

(2.21:1)
Vista Vision
format

(2.36:1)
70mm Full Aperture
format

Figure 9.6 If 35mm photographic slides are converted to standard video or used on a television program produced in the NTSC standard, the photographer must remember that not all of the slide will be visible on the video screen. The 35mm slide is wider than either a 35mm film frame or the video frame, and a small border at the top and bottom of the slide will also be lost from scanning and reproduction. Motion pictures shot in any but the Academy Standard 3:4 ratio will have to be reproduced on standard television by leaving a black stripe across the bottom and the top of the frame, or by losing portions of the film frame on each side of the video frame. The losses are none, or much smaller, if broadcast on the HDTV 9:16 aspect.

UNCLUTTERED BACKGROUND

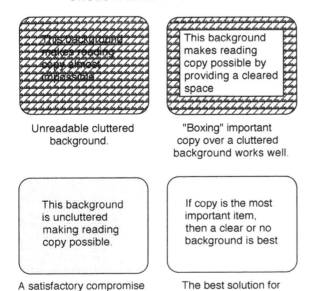

Unreadable cluttered background.

"Boxing" important copy over a cluttered background works well.

A satisfactory compromise is an uncluttered background

The best solution for clarity is no background

Figure 9.5 Any type or important graphic should not be framed in front of a busy background or a background with many small elements. If such a background must be used, the graphic can be framed within a plain box, by defocusing the background, or increasing the lighting contrast so that the important graphic will stand out and be clearly visible.

band of black across the top and the bottom of the frame fills in the areas that are not included in a wide-screen production. At one time letter-box was considered an unacceptable method of showing wide-screen productions, but with the advent of HDTV it is not only acceptable but has become fashionable, with commercials being produced intentionally in letter-box format.

Scanning or Full-Aperture Area

The *scanning area* is the full field of view picked up by the video camera. The *full-aperture area* is the equivalent in film of this area. It refers to the entire field of view recorded on an individual frame of film.

If a graphic illustration or title card is shot live in the studio rather than created as a computer-generated graphic, then it must be framed in the camera so that it is slightly larger than the actual scanning or full-aperture area; this ensures that the edges of the card do not appear in the frame. The scanning area should be about 1½ inches inside the outer edge of a 14-foot 11-inch or 11-foot 8-inch illustration or title card.

Essential Area

The *essential area* of the frame is the safe recording portion of the frame. Graphic information is placed within the essential area, so that it will not be cut off by somewhat overscanned TV receivers or film projector apertures. (Home TVs usually reproduce less than the full camera frame because the horizontal scanning is expanded.) The essential area of the video camera should allow at least a 10% border within the scanning area so that there is no possibility of eliminating essential information. If a graphic image falls within the essential area, an artist can be confident that all key information will be safely recorded and projected.

GRAPHIC FUNCTIONS

Graphic functions can be divided into two categories: digitally created and physically created. In studio, this includes the creation of scenery, props, and backgrounds. Costume design focuses on the creation of costumes for performers, while makeup enhances or changes the facial features and physical appearances of performers. Graphics and illustrations focus on the arrangement of letters, symbols, and visuals within the frame and the creation of complete backgrounds or virtual settings. All three of these aspects of graphic design must be coordinated with one another to effect a consistent and unified approach to all elements that appear within the frame.

Graphic design has three basic functions in a dramatic production: to establish the time, place, and mood; to reflect character; and to reinforce specific themes. A historical time period and setting must be easily identifiable. Costumes, sets, props, and titles denote a specific time and place at the same time that they reflect a specific style or mood. The mood or atmosphere results primarily from the abstract, emotional aspects of design elements and principles. Specific colors and shapes create an emotional mood that can reveal character and reinforce themes. The idea that you can tell a great deal about people from where they live and what they wear can be applied to scenic design. A cold, formal setting or costume reveals a great deal about a character, as does as a warm, relaxed setting or costume. The opening titles warn the audience of the mood, genre, and often the time and location of the production.

GRAPHIC DESIGN

Graphic design, like scenic design, is concerned with structuring pictorial content. Graphic images should be closely tied to overall scenic design, including sets and costumes. For example, the red titles and sepia-toned still photographs (black-and-white pictures with an overall reddish-brown color tone) at the beginning of *Bonnie and Clyde* (1967) foreshadow the violence and bloodshed to come and establish the 1930s setting of the film through costuming and props in each photograph. A good graphic design organizes visual information so that it can be efficiently communicated to viewers. Graphic designs organize many different types of information, including lettering and illustrations. Titles are often the first images presented on a videotape or film, and they must set a context for what is to follow. Graphic titles and illustrations answer questions about who, what, when, where, why, and how or how much. Graphic images often convey information more directly than speech and live-action images. They can boil down complex ideas into simple concepts, which are represented by shapes, words, or numbers. Titles and illustrations can clarify the ideas inherent in more complex, live-action images and speech.

Principles of Graphic Design

The best titles often are very simple. Trying to convey too much information at one time produces ineffective or unintelligible messages. Each image should convey one general thought or idea. Everything presented within that image must contribute to a central theme. A complex array of statistics can often be boiled down to a simple graph or chart. Titles and subtitles that clarify visual information or give credit to contributors must be clear and concise. Good titles and subtitles do not crowd the image, yet title size is often used to convey their relative importance. Simple images are generally more intelligible images. They eliminate confusion and frequently have great aesthetic and emotional impact.

Types of Graphics

Graphics can be divided into two different categories on the basis of their placement and use during production: on-set and off-set graphics.

Off-Set Graphics

Off-set graphics are generated somewhere other than with the live studio camera in the same studio as the production. They may come from a title card, computer-generated image, videotape, or a digital image fed directly into the switcher from a computer.

Computer Graphics

One of the most promising applications of computer technology to film and television production is computer graphics. The advantage of computer graphics systems, like that of the character generator, is that the images do not have to be recorded by a camera and individual frames can be digitally stored. CGs and graphics applications offer a wide range of fonts, font sizes, colors, and backgrounds. Movement, such as crawls, rolls, or digital transitions, is limited only by the particular model of computer. In addition, since the files are stored digitally, they can be called up and used immediately. A large number of files can be entered in advance of a production for insertion at the proper time and place (Figure 9.7).

Figure 9.7 A character generator (CG) is a relatively simple computer graphics machine designed to create lines of type, including numbers, and simple color graphics backgrounds or lines of type to be keyed over other video frames. (Courtesy of Scitex Digital Video.)

A variety of hardware and software systems are currently available for use in video and film production. Most systems allow the operator or artist to control all of the elements of graphic design, including line, shape, and color. Images can be created directly on the screen, using a light pencil, stylus, mouse, or keyboard. The artist can select and control various lines and shapes, as well as image size, color, and placement on the screen. It is also possible to use a stylus to trace a hand-drawn sketch or outline so that it can be computer manipulated and stored in disk form. Some computers have *frame-grabbers*, which allow a single video frame from a camera or VCR to be manipulated by the computer. Some computer software allows graphics programs to be integrated with animation programs to create apparent motion. Images can be placed in disk storage and accessed at any time. A graphics computer that has a standard NTSC video signal output can be fed directly to a VCR or a switcher.

Partially due to convergence, a graphic designer must diversify to learn and use many skills and techniques handled in the past by individual operators. Now a designer must be familiar with all aspects of the field, including basic artistic principles (the same in either analog or digital), typography, photography, motion pictures, video, audio, animation and visual effects (VFX), and Web technology. Basic concepts of design are unaffected by digital technology. The designer still must conceive and develop ideas, and understand graphic principles and solutions, as well as composition, despite the wide scope of tools for exploring graphic concepts faster, cheaper, and over a wider range of solutions.

Graphic Applications

There are two basic types of graphic applications: bitmap and vector formats. Bitmap applications include Photoshop, Painter, and CorelDraw. Bitmap images are made up of a fine grid of individual pixels. Each pixel may be a different color. The combination of pixel color intensities in red, green, and blue will give the desired color, just as the screen on a video monitor provides many different colors from the combination of different intensity of the red, green, and blue guns in the CRT. In order to produce a graphic in bitmap, the application provides a series of tools to modify or edit the arrangement of pixels. Some of the tools are paint brush, pencil, airbrush, cloning, color adjustment, masks, filters, and the ability to build layers with different objects in each unique layer. Bitmap graphics may be as simple as a single frame of type, or as complex as the removal of wires and an unwanted building in a science fiction motion picture like the *Matrix* series (2002-2003).

BITMAP FORMATS

PICT   (Apple Picture) Used only for R-G-B files

BMP   (Windows Bitmap) Used only for R-G-B files

TIFF   (Tagged Image RGB & CMYK or File Format) indexed color Widely used for print. Can be compressed without loosing data

JPEG   (Joint Photographic Experts Group) Best for photos, especially Internet. Compression can reduce file size but with some loss. Should not be multi-compressed.

EPS   (Encapsulated Postscript) Reserved for vector files

GIF   (Graphics Interchange Format) Used only for Web projects

Vector applications include Illustrator and Freehand. The vector graphic is determined by connecting strategically placed points on lines. Moving the lines at the point contact creates mathematical formula determining the shape of the figure. The line may be connected, forming a shape that may be filled with color, textures, or gradients among other aspects. Each object is an individual item in the frame. The curves created by bending the lines into forms are called Bezeir curves. Text can be converted to vector files and shapes and may be grouped and locked together. Layers and filters are available to build special forms and images. Vector files tend to be smaller than Bitmap files.

Type/Font Measurment

- Points (pt) = type height
- Pica = Column width
- Leading = Space between lines
- Kerning = Space between letters
- Dots per inch (DPI) = Resolution
- 12 Points = 1 Pica
- 6 Pica = 1 inch
- 12 pt type = 1/6 of an inch high type
- 72 pt type = 1 inch high type

Typography

The type fonts in computer graphics are based on historical terms spacing used in the print industry. The measurements are points (pt), pica, and inches. 12 points equal 1 Pica. 6 Picas equal 1 inch. So-12-pt type in the print word is 1/6 of an inch. 72 pt is 1 inch. But a computer screen is not necessarily the same size as a graphic printed from that file. Experience leads the designer to know the point size of their fonts, but the sizes are relative to everything in the frame. Computer graphic artists use pts for type size, Picas for column width, and inches for resolution. (dpi) dots per inch. The space between lines is called leading, and the space between letters if adjusted is called kerning.

Searching the Internet

Browsers are applications that provide a means of searching or "surfing" the Internet. Browsers find a page by looking for that page's unique URL (universal resource locator). Once found, it displays that page on the screen using the HTML (hypertext markup language) instructions contained on that page. Depending on the complexity of the page the page will appear instantaneously unless there are complex or moving graphics included. Additional software like QuickTime or RealPlayer may be needed to translate video or Flash for animations. The two major browsers are Netscape and Internet Explorer.

Hypertext Markup Language (HTML)

HTML code is invisible to the viewer of a Web page, but the code is buried within the page file, providing the instructions for the background color, font size, and object positioning in the frame. The code as written appears confusing, but is very logical. Each line is preceded and followed by a "tag" that tells the browser how the line should be displayed. HTML may be written directly using text editors or by using a WYSIWYG (What You See Is What You Get) program like Dreamweaver or GoLive. Graphics for the Web are prepared in an image editor like Photoshop or a layout program like Quark Express or Freehand. Flash and ShockWave programs create animation and sound files to be embedded in a Web page. The speed at which a viewer can download a Web page is dependent on the size of the files and the method the viewer uses to download from the Internet. A 56K modem will be very slow, but any of the broadband systems will download files much more quickly.

Interactivity

Interactivity is a relationship between the computer and the operator. Everything we do on a computer is a form of interactivity since the operator tells (asks) the computer to respond with some kind of an action visible on the screen. Websites offer extensive interactivity with the operator given the opportunity to explore, modify searches, and gain access to files. The Web designer needs to know how to create hyperlinks that connect one page, file, or source with another. The process of creating hyperlinks varies with the application used to create the link text. In essence the application is told to "link" and given an URL as the next item in the link. Java and JavaScript are two leading languages designed to add interactivity to Web pages. Special items such as roll-over buttons, image maps, games, and animated texts may be programmed with a Java application. Other applications such as QuickTime, MP3, Windows Media Player, and RealAudio are used to compress sound and video files to be streamed for Web distribution. Streaming allows a continuous flow of information on the Web to be downloaded and stored on the receiver's computer drives.

Multimedia

Multimedia is the creation of audio and video and graphic programs distributed on a permanent medium rather than on the Internet. The technology used to create multimedia is similar to that of Web pages. The major difference is between the restricted bandwidth of Web pages and the much less restricted bandwidth of CD-ROMs and DVD systems. Multimedia programs produced for distribution on CDs are limited to the playback capabilities of individual computers. DVD multimedia programs deliver full color, motion, and 5.1 surround sound in uncompressed forms. Multimedia programs are produced using video and audio editing applications like Final Cut Pro, Media 100, and Director with animation and graphics added through After Effects and other graphic applications. Editing programs for multimedia are constantly expanding their capabilities and at the same time becoming simpler to operate and cheaper to own.

The primary advantages of computer graphics systems are savings in time and convenience. In preproduction use, storyboards can be quickly and efficiently generated, and then modified immediately prior to actual production to mirror changes. Hard copies can then be printed for camera operators and other members of the production team. During production, illustrations such as charts, graphs, and drawings can be generated quickly and used immediately. Computer-generated graphics provide the background information for weather forecasts. Titles and lettering can be corrected immediately and then added to images to clarify the information they contain. All of this information can then be conveniently stored and accessed during production without using a camera. Images can also be modified efficiently and easily during production. While sophisticated computer graphics systems are still very expensive, low-cost systems, such as those available with many home computer systems, can be inexpensively purchased and integrated into a television production facility.

On-Set Graphics

Set furnishings, props, costumes, and performer makeup are not completely independent elements in the production process. Elements of scenic design interact with each other and many other areas of production to create an overall visual impression. The most important interactions are those between scenic design and each of the following: lighting, performer movement, and camera and microphone placement. Important set elements, such as key props, can be emphasized by lighting them more brightly than other elements. The texture of a rough surface can be accentuated with side lighting, which creates textural shadows in the surface indentations. The color of set elements can be drastically altered by using colored lighting. A colored surface can only reflect wavelengths of light that are present in the light that illuminates it. Different lighting-contrast ratios and lighting styles can enhance a specific mood or atmosphere inherent in the setting.

The most commonly used types of on-set graphics are handheld cards, photographic blowups, and three-dimensional graphic set pieces. Handheld cards are images that a performer holds up to the camera during a scene. The talent controls the timing and placement of this type of graphic illustration.

Still photographs can be blown up or enlarged so that they provide a convenient background or backdrop on the set. Such photographs should have a matte rather than a shiny or glossy surface, so that they do not reflect a great deal of light, and they should be positioned so that no glare or reflection is directed toward the camera lens. Three-dimensional structures placed on the set for illustration purposes are called *graphic set pieces.* A graphic set piece could be an item to be demonstrated, such as a piece of machinery, or an art object. Most on-set graphics can be scanned or shot and recorded ahead of time so that the framing can be precise and the camera is not tied up with a static shot unless it is necessary for the talent to handle the graphic or be part of the action involving the graphic.

Camera cards are usually placed on an easel, which is an adjustable display platform or graphics stand (Figure 9.8). The lights on the easel, which illuminate the card, are normally placed at a 45-degree angle from the card's surface to minimize light reflection in the camera lens. When the cards are attached to the easel by rings, they can easily be flipped, while maintaining perfect registration for the camera.

It is also possible to zoom in to different elements on a card or photograph. This adds dynamic movement to static images. Dissolving from one

GRAPHIC STAND

The stagehand stands behind the stand and drops each graphic on cue from the floor manager

Lamps mounted 45 degrees from the surface on each side with barndoors to control the light

Graphics mounted on stiff board with holes punched to match the rings on the stand

Sturdy, stable base and support

Figure 9.8 A graphics stand is a handy tool to use in the studio to shoot graphics mounted on a stiff board. The lamps should be adjustable to prevent unwanted reflections, and the graphics should be stacked with the first on the bottom and the last on top. All of the boards are held at the top, and they are dropped to the stand one at a time on cue from the floor manager.

Figure 9.9 Keystoning is the effect created by shooting a graphic at an angle rather than straight on. The closer edge of the graphic will appear to be larger, and the farther edge will appear smaller when in reality they are the same size.

card illustration to another is another common technique. The camera should record a card or illustration directly head-on to avoid keystone distortion. *Keystone distortion* exaggerates the size of the top, bottom, left, or right side of a card when the camera positioning is slightly off dead center (see Figure 9.9).

A section of the studio wall that is painted blue or green as the background for a weather report is commonly used as a graphic set piece in television news production. The weather board allows various weather maps and figures to be chroma-keyed behind the weather reporter. A chalkboard on which the talent can write or draw with chalk is also a graphic set piece. During elections, tally boards are entirely digital in operation.

Lettering and Titles

Graphic images can be divided into two additional categories, titles and illustrations, on the basis of the nature of the images themselves. *Titles* are various forms of lettering that either accompany illustrations and live-action images or are presented as written text. They are created electronically on devices called a *character generator* or *graphics generator*. *Illustrations* are visual images, such as charts,

graphs, and pictures. They can be hand-drawn, photographed, or produced with the aid of computer graphics equipment.

Lettering and titles are used to introduce the name of a film or television program and to list the credits or names of people who have contributed in some way to the production. The opening titles of a program are called a *title* or *credit sequence*.

Another common use of titles is to clarify live-action images. Subtitles or name keys are titles keyed in the bottom third of the video or film frame, indicating the person or place being shown. Finally, lettering and titles can be presented as pure text, that is, without any other visual accompaniment (Figure 9.10).

Figure 9.10 To identify key performers the name is typed on the character generator and then keyed over the MCU of the performer below his or her face but high enough in the frame to be visible by all viewers.

Textual materials are used to convey written information in the form of electronic newspapers, advertising, or financial statements.

Credit or Titles

Credit and title sequences present an opportunity for creative, abstract expression on the part of a graphic artist. They are carefully designed to communicate the central message and feelings of a film or television program. The opening credits or title sequence offer the audience an introduction to the basic subject matter of the program. It must arouse the audience's interest, excitement, and curiosity. Titles should integrate well with overall scenic design. Graphic design and lettering styles should be appropriate to the overall subject matter.

Illustrations

Illustrations are drawings, photographs, graphs, charts, diagrams, and maps that provide visualizations of abstract concepts. Charts, graphs, diagrams, and maps are often used to display trends or to unravel complicated ideas or relationships inherent in statistical data. Illustrations can be used redundantly as an accompaniment to verbal descriptions, or independently to add information that cannot be as effectively presented through the written or spoken word.

Photographic Illustrations

Still photographic illustrations, such as slides and prints, should be clear and unambiguous. They should be in sharp focus, have a range of tones from white to black, be of medium contrast, be immediately recognizable subjects, have no extraneous details, and be known objects for scale and size comparison.

Photographic prints can be mounted so that they can be recorded by film or television cameras. Positive prints made from 35mm negative film are normally used. The same source may then be scanned directly into a computer file for manipulation and for instant recall when needed.

Scenic Design

Scenic design is an important contributor to overall characterization and thematic meaning. The first stage of scenic design is analyzing the script to determine what kinds of sets, costumes, and makeup will be required. A script usually provides a clear indication of general time and place, even if it does not describe settings and costumes in detail. Judgments concerning time, place, mood, character, and theme

can only be made after the script has been carefully and thoroughly analyzed. The script itself can be broken down into a list of specific times and places, in much the same way as a breakdown is done for production scheduling and budgeting. A designer can then note the specific psychological mood of the action and characters for each time and place. Finally, more abstract concepts, ideas, and themes that result from in-depth analysis can be integrated with and reinforced by the selection of specific settings, costumes, and makeup.

Set Design

The design of specific physical sets can be conveniently divided into two stages: layouts or floor plans and actual set construction. Design research, layouts, floor plans, and costume sketches are considered *above-the-line expenses*. They are created prior to actual production and before a commitment is made to actual construction, so that changes can be made before more sizable *below-the-line construction* expenses have been incurred. Each stage of design from planning to execution results in a specific two-dimensional or three-dimensional product. By following these stages, a designer refines rough ideas into workable sets that can be efficiently and economically constructed, significantly contributing to overall program effectiveness. Before undertaking the work and expense of set design and construction, some designers may consider the use of a neutral background, called a *cyclorama* or *cyc*. A cyc is a heavy, monochrome curtain that provides a neutral set backdrop. It is convenient to set up in a studio and can be used for many production settings. A cyc will often suffice in many modernist and postmodernist situations (Figure 9.11). Design of computer-generated or virtual sets is done completely within one or more computer programs designed for that purpose. The same amount of research and planning must also precede the actual computer design as is accomplished for a set constructed of physical materials.

During preproduction a designer first draws a rough layout sketch for each set. These preliminary drawings are extremely important preproduction elements. They provide a focus for discussions at preproduction meetings, facilitate the estimation of set construction costs, and serve as a preliminary guide for the actual construction of sets.

A fully scaled floor plan translates actual set dimensions into a proportional ¼-inch or other convenient scale on a piece of grid paper. The designer creates a bird's-eye view of the proposed set in reduced dimensions that are proportional to the actual size of objects on the set. If a wall is to be

Figure 9.11 A sky cyclorama (skycyk) is a plain off-background that may be lit with a variety of different colors or patterns depending on the lighting instruments used. It also represents an infinite or nondescript background if that is called for in the set design. The cyk may be either a drape hung on a continuous rod to allow the drape to be moved and arranged as needed, or hung as a hard cyk with both the corner and the section meeting the floor curved to add to the infinite background.

8 feet long, it will be 2 inches long on the scaled floor plan (eight ¼-inches = 2 inches). Using a fully scaled floor plan, a director can determine if there is sufficient room to move the cameras or talent from one position to another in the set. A fully scaled floor plan can also be used by the lighting director to prepare the studio lighting. The final floor plan layout will include such things as scenery, set pieces such as furniture and props, and set dressings such as curtains. Skilled carpenters and painters translate the drawings into set materials that conform in every possible respect to the designer's original intentions.

Set Construction

Flats are relatively lightweight rectangular boards that are braced and supported by 2×3 inch or 2×4 inch boards on the back so that they are quite sturdy and durable. A variety of devices is used to connect flats together: rope tied over pegs, fastened with metal hinges, or secured with C-clamps. To keep them upright, flats are usually supported by angle braces. *Risers* are hollow rectangular boxes that can be placed on the floor to raise a portion of a set. Risers might be used in a news set, for example, to raise the news desk and seated performers to camera height. Permanent sets are sometimes constructed out of more durable materials. A set that is going to be used day after day, such as for an evening news program, may be permanently secured to the studio floor for added stability. Since set materials are rarely

viewed from behind, carpenters can cut costs by finishing only one side of a set piece and using inexpensive support materials.

Properties

The designer of a more realistic set must also select the necessary furniture and dressings, which fill in the set with objects and materials that add interest, realism, or atmosphere. *Props* or properties are functional furnishings that are integrated into the program. *Hand props* are actually handled by performers, while set pieces are simply interesting, perhaps symbolic, details on the set. Hand props are often used for bits of stage business or action, such as a gun kept hidden from the view of other characters (Figure 9.12). With virtual sets, blue-screen, or chroma key sets, the placement of props is critical since the actual set and environment cannot be seen by the actors or stage crew except by viewing a monitor.

Costume Design

Most television and film productions require costumes and clothing that are selected and designed specifically for one show. For the majority of such productions, the wardrobe person procures costumes from rental houses that specialize in supplying costumes to theater, film, and video productions. In some cases, the clothing will be supplied by clothing manufacturers who want to advertise their products. Higher-budget productions employ costume designers who create original costumes.

In terms of texture, designers know that shiny, highly reflective materials appear much brighter than thick or coarsely textured materials. Bold plaids and

Figure 9.12 Hand props are objects decorating the set that are small enough to be picked up and used by the performers.

COLOR RELATIONSHIPS

OVERLAPPING LIGHTS **SUPERIMPOSED FILTERS**

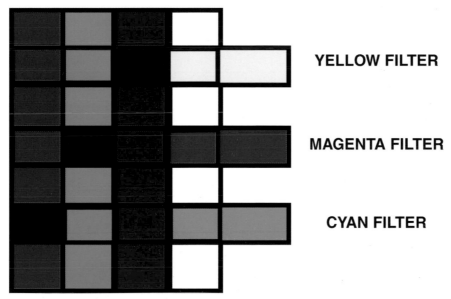

Color Plate 1 The top left illustration shows what happens if pure primary colors (red, green, and blue) overlap, revealing the three secondary colors (cyan, magenta, and yellow); if all three primaries overlap, white light is reflected. The top right illustration shows what happens if white light is passed through filters of yellow, cyan, and magenta: the overlapping areas show red, green, and blue, and the center will have no light passed through since each of the three filters removes one of the three primary light rays. The bottom illustration shows the relationship of the three primary lights as they are passed through filters of the three secondary colors.

COLOR CHARACTERISTICS

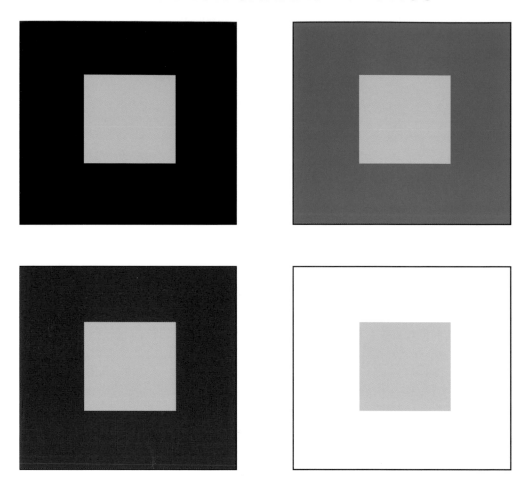

Color is affected by surrounding colors. All of the center patches are the same color, but when surrounded by a lighter color or white it appears darker and if surrounded by a darker color or black, it appears lighter.

white light enters the lens at the prism blocks

red light reflects to the red chip, green light passes straight through to the green chip, and blue light is reflected to the blue chip

Color Plate 2 The four squares of color show how adjacent colors and intensities affect a color. The illustration at the bottom shows light passing through the prisms in a typical three-chip video camera. White light (containing the three primary colors red, green, and blue) passes through the lens and enters the prism blocks. Red light is reflected toward the red chip, green light passes straight through to the green chip, and blue light is reflected toward the blue chip.

EXTERIOR LIGHT & FILTER COMBINATIONS

Exterior lighting-
For film - daylight stock
no filter in place.
For video - 85 filter in place
white balanced
under daylight.

Exterior lighting-
For film - daylight stock
with 85 filter in place.
For video - 85 filter in place
white balanced
under tungsten light.

Exterior lighting-
For film - tungsten stock
with no filter in place.
For video - no filter in place
white balanced
under tungsten light.

Color Plate 3 Operating either a film or video camera under daylight conditions requires proper filters to be in place and proper white-balancing in a video camera. The top photo shows a properly balanced video camera and daylight film in a film camera. The bottom photos show improper combinations of white-balancing in a video camera and mismatching filters and film stock in a film camera.

INTERIOR LIGHT & FILTER COMBINATIONS

Interior Lighting -
For film - tungsten stock
no filter in place.
For video - no filter in place
white balanced
under tungsten.

Interior Lighting -
For film - tungsten stock
with 85 filter in place.
For video - no filter in place
white balanced
under daylight.

Interior Lighting -
For film - tungsten stock
with 80 filter in place.
For video - white balanced
under tungsten light
with 85 filter removed.

Color Plate 4 Operating either a film or video camera under tungsten lighting conditions requires proper filters to be in place and proper white-balancing in a video camera. The top photo shows a properly white-balanced video camera and tungsten film and lighting in a film camera. The bottom photos show mismatching filters and improper white-balancing in a video camera.

stripes call too much attention to themselves. Certain fabric shapes and designs should be consciously avoided by the designer of video costumes and sets because they cause problems during recording. For example, parallel lines that are quite close together, as in herringbone cloth, can cause a moire effect on a video screen. A moire effect is a distracting vibration of visual images caused by the interaction of close-set lines in the materials being recorded and the video scanning lines. In television, the color blue or green, when used for chroma key, is usually avoided in costumes and sets (Figure 9.13).

Makeup

Video and film performers' makeup can be divided into two types: cosmetic and prosthetic. *Cosmetic makeup* enhances the appearance of performers by hiding imperfections, adding needed color, and accentuating their better features, and *prosthetic makeup* transforms the appearance of a performer's face through temporary plastic surgery and other corrective means. Prosthetic makeup can add years to a performer's appearance or entirely transform his

Figure 9.13 Costumes and settings are crucial in the staging of historical films, such as Miramax Films' production of *Restoration* with Robert Downey, Jr., and fellow actors wearing the traditional clothing of the 18th century. (Courtesy of Miramax Films.)

or her physical appearance. Prosthetic makeup gives mobility to the expressive features of an actor and allows him or her some facial versatility in terms of playing many different roles. Prosthetic appliances can be used to make changes in the apparent age, race, nationality, and even sex of an actor. Prosthetic appliances are usually made of foam latex, which can be applied to the performer's face and hands.

Cosmetic makeup enhances the beauty of a performer. It compensates for the heightened awareness of imperfections caused by film and video recording equipment and weak features in a performer's face. It also brings out the best features of a performer's face. Cosmetic makeup hides reddish cheeks and noses, beard lines, freckles, and blemishes. Eyes and lips are the most important aspects of a female performer's face. Makeup can hide or compensate for defects in these facial structures. If a female performer's eyes are too close together, for example, eyeliner can be placed on the outside edges of her lids to make them look farther apart.

Male performers often require makeup to cover beard lines, although many newscasters shave just before they appear on the evening news to avoid whisker stubble. Bright shades of cheek and lip color are generally avoided with males to prevent the appearance of a heavily made-up look. A weak chin can be made more prominent with a subtle accentuation of jaw lines and cheek color. Female performers are usually less concerned or embarrassed about applying makeup than men, but properly explaining the technical need for makeup can help to assuage the timidity of inexperienced performers.

It is possible to hide blemishes and create a consistent overall facial color and texture by simply applying a base or foundation makeup to a performer's face. Gently rubbing with cold cream and numerous tissues will remove makeup. Remember that the purpose of cosmetic makeup is usually to enhance the appearance of a performer, not to call attention to itself unless, of course, a modernist approach is employed. The best way to check a performer's makeup is to test it with a live video camera or a digital camera. If it does not hide blemishes and improve the appearance of the talent, it should be removed and redone. The performer should look natural, except in postmodernist, avant-garde works.

SUMMARY

Graphic design can be approached from realist, modernist, and postmodernist perspectives. Realist sets and design formats depict an actual or general type of place or experience. However, a realist setting can provide an atmosphere that reflects the subjective state of mind or perceptions of a specific character. Modernist designs are relatively abstract and often reflect an abstract conception of space, a subjective feeling, or a state of mind. Postmodernist designs combine a variety of design styles and patterns and emphasize emotional responses and an intentional distortion of realistic visuals.

Scenic design involves three basic design principles: design elements, color, and composition. Design elements include lines, shapes, textures, and movement. Color and contrast are interrelated aspects of design, as are color and shape. Contrasting colors can be used to separate foregrounds and backgrounds, and to create various shapes and they can be used to define specific characters, settings, and themes.

Graphic artists design images that convey information. They use basic principles of design, such as simplicity, proximity, similarity, figure/ground, correspondence, equilibrium, and closure to stimulate viewer interest. Graphic artists select lettering that is highly legible but also expressive. Titles and illustrations are designed and selected on the basis of their appropriateness for specific topics.

Sets are designed to provide an environment for a production. The setting and properties must be practical and utilitarian for both the performers to be able to move and interact, and for the director to be able to place cameras and microphones where they are needed. Makeup is used to hide blemishes and create imaginative characters. Graphic design is an integral part of the overall production process. Graphics can be divided into two categories on the basis of use or placement: on-set and off-set. Graphic images can be divided into two additional categories on the basis of their nature as images: titles and illustrations. Titles are forms of graphic lettering. Illustrations are drawings, photographs, graphs, charts, diagrams, and maps that visualize abstract concepts and ideas. They can be drawn by hand, photographed, or produced electronically with the help of a computer graphics system.

Sets, set furnishings, props, costumes, and performer makeup are not completely independent elements in the production process. Elements of scenic design interact within each other and many other areas of production to create an overall visual impression. The most important interactions are those between scenic design and each of the following: lighting, performer movement, and camera and microphone placement. Sets are usually designed to facilitate the placement and movement of the cameras and microphones, as well as the talent.

EXERCISES

1. Design a realistic room interior on the basis of the description of a setting in a script, short story, or novel. Carefully select and coordinate furniture, props, sets, and costumes so that all of these elements create a realistic impression of time and place. Color and brightness levels of foreground and background elements, sets, and costumes should contrast but not clash with each other. Provide detailed layouts drawn to scale so that the set can be efficiently and accurately constructed. Incorporate elements into the set that are economical to obtain or already on hand, such as specific flats, props, set dressings, and pieces of furniture.

2. Use a cyclorama to create a setting that has no borders, where walls and/or ceilings meet so that space appears infinite. Use the lighting techniques discussed in Chapter 6, "Lighting," to create abstract shapes, colors, and patterns that create a dramatic and unusual sense of space. Discover ways of manipulating the viewer's sense of spatial perspective by simply altering the lighting.

3. Using the description of a specific setting in a dramatic script, short story, or novel, find an existing building that meets the essential criteria needed to represent this place. Assess the difficulties inherent in using this facility from the standpoint of recording, and determine what elements will have to be removed or added to make this an ideal setting.

4. Design a credit or title sequence for a specific production project. Determine how you can best use abstract graphic images and titles to introduce a production, or select live-action images on which titles can be keyed. Select a letter style or font that is consistent with the overall theme, message, and style of your project, and that creates an impression that reinforces the central theme of a drama or the central message of an informational program. It can reflect warmth or coldness, tension or relaxation, simply by virtue of the colors, lines, and shapes it presents. Your project will eventually be shown on a video screen, so be sure to use type sizes that are large enough for titles to be clearly legible. Allow sufficient time for each title to be read twice before another title appears on the screen, unless there are too many credits that must be presented within a relatively short period of time. Remember that a title sequence must effectively introduce viewers to the topic.

5. With the help of a theatre department faculty member, create a prosthetic appliance on a

classmate. Test the effect by shooting a test tape to make certain the effect looks real and accomplishes the desired response in the audience.

6. Arrange six items of different sizes and shapes in a pattern within a single frame. Develop the maximum Z depth effect and follow the rules of composition. Record the arrangement from several different angles to see what creates the greatest depth and at the same time shows the objects to the best advantage.

ADDITIONAL READINGS

Arntson, Amy E. *Graphic Design Basics*, 4th ed. Belmont, CA: Wadsworth Publishing, 2002.

Baker, Georgia O'Daniel. *A Handbook of Costume Drawing*, 2nd ed. Boston, MA: Focal Press, 2000.

Barsacq, Leon. *Caligari's Cabinet and Other Grand Illusions: A History of Film Design.* New York: The New American Library, 1978.

Baygan, Lee. *Techniques of Three-Dimensional Makeup.* New York: Watson-Guptill, 1982.

Birren, Faber. *The Symbolism of Color.* Secacus, NJ: Citadel Press, 2000.

Bordwell, Dave and Kristin Thompson. *Film Art: An Introduction*, 6th ed. New York, NY: McGraw-Hill, 2001.

Bruno, Nicola (Trans. Manfredo Massironi). *The Psychology of Graphic Images.* Mahwah, NJ: Lawrence Erlbaum Assoc., Inc, 2002.

Feldman, Tony. *An Introduction to Digital Media.* New York: Routledge, 1997.

Foley, James D., et al. *Computer Graphics: Principles and Practices*, 2nd ed. Boston, MA: Addison Wesley, 1995.

Graham, Lisa, *Basics of Design: Layout and Typography for the Beginners.* Albany, NY: Delmar Publishers, 2001.

Huffmanm, E. Kenneth and Jon Teeple. *Computer Graphics Applications: An Introduction to Desktop Publishing and Design.* Belmont, CA: Wadsworth Publishing, 1990.

Iuppa, Nicholas V. *Interactive Design for New Media.* Boston, MA: Focal Press, 2001.

Kehoe, Vincent J.R. *The Technique of Film and Television Make-Up Artists for Film, Television and Stage*, revised ed. Boston, MA: Focal Press, 1995.

Kuppers, Harald. *Basic Law of Color Theory*, 2nd ed. Barrons, 1990.

Landa, Robin. *Graphic Design Solutions.* 2nd ed. Albany, NY: Onward Press, 2000.

Lester, Paul Martin. *Visual Communication: Images with Messages.* Belmont CA: Wadsworth Publishing, 2000.

Merritt, Douglas. *Graphic Design in Television.* Boston, MA: Focal Press, 1987.

Nelms, Hennings. *Scene Design: A Guide to the Stage.* New York, NY: Dover Books, 1970.

Olson, Robert. *Art Director: Film and Video*, 2nd ed. Boston, MA: Focal Press, 1998.

Pender, Ken. *Digital Colour in Graphic Design.* Boston, MA: Focal Press, 1998.

Prosise, Jeff. *How Computer Graphics Work.* Emeryville, CA: Ziff-Davis Books, 1994.

Street, Rita. *Computer Animation: A Whole New World.* Gloucester, MA: Rockport Publishers, 1998.

Williams, Robin. *The Non-Designer's Design Book*, 2nd ed. Berkeley, CA: Peachpit Press, 2003.

Wright, Steve. *Digital Compositing for Film and Video.* Boston: Focal Press, 2001.

10 Visual Editing

TOPICS FOR DISCUSSION

- What are the aesthetic approaches of editing?
- What are editing modes?
- How are editing techniques used in digital productions?
- What is the difference between linear and nonlinear editing?
- How does film editing differ from video editing?

INTRODUCTION

The craft of editing consists of selecting, combining, and trimming sounds and visual images after they have been recorded. In the digital age, editing can take place during both production and postproduction. While additional images are being recorded on location, even at great distances from the postproduction site, editing decisions can be shared between editing and production personnel via the Internet or satellite links. Editing can take place sequentially according to the production schedule or the script, or the editing of different sections or different components of a film or television program, such as sound effects, music, dialogue, and title sequences, can be done simultaneously and in parallel. Just as digital editing technologies are replacing analog technologies, parallel filmmaking and editing is replacing serial postproduction. Utilizing parallel editing techniques, directors and editors can continue to refine their editing decisions up until the last minute (Figure 10.1).

Whether they use parallel or serial techniques, editors need to understand basic terms and concepts that are important aspects of editing as a craft. For example, a film or video editor can trim a continuous recording of visual images, usually called a *shot*, by removing unwanted portions at the beginning or end of the shot. Trimmed shots can then be combined with other shots using various transition devices, such as cuts, fade-outs/fade-ins, or dissolves. A *cut* is a direct, instantaneous transition from one shot to the next. During a fade-out/fade-in, the first shot gradually disappears and is replaced by blackness. This is called a *fade-out*. It is followed by the gradual appearance of the second shot from blackness, which is called a *fade-in*. A *dissolve* consists of a simultaneous or overlapping fade-out of the first shot and a fade-in of the second shot. Unlike a fade-out/fade-in, the image never becomes entirely black during a dissolve. *Transitions* generally imply a change of time and/or place from one shot to the next. For example, a cut usually implies a very short, if any, temporal change from one shot to the next, while a dissolve suggests that some time has elapsed. However, a dissolve generally suggests a shorter passage of time than does a fade-out/fade-in.

AESTHETIC APPROACHES

The director's aesthetic intentions regarding combinations of images are fully realized during editing. A good editor is both a practical problem-solver, who comes to grips with the limitations of the visual material that the director has provided, and a creative artist, who sometimes reshapes and improves this material through the use of imaginative editing techniques. Visual images can be combined using principles of editing derived from each of the three aesthetic orientations: realism, modernism, and postmodernism. Few editing situations are guided by one perspective alone. It is often effective to combine different approaches.

Realism

Many techniques used in classical fiction and nonfiction editing that preserve an illusion of reality are basically realist in aesthetic approach. Realist editing preserves spatial and temporal continuity from shot

EDITING PROCESSES

STAGES OF EDITING	MOTION PICTURES	VIDEO or TELEVISION	AUDIO or SOUND
PRELIMINARY	Rough cut and final cut of work print	Off-line non-linear of lower quality tape stock or in a computer	Record each source on separate track of multi-track recorder or physically cut the original tape or enter each track into a multi-track computer program for non-linear editing
FINAL	Conform original film to edited workprint or to digitally edited timecode & KeyKode	On-line linear of original tape controlled by computer following the EDL or on-line nonlinear of original tape	From multi-track recorder or computer dub to stereo tracks in computer to final mix for reproduction

Figure 10.1 The two stages of editing media programs, whether audio, video, or film, follow the same basic pattern. A preliminary stage assembles the material into a tentative order and pattern, and then the final stage completes the editing by trimming and molding the production into its final form (Figure 10.1).

to shot. A smooth, unbroken flow of actions and events from one shot to the next maintains an illusion of continuity in time and space. A movement begun in one shot is completed in the next. A realist approach maintains the consistent directional placement of objects and movements in the scene by following the 180-degree axis rule, as discussed earlier. Directional glances must be consistent from one shot to the next. If one person is looking up at another person in a close-up, then a close-up of the latter should show him or her looking down. Point-of-view shots can be an effective means of enhancing realism and intensifying viewer involvement and identification with specific participants in a scene. Even in a documentary, point-of-view shots can create a "You are there!" feeling that adds to the illusion of reality.

Realist editing also involves eliminating mistakes and clarifying and simplifying the message content. Flubbed lines of dialogue or narration are removed and replaced. Gaps and omissions in coverage are concealed whenever possible. Some mistakes simply cannot be corrected with the material provided. An editor may need to salvage an acceptable combination of images out of bad material, but sometimes bad material simply has to be reshot by the director or eliminated entirely from the final edited version.

Cutting from a moving camera shot to a stationary shot sometimes causes editing problems. If the camera is simply tracking along with a moving subject, cutting directly from a moving camera shot to a stationary one rarely causes problems for the viewer. Cutting from one moving camera shot to another, or from one zoom shot to another moving in the same direction, is usually not a problem either, provided the speed of movement is approximately the same from shot to shot. But cutting from camera movements that are independent of subject movements to stationary camera shots often causes problems. The editor should wait until the camera movement has stopped within the shot before cutting to a stationary camera shot. Also, the use of moving camera shots tends to slow down the action in comparison with stationary camera cuts, such as from a stationary long shot to a medium shot to a close-up. Using stationary camera shots gives the editor more flexibility in terms of editing possibilities. However, moving camera shots can enhance spatial and temporal realism and provide a somewhat smoother, slower, and more deliberate pace.

Realist editing often follows basic patterns of scene construction. A scene or sequence often begins with an establishing long shot and gradually moves closer to the subject as the action intensifies to reveal more intimate details of character and setting. The overall scene and setting can be reestablished with another long shot at the end of the sequence. A variation on this approach is to begin in close-up to arouse interest and attention, and then gradually use more distant shots to establish the setting and orient the viewer. Initial viewer disorientation is gradually overcome and message clarity is eventually reestablished, while interest is added to the scene.

An effective means of enhancing message clarity is to follow a logical cause-and-effect structure when combining images. In a documentary, an editor can begin with the effect or result of certain actions and then present the causes of this event. For example, an instructional sports program about how to perform a specific gymnastic routine can begin with a presentation of the completed routine and then show the type of preparation and practice that goes into perfecting it. Such a sequence can then conclude with a second version of the completed routine, highlighting the various components.

Modernism

A modernist approach to editing often deliberately disrupts spatial and temporal continuity between shots and calls attention to the editing process. Jump cuts, radical shifts in time and place, a rejection of conventional rules of scene construction, directionality, and continuity all focus the viewer's attention on the manipulative powers of the artist and his or her control of the visual medium. A modernist artist is free to experiment with unusual combinations of shots without the constraints of logical clarity or realism. But an artist is not totally free of all constraints and structure. Both aesthetic unity and patterned disruptions of unity are achieved through a conscious and precise manipulation of aesthetic forms.

Modernist approaches to editing often focus on abstract qualities and elements of design within and between shots, such as similarities and differences in shape, color, movement, and texture. Sharp diagonal lines can be juxtaposed with smooth curves and circular shapes. Visual rhythms can be established between shots that are related to audio rhythms in music and sound effects, for example. Modernist approaches to editing are often incorporated into specific sequences within more conventionally realist programming. A dream sequence in a classical Hollywood drama and a poetic sequence of natural beauty in a documentary about the environment incorporate modernist techniques into a more conventional format. Transition devices, such as a dissolve from one scene to the next, can rely on similarities in shape and color between the last shot of one scene and the first shot of the next. Deliberate breaks in temporal and spatial continuity can gener-

ate visual interest through temporary viewer disorientation in a more conventional work of fiction or nonfiction.

Postmodernism

A postmodernist approach to editing can take the form of a collage or pastiche that combines diverse images and sounds and modes of production. For example, documentary and fiction approaches to editing can be combined within a single scene. A dramatic enactment can be staged as a direct cinema interview, as in Mitch Block's *No Lies* (1974), or as a cinema verité documentary about past or even future events, as in Peter Watkins' *Culloden* (1965) and *The War Game* (1966). A documentary, such as Errol Morris's *The Thin Blue Line* (1987), can edit together reenactments of events that occurred in the imaginations of different interviewees and witnesses. Hollywood feature films, such as *JFK* (1991) and *Forrest Gump* (1994), can edit historical documents, such as the Zapruder film of John F. Kennedy's actual assassination, together with an imaginatively staged fictional drama, or in the case of the latter film, can digitally manipulate the image to place a fictional character within the frame of documentary images.

In addition to mixing modes and editing techniques, a postmodernist approach to editing can actively engage the viewer/listener in the process of constructing the artwork. For example, an interactive multimedia production, such as *Explora 1 Peter Gabriel's Secret World* (1993), can allow the spectator to control the audio mixing or editing of various channels of his music within certain parameters determined by the project designer and computer programmers. A postmodernist approach to editing can highlight the impermanent performance aspects of a media production, rather than the completion of permanent perfected texts and works of art. It also encourages the participation of the spectator in the artistic process, rather than reinforcing the controlling presence of the individual artist (modernism) or the artist's transmission and preservation of the natural world or an illusion of a continuous reality (realism).

EDITING MODES

Fiction

Classical Hollywood conventions for shooting and editing fiction films and videos include master-scene shooting and continuity editing. A *master shot* consists of a relatively long duration shot that includes most of the action in a specific scene, usually recorded from a medium- to long-range camera distance. Shooting a master shot allows the actors to achieve some degree of continuity in their performance before the action is broken up into shorter-duration shots with the camera closer to the actors. A master shot provides an editor with continuous coverage of the action. Closer shots can then be inserted into the master shot to intensify the action by revealing a character's facial expressions and gestures. For example, when two characters are talking to one another in a scene, alternating over-the-shoulder, shot/reverse shot close-ups of the two characters (see Chapter 4, "Directing: Aesthetic Principles and Production Coordination") are often inserted into the master shot so that their actions and reactions can be seen more clearly (Figures 10.2A, B, and C).

Continuity editing refers to an editing system that developed in Hollywood and elsewhere beginning about 1910. It consists of a number of shooting and editing conventions that sustain an illusion of continuous time and place within a scene. For example, maintaining the 180-degree action axis or consistent screen direction from one shot to the next sustains the illusion of spatial and temporal continuity (see Chapter 4, "Directing: Aesthetic Principles and Production Coordination"). If a character moves from left to right in shot A but from right to left in shot B, he or she will appear to have dramatically changed direction without any passage of time. This may be perceived as a *jump cut*, that is, a mismatch in spatial continuity suggesting that a gap in time has occurred. When no mismatch in action or gap in time is apparent over a cut from one shot to the next, this is called a *match cut*.

An editor must also be conscious of *eyeline matches*, that is, maintaining directional continuity in terms of characters' looks and glances within a scene. If one character looks screen left in shot A followed by another character looking screen right in shot B, they will appear to be looking at (and perhaps talking to) one another. A common variation on the eyeline match is called a *point-of-view shot*. Here the editor cuts from one character looking in a particular direction to a shot of what they are looking at from their approximate (usually over-the-shoulder) spatial position in the scene. Cutting back to a close-up of a character who has been looking at something in order to see his or her facial expression is sometimes called a *reaction shot*. Point of view and reaction shots not only maintain directional continuity; they can also enhance viewer identification with specific characters' points of view.

A

B

C

Figure 10.2A, B, and C The standard shot series in a scene starts with an LS establishing relationships and positioning in the environment. A tighter MS brings the performers closer. A CU will concentrate the audience's attention on a specific performer.

Nonfiction

Partially or completely staged scenes in nonfiction productions sometimes rely upon the master scene and continuity techniques used in fiction. Variations upon these techniques have also been developed that take into account the difficulties of scripting and staging nonfiction events as well as the use of expository and rhetorical structures that can disrupt spatial and temporal continuity. A variation upon master scene shooting and editing that is commonly used in news and documentary production, for example, is called *A and B roll editing*. "Talking head" interviews constitute the A roll (equivalent to the master shot), while additional recordings of various activities and events that illustrate what the interviewee is talking about constitute the B roll (equivalent to the inserts). The editor inserts B-roll material into the A roll, as the interviewee continues to be heard on one of the audio tracks. A- and B-roll editing adds viewer interest by interspersing rather static shots of a talking head with a wide variety of visual illustrations.

Master scene techniques can also be simulated during the editing of the interview itself. If the camera-to-subject distance or type of shot (long shot, close-up, and so on) varies through the manipulation of a dolly or zoom lens during the recording of the interview, an editor can sometimes change the order in which the interview statements were made by cutting directly from long shot to close-up, such as when a particularly revealing statement is about to be made, to intensify the impact. In this way the basic effect of master scene shooting can be simulated during the editing process by cutting and reorganizing continuously recorded interviews. Viewer interest can be intensified further by then adding illustration materials. Similar techniques are often used with voiceover narration. Either the narration audio is edited first and then images illustrating the narrator's statements are added later, or the visuals are edited first and narration, which explains or complements the visuals, is edited and inserted later.

EDITING TECHNOLOGY AND TECHNIQUES

One of the editor's first tasks is to organize and catalogue all the recordings that the director has provided. The original recorded images are usually dubbed or copied before they are viewed by the editor. Using a copy protects the original recording, which can be safely stored away. Little if any material that has been rejected during actual production will be copied for viewing purposes. The copy or dub of the originally recorded images is repeatedly played back and viewed by the editor. The individual shot and take numbers recorded from the slate at the beginning of each camera take are catalogued or "logged." Time-code or control-track numbers are often logged at this time as well. The editor makes notations to the log, indicating particularly useful or

problematic shots and camera takes. These notations are often extremely useful. (See Figure 10.3.)

One of the best uses of a catalogued list of the individual shots and camera takes that were recorded during production is for the editor to perform a paper edit. During a paper edit an editor simulates the editing process on paper by cutting out each individual shot in a log and placing these shots in the anticipated sequential order of the completed project. A paper edit can also be accomplished using written transcriptions of interviews with accompanying time-code numbers from the original videotapes in a documentary. Performing a paper edit is an effective method of determining whether or not there is sufficient coverage to complete the editing process. It is also an efficient and economical means of manipulating the overall structure of a media production on paper without incurring the expense and labor of actually editing the recorded images themselves. Documentary editors, who rarely have access to an extremely detailed script as a guide to postproduction, often rely upon a paper edit to help them organize the editing process (Figure 10.4).

Digital Nonlinear Editing

Digitizing or Capturing Video and Film
Digital nonlinear editing begins with the digitization of the original videotape or film recordings if the original was an analog recording. Material recorded originally in a digital format may be used as a source in an editing suite, or it can be downloaded to the editor's memory storage system. Because digitizing video and film requires tremendous storage capacity, only those shots and takes that are very likely to be used during editing are likely to be digitized using a computer board or card. A digitizing or capture card or board consists of hardware that rapidly samples electrical signals during videotape playback or film-to-video transfer. These signals carry analog video and audio information, and the capture board converts them to digital information. Capturing video and audio signals requires fairly sophisticated hardware and considerable storage capacity, especially when high-quality images and sounds must be digitized (Figure 10.5).

Computer storage units range from bits to gigabytes. A *bit* is the smallest amount of information a computer can handle. Eight bits make up a *byte*, 1,000 bytes equal a *kilobyte* (KB), 1,000 KB equal a *megabyte* (MB), and 1,000 MB equal a *gigabyte* (GB). It takes slightly less than 1 MB to store just one full frame of video information, depending on the compression ratio of the digitizing system. A full frame of digital video consists of 720 pixels horizon-

EDITING LOG

EDITING LOG

EDITING LOG   DATE _____

LOCATION_____PRODUCTION _____

CAMERA_____ REEL _____

PRODUCER _____ DIRECTOR_____OPERATOR _____

COUNTER	TAKE	DESCRIPTION	REMARKS
00:00:30:00	1	WS-Establishing	Poor pan
00:01:20:13	2	"	Car in BG
00:02:40:28	3	"	Good take
00:04:20:10	1	2-Shot	Bad sound
00:04:50:10	2	"	Good take
00:05:20:15	1	CU-Sam	Framing
00:06:20:15	2	"	Tilt,poor
00:07:20:15	3	"	Delivery
00:08:20:15	4	"	Pix -OK, PoorSound
00:09:20:15	5	"	Good take

Figure 10.3 A production's editing log can be kept by either the director or production continuity clerk. The log indicates precise location of takes, the description of the shot, and a judgment or notation of the take so that the editor will have some guidance as to which takes to consider using during the editing process, regardless of what technology and techniques are used to perform visual editing

EDIT DECISION LIST (EDL)

EDIT#	REEL	DESCRIPTION	VIDEO IN/OUT	AUDIO IN/OUT	TRANSITION
001	3	WS-Ext	00:06:00:20 00:06:02:16	00:06:01:10 00:06:15:04	FI
002	3	MS-Ext	00:00:03:16 00:00:11:04		C
003	5	CU	00:10:02:15 00:11:29:05	00:10:02:15 00:11:29:05	D
004	2	CU	00:19:03:10 00:20:10:28	00:19:03:10 00:20:10:28	D

Figure 10.4 An Edit Decision List (EDL) is a precise listing (usually assembled on a computer) of each edit: its start point and end point, transition, and any special effects or differences in audio and video edit points. This becomes, in essence, a paper edit to be followed by the finale editor.

tal by 480 pixels vertical, or a total of 345,600 pixels (720 × 480) multiplied by 24 bits of color (345,600 × 24 = 8,294,400 bits/8 bits per byte = 1,036,800 bytes or approximately 1 MB per frame).

During digitization, each NTSC analog video frame, which consists of two interlaced scanning fields that add up to 525 scan lines, is converted to a frame of 720 × 480 pixels that can be displayed in a noninterlaced mode on a computer monitor. As mentioned in Chapter 6, "Lighting," there are almost 30 (actually 29.97) video frames in each second of NTSC _video, so it requires about 30 MB to store just one second of full-frame (720 × 480 pixels at 24-bit color), full-motion (30 frames per second) video. Consequently, just one minute of full-frame,

full-motion video would require a storage capacity of 60 (seconds) × 30 MB, or about 1,800 MB (or 1.8 GB), which is a significant amount of storage space. Sixty minutes of full-frame, full-motion video would require a whopping 100 GB of storage space if the material is not compressed first. Most home computers have internal hard disk drives that provide 10 to 100 GB of storage space, and most professional editing systems use a 100+ GB hard disk drive. Obviously, even in the case of relatively large-capacity hard disk drives, some way to reduce the amount of storage space is usually required, especially for editing longer duration projects (Figure 10.6).

The most common forms of storage space reduction used in digital nonlinear editing are compression,

Figure 10.5 A nonlinear editing station consists of a series of monitors for viewing and hearing the material being edited and a computer to store and manipulate the footage. The footage is not actually cut and spliced, but is stored in the computer's memory in the order determined by the editor. Changes may be made quickly, easily, and many times over without damaging the original footage. Once the final edits are satisfactory, the final production can be fed out to either film or videotape for distribution. (Courtesy Scitex Digital Video.)

frame-size reduction, and frame-rate reduction. *Compression* refers to a reduction of the volume of information in order to force it into less storage space. Basically compression reduces the amount of information that must be stored in an individual frame or still image by ignoring some pixel and color information during storage and then duplicating adjacent pixels and colors when the image is displayed during playback. Compression can also be achieved in motion video by storing only the pixels and colors that change from one frame to the next, and then duplicating stationary pixels and colors in subsequent frames during playback.

The volume of information can be reduced in still or motion images by using hardware and software compression, such as Joint Photographic Experts Group (JPEG) and Moving Picture Experts Group (MPEG). JPEG uses intraframe (within a single frame) compression to reduce the volume of information for each frame of video independently of every other frame and is frequently used for still photographs, but it can also be used for motion. MPEG is used exclusively for motion images since it involves both intraframe and interframe (between successive frames) compression. JPEG and MPEG compression are all applicable to digital nonlinear editing. As in videotape format changes, MPEG has been improved upon and there are now several new versions, including MPEG-2 and MPEG-4. MPEG-2 was created as an editing compression scheme, but it included some unwanted artifacts that have been corrected in MPEG-4.

Figure 10.6 The relationships between the measurements of the digital world are all based on the metric system. The amount of memory required for a specific amount of video or film depends on the compression system used. The amount of memory available in computers increases continually even as the price continues to drop.

DIGITAL MEASUREMENTS

Bit = 1/8 Byte	8 Bits = 1 Byte
Byte = 1/1,000 Kilobyte (KB)	1,000 Bytes = 1 KB
KB = 1/1,000 Megabyte (MB)	1,000 KB = 1 MB
MB = 1/1,000 Gigabyte (GB)	1,000 MB = 1 GB

Video frame requires nearly 1 MB

Pixel = smallest element of a picture

Video frame = 640 horizontal pixels x 480 vertical pixels = 307,200 pixels

Color video frame = 307,200 pixels x 24 bits of color = 7,372,800 bits or 921,600 bytes

1 Second of video = 30 frames = 28 MB of memory

1 Minute of video = 1680 MB or 1.68 GB of memory

60 minutes of video = 100 GB of memory

Most consumer computer hard drives are limited to less than 1 GB of memory

Professional computers require increased amounts of memory for nonlinear editing

Both consumer and professional systems use some form of compression to reduce amount of memory required for processing and editing

Compression is usually indicated in terms of ratios, such as 2:1, 10:1, or 15:1. If it requires 1,800 MB of space to store a minute of full-frame, full-motion video, then a 2:1 compression ratio would require 900 MB of storage space, a 10:1 compression ratio would require 180 MB, and a 15:1 compression ratio would need only 120 MB of storage space. Why not use a 15:1 compression ratio all the time? The answer, of course, is that the quality of the images usually deteriorates as the compression ratio increases. The best compression, that is, the least reduction in the quality of images, is usually achieved through a combination of hardware and software compression, rather than through software compression alone.

SAVING SPACE VIA COMPRESSION
One minute of full-motion video = 1,800 MB
Compression = Space
- None = 1,800 MB
- 2:1 = 900 MB
- 10:1 = 180 MB
- 15:1 = 120 MB

Storage space can also be reduced by reducing the image quality, frame size, and frame rates of digitized images. For example, instead of editing full-frame video (720 × 480 pixels), an editor can work with quarter-frame images (160 × 120 pixels). At some point reductions in frame size begin to affect image clarity and visibility. For example, it may be difficult for an editor to see clearly when the frame size of video images has been reduced from 720 × 480 to 180 × 120 pixels, or when images have been compressed by a 15:1 ratio. By the same token, a frame rate of 15 frames per second requires half the storage space as a frame rate of 30 frames per second, but again, the images may seem to flicker or strobe at reduced frame rates, such as when motion video is digitized at 10 or 15 frames per second. So an editor must decide what compression ratio, frame size, and frame rate she or he finds most comfortable and effective while working within the storage capacity limitation of a particular nonlinear editing system. An editor should also allow considerable time to digitize images, since images are frequently digitized in real time; in other words, it takes as much time to digitize images as the duration of the original recordings, and in some cases, more time.

Digital Nonlinear Editing Hardware
Most digital nonlinear editing systems employ computer hardware that is capable of processing and storing vast amounts of visual and audio information. In addition to a video and audio capture card, as

discussed earlier, a nonlinear editing system usually includes a computer processing unit (CPU) with a 2-GigaHertz (GHz) processing system, 800+ MB of random access memory (RAM), a keyboard, a mouse, one or two computer monitors, an NTSC television monitor, a videotape recorder, an amplifier and loudspeakers, and a 80+ GB hard disk drive designed for audiovisual (AV) use. Many professional nonlinear editing systems include a 2+ GHz processing system, 1+ GB of RAM, a 100+ GB hard disk drive, and a high-quality digital recorder featuring SMPTE time code. Professional digital editing systems are used for on-line editing, that is, they can be used to complete the entire postproduction process, including video and audio editing, and can also be used for adding graphics and special effects. These top-of-the-line systems employ a digital video capture card that is capable of capturing on-line or broadcast-quality NTSC digital/HDTV video (Figure 10.7).

Remote Nonlinear Video Editing
As digital cameras and recorders become smaller, record higher-quality signals, and digital nonlinear editing systems have shrunk in size and increased in capabilities, the possibility of digital editing in the field or by long distance is now a reality. Remote Nonlinear Editing (RNLE) gives ENG crews the ability to edit a story as soon as it has been shot by using either the digital camera as the source deck coupled with a small portable editor controller and digital recorder, or by using a small portable editor that contains both built-in digital feed and record decks, monitors, and edit controls. The units are as small as a laptop computer and are capable of cuts-only, versus dissolves and effects, news editing. A second long-distance digital editing system involves editing on location using portable equipment, then sending the edited version through the Internet to the home office where an on-line finished edit can be completed. Both systems involve compressing the signal and some loss of quality, but as technology improves the losses will be minimal.

Digital Nonlinear Editing Software
Digital nonlinear editing software offers several advantages over conventional means of editing film, audiotape, and videotape, including increased flexibility or creativity, as well as potential time and cost savings. A common cliché is that digital nonlinear editing is the equivalent of word processing and desktop publishing for audio, film, and video postproduction. The analogy holds for many aspects of editing that are shared by word processing and various digital nonlinear editing software programs. For

Figure 10.7 The screen of a nonlinear editor reveals the types of transitions available, the segments available to edit, the sound in visual form, time-code information, and running times of the production. Depending on the brand and model of editor, other characteristics of controls also may be visible on the screen. (Courtesy of Apple Computer.)

example, most word processing software allows a writer to cut, copy, paste, and delete words, paragraphs, and pages of text. Digital nonlinear editing affords an editor similar flexibility in terms of instantaneously changing the order and duration of sounds and images. For example, clips of video or audio information can be cut, trimmed, copied, pasted, inserted, and deleted along a time line.

A *clip* is usually the smallest unit of digital video (or audio) information that can be stored and manipulated during editing. It can range from just one frame to an entire movie in duration, but it often consists of a single shot, that is, a continuous camera recording or take. Digitized clips are usually imported (or copied) into a particular editing project file, where they are edited along a time line with other images and sounds. Most editing software provides several windows or screens, including a project window, a time line (or construction) window, a trimming window, a transition window, and a locking window. Different windows can usually be displayed simultaneously on one or more computer monitors. A *project window* usually contains the individual clips in alphabetical order based on the first letters of their written descriptions.

The *time line* or *construction window* displays a time line that contains several video, audio, transition, and superimposition or special effects tracks and indicates the overall duration and order of the edited project. The *viewing window* allows you to view and set the in and out (beginning and ending) points for each clip. The *trimming window* is used for cutting directly (e.g., a straight cut) from one clip to the next. It usually displays the adjoining frames at the cut point between the two clips, allowing the

editor to trim off video frames and/or add additional video frames from one or both clips on the time line. A *transition window* displays dissolves and wipes that can be dragged or copied into the transition track of the time line window wherever two separate video tracks overlap and a transition (other than a straight cut) from the first to the second clip is needed. Finally, a *locking window* allows the editor to lock together or unlock various visual and audio tracks in the time line window, so that they can be cut and trimmed collectively or individually. Images from each motion video clip are often displayed as a series of representative still frames along the time line, while audio is often displayed visually as a continuous, variable area sound track, where high peaks represent loud sounds and rapid fluctuations indicate high-frequency sounds. Clips can be copied and inserted at various points along the time line, and they can also be deleted from the time line and the remaining images and sounds attached to one another. Motion video and still-frame clips can also be placed in preliminary order using a storyboard display that presents one frame from each clip. A storyboard allows an editor to place the clips in rough sequential order prior to trimming precise cut points and adding various transition devices in the time line window.

Every edit made using a digital nonlinear software program is a virtual edit. No digitized material is discarded when clips are trimmed, cut, or deleted along an editing time line, since each clip is stored separately outside the time line window. The time line is in essence an EDL, a listing of all of the shots' in and out cues, durations, transitions, and audio cues. When the project is rendered to either a digital or analog output, the completed sequence will be created from the original digital source material. Every clip stored on a disk drive is instantaneously accessible in its entirety and can be grabbed in the project or clip window and reinserted at any point along the time line. Many alternative versions of a scene or sequence can thus be quickly edited and examined without prematurely eliminating material that may be needed later. Transitions from one shot to another can be previewed, as can the superimposition of titles and various digital video effects without ever actually cutting, discarding, eliminating, or deleting any originally digitized video or audio. The ability to manipulate clips of video and sound along a time line not only adds flexibility to the editing process, but it can also make editing more efficient and cost-effective. Clips can be very rapidly trimmed, cut, inserted, and deleted. Digital nonlinear editing is extremely fast compared to physically cutting and splicing a conventional feature film, for example, and the time it takes to find and insert videotape images and sounds from a source onto a master videotape can be dramatically reduced by using instantaneously accessible digital clips along a time line. The amount of time scheduled for postproduction editing can be significantly diminished, facilitating the editing of projects that require a short turnaround time, such as topical news magazine segments and mini-documentaries. Increased editing efficiency can also translate into cost savings that will affect the overall budget of longer-term projects, when an editor's time and salary can be reduced. Clearly, digital nonlinear editing offers a number of advantages in terms of flexibility and efficiency over conventional videotape and film editing.

Videotape Linear Editing

Videotape linear editing is usually divided into two stages: off-line editing and on-line editing. The difference between these two stages is most clear in productions in which final editing is eventually performed using a broadcast-quality format, such as BetaSP, or any digital format. These original recordings are often dubbed or transferred to a smaller format for off-line editing. This preserves the original recordings while allowing an editor some flexibility to edit and re-edit materials without jeopardizing the quality of the final product. Each duplication of an analog videotape diminishes the quality of the recorded images and sounds. This is why off-line editing is often done in a smaller format, and off-line editing decisions are later performed on an originally recorded larger-format videotape. Off-line editing decisions can be used to guide on-line editing of the larger-format videotape.

Linear Assemble Editing

Linear assemble editing is only used to place the shots in rough sequential order, since it does not provide sufficient editing control to edit exactly from one shot to the next. During assemble editing, both the control track and the visual images from the original recording are transferred to the new assemble-edited version (Figure 10.8). The editor basically follows the script and selects the best takes of each shot, leaving a five-second preroll at the beginning of each camera take, which will allow the videotape to be "up to speed" (precise edits cannot be made from a stationary videotape) when subsequent frame-accurate edits will be made.

Insert Editing

Insert editing (Figure 10.9) allows for precise, instantaneous cutting from one videotape shot to the next. During insert editing the control track from the original recording is not transferred to the edited videotape. Instead, the entire edited videotape is prerecorded with a continuous black signal and constant control track. Specific shots and visual images can then be inserted into the black signal, and playback rate and synchronization is governed by this constant control track. Thus there will be no gap or mismatch in control tracks from one shot to the next during insert editing. In addition to the prerecorded black signal and control track, insert editing usually begins with the prerecording of such information as the tape title; color bars, which are reference bands of colors, including black and white; and a timing or countdown leader, which is a sequential series of numbers of time in seconds used for prerolling the videotape.

ASSEMBLE EDIT

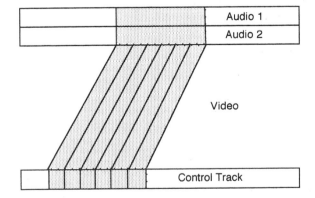

Simultaneous recording of both audio, video, and control track. CANNOT record tracks separately. Does not sync with prerecorded material at end of edit.

Figure 10.8 A video assemble edit involves editing all of the tracks simultaneously: control track, all audio tracks, and the video track.

INSERT EDIT

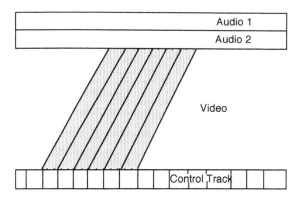

May record audio 1, audio 2, or video tracks individually
or any combination of those three tracks.
DOES NOT re-record prerecorded control track.
Makes seamless edits and exits regardless of track choices.

Figure 10.9 A video insert edit provides the editor with the flexibility to add or change either the audio track or the video track independently or simultaneously. A continuous control track must have been recorded before attempting an insert edit by laying down continuous color bars, a black sync signal, or previously recorded video.

The first shot is inserted after two seconds of black following the number two on the timing leader.

Linear Editing Process

Linear editing systems rarely allow for special effects and transitions other than straight cuts from shot to shot. An off-line editing system has three basic components: two VCRs and an edit control unit. One VCR, called a source, is used to play a prerecorded videotape; the second, called a record, is used to record an edited version of the prerecorded material. The edit control unit is an electronic device that allows the operator to select edit points and to transfer images and sounds from the source VCR to the record VCR. The edit control unit locks the two VCRs together, relying on the videotape control tracks and the servomechanisms in each machine to synchronize the playback and record movements of the two videotapes. If the two videotapes are not synchronized, there will be a gap or mismatch in the video tracking of the recording between two successive shots. One shot might begin somewhere in midframe, such as halfway down the scanning of the image, and the next might begin somewhere else in the scanning of the screen. If two successive shots are not in phase with one another, the image will temporarily flip or break up on the screen when the recording is played back. This problem is similar to that encountered in assemble editing when there is a discontinuity in the control track from shot to shot.

The edit control unit has jog and shuttle controls linked to the source and record VCRs. A *jog control* allows the editor to move a videotape one frame at a time, while a *shuttle control* allows a number of frames of videotape to be moved while the editor searches for the best edit point. Using these controls, the editor locates and still-frames the edit points on the two videotapes. The edit *in-point* on the source videotape is the first frame of the shot following the cut, while the edit in-point on the record videotape is the last frame in the shot preceding the cut. An *out-point*, where the shot to be inserted will end, is usually set by the editor from either the source videotape or the record videotape, but not both, since the edit controller automatically determines the out-point of the other. The edit controller will also automatically preroll the two videotapes the same number of frames in front of the two edit points (usually five seconds), so that they will reach the two edit points simultaneously when the two machines are started at the same time. Most edit controllers allow the editor to preview the cut before it is actually made so that essential material on the record videotape is not accidentally erased and replaced by the material on the source videotape. Once the cut has been previewed, it is a simple matter to actually record the new shot by depressing the edit button. When the precise out-point cannot be known until a subsequent shot will be edited to it, the editor can simply select an out-point that is a safe distance beyond where the next edit point is likely to occur (Figure 10.10).

Figure 10.10 A linear editor controller controls tape decks of quality lower than the original or final format. In many cases a cuts-only editor, rather than an editor, allows dissolves or other effects. An off-line editor may become an on-line editor if the edit controller is used to control the highest-quality level desired by the producer. (Courtesy JVC.)

Time Code

A *time code* is a series of digits that provides an exact reference for each frame. One of the most widely used time codes has been standardized as the SMPTE (Society of Motion Pictures and Television Engineers) time code. It is sometimes added to one of the tracks of the originally recorded videotape, or it is recorded during the vertical intervals between video fields. It consists of an eight-digit series of numbers beginning with either zero (called *zero start*) or with actual clock time in hours, minutes, seconds, and fields (60 per second). Thus, 01:00:00:01 indicates a point one hour and one field into the recording. Separate cassettes or reels of videotape can be differentiated by hours: 01, 02, and so on. The SMPTE time-code system requires a special generator and reader. The time code can actually be viewed in the video image as a "burn-in" time code, which can be helpful during off-line editing to make editing notations, especially when using machines that cannot otherwise read the code, because the code is actually recorded in the picture area of the videotape.

Post Production Techniques

Graphics can be keyed into the image using various types of keys or a downstream keyer into which a character-generated or computer-animated image can be fed.

The presence of the switcher, a video synthesizer, an SEG, and/or a DVE in a computerized editing system allows many different special effects to be created. A variety of wipes, fades, dissolves, and key effects can be accomplished automatically on a post-production switcher. A video synthesizer can manipulate an analog video in ways that are similar to digital effects generated by a DVE. That is, it can convert the component parts of a video signal, such as each color, into separate electrical signals that can be modified by a computer programmer. The height, width, depth, shape, clarity, or position of an image can be changed by turning a dial or flipping a switch. *Solarization* is a technique that relies on a separation between luminance and chrominance information in a video signal. The color can be drained out of the image to produce a high-contrast black-and-white image, which can then be synthetically colored by assigning different colors to different shades of gray.

Digital video signal-processing devices convert the analog video signal into a digital one by using a numerical code and rapid sampling techniques. The digitally coded signal is easier to store and manipulate than an analog one, and image quality is not lost in dubbing. It is possible to create a wide variety of special effects using digital devices, such as a digital video effects (DVE) or a digital video manipulator (DVM). An image or full frame can be continuously compressed to a point of light. It can be expanded, stretched, freeze-framed, pushed off or on, made into an abstract painting-like image, and replicated as multiple images on a screen. The DVE or DVM can also be connected to the video switcher to create automatic chroma key tracking in which the size of the chroma key window can be automatically shaped and positioned. The inserted picture can be proportionately compressed and expanded to fill the window more efficiently and realistically than can conventional chroma key, especially when the main signal camera is tracking or moving, and thereby changing chroma key perspective. These kinds of digital effects can provide an editor with tremendous flexibility in terms of image manipulation during on-line editing (Figure 10.11).

Film Editing

Film editing follows a series of stages similar to videotape editing: from rough-cutting the equivalent of off-line videotape editing, to conforming, the equivalent of on-line editing. The first stage includes viewing a copy of the originally recorded images called the *workprint*, *rushes*, or *dailies*, and selecting

Figure 10.11 A digital effects generator creates a variety of effects not possible with an analog switcher or effects generator. A few of the possible effects are visible on the screen. (Courtesy of Sony Corporation.)

and ordering specific shots and scenes. The final stage involves conforming the original film to the edited workprint. Unlike videotape editing, however, traditional film editing usually involves mechanical processes, such as physically cutting and splicing the film. Also unlike linear videotape editing, conventional film editing is essentially a nonlinear process, since changes can be made in the overall length and order of the sounds and images at any time up to the completion of the rough-cut. Film images can also be transferred to video and digitized so that they can be edited more efficiently with a digital nonlinear editing system, but at some point, the original film must be cut if film prints are going to be made in a film laboratory and projected in a movie theater.

As a result of various postproduction efficiencies, digital nonlinear editing is rapidly becoming the preferred method of off-line film editing or rough-cutting.

Whether a film editor uses traditional mechanical techniques of rough-cutting or digital nonlinear editing techniques, a film editor has a great deal of freedom to experiment with a variety of different takes and shot sequences and durations at all stages of the editing process until the conforming stage.

Screening the Workprint

A film copy made from the originally recorded film is called a *workprint*. During production the film direc-

tor usually specifies which camera takes should be printed, and these selections are noted on the camera report that is sent to the film laboratory (Figure 10.12).

This information is then transferred to a lab report sheet. Because workprinting is expensive, only takes that are likely to be used during editing will actually be workprinted. The editor, director, and producer view each day's workprint, called the *dailies*, in order to evaluate how well things are going. After viewing and approving the footage, the editor catalogues it before beginning a rough cut. An editor will often view the dailies over and over again to get a feel for the production and to stimulate ideas about how images can and should be combined. Sometimes the original film is immediately transferred to videotape and digitized for viewing and editing purposes.

Assemble Editing

The next stage of preliminary film editing is to assemble the individual shots into sequential order. Since films are often shot out of continuity, that is, all shots from one location are recorded at the same time, regardless of when they occur in the script, the editor must assemble the shots into the order specified by the script. During the assemble stage of editing, the entire shot is left intact. As the rough cut progresses and each shot is placed in its proper sequential order, the editor gradually refines the cuts,

Figure 10.12 A camera report form lists all of the pertinent information that the laboratory needs to know in order to properly process the film that it describes. The form indicates which takes are to be printed and includes comments the editor may need to have while editing the workprint.

CAMERA REPORT

Roll No. _____
Page _____ Date _____
Client _____

Production _____
Director _____ Camera Operator _____
Camera _____ Magazine _____ Motor _____
Stock [_____] Rated [I.E. _____]
Print Circled [_____] All [_____] Takes _____

Scene	Take	T-Stop	Remarks

cutting out all extraneous or unnecessary material. Unused shots are called *out-takes*. They are often left on the original camera rolls. The pieces removed from the shots that are actually used are called *trims*. They are frequently stored on the pegs of a trim bin, which is placed near the editing bench. Trims are sometimes spliced back into the film after an editor has tried a specific cut, usually because the cut does not work quite as well as was anticipated. It is therefore unwise to dispose of trims too soon.

Synchronizing the Dailies

The recording and editing of film sound is usually kept physically separate from the recording of film images. Film sound is normally recorded on DAT (digital audiotape), which can be synchronized with the film recorded in a camera, as was described earlier in Chapter 8, "Recording." The audiotape is transferred to magnetic film so that it can be edited in synchronization with the accompanying pictures. One of the first tasks of film editing is to sync up the film visuals with their corresponding sounds so that the workprint can be screened. This is accomplished by finding a common starting point, such as the visual and audio marker at the beginning of each shot provided by a clapstick. Once the visual image of the closing clapstick or slate is linked up with the "clap" sound, the entire shot will be in proper synchronization. The editor cuts together all of the shots in this manner so that they can be screened by the director, producer, and cinematographer while production is still in progress. The editor screens and carefully catalogues this material while preparing for the rough cut (Figure 10.13).

Rough-Cutting

Rough-cutting usually begins with the selection of a master shot containing virtually all the action occurring in one scene. The editor then attempts to insert various matching medium shots and close-ups into the master shot, gradually trimming the shots and refining the edit points throughout the rough-cutting process. An editor must be careful to remove equivalent amounts of picture and sound when trimming a shot, or the film and sound will no longer be in perfect synchronization. If four frames of picture are removed, four frames of sound must be removed. However, an editor can also manipulate the sound track to advantage without completely losing sync. For example, the sound from one shot can be overlapped with the picture of a subsequent shot.

The sound accompanying the subsequent shot is spliced into the sound track in midshot after trimming off a portion of its beginning equivalent in length to the overlap from the previous shot.

Figure 10.13 A flatbed film editor allows the operator to work with two sound tracks and the picture track simultaneously while viewing the picture on the screen. The tracks can be adjusted to sync with the picture while editing.

Synchronous sound effects can be spliced into an existing synchronous sound track or added to a second sound track, then later mixed with the primary synchronous sound track. When additional sound tracks have been added, the editor must then cut out or add in equivalent amounts on all the tracks wherever a general change is made.

Tape Splicing

A tape splicer allows the editor to cut photographic and magnetic film and splice the pieces together with tape. The teeth in the splicer hold the film in precise registration so that accurate, frame-line cuts can be made. The tape is placed on both sides of motion picture film, but only on one side (the base or shiny side) of magnetic film, so that it does not affect the sound track. If film images are taped on both sides, they will form a proper loop as they run through the projector gate and thus avoid jamming or breaking. There are a variety of tape splicers and types of splicing tape available. Some are called *guillotine splicers*, because they cut the tape and punch out the sprocket holes when the editor depresses the handle. Other tape splicers use preperforated splicing tape, which must be carefully aligned with the sprocket holes. Regardless of which type of splicer is used, it is important to make sure that all of the sprocket holes are clear of tape, so that the film can be driven properly by the sprocket teeth in a projector. Straight frame-line cuts are usually made on the picture film, while a diagonal splice or cut line is often used with magnetic film to suppress popping sounds when the magnetic film passes over a head and to reduce head wear.

After all rolls of sound track has been edited together, they are threaded onto individual fullcoat players. All players are locked together with the picture threaded onto a synchronized projector. All of the sound is fed through a mixing board and the operator combines the tracks into one or more final sound tracks on a fullcoat recorder. The conformed film and mixed tracks are sent to the lab where they are combined into a release print for the client's approval (Figure 10.14).

Head Leaders

Film editing begins with the construction of picture and sound head leaders, which are needed to thread up the film on a projector (Figure 10.15). The leaders identify the film by title and provide a common start mark (X) for picture and sound.

Figure 10.14 Fullcoat players and recorders are designed to keep a series of reels of sound tracks synchronized with the final edited workprint during the mixing and dubbing process.

A timing countdown, such as a standard academy leader, normally begins with the number 10 at 10 seconds prior to the film's beginning and ends on the number 2, with an accompanying beep on the sound track, indicating 2 seconds to the start of the film. An opaque black leader appears after the last number of the academy leader, and the film screen is then black for two seconds until the actual film begins. Having established a common synchronization point at the beginning of the film, the editor assembles shots in the order called for in the script (Figure 10.16).

BASIC FILM-EDITING BENCH

A basic film-editing bench consists of a variety of mechanical and electronic devices that make it possible to view the film and listen to the sound track simultaneously. They also allow an editor to maintain perfect synchronization between the visual and audio tracks, to move the film and sound backward and forward, and to physically cut and splice the film images and accompanying sound tracks. A film viewer projects film frames passing through it on a small screen so that they can be inspected by the editor. The sound tracks run over sound heads and are made audible by accompanying amplifiers and speakers. A gang synchronizer locks the film and sound tracks in synchronization with each other. The *gang synchronizer* consists of several sprocketed wheels or hubs on a common drive shaft. A footage and frame counter on the drive shaft keeps an accurate record of the footage and frames of the picture and sound tracks (Figure 10.17).

A set of rewinds is hand rotated to move the film and sound tracks through the gang synchronizer,

LEADER MARKINGS

Picture Head Leader

Figure 10.15 Leader markings are standardized by the film processing industry, but each lab may vary the markings for its own purposes. The magnetic fullcoat and all picture rolls must have leaders spliced to exactly the same length to maintain sound synchronization during the printing process.

Magentic Sound Track Head Leader

FILM ROLL LAYOUT

Head

A Roll

Black Leader   Shot 3   Black leader   Shot 1

B Roll

Shot 4   Black Leader   Shot 2   Black Leader

Sound Track

At least two rolls of pix with shots alternating with black leader and one or more rolls of sound track. Pix shots spliced straight across, sound tracks spliced on an angle.

Figure 10.16 Original film that is edited to be printed is conformed into at least two rolls: "A" and "B." This gives the editor the opportunity to splice alternate shots on each roll so that the printer can perform dissolves, supers, or other effects during the final printing stages. Black leader is spliced opposite the film to be printed unless there is a superimposition or effect. The film splices are made on the frame line, and fullcoat sound tracks are spliced at an angle to avoid "pops" at the edit points.

Figure 10.17 The basic film-editing bench consists of a pair of rewinds, a viewer, a synchronizer, and a supply of reels and spacers for the rewind shafts.

Figure 10.18 The synchronizer on an editing bench is set up with the "A" and "B" rolls threaded along with the workprint as the third roll of film. All are locked in sync by the synchronizer. The shots alternate on the "A" and "B" rolls with black leader spliced between shots in a checkerboard pattern.

movie viewer, and over the sound heads. The take-up reels placed on the rewinds should be equal in diameter so that the picture and sound tracks are driven at the same rate. Spacers are needed to separate both the take-up and the feed reels in conformity with the distance between hubs on the gang synchronizer (Figure 10.18). Clamps are needed to secure the reels to each other so that they can be driven by the common drive or rewind shaft, which is hand operated.

Bench editing is a mechanical process. Although mechanical editing puts everything under the editor's direct manual control, it also suffers from a number of disadvantages, such as difficulty in maintaining a constant speed when driving the film and sound by hand. Manually driven edit benches do not reproduce high-quality pictures and sounds, making evaluation difficult.

Editing Machines

An *upright film-editing machine*, such as a *Moviola Sr.*, interconnects the sound and picture drive mechanism through a common drive shaft. The individual drive mechanisms also can be disconnected so that the sound and film tracks can be driven independently by separate motors. The built-in take-up mechanism is directly above the feed mechanism, thus the name upright editor. The picture and sound playback quality are excellent. There is a variable-speed motor on the picture side and a constant-speed motor on the sound side, used for driving both tracks simultaneously. Additional sound track or picture elements can often be added to an upright machine (Figure 10.19).

Undoubtedly the most convenient film-editing machine that has been developed to facilitate film viewing and mechanical film splicing is the *flatbed editor*, which moves the film horizontally on a

Figure 10.19 The upright Moviola editor has been the standard professional editing tool for many years. It has become less popular as the use of flatbed editors and posting film on video has increased.

table. There are many different types and models of flatbed editors. Some, such as a *Steenbeck horizontal editor*, advance the picture and sound tracks by a mechanical interlock between sprocket drive mechanisms connected to a common motor, while others, such as the Moviola horizontal editor, rely on electronic synchronization of separate motors connected to a common electrical distributor. Some flatbed editors can drive only one picture and one sound track at a time. They are called *four-plate flatbed editors* because they have four take-up and feed dishes or plates. More sophisticated flatbeds have six or eight plates and can run one or two picture tracks and several sound tracks simultaneously in perfect synchronization. The flatbed offers an editor convenient access to all sound and picture tracks because of its horizontal configuration. It often provides a digital counter display of time or footage, a large viewing screen, and a good-quality sound playback and amplification system. Some models allow the sound tracks to be advanced and retarded in relation to the picture, providing added flexibility in finding or manipulating sound/image sync.

A flatbed editor can save a great deal of time in comparison with conventional bench editing. It also allows for more accurate editing by virtue of providing higher-quality picture and sound playback, and a better means of manipulating the sound and pictures independently or together. Splices can be made on a flatbed editor by simply pulling the marked film out to a splicer at the front of the machine. The open projection gate and sound heads on the flatbed allow the splice points to be easily seen and marked with a grease pencil.

Digital Film Editing

If the final distribution medium for a film project is exclusively videotape, original film recordings are often immediately transferred to videotape or digitized for electronic editing. When both film and videotape final copies are needed for different distribution and exhibition outlets, there are several options in terms of postproduction editing. One option is simply to make a film-to-videotape transfer of the completed film (Figure 10.20).

A second option is to edit the film in digital non-linear form and then use the time-code (videotape) and KeyKode (film) numbers generated by the EDL for final film editing or conforming. It is extremely important to use a digital nonlinear editing system that is designed specifically for film editing in order to solve two important problems that can arise: (1) a loss of synchronization between the separately recorded

Figure 10.20 A CCD telecine film-to-video converted. Each film frame is scanned individually, allowing for color correction and filtering in real time as the film is converted to a digital signal. (Courtesy of Philips Broadcast Television Systems Company.)

audio and video tracks, and (2) a failure to accurately convert the frames-per-second speed back to 24 frames per second for film from the digital video, which has 30 frames per second. Audio synchronization can be maintained by using a video-to-film accurate editing program.

The frame-per-second differences between video and film mean that some video frames do not exist on the film, unless the video is recorded at 24p, and then there is a direct correlation between video and film frames and conversion is simple. Computer programs were created in order to convert 24 frames per second of film to 30 frames per second of standard NTSC video. When using standard NTSC video the computer program must be able to recognize which video frames actually have corresponding film frames (using both time code and KeyKode) during editing in order to produce a conformed original film that is properly synchronized with the digitally edited sound track. A project can be shot as film, edited as digital images, and then conformed as film for both video and film distribution. This allows a producer to combine the image qualities and characteristics of film with the editing speed and convenience of digital nonlinear editing. Also, as HDTV equipment and technology improves, shooting a documentary as well as a feature film on HDTV rather than film, editing it digitally, and then transferring it to film for distribution becomes a reality. Through "electronic cinema" such productions could be delivered directly to theaters without leaving the electronic format.

Conforming

Once the film editing decisions have been finalized the original film is conformed to the edited workprint. Conforming is a professional skill that is often performed by a person called a *conformer*, particularly when a negative original must be cut together without error or getting the film dirty. All of the shots from the originally recorded film are permanently spliced into two or more rolls, called A and B (and C, and so on) rolls, using a cement splicer that physically welds two overlapping pieces of film together. During conforming, the individual shots must be divided into two rolls of alternating shots. One difference between 16mm and 35mm conforming is that there is sufficient space between frames in 35mm to be able to make overlapping cement splices on a single roll, although a B roll is required for dissolves, fades, and superimpositions. Individual shots on an A or B roll of 16mm film must alternate with black leader so that overlap splices always overlap into the black leader and are thus invisible when the film is printed. The completed A and B rolls are

printed to a single piece of film, called an *answer print*, at a film laboratory, before a final viewable image is obtained. A film on which picture and sound tracks are "married" together is called a *composite print*.

Marking the Workprint

Because the edited workprint serves as a guide for subsequent editing stages, it must be properly marked with appropriate symbols and designations. A grease pencil should be used to mark the film, since these markings can easily be rubbed off the film if changes are needed. The most commonly used symbols indicate the location of fades, dissolves, superimpositions, extended scenes, and unintended splices. To mark a fade-in, simply separate two lines from a point where the shot is to begin fading. The lines reach the outer edges of the frame where the shot is fully lit. The number of frames covered by the lines should equal the length or duration of the effect. A fade-out is marked by connecting two lines from the outer edges of the frame, where the fade-out begins to the precise point where the scene is supposed to be completely faded out. Again, the number of marked frames corresponds to the length of the effect. At 24 frames per second, a 24-frame fadeout will, of course, last exactly one second.

A dissolve is indicated by placing a fade-out marking on top of a fade-in mark. In this case one shot fades out while another fades in. For a superimposition or double exposure, the basic shot or dominant scene is spliced into the workprint at the beginning and ending points of the effect, but the recessive, superimposed shot is cut into the middle section. A wavy line drawn through the entire sequence indicates a double exposure or superimposition. An extended scene is one that continues despite the fact that the actual footage for this scene is missing in the workprint. A straight horizontal line shaped like an arrow indicates how far the prior shot extends. Finally, unintended splices in the workprint are clearly marked with two short horizontal lines drawn through the splice so that there is no confusion about shot changes at this point in later editing stages (Figure 10.21).

Edge Numbers

Edge numbers are consecutive reference numbers printed onto the edge of original film, either by the manufacturer of the film or by the film laboratory after processing. The latter are usually referred to as *yellow-ink edge numbers*. Edge numbers corresponding to those of the original camera film from which

WORK PRINT MARKINGS

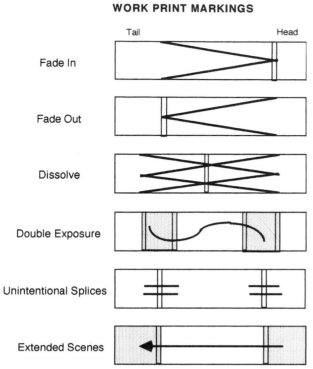

Figure 10.21 Since the workprint film rolls cannot actually have dissolves or effects cut into them, the industry uses standard markings on the workprint to notify the printer at the lab where to place transitions, supers, or double exposures, or where to correct errors that may have been made in the rough cut of the film.

the workprint has been copied can be printed onto the edges of the workprint. After the workprint has been edited, the edge numbers at the beginning and end of each shot are used (much like the SMPTE time code in off-line videotape editing) to select the correct shots from the original film for conforming to the edited workprint. The beginning and ending edge numbers of each shot in the edited workprint are written down so that the corresponding shots in the original film can be pulled and spliced together in their correct order.

Splicing the A and B Rolls

Once the workprint has been edited and marked, the original film from which the workprint was copied must be conformed to the workprint. Instead of editing shots together into a single roll as in workprint rough-cutting, the camera original is conformed into two rolls: an A roll and a B roll. This is done to make the splices between different shots invisible and to allow for special effects, such as fades, dissolves, and superimpositions. The splices are made invisible by using black leader between successive shots on a single roll of film. Thus, where there is a shot on the

A roll, there is black leader on the B roll. The only exception to this rule occurs in conforming fades for negative film, which require clear leader opposite a fade-out. In negative film, black is created by fading light in, not fading it out.

In either case, the two rolls of film are edited in a checkerboard fashion, except for dissolves and superimpositions, where shots are completely or partially overlapped. The individual shots are cement spliced to the black leader. Splices require a slight overlap, so that the two pieces of film can be welded together. To make the splices invisible, the overlap always occurs in the leader area. The emulsion must be scraped off the picture film where it will be bonded to the black leader, so that the two bases come into contact. Film emulsion inhibits the action of the cement. The cement splice provides a permanent bond, and it leaves no unsightly marks.

A conformer prepares the original for splicing by pulling all the shots from the camera original and placing them on individual plastic cores, which are labeled and arranged in sequential order. An alternative approach is to simply pull each shot from its respective camera original roll as it is needed. The conformer makes a complete list of the edge number markings of the edited workprint, and the original camera shots are pulled on the basis of the edge numbers. The film is usually cut with a frame and a half extra at both the head and rail ends of an individual shot, so that there is ample room for overlap.

Conformers usually adopt a standard set of procedures with no variations to avoid mistakes while cutting and splicing original film. Cleanliness is extremely important, because dirt and scratches will show up in the final prints. This problem is aggravated when using negative film, because the scratches and dirt then show up as white marks on the final prints. When all the shots have been prepared for splicing, the conformer places the A and B rolls and the workprint in the gang synchronizer on the editing bench, and proceeds to splice the shots alternately into one of the two rolls, leaving overlaps of specified lengths for dissolves and superimpositions.

Cement Splicing

Cement splicing requires the use of a properly adjusted cement splicer. The proper adjustment and alignment of the cutting blade and arms is crucial to the quality of the splice. The blade and arms should only be adjusted by a trained professional. Cement splicers can be either hot or cold: hot splicers have a heating element that was once needed to speed the drying process; cold splicers do not have any heating element. Today, cement has very little water that must be evaporated, so heating is rarely necessary. It is important to use fresh cement, however, since the welding capacity of cement deteriorates with exposure to air.

To make a 16mm splice, the black leader is positioned with the emulsion side up in the right-hand side of the splicer, by placing the teeth of the splicer in the correct sprocket holes of the leader and then locking down the top portion of the arm. Generally this should leave about 1½ frames of excess leader beyond the cutting edge or blade of the splicer. Raising the blade and then bringing it down over the left-hand arm severs the leader at the proper point. Now the adjacent shot is positioned in the left-hand arm so that the frame line where the splice will occur is placed close to the end of the blade or on the cut line. The emulsion is firmly and evenly scraped off the overlapping portion of the excess 1½ frames of the film so that only the clear base remains. Cement is applied to the scraped portion of the left-hand piece of film, and the right-hand arm is brought down quickly and locked into its welding position. This both cuts off the excess portion of the shot and brings it into contact with the black leader. In five to 10 seconds the cement is completely dried and the spliced film can be removed and inspected. A splice should be able to withstand considerable gentle pulling and twisting. This will ensure that it will not break on the printer. Black leader is never scraped in the cement splicer, unless you are splicing black leader to black leader, as this will cause the splice line to be visible in a frame of picture.

Combining the A and B Rolls

Once the A and B rolls are conformed to the workprint, they are sent to the laboratory so that they can each be printed in succession to a single roll of film, called an *answer print*. The answer print is a test printing of the A and B rolls, after they have been properly timed, that is, after the color and density of each shot has been adjusted by a laboratory professional, called a *color timer*. A composite print marries the A and B rolls together with a sound track so that it can be run in a conventional projector. The composite print usually has an optical sound track, which is advanced ahead of the corresponding pictures by 26 frames in 16mm or 20 frames in 35mm.

SUMMARY

Trimming and combining visual images and sounds define the craft or mechanics of editing, but any discussion of the overall process and art of editing must begin with a consideration of editing stages, systems, modes, and aesthetic approaches. In the digital age, editing occurs during production and postproduction stages, and parallel filmmaking and editing are replacing serial postproduction. The editing process consists of at least two stages: preliminary and final editing. During preliminary editing, images and sounds are repeatedly viewed before they are trimmed and combined, usually using a copy of the original recordings to create a rough cut or off-line edited version. During final editing, the original recordings are on-line edited (video) or conformed (film) into a polished version that will actually be released to viewers and listeners.

Linear editing systems require an editor to add visual images and sounds in consecutive order from the beginning to the end of a piece. Most analog videotape and audiotape editing systems are basically linear editing systems. In nonlinear editing the overall duration of a production can be lengthened or shortened at any time, and images and sounds do not have to be edited in consecutive order from beginning to end.

Classical Hollywood conventions for shooting and editing fiction films and videos include master scene shooting and continuity editing. A master shot consists of a relatively long-duration shot that includes most of the action in a specific scene. Matching close-ups can be inserted into the master shot during editing. Continuity editing refers to an editing system that developed in Hollywood and elsewhere beginning about 1910. It consists of a number of shooting and editing conventions that sustain an illusion of continuous time and place within a scene.

Variations upon master scene and continuity editing techniques have also been developed that take into account the difficulties of scripting and staging nonfiction events, as well as the use of expository and rhetorical structures that can disrupt spatial and temporal continuity. A variation upon master scene shooting and editing commonly used in news and documentary production, for example, is called A and B roll editing. A and B roll editing adds viewer interest by interspersing rather static shots of a talking head with a wide variety of visual illustrations.

Visual images can be combined using principles of editing derived from each of the three aesthetic orientations: realism, modernism, and postmodernism. Realist editing preserves spatial and temporal continuity from shot to shot. A modernist approach to editing often deliberately disrupts spatial and temporal continuity between shots and calls attention to the editing process. A postmodernist approach to editing can take the form of a collage or pastiche that combines diverse images and sounds and actively engages the viewer/listener in the process of constructing the artwork.

One of the editor's first tasks is to organize and catalogue all the recordings that the director has provided. In documentary productions that lack a detailed script, performing a paper edit from a catalogue of shots and camera takes can help an editor efficiently and economically organize the editing process.

There are three types of editing technology and techniques: digital nonlinear editing, videotape linear editing, and film editing. Digital nonlinear editing software offers several advantages over conventional means of editing film, audiotape, and videotape, including increased flexibility or creativity, as well as potential time and cost savings.

A clip is usually the smallest unit of digital video (or audio) information that can be stored and manipulated during editing. It can range from just one frame to an entire movie in duration, but it often consists of a single shot, that is, a continuous camera recording or take. Digitized clips are usually imported (or copied) into a particular editing project file, where they are edited along a time line with other images and sounds. Clips of video or audio information can be cut, trimmed, copied, pasted, inserted, and deleted along a time line.

Videotape editing is usually divided into two stages: off-line editing and on-line editing. Off-line editing is often done in a smaller format, and off-line editing decisions are later performed on an originally recorded larger-format videotape. During assemble editing, both the control track and the visual images from the original recording are transferred to the new assemble-edited version. With insert editing, a portion of one shot can be replaced by another shot. During insert editing, video-only and audio-only edits can be made, as well as video-plus-audio edits.

Film editing follows a series of stages similar to videotape editing. The process begins with rough-cutting, the equivalent of off-line videotape editing that includes viewing a copy of the originally recorded images called the workprint, rushes, or dailies. Film editing also includes selecting and ordering specific shots and scenes with which the original film, edited workprint, and answer print can be conformed to one another. This process resembles online videotape editing. Unlike videotape editing, however, traditional film editing usually involves mechanical processes, such as physically cutting and splicing the film.

Recent developments in digital editing have made it possible to edit film digitally in nonlinear form and then use the time-code (videotape) and KeyKode (film) numbers generated by the EDL for final film editing or conforming. A project can be shot as film, edited as videotape or digital images, and then conformed as film for both videotape and film distribution. Once the film editing decisions have been finalized, the original film is conformed to the edited workprint.

EXERCISES

1. Edit together a short movie trailer or television promotion for a documentary or dramatic feature film, using an existing videotape that is in the public domain, that is, not copyright protected. View the videotape at least twice, writing down the control-track numbers for each shot or sequence that you think you might use in your trailer or promo. Then, using these notes, perform a paper edit of the sequence so that the edited promo, at least on paper, approximates a specific duration, such as one minute or three minutes. Then, using the paper edit, actually edit the sequence on videotape, or digitize the clips that you have selected and edit them using a digital nonlinear editing system. Remember that you are trying to promote the film. Therefore you will want to select sequences that will attract viewers but not disappoint them by setting up false expectations that the film itself cannot fulfill. Basically you want to capture the essence of the film to promote it.

2. Edit your own version of a professionally recorded scene or sequence. Obtain a copy of the original, unedited recordings of a professional-quality production. The American Cinema Editor's (ACE's) annual student editing contest is a potential source of professional recordings or film rushes. After you have edited these shots in film, videotape, or digital form, compare your version with the version actually produced by a professional editor, and determine what you could do to improve your own editing.

3. After completing either #1 or #2, shoot your own five-minute dramatic sequence and edit it on a nonlinear system. If a linear system is available, edit the same sequence using a linear system to compare the differences in ease of editing and the choice of edits.

4. If film equipment is available, shoot and edit the same sequence as #3 on film and compare the two systems.

5. Dub the film from #4 to a digital system and edit the sequence on a computer.

6. Produce an in-studio multi-camera dramatic production by recording the output of all three

cameras as well as the output of the switcher simultaneously. Produce the program as a "live" continuous production without any stopping or reshooting. Take the four tapes and edit them into a comprehensive program using a nonlinear system.

ADDITIONAL READINGS

Bayes, Steve. *The Avid Handbook*, 4th. ed. Boston, MA: Focal Press, 2004.

Benedetti, Robert, ed. *Creative Post Production: Editing, Sound, Visual Effects, and Music for Film and Video*. Boston, MA: Allyn and Bacon, 2004.

Block, Bruce. *The Visual Story: Seeing the Structure of Film, Television, and New Media*. Boston, MA: Focal Press, 2001.

Browne, Steven E. *Video Editing: A Post Production Primer*, 4th. ed. Boston, MA: Focal Press, 2000.

Clark, Barbara, and Susan Spohr. *Guide to Post-Production for TV and Film: Managing the Process*, 2nd ed. Boston, MA: Focal Press, 2002

Compesi, Ronald J. *Video Field Production and Editing*, 6th ed. Boston, MA: Allyn and Bacon, 2003.

Dancyger, Ken. *The Technique of Film and Video Editing*, 3rd ed. Boston, MA: Focal Press, 2002.

Fowler, Jaime. *Editing Digital Film: Integrating Final Cut Pro, Avid, and Media 100*. Boston, MA: Focal Press, 2001.

Gross, Lynne S., and Larry W. Ward. *Digital Moviemaking*, 5th ed. Belmont, CA: Wadsworth Publishing, 2004.

Jones, Stuart Blake, ed. *Film into Video: A Guide to Merging Technologies*, 2nd ed. Boston, MA: Focal Press, 2000.

Kauffmann, Sam. *Avid Editing: A Guide for Beginning and Intermediate Users*, 2nd ed. Boston, MA: Focal Press, 2003.

Levin, C. Melinda, and Fred P. Watkins. *Post: The Theory and Technology of Digital Nonlinear Motion Picture Editing*. Boston, MA: Allyn and Bacon, 2003.

Mamer, Bruce. *Film Production Techniques. Creating the Accomplished Image*, 3rd ed. Belmont, CA: Wadsworth Publishing, 2003.

Millar, Gavin. *The Technique of Film Editing*, revised ed. Boston, MA: Focal Press, 1995.

Ohanian, Thomas A., and Michael E. Phillips. *Digital Filmmaking*, 2nd ed. Boston, MA, Focal Press, 2000.

Rabiger, Michael *Directing Film Techniques and Aesthetics*, 3rd ed. Boston, MA: Focal Press, 2003.

Rowlands, Avin. *Continuity in Film and Video*, 4th ed. Boston, MA: Focal Press, 2000.

Wheeler, Paul. *High Definition and 24P Cinematography*. Boston, MA: Focal Press, 2003.

11 Sound Editing

TOPICS FOR DISCUSSION

- What are the aesthetics of editing sound?
- How does digital sound editing differ from analog sound editing?
- What are the types of sound editing techniques?
- How is film sound edited?
- What techniques are used in mixing sound?
- How is music editing accomplished?

INTRODUCTION

Sound editing is an extremely important stage of postproduction. Sounds can breathe life, realism, emotion, and power into visual images. Sounds can also develop their own form of expression apart from visual images, and they can be edited before, during, or after visual editing. The fact that sounds and images can be edited in tandem or independently of each other allows for considerable flexibility in terms of editing different types of sound and different combinations of sounds and visual images.

Each different type of sound, such as speech, sound effects, and music, can be edited in conjunction with visual images. As noted in Chapter 5, "Audio/Sound," sounds can be synchronous or asynchronous, on-screen or off-screen, and parallel or contrapuntal in meaning with respect to accompanying visual images. Separately edited speech, sound effects, and music tracks can be blended or mixed together to form one monaural sound track or several stereophonic tracks.

Sound editing can be a complex process. It involves combining many different types of sound using various forms and stages of both editing and mixing. From the standpoint of aesthetics, the complexities of sound editing can be approached from three different perspectives: realism, modernism, and postmodernism. Realist sound recording, as discussed in Chapter 5, preserves a feeling of authentic-

ity and accuracy of specific sounds, while realist sound editing preserves a continuity of sounds in time and space. Generally speaking, time flows continuously and sequentially from one sound to the next. There are no apparent gaps or breaks in the audio action.

Realist

Realist sound editing often reinforces realist visual editing. Sounds can follow the lead set by visual images, enhancing, filling out, and reinforcing the images they accompany. Realist sounds are usually synchronous, on-screen, and parallel in meaning with the accompanying images. They rarely develop an independent meaning that competes with the accompanying visual images. Speech, sound effects, and music basically conform to the requirements of specific visuals throughout the editing process. In some situations, such as news and documentary editing, a sound track composed of voiceover narration and interviews may be edited prior to the selection and editing of illustrative images. Nevertheless, sounds and images remain parallel in meaning and complement one another.

Like realist visual editing, realist sound editing emphasizes message clarity. The editor removes mistakes, such as flubbed lines of dialogue or disruptive background sounds, and tries to achieve a proper balance between speech, sound effects, and music. Primacy is usually given to one of these elements at a time, so that the main message is clear and distinct. By simplifying and ordering sounds, an editor avoids listener disorientation and confusion. The space between lines of dialogue or narration is made long enough to allow for a smooth, clear, natural delivery, but short enough to maintain interest and excitement.

News stories and prerecorded interviews in documentaries are examples of situations that often call for a realist approach to editing. A reporter's or filmmaker's voiceover narration or the responses of an interviewee are often edited to maintain better message clarity and flow. In editing narrative fiction, the editor's choices are often restricted by the script, which indicates what lines of dialogue must be used as well as which visual shots must be used at a specific time. But the editor must deviate from the script slightly when problems arise in the original recordings and neither the sounds nor the images can be rerecorded.

Modernist

Modernist sound editing often develops sound as an independent aesthetic element. Continuity of time and space are sometimes disrupted. Sounds may be asynchronous and/or contrapuntal with respect to accompanying visual images, and the audience frequently experiences the thoughts and feelings of the film or video artist, a fictional character in the story, or a social actor within a nonfiction work. In short, modernist techniques develop subjective impressions. Sound effects, for example, can create imaginative impressions of what a character is feeling, thinking, or experiencing rather than an illusion of objective reality or authenticity. The pace and meaning of music can contrast with or counterpoint the accompanying visuals, such as when slow-paced music accompanies rapidly paced visual action. The editor freely develops abstract audio relations and qualities. Modernist sound editing techniques, of course, can be incorporated into realist films and videos to add a degree of unpredictability, generating viewer interest and emotional excitement. The sound in the films of Alfred Hitchcock is a good example of modernist sound editing within generally realist films.

Postmodernist

Postmodernist sound editing offers a pastiche of audio impressions, often mixing documentary, narrative fiction, and experimental modes. Rather than promoting subjective psychological impressions or a realist sense of objectivity, authenticity, and continuity, postmodernist sound editing plunders a variety of genres, historical periods, and previously distinct styles, often generating a feeling of nostalgia for bygone eras and breaking down distinctions between popular and elite cultural forms. Postmodernist editing gives spectators more freedom to explore, respond to, and play with recorded speech, sound effects, and music. It does not reinforce an illusion of reality or the artist's subjective impressions, but instead evokes a sense of free play with sounds and encourages audience participation in the creative

process. This chapter explores a variety of audio editing techniques, some of which reflect postmodernist, modernist, or realist aesthetics that are applicable to digital nonlinear, videotape, magnetic film, and audiotape editing technologies.

DIGITAL NONLINEAR EDITING

Digital nonlinear audio editing offers a number of advantages over analog editing. First, the quality of digital audio does not significantly diminish from one generation to the next, since the binary encoding of audio signals generally allows an editor to maintain a consistent signal-to-noise ratio throughout the editing process. Second, multiple audio tracks can be edited independently or in conjunction with one another. Third, most nonlinear editing programs provide a visual image of a sound track, which indicates fluctuations in loudness and pitch and allows the editor to quickly and easily find and mark precise edit points, such as the beginning or end of specific sounds. Fourth, digital audio can be initially edited in conjunction with visual images, using a relatively simple editing program, and then the same audio can be fine-tuned independently using a separate, more sophisticated audio editing program before it is recombined with the visuals again. The fact that digital audio can be used in different programs without degrading its quality, and that a digital nonlinear edited sound track can maintain exact synchronization with accompanying videotape or film images by using SMPTE time code and/or film KeyKode as common reference points, provides considerable editing flexibility.

Digitizing audio, like digitizing video, requires considerable time and disk space. Audio can be digitized at the time of its original recording, using a separate digital audiotape (DAT), disc recorder, or solid-state device, or an analog recording can be rapidly sampled and digitized during postproduction, either in conjunction with or separately from visual images. Unless the original recording has been digitized in a format that is computer readable, placing the audio information on a hard disk will generally take as long as the real-time duration of the original recording. The sampling rate and bandwidth of an audio signal can be varied during digitization to reduce the amount of storage space that is required. There are two steps to digitizing audio: setting the audio level controls, and setting the audio resolution or quality. Setting the audio level controls avoids distortion and ensures a high signal-to-noise ratio in digital audio, just as it does in analog audio.

The quality of digitized audio and the size of the audio file also depend on the sampling rate and bit depth of the audio. The sampling rate for audio is similar to the frame rate for digitizing video. It measures the number of frequencies into which the sound is broken. The bit depth, which is similar to color depth in visuals, measures the number of tones per sample. A high sampling rate stores and reproduces very high-quality sound. The higher the sampling rate and bit depth, the better the sound quality. Audio sampled at 22 kHz (kiloHertz), that is, at 22,000 cycles per second, and 8-bit resolution (8 bits equal 1 byte of computer information and storage) may be sufficient for monophonic speech and sound effects, but a sampling rate of 44 kHz and 16-bit resolution is probably the minimum required for stereo sound and music, which will require about twice the disk storage space.

Compact disc (CD) audio is normally digitized at 44 kHz and 16-bit resolution. A *bit* is the smallest amount of information a computer can handle. Eight bits make up a *byte*, 1,000 bytes equal a *kilobyte* (KB), 1,000,000 bytes equal a *megabyte* (MB), and 1,000,000,000 bytes equal a *gigabyte* (GB). Thus it takes slightly more than 2.6 MB to store one minute of audio information at 22 kHz and 16-bit resolution (22,000 cycles per second × 60 seconds × 2 bytes = 2,640,000 bytes or 2.64 MB). This is considerably less than uncompressed video information, as discussed in Chapter 10, "Visual Editing." Remember that one full frame of picture requires slightly less than 1 MB. There are 30 frames per second, and thus one minute of uncompressed full-frame video requires 1,800 MB, or about 1.8 GB per minute.

Digital audio, unlike digital video, is not usually compressed when it is digitized, since digitized audio already requires considerably less storage space than digitized video, and audio compression could significantly reduce the quality of the audio signal. *Compression* in audio has two meanings. (1.) Compression refers to a reduction of the volume of information in order to force it into less storage space. (2.) Compression prevents distortion during recording by, for example, reducing the loudness range of a singer, who alternately sings very loudly and very softly. Compression in the second sense is rarely used while digitizing audio that was originally recorded as an analog signal, however.

Digital Nonlinear Editing Hardware

Most digital nonlinear audio editing systems employ computer hardware that is capable of processing and storing vast amounts of audio information. In addi-

tion to an audio capture card, an audio nonlinear editing system usually includes a computer processing unit (CPU) with a 500+ megahertz (MHz) processing system, 250+ MB of random access memory (RAM), a keyboard, a mouse, one or two computer monitors, an audio recorder, an amplifier and loudspeakers, and a 40+ GB hard disk drive designed for audiovisual (AV) use.

Digital Nonlinear Editing Software

Digital nonlinear editing software offers several advantages over conventional means of editing magnetic film audiotape and videotape, including increased flexibility or creativity, as well as potential time and cost savings. Digital nonlinear editing affords an editor flexibility in terms of instantaneously changing the order and duration of sounds and images. For example, clips of audio information can be cut, trimmed, copied, pasted, inserted, and deleted along a time line (Figure 11.1).

A *clip* is usually the smallest unit of digital audio information that can be stored and manipulated during editing. It can range from a fraction of a second to an entire movie in duration, but it often consists of a continuous audio recording or *take*. Digitized clips are usually imported (or copied) into a particular editing project file, where they are edited along a time line with other sounds and images. Most editing software provides several windows or screens, including a project window, a time line (or construction) window, and a locking window. Different windows can usually be displayed simultaneously on one or more computer monitors. A *project window* usually contains the individual clips in alphabetical order based on the first letters of their written descriptions. The *time line* or *construction window* displays a time line that contains several audio tracks and indicates the overall duration and order of the edited project. A *locking window* allows the editor to lock together or unlock various audio and visual tracks in the time line window so that they can be cut and trimmed collectively or individually.

Audio is often displayed visually as a continuous, variable area sound track, where high peaks represent loud sounds and rapid fluctuations indicate high-frequency sounds. Clips can be copied and inserted at various points along the time line, and they can be cut, trimmed, and split into several clips as well as deleted from the time line, leaving the remaining sounds attached to one another. The overall volume of a clip can usually be increased or decreased by adjusting an accompanying volume-control band. Fade-outs, fade-ins, and cross-fades can be created by adjusting the volume band, and

FIGURE 11.1 The screen on a computer running a digital audio editing program shows what the sounds look like in various formats. When editing, an audio editor visually cuts, pastes, and modifies the virtual files as if they were a part of word processing.

sounds can be increased or decreased at will throughout the clip, such as to bring a music track down and under a voice track. Rapid fade-ins and fade-outs of audio clips at cut points from one audio track to another often help to hide digital "popping" sounds, or digital noise, which is sometimes audible at cut points. (Some digital editing systems have programs that facilitate the elimination of digital "popping" sounds in this manner.) Clips can also be filtered, that is, the entire clip can have its frequency response altered. The high-frequency sounds can be reduced and the low-frequency sounds increased in intensity, for example. The reverberation or attack and decay

of a sound clip can also be altered to enhance or diminish echo.

Every edit made using a digital nonlinear software program is usually a virtual edit. No digitized material need be discarded when clips are trimmed, cut, or deleted along an editing time line, since each clip is usually stored separately outside the time line window. Every clip stored on a disk drive is instantaneously accessible in its entirety and can be grabbed in the project or clip window and reinserted at any point along the time line. Many alternative versions of a scene or sequence can thus be quickly edited and examined without prematurely eliminating material that may be needed later. Transitions from one sound track to another can be previewed, as can the filtering of specific tracks without ever actually cutting, discarding, eliminating, or deleting any originally digitized video or audio.

The ability to manipulate clips of sound along a time line not only adds flexibility to the editing process, but it can also make editing more efficient and cost-effective. Clips can be very rapidly trimmed, cut, inserted, and deleted. Digital nonlinear editing is extremely fast compared with physically cutting and splicing a conventional magnetic film sound, for example. The time it takes to find and insert videotape sounds from a source onto a master videotape can be dramatically reduced by using instantaneously accessible digital clips along a time line. The amount of time scheduled for postproduction editing can be significantly diminished, facilitating the editing of projects that require a short turnaround time. Clearly, digital nonlinear editing offers a number of advantages in terms of flexibility and efficiency over conventional videotape, magnetic film, and audio-tape editing.

Digital film sound editing may require specialized software that maintains synchronization between the original film, which is usually recorded at 24 frames per second, and various sound tracks, including the originally recorded synchronous sound. This software or slave system resolves the audio playback to time code, which can maintain synchronization with the original film. Achieving accurate lock to time code allows a film sound editor to benefit from all the advantages of digital sound editing without losing synchronization between the originally recorded film and sound, when the final visual editing will be completed on film, such as for a Hollywood feature film.

LINEAR VIDEOTAPE EDITING

Linear electronic editing of videotape can be divided into two categories: control-track editing and time-code editing. Control-track editing is somewhat less precise than time-code editing. In *control-track editing* each frame of video and audio is counted in terms of pulses in the control track, while in *time-code editing* a sequential numerical code is recorded on the videotape and each frame of video and audio has a permanently coded number that does not change. In control-track editing the frame numbers are sequentially counted from the point at which the VTR counter is zeroed. Most control-track editors slip a bit or skip frames when the videotape is repeatedly stopped and started. Edits are usually accurate to plus or minus two frames in control-track editing, while time-code editing is usually accurate to a specific frame, called frame-accurate.

Control-track videotape editing usually allows for video-only, audio channel one-only, audio channel two-only, audio channels one- and two-only, and audio channels one-and/or two-plus-video editing in the insert mode, as discussed in Chapter 10, "Visual Editing." To insert edit sound onto prerecorded images without erasing those images, the sound must first be recorded on a separate videotape along with a control track. Sound can then be dubbed onto one of the audio tracks or channels of a prerecorded videotape without disturbing the picture or separate audio information on another sound channel. Video can also be added to a videotape without disturbing the prerecorded audio signal. Using synchronized sounds and images originally recorded on videotape, an editor can edit the audio simultaneously within the video, maintaining precise synchronization. Audio editing on videotape can involve a single synchronous sound track on the original videotape or the building of complex dialogue, narration, sound effects, and music tracks (Figure 11.2).

Simple videotape mixing is done by combining two separate audio tracks on a single prerecorded videotape. The two tracks are recorded separately and then played back on a source VCR through a mixer or audio console so that they can be combined onto one track on the record videotape. Mixing videotape audio is limited only by the number of audio tracks and playback machines available.

LINEAR & PCM AUDIO TRACKS

FIGURE 11.2 PCM audio tracks are recorded along with the video in the same slant track. PCM is a digital audio format and may be recorded in short bursts located at the ends of the video tracks. The linear audio tracks can be either analog or digital.

A more expensive alternative to using the control track of a videotape is to use a computerized videotape editor with addressable time codes. The computerized editor can control several video and/or audio sources simultaneously. Sound editing and mixing decisions can be programmed into the computer, which will control the playback and adjust the volume of each different sound source. Any audio or video machine capable of reading the SMPTE time code can be used for computerized editing and mixing. With computer assistance, a complex sound track can be designed, programmed, and mixed automatically on the basis of a mix log that is pro-

grammed into the computer along with all editing decisions (Figure 11.3).

Time-code editing allows an editor to perform more complex mixing of separate audio tracks. For example, the dialogue that is originally recorded and edited on videotape in synchronization with the video images can be dubbed to an audiotape along with other sound elements, such as several music and sound effects tracks. All of the tracks can be mixed down to one track (mono) or two tracks (stereo) on the same multitrack audiotape before the mix down is transferred back to videotape. Music and sound effects can be combined with the dialogue and then

AUDIO EDITING ON VIDEOTAPE

Combining 2 or more audio tracks using
Control Track editing

Combining many tracks from both videotape and
audio sources to one or two tracks on a record
videotape deck through an audio mixer all
controlled by the Time Code edit controller.

FIGURE 11.3 The process of editing audio on videotape provides a very precise means of assembling a variety of different audio sources onto either one or both of the audio tracks on the final edited videotape. The simplest method is to use tracks from two playback decks and mix the audio through an audio mixer. More complex editing can be accomplished by using non-videotape sources mixed with audio from more than one videotape playback deck.

dubbed back to an audio channel of the original videotape in perfect synchronization with the images. A potential problem with multigeneration dubbing and mixing with analog audiotape, however, is that the music or sound effects may be severely degraded in quality by virtue of having been dubbed.

MAGNETIC FILM EDITING

This section is concerned solely with conventional double-system film editing of magnetic film sound. Synchronous film sound is often recorded on ¼-inch audiotape, using a separate synchronous sound recorder. The originally recorded sounds are accompanied by a sync signal element that is recorded on the audiotape along with the primary synchronous dialogue sounds and is used to maintain precise synchronization with the separately recorded visuals. It determines the playback speed of the tape recorder when the film sound is transferred from audiotape to 16mm or 35mm magnetic film. Magnetic film can be physically cut and spliced in conjunction with motion picture film. (Figure 11.4).

Splicing allows an editor to combine sounds in sequential order and to synchronize them with accompanying images. This can be accomplished through physical cutting of magnetic film. If synchronization is not crucial, it may be advantageous to edit sounds initially on conventional ¼-inch tape (to be discussed later in this chapter) since a common film format is not required. Any sounds that are to be synchronized with visual images during editing must first be dubbed to magnetic film. Physically splicing

magnetic film requires several pieces of equipment, including a splicing block and cutting blade, Mylar splicing tape, and some means of locking pictures and sounds in synchronization, such as a gang synchronizer or a flatbed editor. The first step in splicing magnetic film is locating the precise edit points on the two pieces of tape that are to be joined. These points are marked on the base (shiny) sides of the magnetic film with a permanent felt-tip pen. The magnetic film can then be placed in the splicing block so that the proper edit points line up with the diagonal splice edge of the cutting block. Using a diagonal splice line minimizes the chance of creating a "popping" sound when the splice passes over a playback head. A film-splicing block normally has pegs on which the sprocket holes of the film are placed to ensure proper alignment for exact cutting and joining (Figure 11.5).

There are basically two types of film splicers: those that use preperforated Mylar tape laid horizontally across the splice, and those that use unperforated tape laid vertically across the splice. In the latter case, the sprocket holes are punched out as the tape is cut. Both types of tape splicers are available with diagonal splicing blocks for audio cutting and joining, allowing the two diagonally cut pieces of magnetic recording film to be held together with pegs in adjacent sprocket holes so that Mylar tape can be applied to the base side to make a secure splice. The excess tape is cut off by a blade, and the tape joint is smoothed out by rubbing across the top of the splice. The splice should be inspected to see if the sprocket holes are clear and to make sure there are no gaps between the two pieces of audiotape. A tape splice

FIGURE 11.4 Most film soundtracks are recorded on either a ¼-inch reel-to-reel or digital tape deck on location or in the studio. That tape is then dubbed to either 16mm or 35mm magnetic fullcoat film. Several tracks of fullcoat film are threaded on individual fullcoat players and then dubbed through a sound-mixing board to create the final sound mix.

PATH OF FILM SOUND

1/4 inch audiotape recorded in sync with original film footage

DUBBED TO

16mm full coat film

Voice track

Music track

Sound effects track

Multiple tracks of 16mm fullcoat film edited and spliced

DUBBED TO

THROUGH A MIXER

Single final mixed track on 16mm full coat film

FIGURE 11.5 A splicer used to edit sound fullcoat film and workprint film uses a wide clear or opaque tape stretched across the film. The handle is brought down, sealing the tape and punching holes in the tape that is lined up with the sprocket holes in the film.

FIGURE 11.6 A splicer used to edit film to be projected or to assemble "A" and "B" rolls is called a hot splicer. A heating element built into the metal base of the splicer warms the deck of the splicer so that as soon as the acetone is applied to the joint between the film segments, the splice will quickly and permanently bond to create a secure splice. Separate magnetic film tracks are sometimes slugged or interspersed with clear leader, which is completely transparent film with no oxide coating. Using clear leader between recorded sounds is less expensive than using magnetic film, and it also clearly identifies where recorded audio occurs on the roll. Slugging with clear leader simultaneously on all edited sound tracks prevents any continuation of ambient noise or "room tone" and results in patches of completely silent or dead audio. Thus clear leader should only be used with tracks that will eventually be mixed with others.

can easily be redone by simply removing the Mylar tape and putting the two pieces of audiotape back in the splicing block. Note that Mylar splicing tape should never be placed on the oxide side (usually, but not always, the dull side) of the audiotape, where it will interfere with the playback of the recorded sound.

Magnetic film is synchronized with accompanying images by finding the precise frames where the sound of the clapstick is heard on the sound track and seen on the image track for each shot. Once synchronized, magnetic film can be edited frame by frame with the accompanying images. Prerecorded sound effects can be added at the precise points where they mirror the visual action. A crescendo or musical beat can be aligned with a specific action or cutline through physical splicing. To maintain synchronization between the sound and picture once it has been achieved, an editor must add or subtract the same number of frames in both the picture and the sound tracks when any change is required. (See Figure 11.6.)

Synchronizing sounds with film images requires that the sounds be transferred to magnetic film of the same format as the recorded film images. When the sounds and images are in a common format, they can be spliced in complete synchronization. After several different sound tracks, such as separate music, dialogue, and sound effects tracks, have each been independently synchronized with the edited film images, they can be mixed together onto a single master sound track. Each separate synchronized sound track is played back on its own magnetic film playback unit or *dubber*. Dubbers can be synchronized by means of a physical or electronic interlock between drive mechanisms or motors. The dubbers and the magnetic film recorder that will be used to record the master sound track must be driven at exactly the same speed. Each separate dubber can then be fed to a different fader at an audio console or mixer so that they can all be combined.

The output signal of the audio console is fed to a single magnetic film recorder. A synchronous film sound mix is often accompanied by a synchronous playback of the filmed images using an interlocked projector, which is connected to the same electrical signal as the sound playback and record machines. Mixing magnetic film provides precise synchronization between sound tracks as well as between all sounds and the film images.

When synchronization between sounds and images is not crucial, it is often convenient to edit and mix sounds in an audiotape format, such as ¼-inch audiotape. Audiotape editing can then be done using physical splicing techniques. A variety of different audiotape formats can be used for nonsynchronous sound mixing. The resulting mix can be dubbed to the same format as the visual images.

AUDIOTAPE EDITING

Splicing Audiotape

Splicing ¼-inch audiotape requires several pieces of equipment, including a splicing block, a single-edge razor blade, a permanent felt-tip pen, a set of rewinds with a playback head, an amplifier, and a speaker. Sometimes ¼-inch tape is edited while it is played back on a ¼-inch tape recorder with a built-in splicer. The original audiotape recording should be safely stored away after a dub has been made for splicing.

The best procedure for editing ¼-inch audiotape is to find the edit point on one piece of tape by running it over the playback head. This point is then marked on the base side (usually the shiny side) of the audiotape with a permanent felt-tip pen. The tape is then placed securely and flatly in the splicing block with the precise edit point over the diagonal cutline indentation on the block. The tape is severed with a single stroke of a sharp razor blade. Razor blades should be replaced before they get dull. The audiotape is then advanced and the second edit point is marked. The second cut is made in the same manner as the first. After the excess tape has been removed from the splicing block, the two pieces of tape can be butted together and joined by placing a piece of adhesive ¼-inch splicing tape on the base side of the audiotape.

When audiotape will be spliced it is best to maintain as high a tape-to-head speed as possible during initial recording. For music the best editing speed is 15 inches per second, but for voice a tape-to-head speed of 7½ inches per second is usually sufficient to separate most words. It is never advisable to use speeds below 7½ inches per second, since this will make it difficult to separate sounds or produce high-quality recordings (Figure 11.7).

Multitrack audiotape recorders that cannot read time code provide one means of maintaining synchronization between different sound sources that do not need to be synchronized with visual images. Most multitrack audiotape recorders allow the sounds recorded on one track to be played at the precise speed at which the original recording was made, while additional sounds are added on a parallel track. For example, music might be prerecorded on one track. This music could be played back while a singer's voice is recorded on a parallel track. Using this technique, several musicians and singers, for example, can each be recorded at different times and places. Multitrack recorders allow many different sound tracks to be combined, such as those for narration, music, and sound effects. Synchronization between the separate tracks is inherent in the tape since each track is recorded and played back on the tape parallel with the others. Narration can be recorded while the sound effects and music are played back, for example. When each of the different tracks has been properly recorded, they can all be mixed onto a single track. It is important to note that time-code readable multitrack recorders can also be used to maintain synchronization between different tracks, as noted earlier. To initially synchronize sounds with visual images, they are usually edited and mixed in the same format as the accompanying visual images.

Sound Mixing Techniques

Sound mixing combines several different sounds or sound tracks that are running simultaneously. Editing, on the other hand, pieces together sounds in sequence, usually on one sound track at a time. Mixing is a process by which various sound tracks are blended together or combined with each other. Individual sound tracks for speech, sound effects, and music, for example, are first edited into sequential order, often in conjunction with visual images, prior to mixing them together to form one sound track. The volume and equalization or EQ (the attenuation or amplification of specific frequencies) of each different audio channel or track is separately controlled using a fader and EQ controls on an audio console or mixer or within a digital editing program (Figure 11.8).

It is extremely important to maintain a high signal-to-noise ratio in each separate sound track prior to the mix. During the mix, the audio level of one

Spatial Differences in Audiotape Recording Speed

This is one second   worth of copy   at   15   IPS

This is one second worth of copy at 7.5 IPS

FIGURE 11.7 Physically editing audiotape is a matter of finding a space between words or sounds. The more widespread the sounds, the easier and more accurate the editing can be.

The faster the recording speed, the higher the quality of the recording, and for editing purposes, the faster the speed, the greater the distance between words and sounds for easier editing.

VARIOUS AUDIO SOURCES MIXED TO ONE OUTPUT

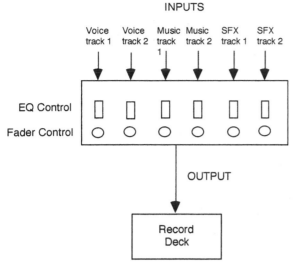

FIGURE 11.8 To combine several audio sources simultaneously, all of the individual sounds are fed through an audio mixer where the individual sounds can be equalized and levels can be properly set in relationship to each other.

sound track can always be reduced. But speech, sound effects, or music that were initially recorded or dubbed at a low sound level cannot be increased in volume during the mix without simultaneously increasing the accompanying noise level, and thereby reducing the quality of the audio. Whenever possible, sounds should be kept at their maximum level until the mix and then adjusted to accommodate other sounds. Properly recorded digital signals will not increase noise level when the levels are changed.

AGCs (automatic gain controls) are sometimes used to maintain consistent audio levels during audio recording and dubbing. This method too often boosts background noise to unpleasant levels during nonspeaking passages. A *peak limiter* reduces excessively loud sounds without boosting background sounds. Both of these devices can affect the setting of maximum mixing levels.

During a mix, the sound editor adjusts the volume of one sound element with respect to another. Sounds can be superimposed on one another, and transitions between sounds, such as fades, cross-fades, and segues, can be created. During an audio *fade*, the *pot* (short for *potentiometer*, a type of volume control) or fader for a sound is gradually turned up or down. A *cross-fade* combines a fade-out on one track with a simultaneous fade-in on another track. A *segue* is an instantaneous change from one track to another. Sound mixes usually involve several playback units channeled through an audio console to a single (monophonic) or dual (stereophonic) track

master tape. The editor or mixer operator must set the proper volume for each playback source and control all special effects and transitions. In digital editing each track is adjusted individually before combining the tracks into a final monaural, stereo, or 5.1 output signal.

A mix is carefully preplanned on a mix log or audio cue sheet. A *mix log* or *audio cue sheet* indicates all the volume and EQ changes and transitions for every sound source the sound mixer must control. It is organized sequentially according to the overall time of the program. Changes in any sound source or the fader assigned to it are then listed under the column devoted to that source, indicating the precise time the change is to occur. The mixer operator consults the cue sheet as a guide to the adjustment of each individual sound source. For example, the opening music may have to be faded in at the beginning of the program, and a narrator's voice may then be faded in over the music a few seconds later. The music may have to be decreased in volume at this point, so that it does not drown out the narration. Forty seconds later, the music may segue to another musical composition, which conveys a different mood or pace. Sound effects may have to be combined with this music, and at certain points, speech, sound effects, and music will probably occur simultaneously. Without a cue sheet, the editor or mixer could easily become confused during a sound mix (Figure 11.9).

Synchronous dialogue is generally recorded simultaneously with accompanying visual images. The sounds and images are then edited at the same time in the same format. When editing synchronous dialogue, an editor must be sensitive to the performance level, intonation, and accuracy of the speaker. Speech sounds that are radically different in intensity or intonation should not be edited together, even though their visual images match. Mistakes in the delivery of lines of dialogue should be removed. Compromises in editing synchronous speech sounds are inevitable, since editing together the best-quality images does not always result in the best-quality synchronous sounds.

The editor is sometimes forced to compromise between image quality and sound quality. An editor must be flexible and creative. For example, it may be necessary to use cutaways, such as a character's reaction to the speech of another character, to cover over mistakes in synchronous dialogue. Two or more portions of the same on-camera speech can be combined to remove missed lines or poor inflection, but unless there are cutaways, visual jump cuts will result. An editor must constantly make decisions on the basis of what is least objectionable, poor-quality sounds or

AUDIO MIXING CUE SHEET

Production _____ Date _____

Producer _____ Director_____ Mixer _____

Track A *Dialogue 1*		Track B *Dialogue 2*		Track C *SFX*		Track D *Music*	
Reel #1		Reel #2		Reel #3		Reel #4	
000	Dead Sync	000	Dead Sync	000	Dead Sync	000	Dead Sync
00:15	Sync pop	00:15	Sync pop	00:15	Sync pop	00:15	Sync pop
00:30		00:30		00:30	Crickets	00:30	Fl Theme
				00:45	Slow fade		
					Hold under		
	Sam:						
01:10	(1st word)		Harold:				▼
	Hi, what's	01:20	Hi back to ya			01:20	FO
			▼				
02:00	(Last word)						
	Thanks, see ya						
					▼		
	Fl=Fade In		FO=Fade Out				

FIGURE 11.9 The audio mixing log provides the mixing operator with a guide as to when to use sound from different tracks. The verbal and timing cues give precise locations for making transitions or adding effects.

poor-quality images, when editing synchronous dialogue and visuals (Figure 11.10).

Looping (which gets its name from loops of film that repeat the same shots over and over) or *automatic dialogue replacement (ADR)* refers to the creation and replacement of lip-sync dialogue in the sound studio during postproduction. The visual images are repeatedly projected onto a sound studio screen while the talent attempts to repeat the lines of dialogue exactly in sync with the lip movements of the on-screen speaker. These newly recorded speech sounds can be used to replace poor-quality original recordings. ADR is often done with the performer trying to speak in unison with the playback (via headphones) of the original, on-set speech, which is used as an audio reference. It is usually less expensive to replace defective dialogue than to reshoot the whole sequence. However, sound studio speech often seems dead and lifeless in comparison with the original recordings with which it must be intercut, unless the sound signal is properly processed. An editor

must pay particular attention to the pace, intonation, and vocal quality of the specific lines of dialogue that are to be inserted within an originally recorded scene.

Nonsynchronous or voiceover narration is frequently used to provide a commentary on visual actions. Voiceover narration can be edited together from audio interviews conducted in the field, or it can be recorded after visual editing in real time with the narrator watching a preliminary edit of the film or videotape and pacing his or her speech to the changing shots and speed of the action. In the former case, the visuals are edited to the narration. In the latter case, the editor's job is to touch up various narration segments so that they coincide with specific visuals and any mistakes are removed. The pace of the narration may need to be speeded up or slowed down during recording or editing to accommodate specific visual sequences. Errors in delivery can sometimes be removed through judicious editing.

There are basically three kinds of sound effects: prerecorded library effects, spot recorded effects, and

MULTITRACK AUDIO MIXING

Drum — Track 1
Bass — Track 2
Piano — Track 3
Lead Guitar — Track 4
Rhythm Guitar — Track 5
Vocal — Track 6
Stereo Left — Track 7
Stereo Right — Track 8

Tracks 1 through 6 are mixed in proper proportions for a stereo mix and re-recorded in sync to tracks 7 and 8

FIGURE 11.10 Several individual audio tracks on a multitrack audiotape can be combined into a single or stereo set of tracks through the process of "ping-ponging." A multitrack recorder can be adjusted so some heads are playback heads and others are set to record. Since they are aligned on one head stack, all of the tracks will be kept in sync.

actuality recorded effects. *Library effects* are catalogued and maintained on phonograph records, audiotapes, or CDs for storage convenience and accessibility (Figure 11.10). *Spot effects* are created in a sound studio to duplicate the supposed off-screen or on-screen source. *Actuality effects* are recorded outside the sound studio. They either accurately reproduce a particular sound or create a vivid sound impression. *Synchronous sound effects* are immediately dubbed to the videotape or film format of the visuals so that they can be edited in synchronization with corresponding visual images.

Library, spot, and actuality sound effects can all be placed in synchronization with visual images.

Once the sound effect is dubbed to the proper format, it is edited into the videotape or film sound track accompanying the visual image. The sound of a door closing or a fist striking a face can be synchronized with the visual image of the action. In videotape editing, the sound effect is usually dubbed to a separate videotape along with a control track or time code so that it can be inserted into the proper videotape frame. In film editing, the sound effect is dubbed to magnetic film, which will correspond frame by frame with the accompanying visual images. In both cases the sound effect is precisely synchronized with its on-screen sound source.

FIGURE 11.11 Sound effects libraries may be recorded on vinyl disks, audiotape, audiocassettes, CDs, or computer floppies.

In digital editing, a computer can be used to find and edit a collection of effects tracks on CD for either videotape or film. Computer storage, retrieval, and control allow a specific sound effect to be quickly accessed and its loudness, pitch, and duration to be altered and used in a variety of ways. For example, a single digitized sound of an airplane can be quickly found on a CD and then manipulated to create the complete illusion of an airplane circling an airport. Using this technique, a collection of basic sound effects can be used to provide an infinite variety of sounds. Each basic sound effect is catalogued and described as a computer file for easy selection and retrieval. It can also be stored digitally on a disk so that dubbing and signal processing does not result in any degradation of quality. Using the SMPTE time code of an edited videotape for reference, a sound effects editor can select, order, and manipulate all the sound effects that will be needed. Once the computer program is created, the sound effects are automatically dubbed, ordered, and processed to the editor's precise specifications.

Music for a film or television program can come from a variety of sources. Library music, which has been prerecorded on a CD, audiotape, or phonograph record, is often used to accompany visual images and other sounds. For public exhibition, the rights to prerecorded music must be secured, as discussed in Chapter 2, "Producing and Production Management." Original music can be recorded in a sound studio for a specific project. It can either be recorded in advance of editing, so that visuals can be edited to the music; or it can be recorded after the visual editing has been completed, so that the performance of the music can be matched to the visuals.

After dubbing prerecorded music to the proper visual format, the editor carefully analyzes it by finding the precise frames where specific musical effects, such as rhythmic beats, crescendos, and changes in pace or tonality, occur. Visual images can then be added to the hard disk, videotape, or film and edited so that shot changes and changes in the intensity of the visual action and pace correspond with the music. Visual images can also be edited in counterpoint to the music, through the use of shot changes and visual tonalities and pacing that contradict rather than complement the music. Synchronizing music to preedited visuals can be quite complicated. Music is usually composed with specific visuals in mind. The tempo of the music may need to be adjusted so that specific effects coincide with the visuals they are intended to accompany. The edited visuals are normally played back while the music is being recorded and are used as visual cues to guide the pace and tempo at which the music is performed.

There are two basic approaches to the problem of mixing music and speech sounds. One approach is to lower the level of the music "down and under" immediately prior to the delivery of a line of dialogue or narration, and then return the music to a normal level after the speech has concluded. A second approach is to keep the music at a consistently low level. If music is mixed at its full value, the speech sounds that accompany it will be difficult to understand. Even when the music is kept at a consistently low level, it is important to have clear and distinct dialogue and narration. An underlying assumption of both of these approaches to mixing music and speech is that the speech must be clearly understood. But it is sometimes necessary to hear the music at its full value, particularly when its pace, intensity, and mood are essential to the establishment of a particular feeling.

Mixing music requires the smooth operation of faders on an audio console or sensitive adjustments within the computer program. The music must have a relatively consistent pace and original recording level at points where it is to be effectively faded in or out or cross-faded with other music, speech, and sound effects. Music that varies in intensity or seems erratic is difficult to fade in and fade out smoothly. Faders should normally be moved very slowly so that one piece of music gradually blends into another piece of music or another type of sound. Sometimes popping on a sudden burst of music can be an effective transition device, a sort of musical punctuation. *Stingers* are short phrases of music, usually characterized by a rapidly descending scale or series of notes, which can also act as punctuation devices. In functionalist and realist situations, music is usually mixed smoothly and gradually with other types of sounds.

SUMMARY

Sound editing can reflect realist, modernist, or postmodernist aesthetics. Realist sound editing preserves continuity in space and time. Modernist sound editing often develops sound as an independent aesthetic element, and subjective sound impressions and abstract audio qualities are often highlighted. Postmodernist sound editing often brings together a pastiche of sounds and audio impressions, borrowing from previous texts and encouraging spectator involvement and textual play.

Sounds can be edited using a digital nonlinear editing system, an analog videotape or audiotape electronic editing system, or by physically splicing analog magnetic film or audiotape. The quality of digital audio does not significantly diminish from one generation to the next, and the editing process is very flexible in terms of instantaneously changing the order and duration of sounds and images.

Conventional film sound editing involves physically splicing magnetic film. Synchronous lip-sync dialogue for film is normally recorded during production using an audiotape recorder, which records both the sounds and a sync signal. The sound track is then dubbed to magnetic film so that it can be edited synchronously with the image. Magnetic film can be physically spliced in conjunction with visual images, and thus synchronization between them is maintained.

Audiotape can be physically spliced in several different formats. Nonsynchronous splicing can be done with ¼-inch audiotape. Multitrack sound recorders allow several different tracks to be recorded in synchronization with each other. A background music track can be recorded and then played back as an accompaniment to a singer whose voice is recorded independently on a separate track. In this way several different types of sounds can be combined on a single reel of audiotape in synchronization with each other.

Sound mixing is a process of blending together simultaneous sounds or sound tracks. This includes transition devices such as fades, cross-fades, and segues. Blending together different types of sounds, such as speech, sound effects, and music, demands smooth and precise operation of the faders on an audio console or mixer. It also requires careful preparation of a mix log, which specifies different audio levels and transitions from one sound track to another. Specific principles of editing and mixing apply to different types of sound, such as speech, sound effects, and music.

Through a technique known as looping or automatic dialogue replacement (ADR), speech sounds can be added to and perfectly synchronized with pre-edited, prerecorded visual images. Voiceover interviews and narration are often edited prior to the selection of illustrative visuals.

There are three basic kinds of sound effects: library effects, spot effects, and actuality effects. Library effects are prerecorded on CDs, phonograph records, and audiotapes. Spot effects are specially recorded in the sound studio, and actuality effects are recorded in the field.

Synchronous film sound mixing requires several interlocked magnetic film source machines, called dubbers. Several audio tracks can then be combined through an audio console or mixer into a single master sound mix on a magnetic film recorder. Film sound can also be edited digitally, but this usually requires specialized software or a slave system that maintains synchronization between originally recorded film and sounds throughout the editing process, when the final editing will be done on film.

EXERCISES

1. Using a shooting script as your guide, prepare a mix log or audio cue sheet for combining all of the various sound elements that will be used in postproduction editing. While precise volume-control settings cannot be known until actual materials are prepared for a mix, virtually all other factors can be anticipated in advance. Try to compose separate and continuous sound tracks or channels on paper for each different type of sound, such as synchronous dialogue, narration, sound effects or background sound, and music. Indicate where one piece of music will cross-fade or segue to another, requiring separate tracks or channels, or where several different sound effects or background sounds must be combined.

A mix log or audio cue sheet will graphically depict the depth and texture of sound by indicating when several types of sounds or sound tracks coexist, such as narration, sound effects, and music. Indicate which type of sound will be dominant if they will not all be of equal intensity. Determine the series of stages sound-track preparation must go through if some types of sound must be pre-mixed prior to the final master mix.

2. Replace some original sound (sound originally recorded with corresponding visuals) with library or spot effects. Grab an audio clip off a CD or digitize an analog audiotape recording of the sound effect. If you are using a digital nonlinear system, use the insert mode; if you are using electronic videotape editing, physically splice the new sounds into the existing magnetic film or audiotape sound track. Compare the edited sound track with the original for sound clarity and consistency.

3. Mix a voiceover narration track with music. Try to make the edits as smooth and indistinguishable as possible. Be careful to maintain consistency in terms of pace and timing in the delivery of narration. Find similar phrases of music on which to make an instantaneous transition from one piece of music to another. Pay careful attention to any discrepancy in terms of audio levels and background sounds when editing together speech, sound effects, or music recorded outside the studio. Fade the music down and under when the narrator is speaking, and fade the music up to its full volume

when the narrator is silent for a reasonable period of time.

4. Dub an existing short dramatic video to a nonlinear system. Use actors to record new dialog by watching the production. Record their audio on a separate system. Once the dialog is recorded, synchronize that audio to the existing video.

5. Add music and sound effects to #4 as needed including footsteps, doors opening, gunshots, or whatever sounds the drama calls for.

6. Dub a favorite music selection to a nonlinear system. Find another recording of the same selection. See if you can edit the two together to make a single selection by combining or alternating cuts.

ADDITIONAL READINGS

Alten, Stanley. *Audio in Media*, 6th ed. Belmont, CA: Wadsworth Publishing, 2002.

Amyes, Tim. *Audio Post Production in Video and Film*, 2nd ed. Boston, MA: Focal Press, 1999.

Derry, Roger. *PC Audio Editing*. Boston, MA: Focal Press, 2002.

Holman, Tomlinson. *Sound for Film and Television*, 2nd ed. Boston, MA: Focal Press, 2001.

Kenny, Tom. *Sound for Pictures: Art of Sound Design for Film and Television*. Vallejo, CA: MixBooks, 2000.

Kirk, Ross, and Andy Hunt. *Digital Sound Processing for Music and Multimedia*. Boston, MA: Focal Press, 1999.

Maes, Jan, and Marc Vecammen. *Digital Audio Techniques: CD-Minidisc, SACD, DVDA, MP3*, 4th ed. Boston, MA: Focal Press, 2001.

Mantell, Harold, ed. *The Complete Guide to the Creation and Use of Sound Effects for Films, TV, and Dramatic Productions*. Princeton, NJ: Films for the Humanities, 1978.

Nisbett, Alec. *The Sound Studio*, 7th ed. Boston, MA: Focal Press, 2003.

Rose, Jay. *Audio Post Production for Digital Video*. San Francisco, CA: CMP Books, 2002.

Rumsey, Francis, and John Watkinson, *Digital Interface Handbook*, 3rd ed. Boston, MA: Focal Press, 2003.

Sennenschein, David. *Sound Design: The Expressive Power of Music, Voice, and Sound Effects in Cinema*. Studio City, CA: Michael Weise Productions, 2001.

Talbot-Smith, Michael. *Sound Assistance*, 2nd ed. Boston, MA: Focal Press, 1999.

Watkinson, John. *Introduction to Digital Audio*, 2nd ed. Boston, MA: Focal Press, 2002.

Yewdall, David. *The Practical Art of Motion Picture Sound*, 2nd ed. Boston, MA: Focal Press, 2003.

12 Animation and Special Effects

INTRODUCTION

Animation and special effects generate visual interest and can be used to create imaginative worlds that defy the physical laws of space and time. Animation simulates movement, allowing cartoon characters to inhabit a unique world and to perform unbelievable actions that would be impossible, if not fatal, for humans. Special effects generate interest and excitement, often allowing futuristic or historical worlds to come to life, dangerous actions and events to be simulated, and live-action characters to accomplish superhuman feats. Digital animation techniques now replace many physical special effects to create realistic-appearing scenes in film and video productions that could not be accomplished in any other manner. The same techniques allow corrections to be made in postproduction to save time and the extra expenses of having to reshoot mistakes made in original shots. Animation on the World Wide Web (WWW) has grown exponentially in the past decade. The first animation film festival held on the Web appeared in 1998. Since then the technology has improved, and there is no doubt that it will continue to improve in the future.

Animation develops imaginative worlds by using single-frame recording techniques to make static images and objects appear to move; whether the medium is digital files, film, or video, the philosophy and basic techniques are the same. By breaking the motion of an object down into its component parts, an animator can control the movements of otherwise lifeless figures and images. Single-frame recordings of static images can create apparent motion when small changes in the positioning of objects occur between successive frames. Thus animation creates apparent changes in position. Only 12 different images may be required for each second's duration of the final sequence, although single-frame versus double-frame animation is always a trade-off between smoothness and cost. The animator's job is to create the desired illusion of movement. Slower movements will require the preparation of more individual frames and smaller changes of position between each frame than faster movements. Time and distance are interrelated. An object that moves a distance of two feet in 24 frames obviously moves more quickly in the final sequence than an object that moves only one foot in 24 frames.

Special effects used to be, and still is, in many ways a highly specialized area of media production. Producing most realistic effects was usually quite laborious and expensive in the past. Today, the widespread use of complex and convincing special effects in low-budget productions has been encouraged and simplified by the availability of relatively inexpensive digital image-processing programs that are built into many video cameras, as well as much digital nonlinear editing and special effects computer software. This chapter provides a broad survey of both traditional and contemporary special effects that are widely used in film, video, and multimedia production.

ANIMATION

Animation is based on an animator's knowledge of time and motion. An animator must be able to break down motion into its component parts so that it can be artificially constructed out of static images. One of the best means of analyzing motion is to examine the individual frames of a live-action film. A live-action motion picture camera, for example, records 24 (25 in Europe) frames every second at standard speed. Each frame represents ¼th (⅟₃₀th in video) of the change in the subject's spatial positioning during one second. By looking at the amount of change that occurs between the successive frames of a live-action sequence, an animator can begin to determine how much change there should be in the position and movement of objects between successive animated frames.

It is not always necessary to record a different image for each film frame, however. A smooth illusion of continuous motion can often be obtained by recording two identical frames of each image or drawing position. Thus only 12 different images will be required for each second's duration of the final sequence, rather than 24 images.

Storyboards and Animation Preproduction

An animated sequence often begins with the construction of a *storyboard*. In this case, the storyboard is a series of sequential sketches that depict the composition and content of each shot or key action in an animated sequence. A storyboard is very similar to a newspaper comic strip. It helps a graphic artist or animator to visualize the entire sequence on paper prior to preparing the final images. The storyboard can be used to communicate the animator's basic idea and strategy to a producer. It can also serve as a blueprint or guide to the actual creation and recording of images. Storyboard images are not as detailed as the actual film or television images will be. They usually consist of simple sketches, line drawings, or photographs. A storyboard simply and clearly communicates the basic idea of a sequence.

Many animators design their storyboards in conjunction with prerecorded music, sound effects, and/or voice tracks. Because timing or synchronization between sound and images is often crucial to the success of an animated sequence, music and sound are initially recorded and analyzed. A log or audio cue sheet is kept of the frame numbers of images where specific sounds occur so that the corresponding images can be perfectly synchronized. A log or audio cue sheet can be combined with the frames of a storyboard. A designer can then tell exactly how many seconds, and therefore how many digital, film, or video frames are required for each storyboard frame. Frames for each point of synchronization between sounds and images can be included in the storyboard so that there is no confusion about precisely where a specific action is to occur. Once the storyboard has been constructed in conjunction with the recorded music and sounds, the actual production phase of animation begins (Figure 12.1).

Types of Animation

Many different types of images and objects can be animated, including hand-drawn illustrations, paper cutouts, puppets, clay figures, still photographs of live actions, and computer graphic images. All of these different forms of animation are based on single-frame recording techniques. It is often helpful to distinguish between flat and plastic animation, as well as between film and digital animation. *Flat animation* two-dimensional (2-D) includes such techniques as cel animation, in which individual illustrations are drawn for almost every frame of a picture. *Plastic animation* encompasses the use of three-dimensional figures, such as puppets or clay figures. Single-frame recording of people and three-dimensional objects is sometimes called *pixillation*. In a sense, all of these techniques or types of animation elevate the animator to the status of director, editor, and scenic designer.

Flat animation refers to the recording of two-dimensional images using single-frame recording techniques. One of the most common forms of flat animation is *cel animation*. *Cels* are individual sheets

EXPOSURE (Dope) SHEET

TITLE_____ SCENE____ ANIMATOR_____ SHEET # ___

FRAME	ACTION	SETTING	LAYERS				BG	CAMERA
			4	3	2	1		

Figure 12.1 An animation exposure sheet, sometimes called a *dope* sheet, includes all of the information the camera operator needs to make the exposures and movements of the cels and which cels to stack in the layer.

of clear acetate on which images can be drawn or painted, usually with ink and opaque watercolors. An ink outline is traced onto each cel from an outline sketch. An outline sketch is made on paper for each cel, and a film or video recording of these sketches, known as a *pencil test*, is often made so that corrections can be made prior to the creation of actual acetate cels. The cel is painted on the opposite side so that the ink lines do not run and so that the rough surface texture of the paint is not apparent. Cels are preperforated with holes at one end so they can be inserted over the pegs of a movable table, called an *animation rostrum*, for precise registration and framing. An *animation stand* consists of a rostrum, lights, and a movable camera platform (Figure 12.2A and B).

A

B

Figure 12.2 A and B Layers of individual cels allow the animator to move some parts of the character or background, but not all at once. Layers of cels also may create a third dimension and sense of depth to the frame. In the top illustration, three individual cels from the left to right: the two space characters, then the moving pattern on the monitors behind the crew, and last the space ship interior as a background. The bottom illustration shows the three cels locked together for the complete frame ready to be recorded.

Cel animation gives the animator or graphic artist complete control over the design of the image. However, drawing each frame individually on a cel can be quite time-consuming and expensive, so many shortcuts are used to conserve time. Because cels are transparent, they can be sandwiched together to combine images drawn on different cels. A background cel can be used over and over again while changes are made in the placement of foreground objects, eliminating the need to redraw the background for each frame. Individual movements of characters' feet, hands, and mouths can be repeated or recycled with different bodies and backgrounds. A series of lip movements synchronized to various consonant or vowel sounds can be used repeatedly rather than drawn individually for each occurrence. To cut costs more drastically, some animators draw only every fourth or fifth frame of recorded film or videotape. This can, of course, lead to rougher and therefore less pleasing animation.

Another commonly used technique for cutting costs and increasing cel-animation efficiency is called *rotoscoping*. In rotoscoping, a sequence is first filmed in live action; the individual frames of the motion picture are then projected on a cel, and an outline of the objects in the frame is drawn and hand-colored. Subjects are normally photographed against a contrasting background so that outlines are clearly visible. The drawn outlines are then colored like standard hand-drawn animation cels. Although rotoscoping makes the production of cels more efficient, it often produces images that are less aesthetically pleasing than hand-drawn animation. The difference between rotoscoped and hand-drawn animation is similar to the difference between naturalistic painting and caricature. A caricature of a person emphasizes or exaggerates characteristic features. In a like manner, hand-drawn cel animation often uses nonrepresentational figures and techniques such as image *squashing* and *stretching* to exaggerate motion. An animator can sometimes create a more vivid impression of motion by exaggerating the compression of objects as gravity pulls them to the ground and then stretching or expanding their shape as they jump or run, temporarily escaping the pull of gravity. Stretching exaggerates acceleration, while squashing exaggerates deceleration. Animated motion is not always a direct copy of live action. These subtle differences in apparent motion become obvious when rotoscoped images are compared with original hand-drawn images. *Motion capture (MoCap)* takes rotoscoping one step further (see explanation under "Motion Capture" later in this chapter).

The illusion of movement in cel animation can be achieved in one of two ways: by drawing a different cel for each change of position of objects within the frame, or by moving the cel itself on the rostrum of the animation stand between recordings. If movement is to be achieved through differences between cels, each cel in the sequence must be placed in exactly the same position within the camera frame by using the registration pegs. On the other hand, if motion is to be achieved by moving the cel, this can be done by using the horizontal and vertical controls of the rostrum. One problem that sometimes stands in the way of physically moving a cel is that the background movement within the two-dimensional image may seem unnatural when it moves at the same rate as the foreground. In live-action photography, the background and foreground seem to move at different rates, providing an illusion of depth and three dimensionality. This problem is sometimes solved by placing the background cels on a separate peg bar, or set of registration pegs, on the same rostrum or table so that they can be moved at a slower speed than the foreground. Virtually all animation stands are equipped with double-peg bars so that backgrounds and foregrounds can be moved independently of one another.

Hand-drawn illustrations are not the only flat images that can be animated. Paper or fabric cutouts and still photographs can also be set into motion. A paper cutout of a person or animal can be constructed so that it has moving body parts. It can then be placed over a variety of backgrounds so that it seems to come alive and move on the screen. A flicker effect can also be achieved by recording frames of colored paper in between frames of specific photographs or illustrations. The change in photographs can be timed to the beat of music. In this way what might otherwise be a boring presentation of static images acquires kinetic energy. Still photographs and printed illustrations, such as magazine images, can be animated through single-frame techniques, such as those used by Frank Mouris in his famous *Frank Film* (1978). Mouris' film is as much a feat of optical printing, discussed later in this chapter, as of animation (Figure 12.3).

Plastic animation refers to the animation of many different types of 3-D figures and objects using single-frame recording techniques. Puppets, clay figures, miniature vehicles, and even still frames of live action can be animated.

Although hand puppets and marionettes are usually recorded in live action so that the mouth and body movements can be synchronized to speech or music, it is possible to animate more rigid puppets and clay figures by moving them slightly between frames.

Unlike the animator of flat, two-dimensional characters, however, the plastic animator must create

Figure 12.3 Frank Mouris specialized in producing films shot single-frame, often using collages of unrelated images shot in sequences as short as two to three frames for a rapid, eye-teasing format.

a miniature three-dimensional world of sets and props within which puppets and figures will move. Careful attention must be paid to minute details. Backgrounds must be painted to scale, and everything must be proportional to the size of the figures. The camera is usually placed in a horizontal position with respect to the scene rather than above it, as with an animation stand. Miniature vehicles, such as cars and trucks, can also be animated through single-frame techniques. Sometimes these animated miniatures are used as a substitute for more costly and dangerous stunts and special effects in live-action films.

An animated three-dimensional figure sequence is shot much like a live-action scene, except that the pictures are recorded frame by frame. More than one camera is frequently used so that action does not have to be repeated for different shots, as in single-camera live-action recording. The animation of three-dimensional objects sacrifices the artist's ability to simulate the blurring effect of photographing live-action figures in rapid movement, and mechanical, nonlifelike movement sometimes results.

Clay or malleable plastic material is often animated so that unique shapes and actions can be recorded. A technique known as *metamorphosis*, in which one figure gradually changes into a totally different form, can be accomplished with clay as well as with images drawn on cels. A famous animated film, called *Clay* by Eliot Noyes, Jr. (1964), shows the evolution of one life form from another using clay metamorphosis. Virtually any shape and type of movement can be constructed using clay or malleable plastic materials.

Human figures can also be animated by a technique known as *pixillation*. Images of human beings can be pixillated by recording one frame, moving the image, and then recording another frame. Pixillation has been used in many films to animate images of human beings so that they seem to perform extraordinary feats. In Norman McLaren's famous film *Neighbors* (1955), two neighbors fight over their adjoining territory. This clever film offers a symbolic treatment of war by presenting a unique abstract image of human behavior and actions. In one scene the human figures hover across the ground with no apparent movement of their limbs. McLaren achieved this image by photographing single frames of his subjects leaping into the air. Only the apex of each jump was recorded, making the people seem to hover over the ground.

Computer Animation

Computer animation programs are used for video and film productions. Virtually all commercials, all newscasts, and most television/cable and film pro grams use some form of computer animation and/or computer graphics. Some animation programs fully integrate graphics programs and animation programs so that still-frame graphic images can be used to create apparent motion. Graphic images can be originally designed on a computer monitor by using various computer commands and devices, such as a light pencil or stylus to draw on a television screen, or an electronic tablet or a mouse to compose images on a computer screen. They can then be colored and manipulated by computer.

Live-action frames can also be grabbed or digitized by some computers for further graphic manipulation and/or combined with computer graphic images. Single-frame graphic images can be stored on disk. These images can be expanded in size for detailed work and then shrunk to a smaller size for actual presentation. The animator can manipulate the colors, lines, shapes, and size of the image. Motion can be created by cycling different movements and using the computer to interpolate intermediate frames of motion between two static frames. An NTSC standard video output can then be fed to a switcher, VCR, or film recorder.

Computer animation programs allow for *interpolation*, another form of animation that uses paths and involves the drawing of lines through 3-D space. Using interpolation, the animator composes the first and last frames of a sequence, referred to as the *keyframes*, and the computer software then creates or interpolates the in-between frames. Even some of the least expensive computer programs can interpo-

late a number of frames. Computer animation allows an almost infinite number of repetitions of the same image. Image cycling is facilitated by simply drawing the first and last frame of a sequence, interpolating the rest, and then recycling this sequence wherever it is needed. It is also possible to make many duplicates of the same image within a single frame.

Rendering is the final step in both two-dimensional (2-D) and three-dimensional (3-D) animation. It is often the most time-consuming and memory-intensive stage of computer animation. The end product of rendering is the creation of a graphics file that can be combined with other graphics files to collectively produce the completed animation sequence. The time and memory required for rendering is often extensive, but it can sometimes be reduced by using shortcuts for color, procedure (mathematical approximations of "natural" patterns, such as marble or clouds), and texture (a graphic drawn on an object, such as a soft drink label drawn on a can) maps applied to images during the rendering process.

The greatest advantages of computer animation are speed and accuracy. Results are immediately viewable. An animator need not wait a day or a week for the film animation to be processed and printed at a laboratory. Images and frames can be quickly designed and accurately copied. They can be stored on disk for long periods of time and used again or redesigned for another animation sequence.

A sophisticated computer animation program can interpolate the three dimensions of a design from a two-dimensional image in much the same way that an engineering or architectural design computer program, such as a CAD program, does. A completely computer-controlled illusion of three-dimensionality can also be obtained in films that combine live-action characters with computer-generated objects and backgrounds, such as *Tron* (1983) and *Who Framed Roger Rabbit* (1988).

The live-action subject is usually recorded against a blue screen or a monochromatic background so that it can be keyed or matted into a computer-generated scene. The availability of these combined animation and special effects techniques has allowed graphic artists to save time and experiment creatively with abstract visual images for film and video (Figure 12.4).

3-D Computer Animation

The differences between 2-D and 3-D computer animation involve the complexities of creating figures with a "Z" dimension. The standard method is to follow the storyboard stage of 2-D drawing with the design and creation of a wireframe model of the

Figure 12.4 The Touchstone production of *Who Framed Roger Rabbit* (1988) combined live-action, cel-drawn animation, and computer animation sequences in a startling yet realistic manner. (Courtesy of Touchstone Pictures and Amblin Entertainment, Inc.)

figure. The wireframe is made up of a series of polygons that approximate the three dimensional shape of the object. The wireframe model is then smoothed and rounded to a more realistic shape by creating the "skin" or outer surface of the object. Textures, shading, and lighting are added to enhance the 3-D effect. The figure must be viewed from all sides to complete the effect. Once the figure is complete, the digital file that represents that figure must then be rendered, just as 2-D animation figures are rendered to a final form that may be output to film or video for combination with background, other figures, added movement; the final form may also be distributed.

Motion Capture

Motion capture (MoCap) is a logical computerized extension of film rotoscoping philosophy. Subjects are wired with sensors located at critical points on the body. The sensors either emit a signal to a remote receiver or are wired directly to a computer with a special program that combines the position of each of the body parts with an animated character. As the subject moves arms, legs, head, or other body parts, the animated character moves the same amount and direction. The movements are accurately recorded in the computer program, allowing the animation to progress in real time as the actor(s) move. The process is not only a rapid means of animating movements, but also the body movements are accurate and realistic. The technology is still under development, and some animation purists do not totally accept MoCap as a legitimate form of animation.

Animation on the Web

Due to the limitations of the delivery systems on the Web, Web graphics and animation must be carefully designed so that they do not exceed the channels of delivery. Full-color, full-sized, moving images do not reproduce well on systems driven by the 56K modems used by many consumers. As systems designed to move data at a higher rate are developed and made reasonable, the quality of animation on the Web will improve. Today Web art borrows from all forms and modes of animation and graphics. Two- and, in limited cases, three-dimensional graphics or animation can be downloaded with patience, plenty of memory, and a speedy delivery system. By comparison to other visual media, Web art will remain somewhat primitive but full of opportunities to experiment and plow new artistic ground.

Film Animation

Film animation requires the use of a camera that records single frames of motion-picture film. The camera is normally suspended above the artwork by mounting it on an animation stand. An animation stand consists of a camera platform attached to vertical poles or columns, so that it can be raised and lowered over the artwork. The camera platform is suspended above a large horizontal table, called a *rostrum*, which can be moved east, west, north, and south. The artwork is secured to this horizontal table by placing the hole perforations in proper registration over peg bars on the table.

The vertical columns and horizontal table of an animation stand allow for a variety of camera movements, such as dollies, zooms, pans, and tilts. During a dolly shot the camera is gradually moved toward or away from the artwork between exposures. For a zoom shot, the focal length of the lens is changed between one exposure and the next. Pan and tilt shots are made by simply moving the rostrum from side to side or from top to bottom between successive frames. A *pantograph* is often attached to one side of the stand so that precise movements can be charted on special graph paper by the pantograph pointer (Figure 12.5).

A *field guide*, which is a transparent sheet that has spacing and framing information etched on it, can be placed over the artwork to adjust the camera frame. The field guide is proportional to the aspect ratio of the film format, such as 1.33:1 or 4:3 for standard 16mm. It provides spacing and framing information for different field sizes. A field size of 11, for example, indicates a field 11 inches wide by 8¼ inches high, while a field size of 4 is 4 inches wide by 3 inches high. Field guides for HDTV and wide-

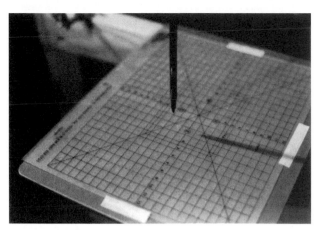

Figure 12.5 A pantograph pointer follows the movement of the animation table on the field. Each movement of the table may be accurately calibrated between exposures.

screen film productions are designed to fit whatever aspect ratio is required for that particular production. A reflex viewfinder is required to frame the image precisely for the camera lens.

The artwork can be evenly lit from above with little glare reflected into the camera by using two lights that are suspended at 45-degree angles to the horizontal table. Backlighting can be provided by a diffused lighting source, such as a light box, placed underneath the artwork on the table. A glass platen is often used over the artwork to keep it flat and in sharp focus. There are often exposure differences between live-action recording and single-frame animation with a film camera. The equivalent shutter speed for single-frame exposure often differs from that used when exposing frames at 24 fps, for example.

A *film animation camera* is normally equipped with special controls for specific animation effects. A variable shutter, for example, can be used to fade out from or fade in to a specific piece of artwork. By rewinding the film to the beginning of a fade-out as indicated by the frame counter on the camera and then fading in on another piece of artwork, a dissolve can be created. Superimpositions can be made by backwinding and double-exposing individual frames.

The efficiency and accuracy of film animation has been greatly increased by the development of computer-controlled animation stands. All of the complex camera movements, such as dollies, fades, focus changes, and movements of the table, such as east/west and north/south pans, can be preprogrammed and computer controlled. As many as 50 different pieces of artwork can be automatically placed in proper registration in sequential order on some computer film-animation stands. Computer control dramatically decreases the setup time. Each

repetition of a specific piece of artwork is recorded at different points on the film. The shutter is simply closed while the frames between them are passed. Thus frames 1, 9, 17, and 25 of an 8-frame cycle or repeated action are recorded consecutively before the artwork for frames 2, 10, 18, and 26 is recorded, until all the frames and artwork have been used. Setup time and operator errors are substantially reduced by having the computer control these operations automatically (Figure 12.6).

Images can be electronically animated by placing a video camera on an animation stand and recording single video frames of the artwork on the table using the same techniques as film animation. An important difference between video and film animation is that the video camera records 30 fps, instead of 24 fps. Single-frame video animation requires the use of a slo-mo (slow motion) recorder or a disk frame-storage unit, rather than a conventional VCR. A *slo-mo recorder* or *video animator* can be used to record individual frames for a 30-second animation sequence. The sequence can then be transferred to conventional videotape. A disk frame-storage or memory unit, such as that used to store pages of text and titles composed on a character generator, can also be used to record individual animation frames. Some memory units have a limited storage capacity, however, and others are capable of storing and immediately accessing hundreds of figures or pages.

One advantage of recording animation electronically is that the results can be viewed immediately. Film animators frequently have to wait several days or longer to see the results of their work. Video animation and film animation can be combined by

Figure 12.6 The control box for an animation stand provides the operator with the means of presetting the number of frames to be exposed on each cel, the exposure time, and all of the other camera controls such as iris setting.

recording a pencil test with a video camera using disk storage of single frames and instantly viewing the results on a monitor so that problems can immediately be uncovered and corrections made. The final cels are recorded with a film camera for optimum quality and maximum storage capacity.

SPECIAL EFFECTS

Special effects can be divided into six basic categories: digital effects, camera effects, optical effects, models, miniatures, and physical effects. *Camera effects* include such features as fast and slow motion as well as single-frame (animation) recording. *Optical and digital effects* run the gamut of image-processing techniques, from *matting* and *keying* (where a portion of one image is replaced by another) to *morphing* (transforming one object into another, which is also called metamorphosis) and *compositing* (placing different layers of images on top of another). *Models* and *miniatures*, when combined with single-frame animation as well as matting and keying effects, can be used to put an object, such as a spacecraft, in motion or to create the illusion of a later century city by placing futuristic buildings into an existing location. Makeup can transform an actor into an android, a zombie, or a werewolf, while physical effects, such as fog, rain, and explosions, can contribute to the emotional mood of a sequence and generate viewer interest and excitement. Each of these different types of special effects is discussed in this chapter. The actual creation of specific effects may require considerable hands-on experience, and in some cases, such as the use of explosive devices, should only be attempted by highly trained specialists.

Digital Effects

Digital image processing has greatly reduced the amount of generational loss in image quality that has traditionally accompanied the creation of conventional film and video special effects. Digital effects can be divided into three areas: transitions, filters, and superimpositions, keys, or mattes; compositing; and morphing. *Transitions* are means of replacing one digital clip, which is usually a single image or shot, with another. *Filters* are means of altering a clip. *Superimpositions, keys,* and *mattes* are combinations of more than one clip that appear simultaneously within the same frame. *Compositing* involves combining different layers of visual information that can each be separately edited and animated using a digital nonlinear editing and an animation program, respectively. *Morphing* or *morphogenesis*

refers to various techniques of transforming one shape or figure into another.

The types of transitions that can be created between one visual clip and another are virtually limitless. Most digital nonlinear editing and special effects programs offer a wide variety of transition devices as well as the capability of modifying the devices and creating custom transitions. Two of the most commonly used transitions are various dissolves and wipes.

During a *dissolve* one clip gradually increases in intensity and visibility throughout the fame while another clip simultaneously decreases in intensity and visibility. In *lap* or *cross dissolves*, one clip fades out at exactly the same rate that another fades in. In an *additive dissolve*, the two clips are combined or added together during the transition. In a *nonadditive dissolve*, the luminance of one clip is mapped onto the luminance of the other. Digital control of dissolves makes it possible to create interesting special effects by allowing the chrominance (color) and/or luminance (brightness) of the clips to be adjusted during the transition.

During a *wipe* one clip is entirely replaced by another clip, beginning in a specific area or several areas of the frame and gradually spreading throughout the frame. One clip can rise like a curtain, while the next is revealed behind it, or one clip can appear to push another off the screen. A wide variety of patterns, from pinwheels to clock hands, can be used to wipe from one clip to the next, and the movements of these wipe patterns or shapes throughout the frame can usually be adjusted.

A variety of *digital filters* allow a clip to be distorted, blurred, sharpened, smoothed, textured, and tinted or colored. Filters can also be used to pan, zoom, reverse motion, slow down, speed up, and flip a clip. The ability to alter the brightness, contrast, and color balance of individual clips allows an operator to function as a timer by smoothing out and eliminating subtle differences in color, brightness, and contrast between successive clips or shots, or to function as a special effects artist by radically altering the original image and generating unusual and interesting effects. For example, all colors except the color red can be removed from a clip so that the entire frame is black and white except those portions of the image that are red in color. A clip can be blurred to simulate the point of view of a character whose vision has been altered. Various mosaic grids of squares or other shapes can be used to create interesting patterns, and an image can be *posterized* by limiting the color spectrum to just a few colors, or it can be *solarized* by blending negative and positive images to create a halo effect. By resizing clips, unwanted areas within the frame can often be eliminated, and zooms and pans can be created on stationary or moving images within a clip.

Two clips can be combined within the same frame by superimposing them upon one another or by using various keys and mattes. Different keys and mattes process visual images differently in order to remove a portion from one clip and replace it with another clip. A *white alpha matte*, for example, removes a portion of a background scene, into which a foreground image, such as a title, which comprises a second clip, can be inserted. The area surrounding the titles is made transparent in the title clip so that the background image fills the nontitle areas.

Compositing refers to combining different layers of visual images. One layer might be a model of a rocket ship moving against a neutral background as though it is taking off. Another might consist of an actual launch site recorded at Cape Canaveral. A third layer might consist of digitally animated images of ice particles falling through space. Each of these layers can be separated, edited, and combined into a composite image using a special effects program. This type of special effect was used to create composite images that simulated an Apollo spacecraft taking off in *Apollo 13* (1995).

Using these same techniques, motion clips, such as moving or talking lips, can be inserted in place of stationary images, such as the stationary lips of a character in the background scene, in order to animate a live-action image. Similar types of digital effects have been used in Hollywood feature films, such as *Forrest Gump* (1994), to allow prerecorded documentary images to be combined with studio recordings and to have historical figures appear to interact with and talk to fictional characters. Various compositing techniques can be used to combine several layers of images—just as superimposition, matting, and keying devices utilize different aspects of the image layer. The chroma or luminance portions of a video signal, or invisible grayscale channels, such as alpha channels, black alpha mattes, and white alpha mattes, may be used to eliminate a portion of one clip and replace it with another clip, combining the two within a single frame.

Morphing or *morphogenesis* refers to various techniques of transforming one shape or figure into another. Morphing can be accomplished in film animation by drawing individual cels that gradually change from one shape or form into another. Digital image processing and animation programs have facilitated the transformation process by allowing the computer to generate the gradual transformation from one figure, such as an automobile, into another, such as a tiger. Digital morphing is accomplished by placing corresponding dots at key points of comparison between two figures and then drawing vectors from the dot on one figure to the corresponding dot on the second figure into which it is being morphed. For example, to morph from one person's face to another's, which occupies the same general size and area of the frame, a series of dots are made by clicking the mouse at primary points of correspondence and transformation from one face to the next, such as around the eyes, ears, mouth, and the outline of the head. Morphing is an effective technique for creating transitions from one image to another, or for altering shapes, forms, and figures and creating imaginative worlds through the use of special digital effects.

Camera Effects

A significant number and range of special effects can be created within a film camera during initial recording. Some film cameras, for example, allow the frames-per-second speed to be altered from the normal sound speed of 24 fps. Recording rates in excess of 24 fps, such as 32, 48, and 64 fps, create slow motion when the processed film is projected at the standard projection speed of 24 fps. Recording rates less than 24 fps, such as 18 and 12 fps, create fast motion. Attaching an *intervalometer* to a film camera allows the frames per second to be significantly reduced to one frame every 1, 2, or 20 seconds, or even every few minutes or hours, to create *time-lapse recordings*, such as images of clouds rolling overhead or flower petals opening and closing throughout the day. Single-frame control of a live-action film camera allows for pixillation effects, which are described earlier in this chapter. Most digital cameras duplicate these same effects, in camera also.

In addition to varying the speed of the images, some film cameras allow fadeouts, fade-ins, superimpositions, and reverse motion to be created during initial recording. The fader control is closed down or opened up at the proper rate, such as one second for a 24-frame duration effect at standard speed, to create an in-camera fade-out or fade-in. The film inside the camera can be rewound with the fader closed, and then the fader is opened up again to superimpose another shot on top of the first one usually with the lens closed down slightly to prevent over-exposure and to make one shot dominant and the other recessive. Reverse motion can be created by turning the camera upside down during initial recording and then reversing the shot end for end, that is, using the beginning of the shot as the end of the shot during editing, which turns the picture right side up and reverses the motion. While more control over these types of effects can be maintained through the use of optical effects during postproduction, some experimental filmmakers prefer to exercise control over these effects during initial recording.

In-camera matte effects can be created by blocking off a portion of the frame during the first exposure, rewinding the film, and then exposing the previously blocked portion of the frame. *Matte boxes* can have half of the frame filled with an opaque black filter, which is then reversed to cover the opposite half of the frame to create a split-screen image. First one side of the frame is exposed, and then the film is rewound and the opposite side of the film is exposed. In-camera mattes, which are finely cut out of metal, can also be inserted behind the lens closer to the focal plane. An actor can then play two different roles within the same camera frame. This is done by first filming the actor on one side of the screen, rewinding the film, and then filming the same actor on the opposite side of the screen. Painted skylines and other scenic additions can be made using the same in-camera matte process by dividing the frame horizontally rather than vertically. Filters can also be placed over a lens, such as a gauze or haze filter, to create a softer image. Cinematographers often carry a variety of transparent materials with them on location that can be used to diffuse the image during recording.

Video cameras can also provide built-in special effects controls. Many of these effects are similar to some of the in-camera film effects described earlier. For example, fade-ins and fade-outs can often be created automatically at the beginning or end of a shot by depressing a fader control. Some cameras allow the speed of motion to be varied to create slow motion, fast motion, and time-lapse recordings. Other in-camera special effects include various forms of digital image processing, such as image patterning, blurring, solarization, and other visual image manipulations and distortions. Again, many of these in-camera effects can also be created during postproduction, such as digital nonlinear editing, although some experimental videographers prefer to create these effects during initial recording.

Optical Effects

One of the advantages of creating special effects during postproduction is that they can often be more carefully controlled at this stage than during the production stage. Mistakes made during production are often very costly if a scene must be reconstructed and actors reengaged. Postproduction special effects are often "added on" to the initial recordings and rarely require the initial scene to be reshot. In the past, in-camera film and video effects were often undertaken to prevent generational loss in terms of reductions in the quality of the image during postproduction, but the advent of digital technologies has virtually eliminated generational loss in the creation of electronic special effects during the postproduction stage.

A variety of optical film effects are still widely used today, including step-printing, traveling mattes, and aerial-image printing. An *optical printer* is needed to create many special effects on film. A basic optical printer consists of a camera and a projector. The two machines face each other, and the lens of the camera is focused on the image from the projector. The camera and projector can be moved toward or away from each other to increase the size of the image. An optical blowup can be created by using a larger-format and a smaller-format projector. Using a smaller-format camera and a larger-format projector creates an optical reduction. The camera and the projector must be precisely positioned so that the full frame of picture in the projector fills the full frame of picture in the camera.

Many effects, such as dissolves, fades, and superimpositions, can be made more easily and less expensively on a conventional contact printer, which brings the original film and the copy into physical contact (emulsion to emulsion) as they pass over a light. A and B roll printing is conventionally done on a contact printer.

More sophisticated optical effects require the use of additional techniques and equipment. *Optical fades* can be made by gradually covering or uncovering the lamp in the projector with a fader bar. Optical fades are usually made with a *taper*, that is, with a logarithmic increase or decrease in light intensity. A taper ensures that the light changes intensity gradually during a fade-out or fade-in. A strictly linear curve, as opposed to a taper, is used for *dissolves* so that scene A fades out at exactly the same rate as scene B fades in. *Optical flips* can be achieved by simply rotating elements within special optical printer lenses. *Freeze-frames* are made by exposing many frames in the camera, while holding the same frame in the projector. *Stretch printing* slows down or retards the perceived action by printing each frame more than once. *Skip printing* is often used to speed up a slow-moving sequence by recording every other frame of the original film.

Wipes, split screens, and optical combinations of animation and live action involve the creation of special *traveling mattes*. *Mattes* consist of special high-contrast, black-and-white images that are made from normal film images or from artwork. For example, suppose a color title must be inserted into a background scene. The two images cannot simply be superimposed on one another, since the colors will bleed together rather than producing solid lettering. A black-and-white high-contrast copy of the titles can be made, so that the black letters will block out the portion of the background image where the colored letters are to be inserted.

The optical printer must have three projectors to do this: one for the background scene, one for the matte (unless the matte and the background scene are *bi-packed*, or run physically in contact with each other in one projector), and one for the color titles. The combination of the three images is then recorded by the camera.

Wipes and split screens can be made from similar traveling mattes, which block out a portion of the screen into which a second image is then inserted. It is possible to combine live action and animation by using traveling mattes in this manner. One sequence can also be recorded against a blue or black screen so that another sequence can be inserted into the blue screen area. Many special effects in science fiction and horror films are achieved by using a blue-screen process. Spaceships are often recorded as they move in front of a blue screen. This blue screen portion of the frame is then used to create a matte that blocks out the area of the frame where the spaceship should appear in a highly detailed background scene with stars in outer space. The spaceship is then inserted as a foreground object into this area.

Aerial image photography combines optical printing and animation by using a film projector with an animation stand. Live-action images can be projected from beneath predrawn cels, so that color titles or animated figures can be combined with live action. The opaque portions of the cel block out the background scene, which is projected underneath it so that the titles are superimposed over the background scene. The combined image is recorded by the film camera suspended overhead. Aerial image photography eliminates the need for special intermediate mattes, such as those that are used during film printing to block out or blacken areas of the frame into which titles and other images are to be inserted. However, aerial imaging requires bright projection illumination.

The choice between doing special effects on film, videotape, or through a digital medium is often a difficult one to make unless it has already been decided to use film or videotape for an entire production. The obvious advantage of digital video is the savings in overall production time. Effects can be set up and viewed immediately, without waiting for laboratory processing. Electronic effects facilities normally have sophisticated computerized editing and switching equipment, so that several images can be run simultaneously. Keys and mattes can be created instantaneously. The purchase or rental costs of these facilities have decreased as their use has increased. Careful preplanning must go into the creation of a special electronic effect prior to entering the studio. Optical film effects are time-consuming to produce, but a very high degree of control and precision can be achieved through multiple passes of the same artwork with film. It is also possible to make sophisticated special effects in films with very low-cost equipment. A basic optical printer, consisting of a simple projector and camera on adjustable platforms, can be purchased for a modest sum, allowing freeze-frames, step printing, superimpositions, dissolves, and many other optical effects to be created.

Models and Miniatures

Full-scale models and reduced-scale miniatures are used whenever a three-dimensional object or setting is needed that either does not exist or when it would be too expensive or dangerous to use an actual object. A miniature may be required for a historical setting that no longer exists, or a full-scale model may be needed for a spaceship that hasn't yet been constructed.

In some situations, such as when the camera must move within the shot, which requires a three-dimensional set to maintain realistic perspective, a painted two-dimensional background cannot be used to create the illusion of a specific location. In this case, a three-dimensional miniature of that location

Figure 12.7 One of the methods of converting a solid object to a digital form is by tracing that form using a 3-D digitizer. The operator traces over all key surfaces of the object with a stylus until a full 3-D image has been transferred to a digital file. (Courtesy of Immersion Corporation.)

can be constructed to allow for camera moves. Usually when actions occur with a miniature, the camera records the action in slow motion to adjust for the difference in time-scale relations between full-scale and miniature environments. Motion must be reduced proportionately to the reduced scale of the miniature. When complicated miniatures and movements are required, it is often prudent to shoot test recordings at a variety of speeds before recording final takes or disposing of the miniature (Figure 12.7).

Effective use of miniatures and models requires careful preplanning, since these types of special effects are often extremely expensive. Similar types of coordination and planning are required, just the same as those that are demanded of an art director, director, producer, and cinematographer during full-scale, live-action production. Drawings are usually prepared and approved before miniatures and models are actually constructed. Problems of linear perspective and scale between live-action, full-scale images with which miniatures may be intercut or combined will need to be worked out during preplanning sessions. Perspective projections and blueprints for miniatures are usually prepared prior to actual construction.

Miniatures are difficult to record not only because of potential problems in perspective, scale, and speed of motion, but also because audience disbelief is often difficult to overcome. Larger-scale, highly detailed miniatures are usually required for longer shot durations, where the audience will have an opportunity to carefully scrutinize them. When smaller, less-detailed miniatures are used, the editor often must keep the shot duration very short to reduce audience scrutiny and to maintain a willing suspension of disbelief. When miniatures are combined with live action, their believability is generally enhanced, provided that there are few if any discrepancies in perspective, scale, and speed of motion.

Miniatures can take advantage of single-frame recording and matting or keying techniques to create apparent motion from stationary objects. A miniature spaceship or airplane, for example, can be recorded against a blue-screen background while it is moved slightly along a suspended, invisible wire between each frame. Later a composite of the background scene and the moving aircraft can be made using photographic or electronic matting and keying techniques. Another advantage of miniatures and models is that they can be used to create inexpensive physical effects, such as various explosions, which would otherwise be too expensive to accomplish using actual objects and locations.

Physical Effects

Physical effects include wind, fog, smoke, rain, snow, fires, explosions, and gunshots. They require the guiding hand of a highly trained professional, especially when their use can endanger the safety of the cast and crew. Wind is usually generated by very large fans or aircraft engines and propellers whose speed and direction can be carefully controlled. Fog is often produced by combining smoke, such as from slow-burning naphtha or bitumen mixtures, and dry ice, which produces carbon dioxide. Most smoke-producing devices use either oil or water-based smoke fluid, which is heated above the boiling point to produce a gas that looks like smoke. Since all smoke is toxic to some degree, it should only be used in well-ventilated areas.

Rain, like wind and fog, is often used to accentuate a mood and atmosphere. Ground-level rainstands and overhead rainheads can be used to produce rain in limited areas, and the surrounding areas can be wetted down prior to shooting to sustain an illusion of a general rainshower. Pumps, valves, hoses, and manifolds (feeding several hoses), and spray heads are used to control the flow of water. When rain effects are produced in a sound stage, it is extremely important to waterproof the floor, to have a means of drainage or water collection, and to avoid any contact between water and electrical equipment, such as lights, which could cause severe injury or even kill cast and crew members (Figure 12.8).

Snow can be created indoors or outdoors using a large, almost silent, wooden-bladed fan, which can also be used for rain effects, and that is called a *Ritter fan*. Plastic snow can be dropped in front of the fan, usually from the top of the left side but never from behind (which would foul the blades and mechanism), by hand or a snow delivery machine. Polystyrene granules can be added to create a blizzard effect. Outdoors a variety of materials, in addition to plastic flakes, can and have been used to create snow, including shaved ice, foam machines, gypsum, salt (on windows and windowsills), and aerosol shaving cream on slippery surfaces.

While fire effects can add excitement and visual interest to a scene, they are also extremely dangerous and should only be created by skilled professionals who know how to contain them. Torches, such as propane torches, are often used to project flames from outside the frame, and fire bars using LPG gas are often used to create and control flames in front of the camera. It is extremely important to have fire extinguishers on hand that can control all three classes of fire: Class A fires, which burn solid combustibles,

Figure 12.8 Most physical effects are the result of special effects crews using machines and chemicals to produce atmospheres and environments critical to the production, such as the Paramount crew on this Western set preparing to create wind. (Courtesy of Paramount Pictures.)

such as cloth, rubber, wood, paper, and many plastics; Class B fires, which burn flammable liquids and gases; and Class C fires, which involve electrical or electronic equipment.

Explosions and pyrotechnics are the most difficult special effects to perform safely. They need to be set up and supervised by experts who are thoroughly familiar with the setting, detonation, and control of explosions and fires, since they are potentially dangerous to cast and crew members. Explosives and pyrotechnics are controlled by the U.S. Bureau of Alcohol, Tobacco, and Firearms. A federal license is needed to use explosives, and information concerning their use can be obtained from the Bureau upon request. Building explosions usually require prebuilt structures constructed of light materials, such as balsa wood or cardboard. Blowing up a vehicle usually requires removing the carburetor and gas tank, while the engine, hood, trunk, and car doors are attached to the car by steel cables to prevent them from flying uncontrolled distances. Most explosions and pyrotechnics require remote detonation.

Bullet hits are created by remote detonation of small explosive devices, called *squibs*, which are positioned over body armor or a hit plate that protects the actor or stuntman. Blood packs, consisting of plastic bags containing corn syrup and red food coloring to simulate blood, and squibs are glued onto the back of the actor's or stuntman's shirt. Wires running down the pant legs are attached to the squibs at one end and to the firing box for remote detonation at the other end. Sometimes the wires have breakaway connectors at the ankles so that the actor or stuntman can break free of the wires just after the bullet hits have been detonated.

SUMMARY

Animation and special effects generate visual interest and can be used to create imaginative worlds. Animation develops imaginative worlds by using single-frame recording techniques to make static images and objects appear to move. Special effects allow futuristic or historical worlds to come to life, and dangerous actions and events to be simulated.

Animation uses single-frame recording techniques to make static images and objects move. By breaking the motion of an object down into its component parts, an animator can control the movements of otherwise lifeless figures and images. Single-frame recordings of static images can create apparent motion when small changes in the positioning of objects occur between successive frames. Animation begins with the construction of a storyboard. A chart or breakdown of the music and/or lip-sync voice is combined with the storyboard so that the animator can calculate the precise order and number of frames that will be needed.

Flat animation is accomplished with two-dimensional drawings and illustrations. One of the most common flat animation techniques is cel animation, in which an individual clear acetate cel is used for each frame. Techniques that can be used to make cel animation more efficient include cycling recurring lip and body movements, drawing a new image for only every third or fourth frame, and tracing the outlines of live-action filmed images, a technique known as rotoscoping. There is a noticeable difference in animation style and effectiveness between rotoscoped animation and hand-drawn cel animation, however.

Plastic animation refers to the single-frame recording of three-dimensional figures and objects. Puppets, clay figures, miniature objects and vehicles, and even still frames of live action (a technique known as pixillation) can be animated. Three-dimensional figures are recorded using techniques that combine animation and live-action recording. The camera is usually placed horizontally rather than vertically with respect to the subject, and a three-dimensional miniature world of sets, props, and backgrounds must be constructed. Single-frame recording allows these inanimate objects to simulate motion and to accomplish seemingly impossible feats.

Computer animation generates images that can be recorded and stored as single frames on disk. Although 2-D computer animation continues to serve certain functions and even full-length features, 3-D computer animation has slowly become the creative leader in feature films and in television shorts. The greatest advantages of computer animation are speed and accuracy. Images can be immediately viewed as well as accurately recorded and rerecorded. Some computers interpolate the in-between frames if the animator simply composes the first and last frames of a sequence. A computer can also be used to interpolate the changes in two-dimensional or three-dimensional objects. Three-dimensional computer animation can be combined with live-action photography, opening up a whole new world of illusion and abstract art to film and television audiences.

Film animation requires a single-frame camera and an animation stand. The animation stand consists of a camera platform that can be raised and lowered and an artwork table or rostrum, which can be moved east and west, north and south. A dolly shot can be created by raising or lowering the camera, and a pan can be achieved by moving the table. A variable shutter on the camera allows fades, dissolves, and other special effects to be accomplished. On the most sophisticated animation stands, a computer controls a complex set of camera and table movements, as well as changes of art. A technique known as aerial image photography combines a projector with the animation stand and camera, so that artwork titles or illustrations on cels can be combined with live-action film images projected from below without requiring more laborious matte printing techniques. A video camera can also be attached to an animation stand, and single frames can be recorded on a slo-mo disk recorder or a disk frame-storage unit.

Special effects can be divided into five basic categories: camera effects, optical and digital effects, models and miniatures, and physical effects. Camera effects include such features as fast and slow motion as well as single-frame (animation) recording. Film recording rates in excess of 24 fps, such as 32, 48, and 64 fps, create slow motion when the processed film is projected at the standard projection speed of 24 fps, and film recording rates less than 24 fps, such as 18 and 12 fps, create fast motion. In addition to varying the speed of the images, some film cameras allow fade-outs, fade-ins, superimpositions, and reverse motion to be created during initial recording. Video cameras can also provide built-in special effects controls, some of which produce effects that are similar to in-camera film effects, such as fades and slow motion.

Digital effects can be divided into five areas: transitions, filters, compositing, morphing, and a combination of superimpositions, keys, and mattes. Transitions are means of replacing one digital clip, which is usually a single image or shot, with another. Filters are means of altering a clip, and superimpositions, keys, and mattes are combinations of more than one clip that appear simultaneously within the same frame. Different layers of images can be digitally combined to create a composite image. Morphing is an effective technique for altering shapes, form, and figures and creating imaginative worlds through the use of special digital effects. A miniature may be required for an historic or futuristic setting that no longer exists or has yet to appear. Usually, when actions occur with a miniature, the camera records the action in slow motion to adjust for the difference in time-scale relations between full-scale and miniature environments. Motion must be reduced proportionately to the reduced scale of the miniature. Models and miniatures, when combined with single-frame animation as well as matting and keying effects, can be used to put an object, such as a spacecraft, in motion or to create the illusion of a later century city by placing futuristic buildings into an existing location.

Optical film effects include step printing, traveling mattes, and aerial image printing. A basic optical printer consists of a camera and a projector. The two machines face each other, and the lens of the camera is focused on the image from the projector. Step printing is often used to speed up a slow-moving sequence by recording every other frame of the original film. Aerial image photography combines optical printing and animation, using a film projector with an animation stand. Live-action images are projected from beneath predrawn cels, so that color titles or animated figures can be combined with live action.

Physical effects include wind, fog, smoke, rain, snow, fires, explosions, and gunshots. They require the guiding hand of a highly trained professional when their use can endanger the safety of the cast and crew. Physical effects, like other kinds of special effects, can significantly contribute to the emotional mood of a sequence and generate viewer interest and excitement.

EXERCISES

1. Construct a storyboard for an animation project. Create frames for each shot that will appear in the completed sequence. Either draw each frame by hand, or use a computer graphics program to compose each one. Make sure that all camera and figure movements are relatively simple to reproduce using an animation stand or a computer animation program. Determine how many individual frames or changes of figure movement and motion from still-frame images will be required. A series of single film or video frames in which recorded objects or materials gradually change their spatial position within the frame are recorded individually and sequentially. When they are played back at normal speed (24 fps in film or 30 fps in video), they produce apparent motion.

2. Do a preliminary test for an animation sequence by creating a series of individual frames such as one animation cycle. Compose pencil drawings for each frame needed to complete a short sequence of actions. Draw the figures and backgrounds on white cards that have an aspect ratio of 4:3. Hold the cards together at the bottom using two fingers of your left hand while rapidly flipping them with your right thumb to simulate the effect of animation and to test the speed of actions you are trying to create. Then, record these cards as

single frames of film or video on an animation stand and assess the results.

3. Project individual frames of live-action film onto a copy stand or a computer drawing tablet in precise registration. Trace the outlines of the figures within the frame. Record these outlines as individual film or video frames. Use this rotoscoping technique to acquire a feeling for how much movement should take place between each animation frame in a purely imaginary animation sequence.

4. Animate cutout paper figures by placing them on an animation stand and moving them slightly between recordings of individual film or video frames. Vary the speed of movement and evaluate the results.

5. Shoot a series of in-camera special effects, such as slow motion, fast motion, reverse motion, pixillation, fade-outs, fade-ins, and split screens.

6. Digitize a short video sequence, divide it into separate clips, and then image process each clip using a variety of transitions, filters, and superimpositions, keys, or mattes using a digital nonlinear editing or special effects program.

ADDITIONAL READINGS

Corsaro, Sandro. *The Flash Animator.* Indianapolis, IN: New Riders Publishing, 2002.

Culhane, Shamus. *Animation from Script to Screen.* New York: St. Martin's Press, 1988.

Fernandez, Ibis. *Macromedia Flash Animation and Cartooning: A Creative Guide.* New York, NY: McGraw-Hill, 2002.

Gallardo, Arnold. *3-D Lighting: History, Concepts, and Techniques.* Rockland, MA: Charles Rover Media, Inc. 2001.

Gordon, Bob, and Maggie Gordon. *The Complete Guide to Digital Graphic Design.* New York, NY: Watson-Guptill, 2002.

Graham, Lisa. *The Principles of Interactive Design.* Albany, NY: Delmar Publishers, 1999.

Griffin, Hedley. *The Animator's Guide to 2-D Animation.* Boston, MA: Focal Press, 2001.

Hoffer, Thomas, W. *Animation: A Reference Guide.* Westport, CT: Greenwood Press, 1981.

Kerlow, Isaac V. *The Art of 3-D Computer Animation and Effects.* Hoboken, NJ: John Wiley and Sons, 2004.

Kuperberg, Marcia. *A Guide to Computer Animation for TV, Games, Multimedia, and the Web.* Boston, MA: Focal Press, 2002.

Laybourne, Kit. *The Animation Book.* New York: Three Rivers Press, 1998.

Maestri, George. *Digital Character Animation*. Indianapolis, IN: New Riders Publishing, 1996.

McCarthy, Robert E. *Secrets of Hollywood Special Effects*. Woburn, MA: Focal Press, 1992.

Miller, Dan. *Cinema Secrets, Special Effects*. London: Apple Press, 1990.

Shaw, Susannah. *Stop Motion: Craft Skills for Model Animation*. Boston, MA: Focal Press, 2003.

Simons, Mark. *Storyboards: Motion in Art*, 2nd ed. Boston, MA: Focal Press, 2000.

Wagstaff, Sean. *Animation on the Web*. Berkeley, CA: Peachpit Press, 1999.

Whitaker, Harold. *Timing for Animation*. Boston, MA: Focal Press, 2002.

Wilkie, Bernard. *Creating Special Effects for TV and Video*, 3rd ed. Boston, MA: Focal Press, 1996.

13 Distribution and Exhibition

TOPICS FOR DISCUSSION

- How does the exhibition of media production compare to retail business?
- What are the technologies used in distributing broadcast signals?
- How are cable and satellite signals distributed?
- How are theatrical and nontheatrical films distributed?
- What part does corporate media play in distribution?
- How has home media distribution changed?

INTRODUCTION

In most media-related business operations, production is analogous to manufacturing, distribution to wholesaling, and exhibition to retailing. A distributor acts as a middleman or intermediary between the people who produce something and those who consume it. Exhibiting film, video, audio, and multimedia productions is similar to running a retail store from which individual consumers buy things. In media production, distribution and exhibition are aspects of postproduction, but producers consider them during preproduction as well (Figure 13.1).

As digital technology advances, it becomes obvious that sending and receiving audio, video, motion pictures, and other digital signals via the Internet will take its place as a major means of distribution and exhibition. Well into the twenty-first century, once digital memory and compression techniques provide high-quality programming and the capability of homes to receive that same quality programs at a reasonable rate, streaming will become practical. The ability of home viewers/listeners to receive a digital signal faster than a 56K modem allows is the key to the success of streaming. Fiber optical lines to the home, increased use of DSL (Digital Subscriber Line) in the home, or wireless Internet systems will allow streaming to become universal. Streaming of video and audio information on the Internet or World Wide Web (WWW) usually takes the form of either Web broadcasting, also known as video or audio on demand, or live Webcasting. Video/audio on demand streaming occurs whenever a computer operator/receiver decides to download prerecorded audio or video information, while live Webcasting occurs at a specific time determined by the sender rather than the receiver.

Distribution and exhibition marketing strategies and technologies will also be affected by a phenomenon known as convergence. *Convergence* refers to the coming together of previously separate technologies, such as computers and television sets. For example, as more and more computer manufacturers, such as Gateway, become involved in audio/video and multimedia technologies, and more and more audio/video product manufacturers, such as Sony, become involved in computer technologies, previously separate entities are coming together. Early examples of convergence include WEB-TV, where WEB searches can be conducted using a conventional TV set, and LCD (Liquid Crystal Display)-TV sets, which can also function as computer screens. As convergence progresses, media producers will need to become increasingly cognizant of new and emerging means and methods of distributing and exhibiting audio, video, and multimedia productions.

The selection of a specific production format or technology and the preparation of a budget must mesh with the anticipated distribution and exhibition technology and outlets. The initial planning for a feature film, for example, may have to consider a wide variety of distribution and exhibition channels and markets, from major theatrical distribution, to

**MOTION PICTURE BUSINESS
COMPARED TO
RETAIL BUSINESS**

MOTION PICTURES	BUSINESS
Producer	Manufacturer
Distributor	Wholesale
Exhibitor	Retail Sales

Figure 13.1 In the motion picture business, the producer is the equivalent of the manufacturer in retail business. The distributor is the equivalent of a wholesaler, and the owner of the theater where the films are screened or exhibited is the equivalent of a retailer.

network broadcasting, cable, DVDs, and nontheatrical or educational distribution to college campuses. Producers must increasingly guard against unwanted and illegal piracy of copyrighted material via miniature video cameras in movie theaters and subsequent Internet streaming. Even a corporate or institutional in-house production is designed with specific types of exhibition in mind. The final product may be sent out as DVD or CD copies or presented "live" via satellite on television monitors or large screens at various corporate locations.

In Chapter 2, "Producing and Production Management," we indicated that specific programs must be targeted for specific audiences. In this chapter we will see how a television or film producer attempts to reach that target audience by selecting the best distribution and exhibition channel(s). Specific projects are tailored for specific forms of presentation in the media, such as cable television or theatrical film, as well as for specific target audiences. A consideration of the technology and economics of distribution and exhibition follows logically from the concern for the audience begun in our study of preproduction. Selecting the best channels requires an understanding of media technology and economics.

TECHNOLOGY OF DISTRIBUTION AND EXHIBITION

Broadcasting, Cable, and Satellite

Broadcasters send video and audio signals to home receivers through the airwaves. Local broadcasters use a limited number of available channels in a restricted broadcast signal range to reach viewers. There are basically two different types of broadcast signals: very high frequency (VHF) and ultra high frequency (UHF). While VHF signals are usually stronger and travel farther than UHF signals, neither can be received with much clarity more than 100 miles away from the transmitter tower.

Television signals use up more area of the electromagnetic spectrum than do radio signals since they carry both video and audio information: about 6 megahertz (6 million hertz) compared with 10 kilohertz (10,000 hertz) for AM (amplitude modulation) radio signals and 200 kilohertz for FM (frequency modulation) radio signals. There are far fewer available television channels than radio channels. Television audio information is broadcast as an FM signal, while video information uses a high-frequency AM signal. There are more UHF channels available (70 channels, from 14 to 83, although the UHF channels above 70 are being phased out and are no longer assigned by the FCC in most locations) than VHF channels (12 channels, from 2 to 13) (Figure 13.2).

After 2006 all local television broadcast stations will switch broadcasting from their original assigned analog channel to a new assigned digital channel. *Until that time*, television stations have the option to broadcast on both channels using two different programs. Cable and satellite operations have to add additional channel allocations to accommodate both the analog and digital channels for each TV station until the analog channels cease to operate.

Broadcast television signals come from a variety of sources. A station can generate a live signal from the studio, or from a remote location in the field, as during a local news broadcast. A prerecorded signal can be played on a videotape playback machine, or a direct feed can come from the network, via satellite or via a telephone line to the station. Whatever its source, an RF (radio frequency) signal is impressed upon a carrier wave so that it can be amplified and transmitted through the airwaves to home receivers. An *RF signal* interweaves the audio and video information and is then decoded by a television receiver. Usually the stronger the wattage of the carrier wave, the stronger the signal and the better the television reception will be. The image quality of conventional broadcast television is limited by the fact that a television station's channel space is restricted to a bandwidth of about 6 megahertz. This bandwidth restriction permits only about 350 lines of analog resolution (more lines of resolution mean better images) in video signals sent to home receivers. By way of comparison, a projected 35mm film image can have 1,000 to 1,200 lines of resolution. High-

THE FREQUENCY SPECTRUM

FREQUENCY	FREQUENCY USE	TYPE OF WAVE
0-10 kHz	Audio	Sound
10 kHz-100 kHz	Experimental, Maritime, Navigation & Comm.	Very Low Freq.
100 kHz-1 MHz	Maritime & Aviation Navigation, Comm. & Ham	Low Freq.
1 MHz-10 MHz	AM B-cast, Ham, Navigation, Industrial	Medium Freq.
10 MHz-100 MHz	Int'l Shortwave,Ham, Citizens, Medical, LORAN	High Freq.
100 MHz-1 GHz	Aviation, TV B-cast, FM B-cast, FAX, Ham, Wx	Very High Freq.
1 GHz-10 GHz	Aviation, STL Microwave, Gov.,TV B-cast, Ham	Ultra High Freq.
10 GHz-100 GHz	Gov., Radio Navigation, Ham, Fixed & Mobile	Super High freq.
100 GHz-1 THz	Experimental, Government, Ham	Extreme High Freq.
1 THz-10 THz	Industrial Photo, Research	Infrared
10 THz-100 THz	Heat Waves	Infrared
100 THz-1 PHz	Heat Waves	Infrared
1 PHz-10 PHz	Light, Heat Waves	Light, Ultraviolet
10 PHz-100 PHz	Ionizing Radiation, Medical Research	Ultraviolet
100 PHz-1 Ehz	Ionizing Radiation, Medical Research	Soft X-rays
1 Ehz-10 Ehz	Ionizing Radiation, Scientific Research	X-rays
10 Ehz-100 Ehz	Gamma Rays	Hard X-rays
100 Ehz-1 ZHz	Gamma Rays	Hard X-rays

The Higher Metric Classifications

Metric Name	Number of units	Common Name
KILO	1,000	Thousand
MEGA	1,000,000	Million
GIGA	1,000,000,000	Billion
TERA	1,000,000,000,000	Trillion
PETA	1,000,000,000,000,000	Quadrillion
EXA	1,000,000,000,000,000,000	Quintillion
ZETTA	1,000,000,000,000,000,000,000	Sextillion
YOTTA	1,000,000,000,000,000,000,000,000	Septillion

Figure 13.2 The frequency spectrum starts with sound frequencies and moves through radio frequencies to light and on to gamma ray frequencies. As communication and computer engineers develop equipment that deals with higher frequencies and greater amounts of memory, the metric system nomenclature of higher numbers will become more familiar.

definition television (HDTV) offers an image resolution that more closely approximates filmed images than conventional broadcast television, but it also requires a much greater bandwidth. Digital broadcast channels are capable of up to six individual signals simultaneously. Only one channel can be watched at a time if the signal is a full *16x9* HDTV signal, but a combination of from two to four channels simultaneously if the signals are standard digital (SD) signals that require less bandwidth than high definition (HD) signals.

A home television receiver has two or three different tuners, one for VHF signals, another for UHF signals, and possibly a third for HDTV broadcast signals. When a specific channel is selected on a tuner, the carrier wave and television signal from a specific station are picked up by the antenna; then the video and audio signals are decoded. A color receiver separates the chrominance channel (red, green, and blue color information) from the luminance channel (black-and-white brightness information). Broadcast television signals are subject to interference from atmospheric conditions, other signals such as CB radios, and poor antenna placements, but they currently reach a larger nationwide viewing audience in the United States than any other means of television distribution. Some local television stations are affiliated with television networks, such as ABC, NBC, CBS, Fox, WB, and UPN; others, which are mainly in major metropolitan areas, are owned and operated (O&O) by these networks (the number of O&Os per network being limited by FCC rules), and still others are independent or nonaffiliated. PBS (Public Broadcasting Service) has member stations in local areas (Figure 13.3).

Satellites are relay stations that orbit the globe and make possible instantaneous communication over vast distances. U.S. satellites are positioned in

SOURCES FOR BROADCAST PROGRAMS

Local station live studio productions

Local station live field (remote) productions

Local live-to-tape productions

Local tape or film series

Independently produced film or tape documentaries

Independently produced film or tape series

Syndicated tape or film specials

Syndicated tape or film series

Animated film or computer specials

Animated film or computer series

Network specials

Network series

Figure 13.3 Broadcast stations must rely on a wide range of sources for their programming. Few stations can produce all of the programming to fill the entire broadcast day without purchasing or leasing programming from a variety of sources.

space so that they maintain a constant position and altitude with respect to land masses on the earth. A satellite's antenna receives signals from the earth's surface and then relays them back to earth. A satellite transmission, like a standard microwave signal used for live-remote ENG transmissions, requires a direct uninterrupted, line-of-sight path between the transmitter and the receiver. But receiver dishes across a wide area on the earth's surface can receive satellite signals if they are properly positioned.

A satellite transmitter or tracking station on the earth is aimed at the satellite's receiving antenna, to which it sends a signal. A transmitter on the satellite relays this signal to a wide area of possible satellite dishes on the ground. Satellites can be used for transmitting live television signals from overseas as well as for coast-to-coast transmission of news and sporting events. Satellites are also used for transmitting cable television programming across the country to various local cable television operators, who distribute the programming along cable wires to individual homes (Figure 13.4).

Home satellite use is growing. In the past, a large (approximately 10 feet in diameter), unsightly analog satellite signal receiver dish needed to be mounted in the yard in order to receive strong, high-quality signals. Digital satellite transmission has dramatically reduced the size of rooftop-mounted receiver dishes to about two feet in diameter, while dramatically increasing the quality of images and sound to include

SATELLITE OPERATION

Figure 13.4 A basic satellite system consists of three parts: a ground station that gathers the programming and transmits the signals to an orbiting satellite, which then retransmits the signals back to individual stations equipped with downlink receivers.

high-definition television signals and CD-quality audio. Regardless of which system, analog or digital, is used, a decoder is needed to receive most services. A dish must be capable of being precisely rotated and positioned, however, to receive signals from more than one satellite.

Cable television distributes television signals from a satellite dish to private homes via coaxial cable or eventually fiber-optic cable (Figure 13.5). Coaxial cable consists of metal wires encased in plastic and/or

CABLE SYSTEM OPERATION

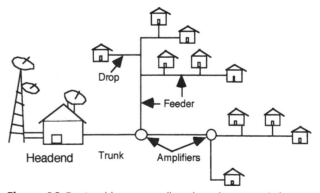

Figure 13.5 A cable system collects broadcast signals from off the air and downlinks programs fed by satellites at the headend. At the headend the signals are modulated onto a series of carrier frequencies that are fed down a single cable. From the headend the signal is fed to trunk lines that feed a fairly large area. Feeder lines take the signal from the trunk line to feed a smaller area, and then the drop is the final line that runs to the individual subscriber.

metal insulators. The insulation makes it possible to send signals over wide areas with minimal interference and loss of signal. Nonetheless, the signal does decrease in strength as it spreads out from main trunk lines. Amplifiers are strategically located in a community to maintain a relatively constant signal strength as the signal passes along subtrunk lines and drops that signal to individual homes.

Optical-fiber trunk lines have significantly reduced signal loss while dramatically increasing information capacity, but it is still quite rare to have optical-fiber connections directly to the home. Some cable lines can be directly connected to a television receiver antenna jack, and others require an intermediate decoder and tuner box. The most sophisticated cable systems allow for two-way or interactive communication between the individual subscriber and the cable operator. Two-way communication can be used for opinion polling and obtaining viewer feedback. In addition to television signals, a cable system can be used to transmit information, such as data for home computers, telephone services, and to serve as a monitoring function for public and private utility companies.

According to the ruling of the FCC, all broadcasting must be in the digital domain once 85% of the potential audience would be capable of receiving digital broadcasts. The goal is for this to be reached by 2006, but more realistically, it will be closer to 2010. All stations have been assigned new channels for their digital broadcasts, and eventually they will stop using their original analog channels. This means that all receivers will need to be delivered equipped with digital capabilities, or an adapter will need to be added to existing receivers. By the middle of 2003, nearly 100% of all American television audiences were served by at least one digital broadcast station. The viewers in only the smallest markets and those not directly served by a local TV station were beyond the reach of a digital station.

High-definition television (HDTV) can produce a high-resolution widescreen video image, which rivals that of film (although most films have somewhat higher resolution and slightly wider widescreen images). HDTV signals require much wider bandwidth than conventional broadcast television signals. Digital satellite and optical-fiber systems facilitate the transmission of high definition on television signals to the home, and the use of HDTV for cable and satellite television, if not broadcast television, is developing quite rapidly. Many media productions are using HDTV for production, even if they are conventionally broadcast or cablecast, to ensure that they will maintain their marketability as HDTV exhibition increases. Eventually HDTV images may

replace film as the preferred theatrical exhibition medium, when high-quality, large-screen HDTV projection devices become economical for theater owners, not just distributors, and raise few piracy problems or concerns for producers and distributors.

HDTV sets have proliferated as the amount of HDTV programming has steadily increased in recent years. A significant number of prime time television programs are currently broadcast in high definition (HD) on all four major commercial networks as well as public television. In addition to network movies and prime time programming broadcast or cablecast in HD, cable movie channels, such as HBO HD and Showtime HD, regularly show movies in HD, and there are also HD science and sports channels on cable, such as the Discovery Channel HD and ESPN HD. To receive these high-definition offerings, consumers need an HDTV set as well as an HD cable box, a satellite receiver, and/or an HDTV tuner. DVD players can play high-resolution video (from MPEG files) by sending component (split signals of high-resolution images) signals to HDTV sets. Coupled with digital surround sound receivers and speakers, large-screen HDTVs can simulate a movie theater experience in the home.

Theatrical and Nontheatrical

Media productions can be distributed to and exhibited in theaters and educational institutions in addition to being broadcast, cablecast, and transmitted via satellite. Theatrical exhibition requires some form of large-screen projection. Electronic projection of large-screen video images is undergoing constant technological improvement and change. Although there are obvious projection limitations inherent in broadcast images, as noted earlier, the use of closed-circuit systems and the development of widescreen HDTV and digital recording is significantly improving the prospects for large-screen electronic projection. The standard cathode ray tube (CRT) monitor used since the beginning of television has been replaced by a variety of flat-screen monitors. A typical flat-screen monitor is less than 5 inches thick and *Rom* can be as wide as 63 inches. Three major types are leading the movement to flat screens; these types are Liquid Crystal Display (LCD), Plasma Display Panels (PDP), and Digital Light Processing (DLP). LCDs started the trend and are used in TV monitors and computer monitors. As technology improved and prices were reduced, plasma display became popular. Complete walls consisting of a single flat screen can be fed a series of different pictures simultaneously. Network control centers use such technology. DLP systems have replaced rear-projection monitors with a series of microchips and high-speed rotating mirrors, which add the chrominance value of the signal. Still in development at this writing are Organic Light-Emitting Diode (ODEO) monitors that may be as thin as 2 inches and use very low voltage.

Most extremely large-screen electronic projection systems project three separate colored light beams, for the red, green, and blue components of the signal, onto an enlarged screen, which may be as wide as 20. These types of projection systems are commonly used in bars, nightclubs, and video-game arcades, and larger screen projection systems are developed for electronic projection in commercial theaters. These electronic projection systems are often used for the live presentation of boxing matches and other exclusive events. The video transmission from the event itself can be carried across telephone lines or satellite relays as scrambled signals, which can then be picked up exclusively by designated theaters. Eventually a digital system of delivery will be used for electronic distribution of theatrical films across the country, once HDTV transmissions, large-screen projection systems, and secure systems for transmission and storage are perfected.

Although digital means of projection are constantly improving, film projection maintains a high standard, which large-screen electronic projection attempts to duplicate. A basic film projection system consists of an intermittent film transport, a bright light source, and a highly reflective screen. The film runs intermittently within the picture aperture or gate area while light passes through each individual frame to illuminate images on a screen. The film movement changes to a smooth, continuous motion over the sound head. Film sound is recorded either optically or magnetically along the edge of the film, and is picked up by a sound head on the projector. The sound is then amplified and sent to a speaker. The most sophisticated feature film soundtracks have six magnetic tracks running along the edges of 70mm film prints, and the separate sounds are channeled to different speakers in the film theater so that the spectator is surrounded by multitrack, stereophonic sound.

Dolby Surround Sound and other 360-degree sound systems that envelop the spectator within a theater are widely used for theatrical projection. Dolby and other noise reduction systems are also frequently used with magnetic film projection systems. A noise reduction system such as Dolby or DBX reduces noise and increases the range of sound frequencies (particularly high-frequency sound reproduction) by selectively increasing the volume or strength of high-frequency sounds during recording, and then selectively reducing this strong signal to a normal level during playback.

Film production can be accomplished using a variety of film formats. Different films require slightly different aspect ratios or aperture dimensions in the projector gate. Widescreen films, such as *Panavision* and *CinemaScope*, require special film apertures, anamorphic lenses, and wider screens. These aspect ratios often exceed 2:1, that is, the image is more than twice as wide as it is high. *Cinerama* uses three separate projectors simultaneously to achieve a widescreen effect. "Standard" theatrical 35mm projection uses an American widescreen aperture of 1.85:1 *(although few theatrical feature films are actually shot or exhibited in this format)*, while standard 16mm is 1.33:1, as is "standard" 35mm film used less and less frequently for television commercials, since this latter ratio corresponds to that of a standard television screen, 4:3 or 1.33:1 (Figure 13.6).

Projectors use a variety of different light sources. The brightest lamps are quartz lamps, HMI lamps, and carbon arc lamps. These light sources are capable of projecting images across wide-open areas at drive-ins and large, major hard-top theaters. Carbon arc lamps require special ventilation because they produce noxious fumes, which could quickly asphyxiate the projectionist in a small projection booth.

COMPARISON OF FILM ASPECT RATIOS

4:3 (1.33:1)
Academy Standard
Television, 35mm 16mm
and S-8mm film formats

(1.85:1)
American Widescreen
format

(2.21:1)
Vista Vision
format

(2.36:1)
70mm Full Aperture
format

Figure 13.6 Film aspect ratios, or the ratio of the width of the picture projected to the height, vary from the Academy standard of 1.33:1 to the 70mm full aperture of 2.36:1. The standard television aspect ratio is 1.33:1, but the standard for ATV is 9:6.

Most multicinemas today use tabletop projectors that run an entire two-hour film without requiring reel changes. These long-run projectors are semiautomatic, but projectionists constantly monitor them during actual operation to prevent damage to the film and to ensure a high-quality image. A single projectionist can monitor several projectors if the images are sent to a group of video monitors. Each projector has a built-in video camera, and all the video outputs are sent to the projection booth, where they can be viewed simultaneously by a single projectionist.

Attempts to revolutionize film exhibition by providing digital satellite or cable transmission of high-resolution, widescreen images to film theaters are continually under development. Such systems offer distributors the potential to save money by delivering films to theaters without the high cost of manufacturing and shipping conventional photochemical film prints. They also pose potential piracy problems via downloading and diverting these signals for the illegal distribution of movies as pirated DVDs or free Internet offerings, if they are not securely encoded and stored.

The problems facing Digital Cinema (DC), formerly called Electronic Cinema (EC), cover a wide range and include undefined standards of compression and resolution, security, reliability, costs, and delivery systems.

SMPTE is working on finding and setting standards with a goal of reaching standards equivalent to the universality of 35mm film. But differences of operation between computer technicians, motion picture technicians, and video technicians have made this a difficult task. Resolution of a typical 35mm film print provides about 2,000 lines of vertical resolution. The best digital projectors of 2004 provide from 1,280 to 1,500 lines of vertical resolution. The difference may not be noticeable to the audience's untrained eye, especially since many film projectors are not operated at their maximum standard. Absolute protection from hackers attempting piracy of the signal can not guarantee protection, regardless of whether the transmission is via satellite, fiber-optics, physical discs, or hard drives. Motion picture systems seldom fail, and computers are expected to periodically crash, which brings into question the stability and reliability of any system developed so far. As of the publication of this text, a reasonable digital projector to serve a medium-sized auditorium costs more than $100,000 and probably will need to be replaced within two to three years. Motion picture projectors cost $10,000 and last a lifetime.

On the positive side, productions may reach theaters two to three weeks earlier, due to the rapid postproduction process in operation if the project is digital from camera to projector. Also, there will be cost savings in avoiding costly printing and delivering of prints to individual theaters throughout the world when a single digital signal may serve several theaters and screens simultaneously. Today a majority of motion picture features are viewed by the audiences on small screens located in multiple-screen theatre complexes. A typical 10,000-lumen digital projector can equal the brightness of a film projected on a small screen.

The final difference between film and a video signal is in the mind of the audience. It has been said that video is what the eye sees and film is what the imagination sees.

Nontheatrical exhibitions often use smaller screens than theatrical exhibitions. Libraries, civic groups, schools, and universities are more likely to use video than film projectors. The use of any type of film in nontheatrical and educational markets has decreased significantly over the past few decades.

VHS videocassettes and DVDs are the most common distribution and exhibition media. Nontheatrical screenings usually involve smaller groups of viewers and significantly less, if any, admission fees than theatrical screenings, reducing the need and demand for high-quality, large-screen projection.

Home Video, Audio, and Multimedia

An expanding market for film and video material is that of consumer videodiscs. Feature films, video albums, and educational or informational programs can be purchased or rented for home or office use. The most commonly used home and office videotape formats are miniDV and D-VHS. Digital 8 records digital video on Hi-8 cassettes, while miniDV records digital video on miniDV cassettes. VHS and D-VHS use ½-inch videotape encased in a cassette, and use helical or slant-track scanning of the tape. Digital 8 cassettes offer a larger capacity than miniDV cassettes, but higher-quality camcorders generally use DV cassettes. Faster recording speeds mean better-quality images and sounds.

Videocassettes that record about 30 or 60 minutes of video material at high speed generally have thicker, more durable tape than 120-minute cassettes and are better suited for production purposes. S-VHS is an improved ½-inch consumer format often used for productions not requiring true professional quality. S-VHS is based on the original VHS system but is not downward compatible; this means an S-VHS tape cannot be played on a VHS machine, although a VHS tape can be played on an S-VHS deck. The

S-VHS signal is actually a composite system made up of three separate signals that must be carried by three separate cables in order to maintain full S-VHS quality.

High-speed ½-inch video images are of very high broadcast quality, exceeded only by the newer digital formats.

Laser disc technology comes in four basic formats: DVDs, CD-ROMs, photo CDs, and audio CDs. A single videotape can hold several hours, a videodisc 1 hour, and a DVD 2 hours of NTSC video. Some discs are permanent recordings. Like phonograph records, they cannot be erased and rerecorded. DVDs are widely used in entertainment markets. DVDs store 8 to 18 GB of digital data, which is sufficient for a feature film and supplementary materials. DVDs can be recorded in five basic formats: DVD-R, DVD-RAM, DVD-RW, DVD+RW, and DVD+R. DVD-R and DVD+R record data only one time, while DVD-RAM, DVD-RW, and DVD+RW can be rewritten or rerecorded hundreds or thousands of times. DVD-RAM was originally used as a recordable storage device for computers but has also been used for editing purposes. There are some incompatibilities between these various DVD formats, such as a DVD+R/RW drive cannot write a DVD-RW or DVD-R disc and vice versa, although a combo drive can write both formats.

CD-ROM is a very powerful information storage-and-retrieval medium for certain multimedia applications. CD-ROMs have a fairly high information-storage capacity of more than 600 megabytes. They can be used very effectively for multimedia applications that do not require full-screen, full-motion video. The speed at which information can be retrieved is limited, making it difficult to use this digital laser-disc technology to record and play back high-quality images. The transfer rate for some CD-ROM technology is about 150 kilobytes per second, which is sufficient for digital CD-quality music and sound, but the transfer rate needed for noncompressed full-screen, full-motion video is approximately 30 megabytes per second. CD-ROMs can be used effectively for still images and for short-duration, partial-screen, compressed or reduced-motion video segments, as well as CD-quality sound.

Photo CDs were introduced by Eastman Kodak for digitizing still images, such as 35mm print negatives and slides. Using a photo CD player, the images can be played on a conventional television set. Since they are compatible with most CD-ROM drives, photo CDs can also be read by computer CD-ROM drives, viewed on a computer monitor, and combined with other digital images and sounds using a digital nonlinear editing or multimedia authoring program.

Laser disc technology, such as videodiscs, CD-ROMs, DVDs, and photo CDs, does not rely on any physical contact between a stylus and a disc. Instead, a narrow beam of laser light tracks across a rotating metal disc, which is encased in transparent plastic. The laser light passes through small holes in the metal disc to produce video images and two separate stereophonic sound tracks. The plastic casing protects the metal disc. Because there is no physical contact with a stylus, there is virtually no deterioration of the disc with repeated use, as there is with stylus tracking. Laser disc technology is also used by audiophiles in the form of compact discs (CDs). The disadvantage of some videodiscs, CD-ROMs, photo CDs, and audio CDs is that they may be permanent recordings and therefore cannot be used for temporary storage and retrieval and cannot be reused. Rerecordable discs may be rewritten as needed.

Recordable CD-ROM technology, CD-R, can be used for temporary or permanent information storage and retrieval. Recordable and reusable laser technology offers a number of advantages over videodiscs, CD-ROMs, photo CDs, CDs, and hard disks in terms of storage. Recordable CD-Rs are similar in size to CD-ROMs (they usually have a gold bottom compared with the silver bottom of a CD-ROM), but they also can be removed, stored, and replaced, serving as an excellent temporary or permanent storage medium. Recordable DVDs are able to record 8 to 18 GB of digital information. Storage of audio recordings on computer hard drives has been facilitated by the MP3 digital compression format, which provides nearly CD-quality sound reproduction with significantly reduced storage size on a rerecordable medium.

Corporate and In-House

Corporate and in-house media technologies are very diverse. A wide variety of the video, audio, and multimedia systems discussed earlier are used by corporations and in-house units. In addition, closed-circuit television and teleconferencing systems are frequently used for corporate and institutional communications.

A *closed-circuit* television system interconnects various recording, transmitting, and receiving devices within a single building or building complex. It can be used to send information from a central location to television monitors in various locations, or to relay information from one room to another, such as the transmission of a surgical operation from the operating room of a hospital to a classroom in the medical school. Closed-circuit television systems are used frequently in government or educational institutions and businesses as well as for arrival-departure displays at airports. The signals are carried to various parts of the building by coaxial cable.

Satellite transmission, optical fiber, and traditional wire-based forms of telecommunications are often used for teleconferencing in corporations and government institutions. *Teleconferencing* refers to "live" or instantaneous group interaction that takes place via simultaneous transmission of video, voice, and/or data from several different locations. Digital video, audio, and data telephonic switching and transmission equipment have greatly facilitated teleconferencing. Images and sounds can be digitally compressed and transmitted around the world or within a limited area to facilitate corporate in-house institutional communication using conventional telephone lines, optical-fiber lines, and/or satellites.

ECONOMICS OF DISTRIBUTION AND EXHIBITION

It is imperative that producers have a basic understanding of the potential markets for a film, television program, or multimedia production. Projects that are initiated without any consideration for, or knowledge of, the economics of distribution and exhibition will rarely if ever reach their target audience. There are many different distribution and exhibition channels, including broadcasting, cable, satellite, theatrical, nontheatrical, home video, audio, multimedia, and corporate and in-house. Each distribution/exhibition channel has different needs, requirements, and economic structures.

Broadcasting, Cable, and Satellite

Commercial broadcasting network television programming in the United States is produced for and by four primary networks, ABC, CBS, NBC, and Fox, as well as three rapidly growing networks, WB (Warner Bros. Television), U/PN (United Paramount), and Spanish language Univision. News, sports, and most daytime programming is originated by the four primary networks themselves. Most primetime evening entertainment programming is produced by a limited number of independent producers and production companies.

Network television programming executives rarely take chances on unproven talent. They depend to a great extent on prior success as a guarantee of future success. Executive producers, such as Aaron Spelling, Michael Crichton, and Steven Bochco, have had repeated commercial success and are in a much better negotiating position with the networks than neophyte producers. Although the networks some-

times take a chance on unproven talent, there is usually some compensating factor, such as a presold property that was popular in another media, or a major star who is willing to play a lead role. To be seriously considered, a producer must put together an extremely attractive package that guarantees some measure of success in terms of attracting a sizable audience.

The economics of commercial broadcast, cable, and satellite television revolve around the selling of audiences to advertisers. Entertainment programming is an indirect product. It provides revenues to the network or the station only when it attracts a large audience with the right demographic characteristics. The broadcast network, local station, cable channel, local cable operator, or satellite channel sells commercial time to advertisers on the basis of the size of the audience it is able to attract. Some advertisers believe that the most desirable audience in terms of demographics is women from 18 to 34 years of age, since they do the bulk of the buying of commercial products at retail stores. But the growing number of 18- to 35-year-old males with disposable income has become a new target of the advertisers as well as Hispanic and other minority demographic groups. Of course, all demographic groups are also sought for specific products and services, and programming is rarely aimed at just one demographic group.

A successful program is one that obtains a relatively high rating and audience share. The rating suggests the percentage of all 80 million-plus television households that are tuned to a specific program. Ratings translate into profit-and-loss figures, since advertisers are charged for commercial air time on a cost-per-1000 viewers basis. A *share* refers to the percentage of television households actually watching TV at a specific time, called *HUT (Households Using Television)*, that are tuned to a specific program. All the shares would add up to 100% (Figure 13.7).

Ratings and shares of television programs are determined by organizations such as A.C. Nielsen and Arbitron, which collect data about what viewers watch by means of diaries kept by viewers or meters attached to home sets. Generally a network program that garners around a 30% share is doing quite well. Good ratings can vary from above 10% in daytime to over 20% in prime time. Shows that consistently fail to achieve these ratings or shares are likely to be canceled in midseason or by the next season.

There are, of course, many factors that can affect a show's ratings. Scheduling is a crucial factor. Some time slots and days of the week are simply better than others in terms of ratings. Audience flow is another important factor. The popularity of the shows that

TELEVISION NETWORK PROGRAM RATINGS

	ABC	CBS	NBC	FOX	UPN	WB
Mon.	7.3/12	8.4/13	8.1/13	3.3/5	2.2/3	2.5/4
Tues.	5.4/8	7.5/12	5.4/8	15.3/23	2.9/4	1.9/3
Wed.	5.6/9	7.3/12	7.1/12	9.7/16	1.3/2	1.9/3
Thurs.	6.4/10	6.7/11	10.2/17	3.5/6	3.6/6	2.0/3
Fri.	4.5/8	5.9/11	8.1/14	2.5/4	1.3/2	2.2/4
Sat.	3.5/6	6.4/12	3.7/7	5.1/9	------	------
Sun.	5.5/9	8.0/13	7.2/12	5.1/8	------	2.2/4
Week Ave.	5.5/9	7.2/12	7.1/12	6.3/10	2.3/4	2.1/3

Figure 13.7 In any one week the number of people or homes watching any one network varies from a share of 4% to 23% (average percentage of TV households using TV at that time). A rating is a program percentage of all TV households.

A typical week of ratings for Spring, 2004. Rankings/Share

precede and follow a specific program directly affects its share and ratings, because audiences often stay tuned to the same channel for a long period of time.

From the independent producer's standpoint, the survival of a show for at least five seasons is crucial to financial success. The amount of money that independent producers are given by the network to produce pilots and series episodes rarely covers the complete cost of production. This strategy is known as *deficit financing*. The producer usually signs a contract at the proposal or initial pilot script stage granting a network exclusive rights to the series for at least five years. The contract specifies the year-by-year increase in network payments for each of the years that a series survives. After five years a sufficient number of episodes have usually been produced for the series to go into syndication.

Syndicated programming, often called *stripping*, is marketed to local stations for morning, early-afternoon, or early-evening broadcast, five days of the week. Independent producers make money from syndication, but they rarely make any revenues from network showings of series. Networks no longer are forbidden by law to directly syndicate their old shows, now allowing the networks a share of syndication revenues. Producers take substantial risks in terms of program development, which only pays off if the program goes into syndication. The

probability of a show lasting long enough to go into syndication is actually quite low, but the success of a single show can pay for many disasters. Now that networks may purchase their own programs, the independent producer must compete with his or her potential clients' own programming.

Syndicated programming generally bypasses the major commercial networks. Syndicated programs are broadcast by network-affiliated local television stations during times of the day when there is no network programming, such as late afternoon and early evening. Independent local television stations show syndicated programming during any time slot, including prime time: 8:00 P.M. to 11:00 P.M. EST. Affiliates may also broadcast syndicated programming during prime time. Each network pays its affiliated stations a fee for broadcasting network programming, although affiliates in very sparsely populated areas may actually receive no fee other than the free use of the programs as a means to attract or draw viewers for the local commercials that are run during local station breaks between shows. An affiliate can, of course, reject the network programming and substitute syndicated or its own local programming. Some major network affiliates have switched networks or combined affiliation with one growing network, such as UPN, and one major network, such as NBC. Of course, an affiliated local station that continually rejects its network's programming or also affiliates with a growing network risks losing its primary network affiliate status. However, because of limited television channel space, local affiliates are usually in a strong bargaining position with the networks.

Affiliates and independents have sometimes banded together to partially finance their own entertainment programming. Although entertainment programming usually comes to a local station through a network or through an independent syndicator, local news, sports, and public service and information programming are usually produced by the station itself. Local news is one of the most competitive and profitable areas of local TV programming. It is important in terms of both the audience it draws to the local news program itself and the audience drawn to the syndicated programming that surrounds the news. During these nonnetwork time slots, local stations sell commercial time to advertisers who pay relatively high cost-per-thousand prices for commercial time, especially in the top 50 local television markets.

Obviously, the economic conditions of commercial broadcast television make it quite difficult for a small, unproven independent film or television producer to sell a single entertainment or informational program to commercial television stations. Television stations are interested in buying or showing a continuous supply of programming, such as a series or even a miniseries, rather than isolated or individual programs. Local stations will often show independently produced documentaries of local or regional interest during slow or weak time slots, such as Sunday morning or Saturday afternoon, but they will rarely pay much, if anything, for this type of programming. An independent producer would do better to find a corporate or individual sponsor for a single program and then guarantee that sponsor a credit line and a certain amount of exposure during slow or off-hours of commercial broadcasting than to try marketing a speculative program to television stations after it has been produced.

Similar kinds of marketing problems plague an independent producer who hopes to market a single program to cable television. Cable operators are often more interested in filling time slots on a regular basis than in buying isolated programs. Nonetheless, there is greater marketing potential for small, independently produced programming through cable television than through commercial broadcasting. The larger number of cable television channels ensures wider access and a greater ability to *narrowcast*, or to target a small, relatively specialized audience. The economic structure of cable television is quite different from that of commercial broadcasting. The cable operator sells specific channels or packages of channels to individual consumers or subscribers, and the program producer and/or supplier often receives a percentage of the subscription fee or commercial advertising revenues. Some channels are allocated to locally produced programs, and they provide community access. They are usually available free of charge to anyone who wants to show programming of community interest.

Producers can advertise their own programs by publicizing a specific program topic and show time and date in print media. Unlike commercial broadcasters, a cable operator will often accept smaller-format, lower-quality video recordings, such as material on ¾-inch videotape that is not of broadcast quality. Network broadcasters, of course, usually demand digital formats or Betacam SP videotapes and 16mm or 35mm films of high quality that meet or exceed NAB (National Association of Broadcasters) standards. Some cable television programming, such as that produced by Turner Broadcasting (superstation WTBS, Atlanta and Cable News Network, CNN, a cable program service), as well as the sports channel ESPN, depends to a significant extent on commercial advertising for its revenues and must meet broadcast standards. Other program channels, such as various movie channels, distribute and sometimes produce expensive entertainment programs and are almost totally dependent on percentages of subscription charges for their revenue.

It is possible to initiate the production and marketing of some cable programs for far less money than is required for commercial broadcasting. Many cable producers are nonunion, and thus can save substantial production costs by paying lower salaries to their personnel. Cable distributors and suppliers have to sell their programming to local cable operators, invest in satellite transmission services, and assume the cost of program advertising. In return, they demand a portion of subscription receipts. It is possible to produce isolated programs on an independent basis for specific cable channels, such as WTBS, or to produce cable programming speculatively for Arts and Entertainment (A&E) or other cable distributors with greater hope of finding a potential buyer than is the case with commercial broadcasting.

Public television is a noncommercial broadcasting distribution and exhibition channel. In the United States it is partially supported by the Corporation for Public Broadcasting (CPB), which was set up by an act of Congress in 1967 that also authorized funds for its operation. The CPB created the current network of public broadcasting stations. There are basically four types of public broadcasting stations: those owned and operated by colleges and universities, such as stations at the Universities of Houston, Wisconsin, and North Carolina; those owned and operated by school systems, such as that in Cincinnati (only 7%); those owned and operated by municipal (state) authorities, such as those in Georgia, New Jersey, and Iowa; and those developed and operated by nonprofit corporations, such as stations in Boston, New York, and Chicago.

Public broadcasting is often threatened by inadequate financial support. Federal budget allocations to the CPB are in constant jeopardy. The pursuit of large audiences through popular programming often attracts major corporate sponsors; however, such sponsorship is sometimes criticized on the basis that it gives these corporations power over noncommercial as well as commercial broadcasting. Some critics charge that on-the-air credits are tantamount to advertising and should not be permitted in noncommercial broadcasting. Public television stations frequently raise money through funding drives. The money they collect is used to fund local productions, to purchase national Public Broadcasting Service (PBS) programming (which they have a hand in selecting), and to defray operating costs. PBS is responsive to member stations who are involved in determining which programs will be nationally distributed. This relationship is quite different from that between commercial networks and affiliates, although the extent to which public stations should be controlled by the national network as opposed to local management is an often hotly debated issue.

Public television programming comes from a variety of sources. Some of the programming is at least partially funded by the Corporation for Public Broadcasting and corporate sponsors at the national level and is then distributed through PBS to its member stations. PBS member stations produce much of the programming that is distributed through PBS to other stations. The largest producers of this type of national PBS programming are PBS member stations in Boston; Pittsburgh; Columbia, South Carolina; New York; Washington; Chicago; and Los Angeles. However, member stations usually produce a series of programs on a specific topic rather than single, isolated programs.

Some programming comes from foreign producers, most notably the BBC (British Broadcasting Corporation). Individual stations themselves often produce a certain amount of local or regional public-interest programming, much of which never receives national distribution. At the local or state level, it is sometimes possible for an independent producer to air an individual program on a PBS station or state

system. Such programs are often independently funded by other sources, although partial funding can come from a PBS station in return for broadcast rights, usually specifying a specific number of airings over a two- or three-year period. The quality standards of PBS are similar to those of commercial broadcast television.

The subject matter and format of PBS programming can be quite different from commercial broadcast programming, although PBS stations have become increasingly concerned about attracting large audiences, which help to generate public financial support. The length of a half-hour PBS program is currently about 26 minutes, compared with about 22 minutes for most programs intended for commercial television stations and cable channels.

Commercial spots are short (often 15- or 30-second) television messages that attempt to sell commercial products and services to consumers. The production of network television commercials and national spot sales is largely controlled by major advertising agencies, such as J. Walter Thompson, Leo Burnett, N.W. Ayer, and McCann-Erickson, who contract with production specialists on a bidding basis. The advertising agency usually develops the basic storyline for a commercial in consultation with the client whose product, name, and/or services are being promoted. The advertising agency also develops a storyboard of hand-drawn images to visualize the spot. The director's job is to capture this idea on 35mm film, HDTV, or Betacam SP videotape. Some creative innovation and play with the basic script idea is allowed with a talented director, but the work of production companies is primarily that of technical and aesthetic execution, rather than of developing creative, original ideas.

The production budget for a network commercial is often extremely high, given the relatively short duration of the final product. It is not unusual to spend from one-half million to one million dollars for a single 30-second network-level spot. The production company must be technically perfect in its execution of the commercial. Sometimes as much as 90,000 feet of 35mm film is shot to produce just 45 feet of final product for a beverage commercial, for example. Major advertisers often contract with a separate individual or company for different aspects of production and postproduction on a commercial, rather than allowing any single production company complete control. Many of the most talented creative producers of network-level commercials work on a freelance basis or have their own production companies.

Local television commercials are often made by television stations or small production companies. Television stations often sell local commercial time to businesses in their area, and then offer to produce the commercials themselves. Small independent production companies sometimes produce the entire commercial for a client, from script to screen. The budgets for locally produced television commercials are quite low compared with network-level commercials. Some are produced on videotape or 16mm film for a few thousand dollars. Only rarely is 35mm film used for the production of local commercials. In the largest local television markets, the production of commercials is handled by major advertising agencies. National spot sales place network-quality spots that are not part of the network schedule on smaller-market TV stations. The costs of commercial production represent but a small fraction of the total advertising budget for the promotion of a product, name, or service. Television time costs are usually much higher than production costs, and many other media besides television, such as magazines, newspapers, and radio, may be involved in a particular advertising campaign.

Public service announcements, or *PSAs*, are the least expensive type of commercial. They are usually shown free of charge in the public interest to help promote public service agencies and nonprofit organizations. While PSAs must meet broadcast standards in terms of technical quality, they are often produced in the most economical format possible, such as DV or ¾-inch videotape. PSAs offer an excellent opportunity for neophyte producers to become involved in a serious production, allowing them an opportunity to perfect their technical competence and to experiment with new techniques.

Theatrical and Nontheatrical

Power in the feature film industry is concentrated primarily in distribution. Major distributors, such as Disney, Paramount, Warner Bros., MGM, United Artists, Columbia, Universal, and Twentieth Century-Fox, receive the bulk of the distribution receipts from feature films. They negotiate with exhibition chains, such as National General and independent theaters, for a split of exhibition receipts. One of the most common splits for a major film is a 90/10 split, which gives 90% of the admission receipts to the distributor and 10% to the exhibitor, above and beyond the latter's fixed operating costs for a specified period of time, such as several weeks. The distributor's percentage decreases gradually over time as the exhibitor's percentage increases. Exhibitors compete with each other for specific films by bidding a specific split and exhibition duration. About 50% of the major U.S. distributors' total theatrical receipts come from foreign distribution.

Distributors also negotiate with television networks, cable television movie channels, and consumer videotape retailers (Figure 13-8). Income from the sale of DVDs, *videocassettes*, and ancillary items now exceeds that of ticket sales in theatres for most feature films and has done so since the mid-1990s.

An average Hollywood-produced feature film today costs more than $20 million to produce. The distributor spends about 30% more than these production costs for advertising, release prints, and other distribution costs. It is virtually impossible to acquire financial backing for even an average budgeted feature film without a major distributor's endorsement. That endorsement usually requires the involvement of previously proven talent, such as well-known stars and directors, in a dramatic production. The distributor then either puts up the money for a production or provides some sort of guarantee to banks, which then finance the cost of production with a loan. Only rarely are independently produced feature films that do not have initial major distributor endorsement later picked up by major distributors. But major motion pictures are being produced in right-to-work states, especially in the South, to lower production costs by avoiding unions and obtaining considerable state and local cooperation.

Low-budget feature films are largely distributed by independent distributors, who do not have as much bargaining power with the largest theater chains and independent theaters as the majors. Of course, a producer can always distribute his or her own film either by negotiating directly with theaters for a split, which is rarely done, or by renting a theater, doing some local advertising, and then receiving any and all gate receipts; this is a technique known as *four-walling*.

Producers negotiate with distributors for a percentage of the distribution receipts. A producer can demand a certain percentage of either the gross receipts or the net receipts (after the distributor has subtracted certain fixed costs), or sell the film outright to the distributor. Obviously a producer who is able to negotiate a percentage of the gross receipts is in a strong bargaining position. The producer must consider a number of factors before deciding on a specific plan, such as the true earning potential of the film, the length of time before real receipts will be received during which interest on loans must be paid, the reliability of distributor accounting, and the hidden costs of production and distribution.

An increasingly important area of negotiations is *ancillary rights* and *commercial tie-ins*, such as toys and T-shirts. Receipts from markets in addition to commercial theaters, such as network and cable

**RANKING U.S. MOTION PICTURES
BY DOMESTIC BOX OFFICE INCOME**

RANK	TITLE	RELEASE	RECEIPTS
1.	Titanic	1997	$600,788,188
2.	Star Wars	1997	460,998,007
3.	E.T. the Extra-Terrestrial	1982	435,110,554
4.	Star Wars I: The Phantom Menace	1999	431,388,297
5.	Spider-Man	2002	403,706,375
6.	Lord of the Rings: Return of the King	2003	377,019,252
7.	Jurassic Park	1993	357,067,947
8.	Lord of the Rings: The Two Towers	2002	341,786,758
9.	Finding Nemo	2003	339,714,978
10.	Forrest Gump	1994	329,694,499
11.	The Lion King	1994	328,541,776
12.	Harry Potter and the Sorcerer's Stone	2001	317,575,550
13.	Lord of the Rings: Fellowship of the Ring	2001	314,776,170
14.	Star Wars II: Attack of the Clones	2002	310,676,740
15.	Star Wars VI: Return of the Jedi	1983	309,306,177
16.	Independence Day	1996	306,169,255
17.	Pirates of the Caribbean: The Curse of the Black Pearl	2003	305,377,624
18.	The Sixth Sense	1999	293,506,292
19.	Star Wars V: The Empire Strikes Back	1980	290,475,067
20.	Home Alone	1990	285,761,243
21.	The Matrix Reloaded	2003	281,596,461
22.	Shrek	2001	267,652,016
23.	Harry Potter and the Chamber of Secrets	2002	261,970,615
24.	How the Grinch Stole Christmas	2000	260,031,035
25.	Jaws	1975	260,000,000

**TOP TWENTY-FIVE FILMS
Actual Domestic Box Office Dollars**
(Not adjusted to 2004 dollars)

Figure 13.8 The calculation of actual dollars earned by motion pictures is a very complex and often mistrusted process. One of the most telling figures is actual box office receipts, but that may not be a fair judgment of a film's popularity because some films are shown in many theaters, others in relatively few. Also, the calculation should be adjusted to today's dollars, which would make many films of many years ago appear to have earned much more than their actual income at the time when they were exhibited. (*Courtesy of The Internet Movie Database, www.imdb.com.*)

television, must be considered. Musical records, books, posters, dolls, toys, clothing, and games that are offshoots of a successful film can make huge profits. Sometimes an especially popular movie star will demand either a large initial payment of several million dollars or a percentage of the gross distribution receipts. The involvement of major stars directly affects not only the production budget but also the producer's negotiations with the distributor and the banks.

The producer and financial backers of a feature film understand that film production is an extremely risky business. Few feature films earn a substantial profit, and most of those that do either are produced on an extremely tight budget for somewhat smaller domestic and foreign markets, or are extremely high-budget films heavily promoted by major distributors. In both of these cases, the successful commercial producer understands the target audience and designs a film and budget that are realistic in terms of audience expectations, preferences, and size (Figure 13.9).

The term *nontheatrical* refers to films and videos that are shown in places other than commercial film theaters. Nontheatrical films and videos are shown by colleges and universities, other educational institutions, civic groups, and other organizations. They are not always exhibited for profit, but often as a cultural or informational service. Although nontheatrical exhibition is usually a nonprofit undertaking, nontheatrical distribution is largely a commercial business. Feature films, for example, are rented to various groups, institutions, and individuals in 16mm film and various video formats for public showing. Renting these works for public showing is often far more expensive than purchasing a home videotape or disc copy, but videotapes and discs, which can be rented or purchased in retail stores, are strictly intended for individual, home use. Higher royalties are demanded for public showings of these films and videos when they are rented from commercial, nontheatrical distributors.

Nontheatrical distribution is not limited to feature films. Individual film and video artists, documentary

**RANKING WORLD WIDE MOTION PICTURES
BY BOX OFFICE INCOME IN US DOLLARS**

RANK	TITLE	RELEASE	RECEIPTS
1.	Titantic	1997	$1,835,300,000
2.	Lord of the Rings: Return of the King	2003	1,047,600,000
3.	Harry Potter and the Sorcerer's Stone	2001	969,600,000
4.	Star Wars I: The Phantom Menace	1999	922,300,000
5.	Lord of the Rings: The Two Towers	2002	921,200,000
6.	Jurassic Park	1993	919,700,000
7.	Harry Potter and the Chamber of Secrets	2000	866,300,000
8.	Lord of the Rings: Fellowship of the Ring	2001	860,700,000
9.	Finding Nemo	2003	853,200,000
10.	Independence Day	1996	811,200,000
11.	Spider-Man	2002	806,700,000
12.	Star Wars	1997	797,900,000
13.	The Lion King	1994	783,400,000
14.	E.T. the Extra-Terrestrial	2002	310,676,740
15.	The Matrix Reloaded	2003	735,300,000
16.	Forrest Gump	1994	679,700,000
17.	The Sixth Sense	1000	001,500,000
18.	Pirates of the Caribbean: The Curse of the Black Pearl	2003	653,200,000
19.	Star Wars II: Attack of the Clones	2002	648,200,000
20.	Lost World: Jurassic Park	1997	614,300,000
21.	Men in Black	1997	587,200,000
22.	Star Wars VI: Return of the Jedi	1983	572,700,000
23.	Armageddon	1998	554,600,000
24.	Mission Impossible II	2000	543,300,000
25.	Star Wars V: The Empire Strikes Back	1980	533,800,000

**TOP TWENTY-FIVE FILMS
World Wide Box Office Dollars**
(Not adjusted to 2004 dollars)

Figure 13.9 Worldwide distribution of motion pictures may triple the gross income as compared to distribution only with the United States. The popularity of films worldwide may also differ from the popularity of films in the U.S. (Courtesy of *The Internet Movie Database, www.imdb.com.*)

producers, and producers of other short informational and educational materials often have their work distributed by a nontheatrical distributor. Nontheatrical distributors who make a profit pass on a certain percentage of their gross receipts to producers. Other distributors are cooperatively organized by independent producers and artists themselves. The New York Filmmaker's Cooperative, for example, passes on a greater share of distribution receipts to individual artists, and keeps only a small percentage of rentals or sales for its own operating costs.

Many commercial nontheatrical distributors, such as Pyramid Films, distribute successful short films. Many of the short subjects they distribute have previously won major awards, such as Academy Awards or major festival awards. One of the best means for beginning producers and directors to find good distributors for short works is to win awards at major festivals and contests. A nontheatrical distributor will often offer winners of major awards the opportunity to use the distributor's promotional and advertising services for a major percentage of the

distribution receipts or offer an outright payment for exclusive distribution rights. These short films are then distributed individually to nonprofit institutions; as packages of shorts to cable television services, such as HBO (Home Box Office); and to colleges and universities. Nontheatrical distributors actively seek projects that have rather specialized audiences or limited markets, since they do not always have to distribute these works through mass media channels such as commercial broadcasting or commercial film theaters.

Home Video, Audio, and Multimedia

An expanding market for film and video productions includes home videotapes and DVDs, audio CDs, and various forms of multimedia, including CD-ROMs. These products are rented and sold to individual consumers. Feature films, popular music with accompanying video images, and informational and educational materials can be marketed in this manner. The individual consumer buys a tape or disc and shows it on his or her own player or computer and monitor. Most entertainment films and videos currently being sold as commercial products were initially produced for distribution to commercial theaters, network television, or cable television. As more consumers possess their own players, more programming will be designed for initial sale to consumers, just like records, books, and computer games in retail stores. Rental and sale of home videotapes has been a rapidly expanding market for entertainment programming for some time. In fact, 1985 was the first year that videotape sales of Hollywood products equaled domestic feature film distribution receipts from theaters.

Emerging new audio recording and duplication technologies have had an impact on audio production and distribution. Recordable CD-ROM technology, CD-R, can be used for temporary or permanent information storage and retrieval, including "burning" or making copies of audio CDs. Storage of audio recordings on computer hard drives has been facilitated by the MP3 digital compression format, which provides nearly CD-quality sound reproduction with significantly reduced storage size. This format has also led to legal complications for some Internet companies, such as Napster, which have facilitated the sharing of audio recordings on individual computers across the World Wide Web, angering some musical artists and recording companies by potentially reducing the size of their markets and royalties on copyrighted materials. Illegal operations such as Napster have been shut down and now have been replaced by share programs that charge a minimum for each shared musical recording. Apple, Microsoft, and AOL, as well as other Internet companies, have joined this expanding field.

The rental and sale of videocassettes and DVDs is an area that can be easily exploited by smaller producers because many videotape and DVD rental and sales outlets are operated as small businesses (although many regional and local markets are dominated by major chains, such as Blockbuster), and distribution is not as tightly controlled as is the theatrical outlet for feature films. Advertising expenses can be substantial, however, and these must be born by the producer who wants to sell videotapes to rental outlets and individual consumers. Most Hollywood films have already had a great deal of publicity and have generated much public interest prior to their availability as videocassettes.

Programming designed specifically for the home videocassette and videodisc market differs in many important respects from programming designed primarily for theatrical distribution. The production of programming for small-screen exhibition raises a number of aesthetic problems. Composition within the frame in a small-screen format must keep key information in the essential area of a TV receiver. Important details cannot be presented on the fringes of the screen, as in a wide-screen feature film production designed primarily for theatrical release. Close-ups are used much more frequently for small-screen productions, and wide vistas and panoramic shots are kept to a minimum. The pacing of entertainment programming intended for television and videocassette distribution is often faster and more action-packed to hold the audience's attention.

At present, using DVDs for mastering is still fairly expensive initially, although the cost of mass duplication is relatively low. Initial recordings and editing are not done on DVD. Videotapes or film recordings are made, edited, and then duplicated on DVD, creating a master pressing or copy from which individual DVD copies are made. Because the cost of this master runs quite high, it is only economical to use this technology when a large number of copies is needed. But the ease, low cost, and simplicity of burning a DVD-R on a typical home computer has made creating DVDs as attractive as burning individual CDs. The high information capacity, relative permanence, and durability of DVDs are all features that make them an ideal information storage and retrieval medium. The low cost of producing numerous copies once the master disc is made makes the disc an excellent means of distributing promotional materials to salespeople or consumers in retail stores throughout the country. When many DVDs are made from the same master, the actual duplicating cost can be as low as $1 to $2 per disc (Figure 13.10).

Figure 13.10 The ability to create quality media productions in a home setting has developed an entirely new distribution network. Now, an individual may record, process, and distribute his or her own work from a relatively inexpensive set of media equipment without relying on any outside organizations.

In terms of direct sales to consumers, the main advantage offered by the sale of a product (rather than the sale of a seat in a theater or time on commercial television) and the relatively low cost of making multiple video copies is that DVDs can be made for and marketed to specialized demographic groups. Distribution channels are not constrained by limited channels of access, as they are in the case of network television and commercial film theaters, where a product must be marketed to a mass, heterogeneous audience. Individual copies can be manufactured and sold to smaller groups of consumers, just as popular rock, country, soul, and classical music can be marketed by the recording industry to smaller groups of people. Individual discs can sell for anywhere from about $10 to $100, depending on the size of the market and the cost of production. As the consumer market expands, independent producers will undoubtedly proliferate, and disc production may become as decentralized as production in the audio recording industry or music business.

Consumer marketing of multimedia products is made somewhat complex by virtue of the diversity of standards in terms of hardware, such as Mac versus PC platforms (a problem that plagued the consumer videocassette rental business early on, when both beta and VHS were fairly common), and the diversity of distribution channels, such as computer retail store sales versus catalogue sales (more Mac-based software and CD-ROMs are marketed via the latter than the former channel, for example). Many CD-ROMs, of course, can be used on both platforms. Publishers finance and market multimedia products, while distributors manage the flow of the product from the publisher to the customer.

Publishers coordinate printing, duplication, and packaging, as well as marketing. Marketing usually involves promotion and advertising, as well as sales. Focus groups may provide responses concerning what potential consumers want and what prices they are willing to pay. Products may then be test-marketed in specific locations before they are mass-marketed across the country. Different pathways to the consumer constitute the distribution channels, such as retail chain stores and catalogue sales. Although the distribution of multimedia products is not as concentrated in the hands of a few major companies as is the case with feature films and network television broadcasting, nonetheless major multimedia publishers are emerging who have distinct advantages in terms of access to capital and distribution channels as well as other means necessary to successfully mass market CD-ROMs and other multimedia technologies to consumers.

Hollywood's involvement in multimedia, for example, has been stimulated by the fact that the videogame business currently generates about the same revenues as the box-office portion of the film industry—over $5 billion per year—and the videogame business is expected to more than double in the next few years. A number of CD-ROMs and interactive videogames have been produced that carry the same titles as Hollywood motion pictures, giving viewers an opportunity to further their involvement with their favorite plots and characters using multimedia. Interactive multimedia divisions of major studios attempt to establish connections between computer games and movies, although important differences still exist between these media. For example, successful interactive multimedia products usually focus upon the user, rather than a Hollywood actor, as the star.

The probability of succeeding in either medium with a particular product remains relatively low, since only about six CD-ROM titles out of every 200 are financially successful. Success and name recognition in one medium can carry over to another. Mass-market CD-ROM production costs average about $500,000, compared with about $20 million for a Hollywood feature film, and Hollywood distributors spend as much as 30% of their total budgets on advertising and distribution, which can translate into significant name recognition for a multimedia product. However, few hit videogames have appeared that are based upon Hollywood films. Some multimedia firms have joined forces with television and music companies to produce arty, experimental stories that draw name recognition from rock groups and successful television programs. A number of other multimedia publishers have focused upon developing CD-ROMs or videogames as an independent art form, relying upon imaginative graphics, animation, and sounds to stimulate the user's involvement and interaction with unique multimedia worlds and characters.

Corporate and In-House

The overwhelming majority of production in the United States is done by corporations and institutions in-house. This is one of the largest and fastest-growing areas of possible employment in production. According to Department of Labor statistics, roughly 193,000 people in this country make their living in broadcast television, while 235,000 people make their living in nonbroadcast television, most of which consists of corporate and institutional production done in-house. At the turn of the century, for example, the largest growth in sales of video equipment came from the industrial/business/institutional market, not the broadcast market.

In-house production by corporations, government agencies, and educational institutions constitutes a special type of distribution and exhibition channel. Much of corporate video production is designed to train and motivate employees, to communicate with employees scattered all over the country or around the world, or to communicate with customers and clients. Different kinds of information can be represented in a more entertaining fashion than might be the case with a brochure or other publication. Sales representatives can be trained in the latest techniques and strategies for selling products. Corporate productions often demonstrate these techniques through dramatizations. Some corporations use videotape facilities to record executive speeches and sales meetings, so that corporate information can be widely disseminated.

Specific products are often advertised and demonstrated in automobile showrooms or department stores using videotapes produced within house. Hospitals and educational institutions often produce programs that are helpful to patients and students. Healthcare information is often disseminated via closed-circuit television or by a mobile VCR unit that can be moved from room to room. Special diets, medications, and surgical procedures that a patient is about to undergo can be clarified and explained better and more efficiently on videotape than in person.

One of the fastest-growing areas of in-house production is the production of instructional DVDs and computer interactive programs and videodiscs for corporate or institutional training. Discs can help students learn an incredible range of tasks at their own individual rate, using a student-controlled player; an interactive video unit, which consists of a computer and a videodisc player controlled by the computer; or an interactive computer with a CD-ROM. The viewer's response can be recorded on a touch pad that controls the operation of the computer and the rate at which new information or questions are presented.

An in-house production unit has varying degrees and types of accountability. The production unit may be directly accountable to management in a corporation in terms of its production budgets and production management. Government agencies and educational units are usually accountable to government or academic administrators. Since the programming that is produced is usually aimed at an internal audience or a specialized audience outside the institution, the means of assessing program success is sometimes quite informal, although sophisticated research into program effectiveness is often done by major corporations. Policy is sometimes controlled by a few individuals. There is usually a specific message to tell, and communication usually takes place in a one-way direction down the hierarchy, although programming ideas sometimes originate from employee, patient, or student suggestions.

Most in-house production units produce videotapes or CD-ROMs that can be played at a time and place that is convenient for the recipient of the information. The in-house producer often has all of the facilities needed to produce a completed product and to internally distribute and exhibit it. Medical schools, telephone companies, and public utilities, as well as government agencies, may have completely outfitted video production units with state-of-the-art equipment, such as digital formats, Betacam SP, or digital videotape recording and editing equipment, as well as high-quality video cameras, lighting, and sound equipment. Small companies and agencies may only have a single miniDV camcorder, a digital tape deck with a monitor, and no sophisticated production or editing facilities.

Individual project production costs are often kept low by having producers, directors, and technical support people on staff who can serve a variety of functions. Personnel who work in corporate or institutional production often have to be more flexible and have a broader range of skills than those who work in a particular broadcast television position. The staff for an in-house production unit is generally quite small. New personnel may be expected to work with slides, audiotape, and film on occasion, as well as videotape. Production costs are usually kept to a minimum as well by using the most economical medium to communicate a specific message. If motion is not essential, a slide and tape show may be a more economical and effective means of presenting the material. Technical information and statistics might be communicated more effectively and inexpensively by writing and illustrating a brochure or a pamphlet. Regardless of the specific medium that is eventually selected, basic writing and production skills are essential qualifications for anyone pursuing a career in the rapidly expanding area of corporate and institutional in-house production.

SUMMARY

The final stage of postproduction is known as distribution and exhibition. Selecting the best means and channels of distribution and exhibition requires an understanding of media technology and economics.

Media producers need to be familiar with the technology used by different distribution and exhibition channels, so that they can tailor the production to specific technological requirements. Broadcasting refers to the transmission of television and radio signals through the airwaves. Cable television distributes video transmissions, often received via satellite dish, to individual homes by way of coaxial cables. HDTV offers the prospect of providing high-quality television images, which can be used by large-screen electronic projection systems in commercial theaters and in private homes.

Theatrical film/electronic exhibition requires some form of large-screen projection. Nontheatrical screenings usually involve smaller groups of viewers and significantly less, if any, admission fees than theatrical screenings, reducing the need and demand for high-quality, large-screen projection. A number of media products are designed or marketed for home, such as DVDs, CD-ROMs, photo CDs, and audio CDs. Corporate and in-house media technologies are very diverse. A closed-circuit television system interconnects various recording, transmitting, and receiving devices within a single building or building complex. Teleconferencing refers to "live" or instantaneous group interaction that takes place via simultaneous transmission of video, voice, and/or data from several different locations.

Producers also need to be familiar with the economics of broadcasting, cable, satellite, theatrical, nontheatrical, home videocassette, videodisc, and multimedia, and corporate and in-house distribution and exhibition. Commercial broadcasters sell audiences to advertisers. Programming is useful to the extent that it draws a large audience with specific demographic characteristics, such as women from 18 to 34 years of age, to commercials aired during a broadcast. Syndicated programming consists of reruns of old network series, movies, and other non-network programming. Public television is partially supported by the Corporation for Public Broadcasting and contributions from corporations, foundations, endowments, and individuals. PBS programming is produced largely by member stations, although some programming is purchased from foreign producers, such as the BBC. Member stations produce their own regional programming as well as programming of national interest that is distributed through PBS. Cable television offers a somewhat better potential market for independent, small-scale productions. However, most cable operators are interested in filling time with continuing series, rather than with isolated individual programs. Commercials are brief messages used on commercial television to sell products, names, and services to consumers. At the national and major local market levels, they are usually produced on 35mm film by production specialists for advertising agencies. At the local level, they are produced by local stations themselves and by small independent producers. Public service announcements (PSAs) are noncommercial messages broadcast free of charge.

Economic power in the theatrical feature film industry resides in the major distributors, such as Paramount, Warner Bros., MGM, United Artists, Columbia, Sony, Universal, and Twentieth Century-Fox. An average feature film distributed by the majors costs above $20 million. About 30% more is spent on advertising and distribution costs. A common theatrical film distribution deal involves a 90:10 split of box-office receipts between distributors and exhibitors. Videocassettes, DVDs, videodiscs, and multimedia products are often marketed to individual customers via video sales/rental stores for home use. They are also used for corporate communications. Consumer marketing of multimedia products is made somewhat complex by virtue of the diversity of standards in terms of hardware. Interactive multimedia divisions of major studios attempt to establish connections between computer games and movies, although important differences still exist between these media. In-house production refers to the production of programming by an organization for itself. In-house production units exist in industry, government, and education, and collectively they represent the largest producer of video programming in the United States. A production unit usually maintains a sufficient staff and supply of equipment to produce a videotape or film completely in-house, using the most economical and efficient medium to communicate with employees, patients, students, and other groups.

EXERCISES

1. Make a list of all the potential distribution and exhibition outlets for a specific production project. Then prioritize this list by arranging the potential distribution/exhibition outlets in a hierarchy from most to least important in terms of the funding sources or your own expectations and potential returns on production investments. Determine the ideal production, editing, and distribution medium (film, video, multimedia, and so on) and format(s) (16mm, VHS, DVD, CD-ROM, and so on) for the most important outlet(s).

2. Calculate the cost of producing a film, video, or multimedia product using this (or these) format(s). Determine if the potential financial investments and returns from the outlets justify these expenses. If not, determine which media and format(s) will work most effectively within the desired distribution/exhibition channels without exceeding potential investments and returns.

3. Consider your potential employment in a particular field of media production, such as corporate, public, or commercial television. What will you need to obtain an entry-level position in this field? In what production capacity do you hope to be employed? Investigate the future employment potential of the field within which you hope to work. Is employment expanding or contracting? How many people are currently working in this field? Talk to someone who is currently working in this area and find out what it is like. Also talk to a personnel officer or director to find out exactly what he or she is looking for and what specific skills are needed. Request a copy of a resume from a previously successful applicant for such a position. Study this resume carefully and compare it with your own.

4. Outline a series of production projects and experiences that will help prepare you for this position and demonstrate your ability to perform a particular or wide range of tasks. Finally, when it comes time to actually seek employment, be persistent. Maintain periodic contact with potential employers, such as contacting them in person once a month for several months. When a job becomes available, it pays to be fresh in an employer's mind.

5. Ask a program director of a television station to let you see an outdated ratings book from your market. Read it carefully and determine where you would place your commercials for maximum effect. Do the same for a local radio station. If this is not possible find old issues of trade magazines like *Broadcasting* or *Entertainment Weekly,* and use the summaries of ratings published in those periodicals.

6. Check to see if one of the larger corporations in your market maintains an in-house production unit. Ask for a tour and find out what they produce, where it is exhibited, and how they budget their operation.

ADDITIONAL READINGS

Albarran, Alan. *Management of Electronic Media.* Belmont, CA: Wadsworth Publishing, 2002.

Alberstat, Philip. *Independent Producer's Guide to Film and TV Contracts.* Boston: Focal Press, 1999.

Alexander, Alison, et al. *Media Economics*, 3rd ed. Mahwah, NJ: Lawrence Erlbaum Associates, Inc., 2003.

Bielby, William T., and Denise D. Bielby. "Controlling Prime-Time: Organizational Concentration and Network Television Programming Strategies." *Journal of Broadcasting & Electronic Media* 47, no. 4, December 2003, 573-596

Brooker, Will, and Deborah Jermyn, eds. *The Audience Studies Reader.* New York: Routledge, 2002.

Croteau, David, and William Waymes. *The Business of Media: Corporate Media and the Public Interest.* Thousand Oaks, CA: Pine Forge Press, 2001.

Dimmick, John W. *Media Competition and Coexistence.* Mahwah, NJ: Lawrence Erlbaum Associates, Inc., 2003.

DiZazzo, Ray. *Corporate Media Production*, 2nd ed. Boston: Focal Press, 2003.

Eastman, Susan Tyler, and Douglas Ferguson. *Broadcast/Cable Programming: Strategies and Practices,* 6th ed. Belmont, CA: Wadsworth Publishing, 2002.

Einstein, Mara. *Media Diversity: Economics, Ownership, and the FCC.* Mahwah, NJ: Lawrence Erlbaum Associates, Inc., 2003.

Jacobs, Bob. *The Independent Video Producer.* Boston: Focal Press, 1999.

Kindem, Gorham, ed. *The American Movie Industry: The Business of Motion Pictures.* Carbondale, IL: Southern Illinois University Press, 1982.

Kindem, Gorham, ed. *The International Movie Industry.* Carbondale, IL: Southern Illinois University Press, 2000.

Lutzker, Arnold. *Content Rights for Creative Professionals*, 2nd ed. Boston: Focal Press, 2002.

Lee, John J., Jr. *The Producer's Business Handbook.* Boston: Focal Press, 2000.

Miller, Philip. *Media Law for Producers*, 4th ed. Boston: Focal Press, 2003.

Ohanian, Thomas A., and Michael E. Phillips. *Digital Filmmaking*, 2nd ed. Boston: Focal Press, 2000.

Redmond, James, and Robert Trager. *Balancing on the Wire: The Art of Managing Media Organizations.* Boulder, CO: Coursewise Publishing, Inc., 1998.

Shanks, Bob. *The Cool Fire: How to Make It in Television.* New York: Vintage, 1977.

Squire, Jason, ed. *The Movie Business Book.* Englewood Cliffs, NJ: Prentice-Hall, 1983.

Wasko, Janet. *How Hollywood Works.* Thousand Oaks, CA: Sage Publications, 2003.

Glossary

1394 See *IEEE 1394, Firewire.*

AAC (Advanced Audio Codec) An advanced version of MP3 also known as MPEG-2AAC.

AAF (Advanced Authoring Format) A file format standard developed by a group of manufacturers and users of editing systems.

ABERRATIONS Disruptions of or imperfections in the light transmission of a lens.

ABOVE-THE-LINE COSTS Production costs relating to producer, director, writers, and stars. See *below-the-line costs.*

A/B ROLL An editing process that uses two separate rolls (cassettes or reels) of tape or film. Each roll contains alternate shots of the sequence, thus enabling the editor to use transitions other than straight cuts between shots.

AC-3 (Audio Coded #3) Also known as Dolby Digital; developed as one of several required audio formats for DVD-Video and ATSC Digital TV.

ACADEMY APERTURE The size of the frame mask in 35mm cameras and projectors (1.85:1) as standardized by the Academy of Motion Picture Arts and Sciences.

ACADEMY LEADER A strip of film containing a sequence of numbers indicating the exact number of seconds remaining before the beginning of a film or videotape.

ACCEPTABLE FOCUS The adjustment of the lens so that the important objects are clear and sharp.

ACTUALITY Reporting of a news story on the actual location.

A/D Analog-to-digital conversion. Also called digitization.

ADAPTATION A relatively faithful translation of a play or piece of literature into a film or television program.

ADDITIVE COLORS The colors used in mixing light and upon which both film and video signals are based: red, blue, and green.

ADI (Area of Dominant Influence) The region covered by ratings of the Arbitron ratings company of one major metropolitan area or area covered by stations covering the same market. Similar to *DMA.*

ADR (automatic dialogue replacement) A process allowing actors to rerecord their lines as they view a playback of their performance.

ADSL (Asymmetrical Digital Subscriber Loop) A digital transmission technology that allows local telephone companies to deliver video services to homes and businesses over copper wires.

AERIAL IMAGE Refilming a projected film image. Other images may be combined using mirrors or single-frame film techniques.

AES/EBU (Audio Engineering Society/European Broadcasting Union) A digital audio standard adopted worldwide.

AESTHETICS The study and analysis of creative works.

AFFILIATE A broadcast station carrying a network's programs, but not owned by that network. See *Owned and Operated.*

AFM (American Federation of Musicians) A union that represents professional musicians.

AFTRA (American Federation of Television and Radio Artists) The union that represents radio and television performers and, in some markets, directors and associate directors.

AIFF (Audio Interchange File Format) A standard file format for storing audio files.

ALIASING A noticeable "jagging" of a computer-created image caused by a sampling rate that is too low.

ALLIGATOR CLIP A light-mounting device consisting of a spring-held clamp that somewhat resembles the jaws of an alligator.

AMBIENT The prevailing location environment; in audio, the background noise present at a location.

AMORTIZATION   Depreciation of the value of equipment and facilities over time for tax purposes.

AMPLIFY   To increase levels electronically.

AMPLITUDE   The instantaneous value of a signal; the electronic equivalent of level or loudness in audio.

ANALOG   Electronic signal that is constantly varying in some proportion to either sound, light, or a radio frequency.

ANAMORPHIC   Optically squeezed widescreen film images, which require special lenses for recording and projecting.

ANCHOR, NEWS   Newscaster who reads the news in the studio; may or may not have written, covered, or reported the story.

ANCILLARY MARKETS   Secondary sales possibilities for a program after it has completed its first run on a network and in the theaters. Also called *back-end*.

ANGLE OF ACCEPTANCE   The angle at which a lens gathers light in front of the camera.

ANIMATION   A process of creating the illusion that inanimate objects are moving.

ANIMATION STAND   The mounting for the animation camera, lights, and table for shooting animation cels. Sometimes called a *rostrum*. (See *cel animation*.)

ANSWER PRINT   The first color-corrected film print returned to the editor from the laboratory to make certain it was printed according to the directions provided.

APERTURE (iris)   The size of the camera lens opening, measured in *f-stops*.

APPLICATION   A computer program designed to permit certain types of work to be accomplished.

ARC   Movement of the camera in a semicircular pattern.

"A" ROLL   The primary roll of film or tape in editing; generally includes the master shots.

ART DIRECTOR   In film and video productions, the person who supervises the overall production design, including sets, props, costumes, settings, and even locations.

ARTIFICIAL INTELLIGENCE (AI)   (1) A computer program that mimics the human mind. (2) In computer games, a method of inserting text-based dialogue.

ASA (American Standards Association)   The rating of a film's ability to reproduce images based on the amount of light required. See *Exposure Index (EI)* and *DIN (European Standard)*.

ASCAP (American Society of Composers, Authors, and Publishers)   One of three major music licensing organizations charged with collecting residual fees due composers and musicians.

ASCII (American Standard Code for Information Interchange)   A universal digital standard for reading binary digits that can be read by almost all computer operating systems.

ASF (Active Streaming Format)   Microsoft's streaming format for *Windows Media* system.

ASPECT RATIO   The mathematical ratio between the vertical and the horizontal measurements of a frame of video or film.

ASSEMBLE EDIT   Sequential arranging of shots in a linear manner. May be accomplished on raw tape without previously recording a control track.

ASSISTANT DIRECTOR (AD)   In film production, the person who helps the production manager break down the script during preproduction and helps the director keep the talent and crew happy during production.

ASSOCIATE DIRECTOR (AD)   In video production, the person who relays the director's commands from the control room to the studio floor, keeps accurate time, and assists the director as needed.

ASYMMETRICAL   (1) In computers, a system that provides unequal send and receive signal speeds. (2) In graphics, a layout with different shapes and sizes on the center dividing line.

ASYNCHRONOUS   (1) A sound that does not match its actual or presumed on-screen source. (2) In computers, signals running at different speeds.

ATM (Asynchronous Transfer Mode)   A high-speed, fixed-packet data standard that works with telephone systems, but not necessarily with LANs or WANs.

ATMOSPHERIC EFFECTS   Environmental special effects such as fog, rain, snow.

ATR (audiotape recorder)   A tape deck based on an analog linear system of recording audio on a plastic-based tape coated with a material that can be magnetized. Generally the tape transport is based on an open-reel system.

ATSC (Advanced Television Systems Committee)   An industry group that sets standards for digital television in the United States.

AVI (Audio Video Interleaved)   A file format similar to MPEG and Quicktime for Windows.

ATTENUATE   To decrease or lower the levels of a signal or parts of a signal.

ATV (Advanced Television)   In the United States, includes digital television and high-definition television.

AUDIO   (1) The sound portion of the videotape. (2) Frequencies within the normal hearing range of humans.

AUDIO CONSOLE   An audio board through which sounds are channeled, amplified, and mixed during production or postproduction. See *mixer*.

AUDITION   (1) An audio circuit designed to allow the operator to hear selected sounds without those sounds being recorded or going on the air. (2) A talent tryout session for directors and producers to watch and listen to prospective performers before casting them in a production.

AURAL   Having to do with sound or audio.

AUTHORING   In interactive writing, the creation of flowcharts or copy for the computer screen.

AUTOMATIC GAIN CONTROL (AGC)   Circuit that maintains the audio or video level within a certain range. Prevents overdriving circuits, which causes distortion, but can increase *signal-to-noise ratio*.

AUTOMATIC LEVEL CONTROL (ALC)   See *Automatic Gain Control (AGC)*.

AVAILABLE LIGHT   Illumination existing at a location; sometimes called ambient light.

AXIS OF ACTION   (Also called 180-degree line) An imaginary line formed by the performer's direction of movement or by drawing a line through major stationary objects. Screen directionality will be maintained as long as the cameras do not cross this line.

BACKGROUND LIGHT   Light used to illuminate the set or background without lighting subjects in front of the set.

BACKLIGHT   Light placed behind the subject, opposite the camera; usually mounted fairly high and controlled with *barndoors* to prevent light from shining directly into the camera lens.

BACKTIME   To calculate the start time of a prerecorded sound track so that it will end at a specified time.

BAFFLE   A panel designed to absorb or reflect sound.

BALANCED MICROPHONE LINE   A mic line that consists of two internal conductors surrounded by isolation and a wraparound ground mesh.

BALL JOINT   The part of a tripod head that can be rotated to level the camera.

BANDWIDTH   Amount or volume of information that can be transmitted though a communications link.

BARNDOOR   Movable metal flaps attached to lighting fixtures to allow control over the area covered by the light from that lamp.

BARNEY   A soft sound insulator placed over a film camera to kill camera noise during synchronous recording.

BARREL   A cable adapter designed to connect two cables ending in similar plugs.

BARTER SYNDICATION   A system of distributing programs in which the syndicator retains a certain number of commercial slots and markets them, keeping the income.

BASE   The shiny side of a piece of film and some tapes. The physical support for either film emulsion or tape oxides.

BASE LIGHT LEVEL   The maximum amount of light required to achieve a recording.

BASE MAKEUP   Makeup that hides blemishes and creates a consistent overall facial color.

BASS   The low-frequency end of the audio spectrum.

BAUD   Number of symbols per second. A measure of data-transmission speed.

BELOW-THE-LINE COSTS   Those production costs of a cast and crew and their work, with the exception of the producers, director, writers, and stars. See *above-the-line costs*.

BETACAM   Half-inch professional videotape format developed by Sony specifically for use in camcorders; has replaced the ¾ U-matic as the predominant news-gathering video format.

BETACAM SP   An improved Sony Betacam format. Uses metal tape but is downward-compatible with Betacam.

BETACAM SX   Digital Betacam format.

BIAS   A high-frequency current mixed into a recording circuit that acts as a carrier of the audio to ensure a linear response.

BI-DIRECTIONAL   Microphone that picks up sound from the front and back but rejects most sound from the sides. The pickup pattern appears in the shape of a figure eight.

BINARY   A number in base 2; an either/or comparison. Computer systems are binary systems.

BIT (binary digit)   The smallest piece of information usable by a computer, either on or off.

BLACK BURST   A composite video signal including sync and color signals, but the video level is at black, or minimum.

BLACK LEVEL   The normal level for pedestal or video black in a video signal. See *set-up*.

BLEED   Space beyond the critical or essential area that may be seen on some television receivers but not on others.

BLIMP   A hard-shell sound insulator placed over a film camera to deaden camera noise during synchronous sound recording.

BLOCKING   Working out talent and camera positions during a rehearsal.

BLOOM   The effect seen when a video signal exceeds the capabilities of the system; white areas bleed into darker areas.

BLOOP   (1) An audible tone recorded simultaneously with a flash of light for the purpose of synchronizing images and sound during editing. (2) To remove specific sounds from a sound track.

BLOW UP   Print a film on a larger format in an optical printer.

BMI (Broadcast Music, Inc.)   One of three major music licensing organizations charged with collecting residual fees due composers and musicians.

BMP (Windows BitMap)   A visual RGB computer format developed by Microsoft.

BNC (Bayonet Neill-Concelman)   A type of twist-lock video connector, now the most common for professional equipment.

BODY MIC   A microphone concealed or hung directly on the body of the performer, sometimes called a *lapel* or *lavalier mic.*

BOOM   Moveable arm from which a microphone or camera may be suspended to allow for movement to follow the action.

BOOST   To raise or increase the level of a signal or portion of the signal.

BOX OFFICE RETURNS   The amount of money paid to theaters for tickets purchased by moviegoers for specific films.

BRANCHING   (1) In a drama, various paths a character may take in action. (2) In multimedia, various paths that a viewer may take by following links on a Web page.

BREAKDOWN SHEETS   A listing of facilities, material, equipment, and personnel needs for production at a specific setting called for in the script, which is filled out during script breakdown.

BRIGHTNESS   The intensity of light.

BROAD   A type of open-faced fill light, usually rectangular in shape.

BROADBAND CARRIER   A high-capacity transmission system used to carry large blocks of information on one cable or carrier: coaxial cable, microwave, optical fiber.

BROADCASTING   The sending of video and audio signals by attaching them to a carrier wave of electromagnetic energy that radiates in all directions.

"B" ROLL   A second roll of film or tape used in editing; usually includes cut-aways and cut-ins.

BSS (Broadcast Satellite Services)   International video satellites on "C" and "Ku" bands.

BUBBLE   Leveling device mounted on a tripod pan head consisting of a tube containing a liquid with a bubble of air trapped inside. Centering the bubble on a circle or crosshair indicates that the pan head is level.

BUDGET   An itemized list of actual or estimated production costs.

BUFFER   A block of computer memory set aside for temporarily holding data.

BURNER   A device to convert digital signals to an optical laser disc, either DVD or CD.

BURN   A condition caused by exposing camera tubes to excessive light levels. An image is retained on the face of the tube that is the negative of the original subject.

BUS   (1) A group of buttons on a video switcher devoted to different sources but sending the chosen signal to a predetermined output: preview, program, or special effects. (2) A wire that carries a series of signals to a common output.

BUZZWORDS   In advertising, phrases or words that have strong appeal and that the audience recognizes.

BYTE   Eight bits; the standard amount of information used to define a single character.

"C" FORMAT   One of three one-inch helical videotape formats specified by the SMPTE. "C" had become the analog production standard for studios in the United States until the development of digital formats.

CABLE RELEASE   A device that allows a film camera to be operated from a distance, often used for exposing single frames.

CAMCORDER   Camera-recorder combination. Designed originally for news coverage, but now becoming popular for *EFP (Electronic Field Production)* and other field productions.

CAMEO   A lighting technique in which foreground subjects are lit in front of a completely black background.

CAMERA CHAIN   A complete video camera unit consisting of a camera, a power supply, a sync generator, a camera control unit, and an encoder.

CAMERA CONTROL UNIT   A series of circuits that provide the signals and controls for operating a video camera.

CAMERA REPORT   A listing of individual camera shots either as they are made in the camera on location, or a listing of shots to be processed by the film laboratory.

CAPACITOR   An electrical device that can store an electrical charge and alter the flow of electronic signals by changing the electrical current passing through it.

CAPSTAN   The rotating shaft that presses against the videotape to keep the tape running at a constant speed.

CARBON ARC LIGHT   An intense light of approximately daylight Kelvin temperature that is emitted by electrically burning carbon rods.

CARDIOID MIC   A specialized unidirectional microphone with a heart-shaped pickup pattern.

CARTRIDGE   A self-contained continuous loop of audiotape or film.

CASE   The upper or lower style of letters. Uppercase letters are capital letters; lowercase letters are small letters.

CASSETTE   Prepackaged container of either audio, videotape, or film containing a specific length of tape or film stock, a feed reel, and a take-up reel. U-matic, Betacam, VHS, DVC tape systems, and Super-8 film all use cassettes.

CASTING   The process of auditioning and selecting performers for a production.

CATHARSIS   An element in drama that functions as an emotional release for the audience.

CATHODE RAY TUBE (CRT)   A television picture tube.

C-BAND The range of frequencies from 4 to 8 GHz used by many satellite companies.

CCD See *Charge-Coupled Device.*

C-CLAMP An attachment device shaped like a "C" that can be used to secure lighting instruments to the grid or to connect flats and other set pieces.

CD (compact disc) A five-inch digital laser disc, generally used for music recordings but also used for computer and video recording.

CD-I (Compact Disc-Interactive) A large-memory CD that can deliver two to 16 channels of video and/or audio and up to 16 hours of audio; designed to provide the programming for interactive systems.

CD-ROM (Compact Disk-Read-Only Memory) A permanently recorded CD disc.

CED (capacitive electronic disc) One type of video disc.

CEL Short for celluloid. The base material used to draw individual animation frames.

CEL ANIMATION The process of drawing and shooting as many as 24 cels per second. Each cel is a drawing on a clear acetate sheet. Cels showing foreground, mid-ground, and background may be layered to give the impression of three dimensions.

CEMENT SPLICE A device with cutting blades and clamps for welding two pieces of film together with cement (often with a warming element).

CHANGING BAG A light-tight black cloth or plastic bag used to load or unload camera magazines with film wound on cores.

CHANNEL (1) A separate audio signal. (2) A separate broadcast signal.

CHARACTER A single letter, number, or symbol used as a means of describing information in a graphic form.

CHARACTER GENERATOR (CG) Computerized electronic typewriter designed to create titles or any other of numeric or alphanumeric graphics for use in video.

CHARGE-COUPLED DEVICE (CCD) (1) Light-sensitive silicon chips. Replaced camera tubes. (2) A solid-state element designed to convert light to electronics; replaced the pickup tubes in video cameras.

CHIAROSCURO LIGHTING Lighting accomplished with high-contrast areas and heavy shadows.

CHIP Semiconductor integrated circuit. Depending on design, can replace tubes, resistors, and other electronic components. This light-sensitive chip, that replaced the camera tube, was the most important development for *EFP (Electronic Field Production).*

CHROMA The color portion of the video signal that includes both hue and saturation.

CHROMA KEY A method of combining two or more levels of pictures from more than one source. The process depends on the background behind the foreground subjects being a solid single color, usually green or blue. A specific type of effects generator ignores the blue or green background so that the foreground subject appears in front of the other signals.

CHROMATIC ABERRATION Visual distortion occurring when different color wavelength bands bend at different angles and intersect at different points behind the lens.

CHROMINANCE (Chroma) The color portion of the video signal.

CHRONOLOGY The timing sequence of events in a story.

CID (Compact Iodine Daylight) Lighting lamp using less wattage than Tungsten and providing near daylight color temperature light.

CINEMATOGRAPHER The operator or supervisor of a motion picture camera; over the years, this term has also been used to refer to those who operate a video camera.

CINEMA VERITÉ Literally "cinema truth," a style of documentary filmmaking in which the camera runs continuously while recording unstaged events.

CINERAMA A widescreen film process (1939–1963) that used three cameras and three projectors placed side-by-side.

CLAMPS Locks placed on the end of a rewind spindle on a film-editing bench to hold the film reels tight on the spindle.

CLAPSTICK A hinged arm on a board used to make a highly visible and audible reference point at the beginning of a synchronous sound film that is to be shot and recorded.

CLEARANCE The process of applying for and receiving permission to use a person's talent, appearance, or property.

CLEAR LEADER Film or tape that has no magnetic or emulsion coating and is thus completely transparent base material.

CLIMAX The decisive point in a drama, where the central conflict becomes so intense that it must be resolved; the central crisis in a drama.

CLIP (1) A single sequence of frames. (2) To cut or restrict.

CLOCK TIME (1) The actual time of day. (2) The reference code often used for *SMPTE* time-code recordings.

CLOSED-CAPTION A form of teletext designed to permit the hearing impaired to read the dialogue and a description of the action of a program. The copy is keyed into a window at the bottom of the frame. A special decoder attached to or built into the receiver is necessary to be able to view the copy.

CLOSED-CIRCUIT A self-contained wired system, as opposed to a broadcast system.

CLOSED SHOP Businesses or industries that require all employees to be members of a guild or a union.

CLOSE-UP (CU) Camera framing showing intimate detail; often a tight head shot.

CLOSURE Psychological perceptual activity that fills in gaps in the visual field.

CMOS (Complementary Metal-Oxide Semiconductor) A solid-state chip that is light sensitive, used as a camera pick-up chip.

COAXIAL CABLE A metal cable consisting of a single conductor surrounded by another conductor in the form of a tube designed to carry high frequencies without loss or distortion.

CODEC A combination encoder and decoder of electronic signals in one piece of equipment.

COFDM (Coded Orthogonal Frequency Division Multiplexing) A modulation system used in both digital television and DAB systems.

COLOR BARS Electronically generated pattern of precisely specified colors for use in standardizing the operation of video equipment.

COLOR CONTRAST Visible differences between adjacent colors, in terms of hue and saturation.

COLOR HARMONY Colors that create a pleasing impression when used or presented together.

COLOR-REVERSAL INTERNEGATIVE (CRI) A color-reversal print of an original negative that produces another negative to be used to make many prints by saving the original negative from the wear and tear of multiple printing passes.

COLOR TEMPERATURE See *Kelvin temperature*.

COLOR TIMING The art of setting the best color and density for the printing of each shot in a film.

COLOR WHEEL Color chips arranged in a dimensional circle to show the relationships between hue (chrominance), saturation, and luminance (brightness).

COMEDY A type of drama characterized by a less serious attitude toward life and an acceptance of its absurdities and incongruities.

COMET-TAILING A lingering afterimage of a bright light or reflecting object passing by the camera.

COMMENTATIVE SOUND Sound that has no visible source and that seems to comment on the visual action.

COMMERCIALS Paid brief messages that advertise products, companies, names, and services.

COMMON CARRIER The FCC's classification of transmission systems open to public use for fees. The operators are not allowed to control the content of the messages. Telephone, telegraph, and some satellite systems are regulated as common carriers.

COMPATIBILITY (1) That two systems can operate together. (2) That a tape recorded in one format can be played back in another. (3) That two different types of signals, such as *NTSC* and *ATV*, can be viewed on the same system.

COMPLEMENTARY COLORS Colors that are opposite each other on a color wheel or that, when mixed together, result in gray.

COMPONENT A signal (often video) in which unique parts are divided and transported or recorded separately. A component video signal may have the luminance and synchronous signals separated.

COMPOSITE A signal (often video) that contains all of the necessary signals in one combined signal. A composite video signal contains both picture and synchronous signals.

COMPOSITE PRINT A single film containing both the picture and sound track.

COMPOSITE SIGNAL A complete video signal, including sync pulse.

COMPOSITING Combining different payers of visual images in a computer graphics or animation program.

COMPOSITION The arrangement of visual elements with the frame.

COMPOUND LENS A lens made of more than one piece of glass or plastic.

COMPRESSED VIDEO A video signal that has repetitive and redundant portions removed, leaving only changes that occur between frames. Allows high-frequency video signals to use less memory and bandwidth.

COMPUTER-GENERATED IMAGERY (CGI) Images created entirely within a computer system.

COMPUTER GRAPHICS Pictorial images and illustrations created on a computer to be used in video and/or film productions.

CONCAVE The shape of a lens that bends light away from the center of the lens, causing the light rays to diverge from each other.

CONDENSER MIC A transducer that converts sound waves by a conductive principle. Requires a built-in amplifier and a power source. Also called electrostatic or capacitor.

CONFLICT A point of contention, disagreement, or competition in a story.

CONFORMING The final film-editing process of actually cutting the original negative into separate rolls and syncing it with the sound for delivery to the laboratory for printing.

CONTACT PRINTER A film-printing device in which original film is placed in direct emulsion-to-emulsion contact with the copy or print being made from the original.

CONTENT The substance of a work of art.

CONTINGENCY FUND Percentage (usually 10 to 20 percent) of a budget added to cover any costly delays or unforeseen production problems.

CONTINUITY (1) A depiction of continuous action. (2) Scripts, especially of commercials. (3) See *script supervisor*.

CONTRAPUNTAL SOUND Sound that is presented simultaneously with visual images but is unrelated or contradictory in terms of meaning or emotional effect.

CONTRAST RANGE Ability of a camera to distinguish between shades of reflected black-and-white light: TV, 30:1; film, 100:1; human eye, 1000:1.

CONTRAST RATIO The ratio of light measurement between the difference of maximum reflectance, as measured with a light meter, and minimum reflectance on a set.

CONTROLLER A specialized computer designed to accurately maintain control over a series of videotape decks during the editing process.

CONTROL TRACK Synchronizing signal recorded onto a videotape to align the heads for proper playback.

CONTROL TRACK EDITING Choice of edit points determined by counting pulses recorded on the tape.

CONVERTIBLE CAMERA A video camera that can be used in either portable field productions or mounted with studio accessories for in-studio productions.

CONVEX The shape of a lens that bends light toward the center of the lens so that light rays converge or intersect at a specific point, beyond which the image is inverted.

COOKIE See *cukaloris*.

COPY The words on a script.

COPY STAND A flat table with lights that illuminate artwork for an overhead camera.

CORE Plastic wheel upon which film can be rolled; unprocessed film placed on cores must be protected from light and loaded in a camera or magazine in complete darkness.

COSMETIC MAKEUP Facial and body makeup designed to hide imperfections and accentuate a performer's better features.

COSTUME DESIGNER The person who designs and supervises the making of clothing for talent.

COUNTDOWN LEADER A section of film or tape with a decreasing sequence of numbers indicating the amount of time remaining before the start of a film or tape.

COUNTER A meter designed to indicate either a position on a reel of tape or film or the amount of tape or film already used. May be calibrated in revolutions, frames, feet, meters, or time.

COUNTERPOINT The simultaneous presentation of two contradictory visual or sound sequences.

CPM (cost per thousand) The cost of exposing viewers to a commercial. Based on ratings of the program in which the commercial is scheduled to run.

CPU (Central Processing Unit) The main circuits that process digital information in a computer.

CRAB DOLLY A four-wheeled camera support on which an operator can sit and operate the camera while it is being moved.

CRADLE The dish on the top of a tripod into which the ball joint of a tripod head or camera mount is placed.

CRANE A relatively large camera mount consisting of a long counterweighted arm on a four-wheeled dolly.

CRAWL Credits or other graphic material moving from the bottom of the frame to the top.

CREDITS Lists of the names and functions of the people who have contributed in some way to a production.

CRISIS An intensification of the central conflict in a drama, usually involving a threat to someone or something.

CRITICAL AREA (essential area) Space occupying approximately 80% of the center of the video frame. This area will be seen with relative surety by the majority of the television receivers viewing that particular program. The 10% border outside of the critical area may not be seen on many receivers.

CROSS-FADE A transition in which one sound source fades out at the same rate as another is faded in.

CROSS-TALK Signal leakage between two channels.

CRYSTAL OSCILLATORS Small bits of quartz that oscillate at an unchanging rate and that can be used to regulate the speed of cameras and recorders.

CRYSTAL SYNC Separate crystal oscillators in the camera and recorder stay in sync without interconnecting cables.

CSI (Compact Source Iodide) Lighting lamp using less wattage than Tungsten and providing near-daylight color temperature light.

CUE (1) Signal to start talking, moving, or whatever the script calls for. (2) To ready material to be played back or edited by running and stopping a tape, film, record, and so on, at a specified spot.

CUKALORIS (cucaloris) A metal filter with cutout patterns designed to be placed in front of or inside of lamps to throw a pattern or mottled shadows. Sometimes called a *cookie*.

CUT (Take) (1) Cue to stop an action, and so on. (2) An instantaneous change in picture or sound. *Cut* is considered a film term and *take* a video term, but they have become interchangeable.

CUTAWAY Close-up shot of an image related to, but not visible in, the wider shot immediately preceding or following it.

CUT-IN Close-up shot of an image visible in the wider shot immediately preceding or following it.

CYCLE Time or distance between peaks of an alternating voltage; measured in Hertz.

CYCLES-PER-SECOND (CPS) The number of vibrations or successive waves of sound passing a specific point in one second.

CYCLING An animation technique for repeatedly using the same movements of hands and feet or other body parts.

D1, D2, D3, D5, D6, D7 (DVCPro), D9 (D-S), D16, SXBeta Digital videotape formats.

D/A Digital-to-analog conversion.

DAB (digital audio broadcast) A wireless digital terrestrial broadcast service. Also known as IBOC/DAB. A digital signal carried on a standard AM or FM radio broadcast.

DAILIES A one-light print of the previous day's film shooting for checking the quality of that day's shooting. See also *one-light print*.

DAM (digital asset management) A movement toward operating digital systems with one central control to allow exchange of files seamlessly between units.

DARS (Digital Audio Radio Services) Proposed satellite digital radio broadcasting.

DAT (digital audiotape) A series of formats designed to record audio in the digital domain, rather than analog. Formats include R-DAT (rotating-head), S-DAT (stationary head), and others being developed at the time of this writing.

DATA Any information used in any project or process, analog or digital.

DAW (digital audio workstation) A combination of software and hardware designed to facilitate the recording and editing of audio signals.

DAYLIGHT SPOOL A metal or plastic reel covering the edges of unprocessed film so that it can be loaded into a camera in daylight.

DBS (Direct Broadcast Satellite) (1) A system of relaying television programs from a satellite directly into the home without being retransmitted by either a cable or TV broadcast station. (2) High-powered, high-band satellite television transmission system.

DECIBEL (dB) Logarithmic unit of loudness. A dB is $\frac{1}{10}$ of the original unit, the Bel.

DECK In media, refers to a machine that plays and/or records audio or video signals.

DEFICIT FINANCING Producing a program at a loss on its first broadcast, depending on making a profit when the program goes into syndication.

DEFOCUS To roll the focus ring of a lens so that the image is out of focus.

DEGREES KELVIN (See *Kelvin temperature*)

DEMODULATION Separation of a program signal from the carrier wave.

DEMOGRAPHICS Characteristics of an audience or group of people in terms of age, gender, income, or other social factors.

DEPTH The illusion of three-dimensionality in visual composition; the "Z" axis.

DEPTH OF FIELD (DOF) The range of distances from the camera within which subjects remain in acceptable focus.

DEVELOPER The chemical solution that brings out the latent image on photographic film.

DGA (Directors Guild of America) Represents directors in both film and television in working conditions and rights.

DIALOGUE Speech between performers, usually seen on camera.

DIAPHRAGM (1) The adjustable opening that varies the aperture size of the lens. (2) The element in a microphone that vibrates according to the pressure waves in the air created by the sound source.

DICHROIC Filters designed to reflect certain colors of light and pass others.

DIFFRACTION Spreading or scattering of light that often occurs around the ball of the iris in the lens.

DIFFUSER Translucent material that breaks up and scatters light from a lighting fixture to soften it.

DIGITAL Binary-based, constant-amplitude signals varying in time. Provides signal recording without noise or distortion.

DIGITAL CINEMA (DC) (formerly called electronic cinema)The distribution and projection of feature film through a high-definition digital video system.

DIGITAL LIGHT PROCESSING (DLP) A rear-screen video display system based on rotating mirrors.

DIGITAL-S A digital video-based tape-recording format.

DIGITAL SIGNAL PROCESSOR (DSP) A circuit designed to change the analog output of a CMSO or CCD chip to a digital signal.

DIGITAL VIDEO MANIPULATOR (DVM) (also called a digital effects switcher) A special effects device that uses digital circuits to create unusual images.

DIGITIZE To create a digital equivalent of an analog image by sampling and converting it to the binary system.

DIMMER BOARD An electrical control center for lighting that alters the voltage to different circuits in a patch board and thus changes the light intensity of the instruments in those circuits, which also affects the color temperature of the light.

DIN (1) Deutsche Industrie Normen: The German standards organization. (2) DIN usually refers to a type of plug-jack.

DIOPTER An adjustable lens allowing the operator to match his or her eyesight with the viewfinder.

DIRECTOR Commands the creative aspects of a production. In the field, makes creative decisions; in the studio, calls the shots on live productions; and in the editing room, provides opinions.

DISH A parabola-shaped antenna designed to receive satellite or microwave signals.

DISCRETE 5.1 AUDIO A six-channel audio-delivery system with speakers placed on the left, right, center, left-rear, right-rear, and including a sub-woofer.

DISSOLVE Transition of one image fading into and replacing another. If stopped at the midpoint, it is a *superimposition*. Also called a lap.

DISTORTION An undesirable change in a signal or either light, sound, or video.

DISTRIBUTION AMPLIFIER (DA) Electronic amplifier designed to feed one signal (audio, video, or pulses) to several different destinations.

DISTRIBUTORS Companies and organizations that rent films to exhibitors and theater owners.

DMA (Designated Market Area) The local ratings area used by the Nielsen Media Research Company.

DOCUDRAMAS A type of historical or biographical drama based on actual events but modified for dramatic and aesthetic purposes.

DOCUMENTARY A nonfiction film or videotape that explores a topic in depth with the purpose of making a specific point.

DOLLY (1) Three- or four-wheeled device that serves as a movable camera mount. (2) Movement in toward a subject (dolly in) or back away from a subject (dolly out).

DOUBLE PERF Film with sprocket holes on both sides or edges.

DOUBLE-SYSTEM RECORDING Recording synchronized sound on a recorder that is separated from the camera that is recording the matching images.

DOWNLINK Transmission path from a satellite to a ground station. Sometimes used to describe the ground station capable of receiving a satellite signal link. See *uplink*.

DOWNLOAD The process of transferring electronic information from one source, circuit, or storage medium to another. Combination of various elements that affect the pace at which actions unfold and the emotional response of the audience.

DRESS REHEARSAL The final rehearsal or dry run of a production with all costumes, props, and other production units prior to the actual recording.

DSL (Digital Subscriber Line) A system designed to allow a standard telephone line to carry digital information at a rate much faster than using a standard digital modem.

DUAL-REDUNDANCY Using two of a single element, such as microphones, in case one of them fails during a critical production.

DUB (1) Copying a recorded signal from one medium to another. (2) Replacing or adding voice to a preexisting recording.

DUBBERS Mechanical/electronic equipment to copy videotape, audiotape, or film soundtracks.

DUPE To duplicate; to make a copy of a tape, film, or disk.

DUPE NEGATIVE A negative copy of an interpositive that is used to make multiple prints of a negative original film.

DV (digital video) Any of several videotape formats for recording a digitized signal.

DVC (digital videocassette) Any of several digital videotape formats.

DVCPro, DVCPro50, DVCPro100 Digital video-based compatible recording formats.

DVD (digital versatile disc or digital video disc) A laser disc capable of storing from 8 to 18 GB of digital information, such as a two-hour movie with eight separate sound tracks and 32 subtitle tracks for international distribution.

DVD-R, DVD+R DVD discs for one-time-only recording.

DVD-RW, DVD-RAM, DVD+RW DVD discs may be recorded multiple times.

DVE (digital video effects) A video switcher used to create digital effects.

DVM (digital video manipulator) See *DVE*.

DYNAMIC MIC Transducer designed to convert sound to electronics by using an electromagnetic coil attached to a lightweight diaphragm.

DYNAMIC RANGE Loudness range from the softest to the loudest that can be reproduced by any system without creating distortion.

EBU (European Broadcast Union) The world's largest professional broadcast and standards-setting association.

EC (electronic cinema) A digital video camera with a high-quality output nearly equaling that of 35mm film.

EDGE NUMBERS Consecutive reference numbers printed on the edge of a piece of film.

EDIT CONTROL UNIT An electronic device that controls the editing manipulations of videotape recordings.

EDIT CUE A cue that activates an edit at a specific point on the tape.

EDIT DECISION LIST (EDL) List of precise locations of edit points. May be generated manually or by computer.

EDITED MASTER The final product of on-line editing.

EDITOR Tape or film specialist charged with assembling stories from footage and recordings to create the final production.

EFP (electronic field production) Single-camera video production taking place at remote locations from the studio.

EFP UNIT A van containing equipment for a single-camera video-recording session at a remote location.

EIAJ (Electronic Industries Association of Japan) Standards-setting organization of Japan. At one time referred to a specific ½-inch open-reel videotape system.

ELECTRET A permanently charged element or capacitor in a condenser mic.

ELECTRONIC CINEMATOGRAPHY (EC) (now called Digital Cinema) Shooting a feature "film" with HDTV cameras and recording on videotape, not film.

ELECTRONIC NEWS GATHERING (ENG) Process of researching, shooting, and editing materials to visually report on occurrences of interest using video cameras and electronic editing specifically for newscasts.

ELECTRONIC PROJECTION Large-screen video-image projection systems, often using multiple monitors or split frames with different images in each frame.

ELLIPSOIDAL A lighting instrument with a mirror reflector in the shape of an ellipse, which produces intense, harsh spot lighting.

EMULSION Chemical layer containing the light-sensitive materials on photography and motion-picture film. The makeup of the emulsion determines how sensitive to light the film is and is rated accordingly.

ENCODING Adding additional signals or data, such as time code and cues of close-caption information, to an existing signal or recording.

ENHANCEMENT A multimedia element such as a link to the World Wide Web.

ENT Abbreviation for interior, a location artificially lit.

EPS (Encapsulated PostScript) A visual computer format used for vector files.

EQUALIZATION (EQ) The manipulation of frequencies to correct or compensate for deficiencies in an electronic signal by boosting or attenuating certain frequencies.

EQUAL TIME The FCC's rule requiring stations to sell airtime to all candidates for a political office if they sell to any one candidate.

ERASE HEAD A device on a recording machine that is used to align all metal particles on magnetic tape prior to recording and in doing so remove any previously recorded signals.

ERROR RATIO (RATE) Measurement of the number of digital errors in a single signal.

ESSENTIAL AREA The area of the full frame within which critical information should fall so that it will not be cut off by a television receiver. See also *critical area* and *safe action area*.

ESTABLISHING SHOT (ES) A shot in which the camera is generally located at a sufficient distance from the subjects to record their actions in the context of their surroundings, thus firmly establishing place, time, and relationships.

EVENT A single activity during an editing session.

EXHIBITORS Film theaters and theater owners.

EXPOSITION A structural element in a drama whereby characters are introduced or settings presented, providing background information and setting a specific mood.

EXPOSURE The presentation of film to light.

EXPOSURE INDEX (EI) A rating of the sensitivity of a specific film stock to light. See *DIN* and *ASA*.

EXPOSURE LATITUDE See *contrast range*.

EXTERIOR (EXT) A setting or location outdoors.

EXTREME CLOSE UP (ECU or XCU) Tightest framing of a shot in a sequence. For example, just the eyes or hands of a subject.

EXTREME WIDE SHOT (EWS or XWS) Widest shot of a sequence. For example, an entire city block or football stadium.

EYELINE MATCHES Editing between shots so that the direction an actor is looking matches.

"F" A type of cable connector for a cable intended to carry a modulated signal or signals. See *RF*.

FACILITIES (FAX) Technical equipment, lights, cameras, microphones, studios, editing rooms.

FACSIMILE (FAX) Transmission of information by optical/electronic system through telephone lines.

FADE-IN OR FADE-OUT A gradual change in signal either from zero to maximum or maximum to zero, in audio, film, or video.

FADER A sliding knob that can be pushed up or down the scale to increase or decrease the audio level.

FADER BAR A movable control for increasing or decreasing the intensity of a video signal on a switcher.

FAST FORWARD A machine operational setting for rapidly advancing tape or film.

FAST MOTION Recording images at a slower speed than normal playback speed so that when played at normal speed the images move faster than normal.

FEDERAL COMMUNICATION COMMISSION (FCC) The U.S. federal government agency charged with the supervision and regulation of all electronic communication media in this country.

FEDERAL TRADE COMMISSION (FTC) The U.S. federal agency that monitors and oversees trade practices in many industries, including radio and television advertising and industrial market structure and competition.

FEED (1) The part of a recording device that supplies tape or film. (2) A source of video or audio information supplied to a station or studio.

FEEDBACK A continuous sound loop from a microphone through an audio amplifier to a speaker that is picked up by the microphone, creating a loud squeal. Feedback also can occur with recording/playback units that form a continuous loop, imitating reverberation.

FIBER OPTICS Glass strands designed to carry communication signals modulated on light waves rather than radio waves.

FIELD One-half of a complete television picture; 265.5 lines of the 525 NTSC system occurring once every 60th of a second. Two fields make a complete frame.

FIELD GUIDE A transparent sheet that indicates the proper field and spacing for character movement and artwork on an animation stand.

FIELD OF VIEW The exact spatial dimensions of the framed image in front of the camera.

FILL LIGHT Soft, shadowless light used to reduce contrast and lighten shadow areas. Usually placed on the opposite side of the camera from the key light and low enough to remove harsh shadows.

FILM (1) Light-sensitive material that is exposed to light in a camera to record visual images. (2) Refers to the whole process of recording, distributing, and viewing images produced by photochemical and mechanical means (excluding video).

FILM PROJECTION The presentation of a film image on a screen by passing light through exposed and processed film in a film projector that is focused by a lens on the screen so that it can be viewed.

FILM PROJECTOR A device that can play back a completed film and project it on screen while amplifying the accompanying sound track.

FILM STOCK The unexposed film described in terms of format, sensitivity, process, and graininess.

FILM-TO-VIDEO TRANSFER Duplicating a film to video through a telecine or flying spot scanner.

FILM VIEWER A device that projects a film image during the editing process.

FILTER (1) A colored or textured semi-opaque element placed between the subject or lens and the focal plane of the camera. (2) A series of electronic elements used to equalize signals.

FINE GRAIN A film stock with small particles that reproduce at a high level of resolution.

FIREWIRE See *IEEE 1394.*

FISHPOLE Handheld expandable mic boom.

FIXING Placing film in a chemical solution that permanently "sets" the developed image as part of the process.

FLAG An opaque piece of material hung between a light and a subject or set to control light or throw a shadow.

FLAT ANIMATION Two-dimensional items used to create animation, usually individual cels or collages of flat objects.

FLASH FRAME An unwanted frame between two edited shots.

FLATBED A horizontal film-editing machine.

FLATS Relatively lightweight background sections that can be lashed together to create a continuous wall in a studio.

FLOODLIGHTS Lighting instruments without lenses that have reflectors and diffusers to spread and soften the light that the lights emit.

FLOOR MANAGER (FM) The director's representative on the studio floor who relays commands to the talent and crew during live or multiple-camera video production.

FLOOR PLAN A scale drawing of the studio used in planning scenery design and construction, lighting, and camera and performer blocking.

FLOOR STANDS Three-legged poles that can be raised and lowered, to which lighting instruments and flags can be mounted.

FLOPPY DISK A flat, flexible magnetic medium designed to store and physically transfer computer data.

FLUIDHEAD A camera mount filled with a fluid that helps the operator create smooth camera pans and tilts.

FLUORESCENT LIGHT Light produced by a fluorescent lamp that creates a soft light that does not produce a specific *Kelvin temperature.*

FLUTTER An audio distortion caused by short and rapid variations in the speed of the reproducer.

FM (Frequency Modulation) Audio broadcasting with a wide frequency range and much freedom from noise.

FOCAL DISTANCE The distance of the subject from the focal plane of the camera.

FOCAL LENGTH The distance from the optical center of a lens to its focal point.

FOCAL PLANE The area behind a convex lens at which the light rays form an inverted image.

FOCUS RING The ring on the barrel of a lens that allows the focus to be changed.

FOOTAGE AND FRAME COUNTER A device that indicates the elapsed tape or film length and duration in feet, frames, or minutes, seconds, and frames.

FOOT-CANDLE (FC) A basic unit of light intensity, theoretically the amount of light from one candle that falls on a one-square-foot board one foot away from the candle.

FORM The method of creating a work of art.

FORMAT (1) A rough outline of a script, often used for newscasts and documentaries. The format is the blueprint for the program, not the word-for-word script. (2) A specific type or size of film, audiotape, videotape, or digital medium. Typical film formats are 70mm, 35mm, 16mm, or S-8. Analog audiotapes are usually described by the width of the tape: ½-inch, 1-inch, 2-inch. Digital formats may be set by the electronics, not the size of the tape. There are more than 20 different analog and digital videotape formats.

FOUR-PLATE FLATBED EDITOR A film editing table with one set of plates for sound, another for picture.

FOUR-WALLING A means by which an independent film producer can distribute and exhibit his or her own film by renting out a theater for a fixed fee.

FRAME (1) Complete video picture, made up of two 262.5 line interlaced scanned fields. There are 30 frames a second in the *NTSC* system. (2) The outline of the available area in which to compose a video picture. Today's NTSC standard is a frame 3 units high by 4 units wide.

FRAME STORE A digital memory device that scans and stores a complete video frame in order to produce some special effects.

FRANCHISE A license granted to a cable TV, *DBS*, or telephone company by a civic unit (city, county) to provide electronic communication services to that unit's citizens.

FREEZE-FRAME Holding the same frame of video or film so that motion is completely stopped.

FREQUENCY Number of complete cycles an electrical signal makes in one second. Measured in Hertz, Hz.

FREQUENCY DISTORTION An unequal reproduction or elimination of some frequencies.

FREQUENCY RESPONSE A measurement of a piece of equipment's ability to reproduce a signal of varying frequencies.

FRESNEL A spotlight equipped with a stepped lens that easily controls and concentrates light.

F-STOP A measurement of the size of opening that allows light to pass through an iris or aperture.

FTP (File Transfer Protocol) A system for transferring digital signals.

FULLCOAT A film stock completely coated with magnetic recording medium designed to record one or more individual tracks of sound. The recording is kept in sync with the picture by the match of the sprockets and recording speed with that of the picture.

FULL-PAGE SCRIPT A script format organized around scenes, in which both the visual and audio information appear in the same paragraphs.

FULL SHOT (FS) An extremely wide shot that takes in the entire setting of a scene or sequence. See also *WS*, *ES*.

FUNCTION To the consumer of art, the reason why it is art.

FUNCTIONAL Referring to sets or lighting. Designed for a specific purpose to serve the needs of the production.

GAFFER Senior electrician on a crew.

GAFFER'S TAPE A strong gray-colored tape used for securing lights and light-mounting devices, among many other objects.

GAIN Amount of amplitude of an electronic signal. Usually measured in dB.

GANG SYNCHRONIZER Several wheels or hubs with sprocketed teeth that hold different reels of film in exact registration frame for frame as they are moved back and forth.

GAP The small distance between the poles of tape heads, usually measured in microns.

GATE The area of the film camera or projector where the film is exposed to light.

GBIT/S Gigabits per second, billions of bits per second.

GELS Flexible sheets of transparent-colored plastic used to create colored light or alter the color temperature of a light source.

GENERAL PURPOSE INTERFACE (GPI) An electronic device controlled by remotely activated electronic switches. With GPI a computer can control a large number of different components from one location.

GENERATION Each level of copies of a medium. The original is the first generation, the next copy is the second generation, and so on. In analog systems each generation adds additional degeneration of the signal.

GENLOCK The process of tying two different synchronous systems together so that a smooth transition may be made between the two. Also necessary when converting computer signals to video and vice versa.

GENRE A type of programming; that is, Western, comedy, and so on.

GIF (Graphics Interchange Format) A computer Web page format.

GIGAHERTZ A measurement of frequency; 1 billion Hertz.

GIRAFFE Small mic boom mounted on a tripod on wheels usually designed for limited mic movement.

GOBO (1) In video, a set piece that allows a camera to shoot through it, such as a window. (2) In audio, a movable sound reflector board. (3) In film, a movable freestanding pattern cutout similar to a *cookie*. (4) On stage, the equivalent of a cookie.

GRAININESS The degree to which grains or crystals of silver halide are visible in a film stock after development and projection.

GRAPHICS   A design consisting of shapes and colors to produce an object of some significance.

GRAPHICS GENERATOR   A digital unit designed to create and combine pictures with type. Sometimes called a paint box.

GRAYSCALE   A multiple-step reflectance intensity scale for the evaluation of a picture. Generally a 10-step scale is used for television, between video white and video black.

GRID   A system of pipes hanging from the ceiling of a studio design to mount lighting instruments.

GRIP   A stagehand, a crew person who moves sets, props, dollies. The head stagehand is the key grip.

GROSS DISTRIBUTOR RENTAL RECEIPTS   The total amount of money paid to motion picture distributors by theater owners for the rental of a particular film.

GUILLOTINE SPLICER   A film tape splicer that uses unperforated tape that it cuts off and perforates in a downward movement of the handle.

GUN   A part of a picture and a camera tube that shoots a stream of electronics at the faceplate of the tube.

HANDHELD CARDS   Illustrations that a performer holds up to a camera during a production.

HANGING MICROPHONE   A microphone suspended from the ceiling or grid.

HARD COPY   Generally refers to a printed copy on paper of a computer output, rather than a floppy disk.

HARD DISC DRIVE   A rigid magnetic disc that is removable or is installed internally in a computer and that stores large quantities of data.

HARD LIGHT   Direct light that creates harsh shadows.

HARDWARE   Mechanical, electronic, or magnetic equipment rather than software, the material recorded, or computer programs.

HARMONIC DISTORTION   Distortion of the primary signal by harmonics of the primary signal, usually caused by overmodulation.

HARMONICS   Sounds that are exactly one or more octaves above or below a specific sound frequency.

HARMONY   The combined effect of playing several consonant tones simultaneously.

HEAD   A pan head supports the camera and is designed to allow both horizontal and vertical movement of the camera.

HEADEND   The cable companies' central control center where incoming signals from off the air, satellites, and other sources are distributed to output lines to the subscribers.

HEAD LEADERS   The beginning leaders placed on film for editing and projection purposes.

HEADPHONES   Small audio transducers mounted on a frame and worn over the head to feed sound to the wearer's ears.

HEADROOM   (1) The space above the head of a person in the frame. (2) The amount of audio or video level that a piece of equipment can handle above the normal 100% modulation without causing distortion.

HELICAL   Videotape with multiple recording heads that records information in long slanting tracks; each track records one field of information.

HERTZ   (Hz) Measurement of frequency. Number of complete cycles completed in 1 second.

Hi8   A semiprofessional 8mm videotape format developed by Sony for the *prosumer* (professional/consumer) market.

HIGH-ANGLE SHOT   A shot in which the camera is placed high above the subject, tending to reduce its size and importance.

HIGH-DEFINITION TELEVISION (HDTV)   One of several subcategories of Advanced TV (*ATV*). Attempt at creating a video system nearly equal to 35mm film in resolution and aspect ratio.

HIGH HAT   A minimal platform designed to mount a pan head allowing for shots close to the ground or to mount the camera on a car, boat, or airplane.

HIGH-KEY LIGHTING   A brightly lit, low-contrast scene created by equal intensities of key and fill light and a low key-to-fill ratio. Also called *Notan*.

HITCHHIKER   A *spider* on wheels.

HMI (Halide Metal Iodine)   A high-intensity, high-color temperature light produced by an energy-efficient HMI lamp.

HOOK   A dramatic device that grabs the audience's attention and secures their involvement in the story.

HORIZONTAL BLANKING   The period of time in a video signal when the electron beam is shut off while the scan returns to start the next line.

HORIZONTAL SYNC   The part of the video signal that keeps all of the equipment synchronized.

HOT SPLICER   A cement splicer with a built-in heating element.

HMI (Halogen-Metal-Iodide)   Lighting lamp using less wattage than Tungsten and providing near-daylight color temperature light.

HTML (Hyperttext Markup Language)   A computer language used for formatting documents to be transferred through the World Wide Web.

HUE   A specific wavelength band of light, such as red, green, or blue.

HUM   Low-frequency noise in audio or video equipment, usually induced by alternating power lines or stray magnetic fields.

HUT (Homes Using Television)   A means ratings companies use to compare audiences for programs by listing the number of TV sets in use at any one time.

HYPERCARDIOD   An extremely directional microphone pickup pattern.

HYPHENATE A performer, crew, or staff member that performs more than one function; for example, Producer-Director.

IATSE (International Alliance of Theatrical Stage Employees) A union that represents stagehands, projectionists, and many other crafts of the television and film industry.

IBEW (International Brotherhood of Electrical Workers) A union that represents crew members in major U.S. markets.

IBOC (In-Band On-Channel) See *DAB*.

ICON A graphic symbol.

IEEE 1394 (FIREWIRE) A low-cost interface to connect digital equipment developed by Apple Computer.

IFB (Interruptable Foldback) A communication circuit that allows the director or associate director to talk to television performers while they are on the air.

ILLUSTRATIONS Stationary visual images such as charts and still photographs.

IMAGE ORTHICON (IO) An early video-camera tube. The development of the IO opened the way for reasonably mobile studio and remote cameras.

IMAGE PERSPECTIVE The apparent depth of the image and the spatial relationships of objects.

IMAGE TONALITY The overall appearance of the image in terms of its apparent contrast and color.

IMAX A widescreen film format shot on 65mm film running horizontally past the lens. The image is 10 times larger than a standard 35mm film frame and is projected on a curved screen.

IMPEDANCE Apparent AC resistance to current flowing in a circuit. Measured in Ohms.

IN-CAMERA EDITING Shooting a sequence of shots on film or videotape so that they do not have to be edited in postproduction.

INCANDESCENT LIGHT Inert-gas-filled electric lamp emitting light and heat from a glowing filament. A typical lamp is the Tungsten-halogen lamp used in most production instruments, as well as the standard household lightbulb.

INCIDENTAL CHARACTERS Minor background figures in a story who often add texture, interest, and depth.

INCIDENT LIGHT Illumination from a light source. Measured in foot-candles or Lux by pointing the light meter at the light source.

INCIDENT METER READING A light meter reading of the intensity of light falling on the subject.

INDEPENDENT A producer, distributor, director, writer, or station that is not affiliated with a network or national company.

IN-HOUSE A production unit that creates programming for the organization or institution of which it is a part.

IN-POINT Starting point of an edit.

INPUT Signal entering a system or an electrical unit.

INSERT A recording of specific actions in a scene to be inserted into a master shot, usually *close-ups*.

INSERT EDIT Assembling a videotape production by adding video and audio signals to tape stock that has already had control track recorded on it. Insert edits also can be made over existing edited tape.

INSTRUCTIONAL PROGRAMS Educational films or videotapes designed as teaching aids for the public, students, or employees.

INTERACTIVE MEDIA Communication systems that permit two-way interaction between electronic stations (video monitors, computers). May depend on stored programs such as games or shopping networks.

INTERCUTTING A relatively rapid alternation between two or more different shots.

INTERIOR (ENT) Setting or location inside of a building or structure.

INTERLACE SCANNING The method of combining two fields of scan lines into one frame.

INTERNEGATIVE A copy of the A and B film rolls onto a single negative film that can be used for printing multiple positive release prints.

INTERNET A public computer network, originally developed by the military, now linking home, education, science, and business computers.

INTERPOLATION An animation technique in computer graphics that allows the animator to compose the first and last frames of an action sequence from which the computer then generates the images in between.

INTERPOSITIVE A print using negative stock of the original negative that then creates a positive image.

INTERVALOMETER A device that allows a video or film camera to take a single frame at preset times, creating a time-lapse series.

INTRO Abbreviation for introduction.

INVERSE SQUARE LAW A mathematical analysis of changes in alternating energy. The amount of energy is inversely proportionate to the change in distance. The formula is easily applied to calculating lighting and audio levels.

IPS (Inches Per Second) Method of measuring the speed of tape, film, or other longitudinal media.

IRIS See *aperture*.

ISO See *exposure index*.

ISDN (Integrated Services Digital Network) A type of dial-up telephone system offering speeds of up to 128 KB per second.

ISOLATED CAMERA A camera that feeds its own videotape recorder and is available for live shots in a multiple camera production, such as an athletic event.

ITFS (Instructional Television Fixed Service) A microwave video-delivery system licensed to educational institutions.

JACK A receptacle for plugs usually mounted on equipment or walls of a studio or control room.

JARGON Terminology and slang of a particular field.

JINGLES Music and lyrics used in commercials that are quickly associated with the product advertised.

JOG CONTROL A circular dial used to either move slowly or rapidly, forward or backward, from one frame or section of an edit to another.

JOYSTICK A level on a video switcher or computer that allows the operator to select specific placement of a wipe, key, cursor, or other special effect or operation.

JPEG (Joint Photographic Experts Group) A compression standard for single frames.

JUMP CUT Any one of several types of poor edits that either break continuity or may be disturbing to the audience.

KELVIN TEMPERATURE Measurement of the relative color of light. Indicated as degrees Kelvin (K); the higher the temperature, the bluer the light; the lower the temperature, the redder the light.

KERNING Measurement of space between letters.

KEY Process of combining two or more images without the background image bleeding through the foreground image. See also *chroma key*.

KEYING or TO KEY Inserting or embedding one video signal into another.

KEYKODE A Kodak film method of labeling individual frames on the film stock. Can be digitized for conforming.

KEY LIGHT Apparent main source of light. Usually from one bright light above and to one side of the camera.

KEYSTONE DISTORTION The effect of object shot at angle rather than square on.

KEY-TO-BACK RATIO A comparison between the amount of light on the subject from the backlight and the amount of light on the subject from the key light.

KEY-TO-FILL RATIO A comparison between the amount of light on the subject from the key light and the amount of light from a combination of key and fill lights.

KICKER A light focused from the side on the subject or on a particular section of the set.

KILL To turn off a light, camera, or audio feed.

KILOHERTZ (kHz) A measurement of alternating energy; 1,000 hertz.

KINESCOPE A film recording of a live or taped video production, now replaced by tape-to-film transfers.

KU-BAND The range of frequencies between 11 and 14 gigahertz increasingly used by communication satellite companies.

LAB REPORT See *camera report*.

LAG Characteristic of a camera tube in which a picture trails its own images as the camera moves. Lag increases with the age of the tube.

LASER (Light Amplification by Stimulation of Emission of Radiation) A single-frequency beam of high-powered light.

LASER DISC A type of video or audio recording made by a laser disc scanning minute holes in a metal disc encased in a plastic covering.

LAVALIER (Lav) Microphone worn around the neck. Also sometimes called a lapel mic when clipped to a tie or the front of clothing.

LAYBACK The process of rerecording a track in sync after it has been modified. Usually refers to audio tracks after *sweetening*.

LAYOVER Transferring the edited sound track to a multitrack recorder for final *sweetening*.

LEAD STORY The most important story of a newscast, usually the first story in the newscast.

LEADING Measurement of space between lines.

LEGAL RELEASE A statement releasing a producer from future legal action, signed by nonprofessional people appearing in or providing materials for a production.

LEITMOTIFS Musical themes associated with specific characters in a production.

LENS Glass or plastic designed to focus and concentrate light on a surface to form an image.

LENS CAP Opaque covering to slip over the end of a lens to protect the surface from damage and to protect the image device from excessive light.

LENS COATING A substance placed on the surface of a lens to reduce the scattered reflection of light entering the lens, which increases the light transmission of that lens. Also used to protect the lens from moisture, scratches, and dirt.

LENS HOOD A device for shading the camera lens from direct sunlight or from artificial light emitted opposite the camera.

LETTERBOX A term describing the presentation of 16:9 format programming on a 4:3 medium that leaves black bands at the top and bottom of the frame.

LEVEL (1) Relative amplitude or intensity. Used to indicate light, audio, video, and other electronic signals. (2) Aligned with the horizon.

LEVELING Adjusting a camera or light fixture to be parallel to the horizon.

LIBRARY EFFECTS Sound effects catalogued and accessible in a prerecorded form on computer discs, CDs, audiotape, or vinyl discs.

LIBRARY SERVER   A storage computer that keeps track of all broadcast elements in a studio or station.

LIGHT   Electromagnetic energy that stimulates receptors in the eyes.

LIGHT-EMITTING DIODE (LED)   A solid-state component that emits light when a small voltage is applied. Useful as a level or operating condition indicator.

LIGHTING DIRECTOR   In video production, the person who designs and supervises the lighting setup. In film, the title is Director of Photography (DP).

LIGHTING INSTRUMENT   The housing within which a light source or lamp is enclosed.

LIGHTING PLOT   A scale outline of a lighting setup on grid paper that represents the studio floor, providing an overhead view of the relationship of lighting instruments to sets and actors.

LIGHTING RATIO   The numerical ratio of the amount of light falling on a subject from the key light against the amount of light falling on a subject from the fill light.

LIGHT METER (exposure meter)   Instrument used to measure the intensity of light. May be calculated in *foot-candles*, *Lux*, or *f-stops*.

LINE LEVEL   Signal amplified enough to feed down a line without fear of degradation. A microphone level is lower than line level; a speaker level is higher.

LIP-SYNC   The process of matching the movement of performers' mouths with the words they are speaking.

LIQUID CRYSTAL DISPLAY (LCD)   A flat-screen monitor based on modulated liquid crystals.

LIST MANAGEMENT   The process of making alterations, trims, or shifting of segments in editing decisions in a computerized editing system.

LIVE ON TAPE   A multiple-camera video production recording as if it were live, but allowing for some postproduction.

LOAD   To transfer date or information to an analog or digital storage device.

LOCATION   Area or site of a production. Usually refers to sites away from studios.

LOCKING WINDOW   A monitor window that allows audio and video to be edited simultaneously.

LOG   Listing of shots as they are recorded on tape.

LONGITUDINAL   Lengthwise; in media, refers to the method of recording audio and control track signals.

LOOPING   The process of rerecording audio during postproduction. Also now called *ADR* (Automatic Dialogue Replacement).

LOUDNESS   Perceived intensity of audio. Depends on the intensity and saturation of the sound, as well as the sensitivity of the listener to a range of frequencies.

LOUDNESS DISTORTION   Disruption in a sound signal caused by overmodulation.

LOW-ANGLE SHOT   A shot in which the camera is placed closer to the floor than a normal camera height. This angle tends to exaggerate the size and importance of the subject.

LOW IMPEDANCE   A type of electrical signal created by most professional microphones and some playback equipment.

LOW-KEY LIGHTING   A lighting aesthetic characterized by pools of light and harsh shadow areas created by minimal fill and a high key-to-fill ratio. Also called *chiaroscuro*.

LPTV (Low-Power TV)   Television stations licensed by the FCC to broadcast using limited power to cover areas or markets not served by major market TV stations.

LUMINAIRE   See *lighting instrument*.

LUMINANCE   The brightness component of a video signal.

LUX   European measurement of light intensity. There are approximately 10 Lux to 1 foot-candle.

MAG TRACK   Short for magnetic sound film track.

MAJOR DISTRIBUTORS (studios)   The largest film distributors, who receive the bulk of the distribution receipts from their films: Disney, Warner Bros., Twentieth Century-Fox, Universal, and Paramount.

MAJOR MARKET   One of the top 100 metro areas in number of TV households.

MASTER   The final product of an audio or video editing session.

MASTER CONTROL   The room to which all video and audio signals of various productions studios are fed for distribution, broadcasting, or recording.

MASTER SHOT   Extended wide shot establishing the scene and often shot during the entire length of the sequence. Intended to be broken down in the editing process.

MASTER TAPE   The final result of an editing session.

MATCH CUT   An edit between two shots that maintain continuity to make the edit almost invisible.

MATTE (traveling or stationary)   An opaque covering over the lens of a camera which allows for reexposure of the covered area later in film or in video to create an irregular shape for a special effect.

MATTE SHOTS   Combinations of different images in the same frame.

MECHANICAL INTERLOCK   A physical connection between different machines or portions of machines that causes them to run at the same speed when driven by the same motor.

MEDIUM CLOSE-UP (MCU)   Relative average framing for a shot. Often framed from the waist up.

MEDIUM SHOT (MS)   Wider than an MCU, often framed head to toe.

MELODY   A series of musical notes or tones that create a structured unit or order.

METAMORPHOSIS An animation technique in which one figure is gradually transformed into another figure of an entirely different shape.

METRONOME   A device used by musicians to provide a regular beat or rhythm.

M FORMAT (M-II, Recam)   Panasonic's professional ½-inch format. Originally sold by RCA as Recam, then upgraded to M-1. No longer manufactured.

MICROPHONE   A transducer that converts sound waves into comparable fluctuations of electrical current.

MICROPHONE BOOM   A long pole to which a microphone is attached so that it can be held just outside of the camera frame.

MICROWAVE   (1) High-frequency carrier for both audio and video signals. Operates only a line-of-sight path. (2) Oven for heating the crew's lunch.

MIC LEVELS   The lower electrical signal strength of a microphone output as compared to line levels of amplified signals.

MIDI (Musical Instrument Digital Interface)   A system designed to allow musicians to connect musical instruments in a digital format.

MIL   A unit of measurement (.001) used to designate tape thickness.

MINIATURE   A three-dimensional replica of a set or prop to be used as a substitute for a full-sized construction. Also called *model*.

MINIDISC   A small audio CD format designed for portable digital audio recordings.

MINI-PLUG   (118-inch) Audio connector designed for small equipment. Scaled-down version of ¼-inch phone plug.

MIRROR SHOTS   (1) The use of two mirrors to make a large periscope that can be used for overhead video camera shots. (2) A partial mirror can be used to combine two film scenes in one take.

MIRROR SHUTTER   A reflective coating on the front of a shutter that intermittently deflects all the light to a reflex viewfinder as the film is advanced in the camera.

MIXER   A piece of electronic equipment designed to combine several signals. Usually refers to an audio board or console.

MIX LOG SHEET (audio cue sheet)   A list of all volume changes, transitions, and equalization changes for a sound mix.

MMDS (Multichannel Multipoint Distribution Service)   A video delivery system using line-of-sight microwave with four or more channels operated by a single company. Often called "wireless cable"; similar to *ITFS*.

MODEL   See *miniature*.

MODELING   Highlighting the appearance of a textured surface through the use of shadows.

MODERNISM   A work of art using factors other than realism to express its concept.

MODULATOR   An electronic component designed to impress one signal on another, usually of a higher frequency.

MODULE   A small device designed to provide a single specialized function.

MODULOMETER (PPM)   A peak reading voltmeter designed to monitor levels of audio signals.

MOIRE EFFECT   A distracting vibration of visual images caused by the interaction of narrow stripes in the design of the material being recorded.

MONAURAL (Mono)   A single track of audio.

MONITOR   (1) To listen to or watch audio or videotapes or off-air programs. (2) Device used to view video signals. Much like a TV receiver, but it is usually much higher quality and generally does not have an *RF* section for off-the-air monitoring.

MONOCHROME   Black-and-white film or video.

MOTIF   Imagery that is repeatedly used in an artistic work to add depth and symbolism.

MOTION CAPTURE (MoCap)   An animation technique used to duplicate movement by fastening electronic or magnetic sensors throughout a body and following them to a computer for recording and manipulation.

MOTION CONTROL   A computer-controlled system for camera or object movements to match other exposures of background scenes for keying in video or double exposure in film.

MORGUE   Library, reference files, or storage for used scripts, tapes, maps, and other reference material.

MOS   (1) Metal oxide semiconductor. A type of camera chip that replaces the camera tube. (2) A film term indicating that a shot was recorded silent, or as the early German film directors said, "Mit out sound."

MOVIEOLA   The traditional mechanical film editor.

MPEG (Motion Picture Experts Group)   A series of video compression standards.

MP3   A highly compressed audio system based on the third level of MPEG. Used to download music from the World Wide Web.

MSO (Multiple System Operator)   A cable company that owns and operates more than one cable system.

MULTICAMERA PRODUCTION (multiple-camera production)   The use of several film or video cameras to record the same action simultaneously from different viewpoints.

MULTIMEDIA   A program combining text, graphics, sound, animation, video, or a combination of any three media.

MULTIPLANE ANIMATION Animation shot on an animation stand that holds several levels of *cels* separated so they may be lit and moved individually. Invented by Ub Iwerks for Walt Disney.

MULTITRACK An audiotape recording with from two to 64 separate tracks recorded on the same audiotape.

MUNSELL COLOR WHEEL A three-dimensional model of colors that shows different color samples by hue, brightness, and saturation.

MUSIC LIBRARIES Collections of musical recordings that require a minimum royalty payment for use on media productions.

NABET (National Association of Broadcast Employees and Technicians) A union that represents crew members and in major markets everyone at an operation.

NARRATE To tell a story or provide a commentary on events.

NARRATION A verbal commentary on the events taking place within a fiction or nonfiction media production.

NARRATIVE A story that is told or narrated by someone.

NARROWCASTING Aiming programs at a specific non-mass market.

NATIONAL ASSOCIATION OF BROADCASTERS (NAB) Professional organization of radio and television broadcasters.

NAT SOUND (natural sound) Ambient sound that exists on location and is recorded as a story happens. Often used as background for a *voiceover*. Sometimes called *wild sound*.

NATURALISTIC LIGHTING Lighting that appears to come from known or presumed actual sources in the setting or location.

NEEDLE-DROP FEES The payment of music or sound effects fees according to the number of times the cut is used rather than a yearly fee.

NEGATIVE A type of film that produces a reversed brightness image when developed.

NEGATIVE/POSITIVE PROCESS A means of producing projectable film images in two steps by first exposing and developing negative film and then printing that negative film on negative stock to produce a positive print.

NET DISTRIBUTOR RENTALS The amount of money a distributor receives from theater rentals of films minus the distributor's own costs.

NETWORK A company distributing programs to stations interconnected but not owned by the network. The FCC defines a network if it distributes at least 15 hours of programming a week to at least 25 affiliates in at least 10 states. Today there are six television networks: ABC, CBS, Fox, NBC, Universal/Paramount, and Warner Bros.

NEUTRAL DENSITY A type of filter that decreases light passage without changing the color value of the light.

NEWSFILM Before small camcorders became practical in the late 1970s, all news stories were shot on 16mm film, edited, and then projected on a film chain or telecine, a projector-camera video combination used to convert film to video.

NIELSEN RATINGS Television audience information researched by the A.C. Nielsen Company, consisting of shares, ratings, and demographics.

NOISE Any undesirable additions to a signal.

NOISE REDUCTION The elimination or diminishing of audio noise by means of signal-processing devices.

NONFICTION The depiction, description, or presentation of actual, unstaged events.

NONLINEAR Editing out of sequence.

NONREFLEX A camera that has a separate viewfinder as opposed to one that allows the operator to look directly through the *objective lens*.

NONTHEATRICAL FILMS Films that are not produced for or shown in commercial theaters. Today, a direct-to-video film can gross more than a major motion picture.

NORMAL LENS A lens that presents an image perspective that approximates the vision of a monocular (single-eye) human. A midrange focal length.

NOTAN A lighting style similar to Japanese watercolors: high key, few shadows, evenly lit.

NTSC (National Television Standards Committee) (1) The organization charged with setting the television standard in the United States in the early days of television. (2) The television standard now in use in North America, much of South America, and Japan.

NTSC COLOR STANDARD The television standard first used in the United States for color TV transmission. This standard uses 525 interlaced lines scanned at the rate of 60 fields and 30 frames per second.

NVOD (Near Video-On-Demand) A pay television system providing programming when requested.

OBJECTIVE LENS The lens on a camera that is used to record the images.

OCCULT BALANCE Choosing colors by intentionally pairing unlike elements.

OFF-CAMERA MICROPHONE A microphone that is invisible to the audience.

OFF-LINE Using the lowest-quality and lowest-cost editing system suitable for a particular project.

OFF-SCREEN SOUND A sound coming from a location not viewed by the audience.

OMNIDIRECTIONAL Microphone pickup pattern that covers 360 degrees around the mic.

OMNIVISION (Also called OMNIMAX) A large film format shot on 65mm film but projected through a fisheye lens on a dome above and around the audience.

OMNISCIENT POINT OF VIEW In literature, a narrative written in the third as opposed to the first person. In media productions, a story told from a relatively objective perspective or camera viewpoint.

ON-CAMERA MICROPHONES Microphones visible to the audience.

ON-LINE Using the highest-quality and highest-cost editing system suitable for a particular project.

ON-SCREEN SOUND Sound emanating from a source clearly seen by the audience.

ONE-LIGHT PRINT A quickly made film copy of the original film processed without adjustments to give the director and director of photography an accurate picture of what was shot and recorded on the film, shot-by-shot.

OPAQUE BLACK LEADER Film leader that is coated with an opaque layer so that light cannot pass through it. Used in *conforming* process to separate shots on the "A" and "B" rolls and as leader before and after the beginning and ending of the film.

OPEN MIC The instruction from the director to the audio operator to bring the *pot* or sounds faded up on a particular mic.

OPERATING SYSTEM Software responsible for controlling the hardware in use.

OPERATOR Person whose main responsibility is to operate equipment; as contrasted with technicians, whose main responsibility it is to install, repair, and maintain equipment; and engineers, whose main responsibility it is to research, design, and construct equipment.

OPTICAL DISK A laser recording medium for digital, video, and/or audio information. A vast amount of data may be stored in a relatively small space and can be designed to record once or record many times. CDs and videodiscs are examples of optical discs.

OPTICAL PRINTER A device consisting of a projector aimed at a camera that can be used to create special effects.

OPTICAL SOUND Sound recorded optically on the edge of film where variations in intensity are recorded as variations in density or the width of the film exposure.

OPTICS/OPTICAL Having to do with lenses or other light-carrying components of a video or film system.

OSCILLOSCOPE Test equipment used to visualize a time factor system, such as a video signal. Shows a technician what the picture looks like electronically. Also may be used to analyze audio or other signals. See also *waveform monitor*.

OUT-POINT The end point of an edit.

OUTPUT Signal leaving a system or electrical unit.

OUT-TAKES Recorded shots that are discarded entirely and do not appear in the final edited version of a media production.

OVEREXPOSURE Excessive exposure of film or video camera to light so that the quality of the image suffers and appears as washed out or overly bright.

OVERHEAD SHOT A shot from a camera that is placed directly overhead. This shot can be duplicated with the use of two mirrors. See *mirror shot*.

OVERMODULATION Adjusting the sound intensity so high that it exceeds the limits of the equipment and causes distortion.

OVERSCHEDULE A production that has exceeded the time limitations specified in the production schedule.

OVER-THE-SHOULDER SHOT (OS) A shot in which the camera is placed behind and to one side of a subject so that the shoulder of that subject is visible in the foreground and the face or body of another subject is in the background.

OWNED AND OPERATED A station actually owned by one of the networks. See *affiliate*.

OXIDE One type of metal coating used on magnetic tape and discs.

PACE A subjective impression of the speed of sounds or visuals.

PACKAGE A marketable combination of production elements such as well-known stars, director, writers, and creative staff.

PACKET A unit of information transmitted as a whole unit between devices.

PAL (Phase Alternating Line) A color television standard used in England and many other countries around the world. It is based on a 625 interlaced line, 25 frames per second system. It is not compatible with the U.S. NTSC standard.

PALETTE A variety of colors.

PAN Horizontal movement of camera, short for panorama.

PANHEAD Mechanism designed to firmly hold a camera on top of a tripod, pedestal, or boom while allowing for smooth, easily controlled movement of the camera horizontally (pan) and vertically (tilt). May be mechanical, fluid, geared, or counterbalanced.

PANSCAN A system of converting widescreen motion pictures to the 3 × 4 television scan area. A print is made by panning across the film, centering on the most important areas of characters.

PARABOLIC MIC A focused, concave, reflective, bowl-shaped surface with a mic mounted at the point of focus. Used to pick up specific sounds at a distance. Commonly used during sporting events.

PARALLAX   The discrepancy between the framed image in an objective lens and the image in a separate viewfinder in a nonreflex camera.

PARALLEL SOUND   Sounds that compliment or have a supporting effect on the visual.

PATCH BAY   A panel with wires connected to equipment in a control room to allow for flexibility in distributing signals to and from amplifiers and mixers. Also called patch board or patch panel.

PATCH CORD   A short cable with plugs on each end designed to interconnect equipment wired to a patch bay.

PAUSE   A mode or function on a recorder or player that holds the medium in position without stopping, but preventing an advance.

PAY CABLE   Cable programming channels that must be paid above the amount for the basic service.

PCM (Pulse Code Modulation)   A digital conversion system.

PEAK PROGRAM METER (PPM)   A standard device for measuring sound intensity of loudness. It measures the peaks rather than the average as is measured in a *VU meter*.

PEDESTAL   (1) Electronic calibration between blanking and black level. (2) Hydraulic, compressed air, or counterbalanced studio camera mount. Designed to permit the camera to be raised straight up or down effortlessly and smoothly.

PENCIL TEST   A film shot of simple sketches of an animation production to check timing and other aspects of the production.

PERAMBULATOR   A large, wheeled, platform-mounted boom that a mic boom operator rides. Capable of swinging a mic over a large area.

PERFORATIONS (perfs)   The sprocket holes at the sides of film or fullcoat. *Single-perf* means sprockets on one side only; *double-perf* means sprockets on both sides.

PERSISTENCE OF VISION   A physical and psychological phenomenon of sight that allows a series of still images to create the illusion of motion. One of the phenomena based upon which the images in animation, motion pictures, and television appear to move.

PERSPECTIVE   The illusion of spatial distance in a two-dimensional medium.

PHANTOM POWER   48 volts required by condenser mic preamplifiers located in the mic. If the mic does not carry its own battery power, may be supplied through the mic line by the mixer or recorder.

PHASE   The relationship of two signals differing in time, but on a common path.

PHASING PROBLEMS   The cancellation of certain frequencies caused by placing microphones too close together when they are picking up the same source.

PHI PHENOMENON   The illusion of apparent motion from rapidly flashing stationary lights and objects used in the animation process.

PHOTOELECTRIC CELL   The transducer in a light meter of a film projector that converts light energy into an electronic signal.

PHOTOFLOOD   Lamp with self-contained reflectors that do not require a lighting instrument.

PHOTOGRAPHER   Originally, a person taking still photographs. In some markets the term was applied to news cinematographers, and even today it sometimes is applied to *videographers*.

PHOTOGRAPHIC FILM   A light-sensitive material, consisting of silver halide particles attached to a flexible support base that yields visual images after proper exposure to light and chemical development.

PHOSPHORS   Light-emitting optoelectronic semiconductors inside a video picture tube.

PICA   Measurement of type horizontal size. 1 Pica = ⅙ inch.

PICKUP PATTERN   The area or space surrounding a microphone within which the sensitivity to sound is the greatest.

PICKUP TUBE   A device that converts light entering a video camera through the lens into electrical signals. Now replaced by solid-state chips.

PICT   A visual RGB format designed by Apple.

PILOTONE   A particular type of sync signal used in synchronous film recording.

PISTOL GRIP   A handheld camera mount.

PITCH   The perception of or human response to different sound frequencies.

PIXEL   A single element of a computer or television picture. Picture resolution may be measured by the number of pixels in a set space.

PIXILLATION   A system of single-frame animation that records only a portion of a live action, creating a floating or jerky movement of subjects.

PLASMA DISPLAY PANEL (PDP)   A flat-screen monitor based on a gas-filled panel.

PLASTIC ANIMATION   Animating three-dimensional objects.

PLATES   The platters on a flatbed film-editing machine that feed and take up film and tracks.

PLAYBACK   The mode or machine operational setting for viewing or listening to a pre-recorded signal.

PLAYBACK HEAD   A magnetic device capable of transforming magnetic changes on a prerecorded tape into electronic signals.

PLOSIVE SOUNDS   Sounds made by the human voice that tend to "pop" a microphone. Sounds beginning with the letters "p" and "b," among others.

PLOT   A scale drawing of the location of a shoot.

PLUG A mechanical connector fastened to the end of a cable. Designed to mate with a matching jack mounted on equipment or on the wall.

PLUMBICON A type of video pickup tube; one of the last developed before being replaced by chips.

POINT OF ATTACK The beginning of a drama that usually generates interest and excitement.

POINT OF VIEW (POV) A camera angle giving the impression of the view of someone in the scene.

POINTSIZE A measurement of the height of type fonts.

POLARIZER FILTER A glass or plastic filter that reduces glare when properly adjusted over a camera lens and/or lights on an animation or copy stand.

POOL FEED A common video or audio feed to supply more than one operation. Often set up for such restricted coverage as presidential appearances or in times of extreme emergencies or tragedies.

PORTABLE LIGHTING KIT A self-contained lighting unit for field production consisting of several lighting fixtures, stands, filters, accessories, and cables.

POSITIVE A type of visual image that reproduces the brightness of the original scene when it is processed or played back.

POSTERIZED Changing a graphic by using a few colors to give the appearance of a printed poster.

POSTMODERNISM Art that depends on the participation of the audience, if not physically, at least in a close mental form.

POSTPRODUCTION The final stage of the production process, during which recorded images and sounds are edited and the production is completed for distribution.

POT Short for potentiometer, a variable resistor used to change the voltage of an audio or video signal.

POWER AMPLIFIER An electronic circuit designed to amplify signals to a high enough level to power speakers or transmit signals over long lines.

POWER PACK Batteries used to power a piece of portable equipment.

PPM See *modulometer*.

PPV (Pay Per View) A cable service paid for on an individual program basis rather than on a monthly basis.

PREAMPLIFIER (preamp) Electronic circuit designed to amplify weak signal to a usable level without introducing noise or distortion.

PREBLACK The process of recording either a black video signal or color bars with a control track on videotape stock in preparation for insert editing that requires a control track prerecorded on the tape.

PREMISE A concise statement that sums up the story or subject matter.

PREPRODUCTION The preparatory stage of production planning prior to actually recording sounds and visual images.

PREROLL The amount of time needed in advance of making an edit or starting a film, audio, or videotape for playback or editing.

PRESSURE PLATE The surface inside a film camera that keeps the film flat in the gate at the *aperture*.

PREVIEW To view an image source without sending it to its assigned destination.

PRIMARY COLORS The basic colors used in lighting and filters: red, green, and blue.

PRIME LENS A fixed focal-length lens.

PRIME TIME In general practice, the television broadcast evening hours programmed by the networks between 8:00 P.M. and 11:00 P.M. for the east and west coasts, and 6:00 P.M. and 10:00 P.M. for the midwest and mountain states.

PRINCIPAL CHARACTERS Friends and foils of the central character(s).

PRINTING The process of making a copy of a film.

PRINT-THROUGH A signal that has bled through from one layer of recording tape to the next.

PRINT-THROUGH EDGE NUMBERS Numbers from the original film that are printed through to the *workprint* by using an edge light during the printing process.

PRISM A glass or plastic block shaped to transmit or reflect light into different paths.

PRODUCER Person in charge of a specific program.

PRODUCTION The stage of the production process during which production materials and equipment are set up and sounds and images are actually recorded.

PRODUCTION DESIGN The coordination of scenic design and other artistic aspects of production, such as lighting.

PRODUCTION DESIGNER The crew person who heads the production design team.

PRODUCTION MANAGER In feature-film production, the person who breaks down the script into its component parts for budgeting and scheduling and who supervises the allocation and use of studio and location facilities.

PROGRAM (1) To set a function of a *pot*, *fader*, or other control. (2) A complete production package ready to be broadcast or distributed.

PROGRESSIVE SCAN A monitor or camera scan system that creates a complete frame with one continuous sweep top-to-bottom and left-to-right. Used in *PAL*, *SECAM*, and computer systems. Proposed as one of HDTV's systems.

PROJECT WINDOW In an NLE monitor, shows individual clips in a pre-determined order.

PROMPTER Device or person that provides the talent with the copy as they work on camera. Copy can be handheld beside the camera, or a signal fed to a monitor mounted with a mirror to project the copy in front of the camera lens so the anchor, for example, can look directly into the camera. This signal may be coming from a black-and-white camera shooting pages of the script or from a signal fed directly from a computer.

PROPERTIES (props)   Functional set furnishings that play a part in a video or film program.

PROPOSAL   A concise summary of a project intended as a sales tool to accurately describe a production and to sell a sponsor on funding.

PROSTHETIC MAKEUP   Makeup and devices designed to transform the appearance of a performer's face or body through temporary "plastic surgery."

PROSUMER   A category of producer and equipment that falls below that of a professional but at a higher level than a consumer.

PROXIMITY EFFECT   A change in the audio pickup by moving the source too close to the microphone; can be used to give the appearance of lowering the human voice.

PSA (Public Service Announcement)   A noncommercial radio or TV spot.

PUBLIC ADDRESS (PA)   Sound-reinforcing system designed to feed sound to an audience assembled in a large room or other space.

PULLDOWN CLAW   The square pin that grabs each sprocket hole of a film in the gate to advance a single frame in the aperture for exposure.

PULLING FOCUS   Adjusting camera focus while shooting.

PURE TONE   A single sound frequency.

QUADRAPLEX (quad)   First practical professional videotape format. Used 2-inch tape pulled across four heads to achieve a high-quality signal. No longer manufactured.

QUARTER-INCH PLUG (Phone)   Audio connector used for many years for high-impedance signals. Still used in some consumer equipment and patch panels.

QUARTZ LIGHT   A Tungsten light source consisting of a Tungsten filament, a quartz housing, and halogen gas.

RADIAL BALANCE   A method of choosing colors by examining their relationship on a color wheel.

RADIO MICROPHONE (wireless mic)   A microphone connected to a small FM transmitter worn by the performer broadcasting a short distance to a receiver connected to the audio mixer. This allows the performer to operate with trailing wires.

RAID (Redundant Array of Independent Disks)   A server made up of a series of interconnected memory storage disks.

RAM (Random Access Memory)   Semiconductor-based memory within a computer or other digital device. Usually deleted when power is removed.

RASTER   The complete sequence of lines that make up the field of lines creating a video picture.

RATING   Estimated percentage of TV households tuned to the same program at any one time.

RAW STOCK   Unexposed film, video, or audiotape that has not been recorded.

RCA   The American corporation that promoted the NTSC video system, the developer of many early television inventions, and the original owner of NBC radio and television.

RCA PLUG (phono)   Audio and video connector designed originally for use only with the RCA 45-rpm record player. Now used as a consumer audio and video connector. Some professional equipment uses this plug for line-level audio. Not to be confused with the phone plug (¼-inch).

REACTION SHOT   Close-up of a character's reaction to events.

READABILITY   The ease of comprehending visual material accurately.

REALISTIC LIGHTING   Lighting that conforms to the audience's conventional expectations of how a scene should appear in "real" life.

REALISTIC SETS   Sets designed to represent a specific or general type of place with which an audience is presumed to have some familiarity, usually filled with "naturalistic" details.

REAR PROJECTION   A projection of a slide or film on a screen behind the performers on a set.

RECEIVER   A television or radio set capable of decoding a broadcast signal.

RECORDING HEAD   A magnetic device that transforms electronic signals into changes in a magnetic field so that sounds and pictures can be recorded on tape.

RECORD MODE   A machine operational setting for recording pictures and/or sound.

REDUCTION   A transfer of film to a smaller format on an optical printer.

REEL-TO-REEL RECORDER   A device that can record and/or play back sounds on an open reel of tape.

REFERENCE WHITE   A white card or large white object in the flame that can be used for white balancing or the proper color adjustment of a video camera.

REFLECTED LIGHT   Illumination entering a lens reflected from an object. Measured with a reflected light meter pointing at the object from the camera.

REFLECTED READING   A light-meter reading of the intensity of light reflected from the subject and/or background.

REFLECTION   A bouncing back of light from an object.

REFLECTOR   A flat or curved surface that light can be bounced off to create indirect light on a set or location.

REFLEX   A type of camera that allows the operator to look directly through the objective lens.

REFRACTION   Light changing direction as it passes through transparent surfaces.

REGISTRATION   The alignment of either electronic or physical components of a system; especially important in tube cameras.

REGISTRATION PIN   A device on some film cameras that holds the film steady while a frame is being exposed to light at the aperture.

RELEASE   (1) Legal document allowing the videographer to use the image and/or voice of a subject. (2) Public relations copy.

RELEASE PRINT   A final copy of a film with sound track that is distributed and exhibited.

REMOTE NONLINEAR EDITOR (RNLE)   An editing station set up in a remote vehicle or suitcase to be used in the field.

REMOTE PRODUCTION   A video production performed outside of the studio.

REMOTE VAN   A large video production semi-trailer containing a virtual studio control room and all of the equipment normally in a video studio for high-level coverage of sports and entertainment events.

REPORTER   A newsperson who is responsible for researching, gathering, and writing news stories. May or may not appear on camera or in the studio.

RESEARCH   The process of investigating and uncovering sources of information about prospective video or film audiences and/or the facts necessary to write a script.

RESIDUALS   Payment made to performers for repeat uses of programs and commercials in which they appear.

RESOLUTION   (1) Ability of a system to reproduce fine detail. In video there are limits imposed by the *NTSC* video system. (2) Overcoming the central conflict in a drama and fulfilling the goals and motivations that have stimulated the dramatic action.

RESPONSE CURVE   A graph of the sensitivity of a piece of audio equipment to different frequencies.

REVERBERATION   The delay between direct and indirect sounds.

REVERBERATION UNIT   A signal-processing device that can create sound reverberation or echo.

REVERSAL PROCESS   A means of producing projectable film images in a single step by using a type of film stock and development process that produces positive images from a single exposure and development.

REVERSE-ANGLE SHOT   A shot in which the camera faces in exactly the opposite direction from that in which it faced in the previous shot.

REWINDS   Rotating spindles on a film-editing bench used to advance and rewind the film.

RF (Radio Frequency)   (1) Those frequencies above the aural frequencies. (2) A type of plug attached to a cable designed to carry a modulated signal.

RHYTHM   The beat or tempo of music or editing that affects the perception of speed or pace.

RIBBON MIC   A transducer using a thin gold or silver corrugated ribbon suspended between the poles of a magnet to create an electrical output.

RIGHT-TO-WORK LAWS   State statutes prohibiting unions from enforcing closed shops or requiring union membership of all employees covered in a contract.

RISERS   Hollow rectangular boxes or platforms to be placed on the studio floor to raise a portion of the set.

RITTER FAN   A mechanical device used to create snow or rain scenes.

ROSTRUM   A movable table with an animation stand on which artwork is placed for precise framing and movement from one *cel* to another.

ROTOSCOPE   A means of producing lifelike animation by filming a subject moving and then projecting each frame under a transparent drawing board and tracing the subject's position.

ROUGH-CUT   The initial selection and ordering of shots and scenes in a production.

ROYALTY FEES   Money paid to composers, authors, and performers for the use of copyrighted materials.

RUB-ON LETTERS   Individual letters that can be transferred to any flat surface to make titles by rubbing on the plastic sheet holding the letters.

RUNDOWN SHEET   A basic outline of a program that simply indicates the time and order of specific segments. See *format*.

RUNNING TIME   Actual program length or duration of a program.

SAFE ACTION AREA   The approximate 90% of the television scanned area that can be reproduced on most home television receivers. Compare this to *critical* and *essential areas*.

SAG (Screen Actors Guild)   The union that represents most film performers.

SAMPLING   Process of taking periodic measurements of a signal.

SANDBAG   A bag filled with sand used to steady lamp stands or other set pieces.

SATELLITE   Geostationary orbiting space platform with transponders to pick up signals from the earth and retransmit the signals back down to earth in a pattern, called a footprint, that covers a large area of the earth.

SATURATION   Intensity of a signal, either audio or video, but especially used as the third of three characteristics of a color video signal. See *hue* and *brightness*.

SCA (Subsidiary Communication Authorization) FCC permission for a company to use subcarriers on existing channels for audio or data transmission.

SCALE The apparent size of objects within the frame.

SCAN LINE A horizontal line of *phosphors* in a television receiver or video monitor, or optoelectronic semiconductors in a pickup tube.

SCANNING AREA The full field of view picked up by the video camera pickup tube.

SCENE A series of related shots, usually in the same time and location.

SCENE SCRIPT A full script without individual shots indicated.

SCENIC ARTISTS Craftspeople who compose detailed sketches, drawings, and set layouts.

SCENIC DESIGN Overall artistic control and coordination of sets, props, costumes, and makeup.

SCENIC DESIGNER In video and film productions, the person who supervises the overall production design, including props and costumes.

SCOOP A lighting instrument with an open bowl reflector that produces soft *floodlight*.

SCORE Music composed for a specific film or videotape.

SCOUTING REPORT A complete report of the facilities available and the equipment needed for a location production at a specific site. See *site survey*.

SCRAMBLING Modifying a video signal so it cannot be received without the proper decoder. Pay cable channels are scrambled.

SCREEN A nondiffusion *scrim* or what films are projected on.

SCREEN DIRECTIONALITY The left-to-right or right-to-left movement and placement of objects in successive two-dimensional images or shots.

SCRIM A metallic or fabric filter placed over a lighting instrument to diffuse and soften the light.

SCRIPT Complete manuscript of all audio copy and visual instructions of a program, whether it is a film, audio, video, or multimedia production.

SCRIPT BREAKDOWN Reorganizing the script in terms of specific settings so that production can be scheduled and an accurate estimate of the budget can be made, in terms of equipment and personnel needs at each setting and on each scheduled day of shooting.

SCRIPT CONTINUITY The dictates of the script, in terms of temporal and spatial details, that must be maintained during production.

SCRIPT OUTLINE A semi-scripted format in which only a portion of videotape or live television program, such as the opening and closing segments, is fully scripted, if other elements are to be ad-libbed. See *format* and *rundown sheet*.

SCRIPT SUPERVISOR The person who maintains continuity in performer actions and prop placements from shot to shot and ensures that every scene in the script has been recorded.

SCRIPTWRITING The process of creating a written outline for a videotape, live television program, audio production, or film.

SEARCH FUNCTION A function on a videotape recorder that allows a specific point on the videotape to be found by moving the tape very slowly.

SEARCH-AND-CUE FUNCTION A machine operational setting that allows a playback machine to search for specific cues on a prerecorded tape.

SDTV (Standard-Definition Television) 525- or 625-line digital television.

SECAM (Sequential Couleur Avec Memoire) The color television system developed by the French and in use around the world in many countries.

SEG (Screen Extras Guild) The union that represents extras, or performers who do not speak on camera or have specific actions to perform.

SEG (Special Effects Generator) A video switcher capable of creating effects as transitions.

SEGMENT A portion of a program or spot.

SEGUE The immediate replacement of one sound source with another.

SELECTIVE FOCUS Using depth of field to direct the viewer's attention to certain areas of the scene by varying those elements in and out of focus.

SELF-BLIMPED A film camera that is completely sound insulated for synchronous sound recording. See *blimp*.

SEL SYNC An internal means of synchronization within an audiotape, which can be used to record consecutive sound tracks in synchronization with each other.

SEMI-SCRIPTED A partial description or outline of a videotape, live television program, audio production, or film.

SEPARATION LIGHT A general lighting term that includes backlights and kickers, which both help to separate foreground subjects and backgrounds.

SEQUENCE Individual shots edited into scenes and individual scenes edited together to make a story.

SERIF Fine lines on the bottom and top of letters of some fonts. Serifs do not show well on scanned media.

SERVO CAPSTAN A *capstan* with an accurate motor that varies the speed of the playback to maintain proper synchronization between a video recorder and playback machine.

SET DESIGNER In large-scale productions, the person who does the actual drawing of set floor plans, elevations, and layouts and supervises the construction of sets.

SET FURNISHINGS Furniture and props that fill out a set.

SETTINGS   Specific exterior and interior places and locations specified in a script.

SET UP   Assemble equipment and people in preparation for rehearsing a production.

SET-UP   Same as *pedestal* and *black level*; electronic calibration between blanking and black level.

SHADING   Adjusting the brightness level, light sensitivity, and color of a video camera.

SHADOW MASK   A series of windows or aperture deflectors inside a television picture tube that prevents electrons from each gun from striking the wrong color light-emitting *phosphors*.

SHARE   Estimated percentage of *HUTs* watching a specific program at one time.

SHARPNESS   A rating of the edge clarity and focus of images reproduced in video or film production.

SHOCK-MOUNTED MICROPHONE   A microphone designed to minimize all vibrations and noise except those inherent in sound waves.

SHOOTING RATIO   The ratio of material recorded during production to that which is actually used in the final edited version.

SHOOTING SCRIPT   A *script* complete in all details, including specific shot descriptions.

SHOT   (1) One continuous roll of the recorder or camera. (2) The smallest unit of a *script*.

SHOTGUN   Ultra-unidirectional microphone designed to pick up sound at a distance by excluding unwanted sound from the sides of the mic.

SHOT SHEET   A listing of all *shots* in the order they are to be made, regardless of their order in the *script*.

SHOULDER HARNESS   A body brace used as a camera mount.

SHUTTER   An opaque device in a film camera that rapidly opens and closes to expose the film to light.

SHUTTLE   Movement of videotape back and forth while searching for edit points. Usually done at speeds faster or slower than real time.

SIGNAL LEVEL   The signal strength of the electrical current from recording and playback equipment.

SIGNAL PROCESSING   Manipulation of the electrical sound signal.

SIGNAL-TO-NOISE RATIO (S/N Ratio)   The mathematical ratio between the noise level in a signal and the program level. The higher the ratio, the better the signal.

SINGLE-CAMERA PRODUCTION   The use of a single video or film camera to record a videotape or film in segments.

SINGLE-PERF   Film with sprocket holes on only one side or edge.

SINGLE-SYSTEM RECORDING   Recording a synchronous sound track within the camera on the same roll of film as the pictures.

SITE SURVEY   A detailed listing of all the information needed to shoot on location at a certain site.

SKEW   Tension adjustment during videotape *playback*. Visible as a "bending" at the extreme top or bottom of the picture.

SKYLIGHT   Indirect sunlight that has a higher color temperature than direct sunlight.

SLANT TRACK   See *helical* scan.

SLATE   Several frames identifying the *shot*, tape, or film reel number, or other logging information. Usually recorded at the beginning of the tape.

SLIDES   Still photographic transparencies that can be projected.

SLIDING TRACK   An overhead light grid to which lighting instruments are attached so that they slide into position along the track.

SLIPPING   Moving a track (usually audio) forward or backward in relationship to the picture or visual.

SLO-MO DISC RECORDER   A video recorder that records live-action images on a rotating disc so that they can be played back in slow motion, such as for game analysis in a sports broadcast.

SLOW MOTION   Recording images at a faster speed than the normal *playback* speed.

SLUG   An identifying name for a news story; usually only one or two words.

SMATV (Satellite Master Antenna Television)   A "private" cable system. Often used by apartment or hotel complexes to serve all of their units.

SMEARING   See *comet-tailing*.

SMPTE (Society of Motion Picture and Television Engineers)   Professional society of members predominantly interested in the technical side of motion pictures, radio, and television. The official organization for setting technical standards for film and video in this country.

SMPTE TIME CODE   A binary code accurately setting hours, minutes, seconds, and frames used to synchronize audio, video, and film media.

SOFT CUT   A very rapid dissolve.

SOFT LIGHT   Indirect, diffused light that minimizes shadows.

SOFTLIGHTS   Large light fixtures that emit a well-diffused light over a broad area.

SOFTWARE   Material recorded on audio, video, and/or computer media. Contrast with *hardware*.

SOFT WIPE   A slight *superimposition* at the point where two images intersect during a *wipe* from one to the other.

SOLARIZATION   A technique that drains the normal color from a visual image and replaces it with artificially controlled colors.

SOP (standard operating procedure)   Predetermined methods of completing a task. Often set by corporate or upper-management policy.

SOUND AMPLITUDE The intensity and height of a sound pressure wave.

SOUND EFFECTS Sounds that are matched to their supposed visual sources during postproduction editing.

SOUND FIDELITY The accuracy or illusion of reality inherent in a sound recording.

SOUND FREQUENCY The rapidity with which air molecules move back and forth in direct relation to the vibrations of the sound source.

SOUND INTENSITY The amplitude of a sound wave, which is perceived as a specific loudness level.

SOUND-ON-FILM (SOF) See *single-system recording.*

SOUND PERSPECTIVE An enhanced perception of distance achieved through the use of different volume levels for near and far sounds.

SOUND PRESSURE WAVE The compression and expansion of air molecules in response to the vibrations of a sound source.

SOUND TEST A test setting of the sound level prior to actual recording.

SOUND UP AND UNDER Instruction to cut the sound in at its proper level and then fade it down to a lower level, where it is still audible but less prominent.

SOUND VELOCITY The speed of a sound pressure wave.

SOURCE MUSIC Music that comes from a source within the actual scene portrayed on screen.

SPACERS Small wheels used to fill the gaps between take-up reels on a film-editing bench so that their spacing matches the spacing of the individual hubs or wheels in a gang synchronizer.

SPATIAL DISTORTION An aural imbalance during stereophonic *playback* or recording that results from a faulty positioning of the sound source.

SPECIAL EFFECTS GENERATOR Electronic device usually installed in the video switcher, which is used to produce *wipes*, *split screens*, and *inserts*.

SPEED OF ACTION The speed of the movement of objects within the frame.

SPIDER An adjustable device into which the spurs of a tripod are placed on a flat, hard surface.

SPLICING Physically cutting and cementing magnetic tape or film while editing.

SPLIT An agreed-upon division of box office receipts between exhibitors and film distributors.

SPLIT-BEAM A reflex viewing system in which mirrors between the lens and the viewfinder eyepiece continuously deflect about 18% to 20% of the light.

SPLIT EDIT An edit made in which the audio and video are assigned separate in- or out-points so that the signals do not start or stop at the same point in time.

SPLIT-PAGE SCRIPT A script that has the visual specification on the left side of the page and the corresponding audio specifications on the right side.

SPLIT SCREEN A special video effect in which one image occupies a portion of the frame and another image occupies the remaining portion.

SPLITTER BOX Device used to feed an input signal to more than one output. Commonly used at news conferences to avoid a jumble of microphones by splitting the feed from one mic to all those covering the event.

SPOT EFFECTS Specific sound effects created expressly for a videotape, live television program, or film in a sound studio.

SPOTLIGHTS Lighting instruments with lenses that sharply focus the light they emit, producing intense, harsh lighting.

SPOT METER A light meter designed to read a very small area of reflected light.

SPOT READING A light-meter reading of the intensity of the light reflected by the subject in a very narrow area as determined by the angle of acceptance of the spot meter.

SPREADER See *spider.*

SPROCKET HOLES The perforations in a piece of film that allow it to be advanced or driven through a camera or projector.

SPROCKET TEETH Metal teeth that drive a piece of film through a camera, projector, or editing device by engaging the sprocket holes.

SPUN GLASS A flexible light diffuser made out of fiberglass.

SPURS Points on the end of a tripod, which can be stuck into soft ground.

SQUASHING AND STRETCHING Animation techniques that exaggerate and caricature motions by accentuating the initial and ending movements of an action, such as running or jumping, to make them seem more active.

STAGE MANAGER The person who supervises the use of studio space, such as the setup and breaking down of sets and props on the studio floor. See *floor manager.*

STAND MICROPHONE A microphone designed to be secured to a mic stand, which can be raised or lowered to conform to the height of the speaker.

STEADICAM A servostabilizer camera mount attached to the operator's body to minimize camera vibrations when the operator moves with the camera.

STEREOPHONIC SOUND Separation of sounds coming from the right and the left during recording and playback, which preserves the directionality of sound sources.

STINGERS Short phrases of music, usually characterized by a rapidly descending scale or series of notes, used as punctuation devices.

STOP MOTION Filming or taping subjects one or two frames at a time.

STORYBOARD A series of drawings indicating each shot and accompanying audio in a production.

STORY TIME The supposed historical time of events presented in a television program or film.

STREAMING A collection of data sent in a sequential fashion through a system used to send audio, video, and other digital signals through the Internet.

STRIKE (1) A command and action to tear down sets, pack up equipment, and clear an area following a production. (2) A work stoppage action in a labor dispute.

STRINGERS Freelance reporters or video/cinematographers who are paid by the story or are retained by a news operation but who are not on full-time staff.

STRIPPING Broadcasting a TV program at the same time of day, five days a week, usually a syndicated program.

STRIP LIGHTS A series of lights connected in a straight line.

STUDIO A controlled, indoor production environment designed expressly for video, audio, or film recording.

STUDIO PRODUCTION The recording of audio, video, or film images inside a controlled production environment.

STYLIZED LIGHTING Lighting that is intended to achieve a special kind of emotional effect or abstract design through nonnaturalistic patterns of light.

STYLIZED SETS Abstract, imaginative settings that reflect an artistic style or give external form to an interior state of mind, such as a specific character's subjective state of mind.

SUBJECTIVE POINT OF VIEW A story told from the perspective of a specific character or participant in the action.

SUBJECTIVE SHOT A presentation of images supposedly dreamed, imagined, recollected, or perceived in an abnormal state of mind by a character or participant in a videotape or film.

SUBPOENA An order of the court to appear as a witness. May include an order to release sources, notes, or original and edited recordings.

SUBTITLES Titles placed in the bottom third of the video or film frame that clarify the image or present the spoken dialogue in written form.

SUBTRACTIVE COLOR The process of using color-absorbing filters to subtract specific wavelengths of light from a white light source and produce the various colors of the visible spectrum.

SUPERCARDIOID A highly directional microphone pickup pattern.

SUPERIMPOSITIONS (supers) Two or more simultaneously fed video signals, stopping a dissolve at the halfway point.

SUPERSTATION A local television station whose signal is satellite delivered to cable systems across the company. WTBS of Atlanta and WGN of Chicago are such stations.

SWEETENING The process of equalizing, setting levels, and mixing voices, music, and sound effects into a master audio recording.

SWISH PAN A rapid horizontal movement of the camera while recording. May be used as a transition device.

SWITCHER (1) In multicamera or postproduction, a device used to change video sources feeding the recording tape deck. (2) The person operating the video switcher.

SYMMETRY The degree to which composition within a camera frame is balanced.

SYNC GENERATOR An electronic device that produces various synchronizing signals necessary for the operation of the video recording system.

SYNC HEAD An additional recording head on a synchronous sound recorder, used for recording the sync signal.

SYNCHRONOUS (sync) Signals locked in proper alignment with each other; sound and picture locked together; all the various video signals in their proper relationship to each other.

SYNCHRONOUS SOUND RECORDER A device capable of recording sounds in synchronization with the images recorded by a film camera.

SYNC SIGNAL A regular wave of electrical current, which can be used as a speed reference for sound and picture synchronization.

SYNDICATED PROGRAMMING Commercial television programs and films that are distributed directly to local television stations, bypassing the major television networks.

SYNOPSIS A short paragraph that describes the basic story line of a script.

TAKES Individual shots of a single action. There may be several takes of the same shot in single-camera productions, from which one will be selected for use in the final edited version.

TAKE-UP The part of a recording device that collects the tape or film.

TALENT Anyone who appears on camera or before the microphone.

TALK-BACK SYSTEM An intercom system in a television studio, used for communication between the creative staff in the control room and the crew on the studio floor.

TALLY LIGHT A light on the top of a video camera that informs the talent and crew which of several cameras has been selected for recording or transmission at a particular time.

TAPELESS RECORDING Recording electronic signals on either optical discs or solid-state media.

TAPE SPLICER A device with a cutting blade and guide for combining different pieces of film or audiotape with transparent tape.

TECHNICAL DIRECTOR (TD) In video production, the person who operates the switcher at the commands of the director.

TELECINE An optical/electronic system of transferring film to videotape. Once called film chain.

TELECONFERENCE A live exchange of video and audio information over a long distance via satellite, microwave, or Web links.

TELEPHOTO Long focal-length lens.

TELETEXT Text and graphics broadcast along with a TV signal for especially equipped TV receivers.

TELEVISION The electronic transmission and reception of visual images of moving and stationary objects, usually with accompanying sound.

TELEVISION QUOTIENT (TV-Q) A popularity index of television performers, which is sometimes used to ensure program success and aid casting decisions.

TEMPORAL CONTINUITY A continuous flow of events without any apparent gaps in time.

TENT An opaque sheet of material suspended over a subject to diffuse and soften the light.

TEXTURE The roughness or smoothness of a surface.

THEATRICAL FILMS Films produced for commercial theaters.

THEME (1) A central concept, idea, or symbolic meaning in a story. (2) A repeated melody in a symphony or other long musical composition.

THREE-OR-FOUR POINT LIGHTING A basic lighting technique that helps create an illusion of three-dimensionality by separating the subject from the background, using *key*, *fill*, and *separation light*.

THREE-SHOT A camera setup in which three subjects appear in the same frame.

THREE-TO-ONE RULE To avoid phasing problems, two or more microphones that are used simultaneously should be placed at least three times as far apart as their subject-tomic distances.

THROUGH THE LENS (TTL) A type of light meter that measures the amount of light actually coming through the lens of a camera.

TIFF (Tagged Image File Format) A visual computer format used in print media.

TILT A vertical pivoting of a camera.

TILT SHOT A camera shot accomplished by moving the camera up and down on a swivel or tilting device.

TIMBRE See *tonality*.

TIME-BASE CORRECTOR (TBC) Electronic device used to lock together signals with dissimilar sync.

Also may be used to correct for phase, level, and pedestal errors in original recordings.

TIME CODE Time-based address recorded on videotape to allow for precise editing. *SMPTE* time code is the one most universally used at present.

TIME CODE EDITING Choice of edit points selected by using sequential code recorded on the tape.

TIME-LAPSE SEQUENCE A visual segment that has been pixilated or compressed in time.

TIMELINE (Construction Window) The monitor window in a NLE showing the chronological arrangement of shots and transitions.

TITLES Lettering recorded within the visual frame that identifies the visual images or adds text to the videotape, live television program, or film.

TITLE SEQUENCE See *credits*.

TONALITY The particular quality or unique characteristics of a musical instrument or voice.

TOPIC RESEARCH The process of gathering accurate information about a prospective program's subject matter.

TRACK A separate tape path.

TRACKING (1) Aligning playback heads on a VCR with the original pattern of video recorded on tape. (2) Movement of a camera to the left or right, usually while mounted on a set of tracks for maximum smoothness and control.

TRAGEDY A type of drama that has a serious tone and often focuses on the misfortunes and problems of life.

TRANSDUCER Any electronic device used to convert any form of energy to another form: a video camera transduces light to video; a microphone transduces sound to electronics; a speaker transduces electronics to sound.

TRANSFER A copy of a recording in which the format is changed.

TRANSFORMER Magnetic voltage or impedance-changing device.

TRANSITION DEVICES Various means of changing from one shot to another to suggest changes of time and/or place.

TRANSISTOR The original semiconductor that replaced the vacuum tube.

TRANSITION WINDOW A NLE monitor that shows transitions available for editing.

TRANSMISSION Moving signals from one to one or more points.

TRANSPONDER A satellite section that receives and retransmits a signal or series of signals on a single frequency.

TRANSVERSE TRACK See *quadruplex*.

TRAVELING MATTE A film matte that moves across the image to create special effects.

TREATMENT   A narrative description of a production. It should read more like a novel than a script since it is intended for a nonmedia person.

TREBLE   High frequencies of the audio band.

TRIANGLE   See *spider*.

TRIM IN/OUT   The process of making small adjustments in the in- and out-points of edits.

TRIMMING WINDOW   The monitor in NEL that shows two shots for creating a straight cut.

TRIPOD   Three-legged portable camera support.

TRUCKING SHOT   A shot in which the camera moves from side to side on a wheeled dolly.

T-STOP   Unit of light transmission for a lens based on actual tests of light transmission.

TUNGSTEN LIGHT   Relatively efficient gas-filled light source of approximately 32,000 degrees Kelvin temperature.

TV-Q (Television Quotient)   A method used to determine the popularity of performers and programs on television.

TVRO (Television Receive Only)   A satellite downlink system that cannot uplink a signal. Home satellite receivers are TVROs.

TYLER MOUNT   A helicopter or airplane camera mount that reduces vibration.

TWO-SHOT   A camera shot including two subjects.

UHF (Ultra-High Frequency)   (1) Frequency band for television broadcasting channels 14 through 69. (2) An older, large, threaded type of video connector.

ULTRACARDIOID   The most directional (narrowest) microphone pickup pattern available; sometimes called a *shotgun* microphone.

ULTRAVIOLET LIGHT   Invisible light that has a shorter wavelength than visible light but can nonetheless affect film and is present in outdoor shadow areas.

U-MATIC   Three-quarter-inch videotape format created by Sony in the early 1970s that revolutionized video news-gathering. Has been upgraded by a compatible U-matic SP format.

UNBALANCED MICROPHONE LINE   A mic cable consisting of a single conductor that is less well insulated than a balanced line and thus more susceptible to cable noise.

UNIDIRECTIONAL   Microphone pickup pattern from a single direction. Comes in a variety of degrees of pickup angle, from cardioid to super unidirectional (shotgun).

UNION AND GUILD CONTRACTS   Agreements regarding salaries, working conditions, and so on, made between various craft, trade, and talent unions or guilds and television, audio, and film producers.

UNSCALED LAYOUT   A bird's-eye view of the studio and set giving a rough approximation of the material that must be constructed.

UPLINK   Transmission path from an earth-based station up to a satellite. Sometimes used to describe the ground station capable of sending a satellite signal. See *downlink*.

UPRIGHT   A vertically arranged film-editing machine.

URL (Uniform Resource Locator)   The address system used to access sites on the World Wide Web.

VARIABLE FOCAL-LENGTH LENS (Zoom)   A lens that can have its focal length changed while in use.

VARIABLE SPEED MOTOR   An electric drive motor whose speed can be varied and controlled.

VECTORSCOPE   Electronic test equipment designed to show the color aspects of the video signal.

VÉRITÉ   The art of filming/recording to create realism without modifying the action.

VERTICAL BLANKING   The period of time that the television electron beam is shut off, while the beam jumps from the bottom of one field or frame to the top of another.

VERTICAL INTERVAL TIME CODE (VITC)   Time address recorded within the vertical interval blanking instead of on a separate linear track.

VERTICAL SYNC   A portion of a television signal that controls the rate of vertical scanning and blanking.

VFX (visual effects)   Also called special effects (SFX).

VHF (Very-High Frequency)   The frequency spectrum includes television channels 2 through 13.

VHS, S-VHS   JVC-developed consumer VCR system; VHS stands for Video Home System. "S" in S-VHS stands for "separate," since it is a semicompatible component recording system, rather than a composite system.

VIDEO   (1) Picture portion of an electronic visual system. (2) All-inclusive term for electronic visual reproduction systems; includes television, cablevision, corporate media, and video recording.

VIDEOCASSETTE   A self-contained set of reels with videotape.

VIDEOCASSETTE RECORDER (VCR)   A machine that can record video and audio signals on cassettes of videotape.

VIDEODISC   An optical disc loaded with video and audio material, most often motion pictures or training tapes or films.

VIDEO ENGINEER   In video production, the person who adjusts or shades the cameras for optimal recording and monitors the videotape recording equipment.

VIDEOGRAPHER   The proper term for the operator of a video camera.

VIDEO METERS   Meters on a videotape recorder that indicate the strength of the video portion of the television signal.

VIDEO NOISE   Static or unwanted light in a video image.

VIDEO SYNTHESIZER   A device that allows an artist to manipulate the analog or digital signal of a video image so that colors and shapes can be creatively altered for special effects.

VIDEOTAPE   Magnetic substance-coated, plastic-based tape used for recording video and audio signals.

VIDEOTAPE EDITING UNIT   An electronic editing system consisting of a playback *videotape recorder* (VTR) or *VCR*, a recorder, and an editing control unit.

VIDEOTAPE RECORDER (VTR)   A device that records audio and video signals on open reels of tape rather than closed cassettes.

VIDEOTEX   An interactive computer graphics database that may be accessed through a modem, cable television, or other lines of electronic communication.

VIDEO-TO-FILM TRANSFER   Copying a videotape on film; was once called kinescoping.

VIDICON   A type of video camera tube that replaced the Image Orthicon. It was lighter, smaller, and more durable and provided higher resolution.

VIEWFINDER   The miniature video monitor mounted on the camera so that the operator can see what is framed by the camera.

VISUAL   The video and picture portion of the program.

VIRTUAL EDIT   An edit location existing only in the software addresses of the edit rather than in a tangible or physical location.

VIRTUAL REALITY (VR)   Video, audio, sensory computer-controlled effects designed to create an artificial environment and/or movement.

VISUALIZATION   The creative process of transforming a script into a sequence of visual images and sounds.

VISUAL STYLE   The particular approach taken by a director to the visual presentation of events in a videotape, live television program, or film, including the selection of specific camera placements, movements, and types of shots.

VOICEOVER (VO)   Story that uses continuous visuals, accompanied by the voice of an unseen narrator.

VOLTS   An electronic measurement of the pressure available at a power source. In North America the standard is 110-120 V.

VOLUME   The measurable loudness of a sound signal.

VOLUME UNIT (VU)   Measurement of audio level. Indicates the average of the sound level, not the peak.

VU METER   The volume unit meter, which indicates the relative levels of sounds passing through a sound system.

WATTS   Measurement of power used in a piece of electrical or electronic equipment.

WAVEFORM MONITOR   An electronic measuring tool; both oscilloscopes and vector-scopes are waveform monitors.

WAVELENGTH   The distance between the crest or valleys of each successive wave of energy in light or sound.

WEDGE   Plate fastened to the bottom of a camera that allows it to be quickly mounted to a tripod equipped with a matched slot.

WGA (Writers Guild of America)   Represents writers in film and television for basic pay, working conditions, and rights.

WHITE BALANCE   Electronic matching of the camera circuits to the color temperature of the light source.

WHITE LEVEL (Gain)   Level of maximum voltage in a video signal.

WIDE ANGLE   A lens with a relatively short focal length and wide field of view.

WILD SOUND   Ambient background sound. See *nat sound*.

WIND NOISE   Unwanted sound caused by air blowing over the pickup elements of a microphone.

WINDOW DUPE   A copy of a videotape that has the *SMPTE* time code recorded so that it is visible in a "window" for viewing, for logging, or locating specific points on the tape during the editing process.

WIND SCREEN   A plastic foam covering placed over a microphone to inhibit wind noise.

WIPE   Electronic special effects transition that allows one image to be replaced by another with a moving line separating the two pictures. Stopping a wipe in midmovement creates a split screen.

WORKPRINT   An edited master recording video or film used in off-line or preliminary editing stages.

WORLD WIDE WEB (WWW)   A distribution information network consisting of Web sites accessed through individual URL addresses offering text, graphics, and sound.

WOW   An audio distortion caused by a change in speed of either the record or playback equipment.

WRATTEN   A series of filters originally designed for photography but adapted for use in cinematography and videography.

WWW (World Wide Web)   An international computer communication network created in Switzerland.

WYSIWYG (What You See Is What You Get)   A description of the comparison of what is shown on the screen and what actually is printed or recorded.

X-AXIS   The plane running horizontally to the camera.

XLR PLUG   Professional audio connector that allows for three conductors plus a shielded ground. Special types of multipin XLRs are used for headsets and battery-power connectors.

Y-AXIS The plane running vertically to the camera.

YELLOW-INK EDGE NUMBERS Edge numbers printed by a laboratory on the film, as opposed to edge numbers placed there by the film manufacturer.

Y SIGNAL See *luminance*.

Z-AXIS The plane running away or toward the camera.

ZERO START The beginning point of *SMPTE* time code on a videotape recording.

ZOOM See *variable focal-length lens*.

Index

Page numbers in *italics* indicate illustrations.

KS2 SCIENCE

Ages 9-11

Peter Riley

PaRragon

Bath · New York · Singapore · Hong Kong · Cologne · Delhi · Melbourne

Educational consultant: Ann Dicks
Illustrated by Rob Davis/www.the-art-agency.co.uk
and Tom Connell/www.the-art-agency.co.uk

First published by Parragon in 2009

Parragon
Queen Street House
4 Queen Street
Bath BA1 1HE, UK

ISBN 978-1-4075-3787-0

Printed in Malaysia

Notes to parents

The Gold Stars® Key Stage 2 series

The Gold Stars® Key Stage 2 series has been created to help your child revise and practise key skills and information learned in school. Each book is a complete companion to the Key Stage 2 curriculum and has been written by an expert team of teachers. The books will help to prepare your child for the SATS tests that they take in Year 6.

The books also support Scottish National Guidelines 5-14.

How to use this book

- Do talk about what's on the page. Let your child know that you are sharing the activities. Talking about the sections that introduce and revise essential information is particularly important. Usually children will be able to do the fill-in activities fairly independently.

- Keep work times short. Do leave a page that seems too difficult and return to it later.

- It does not matter if your child does some of the pages out of turn.

- Your child does not need to answer the questions in complete sentences.

- Check your child's answers using the answer section on pages 60-63. Give lots of praise and encouragement and remember to reward effort as well as achievement.

- Do not become anxious if your child finds any of the pages too difficult. Children learn at different rates.

Contents

Food and the body

The body needs energy. It also needs materials for growth and for keeping the organs working healthily. The body gets all this from food.

Energy-rich foods

There are four groups of energy-rich foods.

Food type		Examples
Sugar	⟶	Biscuits, cakes, sweets, fizzy drinks
Starch	⟶	Bread, pasta, potatoes, rice
Fats	⟶	Butter, cheese, milk, sausages
Oils	⟶	Nuts , fried food, oily fish

Foods for growth and repair

The foods that provide materials for growth (and for repairing cuts and bruises) are meat, fish, eggs, milk, cheese, peas, beans and lentils.

Foods for health

The body also needs nutrients to keep all its organs working well. These are vitamins and minerals. They are found mainly in fruit and vegetables, but also in milk and bread.

DEFINITION

organ A part of the body that performs a particular task in keeping the body alive. For example, the stomach is an organ that helps the body to digest food.

A Make a list of everything you eat in a day. Next to each one write down what the body uses it for — energy, growth or health.

6

Diet and health

Learning objective: To understand that diets can affect health.

A diet must contain a wide range of foods to provide the body with all the energy and materials that it needs. Some diets are unhealthy because they have too much fat and sugar in them.

The body and energy

The body uses most of the energy in food for moving, but it also stores some as fat to keep the body warm. If a diet contains more energy than the body needs, the body stores this extra energy as extra fat. Too much fat can make the body unhealthy.

Making changes

A high-energy diet contains large amounts of sugary and fatty foods. It is easy to change the amount of energy in a diet by changing foods. Sugary snacks like cakes can be swapped for fruit, celery, tomatoes or raw carrot. Fizzy drinks can be replaced with semi-skimmed milk, which also provides vitamins and minerals to help bones and teeth grow well.

B Look at the list that you made in the last activity. Does it contain a large amount of energy-rich foods? Make a list of some healthier options.

DEFINITION

diet The food and drink that you normally eat over the course of a week or a month.

The heart and the pulse

Learning objective: To learn that the actions of the heart and pulse are related.

The heart pumps the blood around the body. At certain places in the body its beating may be felt as a pulse.

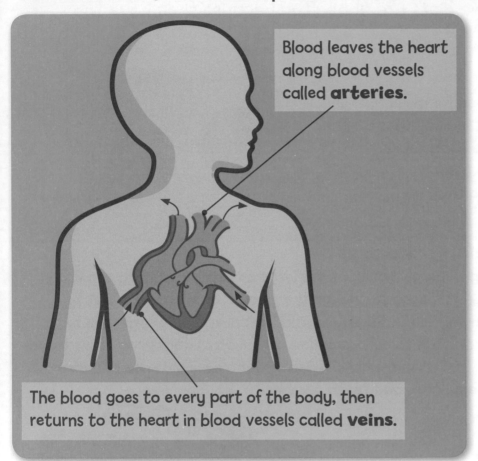

Blood leaves the heart along blood vessels called **arteries**.

The blood goes to every part of the body, then returns to the heart in blood vessels called **veins**.

The pulse

You can find the pulse in your wrist. Hold out your right hand and place the first two fingers of your left hand on the inside of your right wrist. Then press to find the pulse.

The heart and blood

The heart is a bag of muscle about the size of a fist. As the muscles squeeze and relax they make the heart beat. This pumps blood around the body.

DEFINITION

blood vessels
Tubes that carry blood around the body.

Try finding your pulse using the instructions on this page.

A

Fill in the gaps in the paragraph from the word list below.

blood   parts   arteries   vessels   veins   pumps

The heart _____ the blood into the _____ and it travels to all _____ of the body. The _____ returns to the heart in blood _____ called _____ .

Exercise and the pulse

Learning objective: To measure the pulse rate and relate it to exercise.

The blood carries food and oxygen round the body. When we exercise, our muscles work harder. They need more food and oxygen, so the heart beats faster.

Measuring the pulse rate

You can measure how fast the heart beats by counting how many times the pulse throbs in a minute. This is called the pulse rate. A watch with a second hand, or a stopwatch in a mobile phone, can be used as a timer.

How the pulse rate changes

The pulse rate is lowest when the body is at rest. This is found by sitting down and taking the pulse for a minute. You can see how your pulse changes with exercise by walking around for two minutes then sitting down and taking it again. If you keep taking the pulse every other minute for a while the pulse should go back to its resting rate.

HH:MM:SS
00:00:57

B Draw lines to match the pulse rate with the activity. The first one has been done for you.

65   person running

70   person lying down

90   person standing up

120   person walking

Pfew! What happens to your pulse when you exercise?

C Measure your pulse rate when sitting.
Write it here: _____

Measure your pulse rate after walking for two minutes.
Write it here: _____

Predict how your pulse may change after running for two minutes.
Write your prediction here: _____
Measure your pulse rate after running for two minutes.
Write it here: _____

9

Drugs

Certain types of drugs can help the body to recover from illness or injury, but others can make people very unwell.

Helpful drugs

When someone is ill they may take a medicine to get better. Most medicines contain substances called drugs. The drugs may ease pain or help the body to heal or fight infection.

If a child needs medication, an adult should always be in charge!

Harmful drugs

Harmful drugs such as ecstasy, cocaine and heroin damage the brain and heart. Someone who regularly takes harmful drugs is an addict. They may need to take more and more until their health is ruined or they die. Some harmful drugs are taken as tablets, but others are smoked or injected into the body. Drug addicts may share needles, which spreads deadly diseases. People who become addicts can get help and recover.

A

Fill in the gaps in the paragraph from the word list below. (You can use a word more than once!)

drugs	ill	cocaine	killed	medicines

People who are _____ take _____ to get better.

The _____ can contain _____ to help them recover.

Harmful _____ like _____ make people become addicts. Addicts are in danger of being _____ by the _____ they take.

DEFINITION

medication Regular amounts of a medicine (liquid or tablets) taken to treat an illness.

addict A person who feels they cannot survive without taking a certain drug.

Tobacco and alcohol

Learning objective: To know that tobacco and alcohol are dangerous.

Smoking tobacco and drinking alcohol can be extremely harmful.

Tobacco

Tobacco is smoked in cigarettes, cigars and pipes. It contains a drug called nicotine. People who smoke become addicted. The tobacco smoke damages the lungs, causes bronchitis and makes people cough. It contains substances that damage the heart and can cause cancers to develop in the throat and lungs.

Alcohol

Alcohol is found in drinks such as alcopops, beer, cider and wine. It affects the brain and stops people from thinking clearly and moving about properly. When this happens, people are more likely to have accidents. Alcohol is processed by the liver. If large amounts of alcohol are drunk regularly the liver may become fatally damaged. People who become addicted to alcohol are called alcoholics.

B Design a poster to discourage people from smoking or drinking too much alcohol.

DEFINITION

liver A body organ that performs many tasks to keep the body alive.

Parts of a flower

Learning objective: To recognize the different parts of a flower.

A flower has many parts. The parts work together to help the plant reproduce.

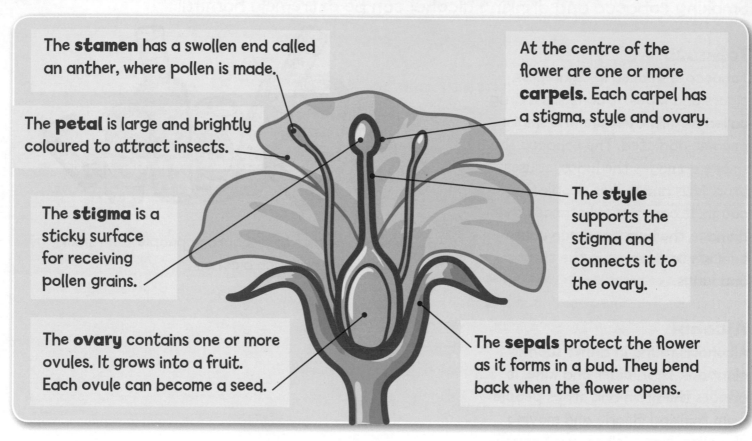

The **stamen** has a swollen end called an anther, where pollen is made.

The **petal** is large and brightly coloured to attract insects.

The **stigma** is a sticky surface for receiving pollen grains.

The **ovary** contains one or more ovules. It grows into a fruit. Each ovule can become a seed.

At the centre of the flower are one or more **carpels**. Each carpel has a stigma, style and ovary.

The **style** supports the stigma and connects it to the ovary.

The **sepals** protect the flower as it forms in a bud. They bend back when the flower opens.

Types of flowers

When you look at different flowers you may find they have different numbers of petals, stamens and carpels. Some plants, such as dandelions, have groups of tiny flowers that bunch together to form flower heads.

A Label this diagram of a flower A to E, using the example above to help you.

A = Petal

B = Style

C = Ovary

D = Stamen

E = Sepal

F = Stigma

G = Carpel

Pollination

Pollination is the movement of pollen from the stamen of one flower to the stigma of another flower of the same kind. Pollen may be carried by insects or the wind.

Insect pollination

Insect-pollinated plants have flowers with large, bright petals and a strong scent. These flowers make nectar, on which the insects feed, near the ovary base. They make small amounts of large spiky pollen, which sticks to the insect's body as it brushes past the stamens to feed on the nectar. The sticky stigma of the next flower the insect visits collects the pollen.

Wind pollination

The flowers of wind-pollinated plants do not have large petals, scent or nectar. They have stamens that hang out of the flower and release a large amount of small, smooth pollen grains. This is trapped by the feathery stigmas of other wind-pollinated flowers, which hang out like a net to catch pollen as it is blown by. All grasses have wind-pollinated flowers.

Look at the flowers in your garden or a local park - try to identify the different parts.

B Tick or cross these boxes - read back through the text on this page for clues.

	Insect-pollinated flower	**Wind-pollinated flower**
Large petals		
Strong scent		
Nectar		
Little pollen		
Lots of pollen		
Smooth pollen		
Spiky pollen		

Forming fruits

Learning objective: To understand that fruits form after fertilization.

A fruit forms from the ovary of a flower after fertilization.

Fertilization

After a pollen grain sticks to a stigma it grows a pollen tube through the style and ovary to an ovule. Substances in the pollen grain travel down the tube and join with other substances in the ovule.

After fertilization

The ovule grows into a seed. This contains a tiny plant and a store of food to help the plant grow. The ovary changes into a fruit around the seed. Other parts of the flower, such as the petals and stamens, fall away but the sepals may stay in place.

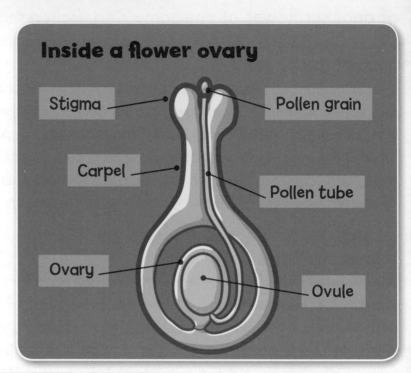

Inside a flower ovary

Stigma

Pollen grain

Carpel

Pollen tube

Ovary

Ovule

Open an apple or tomato. Count the seeds and notice how they are spread out.

A

Match the plant structures on the left with the description of what they do. The first one has been done for you.

Stigma — Turns into a seed after fertilization.

Pollen grain — Makes pollen grains stick.

Pollen tube — Carries a substance from a flower for fertilization.

Ovule — Carries a substance from a pollen grain to an ovule.

DEFINITION

fertilization The process in which a male cell joins with a female cell and makes a new living thing.

14

Fruit and seed dispersal

Learning objective: To know that fruits and seeds can be dispersed in different ways.

The spreading out of seeds from the parent plant is called dispersal. Seeds are dispersed so that they have plenty of space to grow in when they germinate.

Dispersal by the wind

Maple and ash trees have winged fruits. As the fruits fall the wind catches the wings and makes them spin away. The dandelion fruit has a 'parachute', which catches the wind.

Dandelion fruit

Dispersal by animals

Goose grass has fruits covered in hooks, which cling to the fur of passing animals. Succulent berries are eaten by animals, but the seeds pass through their bodies unharmed.

Blackberries

Explosive fruits

When some fruits, such as balsam and lupin, dry they shrink, split open quickly and fling their seeds away.

Lupin pod

B These phrases summarize the main stages in the life cycle of a plant. Put them in the correct order by writing a number (1 to 6) in each box.

- ☐ Plant fully grown.
- ☐ Seedling starts to grow.
- ☐ Plant makes flowers.
- ☐ Seed germinates.
- ☐ Plant disperses fruit.
- ☐ Flowers make fruits.

DEFINITION

germinate When the tiny plant inside a seed bursts out and starts to grow into a seedling.
succulent Soft and juicy.
life cycle The stages in the life of a living thing.

The human life cycle

Learning objective: To know about the different stages in the human life cycle.

From the moment you are born you are growing and changing. In later life you stop growing, but you never stop changing.

The human life cycle is divided into stages.

Baby
A baby cannot do anything for itself. It sleeps most of the time and feeds on milk. After about 6 months a baby learns to sit up, and later to crawl.

Toddler
At about a year old, a baby learns to stand and walk. Toddlers eat a range of foods and begin to learn to talk.

Child
After about two years, a toddler is more skilled at walking and talking — and becomes a child. The child continues to grow and learn many new skills.

Adult
Adults eventually stop growing, but changes continue. As adults get older their hair may turn grey and their skin may become wrinkly.

Adolescent
At about 11 or 12 years girls begin to change into women and boys begin to change into men. The process takes about three years and is known as adolescence.

How do you think you will change in the future?

A Look at photos of yourself as a baby and compare them with how you look now. What are the differences?

Then	Now

Animal life cycles

Learning objective: To compare the life cycles of different animals.

Many animals have life cycles where the young look like smaller versions of the adults. But in some animals the young are completely different from the adults.

Insects

Most baby insects, such as the butterfly, start life as caterpillars or larvae, then change into pupae. Eventually they change again to become adults. This is called metamorphosis.

The **caterpillar** hatches.

It then changes into a **pupa**.

The butterfly lays its **eggs** on a leaf.

The **butterfly** emerges.

Tadpole

Froglet

Frog spawn

Frog

Amphibians

Frogs and toads start life as tadpoles, but as they grow they develop legs, their tails disappear and their head shape changes.

Life cycles and extinction

A life cycle is completed when the adult animal has young, which carry on living after its parents die. If an animal species is rare and the adults are spread out, they may never find a mate. When this happens, the species may die out, or become extinct.

DEFINITION

species A type of living thing. All individuals of the species have very similar features. The males and females can breed to produce young.

B   Put these words in the correct places below.

disappears   jelly   hatches   tail   legs   egg

A frog's _____ is surrounded by _____.
A tadpole _____ from the egg. It has a long _____
and looks like a little fish. In time the tadpole grows _____
and a big head and its tail _____. When this happens it
has turned into a frog.

17

The air we breathe

Learning objective: To learn that air is a real material.

The air in a room cannot be seen or felt, but when you stand in a wind you can feel it and see its effects as it flows by. Air is a real substance. It is a mixture of gases.

Air has weight

This experiment shows that air has weight.

- Two empty balloons are tied to either end of a stick.
- The stick is rested across two boxes so the two ends balance.
- One balloon is inflated and placed back on the stick.
- The stick no longer balances in the centre because the inflated balloon is heavier.

(a)

(b)

Water fills the gaps

Water pools on the surface when the gaps are full.

Air fills the gaps

Pouring water into soil pushes the air out of the gaps between the soil particles. If you measure how much water you can pour into a dish of soil before the water starts to pool at the surface, you can tell how much air was in the soil.

A These pictures show how much water was in a measuring cylinder before and after it was poured onto soil to fill the gaps.

100cm³

60cm³

How much air was in the soil?

DEFINITION

gas A substance with no fixed shape, which flows in all directions and can be compressed, or squashed.

Gases

There are many different gases, and each one has its own properties and uses. The main gases in air are nitrogen, oxygen, carbon dioxide and water vapour.

GAS	PROPERTIES
Oxygen	Oxygen helps us release energy from our food. It lets things burn in it.
Carbon dioxide	We produce carbon dioxide as we release energy from food and breathe it out. Plants use carbon dioxide from the air to make food. Carbon dioxide is squashed into drinks to make them fizzy.
Helium	Helium is the gas used in party balloons. It makes the balloon rise because helium is lighter than air.
Natural gas	This gas is called methane and is made from the decomposing bodies of huge numbers of tiny sea creatures that lived long ago and became covered in rock. Methane is used in gas cookers and fires.

B

Match the gases on the left with the description of their property or use. The first one has been done for you.

Oxygen   Used in some cookers.

Helium   Used to make food by plants.

Natural gas   Lighter than air.

Carbon dioxide   Lets things burn in it.

DEFINITION

decomposing The rotting down of the bodies of dead animals or plants into simple substances such as minerals and gases.

Melting

Learning objective: To understand that solids can change into liquids by melting.

A solid has a fixed shape, but when it reaches melting point it turns into a liquid. The temperature at which a substance melts is measured in degrees Celsius (°C).

Examples of melting

Chocolate can melt in a warm pocket.

Butter melts when it is put on hot food, such as boiled potatoes or toast.

The wax around the wick of a burning candle melts and forms a pool.

An ice cube melts in a glass.

Inside the Earth there are places where it is so hot that the rock melts. (The molten rock bursts through the Earth's surface at the vent of a volcano.)

The melting process

As the temperature of a solid rises close to its melting point, it starts to soften and its shape starts to sag and flatten. At the melting point, the substance flows away.

Reversible change

Melting is a reversible change because, if the liquid substance is cooled down again, it changes back into a solid.

> What do you think would happen to the melted chocolate if you put it in the fridge to cool down?

A

Use these words to fill in the spaces in the paragraph below. You can use the words more than once if you need to.

point   temperature   chocolate   shape
liquid   warmer

A piece of _____ was left on a sunny windowsill. As it got _____ its firm sides started to sag and it began to lose its _____. When the _____ reached melting _____ the chocolate turned into a _____ and dripped off the windowsill.

Freezing

Learning objective: To understand that liquids can change into solids by freezing.

A liquid can change into a solid by a process called freezing. The temperature at which this happens is called the freezing point.

Freezing water

Water freezes at a temperature of 0°C and becomes a solid we call ice. The ice has a fixed shape, which it keeps until it starts to melt again.

Moulding metal

Metals have to be heated very strongly to make them melt. When solid metal is turned into a liquid it can be poured into a mould. As the metal cools, it freezes and becomes a solid again. The solid will have the same shape as the mould the liquid was poured into.

Reversible change

Freezing is a reversible change. If a solid substance is heated up again it changes back into a liquid.

B

Substance	Freezing point (°C)	
Beeswax	64°C	
Water	0°C	
Chocolate	25°C	
Lard	43°C	
Pewter	240°C	

A substance's freezing point is the same as its melting point.

This table shows the freezing points of five substances. In which order do they freeze as the temperature drops from 250°C to 0°C?

Write the order from 1 to 5 in the boxes on the right of the table.

How many would freeze if the temperature fell to just to 30°C?

From liquid to gas

Learning objective: To know that liquids change to gases by evaporation or boiling.

Liquids can change into gases in two ways – by evaporating or boiling.

Evaporation

If water is placed in a saucer, the water at the surface in contact with the air changes into a gas called water vapour. This process of change is called evaporation. The water vapour spreads out in the air. This process continues until all the water has evaporated and formed water vapour.

Conditions for evaporation

Evaporation takes place at normal air temperature but speeds up if the air is warmer or moving fast. Evaporation also speeds up if the air is dry and does not contain much water vapour.

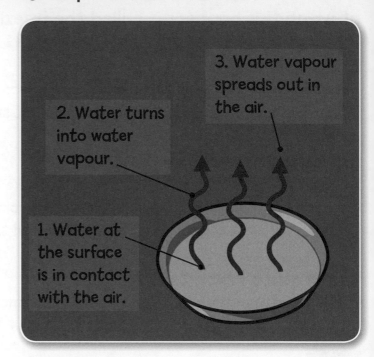

3. Water vapour spreads out in the air.

2. Water turns into water vapour.

1. Water at the surface is in contact with the air.

Boiling

Water boils at 100°C. A gas called steam forms inside the liquid and makes bubbles, which rise to the top and pop into the air.

Evaporation and boiling are reversible changes. Can you explain why this is?

A This table shows the results of an experiment into speed of evaporation in different conditions.

Condition	Time to evaporate (hours)
Cold	10
Hot	2
Still	9
Windy	3
Moist air	12
Dry air	3

What are the best conditions for evaporation to take place quickly?

From gas to liquid

Learning objective: To know that gases turn to liquids by condensation.

Gases can change back into liquids when they cool down in a process called **condensation**. We also use the word condensation to describe the water that forms on the inside of windows in warm kitchens and bathrooms.

Water vapour and steam

You cannot see steam in bubbles and you cannot see it when it enters very hot air. As the water vapour rises from the spout it cools down and condenses on dust particles floating in the air to make the white clouds we also call steam.

Breathing out

There is water vapour in our breath. On a cold day we can see it condense in the air and look like the steam above a kettle. If you breathe out onto a cold drink can from a fridge you will see water droplets form on the can as the vapour in your breath condenses.

Steam cools and condenses to form a cloud of water droplets.

Steam cannot be seen as it rushes out of a kettle spout.

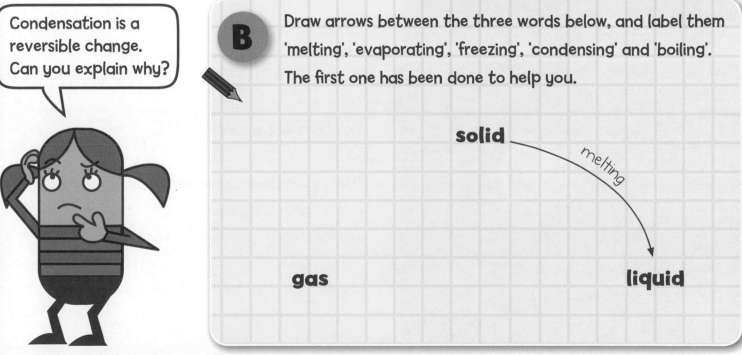

Condensation is a reversible change. Can you explain why?

B Draw arrows between the three words below, and label them 'melting', 'evaporating', 'freezing', 'condensing' and 'boiling'. The first one has been done to help you.

solid

melting

gas

liquid

The Sun, Earth and Moon

Learning objective: To compare the Sun, the Earth and the Moon.

The Sun, the Earth and the Moon are spheres in space.

The Sun
The Sun is a star. It is made of two gases called hydrogen and helium. Inside the Sun hydrogen is changed into helium. This produces light and heat, which spread out through space.

Remember never to look directly at the Sun – it could damage your eyesight.

The Earth and the Moon
The Earth is a planet made of rock and mostly covered in water. The Earth moves anticlockwise around the Sun in an elliptical orbit, once every year. The Moon is also made of rock. It moves anticlockwise around the Earth in an almost circular orbit, once every month. The Sun is many times larger than the Moon, but they appear roughly the same size in the Earth's sky because the Sun is 149,000,000 km from the Earth and the Moon is only 384,500 km away.

DEFINITION

sphere An object with a surface curved round to make a ball shape.
orbit The path taken by one object in space as it moves around another space object.
elliptical Shaped like a slightly flattened circle, sometimes called an oval.

Elliptical orbit

The Earth moves round the Sun.

The Moon moves round the Earth.

A

Do some research and find out the diameter of the Sun, the Earth and the Moon. Match them up below by drawing lines between them.

Earth	1,392,000 km
Moon	3476 km
Sun	12,756 km

Tick the right answer:

The Sun and Moon appear the same size in the Earth's sky because...

a) ...the Moon is nearer the Earth than the Sun. ☐

b) ...the Sun is nearer the Earth than the Moon. ☐

24

The Earth in its orbit

Learning objective: To link the orbit of the Earth with the seasons.

The way the Earth tilts in space and makes its journey around the Sun produces long periods of certain kinds of weather that are known as seasons.

The Earth's axis

The Earth spins on its axis. The axis is tilted just over 23 degrees from vertical and keeps pointing in the same direction as the Earth orbits the Sun.

The hemispheres and the seasons

The equator is an invisible line that runs around the middle of the Earth. The half of the Earth above the equator is called the Northern Hemisphere. The half below it is called the Southern Hemisphere. When a hemisphere is angled towards the Sun it is summer there, and when it is pointing away it is winter. Spring and Autumn occur when neither hemisphere is pointing towards the Sun.

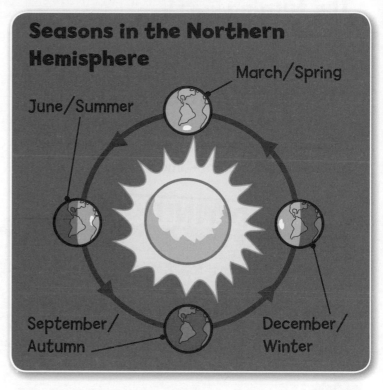

Seasons in the Northern Hemisphere

June/Summer

March/Spring

September/Autumn

December/Winter

B

1. What season is it now? Draw the Earth's position round the Sun and label it.

2. Where will the Earth be in six months' time? Make a drawing and add a label.

3. Draw and label where it will be when it is your birthday.

Day and night

Day and night occur due to the turning of the Earth on its axis.

The turning Earth

The Earth turns round once on its axis every twenty-four hours. During that time, all parts of the Earth spend some time facing the Sun. When a part of the Earth is facing the Sun, it is daytime there. All parts also spend some time facing away from the Sun. When this is happening it is night-time there.

DEFINITION

clockwise The direction taken by the hands of a clock as they move around a clock face.
anticlockwise The opposite direction to that taken by the hands of a clock as they move around a clock face.

The Earth from above the North Pole

The Earth turns in an anticlockwise direction on its axis.

A

Imagine you were above the North Pole in a space ship. Would the Earth below you seem to be turning clockwise or anticlockwise? Write your answer below.

Look at the places marked A, B and C on this picture of the Earth and the Sun. Read the questions, then write A, B or C in the boxes below.

C

B

A

In which place is it midnight?

In which place is it midday?

In which place is it dawn?

The Sun in the sky

Learning objective: To learn how the Sun changes position in the sky.

The Sun appears to move quickly across the sky. This movement is not due to the Sun. The rotation of the Earth makes the Sun appear to move.

The Sun and shadows

As the Sun moves across the sky the length and direction of the shadows change.

Try setting up a shadow stick of your own, and watch how the shadow moves.

The path of the Sun

Sunrise in the east

Midday

Sunset in the west

Sunrise

Midday

Sunset

B Which of these statements are true and which are false? Write T or F in each box.

1. The Sun moves from right to left across the sky. ☐

2. The Sun rises in the sky in the morning. ☐

3. The Sun sinks in the east in the afternoon. ☐

4. The Sun sinks in the west in the afternoon. ☐

5. Shadows point east in the morning. ☐

6. Shadows get longer in the afternoon. ☐

The phases of the Moon

Learning objective: To understand how the phases of the Moon change.

The sunlit areas of the Moon we see change as the Moon moves in its orbit.

As the Moon goes round the Earth the Sun shines on half of the Moon. But from the Earth we can sometimes see only part of the sunlit areas. The sunlit areas seen from the Earth are called the phases of the Moon.

The path of the Moon
The half of the Moon and the part of the Earth facing the Sun are lit up by the Sun.

The phases of the Moon
Some of the phases of the Moon as they appear from the Earth.

A

1. The Moon is said to be waxing as the phases increase in size each night towards a full moon. Which phases occur when the Moon is waxing?

2. The Moon is said to be waning as the phases decrease in size each night towards a new moon. Which phases occur when the Moon is waning?

Look at the Moon in the sky tonight – what phase do you think it's in?

Solar System

Learning objective: To know how the Sun, the Moon and the Earth fit into the Solar System.

The Solar System formed about 5,000 million years ago. It consists of the Sun, the planets (including the Earth) and their moons, asteroids and comets.

Moons

The Earth and Pluto each have one moon. Mars has two, Neptune has 13, Uranus has 27, Saturn has 34 and Jupiter has 63.

Asteroids

The asteroids form a ring, or belt, between the orbits of Mars and Jupiter.

DEFINITION

asteroid A piece of rock left over from the time when the Solar System formed that moves in an orbit around the Sun.

The planets

The Sun is at the centre of the Solar System, and the nine planets move around it.

Uranus

Jupiter

Venus

Pluto

Mars

Sun

Mercury

Neptune

Earth

Saturn

Asteroid belt

B Imagine you were on a space shuttle beyond Pluto and you travelled to the Sun and back. Write down the planets you would pass on your journey and when you would go through the asteroid belt.

* Some scientists now consider Pluto to be a dwarf planet or Plutoid, not a proper planet.

29

Vibration

Learning objective: To learn that sounds are made by vibrations.

A sound is made when something vibrates. A vibration is a to and fro or an up and down movement. Vibrations can move through different materials.

Making vibrations

If a ruler is held firmly over the edge of a table and 'twanged', it vibrates up and down and makes a sound. An elastic band stretched between finger and thumb vibrates to and fro when it is plucked, and it also makes a sound.

Travelling sound

Vibrating objects set up vibrations in the materials around them. When an object vibrates in air, the air around it starts to vibrate. This in turn makes air further away vibrate and the vibration passes through the air as a wave – a sound wave.

The ruler vibrates.

The sound waves pass through the air.

A

Try twanging a ruler over the edge of a table.

This table shows the speed of sound waves through some materials.

Tick the correct box:

Sound travels fastest through... gases ☐ liquids ☐ solids. ☐

Sound travels slowest through... gases ☐ liquids ☐ solids. ☐

30

Loud and soft

Learning objective: To understand about loud and soft sounds.

Large vibrations make loud sounds and small vibrations make quiet sounds. When vibrations pass into some materials they may be absorbed so that little or no sound is heard on the other side. These materials are called sound insulators.

Measuring loudness

The decibel (dB) is the unit used to measure the loudness of sounds. Here are some examples of quiet and loud sounds.

Sound	Loudness (dB)
Road drill	110
Vacuum cleaner	80
Busy street	70
People talking	50
Quiet street	40
Whisper	30
Pin drop	10

Guess how loud it is around you now using the decibel scale. Try it at other times, too.

Sound insulation

Materials can be tested for their sound insulation properties by wrapping them round a sound source, such as a radio, and measuring the distance at which the source sound can no longer be heard.

B

1. How do you think a sound insulation test could be made fair?

2. A radio could not be heard 2 metres away when wrapped in material A and could not be heard 50 centimetres away when wrapped in material B. Which material was the better sound insulator?

DEFINITION

loud sound A sound made by large vibrations that produce large, deep sound waves.

quiet sound A sound made by small vibrations that produce small, shallow sound waves.

Pitch

Learning objective: To know that pitch is how high or low a sound is.

A high-pitched sound is one that sounds like "Ping!" or "Peep!" A low-pitched sound is one that sounds like "Pong!" or "Boom!"

Pitch and loudness

Pitch and loudness do not affect each other. A high-pitched or low-pitched sound can be made either quietly or loudly. Whisper and shout "Ping!" and "Pong!" to check.

Vibration, pitch and frequency

An object that vibrates slowly makes a sound with a low pitch. An object that vibrates quickly makes a sound with a high pitch.

The frequency of a sound is the number of vibrations that pass in a second. Low-pitched sounds have low frequencies and high-pitched sounds have high frequencies. The unit for measuring frequency is the hertz (Hz).

A Here are the frequencies of some common sounds:

Sound	Frequency (Hz)	
Baby's first cry	432	
Bottom C note on piano	32	
Cat's purr	25	1
Chainsaw	4000	
Ordinary Voice	250	
Thunder	40	
Highest note on piano	4096	

Write the numbers 1 to 7 in the boxes to arrange them in order of pitch, starting with the lowest. The first one has been done for you.

How does the pitch change when you change the length of a vibrating ruler?

Musical instruments

Each note of a musical instrument is a different pitch from the others. The notes played on an instrument are changed by varying the way in which the instrument vibrates.

Drums

The pitch of a drum can be raised by tightening the skin, and lowered by loosening it. Small drums have a higher pitch than large drums because the skins are made of less material and vibrate faster when hit.

Stringed instruments

The pitch of a vibrating string depends on its thickness (the amount of material it is made from), its tightness and its length. A long, thick, loose string has the lowest pitch. A short, thin, tight string has the highest.

Wind instruments

The pitch made by a wind instrument such as a recorder is due to the length of the vibrating column inside it. A long air column makes a low-pitched sound and a short column makes a high-pitched sound.

Percussion instruments

These are instruments that are struck to produce a sound. They include drums, cymbals and gongs.

Stringed instruments

The strings of some instruments are plucked, strummed or stroked with a bow. These include guitars, banjoes, violins and cellos.

Wind instruments

The clarinet and flute are woodwind instruments; the trumpet and trombone are brass instruments.

1. Which drum has the lower pitch? Drum A, which has a diameter of 10 cm, or drum B, which is 20 cm across?

2. Which string has the higher pitch? String A, which is long, thick and tight, or string B, which is short, thin and tight?

3. Closing holes on a recorder makes the air column longer. Does this make the pitch higher or lower?

The growing plant

Plants make their own food using energy from the Sun and materials from the air and soil. The food is used for growth and making flowers, fruits and seeds.

Collecting ingredients

The roots soak up water from the soil, and the leaves draw it up the plant. The leaves are covered with tiny holes that let water vapour escape.
As the water escapes into the air, more water is sucked up through the roots. Carbon dioxide from the air also passes in through the holes.

Making food

The water and carbon dioxide in the leaf take part in a non-reversible change when light shines on the leaf. The light gives the water and carbon dioxide the energy to make the change – and food is produced. This process of making food by using light is called photosynthesis. Oxygen is also made in this process. It passes out of the leaf through the holes.

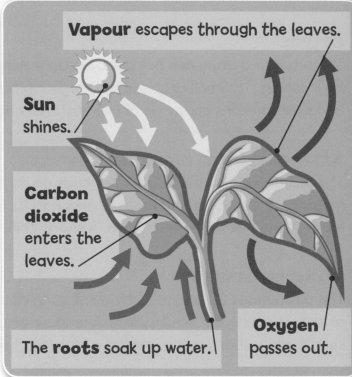

Vapour escapes through the leaves.

Sun shines.

Carbon dioxide enters the leaves.

The **roots** soak up water.

Oxygen passes out.

A

Complete the sentence below using the words from this list:

water   leaf   food   energy   light

When _____ shines on a _____ it provides _____ for _____ and carbon dioxide to be changed into _____ and oxygen.

What do you think happens to the oxygen made by plants?

Where do you think the carbon dioxide comes from for the plant to use?

Roots and soil

DEFINITION

humus The remains of dead plants and animals held in the soil.

Learning objective: To learn that plants take water and minerals from the soil.

The roots hold the plant in the soil. They take up minerals from the soil that are dissolved in the water.

Types of root
There are two main types of root - tap roots and fibrous roots.

Tap roots
A tap root is a long, thick root, which stores food and grows deep into the soil. A carrot has a tap root.

Fibrous roots
Fibrous roots are long, thin and branching and spread out in the soil around the plant. Grass has fibrous roots.

The parts of the soil
The soil is made from rocky particles. The largest particles are pieces of gravel. Sand grains are smaller, silt is smaller still and clay particles are the smallest. All these particles are bound together by humus. The rocky particles and the humus contain minerals that dissolve in water.

Minerals and plant growth
All plants need some minerals to grow healthily. Farmers and gardeners add extra minerals to the soil in the form of fertilizer to help plants grow as healthily as possible.

B

1. How is a tap root different from a fibrous root?

Soil with lots of large rocky particles drains well, but soil with small rocky particles drains poorly.
Here are three soils:
A = gravelly soil   **B = sandy soil**   **C = clay soil**

2. Which soil drains best? ☐
   Which has the worst drainage? ☐

Plant and animal habitats

Learning objective: To learn how plants and animals rely on each other for survival.

Many animals feed on plants, but all animals need plants in some way to help them to survive. Plants depend on animals for survival, too.

Why animals need plants

Plants provide food, habitats and shelter for animals.

Beetle hides in tree bark.

Spider spins web on twigs.

Deer eats grass and shelters under tree.

Bird uses plants to build nest.

Why plants need animals

Bees help plants to spread pollen. Some animals spread fruits and seeds that stick to their fur or feathers, and many animals eat fruits and spread the seeds in their droppings.

Animal droppings also provide the soil with minerals for plant growth.

A Look at the pictures above and answer these questions.

1. Which animals are using plants for shelter?

2. Which animal is using a plant as food?

3. Which animal is using a plant to help it set a trap?

Understanding Keys

Learning objective: To learn how to use a key to identify animal species.

A key is a number of features about organisms set out as questions. As each question is answered you move on to the next one until you identify the organism.

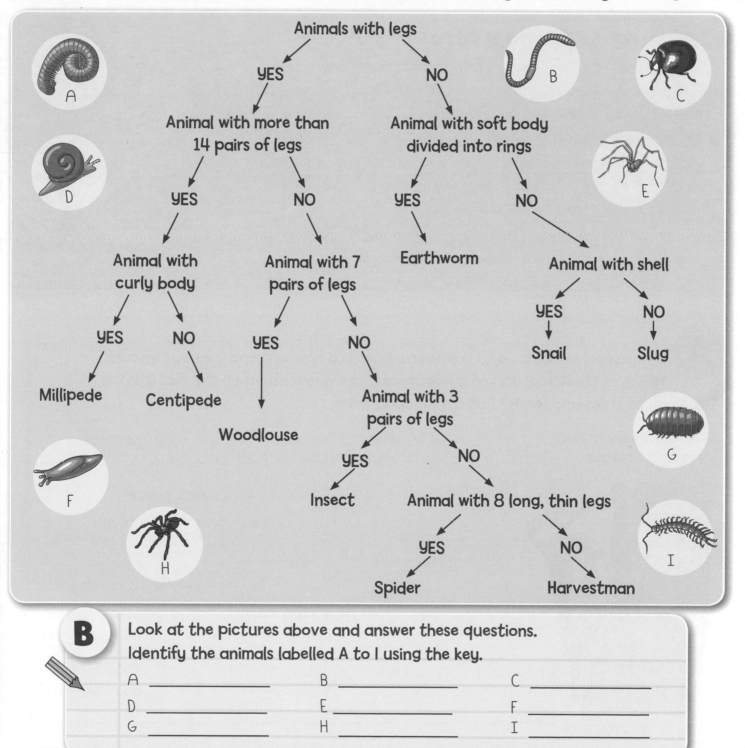

Animals with legs

YES → Animal with more than 14 pairs of legs

NO → Animal with soft body divided into rings

Animal with more than 14 pairs of legs:
- YES → Animal with curly body
- NO → Animal with 7 pairs of legs

Animal with soft body divided into rings:
- YES → Earthworm
- NO → Animal with shell

Animal with curly body:
- YES → Millipede
- NO → Centipede

Animal with 7 pairs of legs:
- YES → Woodlouse
- NO → Animal with 3 pairs of legs

Animal with shell:
- YES → Snail
- NO → Slug

Animal with 3 pairs of legs:
- YES → Insect
- NO → Animal with 8 long, thin legs

Animal with 8 long, thin legs:
- YES → Spider
- NO → Harvestman

B Look at the pictures above and answer these questions.
Identify the animals labelled A to I using the key.

A _____ B _____ C _____

D _____ E _____ F _____

G _____ H _____ I _____

37

Adaptation

Learning objective: To know that living things adapt to survive in their habitats.

Living things have body features that help them to survive in a certain habitat. These special features are called adaptations.

Adapting to a pond habitat

- A fish has overlapping scales and is covered in slime to help it move easily through the water as it swims.

- A frog has webbed feet to push on the water and powerful leg muscles to help it swim quickly. Its eyes are on top of its head so that it can lie safely underwater and pop its eyes above the surface to look for predators.

- The heron has long legs for wading in deep water and a long, sharp beak that is adapted for stabbing frogs and fish.

A A woodpecker holds on to a tree trunk, drills a hole in it and licks out insects. Which of these features of a woodpecker are adaptations to the way it holds on to trees and feeds? Put a ring round them.

Two wings

two eyes

lays eggs

stiff tail feathers

two toes pointing backwards instead of one

chisel-shaped beak

makes a harsh call

strong claws

strong skull

long tongue

feathery crest on head

Food chains

Learning objective: To learn that living things in a habitat are linked by food chains.

Food passes through a habitat along links called food chains.

Link 1
Any part of a plant, such as a seed or leaves, may start a food chain.

Link 2
A plant-eating animal, such as a snail, beetle, rabbit or deer. It is a herbivore, or primary consumer.

Link 3
An animal that eats other animals, such as a spider, frog or shrew. It is a carnivore, or secondary consumer.

Link 4
A large carnivore, such as a fox, owl or heron, which eats smaller carnivores. It is a tertiary consumer.

Prey and predator

An animal that is eaten by another animal is called the prey. The animal that eats the prey is called a predator. A predator is always a carnivore, but prey can be either herbivores or carnivores.

A simple food chain

Lettuce leaf   Slug   Frog   Heron

DEFINITION

herbivore An animal that feeds on plants.
carnivore An animal that feeds on other animals.

B   Make a food chain using these organisms:

beetle   **seed**   **owl**   **shrew**

Remember!
In a food chain, the arrow goes from the food to the feeder.

39

Micro-organisms

Micro-organisms are also called microbes. There are three different kinds of micro-organism - viruses, bacteria and some types of fungi.

Viruses

Viruses cause diseases such as colds, influenza, chicken pox, measles and rabies.

Bacteria

Many bacteria feed on the remains of dead plants and animals and on animal waste. They are essential in recycling the materials from which living things are made. Some bacteria cause diseases like cholera, typhoid and food poisoning — and some can cause tooth decay.

Fungi

Moulds and yeast are fungi. Moulds spread in air as tiny particles called spores. When a spore lands on a suitable surface it grows threads and makes a fuzzy patch that we can see. Moulds are important in recycling materials for living things, but they can make good food turn bad.

Achoo! A cold cannot be cured with antibiotics because it is a virus.

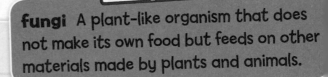

DEFINITION

fungi A plant-like organism that does not make its own food but feeds on other materials made by plants and animals.

A

1. What kind of microbe might give you a cold?

2. What kind of microbe is removed when you clean your teeth?

3. What kind of microbe might be seen growing on an orange?

4. What kind of microbe makes the contents of a compost bin rot?

Living with microbes

Learning objective: To understand that microbes can be either harmful or useful.

Microbes are everywhere – in air, water and on all kinds of surfaces. We can fight or control the harmful ones and use some others to make food.

Preventing and fighting disease

Stop microbes spreading	If you have a cold, cough or sneeze into a handkerchief. Always wash hands before eating. Keep rubbish covered to stop flies getting to it.
Keep clean	Make sure kitchen, cutlery and crockery are clean. Clean your teeth at least twice a day.
Vaccination	Vaccinate against serious diseases.
Medicines	Some infections caused by harmful bacteria can be cured by taking medicines called antibiotics.

Microbes in food

Certain kinds of harmless bacteria are added to warm milk to make cheese and yoghurt. Harmless moulds may also be added to some cheeses to make them 'blue' and add extra flavour.

Yeast is a microbe that is mixed with flour, sugar and water to make dough. The yeast microbes feed on sugar and produce bubbles in the dough, which gives bread its spongy texture and make it rise.

B

What do you think would happen if a bread-making mixture contained only water, flour and yeast?

Dissolving and filtering

Learning objective: To learn that some solutions cannot be separated by filtering.

When some substances are mixed with water, they dissolve in it. Other substances do not dissolve, and they can be separated from the water by filtering.

Dissolving

When a solid dissolves it breaks up into tiny particles that can only be seen with a very powerful microscope. The mixture of water and the dissolved substance is called a solution. If the solid is coloured, like coffee granules, its colour spreads out through the water.

Filtering

A filter can be used to separate a mixture that contains a liquid and solid particles that have not dissolved in it. The liquid passes through the holes in the filter and the solid particles remain behind. A filter cannot be used to separate a dissolved solid from a solution.

Solids trapped in filter.

Filter paper

Funnel

Liquid passes through.

A This table shows the results of an experiment in which different substances were added to water.

Substance	Dissolved
Sand	No
Sugar	Yes
Bath salts	Yes
Flour	No
Custard powder	No
Table salt	Yes

1. Which substances can be separated from the water by filtering?

2. Look at the picture above. Can you describe how a filter works?

Recovering dissolved solids

Learning objective: To learn what happens when water In a solution is changed to gas.

Water is changed into a gas by evaporation and by boiling. If the water contains dissolved solids, they remain behind because they do not change into a gas.

Separation

If a solution is left to evaporate, the dissolved solids will remain behind in the bottom of the container. If a solution is boiled for long enough, all of the water will change to steam, and the solid that was dissolved is left behind.

The liquid evaporates.   Solids are left behind.

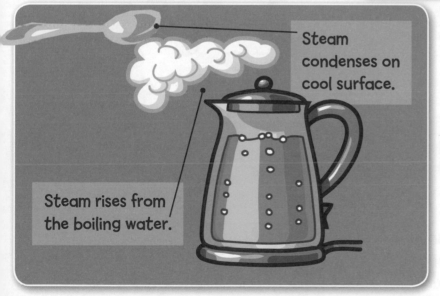

Steam condenses on cool surface.

Steam rises from the boiling water.

Condensation

If a cold surface is held over boiling water, the steam hits it and cools quickly. It condenses and forms a liquid – water. If the steam came from a solution, the condensed water will be pure because none of the dissolved solid will be present.

B Use these words to fill in the spaces in the paragraph below. You can use each word more than once if you need to.

salt   dissolves   boiled   steam   cooling   condensing

When _____ is mixed with water it _____ and makes a solution. If the solution is _____ the water turns to _____ and leaves the _____ behind. The _____ can be turned to water again by _____ it down in a process called _____.

The speed of dissolving

Learning objective: To understand that the speed of dissolving can vary.

The speed of dissolving is affected by the amount of stirring, the temperature of the water and the size of the particles entering the water.

When a solid dissolves

When a solid dissolves it breaks up into tiny particles. These fill up the gaps between the water particles.

Stirring, size and temperature

The effect of stirring can be investigated by adding the solid to the water without stirring and timing how long it takes to dissolve. The experiment can then be repeated with the mixture being stirred slowly, then repeated again stirring more quickly. The results can then be compared.

The effect of particle size can be tested by using caster sugar (small particles), granulated sugar (medium-sized particles), then a sugar lump (large particle) – then comparing the results.

The effect of water temperature can be tested by repeating the experiment using cold, warm, then hot water. The temperature should be taken before the solid is added.

Salt particles in a salt grain

Water particles

Salt particles mix in with the water particles.

Remember!
For a test on the speed of dissolving to be fair, the same amount of solid and liquid must be used throughout.

A

For the tests described above to be completely fair, which of these statements are correct? Tick or cross in the boxes.

1. In the stirring test the size of particles should be the same size. ☐
2. In the stirring test the temperature of the water should be the same. ☐
3. In the particle size test the same volume of sugar should be used each time. ☐
4. In the temperature test the water should be stirred at the same speed each time. ☐

Charts and graphs

Learning objective: To learn how and when to use a bar chart and a line graph.

Some data is best displayed as a bar chart, while other data is best displayed by a line graph.

Using a bar chart
A bar chart is best when the data has a few definite values, such as sugar particle size.

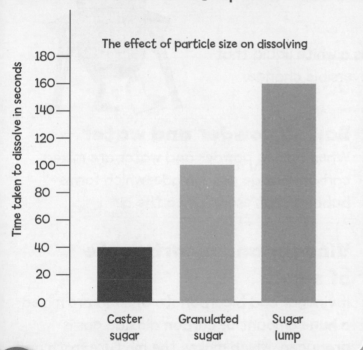

Using a line graph
A line graph is best when the data have a wide range of values, such as temperature.

B

Look at the graphs above and answer these questions.

1. How long did it take for the caster sugar to dissolve?

2. How long does it take for the solid to dissolve at 30 degrees Celsius?

3. What is the water temperature when a solid takes 100 seconds to dissolve?

DEFINITION

data Information, often in the form of measurements, that is obtained from experiments.

45

Irreversible changes

Learning objective: To know that some changes to materials cannot be reversed.

Some changes are irreversible. This means that the materials that took part in a process cannot be recovered easily.

Flour and water

When flour is added to water it makes a sticky dough. The water cannot easily be separated from the flour again afterwards, so the change is an irreversible one.

Plaster of Paris and water

If plaster of Paris powder is mixed with water it makes a white liquid that sets to a hard, solid white plaster. This is another irreversible change.

Ouch! Plaster of Paris is used to make casts for broken arms and legs.

If you make a model volcano with a hole in the centre you can fill it with bicarbonate of soda and vinegar – and create a mini eruption!

Baking powder and water

When baking powder and water are mixed, carbon dioxide gas is made, which forms bubbles that escape into the air.

Vinegar and bicarbonate of soda

If vinegar and bicarbonate of soda are mixed a huge amount of carbon dioxide gas is produced, which makes the mixture froth and fizz before it escapes into the air.

A Which substance:

1. ... makes bubbles of carbon dioxide gas with water?

2. ... makes a sticky dough with water?

3. ... makes a white solid with water?

Heating and burning

Learning objective: To know that heating and burning can cause irreversible changes.

When a substance is heated its temperature rises. If the temperature rises high enough the substance may burst into flame. When this happens the substance is said to be burning.

Heating

When food is cooked irreversible changes take place.
Clay is soft and can be shaped. But when it is heated strongly in a kiln it becomes hard and rigid and cannot be softened again.

Burning

Wood (a solid) burns away to make ash (solid), smoke (tiny solid particles), water vapour (gas) and carbon dioxide (gas). As candle wax burns it changes into carbon dioxide (gas) and water vapour (gas).

B

1. What two things do both wood and a candle make as they burn?

2. Which are reversible and which are irreversible changes? Tick the correct columns.

Process	Reversible	Irreversible
Melting of wax		
Burning of wood		
Baking bread		
Freezing water		
Mixing flour and water		

DEFINITION

kiln An oven or furnace that can generate a very high heat for baking clay into pottery, bricks and tiles.

Look at some meat and vegetables before and after they are cooked. How do they change?

Gravity

Learning objective: To learn about gravity and its relationship with weight.

The force of gravity acts between everything in the Universe, and creates a force called weight.

Gravity and the Universe

The force of gravity acts between every two objects in the Universe. Its effects can only be seen and felt if one of the objects is small (like you) and the other is very large (like the Earth). Gravity acts between the Sun and the planets and keeps them in their orbits.

Gravity on Earth

The force of gravity acts between everything on the Earth's surface and the centre of the Earth. The pull of gravity on your body also makes your body push downwards on things below it. We call this pushing force weight.

When you jump up into the air the force of gravity pulls you back down to the ground again.

Gravity on the Moon

The Moon is smaller than the Earth, and its pull on astronauts who visit it is smaller than the pull of the Earth's gravity. This makes the astronauts weigh six times less than they do on Earth.

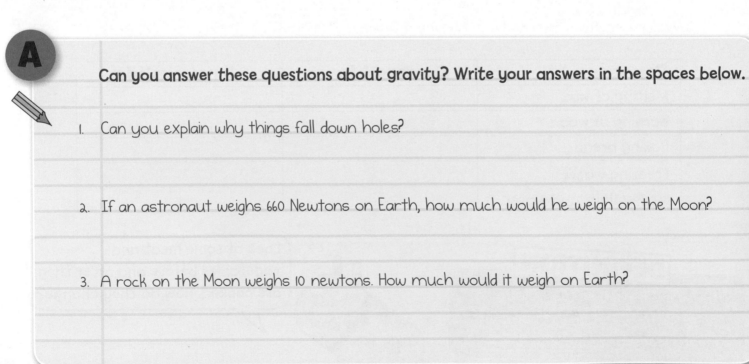

A

Can you answer these questions about gravity? Write your answers in the spaces below.

1. Can you explain why things fall down holes?

2. If an astronaut weighs 660 Newtons on Earth, how much would he weigh on the Moon?

3. A rock on the Moon weighs 10 newtons. How much would it weigh on Earth?

Two forces in action

Learning objective: To know that more than one force can act on an object at once.

If you hold this book, gravity pulls it down and the forces in your muscles push it up.

Force meter

The weight of an object suspended from a force meter makes the spring inside it stretch until its tension force pulls up with the same strength. The weight of the object can then be read on the scale on the side of the force meter.

Tension force pulls upwards.

Weight of object pulls downwards.

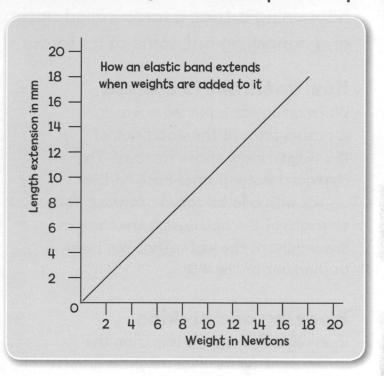

How an elastic band extends when weights are added to it

Length extension in mm

Weight in Newtons

Magnetic force

When a paper clip is put on the end of the magnet it does not fall away, because the pull of the magnetic force matches the pull of gravity.

B

An elastic band was held up and weights were added to it. After each weight was added the length of the elastic band was measured. The results were plotted on the line graph above.

1. What does the graph show?

2. How much is the elastic band stretched when the weight is 6 Newtons?

3. What weight is added to make the elastic band stretch to 12 mm?

4. There isn't a reading for when a 20 Newton weight was attached. Can you guess why?

Upthrust

Learning objective: To learn that water pushes upwards on objects placed in it.

When an object is placed in water it appears to lose weight. What is really happening is that a force called upthrust is pushing against the object's weight and cancelling out some of its force.

How upthrust is caused

When an object is placed in water it pushes some of the water out of the way to make space for itself. This displaced water pushes back on the object with a force called upthrust. The strength of the upthrust is the same as the weight of the water that has been pushed out of the way.

Floating and sinking

If an object's weight is less than the upthrust, it floats. If its weight is greater than the upthrust, the object sinks.

Object pushes water out of the way.

Displaced water pushes back.

A

Six objects were put in water. This table shows their weight and upthrust in Newtons (N).

Object	Weight (N)	Upthrust (N)
1	50	60
2	45	30
3	6	10
4	25	29
5	73	69
6	105	128

1. Which objects floated?
2. What would happen to object 4 if its weight was increased to 35N?

Air resistance

Learning objective: To know that air resistance pushes on objects that move through it.

The strength of the air resistance on an object depends on the size of its surface area pushing through the air.

Gravity and air resistance

When an object falls gravity pulls it down and air resistance pushes upwards on it.

Testing falling spinners

You can make a spinner by cutting and folding a piece of paper and attaching a paper clip to the lower end to help it fall and spin.

1. Mark these lines on a piece of A4 paper.

2. Cut along the solid lines and fold along the dashed lines.

3. Attach the paperclip weight and test your spinner.

The effect of wing size can be investigated by making spinners with differently sized wings then letting them fall from the same height and timing how long they take to reach the ground.

B Three spinners were dropped five times and their falls were timed.

Spinner wing length (cm)	Trial 1 fall (secs)	Trial 2 fall (secs)	Trial 3 fall (secs)	Trial 4 fall (secs)	Trial 5 fall (secs)	Average fall (secs)
3	2	3	4	2	4	
6	4	5	6	5	5	
10	7	8	6	8	6	

1. Fill in the average time for each spinner to fall (add up the fall times of each one and divide by 5).

2. What do the results show?

3. How can the result be explained?

Light rays

Learning objective: To understand that light rays travel from a light source.

Light sources send out light rays which allow us to see. When light rays enter our eyes we see.

Light ray

Light rays travel in straight lines. A light ray can be made by cutting a slit in a piece of card, sticking the card on the front of a torch, then shining the torch across a piece of paper. A light ray is drawn in a diagram as an arrow showing the direction it is travelling.

Light ray and a mirror

If a mirror is placed on the paper and the torch is shone at it from one side, a light ray is seen coming from the mirror. This is a reflected light ray.

Light ray travels in a straight line away from light source.

Light ray hits mirror.

Light ray is reflected.

A In the space below draw a light ray coming from a torch onto a book and being reflected into an eye. Make sure you add the arrows correctly. Also add labels to explain what's happening.

Reflected light

Learning objective: To know that different surfaces reflect light in different ways.

The angle at which a light ray strikes a mirror affects the angle at which the reflected light ray leaves it. The power of a surface to reflect light depends on the material from which it is made.

Comparing angles

Lines can be drawn on paper to show the path of the striking (or incident) ray, the reflected ray and the surface of the mirror. A line called the normal is drawn at right angles to the mirror where the two rays meet. A protractor can be used to measure the angles of the rays from the normal.

Comparing surfaces

The reflective power of different surfaces can be compared by shining a torch on to them and comparing the brightness of the light reflected.

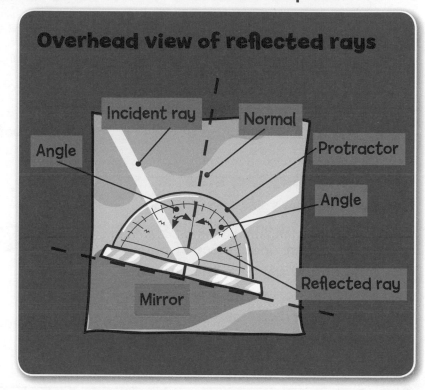

Overhead view of reflected rays

Incident ray · Normal · Protractor · Angle · Angle · Reflected ray · Mirror

B

This table shows the results of two complete measurements and two missing measurements.

1. Can you predict and fill in the missing measurements below?

Angle of incident ray	Angle of reflected ray
20	20
30	
63	63
	77

2. How do the two angles compare? Can you explain why?

Shadows

Learning objective: To learn how shadows form and how their size can change.

A shadow forms when light rays are stopped from travelling. Its size depends on the position of the light source and screen.

How shadows are made

When a light ray strikes an opaque object, its path is blocked. This means there is an absence of light on the other side of the object. We see this as a shadow.

Changing shadow size

The way a shadow's size changes can be investigated by lining up a torch, an opaque object and a piece of paper (the screen). The object is then moved backwards and forwards between the torch and the screen – and the size of its shadow is compared.

Light ray hits object.

Object blocks light.

Shadow falls behind object.

Size of shadow varies.

Object is moved forwards and backwards.

A

Experimental set-up	Width of shadow (cm)
Object halfway between torch and screen	10
Torch moved closer to object	15
Torch moved away from object	7
Screen moved closer to object	9
Screen moved away from object	16
Object moved nearer screen	6

1. Predict the size of the shadow when the object is moved away from the screen. Does it become larger or smaller?

2. How can the size of the object's shadow be increased?

DEFINITION

opaque A material or object that does not allow light to pass through.

screen A surface onto which light is shone.

Shadows and reflections

Learning objective: To be able to compare shadows and reflections.

Shadows and reflections have different appearances.

Shadows

A shadow has an outline. This is made by rays of light, which pass over the edges of the object and shine onto the surface behind. Inside the outline it is dark. No features on the object's surface can be seen in the shadow.

Reflections

When light rays strike a very smooth surface they all change direction together. When the light reaches your eyes you can see a picture in the shiny surface. This picture is called a reflection. Scientists call it an image. The image is a picture of where the light rays came from before they hit the surface. The image is reversed so things on the right side appear on the left. All the features on the object's surface can be seen in the image.

B

Read the statements below. Tick the boxes to say whether you think they are true or false.

1. Shadows are made by opaque objects.   True ☐   False ☐
2. Reflections are made when light is absent.   True ☐   False ☐
3. You can see lots of detail of the object in a shadow.   True ☐   False ☐
4. You can see lots of detail of the object in a reflection.   True ☐   False ☐
5. Another name for shadow is image.   True ☐   False ☐
6. When you wave your left hand in a mirror it looks like
   your right hand is waving.   True ☐   False ☐

7. Write your name on a piece of paper. Easy! Now place a mirror on the paper and look at the paper in the mirror. Try to write your name now. What happens?

Electrical components

Learning objective: To recognize the different components in an electrical circuit.

An electrical circuit is made up of components. Each one has a symbol.

Battery

A battery is also known as a cell. It provides the electricity for the circuit.
The positive terminal of the battery must be connected to a negative terminal.
If they are not connected in this way electricity will not flow in the circuit.

 Wire

Wires conduct electricity between the different components of a circuit.

Lamp

The thin wire in the bulb releases light when electricity flows through it.

open   closed

Switch

When a switch is open electricity cannot flow. When it is closed electricity can flow round the circuit.

Motor

The motor produces a turning movement when electricity flows through it.

 Buzzer

The buzzer makes a sound when electricity flows through it. The red wire must be connected to the positive terminal of a battery for the buzzer to work.

A

Cover the top part of this page. Then, in the spaces below, draw a symbol for:

Motor   Battery   Buzzer   Lamp   Switch

Circuit diagrams

Learning objective: To relate the components of circuits to the symbols in the circuit.

Scientists use the symbols for electrical components to make circuit diagrams. These are accurate records of circuits, which are quick to make.

A diagram of a circuit with a switch, a battery and a lamp.

A diagram of a circuit with a switch, two batteries and a motor.

B

1. Have a go at drawing a circuit diagram for a circuit with two batteries, a switch and a buzzer in the space below.

2. Have a go at drawing a circuit diagram for a circuit with a battery, two lamps in a line and a switch in the space below.

Resistance

Learning objective: To know that electrical components resist the flow of electricity.

All electrical components, except batteries, have wire in them to allow electricity to flow through them. The wire offers some resistance to the electric current.

Wire thickness and resistance

A thick wire has a low resistance to an electric current and a thin wire has a high resistance. The wires used for connecting components have a low resistance but wires in lamps have a high resistance.

DEFINITION

resistance The property of a metal wire that slows down the flow of electricity through it.

Thin resistance wire

Resistance and length

A long, thin wire made from a metal with a high resistance can be used to investigate how wire length affects resistance. The picture on the left shows the loose end of a wire connecting a short length of resistance wire into the circuit. The arrow shows how the loose end can be moved along the resistance wire to increase its length in the circuit. The lamp shines brightly when the resistance is low and dimly when it is high.

A

Look at the circuit diagram above and answer these questions.

1. Will the lamp shine brightly or dimly when a short length of resistance wire is used?

2. Will the lamp shine brightly or dimly when a long length of resistance wire is used?

3. How will the brightness of the bulb change when the loose end is moved to the right?

Batteries and lamps

Learning objective: To know that the brightness of lamps can be changed.

Two 1.5 volt batteries give a voltage of 3 volts.

Batteries supply electricity to circuits, and lamps offer resistance to current flow. The flow of electricity in a circuit is affected by changing the number of batteries or lamps in it.

Batteries and power
A battery's power to generate electricity is measured in volts (V). When batteries are added to a circuit their voltage combines to give greater power.

Lamps and resistance
The high resistance wire inside each lamp lights up when the current flows. If two lamps are joined in a row, or 'arranged in series', the resistance to the current doubles and both lamps shine less brightly. If two lamps are joined side by side, or 'arranged in parallel', the resistance of one does not add to the resistance of the other – both shine as brightly as though they were alone in the circuit.

Two bulbs in series

Two bulbs in parallel

B Have a go at answering these questions about resistance, batteries and lamps.

1. What is the voltage when three 1.5V batteries are put in a circuit?

2. What is the voltage in the circuit when two of the three batteries are taken out?

3. Two lamps are arranged in series in a circuit with one battery. Then a third lamp is added to the series. Do the lamps shine more brightly or more dimly?

Answers

Page 8

A The heart pumps the blood into the arteries and it travels to all parts of the body. The blood returns to the heart in blood vessels called veins.

Page 9

B 65 person lying down, 70 person standing, 90 person walking, 120 person running.

Page 10

A People who are ill take medicines to get better. The medicines can contain drugs to help them recover. Harmful drugs like cocaine make people become addicts. Addicts are in danger of being killed by the drugs they take.

Page 11

B The poster could show healthy people not smoking or drinking too much alcohol and ill-looking people who do. The children could also use sources such as advertisements in magazines to help them with their ideas.

Page 12

A

Page 13 B

	Insect-pollinated flower	Wind-pollinated flower
Large petals	✓	
Strong scent	✓	
Nectar	✓	
Little pollen	✓	
Lots of pollen		✓
Smooth pollen		✓
Spiky pollen	✓	

Page 14

A Stigma makes pollen grains stick.
Pollen grain carries a substance from a flower for fertilization.
Pollen tube carries a substance from a pollen grain to an ovule.

Page 15

B 1-Seed germinates. 2-Seedling starts to grow. 3-Plant fully grown. 4-Plant makes flowers. 5-Flowers makes fruits. 6-Plant disperses fruit.

Page 16

A You have increased in size and your head has got smaller in proportion to your body. The colour of your hair may have changed.

Page 17

B A frog's **egg** is surrounded by **jelly**.
A tadpole **hatches** from the egg. It has a long **tail** and looks like a little fish. In time the tadpole grows **legs** and a big head and its tail **disappears**. When this happens it has turned into a frog.

Page 18

A 40 cm³

Page 19

B Helium - lighter than air.
Natural gas - used in some cookers.
Carbon dioxide - used to make food by plants

Page 20

A A piece of **chocolate** was left on a sunny windowsill. As it got **warmer** its firm sides started to sag and it began to lose its **shape**. When the **temperature** reached melting **point** the chocolate turned into a **liquid** and dropped off the windowsill.

Page 21

B

Substance	Freezing point (°C)	
Beeswax	64°C	2
Water	0°C	5
Chocolate	25°C	4
Lard	43°C	3
Pewter	240°C	1

3 would freeze.

Page 22

A Hot, dry, windy air.

Page 23

B

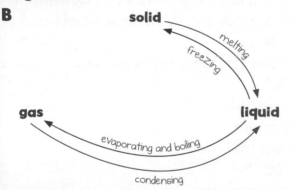

Page 24

A Earth 12,756 km.

Moon 3476 km.

Sun 1,392,000 km.

The Moon is nearer the Earth than the Sun.

Page 25

B The answers to 1 and 2 will depend on the time of year now.

3 will depend on the month in which the birthday takes place.

Page 26

A Anticlockwise. C, A, B.

Page 27

B 1. False, 2. True, 3. False, 4. True, 5. False, 6. True.

Page 28

A 1. Waxing 1 2 3.

2. Waning 5 6 7.

Page 29

B Pluto, Neptune, Uranus, Saturn, Jupiter, Asteroid belt, Mars, Earth, Venus, Mercury, Mercury, Venus, Earth, Mars, Asteroid belt, Jupiter, Saturn, Uranus, Neptune, Pluto.

Page 30

A Sound travels fastest through solids. Sound travels slowest through gases.

Page 31

B 1. By wrapping the same thickness of material around the sound source.

2. B was the best insulator.

Page 32

Professor's question A long piece of vibrating ruler has a lower pitch than a shorter piece.

A 2. Bottom C note on piano.

3. Thunder.

4. Ordinary voice.

5. Baby's first cry.

6. Chainsaw.

7. Top note on piano.

Page 33

B 1. Drum B has the lower pitch.

2. String B has the higher pitch.

3. It makes the pitch lower.

Page 34

A When **light** shines on a **leaf** it provides **energy** for **water** and carbon dioxide to be changed into **food** and oxygen. The oxygen made by plants is used by animals when they breathe in. (Some is also used by plants).

Answers

The carbon dioxide for the plant to use is breathed out by animals. (Plants also make some, and carbon dioxide is also made when things burn.)

Page 35

B 1. A tap root is thicker with fewer side roots, which spread out in the soil. It goes deeper into the soil.

2. Gravelly soil drains best. (A)

Clay soil has the worst drainage. (C)

Page 36

A 1. Beetle and deer are using the plants for shelter

2. A deer is using a plant as food.

3. A spider is using the plant to set a trap.

Page 37

B The animals are A millipede, B earthworm, C insect, D snail, E harvestman, F slug, G woodlouse, H spider, I centipede.

Page 38

A stiff tail feathers, chisel-shaped beak, two toes pointing backwards instead of one, strong claws, strong skull, long tongue.

Page 39

B

Page 40

A 1. A virus might give you a cold. 2. Bacteria are removed when you brush your teeth.

3. Bacteria and fungi might grow on an orange.

4. Bacteria and fungi make the contents of a compost bin rot.

Page 41

B The bread would not have bubbles in it or have a spongy texture. The yeast needs the sugar to feed on and make bubbles.

Page 42

A 1. Sand, flour and custard powder can be separated from the water by filtering.

2. A filter has holes in it that are large enough to let a liquid through, but are too small to let particles of undissolved solid through.

Page 43

A When **salt** is mixed with water it **dissolves** and makes a solution. If the solution is **boiled** the water turns to **steam** and leaves the **salt** behind. The **steam** can be turned to water again by **cooling** it down in a process called **condensation**.

Page 44

A All of the statements are correct.

Page 45

B 1. 40 seconds.

2. 40 seconds.

3. 20 degrees Celsius.

Page 46

A 1 baking powder.

2 flour.

3 plaster of Paris.

Page 47

B 1. water vapour (gas) and carbon dioxide (gas).

2.

Process	Reversible	Irreversible
Melting of wax	✓	
Burning of wood		✓
Baking bread		✓
Freezing water	✓	
Mixing flour and water		✓

Page 48

A 1. The force of gravity pulls them down towards the centre of the Earth.

2. 110 Newtons.

3. 60 Newtons.

Page 49

B 1. How the length of the elastic band extends as weights are attached to it.
2. 6mm.
3 12 Newtons.
4. The elastic band broke.

Page 50

A 1. 1, 3 ,4 and 6 floated.
2. It would sink.

Page 51

B 1.

Spinner wing length (cm)	Trial 1 fall (secs)	Trial 2 fall (secs)	Trial 3 fall (secs)	Trial 4 fall (secs)	Trial 5 fall (secs)	Average fall (secs)
3	2	3	4	2	4	3
6	4	5	6	5	5	5
10	7	8	6	8	6	7

2. The larger the wing the slower the fall.
3. The larger wings have a larger air resistance, which slows down the fall.

Page 52

A An arrow should go from the torch to the book. A second arrow should go from the book to the eye.

Page 53

B 1.

Angle of incident ray	Angle of reflected ray
20	20
30	30
63	63
77	77

2. The angles are always the same. The light leaves the mirror at the same angle at which it struck it.

Page 54

A 1. It becomes larger.
2. Moving the torch nearer object, screen moved away from object, object moved away from screen.

Page 55

B 1. True.
2. False.
3. False.
4. True.
5. False.
6. True.
7. You should find that writing your name is much more difficult to do as the image you are looking at is a reverse of the real view of the paper.

Page 56

A symbol for a:

Motor (M)   battery

buzzer   switch

lamp

Page 57

B 1.   2.

Page 58

A 1. Bright.
2. Dim.
3. From dim to bright.

Page 59

B 1. 4.5 V.
2. 1.5 V.
3. More dimly.

Index